Whores and Highwaymen

Crime and Justice in the Eighteenth-Century Metropolis

Whores and Highwaymen
Crime and Justice in the Eighteenth-Century Metropolis
Gregory J Durston

ISBN 978-1-909976-39-9 (Paperback)
ISBN 978-1-904380-75-7 (Hardback)
ISBN 978-1-908162-19-9 (PDF ebook)
ISBN 978-1-908162-18-2 (Epub ebook)

First published 2012, this paperback 2014 by
Waterside Press Ltd.
Sherfield Gables
Sherfield on Loddon
Hook, Hampshire
United Kingdom RG27 0JG

Telephone +44(0)1256 882250
E-mail enquiries@watersidepress.co.uk
Online catalogue WatersidePress.co.uk

Main UK distributor Gardners Books, 1 Whittle Drive, Eastbourne, East Sussex, BN23 6QH. Tel: +44 (0)1323 521777; sales@gardners.com; www.gardners.com

Cataloguing-In-Publication Data A catalogue record for this book can be obtained from the British Library.

e-book *Whores and Highwaymen* is available as an ebook and also to subscribers of Myilibrary, ebrary, Ebscohost and Dawsonera.

Printed by Lightning Source.

Whores and Highwaymen

Crime and Justice in the Eighteenth-Century Metropolis

Gregory J Durston

WATERSIDE PRESS

Contents

Acknowledgements

I would like to acknowledge the invaluable assistance provided by the staff of the British Library, the Bodleian Library and the libraries of Kingston University and Lincoln's Inn. Thanks are also due to the National Archives in Kew, the City of London Record Office, the Westminster City Archives and the London Metropolitan Archives.

I am grateful to the Principal and Fellows of St. Edmund Hall, Oxford, for their hospitality during the Hilary Term of 2009, my colleagues in the School of Law, Kingston University, for their encouragement, and to Judge Nicholas Philpot, Philippa Russell, and the late Niall Pawsey for advice and assistance with the manuscript.

Gregory Durston
London, August, 2011

Preface

Many aspects of Metropolitan crime, justice and policing in the eighteenth century have been the subjects of intense research over the past 30 years. Numerous distinguished scholars have addressed their minds to, *inter alia*, the incidence and nature of offending, law enforcement, trial procedure and punishment in the London area. However, the resulting monographs and articles have often been chronologically, institutionally, or geographically confined. For example, the City of London has frequently been studied in isolation from Westminster and urban Middlesex, and vice-versa, even though they constituted a single conurbation, unprecedented in size, throughout the century. Additionally, all of these built-up areas have been considered separately from their immediate hinterland, although rural and suburban Middlesex was hugely influenced by its proximity to the Metropolis, and its crime and law enforcement problems were closely linked to that area.

Similarly, the work of the Old Bailey Court has frequently been scrutinised without reference to that of the Metropolis's various Quarter Sessions, let alone the summary jurisdiction of the area's many magistrates and, again, vice-versa, providing a distorted image of Metropolitan crime and justice, whether by focusing excessively on serious but unusual crimes, subject to draconian punishment, or by dwelling on minor offences that were frequently resolved informally. No study has encompassed the whole of the eighteenth century, rather than its first or second moiety or shorter periods.

The aim of this book is to draw all of these threads together by considering both crime and the working of the criminal justice system over the entire Metropolitan area, as well as its immediate hinterland, during the whole of the eighteenth century. In doing so, it provides an overview of how these phenomena interacted and changed during the course of this period. This is particularly important because, as will be seen, many of them were interlinked, often in the most unexpected ways. A change in penal practice might, ultimately, bring about totally unanticipated, and unplanned, changes in the law of evidence. The presence of large state rewards for prosecuting felons helped transform the trial process. As these examples suggest, it was an era in which the law of unintended consequences frequently operated, making a "holistic" approach particularly valuable.

About the Author

Gregory J Durston MA, DipL, LLM, PhD of the Middle Temple and Lincoln's Inn, Barrister-at-Law was born and lives in London. He studied history for his first degree before turning to the law, and qualifying for the bar. He has taught in Law Schools in England and Japan and is currently Reader in Law at Kingston University in Surrey.

For Philippa

PART ONE: CRIME AND THE METROPOLIS

CHAPTER 1

INTRODUCTION

Terms of Reference

This book considers crime, policing and the criminal justice system in the Metropolitan area and its immediate environs during the eighteenth century. Both parameters require definition, even if the latter appears self-explanatory. Although the primary focus is on the years between 1700 and 1800, discussion will, where relevant, extend to the "long" eighteenth century, construed as running from the Glorious Revolution of 1688 to the end of the Napoleonic Wars in 1815. Whatever dates are used, it must always be remembered that such periodisation is inherently artificial. It was a distinguished legal historian, Frederic Maitland, who observed that the unity of all history means that any delineation will necessarily involve tearing a "seamless web".[1]

The Metropolis is taken as constituting the urban conurbation made up of the adjoining cities of London and Westminster, along with the built-up parts of the surrounding county of Middlesex. Some consideration will also be given to Southwark and the other urbanised parts of Surrey that were found south of the Thames, even if there was only one bridge (London) spanning the river during the first half of the period. (Westminster Bridge opened in 1750 and Blackfriars in 1769). This limited expansion to the south, so that Southwark only had 66,000 inhabitants in 1800. Nevertheless, even in 1731, some observers viewed urban Surrey as an integral part of the wider city, claiming that London, taken at its: "...largest extent, comprehends the cities of London and Westminster, with their respective suburbs, and the borough of Southwark, with the buildings contiguous thereto on the south side of the river". By then, the length of continuous built up ground north

1. H. J. Berman, *Law and Revolution: The Formation of the Western Legal Tradition*, 1983, p.49.

of the river, from Hyde Park Gate, on the west side of Grosvenor Square, to Limehouse, in the East, was almost five miles as the crow flies, and rather more by road, while its breadth extended to two and a half miles at its maximum.[2] As will be seen, the whole of the built up area was in a process of constant expansion during the course of the century.

Inevitably, simple structural determinants governed many aspects of the eighteenth-century criminal justice system, especially within the Metropolis, whether it was the sheer pressure of numbers being processed or the inherent limitations on record keeping and communication between public officials at this time. As a result, there are numerous parallels with the justice systems of other large European cities, as well as some marked differences. There are also some interesting similarities between London and eighteenth-century Edo (modern Tokyo) and Peking (Beijing), both of which were major conurbations.

Sources of Information

A variety of primary documentary sources have been used in this study. These include, *inter alia*, depositions, recognisances, indictments, coroners' reports, entries made by the aldermen magistrates of the City of London in their Minute Books, and those made by Middlesex Justices in their notebooks. The advent of the 1731 Act for "Englishing" the law (4 Geo. II, cap. 26), which came into force in March 1733, replaced Latin and Law French with the vernacular on all legal documents, including indictments, informations, commissions and pardons. It also stipulated that they must be written in a clear "common legible hand", rather than traditional court hand. Both of these developments facilitate research for the last two thirds of the century.[3] However, deciphering such records still requires a good command of palaeography. Throughout the eighteenth century, and well after 1733, there

2. M. Gonzales, *London in 1731*, 1888, p.11.
3. D. Horn and M. Ransome, *English Historical Documents, 1714–1783*, vol. X, 1957, p.237. *The Gentleman's Magazine*, 1731, vol.1, p.213, and *The Gentleman's Magazine*, 1733, vol. 3, p.65.

were regular complaints that legal documents were not being written in a readily legible manner.[4]

Printed primary sources

Printed primary sources abound for the eighteenth century, as it was an era of widespread literacy, in which even manual workers could often read to some extent. Literacy levels were also much higher in the Metropolis than in rural areas, so that a clear and growing majority of men in the city could, at least, sign their names by 1700.[5]

The century witnessed the first great newspaper age, something that was encouraged by the permanent lapse of licensing laws in 1695. This was an industry that was centred on London, which had dozens of periodicals by the late 1700s. Some were weeklies, others appeared two or three times a week or, like *The Times* after 1785, came out on a daily basis. By 1792, the capital had at least 14 dailies and a newspaper circulation of 25,000 copies or more, with up to 20 people reading, or being exposed to, each copy.[6] By contrast, Paris was well behind in such developments, not having a regular daily paper until the 1770s.

Crime made popular reading, and newspapers carried a steadily increasing number of reports about Metropolitan felonies. By the late eighteenth century, they probably provided the most important source of popular knowledge about the capital's crimes and its system of law enforcement.[7] In the 1750s, the magistrate Henry Fielding even founded a bi-weekly, the *Covent Garden Journal*, specifically to publicise the work of his Bow Street Public Office.

There was a particularly marked increase in the frequency and depth of newspaper coverage of crime during the last quarter of the century, with *The Times* taking the lead in this respect. This development may have been

4. C. Gery, *Mr. Gery's Case With the Reforming Constables*, 1750, p.1.
5. D. Hay and N. Rogers, *Eighteenth-century English Society*, 1987, p.9.
6. P. King, "Newspaper reporting and attitudes to crime and justice in late eighteenth-and early-nineteenth-century London", 2007, p.74.
7. P. King, "Making Crime News", 2009, p.92.

linked to the *Sessions Papers* becoming more detailed, and legally "complete", after 1775, and so less gripping to a non-specialist audience.[8]

Of course, this process should not be exaggerated. Even in the late eighteenth century, daily newspapers were normally only four pages long, nearly half of which were given over to advertisements. Of the space allotted to news coverage, pride of place usually went to parliamentary reports. This left only limited room for other matters. Nevertheless, the relative ubiquity of newspaper reports on crime allowed the emergence of the phenomenon now described as "moral panic", in which a group or activity becomes defined as a threat to wider societal values, and is presented in an alarmist, stylized and stereotypical fashion by the mass media.[9] For example, the number and gravity of "Mohock" attacks, carried out by wealthy rakes in 1712, was greatly exaggerated, so that a lawyer who cut a man's face after being jostled could be pursued by a furious mob in the belief that he was a member of the gang.[10] The panic led to more vigorous law enforcement against what, in reality, was little more than the steady undercurrent of drunken violence perpetrated by young upper class males.[11] By the 1700s, such panics were a regular feature of Metropolitan life.[12]

As today, newspapers were usually far more interested in crimes involving extreme forms of violence, especially if they resulted in death, than the more "typical" property offences and minor assaults found in the capital. As a foreign visitor noted: "Tragic examples may be read almost daily in English newspapers of poor people met on the road who have been brutally murdered for a few shillings".[13] In 1786, *The Times* was 19 times more likely to report an Old Bailey murder trial than one for simple non-capital larceny. However, the prospect of execution, even for a (non-clergyable) property offence, greatly increased media interest. Because many newspapers were aimed at, and read by, the middling and higher social orders, they also focused on crimes

8. S. Devereaux, "From Sessions to Newspaper?", 2007, p.2 and p.19.
9. See generally, S. Cohen, *Folk Devils and Moral Panics: The Creation of the Mods and Rockers*, 1972.
10. *British Mercury*, March 12 – March 14, 1712.
11. J. Bondeson, "Monsters and Moral Panic in 18th and 19th-Century London", 2001, pp.30-35.
12. D. Lemmings et al, *Moral Panics, the Media and the Law in Early Modern England*, 2009, p.2.
13. C. P. Moritz, *Journeys of a German in England in 1782*, 1965, p.10.

such as forgery which were of special interest to these groups, either because they might be the victims of such offences or because their perpetrators were people of similar backgrounds to themselves.[14] As a result, the overall impression that newspaper reports give of Metropolitan crime is inevitably misleading, though it does have the benefit of being more "victim centred" than the defendant oriented court reports. Offences reported in the latter were necessarily unusual, if only because they had resulted in the capture and prosecution of a suspect, unlike the vast majority of Metropolitan crimes.

Additionally, newspaper accounts are not always very accurate, though some periodicals were more reliable than others. They were based on information provided by a variety of sources, such as court reporters, watchmen, constables, victims and eyewitnesses, not all of them entirely dependable. To this problem might be added considerable journalistic licence, so that one contemporary observer could talk about: "News-Collectors ... inventing stories of rapes, robberies, riots, &c. to fill up the news-papers of the ensuing week".[15] Then as now, journalistic standards and ethics were sometimes poor. For example, in the era's equivalent of a modern tabloid coup, in 1727, a stringer or "news monger" for the *Daily Journal* visited Martin Bellamy, a notorious robber, while he was incarcerated in Newgate prison. He pretended he was authorised to grant Bellamy a royal pardon, under a recent proclamation, in exchange for information about his crimes and accomplices. Bellamy's revelations were then published by the journal.[16]

The freedom of the press to publish highly partisan accounts of notorious crimes before their attendant trials came on, while being largely unfettered by modern notions of contempt of court, sometimes endangered the fairness of Old Bailey hearings. For example, in 1721, one newspaper noted that its competitors had mistakenly claimed that Mary Wilson had confessed to infanticide before her trial for the same crime, thereby making it much more likely that she would be convicted and hanged.[17] In 1782, even the Attorney General complained about prejudicial pre-trial reports, and threatened to

14. P. King, "Making Crime News", 2009, p.112.
15. Anon, *Low-Life: or One Half of the World Knows not how the Other Half Live*, 2nd edn., 1755, p.28.
16. M. Bellamy, *The Life of Martin Bellamy*, 1728, p.9.
17. *Applebee's Original Weekly Journal*, June 3rd 1721. Fortunately, she was still acquitted.

take action. Occasionally, judges would try to redress this risk by expressly warning juries to: "...divest themselves of everything they had heard".[18]

However, as Horace Walpole observed, the London papers: "...though always full of lies, seldom fail to reach the outline at least of incidents".[19] The bare bones of an allegation were likely to be correct, even if the incidental details might not be. Indeed, some modern observers have concluded that, where cases were neither notorious nor "political" in nature, the large amount of information provided by newspapers was usually reliable.[20]

Additionally, and much more dependably, newspapers provide an extremely valuable source of information about contemporary attitudes towards crime, justice and policing, at least amongst literate observers. Of course, as many criminals were illiterate, newspapers do not necessarily reflect the attitudes of those on the "receiving end" of eighteenth-century justice, or the social milieu from which they were drawn.

Old Bailey Sessions Papers

A particularly valuable source of primary information can be found in the contemporary reports of trials at the Old Bailey published throughout this period as the *Old Bailey Sessions Papers*. These first came out in 1674, and quickly became a regular periodical, with editions normally being published eight times a year, following each session of the court. They provided details of all offences that were indicted at the Bailey during the period, i.e. that were not thrown out by a Grand Jury finding that a tendered bill of indictment was unsupported by sufficient evidence to justify it going before a trial jury. What the *Sessions Papers* reported was normally accurate. However, they were usually incomplete accounts of what occurred at trial, so that a failure to mention something cannot be taken as indicative of its absence.[21] Only a

18. J. Hackman, *The Case and Memoirs of the Late Rev. Mr. James Hackman*, 1779, p.i.
19. P. King, "Newspaper reporting and attitudes to crime and justice in late-eighteenth-and early-nineteenth-century London", 2007, pp.19-21.
20. J. Oldham, "Law Reporting in the London Newspapers, 1756-1786", pp.177-178.
21. On their value as records, see J. H. Langbein, "The Criminal Trial Before the Lawyers", 1978, pp.267-272. The most complete collection of the Sessions Papers available has been digitalised and is now available online at www.oldbaileyonline.org. All citations identified as OBSP will refer to this source, full citations being used for manuscript versions of the papers.

relatively small proportion of testimony could be published, even in those hearings that received detailed consideration, and many did not.

This sometimes occasioned confusion, even at the time. For example, after the conviction of John Stanley for murdering his lover in 1723, it was noted that some observers, dependant on these papers for their information, had expressed surprise at the verdict, when they compared it to the result in another, similar, hearing, which had produced an acquittal. However, those who were familiar with the case pointed out that the sessions' papers had not reported evidence of threats made to the dead woman by the defendant some six months before the killing, which were adduced at trial. These appear to have weighed heavily on the minds of the jury when it came to deciding whether Stanley had "malice aforethought" and explained the verdict disparity. The reports also omitted witnesses whose evidence had, rather belatedly, raised the possibility that Stanley was a "lunatic" and so should be subject to an insanity verdict.[22]

Perhaps inevitably, the *Sessions Papers* tended to have a prosecution bias, so that the Crown's case usually looked inherently strong. Defence accounts were sometimes neglected.[23] Another limitation is their changing nature; they went from being populist accounts, focusing on the more eye-catching trials in the 1670s, to quasi-official publications, subsidized by the Corporation of London, at the end of the eighteenth century. During the 1780s, the proceedings also became increasingly cautious about publishing the more salacious details of sexual offences. The difference in levels of reporting between different eras means that comparing accounts of similar crimes is often inherently difficult.

Treatises and biographies

Enormous numbers of legal treatises and criminal biographies, along with private and parliamentary recommendations for social, penal and policing reform, were published during the eighteenth century, as were numerous tracts, broadsheets, ballads and chapbooks about the era's more notorious

22. Anon, *The Life of Mr. John Stanley*, 1723, p.vi and p.vii.
23. R. B. Shoemaker, "The Old Bailey Proceedings and the Representation of Crime and Criminal Justice in Eighteenth-century London", 2008, p.570.

crimes and criminals, all of which will be cited regularly in this book. These are of mixed historical value. Some are largely apocryphal or works of imagination. Others are much more carefully researched. For example, when Daniel Defoe came to write the life of the notorious thief and escapologist John Sheppard his varied source base, men who provided the "most authentick accounts", consisted of several JPs, victims, the principal turnkeys and officers from Newgate and the New Prison, and Sheppard's own confession made to the Reverend Wagstaff, the Newgate ordinary's deputy.[24]

The Newgate ordinary's short biographies of convicts awaiting execution, after being found guilty of a capital offence at the Old Bailey, are similar to many of these pamphlets, but were particularly widely distributed. They were an important perquisite of this poorly paid prison chaplain's office, being commercially sold accounts based on his extensive interviews with the condemned. The ordinary was able to use the threat of eternal damnation to exert pressure on those awaiting execution, and most clerics experienced considerable success in securing information, especially when all hope of a reprieve had been abandoned. This did not necessarily endear them to the prisoners. It was claimed that the Reverend Paul Lorrain was the object of universal scorn, so that a personal friend admitted that he had never heard of more than: "...two people who spoke favourably of him, and those were the printer and publisher of his Dying Speech Papers".[25]

There were also periodic complaints about the slant that the ordinary put on his exchanges with the prisoners. For example, Richard Steele referred to those ministered to by Lorrain as "Paul Lorrain's saints" because their penitence was usually described as "heartfelt". In 1737, another observer referred to the cleric's reports as an "incoherent Magazine of Trash and Scandal" and alleged that the then ordinary, the Reverend John Guthrie, had been determined to blacken the character and memory of one of the men he had ministered to.[26] Nevertheless, although they were certainly not unmediated accounts, there were limits as to how far the ordinary could depart from his

24. D. Defoe, *The History of the Remarkable Life of John Sheppard*, 1724, pp.1-3.
25. Anon (By a German Gentleman), *A View of London and Westminster: or, the Town Spy, etc.*, 2nd edn., 1725, p.37.
26. Anon, *Some Observations on the Trial of Mr. Thomas Carr, Who was Executed at Tyburn, January 18. 1737*, 1737, pp.1-2 and p.8.

subjects' words if he wished them to remain marketable, and their sale was an important part of his income. In 1724, it was claimed that they increased an otherwise modest salary of £60 to one of £100.[27] Even radical historians have been willing to accord factual accuracy to much of their content.[28] Their publication petered out during the 1760s, and stopped altogether in the 1770s.[29] This appears to have been linked to the growth in newspaper reporting and its attendant plagiarism; in 1776, the Reverend John Villette warned that if Metropolitan papers copied his work too swiftly it would not be worth his while to continue, and publication ceased shortly thereafter.[30]

Taken together, and used holistically, all of these primary resources provide hugely valuable insights into crime, law enforcement and the Metropolitan criminal justice system during the period. However, in recent decades there has also been a plethora of secondary work on many of the issues discussed in this book.

Historiography

Eighteenth-century crime and justice has become an important sub-genre within the era's wider social history. As early as 1986, observers could identify a "crime wave" of writing on the subject. This has continued unabated to become a veritable tsunami in recent years. Dozens of books and articles have been published, and numerous Doctoral theses completed, though it should be noted that criminal justice history has a natural tendency towards chronocentrism, that is the assumption that recent scholarship must be

27. B. L., *An Accurate Description of Newgate*, 1724, p.49.
28. See, for example, P. Linebaugh, *The London Hanged: Crime and Civil Society in the Eighteenth Century*, 1991, p.91.
29. The most complete collection of the ordinary's accounts available has been digitalised and is now available online at www.oldbaileyonline.org. All citations identified by the phrase "The Ordinary of Newgate's Account...[date]" will refer to this source, the date referring to the execution of those discussed. Full named citations will be used for manuscript versions that have been consulted. The ordinary also wrote several specific and individually published accounts of celebrated convicts.
30. J. Villette, *A Genuine Account of the Behaviour, confession, and Dying-Words of Daniel Perreau and Robert Perreau*, 1776, p.1.

superior to older work, even where that work provides the "roots" for today's research. Additionally, two superbly annotated websites of primary materials have been set up.[31]

One reason for this present-day interest is the importance of the "long" eighteenth century to the advent of many modern criminal justice institutions and procedures in the Anglophone world. These include, for example, today's adversarial trial, with its recourse to counsel and evidential rules, and the use of penitentiaries. Another explanation is the significance that historians of the era have ascribed to the nation's criminal justice system when seeking to explain why the British state avoided revolution with only a small standing army.[32] The century also straddles the professional focus of both early-modern and modern historians, encouraging analysis.

Academic work on the period has been conducted from a wide variety of perspectives. Legal, social and institutional historians have both crossed swords and complemented each other. Many of these studies raise a key issue; to what extent should historians allow the pre-occupations of today to influence the study of the past? Should they attempt to see the past in its "own terms", rather than through an unhistorical prism of modern values? For example, many of the protections afforded to modern criminal defendants were absent in the 1700s. Does this mean that historians should view the eighteenth-century trial as woefully deficient? Doing so risks producing an anachronistic analysis of the past and transposing modern concerns onto what was a very different society. A failure to do so can result in a Panglossian analysis.

If nothing else, this flood of academic work has, at least, replaced simplistic earlier portrayals of Hanoverian crime and justice with a much more subtle and nuanced picture. In the past, the apparently inadequate institutional response to high levels of offending and disorder was often interpreted as a manifestation of the era's inherent brutality and backwardness, phenomena that were on a par with its poor standards of hygiene. This analysis readily lent itself to a "Whig" interpretation of English social history, in

31. See generally, P. Rock, "Chronocentrism and British Criminology", 2005, pp.473-491. www.londonlives.org and www.oldbaileyonline.org

32. B. P. Smith, "English Criminal Justice Administration, 1650-1850", 2007, p.8.

which gradually increasing pressure for reform was, eventually, manifest in a humanitarian move away from corporal and capital punishments towards the more reformatory process of incarceration. At the same time, crime was gradually tamed by the advent of a professional police force and magistracy.[33] By contrast, research over the past forty years suggests that the eighteenth-century justice system was slightly less brutal, and much less chaotic, than was once thought.[34]

The Whig school of historiography was challenged from a number of positions and perspectives during the 1970s.[35] For example, Michel Foucault saw the era as one in which social control was extended and internalized by the use of imprisonment. Far from being a manifestation of increased humanity, the move from punishment as "spectacle" reflected the priorities of a new bourgeois ruling class, keen to develop a more systematic form of control over the masses, one that would render them amenable to factory discipline. This could be inculcated more easily by an increased emphasis on "reform" rather than selective physical chastisement. As a result, mass imprisonment and the penitentiary replaced the drama of the gallows.[36] Other accounts, written in the same and following decades, were equally radical. Amongst the most influential were those produced by the criminal justice historians based at the University of Warwick (the "Warwick School"). Their work usually stressed the experiences of the poor, or history "from below", and the class bias found in the era's justice system. One of the group, Douglas Hay, suggested that the criminal courts were used to intimidate the population, with the threat of capital punishment being ever-present, even for minor crimes, as a result of the presence of the "Bloody Code" and the withdrawal of benefit of clergy from many offences. However, this was combined with a highly selective implementation of capital punishment in practice, as the Crown issued pardons liberally. It also prosecuted and punished a few members of the upper social orders, to create an illusion of fairness, legal equality and benevolent paternalism. This neutralized lower class dissent, and allowed

33. See, for example, L. Radzinowicz, *A History of English Criminal Law and Its Administration from 1750*, vol. 1, *The Movement for Reform, 1750–1833*, 1948.
34. J. A. Sharpe, "Crime and Punishment", 2002, pp.358-366.
35. P. Baines, "Crime Histories", 2009, p.167.
36. M. Foucault, *Discipline and Punish: The Birth of the Prison*, 1979, pp.305-308.

the upper class to rule in its own interests. Hay went so far as to suggest that this process almost amounted to a ruling class "conspiracy".[37]

This interpretation was vulnerable, in its turn, to the work of legal historians, who considered the primary sources in detail and were swiftly able to identify some fundamental flaws in such an analysis. For example, it did not accord with the realities of court practice, in which many of the people who were vested with discretion were not drawn from the social elite, and where most of the factors considered when exercising discretion were neither arbitrary nor self-interested, but matters that any rational system would take into account.[38]

The bane of modern paradigms has been to take a potentially valuable perspective, and then make it a "catch all" explanation for aspects of the era's deviance or its criminal justice system. Most eighteenth-century observers appreciated that, as a matter of course, those in the: "...superior stations of life should sometimes find means to evade the punishments incurred by infringing the laws of their country".[39] However, the political nation was also well aware of the need to at least appear even-handed when implementing the criminal law. As an MP could observe in 1792, it was axiomatic that the poorest men should have the same treatment from the justice system as the richest, as: "All distinction was unknown in the protection and benefit of the law of England".[40] Such concerns seem to have influenced the outcomes in a number of *causes célèbres* involving upper class defendants, such as the decision not to accept that Lord Ferrers, accused of murdering his valet in 1760, was insane, despite numerous indicia to that effect. The decision not to pardon the Reverend Dodd after he was capitally convicted of forgery, in the face of large-scale petitions for clemency, was influenced by similar considerations. Sometimes, these were expressed quite openly. For example, in 1785, when Christopher Atkinson, a former MP and wealthy corn merchant, was pilloried for perjury, *The Times* noted that there had been concern in some quarters that part of the sentence might be remitted. Instead, it was

37. See generally, D. Hay, "Property, Authority, and the Criminal Law", 1976.
38. J. H. Langbein, "Albion's Fatal Flaws", 1983, p.120.
39. T. Daniels, *The Affecting Case of the Unfortunate Thomas Daniels*, 1761, pp.3-4.
40. W. Cobbett, *The Parliamentary History of England from the Earliest Period to the Year 1803*, London, 1817, vol. xxix, p.1170.

fully carried out, so that the large mob present at the Corn Exchange: "... comforted themselves with reflecting, that though their laws punished with severity the transgressions of the poor, they yet afforded not the smallest shelter to the vices of the rich".[41] However, an awareness of the social implications of their decisions does not necessarily amount to a ruling-class conspiracy.

More recently, Peter King has argued that many historians have placed too much attention on the "black letter" law of Parliamentary statutes that were aimed at addressing criminal justice issues, and on the work of the major criminal courts, especially the Old Bailey and Assizes, and perhaps too little on local, rather than central government, initiatives, and the process by which these were often "shaped from below", sometimes even by those on the margins of political society (though "marginalisation" is always a matter of degree).[42]

41. *The Times*, Nov. 26, 1785, p.2.
42. See generally, P. King, *Crime and Law in England, 1750-1840: Remaking Justice from the Margins*, 2007.

CHAPTER 2

THE EIGHTEENTH-CENTURY METROPOLIS

Introduction

The Metropolitan area was highly singular, if not *sui generis*, because of its size and commercial importance. As might be expected, it also experienced enormous changes, both physical and social, during the course of the eighteenth century. This presents special difficulties to those writing about the era; there is an acute risk that any portrayal will produce an excessively static picture. It also makes any generalisations about the eighteenth century, as opposed to its specific decades, potentially hazardous.

However, a number of general developments *can* be identified as having a major impact on Metropolitan society, including its crime, policing and criminal justice system, during the 1700s. Amongst them were the effects of urbanisation linked to massive population growth, most of it due to migration from outside the London area. Additionally, there was an ongoing decline in what might loosely be termed "communitarianism" on the part of the capital's inhabitants, and an associated increase in social fragmentation. The growing importance of the "middling" social orders was also very significant, not least because it contributed to a major change in cultural values, in which both upper class libertine or rake culture and lower class plebeian culture retreated amongst key elements of the urban population. An increased degree of sensitivity towards crime and disorder was an important manifestation of this phenomenon.

The substantial interdependence of economic, social and institutional phenomena make trying to isolate the individual contributions of these factors to developments in the century after 1688 almost impossible. Many are inextricably interlinked. Indeed, it seems that conjunctures of differing factors were vital to change; it was rare that any single issue lay behind reform. Some of them are associated with what might, very loosely, be referred to as the "impact of modernity", and it has been argued that the century was a vital transitional stage between the early-modern and modern world. As a result, there is a strange juxtaposition of phenomena. Even as Sarah Morduck was being investigated for witchcraft in the Square Mile, at the start of the century, there was growing concern about City brokers spreading false price sensitive information to: "...ground the rise or fall of stocks upon".[1]

As this dichotomy suggests, eighteenth- century London was not a "modern" society, as it would be understood by a twenty-first century observer, but nor is it entirely alien to that observer. It was not yet, generally, a society "of" strangers, though there were many localised exceptions to this general situation, and it was certainly a society "with" many more transients than had previously been the case. As a result, some observers complained that in London and Westminster: "...neighbours hardly know one another; and men live together with as little regard to what each other do, as if they inhabited an extended wilderness".[2] Others alleged that a majority of the inhabitants of Metropolitan parishes could not name their local minister of religion.[3]

Metropolitan Government

Although, by the early eighteenth century, much of the Metropolis had become a single built up area, government remained firmly in the hands of its constituent parts. North of the Thames, these were the City of London ("the City"), the City of Westminster and the County of Middlesex. South of the river, most of the built up areas bordering the Thames were the administrative responsibility of the County of Surrey and its justices, though the City dominated the three manors of the Borough of Southwark, at least for some purposes, the bailiwick being administered by the City ward of Bridge Without, which was situated around the southern end of London Bridge.

---

1. See generally, Anon (By a Jobber), *The Anatomy of Exchange-Alley: Or, a System of Stock-Jobbing*, 2nd edn., 1719.
2. *The Ordinary of Newgate, His Account of the Behaviour, Confession, and Dying Words of the Malefactors who were executed at Tyburn on Tuesday the 9th of July, 1745*, 1745, p.16.
3. Anon, *A Trip Through the Town. Containing Observations on the Humours and Manners of the Age*, 5th edn., 1735, p.2.

Beyond that area, in Bermondsey, Newington and the Clink Liberty, the Surrey justices held full and exclusive sway.[4]

The City

In the City of London, government was vested in the hands of the Mayor, sheriffs, aldermen and common councilmen. All of them were acutely jealous of their ancient privileges and the powers granted by the City's historic Charter. The most important administrative sub-division in the Square Mile was the ward, of which there were 26. Of these, 21 were within its ancient walls, three outside them, and two straddled this fortification. They frequently cut across parish boundaries (there were 97 parishes within the walls), and were themselves sub-divided into numerous precincts. Each ward elected an alderman, who held the position for life, and from whose number the Lord Mayor was chosen for his year in office. Additionally, each alderman had a deputy taken from the Court of Common Council. This body was made up of 210 councilmen, elected annually by ratepayers in the wards, along with the mayor and aldermen. It was sometimes claimed that the government of the City mirrored that of the wider nation, with the Lord Mayor being comparable to the Sovereign, the aldermen to those in the House of Lords and the common councilmen to members of the Lower House.

Southwark

The Lord Mayor and his senior aldermen were JPs for the Southwark area and had the power to hold their own sessions of the peace in this "across the river" ward, once a year. However, this forum dealt with very few cases, and none of any gravity. The influence of the City officials also gradually declined during the course of the century. This was largely the result of pressure from the Surrey magistrates, who also had jurisdiction for criminal matters arising in the Borough, which was an integral part of their own county. By the 1780s, there were complaints that the City's jurisdiction there had been "notoriously invaded" over many years by magistrates from the Surrey Commission.[5]

4. D. Johnson, *Southwark and the City*, 1969, pp.223-224.
5. Anon (By an Inhabitant of the Borough of Southwark), *A Candid Enquiry into the Right of Jurisdiction in the City of London over the Borough of Southwark*, 1787, pp.1-4.

However, the aldermen were usually too busy or infirm to take a very active role there, especially as the charter of 1741, which made all aldermen magistrates for the City, was not deemed to extend to the Borough, where only those who had "passed the chair" (previously been appointed Lord Mayor) could serve. In the 14 years prior to 1801, the City Quarter Sessions in the Borough found only half a dozen indictments, nearly all of them for assault.[6] The Surrey Assizes dealt with all of the area's serious crimes.

Westminster and urban Middlesex

Westminster was, at least nominally, governed by its court of twelve burgesses (seven for the city and five for its liberties), which had been established pursuant to an Elizabethan statute, though the power of this body waned as the century advanced. The burgesses were unelected, being appointed by the Dean and High Steward of Westminster. Additionally, Westminster had its own commission of the peace and bench of magistrates, while also being within the jurisdiction of the Middlesex bench. This fragmentation of political power occasioned considerable administrative confusion. In the 1780s, an observer considering Westminster's overlapping layers of local government could complain about the: "...jarring confusion that must necessarily subsist between several jurisdictions in the same place, ill put together, and invested with discordant and contradictory privileges".[7] Other parts of the Metropolis, that is the built-up areas outside both the Square Mile and Westminster sometimes termed the "out parishes", came under the authority of the Middlesex Justices in the same way in which most other English parishes were dominated by their own county JPs. These included some very large parishes, such as Kensington.

In 1700, there was a significant contrast between the centralised and relatively well-organised government of the City, and the rather atomized, and somewhat *ad hoc*, administration found elsewhere. However, as the century advanced, local government in the rest of the Metropolis began to respond

6. D. Johnson, *Southwark and the City*, 1969, p.263.
7. E. Sayer, *Observations on the Police or Civil Government of Westminster, with a Proposal for a Reform*, 1784, p.13.

to heightened expectations about quality of life issues. In the process, they encountered a number of new problems, especially that of accountability.[8]

The main unifying characteristic of the entire area north of the river, including the still rural parts of Middlesex, was their shared use of the Old Bailey Court to determine serious crimes. However, there was considerable liaison between the Metropolis's various jurisdictions. Suspects arrested in one area, for crimes committed in another, could be returned quite readily for trial. For example, in 1769, when two men who had committed serious offences in Surrey were arrested in Middlesex they were swiftly removed from Newgate by writ of *habeas corpus*, and sent to the Surrey gaol to await that county's Assizes.[9]

Expansion of the Conurbation

The century witnessed a huge expansion in this built-up area. Even by its start, the two cities at the core of the Metropolis, although administratively totally distinct, were physically joined together.[10] All of those parts of the county of Middlesex that were adjacent to the City were also sucked into this conurbation. As a result, in the Square Mile's extra-mural wards, a largely unmarked border, known as the "Line of Separation", ran through the middle of streets in and around places such as Chancery Lane, Hatton Garden and Field Lane.[11] (At a few points there were delineating posts and a chain). This lack of obvious separation occasioned confusion to those in the provinces who sometimes imagined that: "London, Westminster, and Southwark, is all London, because contiguous to one another".[12] However, as early as 1682, the statistician Sir William Petty was willing to use the phrase

8. V. Harding, "Controlling a complex metropolis, 1650-1750", 2001, pp. 29-37.
9. Anon, *An authentic Account of the Trials, Behaviour, and Dying declaration, of the Five Malefactors, Who were executed at Kennington-Common, on Monday the 23rd April, 1770*, 1770, p.4.
10. E. A. Wrigley, "A simple model of London's Importance in Changing English Society and Economy 1650-1750", 1967, p.44.
11. W. Harrison, *A new and universal history, description and survey of London and Westminster*, 1775, p.9.
12. W. Stow, *Remarks on London Being An Exact Survey of the Cities of London and Westminster*, 1722, pp.i-iv.

"City of London" to refer not to the Square Mile, but to the continuous area of "built ground" in the three neighbouring locations.[13]

Over the course of the eighteenth and early nineteenth centuries the expanding Metropolis would also gradually swallow up its penumbra of suburban villages, such as Chelsea and Marylebone, which had, themselves, usually become greatly swollen in size before linking up with the city's outward march. For example, by the 1770s, it could be noted that Islington, lying close in to the Square Mile, was: "...nearly joined to it within these few years, by the number of houses that have been erected".[14] In Middlesex, this process meant that a system of government developed to meet the requirements of a rural environment was forced to do service in very different circumstances, even though: "The same laws which constitute a rural magistracy, to govern the known inhabitants of a country village, answer but very indifferently the purposes of great cities".[15]

Of course, this process can be exaggerated. Even at the end of the eighteenth century much of Middlesex was still rural, although, as early as the 1660s, less than a fifth of the county's inhabitants lived in those parts.[16] Most urbanites remained within relatively easy reach of countryside, one contemporary observer even noting that many Metropolitan vagabonds would sleep under hayricks in the conurbation's neighbouring areas.[17] Throughout the century, Hackney remained a pleasant area of mainly open countryside, providing easily accessible recreation, eating houses and pleasure gardens to all social classes from nearby London, along with mansions and second homes for wealthy, often retired, City merchants. It was not until a rash of speculative building transformed the area during the nineteenth century that it properly joined the Metropolis.[18]

Even so, life in the "undeveloped" parts of Middlesex was frequently dominated by the material and recreational requirements of the capital.

---

13. W. Petty, *An Essay concerning the Multiplication of Mankind*, 2nd edn., 1685, p.8.
14. Anon, *A Description of the County of Middlesex*, 1775, p.174.
15. *The Ordinary of Newgate, His Account of the Behaviour, Confession, and Dying Words of the Malefactors who were executed at Tyburn on Tuesday the 9th of July, 1745*, 1745, p.16.
16. R. Shoemaker, *Prosecution and Punishment*, 1991, p.8.
17. Anon, *Low-Life: or One Half of the World Knows not how the Other Half Live*, 2nd edn., 1755, p.18 and p.82.
18. R. Paley, *Justice in 18th-Century Hackney*, 1991, p.ix.

Most of the county's agriculture was shaped by the need to supply the city with cheese, milk, hay, eggs, fruit and vegetables, while it was littered with the brickworks and gravel pits that supplied raw materials for urban building. Many of its villages, like Southgate, which was only ten miles from the City, followed Hackney in providing wealthy merchants with a convenient country retreat. In exchange, London provided the rural part of Middlesex with a market for its produce and a continuous supply of horse manure and human "night-soil" to fertilize its fields, which were: "...greatly enriched by the compost from the metropolis".[19] As will be seen, the presence of the Metropolis also had a major influence on crime rates in these areas. The constant expansion of the conurbation was the inevitable result of a greatly increased population.

Population Growth

During the eighteenth century, the whole Metropolitan area experienced enormous population growth. One modern estimate suggests a figure of 575,000 inhabitants for the Metropolis in 1700, followed by a relatively slow expansion to 675,500 in 1750, before a huge increase in the second half of the century, which led to a population of 959,000 in 1801.[20] Other estimates place it even higher, especially if urban Surrey is included. Whatever the precise figure, the Metropolis dwarfed other cities in Britain, and became the largest urban area in Europe early in the century, being much larger than Paris, Madrid, or Vienna. By 1722, it was estimated that the circumference of the built up parts alone exceeded 25 miles, so that no Metropolitan coachman could possibly know all of its streets.[21]

Population growth in the City, that is the "Square Mile" (actually 677 acres), both within and without its historic walls (it had several large extramural parishes) was modest, reaching 128,000 from about 125,000 during

19. Anon, *A Description of the County of Middlesex*, 1775, p.167 and p.173.
20. E. A. Wrigley, "Urban Growth and Agricultural Change: England and the Continent in the Early Modern Period", 1985, p.686.
21. W. Stow, *Remarks on London Being An Exact Survey of the Cities of London and Westminster*, 1722, pp.i-iv.

the course of the century, when compared to the expansion that occurred elsewhere in the Metropolitan area. West of Temple Bar, there was more substantial growth. Westminster's population, which was approaching 130,000 in 1700, had reached 165,000 by the time of the first census in 1801.[22] As Westminster grew, fresh parishes were carved out of its existing ones, especially St Margaret and St Martin-in-the-Fields, in the continuation of a process that had started at the Restoration. Thus, St. George's Hanover Square and St. John the Evangelist were established in 1724 and 1728 respectively.[23]

Even more significantly, there was enormous growth in the poorer Middlesex parishes that lay to the east of the City or beyond its northern borders. These were often heavily engaged in brewing, distilling, manufacturing and other forms of industrial and commercial activity. As a result, the City of London, which even in 1650 had contained well under half of the Metropolitan population, held only about a fifth of its inhabitants by 1750, a proportion that was to fall steadily further in ensuing decades.[24]

Mortality

For most of the period, the death rate in London exceeded its birth rate by a considerable degree. Until the final decade of the century, the number of baptisms within the bills of mortality (i.e. most of the Metropolis) was far smaller than that of its burials, something that was especially marked during the era's early years, though a failure to record some dissenter and Catholic births slightly exaggerated the difference. The area was thought by its own inhabitants to produce a much higher infant mortality rate, due to its noxious air and generally unhealthy environment, as a result of which a significantly greater proportion of small children died than in rural areas.[25] So frequent were such premature deaths that some poor people would carry

22. E. Reynolds, "Sir John Fielding, Sir Charles Whitworth, and the Westminster Night Watch Act, 1770-1775", 2002, p.3.
23. E. Sayer, *Observations on the Police or Civil Government of Westminster, with a Proposal for a Reform*, 1784, p.4.
24. V. Harding, "Controlling a complex metropolis, 1650-1750", 2001, p.33.
25. C. Morris, *Observations on the Past Growth and Present State of the City of London*, 1751, p.2.

their dead infants, nailed up in small deal boxes, to fields adjoining the built up area, and then bury them secretly, to avoid the cost of a normal parish interment.[26] Additionally, venereal disease was (rightly) believed to be more prevalent, and periodic epidemic diseases more powerful, than in provincial England.[27] For example, for most of the century it seems that ten per cent of deaths within the Metropolis were the result of smallpox, while many others were occasioned by typhus.[28]

However, after peaking in the middle of the eighteenth century, infant mortality fell sharply for the rest of the era, while that for older children declined during the later 1700s. Adult mortality also fell rapidly, if less spectacularly, after 1750. There were a variety of reasons for this phenomenon, which does not seem to have been closely linked to class prior to the Victorian period. Inoculation played a part but, most importantly, enhanced levels of personal and general cleanliness seem to have been a driving force in this downward trend.[29]

Inward Migration

Despite such improvements, the increase in Metropolitan population was necessarily the result of large-scale immigration from outside the area. London and its environs was a magnet for those from other parts of the country and elsewhere. For most, its attraction was economic; it provided employment, or the means of earning a living (even if nefarious), that was not available elsewhere. As a result, "vast numbers of artisans and labouring people" arrived there, from all parts of the British Isles. Manual work could often be found in the summer months, especially for those, such as carpenters and bricklayers, who were engaged in the building trade. When it was available,

26. Anon, *Low-Life: or One Half of the World Knows not how the Other Half Live*, 2nd edn., 1755, p.21.
27. C. Morris, *Observations on the Past Growth and Present State of the City of London*, 1751, p.2.
28. J. Landers and A. Mouzas, "Burial seasonality and Causes of death in London 1670-1819", 1988, pp.60-61.
29. P. Razzell and C. Spence, "The History of Infant, Child and Adult Mortality in London, 1550-1850", 2007, p.271 and p.288.

rates of pay were much higher than they were in the provinces. However, such employment was highly seasonal, and tended to dry up in the winter. Some new arrivals did not even come in the expectation of "honest" labour. For example, in the 1730s, Joshua Cornwall, a notorious Metropolitan house-breaker had apparently acquired so great a habit of laziness that he found it impossible to continue living in the country. As a result, he went to London: "...that great receptacle of those who are either unable or unwilling to live anywhere else".[30] For others, the capital offered the prospect of adventure. Before gravitating to London in about 1707, Jonathan Wild (1683-1725), an early eighteenth-century Metropolitan criminal mastermind and "thief-taker", had led a fairly uneventful life in Wolverhampton and Birmingham, serving out his time as an apprentice to a buckle-maker.[31] For the destitute, the Metropolis also seemed to offer greater opportunities for begging and more access to institutional relief. One foreign visitor in the 1770s was (wholly mistakenly) convinced that there were very few poor people in London: "... on account of the many charitable foundations, and the immense sums produced by the poor's rate".[32] Others fled to the Metropolis to avoid problems in their parishes of origin. For example, when an unmarried woman gave birth to an illegitimate baby in Egham, the putative father, Thomas Ayres, a local apothecary, immediately decamped to London.[33]

As a result of this combination of attractions and pressures, there were regular influxes of poor Irishmen, along with smaller numbers of Scots, Welshmen and Northerners, as well as many from closer parts of England, such as East Anglia and the Home Counties. Additionally, there were many immigrants from continental Europe, including "swarms of French" (most of them protestant Huguenots) and significant numbers from the Low Countries and Germany, as well as smaller numbers from the Iberian Peninsula (many of them Jews), more "exotic" parts of Europe, and the wider globe.[34]

---

30. A. L. Hayward, *Lives Of The Most Remarkable Criminals,* 1927, pp.420-423.
31. Anon, *The History of the Lives and Actions of Jonathan Wild, Thief-Taker*, 1725, p.2
32. P. J. Grosley, *A tour to London; or, New observations on England, and its inhabitants,* vol. 1, 1772, p.63.
33. E. Silverthorne (Ed.), *Deposition Book of Richard Wyatt*, 1978, p.51.
34. Anon (A Citizen in London), *The Vices of the cities of London and Westminster trac'd from their original,* 1751, p.20.

By the 1730s, one observer thought that there were at least 20,000 Frenchmen in the capital.[35] Even the Danes were numerous enough to have their own coffee shop, while a fashion for black servants led some to complain, in exaggerated terms, about the "swarms of negroes" to be found in London's streets.[36]

This process of inward migration had numerous ramifications. Some immigrants adjusted to urban life successfully, or at least survived in the capital. However, many did not, and joined the ranks of the destitute. As the weather deteriorated, summer arrivals were often "turned adrift" from their seasonal employments and forced to live off their dwindling savings. They would fall into bad company and start to "loiter" about the City. When their money ran out, many would "turn thieves out of necessity".[37]

The Metropolis could be a harsh and unforgiving environment, especially to newcomers. In 1728, a recently arrived boy was found dead from starvation, inside a chest, at a market in Moorfields. He was apparently a: "... poor friendless creature who had wander'd to Town, and having liv'd a long time without lodging or food, had got into that chest for want of a better shelter".[38] Many people in the capital, both male and female, had no accessible kith or kin who could provide assistance in personal adversity, such as unemployment, or whose presence might occasion shame, should they have recourse to crime as a solution to their problems. Significantly, over half of the women indicted at the Old Bailey between 1791 and 1793 had originally come from outside the London area.[39]

Irishmen, in particular, were heavily associated with offending. Some contemporary observers, unconcerned about socio-economic determinants, even speculated as to why, once in England, through some: "...remarkable fatality, the natives of Ireland are more frequently brought to an exemplary punishment than their neighbouring islanders".[40] In an attempt at reducing

35. M. Gonzales, *London in 1731*, 1888, p.192.
36. *Public Advertiser*, 21 September, 1767.
37. Anon (By a Lover of his Country), *The Thief-Catcher; or, Villainy Detected*, 1753, p.43.
38. *London Evening Post*, 27 July, 1728.
39. P. King, "Female offenders, work and life-cycle change in late-eighteenth-century London", 1990, pp.72-74.
40. W. Smith, *An Authentic Account of the Life and Memoirs of Mr. William Smith*, 4th edn., 1750, p.1.

the large numbers of impoverished people arriving from Ireland, an Act of 1713 stipulated that ships' masters who brought them over would face a fine of five pounds per head, and be required to take them back.[41] This statute was hard to enforce and had little effect.

Responses to the Indigent

How could the Metropolitan authorities deal with this influx of impoverished people? One answer lay in a battery of statutory powers. Historically, these had distinguished "ordinary" paupers from vagrants. However, by the eighteenth century, such a distinction was becoming increasingly attenuated, partly because the Vagrant Removal Costs Act of 1700 encouraged parishes to define their paupers as vagrants, so that the cost of removing them fell on the County. There was a plethora of other legislation dealing with the destitute. In 1717, it was claimed that at least 30 Acts had been passed that were, in some way, concerned with regulating the very poor, even if many of them were: "...very difficult to be understood by inferior officers, who were often principally to be concern'd in their execution".[42] A modern estimate suggests that 28 statutes were passed between 1700 and 1824 that affected the regulation of vagrancy.[43]

In theory, many of the arrivals from the provinces could have been removed from the Metropolitan area. Under the Poor Relief Act of 1662 (13 & 14 Car. II c.12), sometimes (if erroneously) known as the Settlement Act, individual parishes had a legal obligation to relieve their own paupers, if they were destitute, with money raised from the local poor rate. Such assistance was usually administered via "out relief", which might involve payment of rent, food, and the donation of cash. This right could be enforced in person, via an application to local justices.[44]

However, a pauper's right to assistance was dependent upon his having a legal settlement in the parish from which he claimed support. This was

41. O. Ruffhead, *The Statutes at Large from Magna Carta to ... 1761*, vol. iv, 1763, p.602.
42. L. Braddon, *The miseries of the poor are a national sin, shame, and charge...* 1717, p.1.
43. N. Rogers, "Policing the Poor in Eighteenth-Century London", 1991, p.128.
44. L. Charlesworth, "Why Is It A Crime To Be Poor?", 1999, p.151.

determined by the 1662 Act, which largely remained in force until 1795 and in a residual form until 1834.[45] The statute was aimed at establishing the parish to which paupers "belonged" and, indirectly, limiting their mobility outside that community. In theory, when a man (or woman) permanently left his parish he had to take a Settlement Certificate, which guaranteed that the parish would pay for his "removal" costs from a host parish if he needed welfare. Settlement was most obviously acquired at birth. Additionally, it might be gained, *inter alia*, by marriage into a parish, being hired there for more than a year and a day, having an apprenticeship with a local resident, or buying/renting property to a certain value within its borders. Settlement ceased in any parish upon acquisition of a legal settlement in another.

Removal was achieved by obtaining an order from two or more JPs. This was usually issued after the magistrates had received a complaint from the overseers of the poor or the churchwardens of the relevant parish, who themselves normally acted after the subject had approached them for relief. The JPs then examined him/her as to residence. A handbook for justices suggested a pro-forma examination in which the vagrant swore that he was:

> ...born and bred up (as he is informed) in the parish of ... and hath not gained a lawful settlement in any parish or place subsequent to the said place of his birth.

Alternatively, it could stipulate a lawful settlement gained since birth, but different to that in which he then resided.[46]

Nevertheless, there were major limitations on the implementation of the 1662 Act. People from outside England and Wales, such as Irishmen and those from the continent, were not properly within its remit. Nor were those who came from "extra parochial" locations, such as the London Foundling Hospital or The Bridewell. The parishes situated around these large establishments

45. A. Browning, *English Historical Documents*, 1660-1714, vol. viii, 1957, pp.464-465. Interestingly, the preamble to the Settlement Act 1662 had expressly mentioned the cities of London and Westminster as being a particular problem when discussing the increase in the nation's mobile poor.

46. J. Higgs, *A Guide to Justices or Modern English Precedents for the Direction of Justices of the Peace and their Clerks*, 2nd edn., 1742, p.228.

were not willing to have their numerous former inmates foisted on them.[47] Even where it did apply, there could be considerable problems in ascertaining settlement, because of the variety of mechanisms by which it could be acquired and (consequently) lost. A removal order could only be issued if it could be established that the pauper possessed a settlement elsewhere.

It was notorious that legal disputes about this responsibility were hugely expensive. Several Metropolitan barristers had significant legal practices that were largely based on settlement actions.[48] Ignoring legal costs, the expense of physically moving vagrants and those being returned under the 1662 Act could also be considerable. Even returning someone to the Home Counties might cost several pounds. In the 1750s, Middlesex tried to economise on the cost of "ragged persons" who were regularly brought to the Clerkenwell House of Correction by local beadles, and marshalled there pending return to their native parishes. They unilaterally reduced the normal allowance of 6d a day to only 2d. As a result, returnees were kept in exceptionally harsh conditions, both in the house of correction and on the journey home. This scrimping led to the death of James Buckland, a man of almost 60, who died one freezing March while awaiting passage. Some complained that the JPs had resolved: "…to starve the poor to save the county expense".[49] Those being passed to and fro between contending parishes would often experience particularly "cruel and severe treatment" in the process.[50]

A statute from 1699 had attempted to enhance the process of removal. It provided that constables were no longer to convey vagrants to the next parish, to be handed over to their counterparts for onward transmission, but, instead, were required to return them directly to their parish of settlement or, if they were from another county, to the nearest parish in the neighbouring shire. In theory, the constables would then have their expenses reimbursed by their local High Constables on the production of appropriate documentation. Unfortunately, this system does not appear to have worked

47. *The Inhabitants of the Parish of Clerkenwell v Bridewell* (1699) 1 Lord Raymond 549.

48. A.N. May, *The Bar and the Old Bailey, 1750–1850*, 2003, p.11.

49. J. Ilive, *A scheme for the employment of all persons sent as disorderly to the house of correction in Clerkenwell*, 1759, p.12.

50. T. Gilbert, *Observations Upon Orders and Resolutions of the House of Commons with Respect to the Poor, Vagrants, and Houses of Correction*, 1735, p.11.

terribly well, requiring further reform in 1713.[51] The Vagrancy Act of that year proposed that passed vagrants be sent back to their place of settlement via a chain of Houses of Correction.[52] This statute was not a huge improvement on its predecessor.

There were also local attempts at enhancing the system. For example, after 1757, Middlesex, like some other counties, had an official "contractor" who was specifically employed to pass vagrants back to their places of settlement from the Clerkenwell House of Correction.[53] In 1760, in a similar attempt at streamlining the system within their own county, the Surrey Quarter Sessions settled on Thomas Buskin as their own contractor. It was hoped that this would reduce the endemic frauds that were being perpetrated by constables who had previously been involved in the process. Buskin, a Southwark man, was paid £250 a year plus 3d. a day per person to go through the county, especially its urban parts, picking up vagrants discharged from Houses of Correction and then moving them in covered wagons: "...according to the directions of their several passes".[54]

Even if a man or woman was sent back to their parish of origin there was no guarantee that they would not swiftly return to the Metropolis. This was a sufficiently common occurrence that a justices' handbook of the era could produce a *pro forma* affidavit to commit an individual to a house of correction who had "returned back to inhabit in our said parish".[55] In 1755, Anne Parker received six months' imprisonment when she was found wandering in the Strand, two weeks after being passed back to Chatham in Kent.[56]

As a result of these problems, both the Settlement Act and the forced return of vagrants seem to have been applied extremely selectively, being largely confined to those who were likely to become an immediate charge

51. J. Kent, "The Centre and the Localities: State formation and Parish government in England, circa 1640-1740", 1995, p.370.
52. N. Rogers, "Policing the Poor in Eighteenth-Century London", 1991, p.140.
53. J. Ilive, *A scheme for the employment of all persons sent as disorderly to the house of correction in Clerkenwell*, 1759, p.12.
54. Anon (Quarter Sessions), *Orders, resolutions, report, and proposals for, and relating to, the passing vagrants in the County of Surrey*, 1760, pp.18-22.
55. J. Higgs, *A Guide to Justices or Modern English Precedents for the Direction of Justices of the Peace and their Clerks*, 2nd edn., 1742, p.217.
56. N. Rogers, "Policing the Poor in Eighteenth-Century London", 1991, p.130.

to the parish, such as the elderly or infirm. Ironically, the system probably worked best in effecting very local returns. For example, when Henry Norris ordered that Samuel Bass and his wife be removed from St John's, Hackney, to Stoke Newington, their place of settlement, the order merely required that a beadle accompany the couple back to their native parish.[57]

In theory, statutory rewards could be issued for arresting vagrants. Initially, these were set at two shillings and, after the advent of the 1744 Vagrancy Act, five and sometimes even ten shillings was available. There were also occasional local initiatives. In 1729, for example, St Martin-in-the-Fields provided that a reward of two shillings would be paid to anyone who found a beggar within the parish who was committed to the house of correction, sent to the local workhouse (if "belonging" to the parish and entitled to relief) or passed back to his parish of legal settlement.[58] However, rewards were normally given at the discretion of magistrates, while constables and beadles were often reluctant to press for remuneration, for fear of attracting popular hostility. As a result, only about one in five arrests resulted in payment.[59]

Significant but not enormous numbers of men and women were "removed" from (and within) the Metropolitan area. In Middlesex, approximately 750 vagrants were "passed" each year in the early 1760s, a figure that rose to over 1,000 in 1790. Even so, it is apparent that many urban justices resisted demands for a more systematic incarceration and removal of vagrants and unsettled people.[60] In many cases, it was easier and cheaper to pay small amounts of casually administered "out-relief", or commit to a workhouse, rather than attempt to enforce a return.

The Workhouses Act of 1723 (9 George 1 c.7) greatly encouraged the spread and use of such institutions within the bills of mortality.[61] It authorised churchwardens and overseers of the poor to construct workhouses where they had the support of their vestries, and to offer accommodation in them as an alternative to out-relief; if it was refused no other form of assistance would be forthcoming. It also allowed parishes to combine as unions to set

57. R. Paley (Ed.), *Justice in 18th-Century Hackney*, 1991, pp.194-195.
58. *London Journal*, 15 March 1729.
59. N. Rogers, "Policing the Poor in Eighteenth-Century London", 1991, p.130.
60. N. Rogers, "Policing the Poor in Eighteenth-Century London", 1991, p.138.
61. A. Browning, *English Historical Documents, 1660-1714,* vol. viii, 1957, pp.464-465.

up workhouses. Numerous establishments were founded in the Metropolitan area over ensuing decades, though their conditions were harsh. In 1732, Matthew Marryot claimed that confining poor people to them was a: "... sort of punishment inflicted on them for no reason but their poverty".[62]

Rise of the Middle Class

Although a majority of the Metropolitan populace could be described as being from the "labouring poor" and, as in the countryside, only a tiny proportion were upper class by any definition, the "middling orders" were very much stronger in the capital than they were in rural areas. Many more skilled artisans, craftsmen, merchants, and shopkeepers were found amongst its inhabitants. Urban areas also tended to contain more finely graded social hierarchies than were found in the country. As the century advanced, both the emerging middle class and the working class were sub-divided into increasingly complex layers. For example, it seems that the final decades of the eighteenth century were important to the emergence of a lower middle class with its own values and consciousness.[63] Similarly, Francis Place noted that, for much of the eighteenth century, the manners of working men had been so similar that they "differed in no material particular". The most skilled members of this class were the most prone to drunkenness, as they had the largest disposable incomes. However, by the 1820s, the difference between skilled workmen and common labourers was as marked as that found between the skilled man and his employer. "Respectability" had grown amongst key sections of the working class, especially its upper echelons, who were, by then, far more: "...orderly and decent, and much more cleanly in their persons".[64]

The Metropolis offered the chance if not, for many, the reality of social mobility and an opportunity to rise to a higher social position. There was published guidance specifically aimed at successful Metropolitan men who

62. M. Marryot, *An Account of Several Work-houses for Employing and Maintaining the Poor*, 1732, Preface.
63. A. Simpson, "The Ordeal of St. Sepulchre's", 2006, pp.368-369.
64. F. Place, *Improvement of the Working People*, 1834, pp.1-6.

wished to behave in the genteel manner that properly matched their newly achieved financial status, so that they could: "...appear in a drawing-room, or before people of the first taste, without fear and trembling".[65] This chance was seized by some elements of the urban population, and undermined traditional notions of hierarchy and subordination, whereby some were placed by: "Him in high stations, others in a low estate. To the former he hath given authority and power, to the Latter he enjoins submission and obedience".[66] Indeed, the foolish desire to live beyond one's station in life became a stock explanation for Metropolitan criminal careers, being blamed for ruining many ordinary people by encouraging them to: "...live beyond what their labour or trade would allow, and by inducing them to take illegal methods to procure money for that purpose".[67]

Although this growing urban middle class was aspirational, it was also fairly vulnerable. The expansion of commerce meant that its members gradually acquired a plethora of valuable goods, such as pewter, silver and timepieces, as well as more traditional items like jewellery. (In 1798, 120,000 watches were made in Clerkenwell alone).[68] The more prosperous of the middle ranks began to fill their houses with bric-à-brac, stocked them with wine rather than ale, and purchased expensive clothes.[69] However, these developments also made their homes potentially lucrative targets for the capital's many burglars and housebreakers. Unfortunately, the middling orders could not afford to defend themselves behind high walls and armed retainers, unlike:

> Rich men [who] had ample means of protecting themselves by their attendants and servants, by riding in their carriages, and by other preventions.[70]

65. Anon, *The Man of Manners: Or, Plebeian Polish'd*, 2nd edn., 1737, p.iv.
66. T. Broughtan, *Serious Advice and Warning to Servants, More especially those of the Nobility and Gentry*, 6th edn., 1763, p.7.
67. A. L. Hayward, *Lives Of The Most Remarkable Criminals*, 1927, p.81.
68. G. Rude, *Hanoverian London*, 1971, pp.120-129.
69. J. Rule, *Albion's People, English Society, 1714-1815*, 1992, p.85.
70. Parliamentary debate in 1792 on the Middlesex Justices Act, in W. Cobbett, *The Parliamentary History of England From the Earliest Period to the Year 1803*, vol. xxix, 1817, p.1467.

Similarly, when it came to the risk posed by highwaymen, they were not like people in:

> ...affluent circumstances [who] are generally attended by servants well armed and are never stopped but when they have omitted this slight precaution.[71]

Of course, they took whatever steps they could to secure themselves and their property. They might keep fierce dogs and have loaded firearms, such as pistols and blunderbusses, readily to hand in their houses, weapons that they were willing to use when necessary. In 1789, for example, an Aldgate merchant's son used a pistol to shoot and kill a burglar. When he subsequently claimed that he thought the intruder was about to rape his sister, the coroner's jury swiftly returned a verdict of justifiable homicide, even though the dead man was nowhere near her room.[72]

Nevertheless, crime remained a matter of acute and growing concern to this class. John Osborn, writing in 1735 about the lives of executed criminals, acknowledged that amongst those who professed to be highly educated such a subject might be viewed with disdain. However, amongst the "middling sort of people" there would be many who would be glad to read about something that was within the "circle of their own comprehension".[73] This concern had political consequences. During the passage of the controversial Middlesex Justices Act of 1792 through Parliament, it was claimed by Lord Grenville that the Bill was not really needed to protect the rich; instead, it was: "...calculated principally for the protection of that class of individuals who had it not in their power to protect themselves".[74] Their influence meant that the era saw a growing demand for effective local government and policing, as expectations of public safety, security and comfort rose.[75] It was also important because, although the plebeian character of many of the criminals who were on the receiving end of the Metropolitan justice system

71. J. W. von Archenholz, *A picture of England: Containing a description of the laws, customs and manners of England,* 1790, p.182.
72. L. James, *The Middle Class: A History,* 2006, p.202.
73. A. L. Hayward, *Lives Of The Most Remarkable Criminals,* 1927, p.9.
74. *The Calcutta Gazette,* 13 December 1792.
75. V. Harding, "Controlling a complex metropolis, 1650-1750", 2001, p.35.

has attracted much attention over the past 50 years, it was the middling social orders that were the prime movers within that system.

Social Segregation

The eighteenth-century Metropolis witnessed a steady decline in the early modern intermixing of urban rich and poor, both on a geographical and a personal basis. The city became more socially stratified and segregated. By the end of the century, it could be observed that those of "rank and fortune" usually resided in the West End parishes, while merchants, bankers and commercial men were to be found in the City. The middle ranks were diffused everywhere in the Metropolis. However, many of the lower orders, made up of labourers and journeymen, resided in the populous parishes to the east of the City, in and around Tower Hamlets, where, even by the 1680s, many of the inhabitants were noted as being impoverished.[76] Concentrations of poor people could also be found in the various parishes to the north of the Square Mile and, south of the river, in Southwark. Increased segregation meant that the labouring poor who lived in the Metropolis were: "...compelled to reside in distinct districts together, for want of cottages, or lodging-rooms, in the more opulent quarters of the town".[77] Commuting to work became increasingly common for both the upper and middling social orders. At the start of the century, even the richest City merchants had often resided within the Square Mile, living near their businesses. However, as the 1700s advanced, many of these men moved their families to the smart and fashionable squares of the West End and travelled to work in a carriage.

This process had many important social consequences. Very significantly, it eroded "vertical" connections between the classes, in which the capital's social components interacted closely with those immediately above or below them in what contemporaries sometimes referred to as the "law of

---

76. Anon, *The Proceedings of His Majesties justices of peace, at the sessions of Oyer and Terminer: held at Hick's-Hall, September the 6th, 1684, for the tryal of the constables, &c. of the hamlets of Spittle-fields, and Bethnal-Green*, 1694, pp.1-4.
77. P. Colquhoun, *An account of a meat and soup charity established in the metropolis in the year 1797*, 1797, p.4.

subordination", in favour of "horizontal" divisions in which the various elements of society had as their primary reference point those of a similar status to themselves. It allowed the development of areas that had a nefarious reputation and identity, many of which would linger into the nineteenth century. In them, criminals could find some degree of protection from the law and public surveillance, receiving support and concealment in networks of alleys that were difficult for law enforcement agencies to penetrate. Amongst these areas, to varying degrees, were the Mint and the Clink in Southwark, and Whitefriars, Alsatia, Spitalfields, Whitechapel, and the Newgate-Cripplegate area, north of the River.[78] A statute from 1724 also noted that many "wicked" people were evading debt in the Middlesex parishes of Stepney and Wapping.[79] In the early century, the area around Drury Lane was infested with prostitutes, bawds, and pimps who attracted other forms of serious crime.[80]

Inevitably, there was growing anxiety about the dangers posed by these increasingly alien parts of the metropolis. Some even argued for the introduction of what, today, might be termed a "surveillance society", in which each house in London's "suspected and beggarly places" would carry a board clearly stating the number, gender and quality of its inhabitants, and would be banded together with several other similar residences, one designated man having a duty to inspect them, and report any changes or suspicious activity.[81]

The general change in social attitudes had other significant consequences. London was, traditionally, the primary centre for the nation's artisan manufacturing. Historically, this had been rooted in the apprenticeship system, whereby young men were bound to a trade for seven years, before they were allowed set up as masters on their own account. During the course of the eighteenth century, there was a clear progression from apprentices residing in their masters' houses to living in separate accommodation, beyond their immediate control. This applied to most occupations, from youths working

78. J. Marriott, "The Spatiality of the Poor in Eighteenth-century London", 2003, p.130.

79. O. Ruffhead, *The Statutes at Large*, 1763, p.533. It also provided that those assaulting men trying to serve process on them could be transported for seven years.

80. F. Poussin, *Pretty Doings in a Protestant Nation*, 1734, p.35.

81. Anon (Philo Patriae), *A Full and Genuine Account of the Murder of Mrs. Robinson, by Elton Lewis*, 1735, p.26.

for skilled craftsmen to clerks training to be attorneys.[82] Many feared that this development actively engendered crime.

Decline in Communitarianism

In part a cause, in part a result, of growing social segregation, there was also a marked decline in what might loosely be termed "communitarianism" at all social levels, in England generally, and London in particular. This was to be one of the most important themes of the era (and in this book). The large amount of unpaid public service performed by laymen, from all but the lowest social strata, had been a vital feature of early seventeenth-century urban life. This stretched from the gentleman acting as a justice of the peace for his neighbourhood, via the "middling" social orders performing the unpaid part-time duty of local constable for a year or two, to ordinary rate payers appearing on lesser juries or serving their turn as nocturnal watchmen. There were a considerable number of other offices to be filled. The result of this tradition of amateur service was that much administration was carried out without cost to either central or local government, something that meant that full-time paid officials, at both the neighbourhood and national level, were few and far between.

A post-Restoration decline in popular willingness to discharge these traditional obligations was to have a profound effect on Metropolitan society. This change was probably motivated by a number of factors, including a general growth in individualism, social segregation, geographic mobility and the pressures of time brought about by an expanding working day. Whatever the reasons, the results were the same in the London area:

> Selfishness so far prevails over the Minds and Dispositions of all Ranks of People, that few or none think themselves under any kind of moral Obligation to serve the Public, unless they are paid for it.

82. C. Brooks, *Lawyers, Litigation and English Society since 1450*, 1998, p.122.

During the "long" eighteenth century, albeit at different times and to varying degrees, the work of watchmen, constables, and urban JPs came to be dominated by financial reward rather than notions of civic duty. As a result, the city's inhabitants began to distinguish themselves from their own government, making them "two distinct bodies".[83] This problem was not special to London. Even eighteenth-century New York experienced a serious shortage of suitable citizens willing to serve as night watchmen, constables, and justices.[84] Nevertheless, it was particularly acute in the capital.

A decline in medieval notions of "communal" policing may also have manifested itself in a more general reluctance to become involved in assisting the criminal justice process without a tangible inducement. In theory, as the jurist William Blackstone noted, any private individuals who were present when a felony was committed were obliged to arrest the criminal involved, and could be fined or imprisoned if he escaped through their negligence.[85] Similarly, if officers attempted to make an arrest, and the suspect resisted: "...all those persons who by chance are present are obliged if the constable desires it to come to their aid".[86] A constable dealing with an affray or assault might also ask any member of the public "within view" to assist him in suppressing it. In all of these situations, a failure to provide assistance was technically an offence. As a result, in 1732, John Bright and Joseph Windsor were summoned to attend petty sessions for failing to assist a headborough who was attempting to carry an arrested man to the New Prison.[87] Nevertheless, by the 1750s, a High Constable could claim that the obligation to render assistance: "...has of late years been treated with contempt by the commonality".[88] Of course, this should not be exaggerated; by modern standards, members of the public were remarkably pro-active in

83. Anon (A Citizen of London), *The Vices of the Cities of London and Westminster, Trac'd from their Original,* 1751, p.9.
84. D. Greenberg, "The Effectiveness of Law Enforcement in Eighteenth-century New York", 1975, p.174 and p.207.
85. W. Blackstone, *Commentaries on the Laws of England,* 1765-9, vol.4, p.289.
86. M. V. Muyden (Ed.), *A foreign View of England in the reigns of George I and George II,* 1902, pp.116-117.
87. R. Paley (Ed.), *Justice in 18th-Century Hackney,* 1991, p.96.
88. S. Welch, *Observations on the Office of Constable,* 1754, p.6.

dealing with crime. However, it seems that this was sometimes contingent on a reward being available, as was often the case by the early 1700s.

Power

In the modern era, the concept of "agency", the degree to which people can influence the course of their own lives and, perhaps, of those around them, has become a central theme in academic discourse. However, no individual or social group in eighteenth- century England, whether rich or poor, was either devoid of agency or an entirely free agent. The poor may have had much less power than the rich, but they were certainly not without influence, even if it did not usually have an expressly political manifestation; popular protest was likely to involve attempts at preserving "traditional" rights as an alternative to those governed by financial exchange.[89]

An awareness of the practical limitations on their own power also placed firm constraints on the "political" nation. In the first half of the century, this encouraged the authorities to enforce the "moral economy", whereby a range of economic crimes were committed by those who drove up the price of corn and other victuals, thereby occasioning: "...uneasiness, discontent, and murmuring, especially among the lower sort of people". Such crimes included forestalling (buying up commodities before they came to market) and other forms of speculation in foodstuffs. Those convicted for a third offence of this type could be pilloried and imprisoned.[90] However, the authorities normally appear to have been careful to ensure that the Metropolis was kept reasonably well supplied with grain and provisions, even in difficult times, making such crimes of limited significance in the conurbation.

In London, the concentration of people and the difficulty of manoeuvre in the confined spaces of an urban environment, combined with the authorities' substantial dependence on relatively poor people for law enforcement, whether as watchmen, substitute constables, or soldiers, placed particularly

89. J. Lea, "Social Crime Revisited", 1999, pp.308-309.

90. J. Gonson, *The Charge of Sir John Gonson Knt. To the Grand Jury of the Royalty of the Tower of London, and Liberties and Precincts thereof*, 1728, p.10 and p.123.

firm constraints on what could, and could not, be done. Illustrations of these limitations on both state and local government power abound. For a very specific example can be considered the situation that developed in 1744, when the leading Metropolitan magistrate, Sir Thomas de Veil, yielded to political pressure to deal with a protest by British servants against the employment of foreign domestics. He arrested three of the protesters, and held them in his house in Bow Street. However, these men were subsequently freed when their comrades stormed the building and released them. So powerful was the "mob" that his successor, Henry Fielding, referred to it as the "fourth estate".

Even more significant was the opprobrium heaped on magistrates such as Samuel Gillam who (very reluctantly) ordered troops to fire on a pro-Wilkes crowd in Southwark, on 10th May 1768, and was subsequently indicted for murder (though acquitted). His treatment may have contributed to the authorities' slow response to the Gordon Riots of June 1780.[91] Ostensibly rallying to support the eccentric Scottish Lord, George Gordon, in his campaign to uphold the Protestant religion, and aided by a slow institutional response, the rioters overwhelmed the City for more than five days, indulging in widespread looting, robbery and arson. There were anti-authority overtones to the riots. For example, both Lord Mansfield's house in Lincoln's Inn and Newgate prison were burnt down. The Lord Mayor, Brackley Kennet, was openly afraid of the crowd: "I must be cautious what I do lest I bring the mob to my house".[92] JPs were also aware of the retribution visited on more interventionist justices, and were intimidated by the demolition of Fielding and Hyde's houses. Many later complained of their "spiritless conduct".[93] The riots were only brought to an end by large-scale military intervention from outside the capital.

91. *The Gentleman's Magazine,* 1780, vol. 50, p.265.
92. I. Gilmour, *Riot, Risings and Revolution: Governance and Violence in Eighteenth-century England,* 1992, p.356.
93. *The Gentleman's Magazine,* 1780, vol. 50, pp.314-316.

The Urban Day

The "long" eighteenth century witnessed a major change in the tempo of urban life. The medieval city had largely shut down in the early evening, after which time there was a well-enforced nightly curfew. This was gradually abandoned as the urban day grew steadily longer; shops became more numerous and opened later, and the number of late entertainments, such as balls and dances, performances at the theatre and opera also multiplied.[94] Additionally, taverns, coffee shops and teahouses seem to have kept progressively longer hours. An analysis of the *Old Bailey Sessions Papers* suggest that, during the 1750s, the witnesses at that court rose shortly after 6 am, began work a little before 7 am, finishing at an average time of 6.50 pm. Although unskilled labourers often finished in the early afternoon, skilled craftsmen, apprentices, and masters might work until seven or even eight in the evening. Most witnesses went to bed shortly before 11 pm.[95]

This expansion of the "active" day into the evenings and night was a European wide phenomenon, and appears to have been particularly marked around the end of the seventeenth century, even affecting the hours at which meals were taken and people slept. It prompted demands for improved nocturnal policing and security so that the extended day could be enjoyed securely. Although the change was the result of a variety of factors, it was partly linked to the advent of moderately effective street lighting in the decades after 1660.

Urban street lighting

Prior to the Restoration, lighting in most urban areas had been confined to requiring householders to place candle lanterns outside their homes. This was often ineffectually enforced, although, in the City, anyone who neglected to do this prior to the Watch coming on duty was supposed to be presented to the Court of Aldermen.[96] However, between 1684 and 1694, and following the

94. J. M. Beattie, *Policing and Punishment in London, 1660–1750*, 2001, p.83.
95. H. J. Voth, "Time and Work in Eighteenth-Century London", 1998, pp.32–33.
96. J. Howel, *Londinopolis*, 1657, p.79 and p.392, and, Anon (A Member of Parliament), *An explanation of the proposed scheme for better paving, repairing, cleaning and lighting the squares, streets,* c.1769, pp.8–9.

lead of Paris and Amsterdam, oil lanterns were introduced to important areas of the Square Mile. As a result, some areas were relatively well illuminated until well after sunset. In 1690, at several places in the City, such a lantern was placed in front of every tenth house so that, together, they: "…all seem to be one great Solar-Light".[97] By the early 1700s, a visiting German, Johann Archenholz, thought that the City was very well lit by continental standards, though this was not necessarily a demanding comparison. Additionally, in London, unlike some continental countries, all available lamps were lit even on nights in which there was a full, or nearly full, moon.[98]

Westminster lagged considerably behind the Square Mile in this respect. However, proponents of improvement there stressed the valuable role of lighting in controlling crime and preventing carriages from crashing in the dark. It was claimed that robberies and assaults were committed during the night that: "…might not be carried on, or the persons escape unobserved, if lamps were placed at proper distances". In 1761 an Act established commissioners for paving, cleaning and lighting the streets of Westminster.

Even in the Square Mile, the new methods of street lighting were only a *relative* improvement. Indicative of this, in a typical evening altercation, a witness could be asked how he could see a knife "at five yards distance". He stressed that it was a bright star-lit night.[99] Night remained by far the most dangerous time for most forms of serious crime, and it was always advisable to avoid side streets after dark.[100] Nevertheless, some people, such as surgeons, midwives, physicians and ministers of religion attending the sick or those who were giving birth, night-soil workers clearing privies, and those going to markets, had no alternative to being out late at night and had to accept the risks that it entailed. For example, in 1726, an apothecary was attacked, robbed and tied up by three armed footpads while visiting a patient in Covent Garden during the small hours of the night.[101] Unfortunately, risk did

97. C. Koslofsky, "Court Culture and Street Lighting in Seventeenth-Century Europe", 2002, pp.745-751.
98. J. W. von Archenholz, *A picture of England: Containing a description of the laws, customs and manners of England*, 1790, pp.178-179.
99. OBSP, *Trial of Antonio da Silva*, 6 May 1761.
100. W. Clowes, *Leigh's New Picture of London*, 1819, p.101.
101. *Weekly Journal, or The British Gazetteer*, 5 February 1726.

not begin at such a late hour. In 1731, an observer claimed that London was: "...notorious for the danger persons are exposed to who walk the Streets after ten at Night".[102]

Alcohol Consumption

The eighteenth-century Metropolis experienced some novel social problems. Foremost amongst them were very high levels of alcohol consumption, which was centred on the Metropolis. This was largely the result of the availability of cheap spirits. The distillation of gin, in particular, had become increasingly prevalent in the city after 1688, its use being popularized by the Court of William of Orange. Unlike brandy, it could be made from domestic grain. Gin consumption accelerated in the 1720s as a result of cheap local production, the spirit often being laced with fruit flavours. According to one estimate (and they are inherently very difficult to make), annual consumption of British spirits grew from 0.36 gallons per capita in 1700, to 1.74 gallons in 1735, and a peak of 2.21 gallons in 1743. After 1743, however, consumption gradually declined to 0.59 gallons per capita in 1771.[103] Gin was qualitatively different to beer (the consumption of which does not appear to have declined significantly), as it seemed to produce a "kind of instantaneous drunkenness". Examples of people drinking themselves to death abounded, such as the beggar who, having obtained a small amount of money, quaffed six quarterns at one sitting in a Portugal Street tavern.[104] For the first time, heavy consumption of alcohol extended to females, one Newgate ordinary urging that the: "...fashionable beastly practice of women's drinking, can't be enough deplored".[105]

Alcohol abuse had numerous social consequences. It seemed to undermine hierarchy and deference, as drunkards would: "...insult and abuse all

102. *The Gentleman's Magazine*, 1731, vol. 1, pp.59-60.
103. J. Warner and N. Her, "Can Legislation Prevent Debauchery? Mother Gin and Public Health in 18th-Century England", 2001, p.379.
104. *Applebee's Original Weekly Journal*, 6 May 1721.
105. *The Ordinary of Newgate, His Account of the Behaviour, Confession, and Dying Words of the Malefactors who were executed at Tyburn on Tuesday the 9th of July, 1745*, 1745, p.20.

persons, without distinction". Inebriates of "inferior rank" would manifest a general disobedience to authority.[106] It was also feared that heavy drinkers, having spent all their money on gin, would steal to support their habit, rather like modern drug addicts.[107] The magistrate Nathaniel Blackerby thought that this was the principal cause of street robbery. Even worse, and perhaps more plausibly, it was claimed that imbibing cheap spirits spawned violent crimes.[108] Alcohol certainly made it much easier for minor disagreements to become vicious, like that between a cobbler and tailor who spent a night drinking together, then quarrelled and fought until one was dead.[109]

Concern about this phenomenon led to a coalition of reformers and pressure groups, including the Metropolis's two main benches of justices, the Royal College of Physicians, and the Middlesex Grand Jurymen, campaigning for action to be taken. This initially saw fruit in an Act of 1729, which placed a duty of five shillings per gallon on spirits, a £20 license fee for retailing them, and a fine of £10 for those caught hawking gin in the streets. This statute was widely evaded, leading to its repeal in 1733.[110]

However, gin production continued unabated. A report commissioned by alarmed Middlesex JPs in 1736, and based on information provided by the High Constable for Westminster, suggested that in the Middlesex part of the Metropolitan area alone there were 7,044 houses and shops where gin and brandy were sold. It was assumed that many other establishments had been overlooked. In some areas, one in six houses were involved in the trade.[111] This report led to the passing of the Gin Act in the same year, which attempted to regulate the industry, though its numerous failings also required repeal within a fairly short period. Although the problem abated during the latter

106. N. Blackerby, *The Speech of Nathaniel Blackerby Esq... On Saturday, April 1. 1738, To the Justices, High Bailiff, High Constable, and Petty constables of the City and Liberty of Westminster*, 1738, pp.3-4.

107. T. Wilson, *Distilled spirituous liquors the bane of the nation being some considerations humbly offered to the legislature...*, 1736, p.vi and p.xi of the Appendix.

108. *The Times*, June 25, 1785, p.4.

109. *Weekly Journal, or the British Gazetteer*, 27 June 1730.

110. J. White, "The Slow but Sure Poyson: The Representation of Gin and Its Drinkers, 1736-1751", 2003, p.40.

111. T. Wilson, *Distilled spirituous liquors the bane of the nation being some considerations humbly offered to the legislature*, 1736, p.vi and p.xi of Appendix.

part of the century, observers in the 1780s were still complaining about the number of Metropolitan gin shops and the manner in which they inflamed: "...bad men and women to commit every species of wickedness".[112]

112. J. Dornford, *Seven Letters to the Lords of the Privy Council, on the Police*, 1785, p.ix.

CHAPTER 3

METROPOLITAN CRIME

Definitions of Crime

What is a crime? In the modern era, this has been the subject of much jurisprudential debate, with definitions that stress its special characteristics when compared to a civil wrong. For example, that it is normally dealt with by an action brought in the name of the state, rather than an individual, is usually heard in a specialist court, and that the court's decision is primarily designed to punish the law breaker rather than compensate his victim. Similar definitions were reached in the eighteenth century. Thus, according to one contemporary observer, criminal actions were aimed at producing: "…some penalty or punishment in the party sued, be it corporal or pecuniary, and are called actions penal".[1] Even so, the dividing line between civil and criminal actions was not always as precise as it is today. For example, "criminal conversation", in which the cuckolded male victim of his wife's adultery could sue her paramour for compensation, the measure of which was influenced by a variety of factors, was a civil action despite its name.

As in the modern era, there appears to have been a distinction in the eighteenth-century mind between administrative or regulatory offences that were *mala prohibita* and those, like murder, that were *mala per se*. In the 1750s, for example, fishermen in the lower Thames were punished for throwing out nets from their boats that would catch undersized fish, contrary to an Act of Parliament and in "Defiance of the Laws of Conservancy".[2] It is unlikely that they, or their neighbours, viewed such matters as being quite

1. J. Impey, *The New Instructor Clericalis, Stating the Authority, Jurisdiction, and Modern Practice of the Court of King's Bench*, 1782, p.5.
2. Anon, *Low-Life: or One Half of the World Knows not how the Other Half Live*, 2nd edn, 1755, p.84.

the same as mainstream crimes, though it is (and was) not always easy to distinguish between the two.

Legal Classification of Crimes

Legally, the era's crimes can be divided into several, sometimes overlapping, categories. For example, summary offences—petty crimes that were triable by magistrates sitting on their own—can be distinguished from indictable offences, more serious crimes that could only be prosecuted on indictment before a jury. The former were of steadily growing significance during the period. The latter, determined by what might be called the "traditional" method of English fact adjudication, encompassed a wide range of offences, of different degrees of seriousness. Indictable offences can be further subdivided into treason, felony and misdemeanour.

Treason

Treason was, primarily, a political crime, and would be of little significance to this study, but for the fact that it also encompassed offences against the national currency, or "coining". These included, for example, gilding base metal coins so that they could be passed off as gold or silver currency, and "clipping" coins by filing off small amounts of precious metal from their rims. Because coining was classified as treason, it was unclergyable. Additionally, its execution ritual was slightly different for men, and very different for women, who made up a significant proportion of those indicted for the crime.

There were several hundred prosecutions for coining at the Old Bailey during the 1690s, a period when the national currency was under constant attack because of a disjuncture between face and bullion values.[3] The milling and stamping of coin edges seems to have greatly reduced the incidence of such crimes, which declined markedly after this period. Even so, during the eighteenth century, more than 400 people came before the Old Bailey accused of various coining and currency offences, including "uttering" (passing forged money). Despite its name, and (again) its unusual punishment

3. N. Tosney, "Women and 'False Coining' in Early Modern London", 2007, pp.105-107.

regime for women, "petty treason", the murder of a husband by his wife, or a servant/subordinate of his/her immediate superior, such as the killing of a rector by his curate, or a master by his apprentice, was technically a felony.[4]

Mainstream indictable crimes were classified as either (serious) felonies or (less serious) misdemeanours. Such gravity-based distinctions in offence classification were certainly not unique to England. A somewhat similar division, between *grand* and *petit* criminal cases, was found in France.[5]

Felony

Felony encompassed the most serious criminal offences, all but one of which attracted the death penalty, although the misleadingly named privilege of "benefit of clergy" meant that this was often more of a theoretical, rather than a real, danger (see below). The single exception to this general rule was petty larceny, the theft of goods worth less than a shilling, which was a non-capital offence, though still technically defined as a felony; it was frequently treated, on a *de facto* basis, as a misdemeanour.

Benefit of clergy

Felonies were themselves subject to a very important sub-division, so there were: "...two sorts; one which for the first offence is allowed clergy, and another that is not".[6] This was a distinction of crucial significance to the entire criminal justice system. Benefit of clergy was a relic of the Church-State struggles of the medieval period whereby offending clerics could escape temporal punishment after conviction by insisting on being handed over to the ecclesiastical courts. During the late medieval period, requirements that claimants be tonsured and in ecclesiastical dress had gradually been abandoned and literacy had become the sole test for clerical status, so that numerous laymen were able to claim it, once an ability to read was no longer confined to the clergy. As a result, the privilege had been transformed into a mechanism whereby many laymen could obtain clemency for some types of felony, so mitigating the "death for felony" rule. This was especially the case

4. M. Dalton, *The Country Justice*, 1655, p.295.
5. S. G. Reinhardt, "The Selective Prosecution of Crime in Ancien Régime France: Theft in the Senechaussee of Sarlat", 1986, pp.4-6.
6. G. Jacob, *Everyman His own Lawyer*, 4th edn., 1750, p.434.

as, by the 1690s, any pretence to the literacy qualification being a real test, rather than a legal fiction, had also largely been abandoned. By then, when a convict had the right to ask for clergy the courts would rarely require him to do more than repeat a few words of the requisite scriptural text (the "neck verse"), these often being whispered to him, *sotto voce*, by a court chaplain.[7] Women were allowed to claim an identical privilege, without any requirement of being able to read, by dint of two seventeenth-century statutes. The by then almost pointless reading test was finally abolished for men in 1706 (5 Anne c.5), everyone becoming entitled to benefit of clergy, whether literate or not, where it still existed.

However, after 1487, laymen (i.e. those not in holy orders) were limited to claiming the privilege on just one occasion. This change prompted the introduction of branding, to prevent convicts claiming clergy a second time. This was usually done on the brawn of the thumb, though, for a short period between 1699 and 1706, branding was on the cheek. (The temporary change in bodily position appears to have been aimed at enhancing its deterrent value).[8] Internationally, such marking of serious criminals was not uncommon. For example, in eighteenth-century Japan, many convicts were subject to tattooing as part of their punishment.[9]

In reality, and whatever had been the situation in earlier periods, eighteenth- century English laymen often made more than one claim for clergy, either because the branding had been done in a perfunctory manner, and faded away, or because it was being quietly ignored in a society in which it was no longer considered acceptable to hang large numbers of people for relatively minor crimes. By the early 1700s, the ineffectualness of branding may have been further increased by the development of a practice whereby, on paying a small sum, some convicts were allowed to have their iron dipped in cold water before being touched by it.[10] As a result, shoplifters who were convicted of a clergyable felony, having previously been found guilty of a

7. M. Misson, *Memoirs and Observations in his Travels over England*, 1719, pp.17-18.
8. J. M. Beattie, *Crime and the Courts*, 1986, p.144.
9. D. E. Wright, "Female Crime And State Punishment In Early Modern Japan", 2004, p.14.
10. M. V. Muyden (Ed.), *A foreign View of England in the reigns of George I and George II*, 1902, p.125.

similar offence, could escape execution. Many clergied thieves would also use aliases to make subsequent identification harder.[11]

Typically, Elizabeth Brown, condemned to death in 1717 for picking pockets, admitted that she had been clergied on at least three occasions over the previous 12 years, being: "…twice burnt in the cheek; [and] after that, was of late burnt in the hand and sent to the bridewell in Clerkenwell".[12] Roderick Awdry had been clergied three times by the time he was executed in 1714, despite being just sixteen years of age. By the time branding was formally brought to an end, in 1779 (19 Geo. III c.74), it could be noted, with considerable understatement, that the process had "often been disregarded and [was] ineffectual".[13] (After this date, clergied offenders could be whipped or fined instead of being branded).

However, the rule that limited laymen to a single claim was preserved, if only very rarely applied, throughout the eighteenth century, even after 1779. In 1749, for example, Robert Davie was sentenced to death for simple grand larceny after it transpired that he had claimed clergy a decade earlier for a similar crime. He had denied this, but evidence was called leading a jury, specially empanelled to determine the matter, to find for the King on this issue. As late as 1785, James Scott, convicted of a clergyable form of coining, was also sentenced to death after the Crown was able to prove that he had a previous conviction, for a similar offence, for which he had already claimed the privilege. To establish this, they called the celebrated Bow Street Runner, John Townsend, who had been present on the earlier occasion, to give evidence. Perhaps significantly, Scott's death sentence was respited.[14]

Even as the prerequisites for clergy (literacy and no previous claim) were either abandoned or applied much less strictly, many serious, and some middle ranking, felonies were being withdrawn from the privilege altogether. As a result, it was granted more willingly, but for fewer and fewer offences.

---

11. Anon, *The Great Grievance of Traders and Shopkeepers, by the Notorious Practise of Stealing their Goods out of their Shops and warehouses by persons commonly called shop-lifters*, c.1720, p.1.
12. *Weekly Journal or British Gazetteer*, March 23rd, 1717.
13. *Morning Chronicle and London Advertiser*, 11 May, 1779.
14. OBSP, Trial of James Scott et al, 19 October 1785.

Withdrawal of clergy

Historically, all common law felonies had attracted clergy, as it was deemed to be: "…granted where it is not expressly taken away by statute".[15] From the Tudor period onwards, a series of parliamentary Acts had withdrawn it from many serious offences, such as murder, rape, sodomy, burglary and robbery, or created new, and very specific, felonies that did not attract the privilege. Even so, until the Restoration, the theft of goods worth more than a shilling (simple grand larceny) was clergyable in most circumstances, although pick-pocketing had been withdrawn from its ambit during the Elizabethan period.

However, in the decades after 1660, a fresh wave of statutes withdrew clergy from several other forms of theft. These included, *inter alia*, shoplifting and thefts from warehouses and stables to the value of five shillings or more (1699), and theft from a house or out-house to the value of 40s, even where there was no break-in (1713). Sheep stealing (1741), cattle theft (1742), theft from a ship in a navigable river or wharf of goods valued at forty shillings or more (1751), and theft from the mail (1765), all gradually followed.[16] Not everyone approved of such developments, which meant that, ostensibly, many thieves were in the: "…eye of the law upon the same foot with murderers".[17]

Of course, it was always open to prosecutors to indict for simple grand larceny (a clergyable offence) rather than a specific unclergyable form of theft. More significantly, juries could still convict for such a crime, even if an unclergyable theft had originally been charged. Arguably, after 1718, this course was more attractive than had hitherto been the case, as the Transportation Act of that year had made expulsion to America, and forced labour once there, the "normal" punishment for grand larceny. Those convicted of this crime would no longer be clergied and released. This had normally been the situation before 1706 and remained the case where the court did not invoke a statute from that year (5 Anne, c.6) to sentence a clergied offender to up to two years' hard labour in a house of correction. For an example of the 1706 Act's operation, can be considered the batch of 36 Old Bailey convicts, who were clergied in 1713. After being burnt in the hand, all were

15. G. Jacob, *Everyman His own Lawyer*, 4th edn., 1750, p.434.
16. J. M. Beattie, *Crime and the Courts in England 1660-1800*, 1986, pp.144-145.
17. Anon, *Hanging Not Punishment Enough*, 1701, p.5.

sent to hard labour at the Clerkenwell Bridewell.[18] However, such sentences were not invariably imposed, and where they were, not necessarily for the full two years. Thus, Elizabeth Brown received 12 months hard labour in bridewell after being clergied.[19] In many cases, the Act was not applied at all between 1706 and 1718, and it was largely abandoned in favour of transportation afterwards.

Unclergyable forms of theft

Pickpocketing

The oldest unclergyable form of grand larceny was the offence of "pick-pocketing", which involved "privately" (secretly) stealing goods from another's person that were worth more than a shilling. William Blackstone thought that this was due to the ease with which the offence could be committed.[20] Picking pockets of goods below a shilling in value remained petty theft and thus, of course, not even potentially capital.

However, it was vital that pick-pocketing be committed without the victim's knowledge if it was to be more than simple theft. It remained clergyable if: "...openly done before the person's face".[21] Even at the start of the period, overtly "snatching" goods worth more than a shilling from the person was not enough, as it was not done "secretly". However, as the eighteenth century advanced, the technical requirements for the offence came to be interpreted ever more strictly. In a case from 1731, it was held that privately stealing could only extend to a principal in the first degree, so that the: "...hand alone which takes the property can be guilty of the offence". This meant that where, as occurred during a scuffle in the Prince William Tavern that year, it became impossible to ascertain which of the defendants had taken a banknote of a hundred pounds, none could be convicted of the unclergyable offence.[22]

---

18. *British Mercury*, September 23rd, 1713. The convicts swiftly fell upon the prison's keepers and attempted to escape.
19. *Weekly Journal or British Gazetteer*, 23 March, 1717.
20. W. Blackstone, *Commentaries on the Laws of England*, 1765-1769, vol. 4, p.241.
21. A L. Hayward, *Lives Of The Most Remarkable Criminals*, 1927, p.8.
22. *R v Baynes and others* (1731) 1 Leach 7.

By the final decades of the century, an accretion of case law also defined it as only happening in those situations in which the theft occurred without constructive "knowledge" on the part of the victim, and without him having been grossly careless in his conduct; for example, by being drunk or asleep with a prostitute when the theft occurred.[23] Thus, in a case from 1782, Thomas Sheridan visited a public house with the defendant then returned to his lodging where he fell into an intoxicated sleep and she stole his watch. The court ruled that this did not constitute stealing "privately" as the statute was intended to protect property which people could not secure by "proper vigilance and caution".[24] Even more significantly, in 1778, two women who had taken items from a sleeping cabman who was waiting outside a brothel were acquitted, as it was held that the statute was intended only to protect "persons in public meetings and places of proper resort".[25] In both these cases, the defendants were merely found guilty of grand larceny.

As a result of these developments, when it came to picking pockets, a thief who had been indicted for "privately stealing from the person" under the Elizabethan statute could receive four possible verdicts: guilty of the full, unclergyable, offence; guilty of the clergyable offence of simple grand larceny; guilty of petty theft, the stolen items having been valued at less than 12d; or not guilty of any offence. To take the 253 cases prosecuted as pocket picking in the 10 years from January 1730 to December 1739, 116 produced outright acquittals, while 131 defendants were found guilty of some form of crime. However, 95 of these were only convicted of petty theft. Interestingly, most of these convicts were sentenced to transportation, rather than a whipping, suggesting that the trial judge was keen that the court not be too lenient. Of the remainder, it seems that only 23 of those indicted under the Act were found guilty of the full offence and sentenced to death. Most of the rest were found guilty of simple grand larceny (for which transportation was the usual disposal), perhaps because the theft was not deemed to have occurred secretly or from the person. Thus, only slightly more than two defendants a year were sentenced to death after being convicted of picking

23. D. Palk, *Gender, Crime and Judicial Discretion*, 2006, pp.69-70.

24. *R v Gribble* (1782) 1 Leach 222.

25. OBSP, Trial of Mary Reading and Mary Jones, 9 December 1778.

pockets during the 1730s. Several of these men and women would have had their sentences commuted, and merely been transported as a condition of their reprieves.

Shoplifting

The "Shoplifting Act" of 1699 made the offence of "privately stealing" goods worth five or more shillings from retail premises a capital offence. Its enactment reflected concern at an apparent growth in retail theft in the Metropolitan area, at a time when shops had replaced peddlers and open markets for the sale of durables and semi-durables, such as cloth and clothes. However, prosecutions under the 1699 Act appear to have been comparatively rare, compared to the huge number of cases that must have occurred throughout the Metropolis.[26]

Even when prosecutions were brought under the statute, acquittals or convictions for lesser offences such as petty theft or simple grand larceny were usually returned, many juries finding an accused person guilty of simple grand larceny to the "value of 4s. and 10d" (this sum being almost a "ritual" one in many situations) or petty theft to the value of 10d. It seems to have become increasingly easy to return such lesser verdicts as the century advanced, because the definition of shoplifting set out in the 1699 Act, like that of pickpocketing, was interpreted progressively more strictly by the courts.

Of 294 cases indicted under the 1699 Act during the 1730s, 231 resulted in convictions for *some* form of theft. However, in 149 of these, defendants were found guilty of stealing goods to the value of less than five shillings, and so were guilty of simple grand larceny, while another 61 were convicted of petty theft, the items stolen being valued at under a shilling. During the entire decade, only 11 defendants were convicted of the full offence and sentenced to death, which penalty was also subject to post-conviction commutation in some cases. Although a small number of such prosecutions, like that of

26. T. C. Whitlock, *Crime, Gender and Consumer Culture in Nineteenth-century England*, 2005, p.130.

Mary Jones in 1771, produced convictions for the full offence until late in the century, there were usually "special factors" involved.[27]

Theft from Domestic Premises

Theft from domestic premises of goods worth more than 40 shillings was withdrawn from clergy by statute in 1713 (12 Ann, c.7). This Act was, in part, passed to deter "wicked and ill-disposed servants" who stole from their employers, though it was not confined to them. There was particular concern, that domestic staff might facilitate the entry of other criminals into the houses in which they worked.[28] Immediately prior to this legislation, Jane Roberts and her male friend John Daley had been accused of burglary from the house of Sarah Cross, where Roberts worked as a maid. While her mistress was out one night, Roberts answered Daley's knock at the front door without first asking who was there. Daley and another man then entered and proceeded to bind and gag two other servants before ransacking the premises and stealing more than £30 of silverware and other valuables. When examined by the Lord Mayor, Roberts claimed that Daley "made love to her, and drew her in".[29] However, although accused of the unclergyable (and so capital) crime of burglary, they were acquitted of this count and found guilty of the lesser offence of simple grand larceny, for which they were duly clergied, branded and released. Presumably, the fact that Roberts had invited the men into the house raised a doubt about whether it was (legally) a burglary. The new Act would have allowed her to be executed.

Once again, capital prosecutions under the 1713 statute met with only limited success. During the 1730s, there were about 635 indictments for the crime, producing about 410 cases in which the defendant was found guilty of some type of offence. Nevertheless, in only 70 of these was a conviction secured for the full offence, and an accompanying death sentence passed (again subject to possible commutation). In dozens of others, the jury simply

27. OBSP, Trial of Mary Jones, 11 Sept 1771. A. Marks, *Tyburn Tree its History and Annals*, 1908, pp.255-257.
28. P. Humfrey, *Female Servants and Women's Criminality in Early Eighteenth- century London*, 1998, p.74.
29. OBSP, Trial of Jane Roberts, 25 February 1713.

returned a verdict of theft to the non-capital value of 39 shillings (simple grand larceny).

Rationale for clergy

An examination of benefit of clergy during the eighteenth century produces an apparently contradictory picture. More offences were made potentially capital (by withdrawal of clergy), but, at the same time, these were not usually enforced, exceptional situations apart, and gradually became subject to strict extra-statutory legal limitations as a result of case law. At the same time, the ability to claim clergy, where it still applied, became universal for first offenders and was tacitly allowed for most others. This paradox formed part of the basis of Douglas Hay's notion of a ruling class "conspiracy", and certainly invites the question as to *why* Parliament passed such statutes in the first place? There were probably several reasons. Most importantly, it gave extra discretion to the courts to deal adequately with a handful of "hard" cases. It also made a statement, allowing Parliament to be seen to be "doing" something about a case that had caught the public eye and become a *cause célèbre.* Many MPs had a simple faith in the deterrent value of the "headline" potential punishment, irrespective of how often it was applied. For example, the preamble to the 1713 statute suggested that it was necessary to create a capital offence to cover these situations, as people were being actively: "... incouraged [sic] to commit robberies in houses by the privilege, as the law now is, of demanding the benefit of clergy".[30]

Petty theft

Petty theft entailed stealing goods worth less than a shilling, and was the only felony for which a death sentence could not be passed under any circumstances. The traditional punishment for this crime was a flogging, though it could attract a sentence of transportation after 1718. The offence had originated in a statute of 1278, introduced in response to cases in which men had been put to death for stealing items worth as little as 4d.[31] Of course, inflation had greatly reduced the value of a shilling by the eighteenth century.

30. O. Ruffhead, *Statutes at Large*, vol. iv, 1763, p.602.
31. S. McGlynn, "Violence and the Law in Medieval England", 2008, p.56.

In the Metropolitan area, petty larceny was only rarely prosecuted in its own right during the eighteenth century, especially its early decades, though it must have been very common. It was not indicted very often at Metropolitan Quarter Sessions during the first half of the period, and there were only a little over 800 indictments for the crime at the Old Bailey, an average of about one per sessions, during the course of the century. Perhaps surprisingly, in most of these cases, the decision to proceed for petty theft appears to have been a genuine reflection of the stolen item's value, rather than an attempt at limiting the penal consequences for the defendant, or pre-empting a jury's likely decision to down-value the goods taken. For example, linen handkerchiefs worth only a few pence crop up regularly in the reports. Why these particular cases came for trial at the higher forum is difficult to ascertain.

Significantly, the distribution of petty theft cases at the Old Bailey over the course of the century was by no means uniform. There were less than 30 indictments during the first quarter of the period, just over 100 cases in the second, more than 450 in the third quarter, and over 250 in the final 25 years. Because it was sometimes prosecuted at Quarter Sessions, drawing too much significance from this evolving pattern is inherently dangerous. It might simply reflect changes in the distribution of work between courts. Nevertheless, the Transportation Act of 1718, which allowed a sentence of transportation to be imposed on those found guilty of petty theft, *may* have meant that magistrates were more willing to commit for trial on indictment, rather than sending a petty thief to the bridewell as a disorderly person, as was common early in the century. Alternatively, they may, previously, have been reluctant to commit such cases for trial on indictment, knowing that a guilty verdict would simply increase the number of people who were to be whipped in public, something that had increasingly significant public order implications. It might also be indicative of a more general change in attitude towards using committal to a bridewell or house of correction as a way of dealing with those who perpetrated mainstream criminal offences.

Misdemeanours

Misdemeanours were less serious crimes, whether common law or statutory, though to modern eyes a few appear misclassified. For example, abducting infants for commercial purposes (a crime that was traditionally associated with gipsies) was only a misdemeanour, for which the pillory was the normal punishment, even though many urged that it be made a capital felony, given the enormous distress it occasioned.[32] Misdemeanours included most assaults and public disturbances, many lesser frauds, perjuries, and some forms of receiving stolen goods. For much of the period, some of these offences, especially assaults, though technically criminal, were viewed almost as quasi-civil matters. Nevertheless, they were always tried on indictment (by a jury), unless statute made them summary offences. They did not carry the death penalty, their normal punishments being fiscal, corporal or, more rarely, custodial.

Crime Rates and Patterns

Assessing change in the incidence of crime is fraught with difficulty. Contemporary perceptions as to the direction in which crime rates are moving are often unreliable. Most eras produce large numbers of people who feel that they are living amid deteriorating security, and eighteenth-century London was no exception. Nevertheless, one general improvement can be noted during this period: there was a significant decline in the incidence of very serious violence.

Lethal Violence

Aggression and violence appear to be innate to human beings, as they are found in nearly all societies, during all historical periods. For this reason, if no other, it is likely that they serve an evolutionary purpose.[33] However, levels and degrees of violence differ enormously between different societies and eras, suggesting that they are socially and culturally determined to a very significant degree. This appears to be more important in deciding the incidence of violence than any innate biological factors.

---

32. *The Times*, 12 June, 1789, p.3.
33. J. Carter Wood, "The Limits of Culture?", 2007, p.106.

Although it can be difficult to distinguish long-term trends from short-term fluctuations, one Metropolitan (and national) trend is reasonably clear: potentially lethal violence, as manifest in the murder rate, declined markedly during the 1700s. This was not a new phenomenon even then. The eighteenth century was situated within a long period of rapidly declining European homicide rates that ran from the late medieval period to the first half of the twentieth century. An especially marked fall occurred after the middle of the seventeenth century. These changes are particularly important, as crimes involving homicide have an almost uniquely high level of both reporting and prosecution. As a result, it is almost the only crime that allows for reliable estimates in a historical context. However, murder rates act as more than an index to that crime. They provide an indication of the incidence of very serious assaults.[34] Frequently, it is just chance factors, such as the availability of ready assistance or the presence of an effective weapon, that distinguish the two.

In England as a whole, it seems that there was an average of 2.3 homicides per 100,000 head of population during the first half of the eighteenth century. In the second half, however, it dropped to only 1.4.[35] This rate of decline was probably exceeded in the Metropolitan area.[36] Most observers accept that there was at least a halving, and probably a quartering, of the per capita rate of homicide in and about the capital during the course of the century. A selection of statistics is indicative. At least 118 males were convicted of the full offence of murder at the Old Bailey in the first half of the century (perhaps about 125, given gaps in the *Sessions Papers*). The figure was only 123 in the second 50 years of the period, despite an increase of well over 50 per cent in the Metropolitan population over the same time. More specifically, during the 1720s, 87 people were convicted of murder at the Old Bailey. By the 1780s, this had fallen to only 33 individuals for the decade. If all murder prosecutions for these decades are considered, irrespective of verdict, the figures are proportionately similar, 160 and 68 people respectively. The fall

34. P. Spierenburg, "Democracy Came Too Early: A Tentative Explanation for the Problem of American Homicide", 2006, p.104.
35. M. Eisner, "Modernization, Self-control and Lethal Violence", 2001, p. 629.
36. R. Shoemaker, "Male Honour and the Decline of Public Violence in Eighteenth-century London", 2001, pp.190-193.

in homicide rates over the century does not appear to have shown an even decline. The *Old Bailey Sessions Papers* suggest, for example, that there was a particularly significant fall in both prosecutions and convictions during the 1730s, when compared to the 15 years after 1715 (the first year for which the *Sessions Papers* are complete).

These figures are important because the Old Bailey dealt with nearly all killings in the Metropolis; the small number of those tried for homicide at the Court of King's Bench, the only other competent forum, was not statistically significant. Additionally, there is nothing to suggest a decline in the proportion of homicides prosecuted *vis à vis* killings actually committed, and most academics are of the opinion that improvements in medical technology did not have a major impact on a victim's chances of surviving a serious wound before the late nineteenth century.[37] As a result, it seems that these figures reflect real trends in lethal violence within the Metropolis, and signify a major decline in the capital's murder rate.

This process frequently went unnoticed by contemporary observers. In 1752, it was claimed that the fact that murder had, in recent years: "…become much more frequent in this kingdom, than it was ever before known to be, is too sad a truth to be disputed".[38] The preamble to the Murder Act of that year made the same point. Even Henry Fielding, who was in a better position than most to make an informed estimate, was persuaded that no one could deny that the English murder rate had increased to a "deplorable degree".[39]

Nevertheless, such a fall in the homicide rate made England, including the Metropolis, a markedly different place to many other parts of Europe, and some European cities, though they, too, often witnessed a major decline in lethal violence. For example, it seems that the Irish homicide rate during the 1730s was about four times that in England. However, it was England not Ireland that was unusual.[40] Strict laws against premeditated homicide were enforced against all social classes, so that a French visitor could observe,

37. M. Eisner, "Long-Term Historical Trends in Violent Crime", 2003, p.95.
38. Anon, *A Warning Piece Against the Crime of Murder*, 1752, p.i.
39. H. Fielding, *Examples of the Interposition of Providence in the Detection and Punishment of Murder*, 1752, p.7.
40. N. Garnham, "How violent was eighteenth-century Ireland?", 1997, pp.390-391.

albeit with some exaggeration, that: "London is the only great city in Europe where neither murders or assassinations happen".[41]

Murder in the course of instrumental crime, such as robbery, was particularly rare. Even Sir John Fielding conceded that English highwaymen would only kill if forced to such a measure.[42] Another contemporary observer felt that this reluctance to take life, when compared to robbers from other countries, was proof that the "spirit of humanity is natural to our nation".[43] It was also something that foreign visitors found surprising. When Thomas Neave's gang robbed a French Huguenot parson the cleric immediately pleaded for his life, mistakenly assuming that they were of the: "...same barbarous Mould and Stamp with the French collectors on the High-way".[44] In 1782, a visiting German thought (somewhat implausibly) that some highwaymen did not even load their firearms.[45] This reluctance to spill blood may have affected popular responses to such crimes. Several contemporary observers claimed that there were instances of gentlemen, accompanied by up to six or seven servants, being successfully robbed, without resistance, by a single armed highwayman.[46]

Why did this apparent decline in very serious violence occur? Because it happened in the absence of an organized police force, modern studies have usually attributed it to a rise in popular intolerance for such behaviour. Various explanations as to *why* such a cultural softening of manners should have occurred have also been proposed. In the early twentieth century, for example, Max Weber argued that Protestantism, emphasizing sobriety and the cultivation of shame, had a major disciplinary effect on popular behaviour. Other observers have focused on the rise of modern individualism, characterized by a disengagement from some of the social demands of the wider

41. P. J. Grosley, *A Tour to London: or, New Observations on England, And Its Inhabitants*, 1772, vol.1, pp.61–2, and p.67.
42. J. Fielding, *A Brief Description of the Cities of London and Westminster*, London, 1776, p.xxxii.
43. J. Brown, *Estimate of the Manners and Principles of the Times*, 1758, p.15.
44. T. Neaves, *The Life of Thomas Neaves, The Noted Street-Robber*, 1729, p.17.
45. C. P. Moritz, *Journeys of a German in England in 1782*, 1965, p.10.
46. A. Moreton, *Second Thoughts are best: or, a Further Improvement of a Late Scheme to Prevent Street Robberies*, 1729, p.24.

society, especially if they required recourse to violence. These changes were encouraged via the new medium of cheap print.[47]

In the 1930s, Norbert Elias provided the most persuasive analysis for the trend, with his emphasis on the process of modernisation whereby the state gains a monopoly of power, taxation and legitimate violence, disarming its powerful members and neutralising their more aggressive impulses in the process. As a result, individuals develop a stronger degree of self-control.[48] This explanation has been highly influential on recent scholarship examining the decline in lethal violence.[49] The emerging commercial, bourgeois, middle class, market oriented society that characterised Georgian London prized restraint in resolving interpersonal disputes.[50] This produced a broadening definition of what constituted "violence", along with stricter laws against such behaviour. The "civilising process" attacked cultural mentalities that tolerated high levels of impulsivity, personal retribution, and the community's control of cultural boundaries through violence.[51]

A number of more specific aspects of the eighteenth-century reduction in serious violence have been considered as part of this process. For example, most of the fall in homicide rates is (inevitably) explained by a decline in male killings. It has been claimed that this was, in large part, the result of changing attitudes towards notions of honour.[52] This meant that, after the mid-seventeenth century, verbal aggression slowly lost some of its power to prompt lethal responses.[53] Honour had been a form of capital in early modern society, the loss of which could not be lightly countenanced. Even at the start of the eighteenth century, it was still often "fetishised" so that minor slights, such as accidental jostling, might produce quite disproportionate

47. M. Eisner, "Long-Term Historical Trends in Violent Crime", 2003, pp.130-132.
48. M. Eisner, "Modernization, Self-control and Lethal violence", 2001, p. 629.
49. See, for example, P. Spierenburg, *A History of Murder: Personal Violence in Europe from the Middle Ages to the Present*, 2008.
50. J. Warner, "My Pappa is out, and my Mamma is asleep", pp.563-564.
51. J. Carter Wood, "Self-Policing And The Policing Of The Self: Violence, Protection And The Civilizing Bargain In Britain", 2003, p.127.
52. R. Shoemaker, "Male Honour and the decline of public violence in eighteenth- century London", 2001, pp.190-193.
53. M. Eisner, "Long-Term Historical Trends in Violent Crime", 2003, pp.130-132.

levels of violence in response (often the hallmark of an "honour" culture).[54] Unsurprisingly then, it has been argued that the dramatic decline in the Metropolitan homicide rate during the eighteenth century was the result of new understandings of masculinity.[55]

As honour became a private rather than a public quality, there seems to have been a decline in the general male "prickliness" that had often led to killings at the start of the period. A growing proportion of men felt able to follow the example of George King, who had recourse to the law, rather than his own mettle, when dealing with a man who started: "...pissing on him [and] challenging him to fight".[56] Significantly, after the 1730s, gentlemen very slowly stopped wearing swords in public, unless they were military officers. In 1752, it was even suggested that a law be passed forbidding people from carrying hidden weapons or publicly wearing swords and hangers, without a special licence.[57] This development also had situational benefits in preventing lethal violence. For example, before this trend was well advanced, a link boy, lighting two "gentlemen" on their way home along The Strand, was accused of going too slowly by his customers, and stabbed in the back, dying of his wounds a couple of days later.[58] The change in attitudes to violence, and the general absence of swords, would have made such an incident very much less likely by the end of the century.

Non-Lethal Violence

Despite the decline in homicide rates, the post-medieval civilising offensive had a long way to run at the end of the eighteenth century. Many forms of violence were still socially accepted methods of resolving interpersonal

54. P. Spierenburg, "Democracy Came Too Early: A Tentative Explanation for the Problem of American Homicide", 2006, p.3.
55. R. Shoemaker, "Male honour and the decline of public violence in eighteenth- century London", 2001, p.190 and p.193.
56. R. Paley (Ed.), *Justice in 18th-Century Hackney*, 1991, p.59.
57. C. Jones, *Some Methods Proposed Towards putting a Stop to the Flagrant Crimes of Murder, Robbery, and Perjury*, 1752, pp.5-6.
58. *Original Weekly Journal*, 21 February 1719.

disputes, amongst all social classes.[59] Additionally, attitudes to violence, and rates of change in those attitudes, were not uniform. It seems that elements of the middling social orders became more fastidious about its use rather earlier than many working, and even upper class, men. Rake and libertine violence persisted amongst the latter until well into the century. As late as 1760, when a prostitute died after being cut by three men, observers could note that it was: "...very usual for young gentlemen to be making passes with their swords, at anything that is near them".[60] Unsurprisingly, in the same decade, Saunders Welch could complain of the "bad examples of too many in higher stations".[61] Similarly, it was not until the 1800s that routine, low level, and especially domestic working class violence became a matter of serious concern to the political nation.[62]

To foreigners, Londoners, like Englishmen generally, were associated with public fist fighting in the streets. Some continental visitors even believed that this, like cockfighting, was an inherent part of the national character, and an aspect of the: "...well-known taste of the English for combats of men and animals".[63] Crowds would often encourage youths who were at odds with each other to resolve their differences by fighting. Inevitably, this sometimes had tragic consequences. In 1726, for example, Richard Pritchard was tried for murder, after William Fenwick, his opponent in a pre-arranged bare-knuckle boxing bout, died of his injuries.[64]

However, such conflicts were not entirely devoid of regulation. Like the (much rarer) upper class duel, proletarian fights were often subject to informal rules, which were widely followed and had considerable importance in any ensuing criminal proceedings. Frequently, only fists and head butting

---

59. J. Warner, "Violence against and amongst Jews in an Early Modern Town: Tolerance and its Limits in Portsmouth, 1718-1781", 2003, p.429.
60. Anon (By one of the Jury), *The True and Whole Proceedings of the Coroner's Inquest at St. Mary-Le-Bonne; On Saturday, October the 11th, 1760. Touching the Death of Ann Sharp.* 1760, pp.3-24.
61. S. Welch, *A Proposal to render effectual a Plan to remove the nuisance of Common Prostitutes from the streets of this Metropolis*, 1758, p.48.
62. M. Wiener, *Men of Blood: Violence, Manliness, and Criminal Justice in Victorian England,* 2004, pp.9-12.
63. M. Grosley, *A Tour to London: or, New Observations on England, And Its Inhabitants*, 1772, pp.51 and 62.
64. *Weekly Journal, or The British Gazetteer*, 12 February 1726. *OBSP, Trial of Richard Pritchard, 2nd March, 1726.* Wagers had been laid on the fight's outcome.

were allowed. Certain other blows were proscribed and, sometimes, even "rings", rounds and seconds would be employed. These conventions occasionally received official recognition. In 1819, Mr. Justice Best publicly deplored an Un-English change in manners on the part of the "lower classes" that was manifest in their increased willingness to use knives rather than fists. Even foreign visitors alluded to them. For example, in about 1760, one Portuguese sailor, involved in a violent altercation with a blade-wielding colleague, apparently told him: "...I'll box you in the English way, and reprimanded his countryman for taking the knife out".[65]

Any deaths that resulted from even vaguely consensual fights, conducted on roughly "even" terms, within culturally defined limits, were very unlikely to produce murder convictions, and sometimes did not even lead to prosecutions. At most, they would normally result in manslaughter verdicts followed by a claim of clergy and discharge. Frequently, they produced outright acquittals. In Pritchard's case, although the killing produced a prosecution that survived a Grand Jury's scrutiny, he was swiftly acquitted at trial.[66] Similar results followed duels fought by members of the upper social orders, provided the widely acknowledged rules of such engagements had been followed. Even in the late eighteenth century, judges ensured that strict legal theory was often ignored in these cases.[67]

Assault and the Law

For much of the 1700s, non-lethal violence was accorded relatively little significance by the criminal justice system. Prior to the nineteenth century, most incidents of violence that did not result in death were tried at Quarter Sessions as misdemeanours. Even if they were heard at the Old Bailey, the legal status of the crime usually meant that any punishments imposed were very limited. For example, in 1703, Thomas Fishe was tried for simple

65. OBSP, Trial of Antonio da Silva, 6 May 1761.

66. *Weekly Journal, or The British Gazetteer*, 12 February 1726. OBSP, Trial of Richard Pritchard, 2 March 1726.

67. See generally, S. Banks, "'Very Little Law in the Case': Contests of Honour and the Subversion of the English Criminal Courts, 1780-1845", 2008, pp. 575-594.

assault (a misdemeanour) after he attacked a man with a knife and attempted to cut his throat. He pleaded guilty and was merely fined and discharged.[68] Ninety years later, a newspaper could still note that it was incongruous that a man had received only six months imprisonment for stabbing another in his side, while a: "...poor wretch is shortly to suffer death in the Metropolis for stealing a pair of shoes".[69]

Only a handful of the gravest, and most specific, non-lethal assaults were legally classified as felonies. Amongst the most important of these was that created by Lord Coventry's Act (22 & 23 Car. II), whereby an unclergyable felony was committed if anyone with 'malice aforethought', and after lying in wait, cut out a man's tongue, put out one of his eyes, slit or cut off his nose, or otherwise inflicted very severe injury: "...with intent to maim or disfigure him". Sir John Coventry, an MP, had angered members of the court party during a parliamentary debate in 1670, as a result of which he had been dragged from his carriage, and had his nose slit to the bone. The Act was one of its results.

Nevertheless, the legal prerequisites for this crime were highly technical, and strictly applied, so that it was rarely indicted.[70] At the Old Bailey, there were only about half a dozen prosecutions for the offence during the entire eighteenth century, and the courts were fastidious about insisting that all its prerequisites were made out. For example, in 1763, William Lee was acquitted after taking a razor to his wife's neck because, although the facts of the case were proved beyond doubt, his crime: "...did not come within the description of the Act of Parliament, commonly called the Coventry Act, which is for maiming the face".[71] In Thomas Tickner's case, a conviction under the statute was referred to the twelves judges who concluded that it did not show "sufficient evidence of lying in wait".[72] However, Thomas Mills was convicted and sentenced to death for the crime in 1783, after attacking a man, and slitting his nose, in what appears to have been some kind of revenge attack. In this case, the court was careful to warn the jury that the

68. OBSP, Trial of Thomas Fisher, 13 October 1703.
69. 'Inequality of Punishment' in *The Observer,* 20 January, 1793.
70. W. Blackstone, *Commentaries on the Laws of England*, 1765-1769, vol. iv, p.207.
71. OBSP, Trial of William Lee, 6 July 1763.
72. *R v Thomas Tickner* (1778) 1 Leach 187.

defendant's state of mind was crucial, and that simply assaulting someone and bisecting their nose, without the requisite intention: "...would still remain a great misdemeanor only".[73]

The problems faced by the authorities when dealing with Rhynwick Williams are indicative of this marginalisation of serious but non-lethal violence, even late in the century. Williams, supposedly the "London Monster", had committed a series of assaults that involved slashing women's buttocks with a blade. By the time he was arrested in 1790, the crimes had achieved widespread notoriety in the London newspapers and there was a strong desire that their perpetrator should stand trial for felony, rather than the lesser species of crime. However, with the best will in the world, it was felt to be impossible to bring him within the ambit of Lord Coventry's Act. Specialist provisions within the Black Act of 1722 were also considered, but again to no avail. Ultimately, the authorities settled on a very obscure, and never previously enforced, "Bloody Code" statute from 1721 that had forbidden cutting or defacing clothes in the street. This Act had been aimed at weavers who were, allegedly, pouring *aqua fortis* on the clothes of people wearing foreign (rather than English) made textiles. Although Williams was duly found guilty of this offence at the Old Bailey, the legal basis of his conviction was immediately considered dubious, and was reviewed by the twelve Westminster judges, who concluded that it was wrong.[74] As a result, he was returned to the Old Bailey to be told that the law had been: "...strained beyond its bounds to render me a felon; that my case came only within an action of assault". He was then remanded in custody to await trial for this misdemeanour at Hick's Hall, where he was duly convicted.[75]

A major process of *legal* change, in this respect, would only begin with Lord Ellenborough's Act of 1803, which effectively created new capital crimes of attempted murder and very serious violence, building on an older Irish statute. The 1803 Act contained a range of specific offences, including one that made it a capital offence to do grievous bodily harm, shoot at, stab, or cut another person with intent to murder, maim, disfigure or disable them.[76]

73. *R v Thomas Mills* (1783) 1 Leach 259.
74. J. Bondeson, *The London Monster*, 2000, p.92.
75. R. Williams, *An Appeal to the Public, by Rhynwick Williams*, 1790, p.vii.
76. P. Handler, "The Law of Felonious Assault in England, 1803 – 61", 2007, p.188.

However, before the end of the eighteenth century, a change in legal attitudes towards ordinary (i.e. misdemeanour) assault had also become discernible.

For much of the period, it seems that the primary aim of a complainant when bringing an assault indictment at Quarter Sessions was to secure compensation, or some other form of redress, rather than the punishment of their assailant. If the parties agreed terms, whether they involved financial payment or, less commonly, a public apology, the defendant might receive a nominal fine of a shilling, after pleading guilty. For an example can be considered a case at the Guildhall Sessions in 1766, in which a tradesman was tried for assaulting his wife. Both parties were legally represented, and after several witnesses had been heard the matter was compromised when the defendant agreed to pay his wife six shillings a week as separate maintenance, so allowing her to live apart from her husband.[77] As a result, there were considerable affinities between civil and criminal proceedings in this context. Prosecuting assaults by indictment was less expensive than bringing a civil action for battery, though such actions were also fairly common, and allowed the prosecutor to present evidence that would be inadmissible at a civil hearing, such as his own sworn testimony. Magistrates tended to treat all but fairly serious cases of interpersonal violence as being quasi-civil matters.

Nevertheless, it seems that a major transformation in attitudes towards low-level, non-lethal, violence took place in the second half of the century. By its final decades, tolerance for such behaviour was much smaller in English courts than had previously been the case. Although the great majority of assaults were still being processed summarily, a significant minority resulted in public trials in which ritual confessions and nominal fines were no longer the expected outcome. People convicted of interpersonal violence were increasingly subject to legal procedures and sanctions that were similar to those faced by petty thieves. Pleas of guilty became less common. Assault moved decisively away from the civil, towards the criminal, sphere, even though there were no formal changes in the law, as attitudes towards violence changed.[78]

77. *The Whitehall Evening Post; or, London Intelligencer*, 18 September 1766.

78. P. King, "Punishing Assault: The Transformation of Attitudes in the English Courts", 1996, p.72.

The Incidence of Property Crime

Unlike homicide, but like low-level violence, determining the incidence of property crime is very difficult, though it was by far the most common form of criminal activity prosecuted in the Metropolis. More than 90 per cent of Old Bailey indictments involved such offences. Some modern academics have drawn cautious conclusions from changing indictment levels for property crimes, and argued that they provide some guidance to variations in 'real' rates of criminality.[79] Others have been acutely sceptical of their value as the 'black figure' of unreported crime poses even more of a problem when considered in an historic context than it does today. Differing levels of public sensitivity, manifest in the willingness of victims to prosecute, and policing effectiveness, displayed in the number of thieves caught, are likely to make formal prosecutions a fairly unreliable indicator of the overall level of crime. This has even led some modern observers to attempt retrospective victim surveys using contemporary diaries.

Whatever the precise incidence of crime, many contemporary observers, like John Dunton, thought that: "No Kingdom can match England for Pick pockets, foot pads, house-breakers, and highwaymen".[80] Although he was prone to hyperbole, this view was widely shared. In 1785, for example, Martin Madan was persuaded that crime levels in England were so notorious across the Channel that, on one occasion, when a Parisian family were the victims of burglary, the master of the house claimed they had been assailed "par less rossignols Anglais".[81] The Metropolis was considered the epicentre of English offending, even allowing for its size, being: "…more pester'd with low villany, than any other place whatever, the proportion of bignes between them not left unconsider'd".[82]

Whether this reputation was entirely deserved is another matter. The visiting Frenchman Pierre-Jean Grosley noted that, although constantly warned

79. D. Hay, "War, Dearth And Theft In The Eighteenth Century: The Record Of The English Courts", 1982, p.158.

80. J. Dunton, *The Shortest Way With Whores and Rogues: Or a New Project for Reformation*, 1703, p.19.

81. M. Madan, *Thoughts On Executive Justice*, 2nd edn., 1785, p.4.

82. B. De Mandeville, *An Enquiry into the Causes of the Frequent Executions at Tyburn*, 1725, p.3.

about the dangers of Metropolitan crime by native Londoners, and despite very lax personal security, he had not become a victim during his own stay. Indeed, much of what he saw there, such as valuable pewter tankards being left outside taverns to be picked up later in the day, led him to suspect that property crime was much less common in the capital than many thought.[83] Some decades later in the century, another continental visitor, Johann Wilhelm von Archenholz, also thought that foreigners exaggerated London's crime problems, largely because they were unable to separate the normal security of the city from that of the arterial roads surrounding it. Those who dwelt on the highwaymen who operated near the capital, who *were* a real problem, would: "...imagine that it is the worst regulated metropolis in the world". However, when it came to the conurbation itself, Archenholz thought that London was as well governed as any city could be, given the high level of personal freedom enjoyed by its very large, and diverse, number of inhabitants.[84]

Obviously, there were numerous serious crimes in the Metropolitan area, because they were the: "...natural consequences of an increased population and an enlarged commerce". The apparently high level of offending had to be seen in relation to the area's huge population.[85] As Daniel Defoe observed of London and Westminster: "Crimes ever were, and ever must be unavoidably frequent in such populous Cities as yours are".[86]

According to this analysis, what was extraordinary was not the amount of crime, but that the many poor people living in close proximity to, and acutely aware of, the "luxurious and effeminate" lives of the Metropolis's great and wealthy, had not entered into a general conspiracy to plunder them.[87] These observations must be borne in mind when considering the

83. P. J. Grosley, *A tour to London; or, New observations on England, and its inhabitants,* vol. 1, 1772, pp.49-50.
84. J. W. von Archenholz, *A picture of England: Containing a description of the laws, customs and manners of England*, 1790, p.178.
85. Anon (By a Citizen of London), *Observations on a Late Publication: Intituled A Treatise on the Police of the Metropolis*, 1799, p.iii.
86. D. Defoe, *The History of the Remarkable Life of John Sheppard*, 1724, pp.1-20.
87. J. W. von Archenholz, *A picture of England: Containing a description of the laws, customs and manners of England,* 1790, p.179.

'consensus' view on Metropolitan security that historians have discerned as gradually emerging after 1700.

It is, perhaps, also revealing that a frequent trope in eighteenth-century London was the naïve countryman who came up to town and fell victim to the capital's cunning felons. In an era of limited communications, this was also a very real risk. Newcomers, especially those from rural areas, could be totally oblivious to the city's snares and dangers. As a result, visiting farmers regularly featured amongst those who were robbed or swindled in the city. For example, in 1737, Sir Richard Brocas committed two tricksters to Newgate for: "…cheating a countryman of half a guinea at cutting of cards". A concerned member of the public had seen the pair lure the rural visitor into a tavern, and called a constable to rescue him.[88] Long-term residents of the city were likely to be much more aware of its risks. Nevertheless, some observers have concluded that levels of property crime were increasing by the end of the century, even if the number of highwaymen was declining at the same time, due to infrastructure change.[89]

Female participation in crime

Women were disproportionately involved in Metropolitan crime, compared to their rural counterparts, especially in the early part of the century, when they made up over a third of the Old Bailey's caseload.[90] The proportion of felonies committed by women then gradually declined, though as late as the period between 1780 and 1808, 53 per cent of pickpockets tried at the Old Bailey were female.[91] A variety of reasons have been advanced for this phenomenon, ranging from the special economic pressures women faced

88. *London Evening Post*, 22 October, 1737.
89. D. Bentley, *English Criminal Justice in the Nineteenth Century*, 1998, p.16.
90. M. Feeley and D. L. Little, "The Vanishing Female: The Decline of Women in the Criminal Process, 1687-1912", 1991, p.719.
91. D. Palk, *Gender, Crime and Judicial Discretion*, 2006, p.69. Women tended to commit their offences at night, often targeting drunken men who were seeking a sexual encounter. Male pickpockets were more likely to work the streets in traditional 'cut-purse' fashion.

in the capital, to the unusual social freedoms they enjoyed in the same environment.[92]

Juvenile participation in crime

Youth crime was seen as a special Metropolitan problem, as juveniles were heavily represented amongst felons in the London area. In 1729, it was noted that of the 20 people admitted to the New Prison over the previous eight days, most had been "meer children".[93] There were regular complaints about: "Boys of seven or eight years old, taken in robbing a shop; and some of 13 or 14 robbing in the streets".[94] In 1730, Sir John Gonson issued warrants to search night-houses around Covent Garden and the Strand that were thought to harbour a gang of boys, 30 strong, who picked pockets in the local area. Eight of the most notorious were arrested, the oldest of them not more than 13 years of age.[95] In April of the following year, six boys aged between 11 and 15 years old were arrested in a house in Chick Lane for being notorious thieves and pickpockets.[96] After the mid-century, several private initiatives were specifically set up to deal with juvenile criminals, among them being the Marine Society (1756), the Philanthropic Society (1788), and, though it was not exclusively for youths, the Refuge for the Destitute (1804).

Juveniles and the law

Legally, it was: "...clear that an infant above fourteen and under twenty-one is equally subject to capital punishments, as well as others of full age". (The age of majority was 21). However, at common law, the age of legal responsibility was just seven years. Below this age a child could not be guilty of felony: "...whatever circumstances proving discretion appear". Those of this age and above, but under 14 could, in theory, be convicted and executed, if

92. See generally, G. Durston, *Victims and Viragos*, 2007.

93. *London Journal*, 20 December 1729.

94. *The Gentleman's Magazine*, 1731, vol. 1, pp.59-60.

95. *Grub-street Journal*, 29 July, 1730.

96. *London Evening Post*, 10 April, 1731.

they were found to be *doli capax* when offending, and so capable of discerning right from wrong.[97]

Nevertheless, most juveniles, even those over 14, were considered to be too young to be prosecuted and, even more so, executed, in large numbers, especially given the comparatively trivial nature of many of their crimes. Extreme youth was sufficiently unusual that it was almost invariably the subject of comment by the authors of the Sessions Papers, making them a fairly reliable indicator of the age of non-adults who were prosecuted at the Old Bailey. Between 1700 and 1799, the Sessions Papers record that 103 children under the age of 14 were tried at that court (a few cases are missing for the first 14 years of the period). One of the 103, ten-year-old Susannah Pain, was tried and acquitted on two separate charges of theft, at different sessions, within the space of six months.[98] Perhaps surprisingly, such prosecutions became more, rather than less, common as the century advanced. There were 25 cases between 1700 and 1749, 13 between 1750 and 1774, and 67 in the last quarter of the century. On average, just over one child a year was prosecuted at the Bailey during the era.

However, most of the 103 juveniles were 'older' children, aged 12 or above. Only 15 were under the age of eleven, and of these, only one was eight years old, while just two were nine. Only 16 of the total were female. Sixty-nine were found guilty of an offence, even if it was a less serious one than that originally charged (often the case). Only 15 children under the age of fourteen, nine fifteen year olds, 12 sixteen year olds, 22 seventeen year olds, and 28 eighteen year olds, were capitally convicted at the Old Bailey during the course of the century. Given that the average age of puberty in the eighteenth century was almost two years later than it is today, many of these defendants really were childlike in appearance: slight of stature, beardless, high pitched in voice and (in the case of girls) bosom free.[99]

Even where they were sentenced to death, children would nearly always be reprieved prior to execution. Sixteen seems to have been the youngest

97. M. Hale, *The History of the Pleas of the Crown*, updated by G. Wilson and S. Emlyn, vol.1, 1800, p.31 and p.24.
98. OBSP, Trial of Sussanah Pain, 8 December 1762 and 23 February 1763.
99. R. H. Sprinkle, "The Missing Politics and Unsettled science of the Trend towards earlier Puberty", 2001, pp.45-47.

age at which eighteenth-century defendants were ever hanged for property crimes (as opposed to murder or rape), and such cases were exceptionally rare. Although there are occasional media reports of younger offenders being executed, there is only one Metropolitan case of a defendant who was sixteen years old being hanged that is also confirmed by the ordinary in his *Account*. In 1717, Edward Elton, from Holborn, was executed for a housebreaking, during which he had taken some clothes and linen. He claimed to be 16, though it is possible that he was a little older. It is not obviously apparent why he received such a severe disposal. A few other youths in their late teens were also hanged. However, the great majority of those executed for property crimes were in their twenties and thirties. Perhaps surprisingly, the cases for which many of the 103 children were prosecuted were not particularly serious examples of their type. For example, Elizabeth Armstrong ('Little Bess') was accused of stealing two silver spoons after climbing into a house through an open window. She had older accomplices, to whom she passed the spoons, perhaps explaining the decision to indict her.[100] Even stranger, in 1792, William Causeway, aged 12, was accused of stealing four metal watch chains worth only two shillings.

The Metropolis and its Environs

The Metropolis had a huge impact on the shires that either bordered or were near to it. For example, in Surrey, Kent and Essex those parishes that were close in to the capital had by far the highest indictment rates in their counties. Of course, prosecution rates and crime rates are not necessarily the same thing. The ready presence of magistrates in these more populated areas undoubtedly encouraged recourse to the courts, where it would not otherwise have occurred. Nevertheless, it does seem that the proximity of the Metropolis had a real impact on the incidence of offending in these areas. They provided readily accessible targets for Metropolitan criminals travelling outwards, and to 'local' thieves who were attracted to crime by the ease with which stolen items could be liquidated in the nearby capital.

100. OBSP, Trial of Elizabeth Armstrong, 14 July 1731.

In the late eighteenth century, the authorities in suburban Surrey villages regularly complained that their proximity to the Metropolis was leading to high levels of offending.[101] Similarly, many of the burglaries that were prevalent in southwest Essex appear to have been committed by Metropolitan offenders. The capital's closeness to the countryside also meant that some decidedly bucolic crimes could be centred on the Metropolis. For example, cattle theft was common in the dairying region around Epping.[102] Patrick Bourke and George Ellis specialised in killing sheep in fields near to the built up area, whether they were in Middlesex, Kent or Surrey, and then stripping the carcasses of fat, which they sold on to a tallow chandler in Southwark. They slaughtered 126 animals before being caught and executed in 1744.[103] In the latter part of the eighteenth century, it was claimed that equine slaughter houses had also been set up in and about the Metropolis, to which stolen horses taken from the capital or its adjacent rural parts could be taken and killed, after which their flesh, skin and fat might be removed and sold; together, these were usually worth about 30 shillings.[104]

Unsurprisingly, the incidence of highway robbery in the counties around the Metropolis was particularly high. Many highwaymen resided in the capital while foraying outwards, and those who were arrested were often captured 'in town'. According to John Fielding, most of the highwaymen who operated within 20 miles of the capital retired to London for shelter.[105] The conurbation provided them with anonymity and so was the: "...best forest for such beasts of prey to shelter in".[106] For example, John Everett and Richard Bird were based there during the 1720s, when committing robberies in Middlesex, Essex, Surrey and Kent. Similarly, in the 1770s, it was alleged that William Field frequently committed four or five robberies a night in London's environs, before taking his booty into the Metropolis for disposal.[107]

101. P. Rawlings, *Policing: A Short History*, 2002, p.67.
102. P. King, *Crime, Justice, and Discretion in England 1740-1820*, 2003, pp.140-142.
103. *The Ordinary of Newgate, His Account of the Behaviour, Confession, and Dying words ... Who were executed at Tyburn, on Monday the 24th of December, 1744*, 1744, pp.30-31.
104. M. Madan, *Thoughts On Executive Justice*, 2nd edn., 1785, p.42.
105. J. Fielding, *A Plan for Preventing Robberies Within Twenty Miles of London*, 1755, p.9.
106. Anon, *News from Newgate Or, a true Relation of the manner of taking Seven persons, very notorious for Highway-men, In the Strand*, 1677, pp.4-5.
107. J. L. Rayner and G. T. Crook (Eds.), *The Complete Newgate Calendar*, vol. IV, 1926, pp.95-96.

The notorious Dick Turpin was a member of a Westminster-based gang during the 1730s. The former Whitechapel butcher would meet associates such as Samuel Gregory in Drury Lane taverns, where they would agree on targets in more remote parts of Middlesex. Typically, one winter afternoon they met at the Black Horse tavern and then rode to another public house in Edgeware from whence they set out to the house of a wealthy local farmer. Once there, they forced entry, beat and tied up the occupants, and attempted to torture them into providing information about their valuables. They then stole cash, plate and linen, some of which were later recovered in Thieving Lane in Westminster.[108]

Many highwaymen even used horses hired from Metropolitan livery stables to commit their crimes.[109] Thus, when a prospective robber complained to Jonathan Wild that he had neither horse nor weapons, or money to buy them, the latter merely told him where he might rent them. James Smith, having decided to 'go on the road', hired a horse and set off for Finchley Common with a pair of pistols and a long knife. On his very first day, he carried out three lucrative robberies.[110] It was for this reason that Sir John Fielding urged stable keepers to take precise details of those who took their animals.[111]

Highwaymen often sought commercially busy roads that passed through lonely spots near the capital, such as Hounslow Heath in Middlesex and Black Heath in Kent. John Everett favoured the former, along with Epping Forest.[112] Farmers going to and (even better) from market made particularly attractive targets, as they would often be carrying large amounts of cash. Thus, John Bowden was robbed on the Edgeware Road while returning to Watford from Smithfield Market. His assailant, the highwayman Thomas Twinbrow, immediately rode off towards London.[113] Those who were moving

108. R. Turpin, *The Genuine History of the Life of Richard Turpin, The Noted Highwayman*, 1739, pp.9-11.
109. J. Fielding, *A Plan for Preventing Robberies Within Twenty Miles of London*, 1755, p.9.
110. Anon, *The Remarkable Life of James Smith, A Famous Young Highwayman*, 1756, p.3.
111. J. Fielding, *Extracts from such of the Penal Laws, As particularly relate to the Peace and Good Order of this Metropolis*, 1762, p.306.
112. J. Everett, *A Genuine Narrative of the Memorable Life and Actions of John Everett*, 1730, pp.6-7.
113. W. Peers, *The Genuine Lives of Christopher Johnson, John Stockdale, and William Peers*, 1753, pp.29-30.

between the capital and its satellite villages were also vulnerable. In 1730, a gang of ten robbers infested the roads between London and Islington until captured in bed in a public house near Windsor.[114] Highwaymen could almost operate within the Metropolis itself. On a moonlit night in November 1749, Horace Walpole was attacked while travelling in his coach through Hyde Park.[115] With good horses, such robbers could be back in the capital within minutes of their crimes. As a result, there were suggestions in the 1720s that parties of armed horsemen be stationed at the borders of the city so that they could escort travellers in exchange for a small payment.[116] Additionally, some provincial highwaymen, though not based in London, would hide there when closely pursued in the counties where they normally operated.[117]

Professional Crime

London seems to have been almost the only place in eighteenth-century England that witnessed a significant level of organised crime.[118] This appears to have got worse during the first half of the period, when men like Edward Burnworth led fairly substantial criminal gangs. They were often ruthless, being prepared to murder thief-takers and prosecution witnesses. By the 1750s, Henry Fielding was convinced that the Metropolis contained a criminal gang that was almost a hundred strong, with designated officers and a treasury. They were supposedly adept at disguise and armed with every method of evading the law, should they be caught, whether by physically escaping from custody, bribing and threatening prosecutors into dropping charges, or procuring large numbers of false witnesses to support bogus alibis.[119] Although this may have been an exaggeration, much of the Fielding brothers' most taxing work involved breaking up various Middlesex gangs.

114. *Grub-street Journal*, 23 July 1730.
115. P. Toynbee (Ed.) *The Letters of Horace Walpole*, 1905, vol. I, 1905, p. xl.
116. A. Moreton, *Second Thoughts are best: or, a Further Improvement of a Late Scheme to Prevent Street Robberies*, 1729, p.24.
117. G. Spraggs, *Outlaws and Highwaymen: The Cult of the Robber in England from the Middle Ages to the Nineteenth Century*, 2001, pp.89-90.
118. J. McMullan, *The Canting Crew: London's Criminal Underworld 1550-1700*, 1984, pp.21-23.
119. H. Fielding, *An Enquiry into the causes of the Late Increase of Robbers*, etc., 1751, pp.2-3.

There were 'criminal families' in the capital, where nearly all male, and some female, members, were offenders. For example, it was claimed that the expert pickpocket William Cox had 'trained' as a career criminal from birth, so that, before his early death by hanging in 1773, at the tender age of 20, he had stolen money and goods worth over £10,000. His first offence occurred when his father held him over some iron railings to steal a silver tankard from a window. All of his family and immediate relatives, apart from his mother, were noted for their criminal activities.[120] Many of the specialised criminal techniques and confidence tricks practised by such people were common enough to have acquired popular names, such as 'Buttock and Twang'.[121] Sophisticated counterfeiting offences (rather than simple 'clipping') seem to have been committed by particularly ruthless, professional, gangs.

Nevertheless, most modern commentators feel that the notion of a distinct Metropolitan 'underworld' is largely a literary construct. Then as now, ascribing a structured hierarchy, offence specialism, and complicated stratagems to criminals made for popular reading, especially when it could be combined with an associated cant or 'thieving' language. Thus, in the 1720s, it was alleged that the capital abounded with 'sneaking budges', 'bulking files', 'knowing fellows', and 'ripping coves', amongst many others, each with their own criminal specialism and a hierarchy of status, dependant on their skills.[122] Such reports, although making good copy and usually having a kernel of truth, were greatly exaggerated. It is unlikely that many poor Londoners distinguished 'snabblers' who stole hats at night, from 'merry-coves' who, while singing ballads, 'cased' vulnerable houses.[123]

More importantly, professional criminals were never 'typical' of members of the Metropolitan underworld. Even in the early 1700s, there was a widespread perception that the capital's criminals were largely drawn from the poorest sections of society, and that many were based in and around the

120. Anon, *A Genuine Account of the Life, Robberies, Trial and Execution of William Cox*, 1773, pp.3-16.
121. Anon, *Hell upon Earth: Or the most Pleasant and delectable History of Whittington's Colledge, otherwise (vulgarly) called Newgate*, 1703, p.2.
122. Anon, *The Life and Glorious Actions of the most Heroic and Magnanimous Jonathan Wilde*, 1725, p.13.
123. Anon, *The History of the Lives and Actions of Jonathan Wild, Thief-Taker*, 1725, pp.16-23.

streets. It was feared that the thousands of impoverished people who, under the pretence of blacking shoes, moved about the City and its suburbs, were particularly prone to crime.[124] Similarly, De Mandeville was convinced that the City abounded with loose, idle and dishonest poor people, and that it was this that engendered the higher levels of crime found in the capital.[125]

This identification of a criminal "class" became progressively stronger as the century advanced, and crime ceased to be a phenomenon that was associated with 'everyman' and his ability to succumb to sin and came to be seen as the preserve of a distinct social group. Late in the century, Pierre-Jean Grosley identified a section of the Metropolitan working class, made up of porters, sailors, chairmen and day-labourers, as being particularly crime prone. He claimed that its members were markedly different even to the lower class of artisans found in the capital.[126] However, the process whereby conventional property crime became a lower class phenomenon was matched by a growth in what, today, would be termed "white collar" crime.

White Collar Crime

White Collar crime became far more prevalent as a result of the opportunities provided by the commercial revolution of the era. This posed enormous problems. At the start of the century, there were gaps in the penal code and, by the standards of the time, inadequate punishments for such offences. To address this problem, fraud was raised in status from a misdemeanour to a felony, in many situations, and prosecuted more frequently. As a result, a century that had begun with the occasional indictment for witchcraft witnessed numerous prosecutions of a distinctly modern hue. For example, John Rice, executed for forgery in 1763, had been a City stockbroker and lived an opulent lifestyle. Unfortunately, his ambitions outrunning his means, he had been driven to that "species of gaming called speculating in the stocks". This had resulted in his losing £60,000, and led him to forge a power of

124. A. Moreton, *Everybody's Business is Nobody's Business*, 5th edn., 1725, pp.1-34.
125. B. De Mandeville, *An Enquiry into the Causes of the Frequent Executions at Tyburn*, 1725, p.2.
126. M. Grosley, *A Tour to London*, 1772, p.84.

attorney for one of his client's assets.[127] In 1752, Moses Moravia and John Manoury were convicted of deliberately sinking a ship that they owned, and then claiming on its insurance policy.[128] Widespread corruption, especially during Sir Robert Walpole's venal era (1721-1742), was also an apparently intractable problem until relatively late in the century.

127. OBSP, Trial of John Rice, 13 April 1763.
128. OBSP, Trial of Moses Moravia and others, 25 June 1752.

CHAPTER 4

ATTITUDES TOWARDS CRIME AND POLICING

Concern about Metropolitan Crime

It is frequently claimed that Georgian London was subject to unprecedented concern about crime.[1] Whatever the "true" incidence of offending, there is considerable evidence for widespread anxiety. It was manifest in regular complaints, from a variety of bodies and individuals, about the dangers posed by the city, and by a widely expressed view that Londoners were living in a markedly less secure environment than their forbears. In 1718, for example, Charles Hitchin, the City marshal, lamented that in a city that was formerly famous for its good order, people were afraid to go out, especially after dark, for fear of being attacked. Even taking a coach was insufficient to prevent them being: "...assaulted, cut and robbed in the publick streets".[2] In 1731, it was claimed that only a few years earlier, London had been as: "...remarkable for the safety of its inhabitants, as it is now notorious for the danger Persons are exposed to who walk the Streets after ten at Night".[3] Daniel Defoe feared that acute danger was not confined to the evening, and noted that several robberies have been committed in the middle of the day.[4] It was not just the Square Mile. It was alleged that hardly a night passed in neighbouring Westminster without an outrage being committed, and that no one stirred there after dark without being afraid.[5]

1. D. Lemmings, "Criminal trial procedure in eighteenth-century England: the impact of lawyers", 2005, p.73.
2. C. Hitchin, *A True Discovery of the Conduct of Receivers and Thief-Takers in and about the City of London*, 1718, pp. 7-8.
3. *The Gentleman's Magazine*, 1731, vol. 1, pp.59-60.
4. D. Defoe, *Street-Robberies, Considered: The Reason of their being so Frequent, with Probable means to Prevent 'em*, 1728, p.49.
5. N. M., *A Letter to a Member of Parliament, Concerning the Bill for Regulating the Nightly Watch in the City of Westminster*, 1720, p.26.

A decade later, the author of a dystopian view of the Metropolis as a whole complained about the horrible scenes of street-robbery and murder found in the capital, so that people were: "...almost under the necessity of carrying pistols instead of prayer-books to their parish churches".[6] Such fears continued to resurface periodically for the rest of the century. For example, there was an upsurge of concern in the straitened 1780s. When introducing the ill-fated Police Bill of 1785, the Solicitor General was adamant that no Londoner who travelled after dark could be unaware of the pressing need for reform.[7] Ironically, only a year after their own opposition brought an end to the 1785 Bill, the mayor and aldermen of the City petitioned George III about the "rapid and alarming increase" of crime in and about the Square Mile, allegedly evidenced by a 25 per cent increase in trials at the Old Bailey Sessions over the previous decade.[8]

However, the extent to which such anxieties reflected the feelings of "ordinary" Londoners, let alone reality, is hard to establish. Growth in the printed media undoubtedly fanned middle class fears. Graphic and frightening stories about crime constituted an important part of the diet of most newspaper readers.[9] In a large city like London, it was not difficult to find plenty of genuine incidents to provide gruesome copy, and such reports undermined confidence in the Metropolitan policing system. Readers were often left with the impression that crime was committed at will, in a random manner. Reassuring accounts that stressed the inevitability of punishment declined steadily during the period.[10]

Additionally, a fear that one is living in an era of deteriorating security appears to be innate to human beings. Certainly, some eighteenth-century claims have a distinctly cyclical quality. For example, the jurisprudential writer Martin Madan's concern during the 1780s that the Metropolitan criminals of his day were becoming so audacious that even the daylight hours had become dangerous is identical to Defoe's fear about the same issue voiced

6. Anon, *Hell Upon Earth: Or the Town in an Uproar*, 1729, pp.1-2.
7. *The Gentleman's Magazine*, 1785, vol.55, p.962.
8. *The Gentleman's Magazine*, 1786, vol. 56, pp.263-264.
9. P. King, "Newspaper reporting and attitudes to crime and justice in late-eighteenth-and early-nineteenth-century London", 2007, pp.73-112.
10. E. Foyster, "Introduction: Newspaper Reporting of Crime and Justice", 2007, pp.9-12.

six decades earlier.[11] Even at the time, it prompted Sir Samuel Romilly to describe Madan's work as ludicrously exaggerated and primarily aimed at exciting the fears of his "timid readers".[12]

By contrast, and as already noted, throughout the era there were also many informed observers willing to say that the Metropolis was not especially dangerous or crime prone. As one observer noted at the end of the period, a visitor to London would imagine from the numerous published reports of serious crime that it was a very dangerous place. However, while acknowledging that it contained thousands of criminals, he felt that it was a matter of "especial surprise" given its size that so few robberies and burglaries were committed in its streets and warehouses.[13] The celebrity status accorded to some prominent eighteenth-century Metropolitan criminals, especially highwaymen, a phenomenon that was at its peak in the 1720s, is also significant. For the half century after 1720, the concept of the polite and gallant "gentleman" highwayman was widespread.[14] Crowds of people, including those from the upper social orders, visited Newgate to see felons like James Carrick (1722) and James Maclaine (1750) who were the epitomes of such men.[15] Such respect was even extended to some less patently glamorous felons. This does not appear to be obviously indicative of a society in which the threat posed by crime evinced universal fear. Even Bernard De Mandeville accepted that men who were watchful when abroad, and who avoided crowds, being drunk in public, having connection with street-walkers, being out late at night, and who were careful to check that their locks, bars and shutters were all in place at home, were markedly less likely to be victimised.[16] Robbers looked for the timid or unwary, and those who were dissolute, drunken or off the beaten track. They would very seldom interfere with a man who took basic precautions and avoided suspicious company and places.[17]

11. M. Madan, *Thoughts On Executive Justice*, 2nd edn., 1785, p.5.
12. Sir S. Romilly, *Observations on a Late Publication, Intituled, Thoughts on Executive Justice*, 1786, pp.10-12.
13. W. Clowes, *Leigh's New Picture of London*, 1819, p.101.
14. See generally, R. Shoemaker, "The Street Robber and the Gentleman Highwayman: Changing Representations and Perceptions of Robbery in London, 1690-1800", 2006, pp.381-405.
15. A. McKenzie, *Tyburn's Martyrs: Execution in England 1675-1775*, 2007, p.105.
16. B. De Mandeville, *An Enquiry into the Causes of the Frequent Executions at Tyburn*, 1725, p.10.
17. W. Clowes, *Leigh's New Picture of London*, 1819, p.101.

Legitimacy and the Criminal Law

How much general agreement was there in the eighteenth-century Metropolis as to what was properly criminal, and so deserving of punishment? The degree to which the law had popular legitimacy and support amongst the "lower orders" has been a hotly disputed topic amongst social historians over the past 50 years. It is not simply an academic question. Legitimacy provides a reservoir of goodwill that allows those with power to go against what elements of the public might want in any particular situation without suffering seriously adverse consequences.

There have been several academic attempts at distinguishing between different forms of eighteenth-century crime in this respect. These have usually produced a taxonomy of offences in which some had widespread popular support, others were ascribed almost no legitimacy at all by poorer people, while, in between, there were crimes which might be condemned to a greater or lesser degree, depending on the circumstances in which they were committed.

Not all felonies, let alone misdemeanours, were viewed as inherently bad by large sections of the population. Popular attitudes towards crime, sometimes amounting to an unwritten code, could be quite distinct from the laws of the land.[18] Of course, many crimes, such as murder and rape, were outlawed by both codes. However, *some* offences were actively condoned by poorer people, though how much behaviour fell within this category is very hard to establish.[19] In rural and coastal areas it might encompass offences such as poaching, smuggling, disorder in the course of food riots and, towards the end of the period, the "theft" of crops committed in the context of post-harvest gleaning. In an urban and suburban environment, it might include the "theft"of work materials by employees in manufacturing, construction or the docks. Many thought that some such appropriations were legitimate and traditional work perquisites that were being criminalised by powerful vested interests.

18. E. Thompson, *The Making of the English Working Class*, 1968, p.64.
19. J. Rule and R. Wells, *Crime, Protest and Popular Politics in Southern England 1740–1850*, 1997, p.154.

In between these extremes, it is hard to know how far popular legitimacy extended down the criminal code, as members of the "lower orders" have left comparatively few written records of their own. It is impossible to establish how many people shared the views of the highwayman James Shaw, who could not, apparently, be persuaded that there was anything very criminal about taking the superfluous cash of those who lavished it on "vanity and luxury".[20] However, much appears to have depended on contextual factors. Non-violent theft from an extremely rich man might be viewed very differently to the robbery of a poor one.

Some indication of popular concerns can be evinced from the public reaction to the perpetrators of various forms of crime, whether at the Tyburn gallows or the pillory, which was *relatively* discriminating. Indeed, some observers felt that the mob was "pretty just" in its treatment of those being pilloried. Only those viewed as particularly reprehensible were subjected to the severest treatment. Unsurprisingly, people convicted of heinous crimes faced popular opprobrium. For example, in 1735, a group of notorious murderers on their way to Tyburn were pelted with dirt whilst being tied up to the gallows.[21] When it came to less draconian offences, there was often extreme hostility towards those who were guilty of perjury, forgery, and "scandalous practices" (sexual offences).[22]

Perjury, though legally only a misdemeanour, could have terrible consequences and was often acutely resented as a result. For example, when George Wood, a bailiff's officer, was pilloried in Fetter Lane for the crime he was "severely treated by the populace". As well as throwing dirt and rotten vegetables (normal practice in such situations) they also pelted his face with stones and broken glass, so that he was almost dead by the time he was taken down.[23] Nevertheless, even the mob's treatment of perjurers was relatively discriminating. Thus, in 1763, three tearful and fairly elderly men pilloried opposite Westminster Hall for giving false testimony in an action relating to the rights to an estate in Leicestershire elicited: "...such compassion from the populace, that they treated them with the greatest lenity, and

20. A. L. Hayward, *Lives Of The Most Remarkable Criminals*, 1927, pp.67-71.
21. *The Old Whig*, 2 June 1735.
22. M. Gonzales, *London in 1731*, 1888, pp.156-157.
23. *The Old Whig*, 5 June 1735.

some money was collected for them".[24] They may have viewed it as a family argument between rich men.

Sexual "perversion", whether homosexuality, bestiality, or cross-dressing, attracted acute hostility. Those who were involved in the organization of prostitution, such as bawds, pimps and "bullies" were also unpopular, though this did not normally extend to the prostitutes themselves. In 1719, when two women were pilloried in Charing Cross for keeping notorious bawdy-houses, they were treated with the: "...highest resentment of the mob on those occasions, in showers of rotten eggs, dirt, &c".[25] The pillorying of (attempted) sodomites was especially harsh. One foreign observer felt that the English viewed the crime with so much abhorrence that the: "...fury of the populace is unbounded".[26] Thomas Blair died as a result of this treatment in 1743. Daniel Lobley met a similar fate, for the same crime, in 1763.[27] When Theodosius Read and William Smith were pilloried at St Margaret's Hill, their treatment by a crowd of several thousand was so brutal that one died after 30 minutes, while still in the apparatus, and the other expired from his injuries shortly after being taken down.[28]

The abuse of the powerless also excited anger amongst poorer Londoners. This can be seen in cases involving parish apprentices "put out" into the care of local people who for a small premium took them into their households and, in theory, taught them a trade. This spared the parish the expense of raising orphans, bastards and the infants of the indigent.[29] In 1767, Elizabeth Brownrigg was executed amid popular rejoicing for murdering her maid.[30] The following year, Sarah Metyard and her daughter attracted the same hostility before they were hanged for a similar crime. Some other crimes, such as coining, were also generally unpopular. When forged coins were passed, they could end up in the hands of poor people who would either have to commit an offence to get rid of them (uttering), or accept a financial loss.

24. P. Bartlett, "Sodomites in the Pillory in Eighteenth-century London", 1997, p.554.
25. *Weekly Journal, or, British Gazetteer*, 27 June 1719.
26. J. W. von Archenholz, *A Picture of England*, vol. 2, 1789, pp.102-4.
27. P. Bartlett, "Sodomites in the Pillory in Eighteenth-century London", 1997, p.559 and p.564.
28. *Morning Post, and Daily Advertiser*, 11 April 1780.
29. A. M. Kilday and K. Watson, "Child Murder in Georgian England", 2005, pp.40-46.
30. *The Gentleman's Magazine*, 1767, vol. 37, p.419 and p.433.

This explains why Barbara Spencer was stoned by a mob while praying before her execution.[31]

By contrast, and perhaps unsurprisingly, taxes and, even more so, duties, seem to have been unpopular among the general populace, and those punished for failing to pay them were often dealt with sympathetically. For example, in 1738, a man who was pilloried for defrauding the Crown of the duty payable on soap was treated "very quietly" during his time in the apparatus. When taken down, he bowed to the attendant mob.[32]

However, none of these cases provide an indication as to popular attitudes to conventional property crimes such as theft, fraud, and housebreaking, which made up the vast majority of serious indictable offences. Responses to these offences were often hostile. For example, in 1739, an Irishman being pilloried at Bishopsgate for defrauding a pawnbroker of several guineas by passing off plate as solid gold was "severely pelted by the populace".[33] Pawnbrokers were not generally popular, and, unless the incident occurred during one of the period outbreaks of anti-Irish feeling, it is hard to explain. Similarly, in 1785, a woman whose valuable timepiece had been stolen by a coachman in Bedford Square came under considerable pressure from the "mob" to indict him. To their indignation, she let him go, though they successfully prevented her from giving him a gift of money.[34]

Reform Movements

The era witnessed a major change in social attitudes towards crime, disorder and immorality amongst key elements of society. These changes appear to have accelerated rapidly in the decades after 1780, when what have been termed "middle class" values became increasingly prevalent amongst key sections of the urban populace. The century witnessed a progressively stronger reluctance to accept crime and disorder as an inevitable result of man's fallen state and the sum of individual pathologies, and a greater willingness to see

31. *Weekly Journal or British Gazetteer*, July 15th, 1721.
32. *Old Commonsense: Or, the Englishman's Journal*, 23 September 1738.
33. *Old Commonsense, or, the Englishman's Journal*, 2 June 1738.
34. *The Times*, 13 September 1785, p. 3.

it as a potentially remediable social problem. Nowhere was this more manifest than in the Metropolis.

Such attitudes took many forms, both conservative and liberal, whether manifest in the work of the Reformation of Manners movement or Thomas Coram's campaign to establish a foundling hospital for infants who were exposed on the capital's streets. Some men, such as Sir John Gonson, supported both approaches. This change in attitudes slowly prompted a greater willingness on the part of the political nation to pay for law enforcement, to demand that it be effective, and to accept that it might affect some long cherished rights and freedoms in the process.

Reformation societies

The first of the Societies for the Reformation of Manners was established in 1690 in Tower Hamlets, being supported by a Royal Proclamation against vice and a letter sent from the Queen to the Middlesex justices (in July 1691) urging them to enforce the laws against swearing, Sabbath violation, and various forms of disorderly conduct.[35] This eventually resulted in their meeting at Hick's Hall to formulate a plan of action aimed at ensuring that taverns and coffee houses were closed on the Sabbath.[36] During the ensuing two decades, the original society was followed by dozens of similar associations in the London area.

The funeral of John Dent, a murdered reforming constable, is indicative of the level of establishment support behind the initiative in the early years of the century. Dent's coffin was carried by a large number of prominent gentlemen. The procession was led by twenty beadles, and followed by a dozen constables, 20 clergymen, twelve Westminster JPs and two aldermen from the City.[37] Inevitably, of course, many people joined the societies for political reasons, rather than out of genuine sympathy with their objectives. For example, in 1727, when Charles Hitchen, a corrupt deputy City marshal, was prosecuted for sodomy, it was noted that he had always been a: "… very busy and active Fellow for promoting the Reformation of Manners".[38]

35. J. Woodward, *An Account of the Societies for Reformation of Manners*, 1699, p.7.
36. *The Post Man*, 3-5 March 1698.
37. *Post Boy*, 26-29 March 1709.
38. *Mist's Weekly Journal*, 15 April 1727.

Nevertheless, most of their members, such as Sir John Gonson, a highly active JP who would eventually become the chairman of the Westminster Sessions, were motivated by a genuine commitment to the cause.

Very significantly, the societies did not confine themselves to moralising. Political pressure from their members contributed to the decision to end some of the traditional, but extremely unruly, fairs and entertainments found in the Metropolitan area, such as that marking St. Bartholomew's Day. Encouraged by this, the Grand Jury of Middlesex then moved against the Mayfair, on the grounds that it was immoral, a public nuisance, and likely to produce breaches of the peace.[39]

Even more importantly, the societies actively prosecuted offences of immorality, with a view to inspiring the: "...laws against prophaneness with terror".[40] It was a constant source of irritation that, although the criminal law was on their side, it was very rarely applied in practice.[41] In *theory*, if constables and church wardens fulfilled their oaths of office properly they would take action against every form of low level disorder found in their parishes, whether drunkenness, cursing, prostitution or gambling.[42] In reality, this almost never happened. JPs were equally selective. In 1730, Francis Hare told a meeting of the Society that magistrates had: "...neither eyes nor ears to see offences".[43] For their members, actively prosecuting offenders was seen as a moral duty and even an expression of love towards sinners who were otherwise bent on destroying their own souls. Early intervention via criminal sanctions would prevent their "mad careers" progressing from drunkenness to capital offences.[44] Indeed, one newspaper correspondent suggested that actively prosecuting moral offences was almost the only way

39. Anon, *Reasons for suppressing the yearly fair in Brook-field, Westminster; commonly called Mayfair*, 1709, p.36.
40. J. Denham, *A Sermon Preach'd to the Societies for Reformation of Manners, at Salter's-Hall, On Monday, June 29, 1724*, 1724, p.1.
41. J. Woodward, *An Account of the Societies for Reformation of Manners*, 1699, pp.2-3.
42. Anon, *An Enquiry into the Causes of the Encrease and Miseries of the Poor in England*, 1738, p.47
43. P. Bartlett, "Sodomites in the Pillory in Eighteenth-century London", 1997, p.564.
44. F. Grant, *A Vindication of Informers of the Breaches of the Laws Against Prophaness and Immorality*, 1701, pp.6-7.

by which: "…persons in the lower ranks of life can do any considerable service to the public".[45]

As a result, individual members of the societies would pass on information to local magistrates, with the societies providing funds to pay for prosecutions or even bringing them in their own right. To expedite such prosecutions, the societies also established networks of moral guardians in London, with four stewards being appointed in each ward of the City, two for every parish, and a committee being set up whose business it was to record the names and addresses of those who were guilty of offences of immorality. As a Lord Chief Justice later noted of their successors, they often acted: "…like a new sort of grand jury, who meet once or twice in a week, and take upon themselves to present, correct, reform, and commence prosecutions".[46]

At their peak, the societies were very active. In the cities of London and Westminster alone, they prosecuted 2,003 people in the year running from the 1st of December 1717. Of these, 1,253 were for "lewd and disorderly" practices (largely prostitution), 492 for exercising their trades on the Sabbath, and 202 for swearing and cursing in public.[47] The movement's financial resources led their targets to complain of the difficulty of getting justice when an individual had to: "…oppose a Society, or stake a single fortune against a general subscription!"[48] However, their work was not purely an exercise in policing the poor. Prostitutes' clients were sometimes targeted, so that well-to-do people were also troubled by their campaigns.[49]

Many members of the societies, like the unfortunate Dent, became highly interventionist local constables. Thus, in September 1730, a dozen disorderly men and women were arrested in several night houses by "informing constables".[50] The societies also tried to facilitate a more professional and efficient approach to prosecuting crime by issuing blank, pro forma, printed warrants, for commonly occurring offences. These would merely require the

45. *London Chronicle*, 3-5 June 1762.
46. *Leeman v Allen and Others* (1763) 2 Wilson K.B. 160.
47. *White-hall Evening-Post*, 13-15 January, 1719.
48. C. Gery, *Mr. Gery's Case With the Reforming Constables*, 1750, p.1.
49. J. Hurl-Eamon, "Policing Male Heterosexuality: The Reformation of Manners Societies' Campaign Against the Brothels in Westminster, 1690-1720", 2004, p. 1017.
50. *Grub-street Journal*, 17 September 1730.

name, crime and place of abode of the suspect to be completed by the JP It was hoped that this would make life easier for magistrates and their clerks, who: "…when they happen to be no hearty friends to these proceedings, will have the less occasion to be prejudiced against them". The society proposed that the warrants be issued to the "best disposed" constables (some of them members of their own organization) to be enforced.[51]

However, although several judges joined the organization, there was also considerable judicial caution, and occasional overt hostility, about much of its work. Thus, Lord Chief Justice Holt declared that he was as much in favour of reformation as anyone but that it had to done be "in a legal manner". In May 1726, damages of £20 were awarded in a civil action against the High Constable of the Holborn Division, and a prominent member of the Society, for arresting a young gentleman in Westminster Abbey and detaining him for two days in the Gatehouse Prison.[52]

The impetus behind the first wave of societies appears to have petered out in the 1740s, probably for generational reasons and as a result of hostility towards their use of informers to enforce the unpopular 1736 Gin Act. Nevertheless, the perceived need for their existence did not disappear, and led to their re-establishment in London in 1757, though they never approached their previous numbers. According to John Wesley, this second initiative originated on an August Sunday that year, when a small group of men meeting for prayer fell to complaining about the widespread profanation of the Lord's Day, especially in the area around Moorfields. Resolving to take action, they consulted Sir John Fielding for advice. With his help, they decided to set up a new society for the reformation of manners. Although it initially distributed reforming pamphlets, it swiftly followed its predecessor in taking more direct action. In the five and a half years between August 1757 and August 1763, John Wesley claimed that they conducted more than 10,588 prosecutions.[53] These included large numbers of actions for brothel keeping, prostitution, and Sabbath breaking, with smaller amounts for gaming, profane swearing and selling obscene prints.

51. J. Drury, *An Account of the Progress of the Reformation of Manners*, 1701, pp.10–11.
52. *Weekly Journal, or The British Gazetteer*, 28 May 1726.
53. J. Wesley, *A sermon preached before the Society for reformation of manners, etc.*, 1763, pp.1–12.

This revived reform movement came to grief fairly swiftly, after an adverse verdict from Judge Charles Pratt. Taking the opportunity to show his "dislike towards these reformers", Pratt refused to set aside as excessive a jury award of £300 damages made against several reforming constables on a charge of assaulting and falsely imprisoning the keeper of an alleged brothel, the Rummer Tavern, even though it had only been for a few hours, and done in good faith (if rather carelessly).[54] This proved a deathblow to the society's funds, especially when accompanied by the action's considerable legal costs. The society limped on under its debts until 1765, when it disintegrated.

Nevertheless, this was not the end of organized reform movements. After 1787, William Wilberforce persuaded King George III to issue a proclamation against vice and immorality (rather as William III had done in the previous century), and then founded a voluntary organization to put its aims into effect. This resulted in the Proclamation Society, which attempted, in particular, to suppress blasphemous and indecent literature. In 1795, James Roach, the publisher of *Harris's List*, describing Metropolitan prostitutes and their services, was prosecuted by the society and sent to Newgate for a year. The Proclamation Society recruited relatively small numbers of prominent members of the "establishment", whether peers or churchmen. However, it was followed by the Society for Suppression of Vice, established by Thomas Bowdler and other likeminded men in 1802, which recruited a more numerous and middle class membership. Its initial goals were to prevent the profanation of the Lord's Day, prosecute blasphemous publications, bring the trade in obscene books to a halt, close disorderly houses and suppress fortune tellers.[55] Both organizations were heavily influenced by the evangelical theology of the era.[56]

54. *Leeman v Allen and Others* (1763) 2 Wilson K.B. 160.
55. *The Morning Chronicle*, 1 December, 1802.
56. M. J. D. Roberts, "The Society for the Suppression of Vice and Its Early Critics, 1802-1812", 1983, p.160.

CHAPTER 5

EXPLANATIONS FOR METROPOLITAN CRIME

Introduction

Eighteenth-century London was a diverse society and it produced a correspondingly broad range of thought on crime and disorder. There was never a consensus of opinion. Instead, different schools of thought waxed and waned in strength, moving from the peripheries to centre stage, and vice versa, gaining or losing adherents, but rarely being entirely extinguished and never being totally dominant.

Speaking very broadly, and as in the modern era, there were two overarching attempts to explain crime. To many, it was the result of innate human wickedness that had been allowed to flourish by an individual's failure to resist the snares of the devil. By contrast, others were more sensitive to structural determinants, such as poverty and unemployment. These approaches were not mutually exclusive, and many observers ascribed significance to both, believing that crime was the inevitable consequence: "… either of the wants, or the depravity, of the lowest part of the human species".[1] Both factors could operate simultaneously in individual felons. It was accepted by many proponents of the role of original sin that the Devil did not operate in a social vacuum, and was likely to make work for idle hands. Conversely, most of those who ascribed significance to poverty did not preclude an important role for human agency.

1. D. Defoe, *The History of the Remarkable Life of John Sheppard*, 1724, pp.1–20.

Immorality

Many eighteenth-century observers thought that crime was largely the product of the: "…almost total want of morals, and dissoluteness of manners of the common people".[2] A progressive moral deterioration, initiated by the commission of minor sins, such as Sabbath breaking or the excessive consumption of spirits, which ultimately culminated in the commission of capital felonies like murder and robbery, was an especially popular explanation for crime, particularly in the century's early decades. It was an analysis that the Newgate ordinary traditionally, and enthusiastically, endorsed in his published accounts of the lives of condemned prisoners. For example, according to the Reverend John Guthrie, Thomas Homan, who brutally murdered an elderly woman during a bungled burglary, had initially stolen small amounts from the baker to whom he was apprenticed, married before his articles were finished (forbidden for apprentices), frequented skittle grounds, played cards and kept the "basest company" before progressing to homicide.[3]

John Addison's criminal career was another classic example of such a progression. It appears to have commenced when he abandoned his apprenticeship to a butcher in Southwark three years early. He then started to mix with bad company and, in particular, the proverbial "lewd women" who were commonly believed to lure young men into offending. To support his irregular lifestyle he drifted into crime, going from petty thefts to picking pockets and shoplifting, then burglary and housebreaking, before arriving at highway robbery, for which he was eventually hanged.[4]

This type of criminal career progression was such a cultural trope that it formed the underlying theme for the life of Hogarth's "Idle Apprentice", a series of prints from 1751. The bad apprentice's journey to the gallows begins when he neglects his master's business and gambles in a churchyard during divine service (see the plate section). It was thought to be highly unusual

---

2. S. Welch, *A Proposal to render effectual a Plan to remove the nuisance of Common Prostitutes from the streets of this Metropolis*, 1758, p.48.
3. J. Guthrie, *The Behaviour, Confession, and Dying Words of Thomas Homan, who was Executed on Thursday the 18th of this Instant November*, 1742, p.5.
4. Anon, *An account of the life, birth, death, parentage, and conversation, of Mr. John Addison, a most notorious highwayman*, 1711, p.4.

for a mature man, who had previously led an honest life, to suddenly commit a serious offence. It was this that made John Austin's behaviour all the more remarkable. He had been born to honest parents and reached the age of 37, working as a gardener, without the slightest blemish on his character, other than packing up plants for a Monday market on the Sabbath. In 1725, he was arrested for knocking down a man in Stepney Fields with a club and robbing him of his coat. While awaiting execution he was asked how a man of his character, in well-to-do circumstances, came to behave in such a manner, and could only reply that he had been disturbed in his mind and had committed the robbery from a "sudden impulse".[5]

The notion of progressive moral deterioration had important implications for crime control. Any form of policing that offered early intervention in the careers of offenders might break their downward cycle. As a result, men like Patrick Colquhoun sought the: "Meanes of embarrassing and checking the Progress of crimes in these First Stages". The notion of a slippery slope of offending also received official support. Late in the century, Henry Dundas, the Home Secretary, speaking in support of the Middlesex Justices Act 1792, reminded his fellow MPs that "rogues reached the gallows by degrees". They frequently started as pickpockets in their early teens, became emboldened by their initial thefts, and used the proceeds of these crimes to buy a horse with which they took to highway robbery.[6]

However, even then, many felt that it was superficial to: "...see the source of all our public miscarriages in the particular and accidental misconduct of individuals". Although such an analysis was attractive, because it allowed the public to feel that they had no responsibility for what occurred around them, it was more convincing to identify "permanent and established causes" for offending.[7]

5. A. L. Hayward, *Lives Of The Most Remarkable Criminals*, 1927, p.292.
6. Anon (By a Friend to the Constitution), *Observations on the Duty and Power of Juries, as established by the Laws of England*, 5th edn., 1800, p.448.
7. J. Brown, *An Estimate of the Manners and Principles of the Times*, 7th edn., 1758, pp.5-6.

Structural Determinants

Even at the start of the eighteenth century, many Metropolitan observers attributed crime to social hardship and environmental stress. In 1701, a newspaper could applaud proposals that were aimed at dealing with indigence and other root causes of crime, rather than waiting for draconian punishment to become necessary.[8] Such an approach would put a stop to the many robberies: "...occasioned by the number of idle people".[9] By the end of the century, far more people were willing to acknowledge the impact of the urban environment, including its lack of regular well paid work, on offending. Thus, a Middlesex magistrate, writing in 1787, was well aware that many of his contemporaries attributed an apparent rise in metropolitan crime not, as he did, to excessive lenience in the criminal justice system, but to the: "... great number of soldiers and sailors discharged since the last war, together from [with] the want of employment for a large body of artificers, joined to the dearness of all kind of provisions and the heavy taxes".[10] In 1801, even a French visitor could note that, in London: "The high price of provisions contributes to multiply those crimes which originate in distress".[11]

Necessity, and the attendant desire to provide for a family that would otherwise go without, was also regularly advanced at trial as an explanation for offending, being the most common plea in mitigation, even though it was not a legal defence.[12] Such pleas were tendered in both minor and serious crimes. For an example of the latter can be considered the case of Richard Arnold, a 33-year-old man from Leicestershire, who had come to London, married and had two children. Although an industrious worker, who had been in regular employment for many years, both he and his wife fell chronically ill, which rendered them incapable of any form of labour. Arnold resolved to deal with his financial problems by resorting to highway

8. *The Post Angel or Universal Entertainment*, 1701, vol.1, issue 4, p.260.
9. Anon, *A Method Proposed to prevent the many Robberies and Villainies Committed in and about the City of London*, 1752, p.14.
10. Anon (By a Magistrate), *Some Hints Towards A Revival of the Penal Laws*, 1787, p.9.
11. M. De Calonne, *Proposal for Preventing Highway Robberies in the Environs of London; or, an Account of the Marechaussee in France*, 1801, p.9.
12. A. L. Hayward, *Lives Of The Most Remarkable Criminals*, 1927, p.427. D. Rabin, "Searching for the Self in Eighteenth-century English Criminal Trials, 1730-1800", 2003, p.93.

robbery, despite being very sick. He rented a one eyed (and correspondingly cheap) horse in Moorfields and attempted to stop travellers on the road near Ealing. He was captured during his very first, and rather amateurish, crime. While awaiting execution he told the ordinary that he had had no contact with other felons and was forced to robbery because he and his wife had: "…nothing to supply their wants, but both ready to perish, knowing no remedy, which drove him to this desperate and unhappy course".[13] At the opposite end of the scale of gravity, even a rabid critic of immorality knew that most London streetwalkers "whore[d] for bread".[14] If they were unable to find customers, they might be forced to pick pockets "for the ensuing day's sustenance".[15] There was even some official sympathy for those in this situation, although it was often difficult to: "…judge of the reasonableness of such an excuse".[16]

There appears to be *some*, albeit limited, statistical linkage between the incidence of property crime and dearth during the eighteenth century. Several modern observers have reached the tentative conclusion that it was, to some degree, a response to general economic adversity. For example, spikes in indictment rates at the Old Bailey in the early years of the eighteenth century, such as that which followed the very poor harvests of 1709 and 1710, suggest some relationship between the number of charges being laid and standards of living.[17] Similarly, the Old Bailey witnessed a major increase in the number of people charged with theft during the 1780s, which also saw considerable hardship. Both 1782 and 1783 produced poor harvests and an economic slump. There was another severe recession in 1788, which was aggravated by the harsh winter at the end of that year. According to some estimates, real wages in London fell by 11 per cent during the decade.[18]

---

13. J. Guthrie, *The Ordinary of Newgate, His Account of the Behaviour, Confession, and dying Words of the Malefactors who were Executed at Tyburn, On Monday the 22d of November, 1742*, 1742, p.6.
14. J. Dunton, *The Shortest-Way with Whores and Rogues*, 1703, p.41.
15. Anon, *Low-Life: or One Half of the World Knows not how the Other Half Live*, 2nd edn., 1755, p.17.
16. A. L. Hayward, *Lives Of The Most Remarkable Criminals*, 1927, p.427.
17. J. M. Beattie, "Crime and inequality in eighteenth-century London", 1995, p.121 and pp.131-132.
18. L. Mackay, "Why they stole: women in the Old Bailey, 1779-1789", 1999, pp.623-639.

However, as already noted, treating the incidence of prosecution as a reliable indicator of the level of property crime is fraught with difficulties. If only one in ten crimes committed was actually prosecuted, indictment levels would be ten times as sensitive to changes in the proportion of victims who chose to bring a prosecution as they were to changes in the absolute level of offences. Moral panics caused by dearth and the demobilisation of soldiers could explain increasing indictment rates, as much as the effects of hardship. As a result, it has also been argued that in only a handful of years can any real correlation be shown between the number of thefts prosecuted and levels of economic adversity.[19]

Need and Greed

On a personal basis, it is hard to determine the position of the "typical" Metropolitan offender on the need/greed scale. Although poverty might help to explain the relative vulnerability of different social groups to being indicted for theft, it is not, on its own, an entirely satisfactory explanation for crime. There were rich thieves. For example, the notorious highwayman James Smith had received and inherited significant sums of money from relatives, including a legacy of £300. Nevertheless, he found this inadequate to fund a grossly extravagant lifestyle in which he spent large amounts of money on the more expensive sort of Metropolitan "lady-bird".[20]

Of course, and very importantly, need and greed were not mutually exclusive. For example, it was noted that William Allison, a poor countryman who was executed at Tyburn in September 1726, had been induced to commit his crime: "...partly through covetousness, and partly through want".[21] This probably applied to a high proportion of those who were convicted at the Old Bailey. They were poor, but not destitute, deprived of the little luxuries that they could see all around them in the Metropolitan environment, but not starving. Many ordinary labouring men, especially those with families,

---

19. P. King, *Crime, Justice, and Discretion in England 1740-1820*, 2000, p.12 and p.166.
20. Anon, *The Remarkable Life of James Smith, A Famous Young Highwayman*, 1756, p.3.
21. A. L. Hayward, *Lives Of The Most Remarkable Criminals*, 1927, p.381.

could only obtain a bare subsistence via the most "unintermitting exertions". They lacked any real domestic comfort and would have to accept extreme self-denial to make ends meet.[22] Some foreign visitors detected a "bleakness" about life for the London poor that went beyond financial comparison with those of other countries, although they were also shocked by the numbers who perished from diseases produced by exposure to cold and inadequate and unwholesome food.[23] In these circumstances, property crime could appear attractive, if only because there would always be people who were not willing to: "...encounter poverty with honest labour".[24]

For many Metropolitan criminals, their way of life was not an identity, merely an expedient, being interspersed with poorly paid, unskilled, frequently seasonal, but still legitimate forms of work. Numerous felons who might have ended their careers at the gallows, or by being transported to America, left their nefarious existences and returned to "normal" life, because the risks came to seem excessive or because they had discovered alternative, and legal, forms of income. Thus, just before his execution at Tyburn in 1723, the highwayman William Duce wrote a letter to a former associate who had: "...retired and lived honestly and privately, [and] was no longer addicted to such courses".[25] John Dyer, who was hanged at Tyburn in 1729, had fallen into crime in his native Wiltshire, but initially "liv'd very honest" after moving to London. He worked for shoemakers in Holborn for over eighteen months, before reoffending.[26] Eighteenth-century observers saw a relatively small difference between the thieves who were transported to America and those from a similar social milieu who went there as voluntarily indentured labourers. Taking account of other factors (an inherently difficult task), it seems that the cost of voluntarily indentured labour worked out at 2.44 pounds sterling a year, compared to 1.93 for that of convicts. Thus, there was only a 21 per cent discount for their "criminality".[27]

---

22. Anon (By a Citizen of London), *Observations on a Late Publication: Intituled A Treatise on the Police of the Metropolis*, 1799, p.26.
23. M. A. Espriella, *Letters from England,* vol.1, 3rd edn., 1814, p.302.
24. Anon, *A Method whereby Criminals liable to Transportation may be render'd not only useful but honest members of the publick*, 1727, p.3.
25. A. L. Hayward, *Lives Of The Most Remarkable Criminals,* 1927, p.121.
26. J. Dyer, *A Genuine Narrative of the Memorable Life and Actions of John Dyer*, 1729, p.18.
27. F. Grubb, "The Market Evaluation of Criminality: Evidence from the Auction of British

However, once people had become involved with the criminal justice system, the chances of a successful return to ordinary life declined sharply. In an anticipation of the "labelling theory" that was to become popular in the 1960s, some observers noted that former convicts, especially those who had been in prison, were usually viewed as infamous characters, whether by reputation or on enquiry, so that: "...none who know them will employ them". At the same time, charity, whether parish or private, could also be "very cold" towards those who were physically able to work. As a result, healthy former criminals were often forced to steal rather than face starvation.[28] This was one reason that the temporary expedient of branding clergied thieves on the cheek, rather than on the brawn of their thumbs, employed between 1699 and 1706, was abandoned: "...it excluded them the society of the just, and left them destitute thereby of the means of getting an honest livelihood".[29] It was also part of the reason that branding on the thumb was finally abolished altogether in 1779. It fixed convicts with a "lasting mark of disgrace" that prevented them from securing legitimate employment.[30]

Opportunity to Offend

Contemporary observers, like William Paley, often focussed on the increase in criminal potential found in the expanding Metropolis, something that could: "...multiply crimes by presenting easier opportunities". As London became a world city of international commercial importance, and its population required ever more produce to sustain themselves, goods of all descriptions, whether luxury items or the basic necessities of life, were traded in huge quantities. Increased general wealth necessarily added to the value of property that was in circulation, providing further opportunities for crime and encouraging offending.[31] As a magistrate observed, in a commercial

---

Convict Labor in America, 1767-1775", 2001, p.298.

28. L. Braddon, *The miseries of the poor are a national sin*, 1717, p.12.
29. Anon, *A Method whereby Criminals liable to Transportation may be render'd not only useful but honest members of the publick*, 1727, p.7.
30. *Morning Chronicle and London Advertiser*, 11 May 1779.
31. L. Zedner, "Policing Before and After the Police", 2006, p.85 and p.78. Sir J. Fielding, *Extracts*

nation like England: "...offences will naturally increase in proportion as our trade increases".[32] However, there were fears that increased amounts of wealth had malign effects that went beyond providing simple opportunities for crime. In particular, there was concern that it had a corrupting effect on the wider society.[33]

The Effects of War on Crime

There was a well-established correlation between war and a reduction in criminal prosecutions in the London area during the eighteenth century, while the end of major conflicts saw an equally marked increase in Metropolitan indictments. This link appears to have waned in the early 1800s. The connection was as noted by contemporary observers as it has been by modern academics analysing prosecution rates. Thus, in the early 1720s, when the Metropolis faced an apparent crime wave, it was claimed that: "...most wish'd for a War, to rid the country of such vermin, who were continually doing mischief in some place or other".[34] Over half a century later, in June 1777, a Metropolitan newspaper could note that since the outbreak of the American War of Independence: "...robberies in general are something less frequent".[35] Similarly, in 1791, it was pessimistically expected: "...from the discharge of men from the Fleet, that great depredations will be committed this winter".[36] At the end of the eighteenth century, the Surrey justices anticipated that demobilisation might require that their newly built gaol in Newington be filled to its capacity.[37] On a less anecdotal basis, in 1812, it was claimed that a detailed breakdown of Metropolitan execution rates since 1749 showed that hangings had decreased during hostilities and risen

from Such of the Penal Laws, As Particularly relate to the Peace and Good Order of this Metropolis ... to which is added...a short Treatise on the office of Constable, 1768, p.8.

32. Anon (By a Magistrate), *Some Hints Towards A Revival of the Penal Laws*, 1787, p.6.
33. Anon (By a Friend to the Constitution), *Observations on the Duty and Power of Juries, as established by the Laws of England*, 5th edn., 1800, p.13.
34. Anon, *The History of the Lives and Actions of Jonathan Wild, Thief-Taker*, 1725, p.A3.
35. S. Devereaux, "The Making of the Penitentiary Act, 1775-1779", 1999, pp.423-424.
36. *The Times*, Oct 11th 1791, p.3.
37. C. W. Chalkin (Ed.), *Surrey Gaol and Session House, 1791-1824*, 2009, p.xxi.

in peacetime.[38] According to a modern estimate, warfare saw a fall of up to a third in indictment rates.[39]

This connection was particularly important, because the eighteenth century was a period of regular conflict. The era began with some of the consequences of the large-scale demobilisation of 1697 that marked the end of the War of the League of Augsburg still in effect. This was swiftly followed by the War of the Spanish Succession (1701-1714), which saw the army soar from a shell of only 8,000 troops, and released 157,000 men at its conclusion, and the War of the Austrian Succession (1740-1748), which ultimately produced 79,000 ex-servicemen. The mini crime wave that Henry Fielding was forced to address was part of the aftermath of the Seven Years War, which ended in 1763, discharging 160,000 men into society.[40] There was another massive demobilisation of at least 130,000 soldiers and sailors (possibly as many as 160,000) after the American War ended in 1783, which saw a particularly marked increase in the number of people charged with theft.[41] The last years of the century saw the impact of the French Revolutionary War.

The correlation between war and criminal prosecutions appears to have been multi-faceted. To a significant extent, variations in indictment rates during and after hostilities can be explained by changing reactions and responses to potentially criminal actions, on the part of victims and magistrates, rather than any "real" change in offending rates. There may well have been an increased willingness to indict suspects after a conflict, in a system that was largely based on private prosecution. In Essex, for example, alarmist newspaper reporting of the expected crime wave that would follow the impending peace of 1783 may have prompted victims to begin initiating formal prosecutions in greater numbers *before* the troops returned from America.[42]

There was also a greater willingness to divert suspects from the criminal justice system by requiring or allowing them to enlist, rather than facing trial, while hostilities were ongoing. After 1689, the English/British

38. J. Neild, *State of the Prisons in England, Scotland, and Wales*, 1812, p.635.
39. P. King, *Crime, Justice and Discretion in England 1740-1820*, 2000, p.154.
40. J. Marriott, *The Spatiality of the Poor in Eighteenth-century London*, 2003, p.131.
41. L. Mackay, *Why they stole: women in the Old Bailey, 1779-1789*, 1999, pp.623-639.
42. P. King, *Crime, Justice and Discretion in England 1740-1820*, 2000 p.169.

Army contained increasing numbers of criminals, due to these recruitment practices. As this process frequently occurred after suspects had been apprehended, but before an indictment was brought, the accused man might not show up in any criminal statistics. Occasionally, it was even done on a private basis, between crime victim and detained suspect, without any formal involvement by the state. At others, it was done after the authorities had been involved but before trial. Thus, when Samuel Holland was caught stealing a small amount of lead pipe from the house of Saunders Welch, in 1741, he was questioned by his victim while being held in a nearby watch-house. On Holland's begging for mercy, Welch was initially willing not to press charges on condition that he enlisted in a foreign garrison and, on his consenting to this, a recruiting sergeant was sent for. However, when it was realised that the thief was an Irishman by origin (these not being recruited in London at this time), this option was withdrawn, and he was subsequently prosecuted to conviction.[43] Thomas Hunter, a burglar who was committed to Newgate pending trial, was more fortunate. He avoided his hearing, while in custody, by agreeing to enlist in a regiment of marines, albeit that it was an indulgence that he swiftly abused.[44] Similarly, in 1766, a young pick-pocket who had been carried before the sitting alderman at the Mansion House asked to be sent to India. His request was complied with, and he was temporarily committed to Clerkenwell Bridewell.[45] Presumably, he was then put into the military service of one of the "European" regiments of the Honourable East India Company.

Of course, many felons were recruited *after* conviction. At the start of the eighteenth century, a few who had been found guilty of clergyable offences and who were illiterate would still offer to enlist before sentence was passed, rather than risk failing the reading test for benefit of clergy (the test was abolished in 1706).[46] More commonly, men were enlisted post-conviction as a result of the Mutiny Act of 1702, amongst other provisions, which allowed

43. OBSP, Trial of Samuel Holland, 28 August 1741.

44. P. Lorrain, *The Ordinary of Newgate, his Account of the Behaviour, Confessions, and Last Speeches of the Criminals that were executed at Tyburn, on Wednesday the 21st June, 1704*, p.2.

45. *The Whitehall Evening Post; Or, London Intelligencer*, 28 October 1766.

46. Anon, *Hell upon Earth: Or the most Pleasant and delectable History of Whittington's Colledge, otherwise (vulgarly) called Newgate*, 1703, p.10.

the pardoning of capital offenders who agreed to join up. For example, in October 1771, a group of five convicts, including Robert Parker: "...received his majesty's free pardon, on condition of entering as marines".[47] The number of such men increased greatly once hostilities were underway. In 1776, among 600 recruits to the Royal American Regiment being sent to Florida in a flotilla of ships, there were many who had been pardoned from transportation on condition of enlisting. (Several of them tried to escape while their ship was sailing down the Thames).[48] Similarly, in 1794, Oliver Minton and George Duffey, sentenced at the Middlesex Quarter Sessions to a year's imprisonment in Newgate for assault, were pardoned and released from custody on condition of enlisting in the Eighth Regiment of Light Dragoons.[49] These cases do, of course, show up in indictment rates.

In all cases, whether recruitment took place before or after conviction, offenders were taken out of circulation. When peace returned, they were discharged and may have returned to their previous lives, helping to explain post-disbandment crime waves.[50] Thus, it was noted in 1785 that, during the then recent war in America:

> ...many abandoned characters were sent among our soldiery and seamen; and as a great number of those are now discharged ... it serves to increase the number of such as live by unlawful means.[51]

The training and brutalisation that some of these men received during their service could only exacerbate matters. For example, the highwayman John Thomson had served aboard a warship, in the course of which he had seen numerous fierce engagements and helped take many prizes, so that he had become accustomed to blood and plunder. When he returned home to

47. *Middlesex Journal or Chronicle of Liberty*, 19 October, 1771.
48. *Morning Post and Daily Advertiser*, 30 March, 1776.
49. NAHOCR700000001 Document at www.londonlives.org Last accessed 17 February 2011.
50. J. Childs, "War, crime waves and the English army in the late seventeenth century", 1997, p.9 and p.13.
51. J. Dornford, *Seven Letters to the Lords of the Privy Council, on the Police*, 1785, p.19.

London, instead of adopting an honest way of life, he endeavoured to: "... procure money at the same rate by land which he had done at sea".[52]

War also reduced the incidence of crime by allowing the authorities to remove elements of the wider "street population" that provided the milieu from which many criminals sprang. At the outset of hostilities marginal members of Metropolitan society were forcibly recruited into military or naval service. Thus, in March 1701, it was noted that press warrants were given out for: "...taking up all the lusty vagrants who can give no account of themselves, and are able to serve His Majesty".[53] These warrants also reduced the need to press ordinary men into the navy, something that was extremely unpopular, politically sensitive, and often of dubious legality.[54] To put this onto a regular basis, a series of statutes extended the power of magistrates to: "...seize and send for soldiers, all such able bodied men, as they may call *idle* and *disorderly*". The most important of these was set out under the Act for Raising Recruits (the "Pressing Act") of 1704. Under this statute, Parliament authorised justices of the peace to conscript able-bodied men who had no visible means of support. In practice, it allowed the forced recruitment of vagrants and the unemployed. Inevitably, its wording gave considerable latitude to magistrates when it came to determining what constituted lawful employment. Many argued that idle and disorderly were: "...such vague expressions, as a ministerial Justice of the Peace may construe as he pleases".[55] As a result, in George Farquhar's *The Recruiting Officer*, of 1706, "Thomas Appletree" declares that he would rather be a JP than an emperor, because: "...since this pressing Act they are greater than any Emperor under the Sun".[56] It was in executing a warrant to impress such able vagrants for military service, in the Covent Garden area, that the reforming constable John Dent met his death in 1709.[57] As a youth, Jonathan Wild was considered to have been at risk of being pressed in this manner, because he was an "idle

52. A. L. Hayward, *Lives Of The Most Remarkable Criminals,* 1927, pp.75-76.
53. *English Post,* 28 February–3 March, 1701.
54. N. Landau (Ed.), *Law, Crime and English Society, 1660-1830*, 2002, pp.79-81.
55. A. E. Simpson, "The Mouth Of Strange Women Is A Deep Pit'", 1996, p.59.
56. K. J. Gardner, "George Farquhar's The Recruiting Officer: Warfare, Conscription, and the Disarming of Anxiety", 2001, pp. 43–61.
57. T. Bray, *The Tryals of Jeremy Tooley, William Arch, and John Clausson, Three Private Soldiers for the Murder of Mr. John Dent, Constable,* 1732, p.4.

drunken fellow". Fortunately for Wild, if not for Metropolitan society, he was double jointed and had a remarkable ability to dislocate his hip–bone at will, so that he successfully feigned lameness whenever a recruiting party came by.[58] In 1708, JPs alone delivered 1,493 men to 57 infantry battalions.[59]

Many observers thought that the wartime power to force vagrants into the military was so valuable in reducing crime in the capital that they regretted its lack of general availability. In 1732, it was claimed that if constables had such a power during: "…times of peace as well as war, so as to enable them to impress all disorderly persons, not capable of giving a satisfactory account of themselves, many foot-pads would be taken up".[60]

However, it is also possible that the correlation between war and crime reflects a real reduction in the level of Metropolitan offending during hostilities for reasons *other* than criminals being taken out of circulation. It could be explained by the greater employment opportunities afforded to the poor, with large numbers of men being given work in war industries, or facing less competition when seeking employment because others had been recruited to the military. As a result, fewer poor people were in extreme need, and so under pressure to steal.

The link between hostilities and offending levels was not unique to London; it occurred throughout eighteenth-century England. For example, Suffolk, like nearly every English county, saw indictment rates rise rapidly after the American war ended in 1783.[61] However, the connection was particularly marked in the Metropolis, for a variety of reasons. Sailors were often paid off there or had to go to there to secure their prize money. Similarly, many discharged soldiers were demobilised at the southern ports or came from regiments that had been disbanded en masse in the Southeast, with only very modest payments to cover their return to civilian life. They naturally gravitated towards the capital. The magistrate Henry Zouch felt that

58. Anon, *The History of the Lives and Actions of Jonathan Wild, Thief-Taker*, 1725, p.2.
59. J. Childs, "War, crime waves and the English army in the late seventeenth century", 1997, p.9 and p.13.
60. R. King, *The New Cheats of London Exposed*, 1732, p.22.
61. P. King, "Legal Change, Customary Right, and Social Conflict in Late Eighteenth- century England: The Origins of the Great Gleaning Case of 1788", 1992, p.9.

discharged servicemen were the most troublesome people he had to deal with and deplored the public failure to assist them.[62]

Receivers

One reason that crime flourished in and about the Metropolis was the comparative ease with which stolen goods could be liquidated. London provided easy access to receivers, both small-scale dealers, often operating from the cover of legitimate businesses such as pawnbrokers' establishments, second-hand garment sellers or taverns, and those who dealt on a larger, even-quasi commercial, scale. Some of the latter had links to parts of the continent, with Holland being particularly favoured.

According to the *Sessions Papers*, about 2,000 people were prosecuted at the Old Bailey for the crime during the century. However, because it was often only a misdemeanour, it was also sometimes indicted at the various Quarter Sessions held in the Metropolis. Receivers were extremely difficult to convict (as they often are today) despite legislation facilitating such prosecutions in 1691, 1702 and 1706. Only a relatively small proportion—just over a quarter—were found guilty at the Old Bailey, a significantly lower rate than for most other offences, and reflecting the fact that to: "...prove that a person receives stolen goods, knowing them to be stole, is a difficult matter". It was not enough that someone had purchased, or allowed someone to pledge, stolen goods in slightly dubious circumstances; the defence of innocent mistake was regularly, and successfully, advanced. Pawnbrokers were well aware of this. In the 1740s, a group of 50 of them were rumoured to have banded together to produce a common fund of £300 to finance the legal fees of any of their members accused of knowingly receiving stolen goods.[63]

62. H. Zouch, *Hints Respecting the Public Police*, 1786, p.11.
63. Anon (By an Impartial Hand), *A Plain Answer to a late Pamphlet, intitled, the Business of Pawnbroking stated and defended*, 1745, p.4 and p.6.

Pawnbrokers

Pawnbrokers were an essential part of the urban economy. Marginalised Londoners had such frequent recourse to them, albeit at extortionate rates of interest, that it was claimed their regularly pledged clothes could: "...almost go to pawn alone by themselves". However, although they had numerous customers amongst the poor, they had few friends, many feeling that they grew: "...fat on fraud and oppression, as a toad on filth and venom". It was widely appreciated that many criminals resorted to pawnbrokers, who would often act as a de facto "treasurer of the thieves exchequer".[64]

Nevertheless, the number of pawnbrokers who bought stolen goods deliberately was a matter of considerable debate. Perhaps unsurprisingly, members of the trade argued that most of them were reputable and honest, and that it was just a few "bad apples" who gave them such a poor reputation. Certainly, some pawnbrokers *were* careful about what they purchased or took as security for a loan; pawning goods to realize the proceeds of a crime could be a highly dangerous moment for thieves. For example, in 1707, Herman Bryan was caught after attempting to sell part of the proceeds of a burglary to a goldsmith named Acton. Acton became suspicious when Bryan asked for only eight pounds for a gold case and chain that were clearly worth at least £50; he "stopped" them (i.e. held them) pending enquiry, which revealed them to be stolen.[65]

To reduce the risks of this transaction, experienced criminals who had made a good "haul" would normally divide up the proceeds and pawn them with a variety of different businesses. In 1738, in an extreme illustration of this phenomenon, two pickpockets who had stolen a single pocket watch disposed separately of its gold chain, outer and inner case, with three different businesses.[66] Some would sell off very valuable items outside the London area; occasionally they would go as far as the Low Countries to do so. In 1727, when Thomas Neaves's gang stole nine silver watches, and one gold

64. S. H. Misodulus, *The young-man's counselor or the way of the world displayd; in several profitable essays, serious and comical*, 2nd edn., 1713, pp.119-121.
65. P. Lorrain, *The Ordinary's Account of the Life and Conversation, Birth, Parentage and Education of John Herman Bryan, The Switzer*, 1707, pp.3-4.
66. *Old Common Sense: Or, the Englishman's Journal*, 11 February 1738.

timepiece, from a watch-smith's shop window, they pawned those made of the lesser precious metal with a variety of Metropolitan brokers. However, Neaves went all the way to Shrewsbury to dispose of the gold timepiece, selling it there for eight pounds before returning to London.[67]

Nevertheless, many pawnbrokers were unscrupulous. It was frequently alleged that they would accept goods in obviously suspicious circumstances, knowing that the items being tendered must have been stolen, and advancing only a tiny proportion of their true value as a result. Thus, they might lend servants, porters or prostitutes: "…ten guineas upon a diamond ring, &c. that is worth fifty guineas, without any inquiry".[68] This would be done in the certain knowledge that their clients would not return, as: "Thieves and Pickpockets (their chiefest customers that bring the lumping bargains) never intend to redeem".[69] Such items could then be sold on at a large profit.

Pawnbrokers were regularly criticised by judges sitting at the Old Bailey and Metropolitan magistrates. Thus, in 1766, a pawnbroker who had taken, as a security, a silver milk-pot from a maid who had stolen it from her master, was reprimanded by Sir Richard Glynn, the sitting alderman at Guildhall, for receiving things of:

> …such a value from a woman so meanly dressed as such who brought them to him, as there could be no probability of their being their own.[70]

It was not just valuable items that were "recycled" by this means. Early in the eighteenth century, one observer felt that the vast majority of the huge number of second-hand silk handkerchiefs that were offered for sale in the Metropolis were put into circulation by pick-pockets, who would be paid just a few pennies for them by pawnbrokers. These could then be sold freely, being so similar they could not be identified. He proposed that any broker selling second-hand silk handkerchiefs be presumed "guilty of the

67. T. Neaves, *The Life of Thomas Neaves, The Noted Street-Robber*, 1729, p.14.
68. Anon (By an Impartial Hand), *A Plain Answer to a late Pamphlet, intitled, the Business of Pawnbroking stated and defended*, 1745, p.6.
69. S. H. Misodulus, *The young-man's counselor or the way of the world displayd; in several profitable essays, serious and comical*, 2nd edn., 1713, p.121.
70. *The Whitehall Evening Post; or, London Intelligencer*, 13 September 1766.

said crime of buying stolen goods".[71] The theft of such items was sufficiently common that boys who specialised in picking pockets of handkerchiefs had their own cant name ("clout-files").[72]

71. J. D. Gent, *An Humble Proposal to Prevent the Beginnings of Theft, viz. The Picking Pockets of Handkerchiefs*, c.1720, p.1.
72. Anon, *The History of the Lives and Actions of Jonathan Wild, Thief-Taker*, 1725, p.16.

CHAPTER 6

CRIMINAL LAW AND PROCEDURE

Introduction

The criminal justice system was more central to life in the Metropolis than it was in the provinces, even allowing for the relative difference in size and crime levels. There were probably two reasons for this. Firstly, it seems that members of the smaller, more stable, and intimate societies found in rural England were less likely to have recourse to criminal prosecution as a way of controlling their more wayward members, than those in the densely populated, socially variegated, and more transient communities found in the Metropolis. Secondly, London provided much easier access to the criminal justice system than rural areas.

Lack of Informal Controls

Formal law enforcement is merely one type of social control, and its extent and significance often varies inversely to the effectiveness of others.[1] It may be an age-old truth that there is: "...no other way to protect the innocent, but by punishing the guilty".[2] However, in rural parts this could be achieved via mechanisms other than the courts. Unfortunately, many of these, such as being ostracised by neighbours, were relatively ineffective in the Metropolitan area. By default, this made the criminal law of much greater importance in controlling the interpersonal dealings of Londoners.

Extra-legal controls have many advantages over those imposed by the criminal justice system. Informal sanctions are more nuanced and graduated,

1. M. Strathern, "Discovering 'Social Control'", 1985, p.111.
2. D. Defoe, *The History of the Remarkable Life of John Sheppard*, 1724, pp.1-20.

and their implementation is not contingent on formal proof or even, in many situations, physically securing a suspect. In the criminal justice system, even if a suspect is detained, a court will have to be persuaded to an appropriate standard that he is guilty before a legal punishment can be imposed. The absence of informal controls made the criminal justice system far more of a presence in the lives of Londoners. Additionally, law enforcement in the capital was far more "visible" to ordinary people. For example, many thousands would witness a hanging, whereas, in predominantly rural areas, very few would ever see an execution, unless they lived near to a county gallows.

Ease of Access to the Law

The second explanation for the increased recourse to the criminal justice system in urban areas turns on simple availability. In a world where many aspects of a criminal prosecution had to be actively sought out, and then paid for, by members of the public, many people inevitably developed a "consumerist" approach towards the law. Convenience and cheapness were prized. Easy, regular and reliable access to an affordable court was likely to produce much larger numbers of men and women who were willing to seek its protection, and look to it for redress, than would otherwise have been the case. By contrast, if a court or judicial officer, such as a magistrate, was a long way away, expensive, or difficult to find, there was likely to be much greater popular reluctance to have recourse to his services. It was sometimes claimed that the decline of the country's historic leet courts, in favour of the JPs' various summary jurisdictions, was partly linked to the latter's willingness to keep "open shop" and make themselves familiar to a public that: "... love[d] to buy law, one would think, as they do any other commodity".[3] This explains, in part, why urbanites were more likely to use the criminal courts than their country cousins. In the provinces, and even the Home Counties, there was a significant correlation between use of the criminal courts and a complainant's proximity to those forums. In the Metropolis, a JP or alderman magistrate could usually be found close to hand and, increasingly as

3. J. Ritson, *The Jurisdiction of the Court Leet*, 2nd edn., 1809, p.xix.

the century advanced, at set hours in a set place. Additionally, any ensuing judicial proceedings would also take place nearby; prosecutors would never have to make the substantial journeys to Assizes or Quarter Sessions that occurred in many rural areas.

Criminal Procedure

The "typical" serious criminal case being processed in the Metropolitan justice system went through a number of stages. Firstly, there would be the detention of a suspect, who would often be caught "red-handed" by his victim, perhaps assisted by members of the public during the day or watchmen at night. Alternatively, the suspect would be held by a constable, acting on a justice's arrest warrant (this officer would often be accompanied by the complainant).

Production before a magistrate would then usually follow, either at the justice's house or, after the early decades of the century, at a rotation office, such as that established at Bow Street in Middlesex, or the Justice Room at Guildhall in the City. Once there, the suspect would be examined by a magistrate, whether City alderman or Middlesex/Westminster JP Obviously weak cases would be thrown out, and suspects in the remainder committed to prison (or bailed) to await their trials. The documentation assembled would then be sent on to one of the Metropolitan Quarter Sessions, where the indictment would be drawn up and a Grand Jury would determine whether there was a case to answer. If they found a "true bill", proceedings would move on to the Old Bailey, where the trial would be conducted after the defendant was produced from Newgate or answered to his bail. If convicted (and many were not) he would be sentenced to death (though this might later be reprieved), transportation, or a lesser penalty, depending on the gravity of the offence. Middle and lesser ranking, but indictable, cases might go through a similar process but would be tried at Quarter Sessions.

Attrition

The inefficiency of contemporary policing and the high degree of discretion found within the system meant that only a small number of serious criminals were likely to be prosecuted to conviction, and even fewer would receive condign punishment. This was a matter of complaint throughout the century. In 1727, for example, it was observed that out of:

> ...ten thefts committed hardly one is discover'd and of ten discover'd scarce one is prosecuted to conviction, and that of three convicted rarely above one is executed.[4]

In the same decade, Metropolitan retailers complained that a combination of compounding, and the reluctance of victims to go to the trouble and expense of prosecuting detained shoplifters, meant that only one in ten of those apprehended for the crime were actually brought to court, while considerably fewer were found guilty.[5] At the century's end, others could still condemn the way in which death penalties were being commuted after trial, given the: "...great difficulty of bringing offenders to justice, of substantiating their crimes, and of identifying their persons".[6]

Many felons were not even apprehended. James Smith, a youthful highwayman in and about the Metropolis during the 1750s, told the chaplain attending him before his execution on Surbiton Common that he had committed 106 robberies prior to his arrest. He was adamant that he had never fallen into the hands of the law before being caught and convicted of the crime for which he eventually "suffered".[7] Even where a felon had been apprehended, and his victim had involved the authorities, the attrition rate was enormous. Much appears to have occurred early in the process and thus is often either inadequately documented or not recorded at all.

To take an extreme example, during her 24-year criminal career, Charlotte Walker, a habitual thief and prostitute from Holborn, survived eleven trials

4. Anon, *A Method whereby Criminals liable to Transportation may be render'd not only useful but honest Members of the Publick*, 1727, pp.3-4.
5. Anon, *The Great Grievance of Traders and Shopkeepers*, c.1720, p.1
6. *The Crisis*, 12 August 1792.
7. Anon, *The Remarkable Life of James Smith, A Famous Young Highwayman*, 1756, pp.6-7.

at the Old Bailey before finally being convicted and transported to Australia in 1801. Even more remarkable, these trials were just the tip of the iceberg of her involvement with the criminal justice system. She was discharged by a Grand Jury on at least a dozen occasions, indicted but discharged without trial on two others, and arrested then released without further action at least 15 times; almost certainly, many more instances have not been recorded. How many incidents occurred in which she was detained but the authorities were not involved, with her victims negotiating a return of their missing goods or cash, being bribed into not prosecuting, or administering summary chastisement before releasing her, can only be guessed at.[8]

Charlotte was in a slightly favoured position. She was a woman, and women were more likely to receive benign outcomes from both complainants and the criminal justice system than their male counterparts. Additionally, many of her victims were her clients, and frequently intoxicated. Such men received little sympathy from either magistrates or jurors. Furthermore, she had a strong native intelligence, allowing her to produce convincing defences in a forensic environment. Perhaps most importantly, she was careful about what she stole and the speed with which she disposed of stolen items. Nevertheless, although few were quite as lucky as Charlotte, she was certainly not unique. At about the same time, and during a long criminal career that was largely spent in the London area, the Irish pick-pocket George Barrington also survived numerous arrests, with victims refusing to prosecute, magistrates to commit for trial, Grand Juries to find a true bill, prosecution witnesses to appear, or trial juries to convict.[9] Similarly, John Rann, a highwayman executed in 1774, was rumoured to have escaped conviction as many as a dozen times, though his biographer thought that he had only been indicted (and acquitted) on three earlier occasions before his final, fatal, appearance at the Old Bailey.[10]

---

8. M. Clayton, "The Life and Crimes of Charlotte Walker, Prostitute and Pickpocket", 2008, pp.4-8.
9. G. Barrington, *The Life and Extraordinary Adventures of George Barrington*, c.1795, pp.1-8. He was eventually convicted and transported to Botany Bay.
10. Anon, *A Genuine Account of the Life of John Rann, Alias Sixteen-String Jack*, 1774, p.9.

The Growth of Legalism

English procedural law, both criminal and civil, was highly technical throughout the eighteenth century. This meant that there should have been considerable scope for avoiding its reach by finding a defect in the process. The visiting Frenchman Pierre-Jean Grosley was convinced that the "most idle and ridiculous quibbling" was permitted in criminal courts.[11] Many English observers claimed that they could provide accounts of thieves being acquitted on a technicality, even though: "...no one in court believed them innocent".[12] They would focus on cases such as that of the London-based master criminal Dick Swift, who apparently avoided execution for returning prematurely from transportation because the copy of his earlier conviction, adduced at the Coventry Assizes, mistakenly stated that he had received 70 rather than 72 pounds of candles.[13] The same precision was, in theory, necessary in many other legal documents, including some of those drawn up by JPs. As a contemporary observer candidly accepted, given the "numberless and extensive powers" vested in magistrates, it was inevitable that they would make legal mistakes on a regular basis. In theory, these were vulnerable to review by the superior courts, even though those forums normally did: "...what they could, consistently with the law, to support the acts of the Justices".[14]

Nevertheless, in *practice*, over much of the country, such legal review, like the taking of points of law at trial, was extremely rare, being a hypothetical risk rather than a real danger. As a result, legal theory and practical reality parted company to a very significant degree, and had done for centuries.[15] This process was assisted by the rule that normally denied a defendant a copy of his indictment, which meant that he might not notice one of the many potential defects that would otherwise render it "bad and of no effect".[16] Even

---

11. M. Grosley, *A Tour to London: or, New Observations on England, and its Inhabitants*, vol.3, 1772, p.34.
12. Anon (By a Magistrate), *Some Hints Towards A Revival of the Penal Laws,* 1787, p.11.
13. W. Jackson, *New Newgate Calendar: or, Villany displayed, in all its branches,* vol. iv, 1795, p.298.
14. T. Woodford, *A Discourse Concerning Some of the most important Branches, and Parts, of the Office of the Justices of the Peace*, 1749, p.iii.
15. J. S. Cockburn (Ed.), *Crime in England 1550-1800*, 1977, pp.65-68.
16. *World and Fashionable Advertiser*, 1 February, 1787.

so, the most important explanation for this divergence was that criminal proceedings in serious matters were largely unlawyered, both prior to and at trial, while most laymen were totally ignorant of the law. The judicial figure was normally the most legally knowledgeable person in the process.

However, London was *slightly* different in this respect. The close proximity of the capital's trial courts and justices to the centre of government, to the Court of King's Bench, and the scrutiny of the nation's newspaper industry, seems to have reduced the extent to which theory could part from reality. Most importantly, more lawyers became involved in the process, and there was greater popular legal knowledge. Together, these help to explain a marked increase during the course of the eighteenth century in what might, loosely, be termed "legalism", this being a somewhat less loaded term than referring to the "Rule of Law". It can be defined as a desire or insistence that the agents of local and national government conform to the letter of the law, and its established rules and procedures, when acting, and have legal authority for that action.

Metropolitan Lawyers

London was a highly lawyered society. Obviously, it was home to all of England's "senior" legal professions, whether barristers, serjeants or doctors at law. More significant, however, was the presence of numerous members of the lower branches of the profession, such as attorneys and solicitors. The city was a legal honey pot. By the 1670s, Sir Matthew Hale could complain that many lawyers were being: "...drawn up to London, so that there are scarce any left in the country".[17] During the eighteenth century, it seems that more than a third of the country's attorneys practised in the Metropolitan area. In 1731, there was one formally registered attorney to every 383 inhabitants in the Metropolis (1,533 lawyers), compared to one for every 1,290 people in the provinces. Urban parts of Surrey were equally well provided for, 25

17. D. Lemmings, *Blackstone and Law Reform by Education: Preparation for the Bar and Lawyerly Culture in Eighteenth-century England*, 1998, p.217.

of that county's 70 attorneys being found in Southwark.[18] Similarly, 1,087 of the 3,127 attorneys mentioned in the unofficial *Law List* of 1775 could be found there (many practising lawyers were not mentioned in the list).[19]

Even these figures are misleading, as there were numerous individuals who provided legal advice for remuneration without being formally registered. The constant demand for legal services at affordable prices had spawned "sham-lawyers". These were men who after a cursory study of the most basic legal textbooks, such as Burn's *Justice of the Peace*, set themselves up as legal advisers.[20] They were the urban equivalent of the rural "hedge solicitors".

Members of these "lower" legal professions provided a range of services. A considerable number were centred on the seamier sides of Metropolitan life. For example, some solicitors made their livings by providing help to debtors. More relevant to this book, many others were involved in criminal work, whether by "managing" prosecutions for crime victims or by advising defendants. As a result, they were often called "Newgate Solicitors", because they touted aggressively for business around that court. There were regular complaints about what might now be termed "ambulance-chasing" lawyers who, when a crime was reported in the newspapers, would immediately contact the victim, offering to prosecute the matter on their behalf for a fee, and warning them of the dangers of being a litigant in person.[21] Many made reasonable livings from criminal work. One contemporary observer claimed that he had seen a hundred Newgate solicitors at a time:

> ...scouring amongst their clients, the whores and thieves at Hick's Hall, at a Sessions, and some of them in pretty good habits too".[22]

18. P. Aylett, "A Profession in the Marketplace: The Distribution of Attorneys in England and Wales 1730-1800", 1987, p.2.
19. V. Belcher, "A London Attorney of the Eighteenth Century: Robert Andrews", 1986, p.40.
20. G. Parker, *A View of Society and Manners in High and Low Life*, 1781, p.25. It is also a phenomenon that has been witnessed in the modern inner city.
21. Anon, *Directions for Prosecuting Thieves Without the Help of those False Guides, The Newgate Solicitors*, 1728, p.3.
22. E. S. (Gentleman in Prison), *A companion for debtors and prisoners, and advice to creditors in ten letters*, 1699, p.16 and p.37.

Several Old Bailey solicitors, who were also active at Metropolitan Quarter Sessions, lived entirely on the proceeds of the services that they provided in criminal matters.[23]

In 1699, one informed observer claimed that such lawyers were usually once prosperous men who had exhausted their estates in litigation, but gained a working knowledge of the law in the process, or former bailiffs. (Jonathan Wild learnt a considerable amount of law by associating with the latter). Significantly, in 1717, a witness at the Old Bailey, seeking to explain how he had come by various sums of money, claimed that they were from his different employments, which he appears to have viewed as being on a par with each other; he had worked: "…sometimes as a weaver. Sometimes as a solicitor at law, and sometimes in stock-jobbing, &c".[24]

Even ignoring extreme cases, like that of William Wreathock, a Hatton Garden attorney who led a gang of robbers in the 1730s, many of these marginal legal professionals were not entirely reputable. In theory, even then, there were professional restrictions on their conduct when engaged in preparing prosecutions and defence cases. For example, they could encourage potential witnesses to give evidence, and save court time by discussing the potential relevance of their testimony prior to trial, asking: "…whether they have anything to say to this or that point". However, a solicitor was not supposed to suggest an answer or, even worse, bribe witnesses as to what they should say in court.[25] Nevertheless, it was frequently alleged that such lawyers were adept at perjury and "stitching" cases together.[26] According to Sir Thomas de Veil, Newgate solicitors would often use legal technicalities and dubious practices to "extricate notorious offenders out of their difficulties".[27]

Of course, the impact of lawyers can be exaggerated. In a society that was devoid of any form of legal aid, only offenders who were better off,

23. Anon, *Directions for Prosecuting Thieves Without the Help of those False Guides, The Newgate Solicitors,* 1728, p.12.
24. OBSP, Trial of Thomas Panting, 11 September 1717.
25. Anon, *Seasonable cautions for juries, solicitors and witnesses, to deterre from man-catching,* 1681, p.3.
26. E. S. (Gentleman in Prison), *A companion for debtors and prisoners, and advice to creditors in ten letters,* 1699, p.16 and p.37.
27. Sir T. Deveil, *Observations on the Practice of a Justice of the Peace,* London, Edward Withers, 1747, pp.4–5.

professional criminals (especially if associated with a gang), or who had many friends, were able to take advantage of high-level advice from counsel with a view to finding legal loopholes. The destitute were normally denied access even to Newgate solicitors. As was noted in Parliament in 1792, the lower classes seldom had the means to apply "for redress against abuse of power".[28] However, there is also considerable evidence of a substantial degree of legal competence and knowledge amongst non-polite, and sometimes even marginally literate, elements of eighteenth-century society, whether war widows, sailors' wives, free miners or, sometimes, urban criminal defendants.

Popular Legal Knowledge

The era witnessed the flourishing of "self help" legal manuals aimed predominantly, though not entirely, at a non-professional market.[29] Giles Jacob, for example, was a prolific author of such manuals, including the enormously influential *New Law Dictionary*, which reached a substantial audience throughout England and colonial America.[30] Although Jacob's most successful work, it was just one among many practical legal books that he produced in the early decades of the eighteenth century.

The London area's large population also meant that it was easier to find a layman who "knew" about the law than would have been the case in rural areas. There were regular contemporary reports of prison inmates in the capital's gaols discussing the finer details of criminal law prior to their hearings. It is safe to assume that, in the Metropolis at least, some of those who were likely to find themselves on the wrong side of the criminal law, such as habitual thieves, gained enough acumen to "play" the system or at least to avoid some of its more obvious pitfalls, such as making admissions to examining justices. Indicative of this dissemination of legal knowledge can be considered a case from 1789, in which a constable and an excise officer

28. W. Cobbett, *The Parliamentary History of England from the Earliest Period to the Year 1803*, 1817, vol. xxix, p.1465.
29. W. Prest, "Lay Legal Knowledge in Early Modern England", 1999, pp.310-311.
30. J. Rudolph, "That "Blunderbuss of Law: Giles Jacob, Abridgment, and Print Culture", 2008, pp.196-215.

arrested a "poor man" who made and sold lace. He was held in the Highgate "cage" overnight, and then taken to the Custom House in London. Once there, he was swiftly released, as he was entitled to sell any lace that he had personally made. He immediately responded by taking the constable and excise man before a magistrate, for false imprisonment.[31]

The Impact of Legalism

Legalism was combined with, and linked to, a decline in the hitherto fairly "robust" approach to the periodic miscarriages of justice that had marked Stuart felony trials. At the start of the period, the Reverend George Stanhope candidly observed of perjured prosecution witnesses that experience showed the: "...most unblemish'd innocence not always to be sufficient protection against them".[32] In the early 1700s, the political nation appears to have been relatively sanguine about the risks of mistaken capital conviction and execution. They themselves were unlikely to be on the receiving end of such treatment, as they rarely constituted defendants in felony cases, at least until fraud was made a felony (something that probably contributed to new attitudes). This gradually changed.

Of course, this was still relative. To the end of the period, official action was very poorly regulated by modern standards, and often highly arbitrary as a result. Nevertheless, at all levels, the century between the Glorious Revolution and the onset of the French Revolution saw an increased insistence on legal niceties. The impact of this on high profile cases has been well marked, not least because it was manifest in defendant-protecting statutes such as the Treason Act of 1696. However, it also had a much wider, if more gradual, impact on more mundane felonies. Even if only a very few cases resulted in legal actions in the Court of King's Bench to enforce strict legal rights, this, combined with the increased presence of lawyers and legally

31. *The Times*, 22 Oct, 1789, p.3.
32. G. Stanhope, *The Duty of Witnesses. A Sermon Preached at the Summer Assizes Holden at Maidstone in Kent... August the 5th*, 1701, p.22.

articulate members of the public, influenced the way in which officials went about their business.

For watchmen, constables, and magistrates, it could produce a challenging working environment, and placed limitations on their actions. In 1754, Saunders Welch, drawing on eight years' experience as High Constable for the Holborn Division, warned constables about the dangers posed by: "... low solicitors, who are for ever watching their conduct, and ever preying upon either their ignorance or rashness".[33] Parish officers could be sued if they acted *ultra vires*. So serious was this risk that, in 1730, the King agreed to fund the defence of all officers in Westminster, having been made aware that they were being burdened by: "...vexatious prosecutions, that are frequently commenced against them, upon the least mistake in executing of their office". Sometimes, Sir John Gonson claimed, they did not even need to have made a mistake to become the subject of such malicious legal actions.[34] Such legal actions might not have had enormous prospects of success.[35] However, those on the receiving end of them could be put to considerable trouble and expense, even if they were ultimately exonerated.

As the eighteenth century advanced, both magistrates and the courts seem to have placed more importance on legal niceties and employing "correct" procedures. Practices that had been widespread at the start of the century came to seem less than ideal. The rise of "legalism" in the Metropolitan area will be one of the themes of this book.

The Role of Discretion

A considerable element of discretion has always been present in the English criminal justice system. Even in the modern era, victim surveys suggest that many serious offences are not reported to the police, especially where there will not be an ensuing insurance claim. Nevertheless, the eighteenth

33. S. Welch, *Observations on the Office of Constable*, 1754, p.5 of the Introduction.

34. *London Journal*, 11 August 1730.

35. E. Bachiler, *To his Highness Oliver Lord Protector of the Commonwealth of England*, 1655, pp.6-8 and p.20.

century is considered to have been a "Golden Age" for discretionary justice. This was found at all stages of the criminal process.

In the 1700s, and as today, the victim's involvement marked the point of maximum discretion. However, unlike today, a swift 999 or (in America) 911 call did not lead to the victim abdicating his primary role and responsibility in the matter. The decision to prosecute (and for what) was left very largely in his (or her) hands. Additionally, both examining magistrates and Grand Juries had considerable discretion as to whether to allow matters to proceed to trial, while jury nullification and mitigation was at its peak, and there was huge discretion vested in the judiciary and the executive to award capitally convicted defendants reprieves from execution.

A myriad of different considerations could be, and often were, factored into verdicts, reflecting matters as diverse as personal culpability, the gravity of the offence, and the need, at a particular time, to set a deterrent example. More arcane extra-legal considerations could also go into the equation where appropriate. These might include, for example, a realistic understanding of the economic position of the single mother of small children or disapproval of a retailer who had been lax about the security of his premises. Thus, there was a marked tendency in shoplifting allegations towards showing lenience in cases where goods had been positioned temptingly outside a shop, or in which large crowds had been attracted by a sale involving heavily discounted prices.[36]

Taken together, these factors sometimes produced highly inconsistent results in legally almost identical situations. An apprehended thief might experience anything from some Anglo-Saxon expletives, accompanied, perhaps, by a beating or a ducking, followed by release, to prosecution to conviction and subsequent execution. William Newcomb, for example, who was eventually executed at Tyburn for burglary, might have met his death three years after he had been apprenticed to a shoemaker, when he stole a very considerable sum of money from his master. Nevertheless, this man: "...having a respect for his family, put him away without prosecuting him".[37] Similarly, in 1739, after several pickpockets who had been "very

36. D. Palk, *Gender, Crime and Judicial Discretion, 1780-1830*, 2006, p.46.

37. A. L. Hayward, *Lives Of The Most Remarkable Criminals*, 1927, p.522.

busy" amongst the crowd assembled to watch a man being pilloried at the Royal Exchange had been arrested, most of them were committed to the City Compter for formal prosecution. However, two of them were merely subjected to the "horse pond law", and were ducked instead.[38] Selection for draconian example was more random for some offences than others. Sodomy seems to have been a fairly extreme example of this process, and so provides a particularly valuable illustration of the exercise of discretion.

Sodomy and discretion

By the start of the eighteenth century, London had a distinctive homosexual sub-culture. There were fairly well known "molly houses", where homosexual men could meet, and walks within the Metropolis that were notorious homosexual cruising grounds.[39] Even so, throughout the period, consensual sodomy between men was a capital offence for which they could be hanged. Indeed, it was, ostensibly, one of the worst crimes in the criminal canon. At the start of the century, it could seriously be proposed that a convicted sodomite might have his genitals cut off and burnt by the common hangman or, alternatively, be placed in a tub and have: "...liquid and burning Brimstone poured down upon him till he expires".[40] Nevertheless, the number of men who were prosecuted, let alone hanged, for the offence was extremely small. Even in 1695, an observer could note that sodomy "fills not the black warrant".[41] Almost a century later, it was still: "...very uncommon to see a person convicted, and punished for this crime". Numerous eighteenth-century Metropolitan homosexuals, arrested in apparently compromising circumstances, were discharged without formal legal action being taken, charged with the inchoate offence of "assault with sodomitical intent" or acquitted of the full offence at trial. Even if convicted, they might be reprieved prior to execution.

Doubtless, many practising homosexuals took great care not to be found out, and: "... never yield[ed] to such a brutal appetite but with the utmost

38. *Old Commonsense, or, the Englishman's Journal*, 2 June 1738.

39. P. Bartlett, "Sodomites in the pillory in Eighteenth-Century London", 1997, p.559 and p.564.

40. J. Dunton, *The Shortest-Way with Whores and Rogues*, 1703, p.35

41. C. Jones, *Some methods proposed towards putting a stop to the flagrant crimes of murder, robbery, and perjury*, 1752, p.20.

precaution".[42] To an extent, the technical and evidential requirements necessary to prove sodomy also facilitated the low conviction rate; eyewitness evidence of penetration was normally required. As a result, men such as John Painter and John Green were only indicted for the inchoate offence when watchmen found them in the porch of Stepney Church, late one summer night, while in each other's arms, and naked from the waist down.[43] However, these factors, on their own, do not come close to explaining the low incidence of convictions.

Most adult male eighteenth-century Londoners were "men of the world". They knew that these things went on in their society and, whatever they might say in public, were often prepared to adopt a "live and let live" approach to such behaviour, *provided* it was very discreet, consensual, and confined to adults. Such an accommodating attitude appears to have extended to many parish officers. For example, in 1749, Richard Spencer invited a seventeen year old apprentice to drink beer with him, asked him about the size of his genitalia, then touched and kissed him, before the apprentice forced him away and fetched a constable. Initially, this officer was willing to deal with the matter entirely summarily, insisting that Spencer pay for the beer consumed, calling him a "blackguard and rascal", kicking him a couple of times on the backside and throwing him out of the pub. Unfortunately for Spencer, this did not satisfy the apprentice, who ran after him and, with assistance from passers by, detained Spencer before insisting that the constable instigate formal proceedings.[44]

Caution about such matters was shared by many of the capital's magistrates. When the Society for the Reformation of Manners sought to prosecute sodomites during the 1720s they found considerable difficulty in getting their cases to court. For example, after a raid on Margaret Clap's "molly house", over 40 alleged homosexuals were arrested, but only a handful indicted.[45] The society was convinced that this was because the justices were unwilling to allow such charges to proceed in large numbers. Some statistical evidence supports their analysis. Of 16 sodomy-related offences found in the records

42. J. W. von Archenholz, *A Picture of England*, vol. 2, 1789, pp. 102-4.
43. OBSP, Trial of John Painter and John Green, 30 August 1727.
44. OBSP, Trial of Richard Spencer, 5 July 1749.
45. OBSP, Trial of Gabriel Lawrence, 20 April 1726.

of the Guildhall Justice Room during the second half of the eighteenth century, just six were sent for trial.[46]

As a result, between 1700 and 1799, only 60 men were prosecuted, and just 23 capitally convicted, of the full offence at the Old Bailey, and five of these came from the raid on Margaret Clap's house. Several of the 23, like Samuel Taylor and John Berry, caught red handed committing sodomy in a public convenience near the Strand, were ultimately reprieved from execution. In this case, Serjeant Urling, the deputy recorder of the City, immediately recommended the two men to mercy when making his report (in person) to the King in Council at St. James's.[47] Judges and jurors were, it seems, reluctant to see homosexuals convicted and hanged in large numbers, despite the horror that their crimes supposedly evinced.[48] Londoners *may* have been more "liberal" in this regard than their provincial cousins. As late as September 1806, for example, five men convicted of sodomy at the Lancashire Summer Assizes were executed.[49]

Limits to discretion

However, although there was a very large degree of discretion in the eighteenth-century justice system, it is also possible to exaggerate it, especially in a Metropolitan context. Discretion was not exercised in a cultural or situational vacuum and was not unfettered. Numerous individuals and bodies had agency in the process, but none were entirely free agents. Legal, social, and cultural constraints, along with customary expectations, shaped behaviour.[50] Even the victim/complainant, probably the freest agent in the process, might come under social pressure to prosecute or not, as the case might be.

Most importantly, in a system premised on discretion and tailor-made judgments it is necessary for victims, magistrates and the courts to be able to make a reliable assessment of a suspect. Was he a previously upright and

46. P. Bartlett, "Sodomites in the pillory in Eighteenth-Century London", 1997, p.564.
47. *Daily Gazetteer*, 3 March 1738.
48. N. Murray Goldsmith, *The Worst of Crimes: Homosexuality and the Law in Eighteenth-Century London*, 1988, pp.34-36.
49. H. G. Cocks, "Safeguarding Civility: Sodomy, Class And Moral Reform In Early Nineteenth-Century England", 2006, pp.121-123.
50. P. King, *Crime, Justice and Discretion in England 1740-1820*, 2000, p.355.

useful member of the community who had succumbed to temptation or sudden hardship, or a habitual criminal who was simply acting in character? Answering these questions requires both accurate information and sufficient magisterial and forensic time to consider it. In the smaller, more stable, and "face to face" communities of provincial England, character could usually be determined with some degree of accuracy and reliability. In the Metropolis, with its significantly immigrant, and much more transient, population it was very much harder to carry out such an assessment, making a justice system that was contingent on such extrinsic factors more of a lottery, and so less attractive. Additionally, even where reliable information as to reputation was available, the sheer pressure of business in a densely populated urban area reduced the scope for weighing it up in a careful and measured manner at both the pre-trial and trial stage of proceedings.

In rural areas, considerable informal pressure could also be brought against crime victims by relatives, friends and neighbours of the accused not to prosecute a local man. Local vestries would know that they would be required to provide poor relief to the family of a breadwinner who was incarcerated, transported, or executed. Additionally, there was more scope for "arrangements" to be made instead of proceedings being brought. For example, a local labourer who was caught stealing from a farmer could arrange to do work on his victim's land, in lieu of being indicted. In a more transient environment such pressures were much less likely to be present, and non-fiscal settlements were less practicable.

As a result, key figures within the Metropolitan justice system, ranging from examining magistrates to trial jurors and judges, had recourse to what might be termed "standard procedures" or disposals in many commonly recurring situations. These were used by parish officers, magistrates, judges and jurors. They were not necessarily followed, for a myriad of different reasons, but constituted the de facto "default" position. They were not precise, and changed gradually over time, as they were transmitted across generations of men. For example, executive, judicial, jury and even victim decisions were heavily shaped by the notion that it was young, mobile, often rootless, and frequently single, men who constituted the greatest criminal threat, especially in the Metropolis.[51] At the same time, such men were perceived as having less excuse for having recourse to crime, on the basis that they were the most equipped to labour, and frequently had few, if any, dependants. Unsurprisingly, they were also the most likely to be prosecuted to conviction and execution.

Furthermore, after the mid-eighteenth century, the flexibility occasioned by a high degree of discretion was increasingly seen as "unfair", as a sign of systemic inefficiency and a lack of institutional professionalism, encouraging change. This pressure for reform would gather pace towards the end of the period and culminate in a reformed criminal justice system, one in which there was an attempt to produce a milder, more finely calibrated and graded, but consistently enforced, penal regime.

Reluctance to Reform

Reform in all of these areas was usually a matter of political inclination rather than simple viability. Had there been the will to change policing and the justice system within the Metropolis, in a certain direction, it could have been put into effect at any point during the century. Where national survival or the nation's vital interests were at stake, the country could and did bring enormous resources to bear. Between 1688 and 1815, England and (after 1707) Britain, developed a powerful "fiscal-military" state, capable of raising large amounts of revenue to finance its armies and navies during an era of frequent and intense conflict. This required the efficient collection of taxes and excise, which in turn prompted the development of powerful bureaucracies, and led to the establishment of important quasi-government institutions, such as the Bank of England (founded in 1694).[52]

There were several reasons why such dynamism was not shown over law enforcement. Economy was one of them. A reluctance to spend money, whether at a national or local level, was palpable. As contemporary observers

51. P. King, *Crime, Justice and Discretion in England 1740–1820*, 2000, p.217.
52. D. Phillips, "A 'Weak' State? The English State, the Magistracy and the Reform of Policing in the 1830s", 2004, p.873 and p.877.

freely accepted, proposals that were made with a view to enhancing security or dealing with vagrants were likely to run into the response that: "... national debt, and taxes, are already very burthensome to the subject".[53] Even Sir John Fielding was reduced to writing regular importuning letters to his patrons, reciting alarmist litanies of criminal incidents in the Metropolitan area, and begging for further funding for his Bow Street project. For example, in a letter from 1764, written to the Secretary to the Treasury, he lamented his lack of personal opportunity to persuade Lord Grenville, the First Lord of the Treasury, of the: "...amazing importance of the police to government". He urged that the public good occasioned by an effective police should be an exception to the general (and laudable) rule of avoiding expense to the Crown.[54] In 1792, MPs considering the proposal in the Middlesex Justices Bill to establish stipendiary magistrates in the Metropolitan area were acutely alarmed at the £20,000 that, it was thought, would be required to fund such a development (as well as the novel patronage it would give to the government). Proponents of the legislation freely conceded that they would have preferred a Bill that was more extensive when it came to policing, but accepted that such a Bill would have failed: "...on account of the expense of a complete system".[55]

However, cost, on its own, is not a sufficient explanation; the Royal Navy was very expensive. Just as important was a fear of the political implications of introducing an enhanced policing and justice system. Although the state became powerful, it was in discreet areas. Unlike major continental countries, such as France and Prussia, which were associated with overbearingly strong and centralised forms of government, the virtue of England was its minimal government, which did not (and could not) interfere excessively in the lives of its "freeborn" subjects.[56]

As will be seen, such emotions were powerful, and long lasting, being regularly reiterated throughout the eighteenth century and reinforced during the

53. Anon (By a Lover of his Country), *The Thief-Catcher; or, Villainy Detected*, 1753, p.47.
54. D. Horn and M. Ransome, *English Historical Documents*, vol. X, 1714-1783, 1957, pp.279-280.
55. W. Cobbett, *The Parliamentary History of England From the Earliest Period to the Year 1803*, 1817, vol. xxix, p.1195 and p.1464.
56. D. Phillips, "A 'Weak' State? The English State, the Magistracy and the Reform of Policing in the 1830s", 2004, p.873 and p.877.

Napoleonic wars. Thus, the objections to the 1785 Police Bill were couched in the language of constitutional rights, whatever ulterior motives lay behind them. Within days of its presentation, the sheriffs of the City appeared before the Bar of Parliament to present a petition outlining their implications for civil liberties and the historic privileges of the Square Mile. The aldermen were particularly alarmed at the destruction of the constitutional rights of many thousands by a: "System of Police altogether new and arbitrary in the extreme". Additionally, they felt that it would needlessly create officers vested with dangerous powers who would be exempted from existing legal controls.

Nevertheless, Metropolitan observers were also the first to challenge such notions. London was many years ahead of the provinces in the willingness of key elements of its population to contemplate major change. In 1785, for example, Josiah Dornford felt that losing some "freedoms" would be a very acceptable price to pay for enhanced security, and that it would be: "...better to have our lives and properties preserved, even by arbitrary police, than not have them preserved at all".[57] Many observers felt that the Metropolis's problems were the inevitable result of applying the same form of government to a city as was used in the countryside.[58] Unfortunately for the proponents of such views, anything established in the Metropolitan area was likely to provide a precedent for the rest of the country, something that was widely appreciated at the time.

57. J. Dornford, *Seven Letters to the Lords of the Privy Council, on the Police*, 1785, p.xi.
58. E. Sayer, *Observations on the Police or Civil Government of Westminster, with a Proposal for a Reform*, 1784, p.17.

PART TWO: POLICING

CHAPTER 7

POLICING THE METROPOLIS

Introduction

For much of the eighteenth century, London witnessed a heated debate between elements of the "political nation", ranging from members of parish vestries to government ministers, who felt that it was necessary to enhance Metropolitan law enforcement, and a ground swell of opposition, from all social quarters, to the creation of any form of strengthened police force. The former were motivated by anxiety about Metropolitan crime levels and popular disorder, combined with a growing feeling that the capital's problems were not caused by the: "...more than ordinary depravity of the people, but the absurdity of the police".[1] They were concerned that crime flourished because of the "too remiss execution of the law".[2] By contrast, opponents of change were driven by a fear of government interference with traditional English political liberties, as enshrined in the 1688 settlement, a diminution of the influence and patronage of local power elites, and the likely increase in expense occasioned by any change.

However, the eighteenth-century ruling classes were not invariably opposed to police reform. There may have been strong resistance to centralized policing, but locally controlled reforms attracted much less opposition, and the history of such reforms stretches back to the early 1700s.[3]

1. Anon (By a magistrate), *Some Hints Towards A Revival of the Penal Laws,* 1787, p.13.
2. S. Welch, *A Proposal to render effectual a Plan to remove the nuisance of Common Prostitutes from the streets of this Metropolis*, 1758, p.48.
3. E. Reynolds, "Sir John Fielding, Sir Charles Whitworth, and the Westminster Night Watch Act, 1770-1775", 2002, p.1.

Reformers

A succession of men made proposals for major police reform over the course of the century. They included Daniel Defoe, the magistrates Henry and John Fielding, and Patrick Colquhoun. It is sometimes suggested that the importance of such men has been exaggerated in the "Whig" narrative of policing history.[4] However, it should not be underestimated. Colquhoun would not have been called to give evidence before several parliamentary select committees if this had been the case. Nevertheless, it *is* true that they were highly partisan and proselytising men with a "mission", and views that were not the subject of overwhelming, let alone universal, support. As late as 1785, there were those who believed that, far from needing major change, London was already much better policed than the countryside. Indeed, some complained that, due to the rigorous prosecution of criminals there, many of the capital's "abandoned wretches" were leaving the city and carrying out their depredations in adjacent rural areas.[5]

The Concept of a "Police"

Even late in the eighteenth century, the very word "police" (from the Greek *politeia*) was relatively new. Originally, it did not mean a uniformed force employed by the state to impose order, but a more general system of government, the task of which was to regulate broad aspects of communal existence.[6] In England, the word had not been used at all by Henry Fielding, though his half-brother, John, employed it in 1758. It was used only a dozen or so times in classical eighteenth-century English literature, and then often in connection with France, by well-travelled writers such as Laurence Sterne and Tobias Smollett. However, it was in regular political use by the 1780s. In 1781, Richard Sheridan observed to Parliament that, although it

4. R. Paley, "An imperfect, inadequate and wretched system? Policing London before Peel", 1989, p.97.
5. Anon, *Internal Police of the Kingdom Very Much Neglected*, 1785, p.951.
6. F. M. Dodsworth, "The Idea of Police in Eighteenth-century England", 2008, p.583.

was not an English word, he was confident that gentlemen would understand what it meant.

At this time, it still encompassed matters as diverse as the penal system, moral exhortation, alcohol licensing, poor law relief, and the provision of rewards for the detection of crime. In 1763, Adam Smith declared that the word meant the regulation of inferior parts of government, including cleanliness, security and "cheapness or plenty". He was almost embarrassed to consider something so "mean" as the details of the city guard, as the greatest safeguard against crime was not officers but prosperity.[7] In 1785, Jonas Hanway discussed reform of the capital's constables in less than half a dozen pages of his otherwise substantial work, *The Defects of Police*. He was equally concerned with creating appropriate types of workhouse, and felt that the poor law constituted a considerable "part of our police".[8] Even Patrick Colquhoun, writing in 1796, had had *relatively* little to say on a full-time centralised body of men entrusted with policing.

Gradually, however, a transitional stage developed in which the word acquired two separate meanings; namely, the general arrangements made to ensure that the inhabitants of a city or borough obeyed the law, and, separately, the force of peace officers employed for that purpose, though it only fully acquired its modern connotations after 1829. Even so, as a foreign visitor noted in the 1780s, this did not mean that such an establishment was absent, although the English did not have a: "...single word in their whole language to express what we term the police".[9]

Other Parts of the British Isles

It should, perhaps, also be noted that although its size and social problems meant that the Metropolitan area was at the forefront of policing reform during the century, it was not alone. For example, several Scottish cities were eventually given parliamentary authorisation, via private Acts, to form police

7. A. Smith, *Lectures on Justice, Police, Revenue and Arms: reported by a student in 1763*, 1984, p.234
8. J. Hanway, *The Defects of Police*, 1785, p.142.
9. J. W. von Archenholz, *A picture of England: containing a description of the laws, customs, and manners of England*, 1790, p.178.

forces, among them being Aberdeen (1795) and Glasgow (1800), though these tended to build on existing policing traditions. Patrick Colquhoun drew upon, and was influenced by, the developments that were taking place in his native Glasgow.[10] The 1786 Dublin Police Act (27 Geo. III c. 24 Ireland), which produced a uniformed, paid, professional force that lasted until 1795, and a successor force created by the 1795 Dublin Police Act (39 Geo. III c.56 Ireland) also provided an important precedent for English reformers.[11]

The Medieval Policing Legacy

Until the end of the eighteenth century, Metropolitan policing was largely the responsibility of an amalgam of the historic parish constables, night watchmen, beadles and (in the City) marshalmen with the important (but very modest in scale) policing innovations of the second half of the era. Traditional forms of local policing still had primacy in 1800. Typically, in the parish of St Clement Danes, in 1737, there were eight constables, two beadles and 28 watchmen to police a population that was (probably) around 10,000 people.

The system's roots were ancient, and had evolved in a society that was overwhelmingly rural, largely static, and usually lived in small and intimate communities. Its form inevitably reflected these features. Although not a rural society, medieval London had shared many of these characteristics. The city's relatively small size meant that a slightly modified version of the national system remained viable, especially as there were usually soldiers in the Tower available to supplement the local policing agencies in emergency. This historic system had been formalised in 1285, during the reign of Edward I, by the Statute of Winchester, which laid the foundations for an urban watch system making its use widespread in cities, boroughs and towns. There was an equivalent statute, specifically passed for the City of London in the same year. Many of the structures it laid down remained in force until the nineteenth century, albeit with considerable amendment.

10. See generally, D. G. Barrie, "Patrick Colquhoun, The Scottish Enlightenment And Police Reform In Glasgow In The Late Eighteenth Century", 2008, pp. 59-79.
11. S. H. Palmer, *Police and Protest in England and Ireland 1780–1850*, 1988, pp.27-29.

Problems with Policing

The preamble to the 1829 "Act for improving the Police in and about the Metropolis" (10 Geo. IV, c.44), which founded the modern Metropolitan Police, identified problems with the quality, numbers, jurisdiction, control and supervision of London's law enforcement officers. By then, this was very well trodden ground. Such concerns had been constants in the debate on police reform for decades, being repeated, almost *ad nauseam*, from early in the previous century. For example, when giving evidence in 1772 to the Committee appointed to enquire into Metropolitan burglaries and robberies, Sir John Fielding complained that the watch were too few in number, their pay insufficient to attract men of quality, that they were too divided and their parish jurisdictions too circumscribed. By 1785, Jonas Hanway could opine that such complaints were a "hackneyed theme". He, too, believed that an enhancement of standards amongst individual officers, a general unification of policing jurisdiction throughout the London area, a localised expansion of resources where it was inadequate, and an effective command hierarchy to ensure that the system functioned properly were all necessary.

Validity of Criticism

These criticisms continue to underlie the "Whig" version of police history, in which 1829 brought "order out of chaos". However, it is clear that dissatisfaction with the watch and constables was as much based on raised expectations, as on any deterioration in the old policing system, which was, in reality, considerably improved over the course of the eighteenth century. Although the system's faults never came close to being entirely resolved, progress was made in many individual parishes towards producing more effective local forces. Thus, John Beattie has described the steps taken in the Square Mile to meet the challenge of crime and disorder during the first half of the era, while Andrew Harris has considered the same area at the end of the eighteenth century. In Westminster and urban Middlesex, Elaine Reynolds has identified some of the defining characteristics of "modern" policing as being present in the reformed watches of the more well-to-do West End parishes by the middle of the period. Many features of the "new" (post-1829) police accorded with what might be termed existing "best practice". As a result, Reynolds has argued that modern "professional" policing has its beginnings in various private parliamentary Watch Acts of the mid-1730s. These put the financing of the local watch on a formal and secure basis and introduced or expanded the use of defined beats for watchmen, uniforms, stands where they could readily be found, and enhanced forms of supervision and discipline. Some other Metropolitan parishes copied these reforms, in so far as they were willing to incur the additional expense.[12]

Paris and Continental Cities

Foreign visitors frequently remarked that London differed from most continental capital cities, especially Paris (its nearest rival), in not possessing a military-style force, whether mounted or on foot, to prevent serious crime. Instead, the: "...only watchmen you see is a man in every street carrying a stick and lantern".[13] Many reform-minded Englishmen looked enviously towards Europe and, in particular, France, which had been famous throughout most of the eighteenth century for its comparatively vigorous, and supposedly effective, police system. In 1763, a distinguished English visitor was impressed by the hierarchy, professionalism, specialism and sub-division of responsibility found in Parisian policing, with its *lieutenant de police* heading an organisation that had a military-style watch consisting of both a 400 man *guet a pied*, made up of disbanded infantry soldiers, and a 220 man *guet a cheval*, formed from former cavalrymen, who patrolled by day and night. Additionally, the *lieutenant de police* commanded several dozen commissaries, a form of full-time magistrate and investigator, with inspectors to assist their work by informing them of all "abuses and irregularities" committed within their districts. Furthermore, there were numerous government spies, as well as 50 "exempts de police" tasked with enforcing the observance of

12. E. Reynolds, *Before the Bobbies. The Night Watch and Police Reform in Metropolitan London, 1720–1830*, 1998, pp.4-5.
13. M. V. Muyden (Ed.), *A foreign View of England in the reigns of George I and George II*, 1902, p.68.

public regulations, other men specifically detailed to supervise the public theatres, and a force of "archers" whose function was to arrest vagabonds, beggars and loose women found in the streets. All of these bodies, it was alleged, worked in harmony, so that even the most audacious criminals could not evade the law. It was all very different from London, with its amateur constables and JPs, attempting to carry on their businesses and trades at the same time as fulfilling their offices, being entrusted with a very wide range of responsibilities, and often not communicating effectively with each other.[14]

Similarly, in 1792, another English observer claimed that, prior to the Revolution, whatever other problems France might have had with its government, its capital's police was "certainly admirable", and its streets and highways were usually safe for travellers.[15] The central offices of the Parisian Police had employed more clerks during the second half of the eighteenth century, and become increasingly bureaucratic. By the 1780s, they were taking steps to cross-reference files to see whether a suspect had a previous criminal record, to link crimes committed in different parts of the City, and to trace stolen goods[16] (This development was mirrored in London to a modest degree after 1781). Other Englishmen were more mindful of the alleged strengths of the Dutch system, and the apparent orderliness of Amsterdam; national prejudices were less acute than when extolling the French system.[17]

Whether this admiration for continental cities was entirely warranted is debateable. Paris was probably slightly more secure and better policed than London prior to the Revolution, and its main arterial routes were certainly safer than their Metropolitan counterparts. Nevertheless, during the period between 1760 and the Revolution it seems that propertied Parisians, like their London counterparts, became increasingly alarmed at the level of crime and disorder found in their city.[18] English visitors were often dazzled by the military image and centralization of the Parisian police, perhaps taken in by a deliberately cultivated myth about the effectiveness of its spies and their general omniscience. In reality, the police had only a tenuous control

14. Sir W. Mildmay, *The Police of France*, 1763, pp.43-63.
15. *The Crisis*, 16 August 1792.
16. D. Garrioch, *The People of Paris and their Police in the Eighteenth Century*, 1994, p.513
17. A. Becket, *A Trip to Holland*, vol. 2, 1785, p.142.
18. R. Andrews, *Law, magistracy, and Crime in Old Regime Paris, 1735-1789*, vol.1, 1994, p.42.

of much of the city. Their numbers were quite small for the area and populace they policed, making them highly dependant on public support where they operated effectively. In the face of major popular disturbances, strong resistance or hostility they often melted away. Many of their members were, like London watchmen, not in the first flush of youth, averaging about 40 years of age. Additionally, members of the Guard were extremely badly paid, working a single 24-hour shift every other day and, like London watchmen, usually holding a second job, and often working as labourers when out of uniform. Like their English counterparts in the watch, there was a high turnover of men.[19] Indeed, in many respects it was France's rural (rather than its urban) police, the *marechaussée*, which was markedly superior to its English counterpart.[20]

Despite this, an awareness of, and admiration for, the quasi-military model found on the continent encouraged periodic suggestions that the City of London militia regiments, or other part-time Metropolitan military formations, double up as watchmen. This seemed to offer a number of advantages. It would reinforce national defence while greatly enhancing local security. Furthermore, because it would "kill two birds with one stone", it held out the potential for being cost-effective (always a vital consideration). It also provided a ready-made hierarchy that could transcend local boundaries, and would provide a powerful and disciplined force for dealing with riots and disturbances (another perennial concern). Nevertheless, even the most admiring Englishmen were normally obliged to accept that the quasi-military Parisian model would not be acceptable in London, given the national political culture and character: "The Police of Paris is that of a Garrison. Her watchmen are soldiers and every street has its barrack".[21] As a result, English observers normally suggested that aspects of the French system, rather than its entirety, should be copied in the Metropolis.[22]

---

19. D. Garrioch, *The People of Paris and their Police in the Eighteenth Century*, 1994, pp.515-516 and p.523.
20. I. A. Cameron, "The Police of Eighteenth-century France", 1977, p.47.
21. *The Times*, Nov 10, 1801, p. 2.
22. Sir W. Mildmay, *The Police of France*, 1763, pp.43-63.

The "Professional" Police of the 1700s

The "traditional" Metropolitan policing arrangements of parish constables, watchmen and beadles, were gradually supplemented by piecemeal reforms during the second half of the eighteenth century. These added limited "professional" forces to the capital's law enforcement officers. They eventually included the Bow Street Runners (operational from the 1750s) and the various patrols that also operated out of Bow Street.[23] These included a "Foot Patrole", established on a permanent basis in 1790 by Sir Sampson Wright during his tenure as chief magistrate (1780-97), and operative throughout sixteen districts of central London during the hours of darkness before 1 am. It numbered 60 men in 1800.[24] A short-lived horse patrol was introduced during a crime panic in 1763, on the advice of John Fielding. It was abandoned the following year when the government withdrew funding (it was revived in 1805). The generally sound reputation of the Bow Street Runners and members of the patrols was one reason that there were few objections to attaching salaried officers to the new police offices in 1792.[25] Six professional constables were initially attached to each office, their numbers subsequently increasing to twelve. To this group must be added the men attached to the Thames River Police, formally established in 1800, having been started as a private venture by West India merchants in 1798. It was intended to prevent crime in and around the Port of London. Nevertheless, the total number of professional constables remained very small. As a journal correspondent pointed out to "sarcastic" critics of the 1792 reforms, although the constables attached to the police offices established that year had experienced considerable success against pickpockets, the three offices to the West of Temple Bar had only 36 men between them to police an area of a hundred thousand homes and half a million people.[26]

These new forces worked in a variety of ways. The Bow Street Runners, and, to a lesser extent, the salaried constables attached to the 1792 police

23. L. Radzinowicz, *A History of English Criminal Law and its Administration from 1750*, vol.3, 1948-56, pp.56-57.
24. D. Bentley, *English Criminal Justice in the Nineteenth Century*, 1998, p.5.
25. J. M. Beattie, "Garrow and the Detectives", 2007, pp.5-23.
26. *The Gentleman's Magazine*, 1793, vol. 63, p.604.

offices emphasised detection, though the latter body conducted a small amount of preventative patrolling, along with the enforcement of warrants. By contrast, the various state-funded "patrols" (foot, horse and day) emphasised overt mobile urban surveillance and thus were primarily a preventative force, like the traditional parish watch.

Police and the Political Nation

In theory, a constable, and the watchmen who derived their authority from him, knew that men of "any degree [we]re subject to his power".[27] In practice, when dealing with members of the upper social orders, a degree of circumspection was prudent, and usually manifest by both constables and watchmen, "reforming" officers sometimes excepted. Thus, in the 1790s, when a young gentleman who had been walking with a high-class prostitute was arrested by a watchman, and brought back to the watch-house, the constable of the night swiftly discharged them both and: "...reproved the watchman for not knowing his duty". By contrast, a homeless girl who was detained at the same time was put in the watch-house cell overnight and then committed to the bridewell.[28] Constables and watchmen who attempted to apply the law to their social superiors sometimes got their fingers burnt. For example, in 1752, a Covent Garden watchman was bound over to the Middlesex Quarter Sessions by Henry Fielding for assaulting (or arresting) a gentlewoman in the street and threatening to drag her to the Roundhouse Prison.[29]

Nevertheless, confrontations were sometimes unavoidable, if only because of the frequent presence on the streets of young fighting-drunk members of the upper classes who wished to finish their evenings by putting the watch "to flight".[30] Young "rakes" would beat and abuse watchmen as they came "reeling from the taverns".[31] Although the Mohock threat of 1712 was greatly

27. W. Fenner, *The Compters Commonwealth*, 1617, p.52.
28. J. Fielding, *The New London Spy*, 1790, p.44.
29. *The Covent Garden Journal*, 25 February 1752.
30. J. Fielding, *A Brief Description of the Cities of London and Westminster*, 1776, p.xxx.
31. P. J. Grosley, *A Tour to London or, New Observations on England, And its Inhabitants*, 1772, vol.1, pp.48-49.

exaggerated, the only six men to be prosecuted stood trial for assaulting a watchman. They had been "well beaten" in their turn by the watch on arrest.[32] As this suggests, not all parish officers were intimidated by the upper orders.

Anonymity of Parish Officers

The "traditional" English policing system had been premised on a face-to-face society in which those who held public office, whether constables or watchmen, were known to those upon whom they exercised authority. Population growth and mobility meant that this had ceased to be the case in much of the Metropolitan area by 1700. This occasioned numerous problems. Amongst them was that miscreants could successfully impersonate law officers. As early as 1674, a group of men dressed up one of their number in a: "...Gown, Cap, Staff and all the formalities of a constable, the rest being put into a suitable Garb, and [then] reverently attending him as his watchmen". During the night, they passed, without challenge, several other watches, giving and receiving the: "...usual complement, Good Night Brother, to the Constable". They then used their cover to gain access to residential premises where they could steal goods or cash, under the guise of searching for coiners who, they claimed, might have taken refuge there. Once inside, they took more than seven pounds worth of coins, from one house, on the pretence that it needed to be examined for forgery. They even issued a receipt for the cash in the name of a local JP This ploy was then repeated at a nearby alehouse, where they purported to be looking for stolen plate, taking £20 worth of the establishment's own plate for later "examination". It was only when they attempted the same stratagem at a canny shopkeeper's premises that suspicion was aroused and they were arrested.[33]

By the early eighteenth century, impostors were regularly pretending to be parish officers in parts of Westminster, well aware that people no longer took it for granted that they could recognise their local constables and watchmen. At about the same time, the City of London was forced to experiment with

32. *British Mercury*, March 12–March 14 1712.

33. Anon, *The Counterfeit Constable and the Wicked Watch*, 1674, pp.5-7.

a system of monthly, and secret, "watchwords", allowing watchmen from neighbouring wards to identify each other in the dark. Clearly, voice recognition was no longer enough. The most common single form of imposture prosecuted at the Westminster Quarter Sessions between 1685 and 1720 was that of "pretend" law officers. There are at least 17 references to a total of 29 men who falsely claimed to be constables, Marshalsea or sheriffs' officers. Some would carry a staff or other badge of office; others simply relied on a convincing demeanour. Frequently, they would extort money in lieu of "arresting" those they targeted. Others might try to intimidate streetwalkers into providing sexual favours or bribes. As even official law officers were notorious for their venery, such behaviour did not necessarily arouse suspicion.[34] This phenomenon continued into the late eighteenth century, if on a smaller scale. For example, in 1775, the Guildhall Court committed Edward Russell to a month's hard labour in the bridewell. He had pretended that he was employed by the City marshal and took several people into custody "with an intent to extort money from them".[35]

Fragmentation of Policing

Before 1829, there was no Metropolis-wide police "system". Constables and watchmen in Middlesex and Westminster usually had no legal jurisdiction beyond their own parishes, and could not normally operate "out of area", at least in theory.[36] Those from the City could not act outside the Square Mile, though constables there had one major advantage over their cousins in Middlesex and Westminster. Their legal jurisdiction extended to the City's limits as a result of the 1663 Night Watch Act, passed by the Square Mile's Common Council. This meant that: "In London, a Constable is not only a Constable within his precinct, but over all the ward and city".[37] In

34. J. Hurl-Eamon, "The Westminster Impostors: Impersonating Law Enforcement in Early Eighteenth-century London", 2005, pp.461-464.
35. *Middlesex Journal*, April 20-22 1775.
36. J. Ritson, *The Office of Constable*, 1791, p.2.
37. J. Paul (Barrister), *The Compleat Constable*, 1785, p.6, and Anon, *The Complete Parish Officer*, 1772, p.11.

practice, however, even City constables rarely operated outside their allotted areas, and in the heavily sub-divided City of London, with its myriad of wards, small parishes and precincts, these were often very small. Indeed, in an attempt to address this problem in the early 1760s, the Court of Aldermen approved the appointment of members of the (refounded) Society for the Reformation of Manners as extra constables, with specific encouragement to act anywhere in the City, instead of being given a highly localised responsibility, as ordinary constables were.[38]

In some ways, the gradual proliferation and accretion of new, small, professional forces in the second half of the eighteenth century served to exacerbate the general lack of "system" in Metropolitan policing, especially as co-operation between them and the traditional system of watchmen and constables, on which they were superimposed, was often woefully deficient. For example, William Blizzard, surgeon to the (part-time) Honourable Artillery Company, noted that, in the early 1780s, after a notorious murder and continual robberies and acts of violence on the roads near Islington, a party of men from his regiment, accompanied by peace officers, spent many nights in a "spirited search" for those involved. Although they arrested several suspicious people, and took them before a magistrate, he: "...rebuked them for meddling with a business, which, he said, his own people much better understood".[39]

The fragmentation of policing occasioned more general problems. It produced an acute parochialism, both literally and metaphorically, amongst constables and watchmen. Even if individual parishes established effective watch systems they could not usually act in "mutual concert and co-operation" with others.[40] Fragmentation meant that in the case of a major and sudden emergency there were often only limited policing resources available. For example, one night in 1730, four prostitutes were rescued from the hands of a constable and his watchmen after a group of men, armed with sticks,

38. J. Innes, *William Payne of Bell Yard, Carpenter c1718-1782*, nd, p.19.
39. W. Blizard, *Desultory Reflections on Police: with an essay on the means of preventing crimes and amending criminals*, 1785, p.23.
40. G. B. Mainwaring, *Observations on the present state of the Police of the Metropolis*, 1821, p.22.

came to the women's assistance and: "...beat the watch and Constables to such a degree that they were obliged to release them".[41]

It also led to attempts to "off-load" responsibility for nuisances and other minor public order problems onto neighbouring parishes and jurisdictions. For a typical illustration can be considered a case from 1735 in which watchmen from St. James's parish found a drunken woman in the Tyburn Road. Instead of dealing with the situation themselves, as they should have done, they simply dragged her into neighbouring St. Anne's parish, and left her there, where she eventually died from alcohol poisoning. Perhaps unsurprisingly, it was feared that this would: "...cause a dispute at law between the two parishes".[42] In 1785, it was noted that a simultaneous campaign against prostitutes in both the City and Westminster meant that each was attempting to drive them into the other's jurisdiction, so that these: "...wretched women must seek an asylum in the arms of old father Thames".[43]

Both criminals and rioters appreciated that the major jurisdictional boundaries within the Metropolis added to the conurbation's policing problems. They would sometimes take advantage of the borders between the City, Middlesex and Westminster to avoid arrest. Thus, during the Wilkite and Gordon riots, in 1768 and 1780, crowds assembled at Moorfields, on the border between the two "cities", moved from one to the other, to avoid the attentions of their respective magistrates.

Fragmentation also led to severely unequal policing provision throughout the Metropolitan area. London's social stratification meant that many poor vestries did not have the means to introduce the reforms pioneered by their richer neighbours. Even allowing for differences in their size, the variation in the distribution of Westminster watchmen in the early 1770s was extreme. For example, St. James had 56 men and St. Mary Le Strand only two.[44] Urban Middlesex was the same. In 1811, Bethnal Green had 18 watchmen, two inspectors and a beadle for 33,000 people, whereas neighbouring Shoreditch had 75 watchmen and six patrolmen for 44,000 inhabitants,

41. *Grub-street Journal*, 30 April 1730.

42. *The Weekly Oracle: or, Universal Library*, 18 January 1735.

43. *The Times*, 7 November, 1785, p.3.

44. C. Whitworth, *The Draught of an Intended Act, For the better Regulation of the Nightly Watch and Beadles within the City and Liberty of Westminster*, 1773, p.2.

almost three times as many on a per capita basis.[45] Even the City, although slightly better in this regard, did not have a proportionate distribution of officers, the three large (and relatively poor) extra-mural parishes being notably under-staffed.

Exceptions

As a result of the fragmentation of legal authority, constables were periodically reminded to be careful not to do any act as constable, outside their respective parishes: "...except you are especially appointed by a warrant, or in aiding your high constable in the discharge of his duty".[46] However, as this comment suggests, there were a few exceptions to the general rule. For example, constables could sometimes act under the authority of a specific warrant, even if outside their own parish. Thus, in February 1726, seven constables accompanied by watchmen, and armed with a Lord Mayor's warrant, attempted to arrest the landlord of the Goat and Buffler tavern in Fleet Street, for keeping a common gaming house.[47]

More importantly, both constables and watchmen might be gathered together for special public order or policing functions, "on extraordinary occasions", whether in an active role or as an emergency reserve. This was an ancient practice and was covered by special legal authority, as it would inevitably require officers to act "out of area". Usually, this authority came from their High Constables, who had the power to act anywhere in their own divisions, unlike their parochially confined inferiors. However, and vitally, when petty constables accompanied a High Constable on a specific operation, they shared his legal authority, and so were empowered to act outside their parishes without themselves being *ultra vires,* as a:

> ...high constable has the same authority in every parish in his division as you have in your separate parishes; and you partake of that authority when you are with him".[48]

---

45. R. Paley, "An imperfect, inadequate and wretched system? Policing London before Peel", 1989, p.103.
46. S. Welch, *Observation on the Office of Constable*, 1754, p.38.
47. *Weekly Journal, or The British Gazetteer,* 5 February 1726.
48. Anon, *An Essay on the Office of Constable*, 2nd edn., 1758, p.40.

This allowed the concentration of constables to address specific urban problems. For example, in 1725, Mr. Jones, the High Constable of the Holborn Division, led a large group of constables against gaming establishments at Belsize, arresting six men after a major affray.[49] In 1730, a dozen JPs who had met at the Covent Garden vestry sent their High Constable together with a large number of petty constables to execute warrants against local disorderly houses.[50] Similarly, in the 1750s, it was noted that High Constables "attended by their several petty constables" would sometimes visit taverns in Middlesex villages close to the Metropolitan area, such as Chelsea, Islington and Stepney, to ensure that they were not open on the Sabbath.[51]

In Middlesex, the presence of High Constables also meant that constables could be assembled in large numbers, from surrounding parishes, to deal with the crowds that gathered around a pillory, or to follow the procession to the Tyburn gallows from Newgate. Thus, at the execution of the notorious Lord Ferrers, in 1760, a High Constable preceded a very large body of Middlesex constables: "...the greatest probably that had even been assembled together upon any occasion".[52] Similarly, more than 300 constables were on duty in 1785, when Christopher Atkinson, a former MP, was pilloried for perjury in Mark Lane, as it was anticipated that an enormous and hostile mob would gather to watch the event.[53] However, even this form of co-operation was not universal. For example, by long custom, constables appointed by the Leet Court in the Savoy confined their activities to the borders of their Liberty (about half of the Strand), evincing a marked reluctance to assist in policing public executions, the pillory, proclamations, processions and coronations. By the latter decades of the eighteenth century, this occasioned considerable annoyance to the Middlesex justices.[54]

Of course, whatever the theory, the realities of policing meant that practice was sometimes different, especially between conjoined jurisdictions.

---

49. *The London Journal,* 25 August 1725.
50. *Grub-street Journal,* 23 July 1730.
51. Anon, *Low-Life: or One Half of the World Knows not how the Other Half Live*, 2nd edn. 1755, p.48.
52. L. Shirley, *An Account of the Execution of the Late Laurence Earl Ferrers*, 1760, p.6.
53. *The Times,* 26 November, 1785, p.2 and 30 November, 1785, p.3.
54. R. Somerville, *The Savoy; Manor: Hospital: Chapel*, 1960, p.183.

Thus, in 1709, a Westminster constable named Brey gave evidence that in his many years of experience, the officers from his parish had frequently acted in neighbouring parishes or liberties. Conversely, their constables had often entered his parish without local officers "molesting" them. However, this could have serious consequences if something went wrong. Lord Chief Justice Holt was adamant that Brey's acting out of his constablewick produced a "confusion of jurisdictions". It helped the judge conclude that the arrest that had prompted the killing of an officer was unlawful, something that, in turn, had an enormous impact on the legality of the defendants' behaviour. At Holt's suggestion, the jury returned a special verdict.[55] In due course, this was considered by the 12 judges sitting together at Serjeants' Inn (Holt amongst them) who decided, by a narrow majority, that the defendants should be acquitted of murder and merely convicted of manslaughter, something that allowed them to walk free.[56]

Amelioration

The problems occasioned by fragmented policing led to various attempts, throughout the eighteenth century, to promote liaison and co-operation between and within the capital's various parts. Thus, in September 1744, Mr. Jones, the City's deputy marshal, was sent to see Sir Thomas de Veil, the leading Middlesex JP, immediately after the Lord Mayor and aldermen had been informed by the City marshals that they had been: "...disappointed in their endeavours to bring some audacious robbers to justice, by their running out of the City Liberty into the County". De Veil agreed to the deputy marshal's request for assistance from Middlesex peace officers and told him that: "Directions should be given to their Officers to act at all times in conjunction with those of the City". Subsequently, the City authorities wrote to the Westminster JPs asking them to ensure that their officers were vigilant about dealing with a criminal gang that had been active in the Square Mile but which was based in the neighbouring city.[57] Similarly, in 1754, Saunders Welch urged Metropolitan constables to co-operate,

55. T. Bray, *The Tryals of Jeremy Tooley, William Arch, and John Clausson, Three Private Soldiers for the Murder of Mr. John Dent, Constable...*1732, p.8 and p.26.
56. *Post Boy*, 29 November–1 December 1709.
57. *The Gentleman's Magazine*, 1744, vol. 14, p.505.

so producing: "...a perfect union among yourselves, a ready and cheerful assistance of one another".[58]

Proposals for Reform

Numerous plans were advanced during the eighteenth century to reduce London, or at least its main component parts, to an integrated policing system and so ensure that the area's: "...constables and the numerous, but useless, watchmen, be put under some new and efficient regulation".[59] For example, as early as 1751, the introduction of a Westminster wide body, to supervise the individual parishes and monitor their policing performance had been mooted.[60] In 1755, a proposal to Parliament had suggested that Westminster be divided into 26 wards, policed by 13 companies of 24 watchmen. These would be under the supervision of four mounted night marshals (as well as the parish constables). Similarly, in a paper delivered to the Police Committee of 1772, Sir John Fielding proposed that the "whole direction" of the watch in Westminster ought to be put under one commission, made up of the city's magistrates. Other plans were more ambitious, extending to the entire Metropolitan area. In 1785, Jonas Hanway proposed that the Metropolis be divided into four divisions, each under the supervision of "principle justices" who would be responsible for circa 150,000 people. Each of these would be subdivided into four, containing about 35,000 inhabitants, and headed by a salaried sub-justice. These would be further divided into two, each led by a head constable. These officers would preside over six divisions, headed by a constable.[61]

In the same year, the not dissimilar, and very radical, London and Westminster Police Bill was introduced into Parliament by William Pitt's Solicitor General. Aimed at the "Prevention of Crimes and the Speedy Detection and Punishment of Offenders against the Peace in the Cities of London,

58. S. Welch, *Observations on the Office of Constable*, 1754, p.3.
59. *Gentleman's Magazine*, vol. 63, 1793, p.604.
60. Anon (A Citizen of London), *The Vices of the Cities of London and Westminster. Trac'd from their Original*, 1751, pp.30-31.
61. J. Hanway, *The Defects of Police*, 1785, p.238.

Westminster and the borough of Southwark", it advocated a single police district for the entire Metropolis, with a force of permanent constables replacing the locally controlled system of JPs and parish officers. It stipulated that the area would be sub-divided into nine police divisions. Three government-funded Commissioners of Police would be selected to preside over the system and would, in their turn, appoint nine stipendiary magistrates, who would keep regular hours at public offices in each division. Each division would also have a chief constable and armed petty constables acting on his orders. Constables would patrol the streets full-time, both on foot and on horseback. The nine chief constables would receive orders from a High Constable, directly under the authority of the police commissioners. Vitally, all petty and high constables were to have full powers "over the whole jurisdiction".[62]

To allay concern, the Attorney General suggested, rather implausibly, that this was not a new system at all, but "merely a bill to give a more vigorous operation to the old".[63] Despite such assurances, it met bitter opposition, especially from the City. Proponents of the Bill claimed that the Square Mile's aldermen had been influenced by a garbled version of the proposed Act rather than the one presented before Parliament. Additionally, it was pointed out that opposition from aldermen and the Middlesex JPs, especially the Trading Justices, was unsurprising, as a measure whose:

> ...object was to deprive many gentlemen present of great emoluments, and all of some supposed importance, was not likely to have a numerous body of voluntary advocates".[64]

Nevertheless, the 1785 Bill failed. By contrast, the 1786 Dublin Police Act (27 Geo. III c. 24 Ireland) was successfully passed into law. It provided what was, essentially, the same police scheme, appropriately scaled down in size.

The failure of the 1785 Bill did not bring an end to proposals for reform. Ironically, shortly after their opposition helped to wreck it, the Mayor and Aldermen of London were considering reform of their own. In November

62. *The Times*, 30 June 1785, p.3.

63. *The Gentleman's Magazine*, 1785, vol. 55, pp.962-963.

64. Anon, *Defence of the Police Bill, in Answer to a Charge Delivered By W. Mainwaring Esq., A gentleman of Westminster*, 1786, p.3.

1785, they discussed a plan whereby a nightly force of 30 horse and 20 foot, drawn from a larger body of 150 men, and based in Guildhall, would supplement watch and constables in the Square Mile.[65] More modestly, the 1798 Police Committee recommended that there be a central board to supervise the different policing establishments of the Metropolis, though, to Colquhoun's dismay, this was not implemented. Major reform would wait until 1829, and would then exclude the Square Mile.

65. *The Times*, 9 November 1785, p.2.

CHAPTER 8

CONSTABLES

Introduction

Constables and headboroughs were the most important law enforcement officers found at parish level. Headboroughs were assistant constables, vested with most of the powers of the principal holders of that office.[1] Traditionally, both were part-time, untrained, and unpaid men, temporarily appointed to enforce the law in their own parishes. They did not wear a specific uniform, being attired in their normal workaday clothes, although they sometimes carried a tipstaff or "painted rolling-pin", which was a constable's badge of office in the City and parts of Middlesex. This might be shown to prison authorities and members of the public in situations where an officer was attempting to exercise his legal powers.

Such "traditional" types of parish constable were accompanied or joined by other officers, fulfilling a broadly similar function, during the course of the century. By the end of the era there were five further types of constable in the Metropolis: paid substitutes or deputies for those properly appointed to the office; those attached to the Bow Street Office; those attached to the police offices established in 1792; special constables sworn in for emergencies, and officers belonging to the Thames River Police.[2] Nevertheless, the traditional type of constable, and those deputising for him, were by far the most common throughout the period.

Parish constables were: "...bound to perform their office gratis".[3] Although they did not receive a salary, they could recover expenses that were necessarily incurred in the course of their duties and received a small set fee for

1. R. Gardiner, *The Compleat Constable*, 4th edn., London, 1710, p.5.
2. P. Colquhoun, *A Treatise on the Functions and Duties of a Constable*, 1803, p.xii.
3. R. Gardiner, *The Compleat Constable*, 4th edn., London, 1710, p.7.

performing certain specific tasks. These were not of a size to motivate most men. Although constables might be paid 4d. for enforcing an arrest warrant, no respectable shopkeeper or tradesman would: "...neglect greater advantages [from their businesses], to get a groat in the service of the community".[4] Occasionally, officers might be rewarded more generously, on an *ex gratia* basis. In 1741, for example, Jonathan Bellamy, the constable of St. Bride's, noted that he had been given a guinea for apprehending a suspect pursuant to an arrest warrant.[5] In 1785, the City marshal was ordered to pay the 350 or so officers who had been in attendance when Christopher Atkinson was pilloried five shillings each as an: "...encouragement for constables to do their duty for the future".[6] Additionally, of course, it was inherently more likely that they would secure a share of the large state (and private) rewards available for apprehending felons than would ordinary members of the public. Several, like the headborough Alexander Forfar, seem to have used their official position to help them operate as thief-takers.[7] Nevertheless, the prospects of such remuneration were too remote to prove a major attraction for most of the men appointed.

Appointment of Constables in Middlesex and Westminster

Traditionally, constables and headboroughs were elected to their office for a year or (much more rarely) two, by the jurors of their local leet court. For example, in Westminster, they were chosen by selecting half the men from a group of 160 summoned by the Dean of Westminster to a leet court (effectively a manifestation of the Court of Burgesses) held on the first Tuesday after Michaelmas. Even the unsuccessful 1720 Bill for the reform of Westminster watchmen expressly reserved the right to select constables to this body.[8] As a result, Westminster was supposed to have 80 constables, shared

4. Anon (By a Lover of his Country), *The Thief-Catcher; or, Villainy Detected*, 1753, p.46.
5. OBSP, Trial of John Thobalds, 5 April 1741.
6. *The Times*, 26 November, 1785, p.2 and 30 November 1785, p.3.
7. OBSP, Trial of Ann Collier, 5 December 1744.
8. N. M., *A Letter to a Member of Parliament, Concerning the Bill for Regulating the Nightly Watch in the City of Westminster, and Liberties thereof*, 1720, p.2.

out amongst its various parishes, ranging from the 14 men who were assigned to St Martin-in-the-Fields to the two individuals serving St. Mary-le-Strand.[9] A broadly similar situation prevailed in other parts of Middlesex.

However, by the eighteenth century, this traditional system of appointment had been in decline in many parts of England, including Middlesex, for decades. Sometimes, a leet jury would merely confirm the nomination of a local parish vestry rather than actively selecting the men appointed. Where leet courts were altogether absent, as was often the case by 1700, especially in urban areas, constables might be chosen directly by their vestry. Additionally, in 1662, magistrates were authorised by statute (13 & 14 Car. 2, c. 12) to fill vacancies if a leet had not been held, a constable had died in office, or an officer had left his parish suddenly.[10] Where leets did still sit, it was often only on an intermittent and irregular basis. As a result, by the early eighteenth century, serving constables in Middlesex, who had finished their year in office, would frequently have to petition the Justices to appoint a man in their place, on the grounds that there was no prospect of a leet court being held that would release them (in many areas, constables could not leave office until a replacement had been appointed).[11]

Even where surviving leet courts still appointed constables, JPs acquired considerable powers over the officers selected. For example, two magistrates could remove a man from office if he proved unsuitable, and appoint someone else in his stead, on receiving a formal complaint.[12] Additionally, magistrates would normally administer the oath of office to constables.[13] Thus, in 1712, when Thomas Batt was elected as a constable by the Leet Court of the Savoy Manor in Westminster, he was required to appear before a Middlesex JP to be "...duly sworn into the said office".[14]

Inevitably, given the considerable overlap in their jurisdictions in this area, there was often considerable tension between magistrates and leet

9. J. Paul, *The Compleat Constable*, 1785, p.7.
10. J. R. Kent, "The English Village Constable, 1580-1642", 1981, pp.34-35.
11. E. G. Dowdell, *A Hundred Years of Quarter Sessions, The Government of Middlesex From 1660-1760*, 1932, p.18.
12. J. Shaw, *Parish law: or, a guide to justices of the peace, ministers, churchwardens*, 1733, p.327.
13. *The Case of the Constables of Milborn Port* (1740) 93 E.R. 118.
14. J. Ritson, *A Digest of the Proceedings of the Court Leet of the Manor and Liberty of the Savoy*, 1779, p.6.

courts. In the early 1720s, for example, Westminster JPs and the Court of Burgesses regularly clashed over the appointment of constables, just as they did over the watch. The Justices thought that the men being selected by the burgesses were often deficient in quality.[15]

Appointment of Constables in the City

In the City of London, the appointment process was rather different. The inhabitants of the precincts in each of the 26 wards within the Square Mile would nominate constables on St. Thomas's day. These men would then be approved or rejected by the wardmote, ancient bodies consisting of 12 or more men of "repute and known integrity" (As well as appointing constables, they would inquire into officers who were remiss in carrying out their duties).[16] If a constable's appointment was approved by the wardmote he would be sworn into office before the Court of Aldermen. By the latter stages of the century, the Corporation of London was also appointing a considerable number of "extraordinary" peace officers, with all the legal powers of normal constables, in addition to these traditionally appointed officers.[17]

The number of men selected for the office by ward or parish varied over the years. In the City, for example, it had been laid down in 1663 that there should be 237 constables, their numbers closely, but not precisely, linked to the number of precincts in the Square Mile. There was a huge variation in per capita provision. At the extremes, Cripplegate Without had more than ten times as many houses per officer as Billingsgate.[18] Numbers were periodically revised over ensuing years.

15. Anon, *An Account of the Endeavours That have been used to suppress Gaming-Houses*, 1722, p.9.
16. J. Howel, *Londinopolis*, 1657, p.79 and p.392, G. Jacob, *The Laws of Appeals and Murder*, 1719, p.5. They would also inquire into breaches of the peace, tavern-licensing regulations, suspected felons who were resident within their wards, and breach of fire regulations.
17. P. Colquhoun, *A Treatise on the Functions and Duties of a Constable*, 1803, p.x.
18. J. M. Beattie, *Policing and Punishment in London, 1660–1750*, 2001, p.116.

Qualifications and Qualities

There was near universal agreement that constables should be:

> ...honest, understanding and able men, and to be men of substance, and not of the meaner sort, and resident where chosen.[19]

In the City of London, they could not be in receipt of alms, and were supposed to be over 21 but less than 70 years of age, though there were several reported cases of older men being selected. They had to be in possession of their mental faculties, not "ideots", physically healthy, rather than being sick or "feeble with old age", and living permanently in the parish that selected them, rather than simply owning land there. Men whose occupations would regularly take them away from home (and thus their parish), such as itinerant workers, were not considered appropriate. It was also not thought to be a suitable position for poor men, because they were usually:

> ...ignorant and fearful and less able to attend this office; their necessity requiring them to mind their own trade and employment.[20]

English Jews could (and sometimes did) serve as constables in the Metropolitan area, but naturalized foreigners were exempt, as were some other men, whether at common law or as a result of an express statutory provision. Amongst them were clergymen, City aldermen, lawyers and those actively serving in the militia, along with a considerable number of other, more arcane, professions and occupations. In London, for example, surgeons and members of the Company of Apothecaries were spared by statute from service.[21] Although, nationally, publicans were not formally exempt from serving, it was generally thought that they should not be nominated to the office, as one of a constable's primary duties was to police such individuals.[22] Indeed, in 1683, the Middlesex Grand Jury resolved that no peace officers should be

19. J. Shaw, *Parish law: or, a guide to justices of the peace, ministers, churchwardens*, 1733, p.327.
20. R. Gardiner, *The Compleat Constable*, 4th edn., 1710, p.7.
21. J. Paul, *The Compleat Constable*, 1785, p.2 and p.4.
22. Anon (The Society for the Suppression of Vice), *The Constable's Assistant,* 1808, 2nd edn., p.14.

permitted to keep alehouses during their time in office. Similarly, in 1712, the Middlesex Justices issued an order to High Constables to warn leet stewards not to appoint alehouse keepers as constables.[23] Anyone involved in purveying alcohol was legally exempt from service in Westminster.

In some parts of the country, a customary system of rotating the position between the inhabitants of designated houses seems to have developed, and been legally recognised.[24] Where such a system was used by a Middlesex parish, the county's justices, sitting at Quarter Sessions, would usually discharge men who petitioned them after being selected out of turn.[25] They would also exempt those who had another valid reason (medical etc.) for not serving.

In the City of London, the Court of Aldermen had this function, deciding whether men were in sufficiently poor health, or frequently enough absent on business, to be excused from service, if they challenged their election. Thus, in 1784, when Samuel Stephens was appointed by St. Sepulchre in Farringdon Without, he successfully petitioned to be excused, with the aid of a physician's report, on the basis that his asthma and a persistent cold meant that if he was required to take his turn sitting up as constable of the night, it would "endanger his life".[26]

In some places, there were also formal restrictions (as opposed to informal customs) preventing those who had served in the recent past from having to do so again, within a set period of time. In Westminster, for example, no one was compelled to serve as a constable more than once every seven years by statute (29 Geo. 2. C. 25).[27] Those who had been awarded a "Tyburn ticket" for prosecuting certain types of felon to conviction, or purchased such a certificate (it could be sold on once) were also exempt. Nevertheless, many men who argued that they could, legitimately, refuse to take on the office, had their claims rejected by the JPs and aldermen. A few sought to

23. E. G. Dowdell, *A Hundred Years of Quarter Sessions*, 1932, p.18.
24. T. Barlow, *The Justice of Peace: A Treatise Containing the Power and Duty of that Magistrate*, 1745, p.139.
25. E. G. Dowdell, *A Hundred Years of Quarter Sessions*, 1932, p.25.
26. A. Harris, *Policing the City: Crime and Legal Authority in London, 1780-1840*, 2004, p.18
27. J. Trusler, *The London adviser and guide*, 1786, p.59.

challenge these decisions via litigation in the higher courts, though this was usually prohibitively expensive.[28]

Traditionally, the property and residence requirements of the office meant that constables were drawn from elements of the capital's "middling" social orders, that is its petty bourgeoisie. This was largely made up of small shopkeepers, skilled artisans, and tradesmen. For example, in the Liberty of the Savoy in Westminster, constables included Benjamin Walwyn, who was a glover, and Michael Connor, a peruke maker.[29] In the City, a Mr. Howard, a Long Acre constable, was a coach-maker.[30] John Townesend, a Hackney (Middlesex) constable in the 1730s, was a local master builder.[31]

It has been argued that this social group probably formed little more than seven per cent of the adult male population of the metropolis, perhaps totalling something over 12,000 men at the end of the eighteenth century, though some estimates place it a little higher. Such men also frequently served as churchwardens and overseers of the poor in their parishes.[32] Indeed, some handbooks for constables would also contain descriptions of the powers and responsibilities of these officers, on the assumption that the same man would be likely to serve in some or all of these positions during the course of his adult life.

Unpopularity of the Office

Throughout the eighteenth century, numerous Metropolitan men were acutely reluctant to take on the unpaid and sometimes onerous duty of constable. It involved considerable trouble and inconvenience, some danger, and the opportunity to make neighbourhood enemies. Frequent nocturnal duty, as part of the rota required to serve as "constable of the night", was

28. See, for example, *The King v Clerke* (1664) 1 Keble 933.
29. J. Ritson, *A Digest of the Proceedings of the Court Leet of the Manor and Liberty of the Savoy*, 1779, pp.7-8.
30. *Weekly Journal or British Gazetteer*, March 10 1722.
31. R. Paley (Ed.), *Justice in 18th-Century Hackney*, 1991, p.143.
32. L. D. Schwarz, "Income distribution and social structure in London in the late eighteenth century", 1979, pp.250-259, and J. Innes, *William Payne of Bell Yard, Carpenter c1718-1782*, nd, p.13.

particularly fatiguing. It could affect the appointee's ability to perform his regular work the following day. In the early 1700s, for example, the satirical writer New Ward described being caught, with others, tippling late at night by a City constable, who was a tailor by trade. They were held overnight in the Poultry Compter. The following morning, the arresting constable returned to the prison in his work clothes, having come straight from his business, with his sleeves still punctured by needles. He then escorted them to the Guildhall Justice Room. More conveniently, for Westminster and Middlesex constables, "night-prisoners" detained at the Clerkenwell Prison would often be taken before a magistrate by one of the two deputy turnkeys at the gaol.[33] Nevertheless, even then, the constable would still have to attend the hearing to give evidence.

Perhaps unsurprisingly, many men would have recourse to petty bribery to avoid being selected, and would: "...caponise the whole Neighbourhood at Michaelmas to stave off the Constableship".[34] Where chosen, many others paid the designated fine for refusing office. Thus, in the Liberty of the Savoy, men were regularly amerced between £2 and £10 for refusing to accept the position without a reasonable excuse. Others were fined lesser sums for being slow to take up the office, after being duly appointed.[35] After the mid eighteenth-century, those refusing to serve in Westminster would be amerced £8 by statute (29 Geo. 2. C. 25).[36]

A reluctance to serve in this capacity was not unique to London, or even England. In eighteenth-century New York, for example, many men accepted a fine in lieu of service as constables.[37] However, it was particularly acute in the Metropolis. Nevertheless, an appointee could escape being fined if he could find an acceptable deputy to take his place. Realistically, this meant

33. J. Ilive, *Reasons offered for the Reformation of the House of Correction in Clerkenwell*, 1757, p.36. They would also take already incarcerated suspects for further examination where necessary.
34. Anon (Tom Tattle), *A Letter from Tom Tattle A Literate Watchman of Westminster to his Brother Jack Drydrub*, 1720, p.6.
35. J. Ritson, *A Digest of the Proceedings of the Court Leet of the Manor and Liberty of the Savoy*, 1779, pp.7-8.
36. J. Trusler, *The London adviser and guide*, 1786, p.59.
37. D. Greenberg, "The Effectiveness of Law Enforcement in Eighteenth-century New York", 1975, p.179.

providing, and paying for, a substitute (still usually cheaper than paying the appropriate fine).

Substitutes

The power to deputise the office of constable, by appointing a substitute, appears to have gradually emerged during the seventeenth century. It had long been recognised that although a constable could not appoint someone to cover his whole duty, he might deputize a man to do: "...many things under him, and in his name, that relate to his office".[38] For example, during his period of service, a constable could assign someone to cover for him "in case of sickness or other misfortune".[39] However, according to the traditional analysis, the duly appointed constable was still personally responsible, and legally accountable, for anything untoward that happened during his year in office.[40] Late in the seventeenth century, statutory provision was made for dissenters who had been chosen as constables to deputize if they wished (1 W. and M. c.18).[41]

Gradually, from these roots, the practice spread to ordinary, healthy, Anglicans who did not wish to carry out the duty in person, and those who acted as their substitutes acquired legal responsibility for their performance in office. By 1663, it had been accepted that a deputy who was a 'fit' person could be sworn in and would be personally answerable for any failings, even if this was: "...rather a toleration than law".[42] (This was allowed because the office of constable was ministerial, rather than judicial).[43] By the start of the eighteenth century, it was well established that healthy men could appoint deputies.[44] Many did so. By then, such substitutes, provided they

38. R. Gardiner, *The Compleat Constable*, 4th edn., 1710, pp.9-10.
39. E. W., *The Exact Constable*, 1663, pp.11-12.
40. R. Gardiner, *The Compleat Constable*, 4th edn., 1710, pp.9-10.
41. J. Shaw, *Parish law: or, a guide to justices of the peace, ministers, churchwardens*, 1733, p.327.
42. E. W., *The Exact Constable*, 1663, pp.11-12.
43. R. Gardiner, *The Compleat Constable*, 4th edn., London, 1710, p.9.
44. J. Shaw, *Parish law: or, a guide to justices of the peace, ministers, churchwardens*, 1733, p.327.

were considered to be fit persons, were always sworn into office on their own account and personally liable for any faults and failings during their year of service.[45]

The incidence of substitution increased steadily throughout the eighteenth century, in part, it seems, because the constable's position became more onerous, as the urban day lengthened and it acquired extra duties. As a result, by 1779, in many areas: "The practice of swearing in substitute constables is of late years become so common as even to be regarded as a matter of course".[46] Additionally, substitution appears to have been more popular with other potential candidates for the office, because, where a fine was paid, they were more likely to: "...be obliged to serve the office before their regular turn".[47] (Some fines were used to pay for constables, so that this did not occur).

Although the rate of substitution grew steadily during the course of the eighteenth century, its incidence differed greatly between the City, Westminster and urban Middlesex, and between the individual parishes and wards within these areas. Unsurprisingly, the level of substitution was much higher in richer parishes than in poorer ones. Within the City, between 1728 and 1731, its incidence varied from zero in the very poor ward of Cripplegate Without, up to 94 per cent in affluent Cornhill and Limestreet.[48] These differences largely reflected the relative wealth of their inhabitants, although some wards were inherently more willing to allow appointees to deputize than others.

By the latter years of the eighteenth century, it had become "customary practice" in London to hire a substitute.[49] In 1796, Patrick Colquhoun estimated that only 98 of the 243 constables in the City were householders fulfilling their duty in person. However, in other, poorer, parts of Metropolitan Middlesex and Westminster, especially during the early decades of the eighteenth century, the level of personal service was very much higher;

45. R. Gardiner, *The Compleat Constable*, 4th edn., 1710, p.10.
46. J. Ritson, *A Digest of the Proceedings of the Court Leet of the Manor and Liberty of the Savoy*, 1779, pp.7-8.
47. C. Halifax, *The Constable's sure guide; or every constable his own lawyer*, 1791, p.6.
48. J. M. Beattie, *Policing and Punishment in London, 1660-1750*, 2001, p.148.
49. C. Halifax, *The Constable's sure guide; or every constable his own lawyer*, 1791, p.6.

in some, it was almost universal. A few substitutes made a virtual career out of their voluntarily adopted duty, while others worked for several years. For example, James Prior served as a constable for the Bassishaw ward of the City every year between 1778 and 1807, before becoming its beadle. Of the 22 men who served in the ward of Broad Street between 1785 and 1794, 14 held office more than once, and ten served four or more times.[50]

Quality of substitutes

The quality of substitutes was a matter of permanent concern to the authorities. Of course, there were *some* benefits to the system in terms of professionalism. Because many men served for years on end, they acquired considerable experience and knowledge. Against this, the fee that substitutes received from those originally selected was very modest, normally just a few pounds, so that they were often of low quality. Although deputies had to be approved by various parish and local bodies, they were nearly always poorer, and socially inferior, to the men whose places they took. Even at the start of the nineteenth century, observers were lamenting that far too little attention was paid to their character and impact on the capital's policing system. It was claimed that any man who, for a few guineas, would accept the office could, by definition, be: "...presumed to be unfit for the situation". By contrast, it was just those prosperous people who were most "respectable", and so best equipped to serve, who would almost always find a replacement.[51]

Conflicting Pressures on Constables

Constables were in an inherently awkward situation. They were answerable to area magistrates, and tasked with enforcing the law. However, they also had to live with, and mediate between, local people. If they violated community values they might face hostility from their neighbours, to whom they were accountable at meetings of the parish vestry. In some situations, the wisest policy was to "see no evil, hear no evil". As a result, there were regular cases

---

50. A. Harris, *Policing the City: Crime and Legal Authority in London, 1780-1840*, 2004, p.20.
51. Anon (The Society for the Suppression of Vice), *The Constable's Assistant*, 2nd edn., 1808, p.13.

of constables failing to carry out their duties. For example, in the 1680s, many of the poor people living in Tower Hamlets worshipped in the area's numerous "secret" but widely known conventicles for dissenters. Even so, local parish officers refused to make any discovery of these establishments or to execute justices' warrants against them. This forced area magistrates to use private informers to locate them, and then to suppress them in person. Eventually, a large number of local constables were fined and, in some cases, pilloried, by the Middlesex Quarter Sessions for their failings in this regard.[52] Similarly, in 1722, it was claimed by a group of activist JPs that the corruption and inaction of local constables had been responsible for the initial failure of their campaign against Westminster's gambling houses, this reflecting the: "Constables Insolence towards them, and their Friendships with the Gamesters". As a result, several officers were bound over or committed to prison for refusing to serve arrest warrants on their neighbours and for alerting suspects about forthcoming raids.[53]

Such concerns also resulted in constables swearing in their returns that their parishes were free from certain forms of deviance, when this was transparently not the case. This prompted one observer to note that he must be mistaken in imagining there were any brothels within the purlieus of St. Paul's, Covent Garden, as the: "...Constables, who have the utmost detestation of perjury, so clearly demonstrate by their oaths".[54]

Operation

Except when taking a turn to supervise the night watch or after being mobilised by their High Constables for crowd control, parish constables were specifically summoned to perform particular duties as and when they were needed, whether by a member of the public or a local magistrate. For

52. Anon, *The Proceedings of His Majesties justices of peace, at the sessions of Oyer and Terminer: held at Hick's-Hall, September the 6th, 1684, for the tryal of the constables, &c. of the hamlets of Spittle-fields, and Bethnal-Green*, 1684, pp.1-4.
53. Anon, *An Account of the Endeavours That have been used to suppress Gaming-Houses*, 1722, p.5 and p.9.
54. Anon, *A congratulatory Epistle From a Reformed Rake*, 1758, p.15.

example, the highwayman James Whitney was held after an acquaintance spotted him entering a house in Hounsditch and fetched constables from Aldgate to arrest him.[55] On another occasion, when a constable returned to his house with a female guest, she took the opportunity to steal his valuables after he was suddenly called away on duty.[56]

Finding a constable in an emergency could be difficult, especially for those who were not from the same parish as the local officer and unfamiliar with where he lived. For this reason, constables in London were required to place both the King's Arms and the Arms of the City over their doors, or, if they lived in an alley, at its street-end, to show that an officer resided there.[57] This requirement seems to have replaced a slightly earlier custom, whereby both London and Middlesex constables would have: "…staves and painted Lattis, set or nailed up at each of their Doores".[58]

Constable of the Night

Constables would have to take regular turns serving as the "constable of the night" for their parish or ward. Sometimes, this might have to be done on a weekly basis. The duty would require them to spend the night awake at the watch-house, so that they could supervise the watch and consider what action to take with regard to those arrested during the hours of darkness. Constables were considered to be more competent at judging the: "…propriety of detaining them or setting them at large than the class of persons usually employed as watchmen".[59] Thus, John Penny was on duty when Elizabeth Morris was brought to his watch-house, after being found carrying a bundle and a box. Penny asked her to send for somebody to vouch for her reputation, which she did, two women arriving and saying that she was

55. Anon, *A Full and True Account of the Apprehending James Whitney*, 1692, p.1.
56. OBSP, Trial of Elizabeth Morris, alias Mary Tipping, 4 December 1724.
57. J. Trusler, *The London adviser and guide*, 1786, p.59.
58. S. Dixon, "Quakers and the London Parish 1670-1720", 2007, p.237.
59. J. W. Willcock, *The Office of Constable*, 1827, p.121.

an honest woman and the goods were her own. Despite this, Penny took Morris before a justice the following morning.[60]

Additionally, constables would often inspect the watch before they went on duty, and during the course of the night. It would appear that most discharged the latter duty by sallying forth from their watch-houses to make a circuit of their ward or parish, checking that its watchmen were set and alert. In the City of London they were, theoretically, required to do this at least twice a night.[61] Two circuits also appear to have been the pattern in eighteenth-century Westminster, although the beadle often carried out one of these. Each circuit could take up to an hour, depending on how much time was spent speaking to individual watchmen; frequently, it was much less.[62] For example, in June 1793, Francis Palmer, a Chick Lane constable, noted that while "going my Rounds", at about two o'clock in the morning, he met the nefarious Sarah Laycock in Black Boy Alley. Palmer was alone at this point as he had: "...left the Watchmen at their Stand".[63]

When William Bird, the keeper of the St Martin's roundhouse, was tried for murder in 1742, a series of men who had served as constables of the night in that parish were called to give evidence about overnight practice in the gaol. Mark Coney noted that, before going home in the early hours, he would normally put the less well-behaved prisoners into the holding cell, while the others would be allowed to remain upstairs. Usually, there would be no more than seven or eight of them, as there had been no concerted campaigns against streetwalkers and vagrants during his year in office. According to John Chambers, who had served two years earlier, the constable normally left between 4 am and 5 am, shortly before the watch went off duty. (The following morning, Bird would take those held overnight before a Justice).[64]

Unfortunately, as was noted in 1728, once inside a watch-house many constables did not make much of an effort to check-up on their watchmen, preferring instead to: "...guzzle till their time of going home comes".[65] Little

60. OBSP, Trial of Elizabeth Morris alias Mary Tipping, 4 December 1724.
61. Anon, *The Complete Parish Officer*, 1772, p.12.
62. J. Paul, *The Compleat Constable*, 1785, p.6.
63. OBSP, Trial of Mary Rosum, 29 June 1743.
64. OBSP, Trial of William Bird, 13th October 1742.
65. D. Defoe, *Street Robberies Consider'd*, 1728, p.60.

had changed over 25 years later. Saunders Welch demanded that constables show more activity, rather than: "...drinking or sleeping in the watch-houses, or going off your station at improper times".[66] A decade further on again, it was noted that, at about three o'clock in the morning, it was common to see inebriated constables of the night, who had got through their duty by drinking in their watch-houses, being: "...led by the watchmen to their several habitations".[67] Some even brought friends along to keep them company and admire their exercise of power and authority.[68] A few diverted themselves in an even more inappropriate manner. Francis Palmer met a prostitute while on duty, went drinking with her, and claimed that his pocket was picked by one of her colleagues. Palmer later admitted that he thought that as duty: "...Constable, I was very safe; I was not afraid; I thought they would not offer to rob me".[69]

Control of Constables

Given that the office was often extremely unpopular, either being filled by men who had no wish to carry it out in person, but who could not afford the alternatives, or by paid substitutes of often dubious quality, it is, perhaps, not surprising that it was not always conducted with great enthusiasm. To encourage them to withstand both local social pressures and the attractions of indolence, constables could be subjected to a large array of fines and other punishments if they failed to carry out their duties properly.

Historically, they had been disciplined by their local leet courts.[70] As these forums fell into abeyance, magistrates had become increasingly involved in the process. Parliament also gave them new statutory powers to punish errant officers. For example, one Act (10 Geo. 2. C.22) provided that: "Constables in the City of London misbehaving shall forfeit 20s". Such cases could be

66. S. Welch, *Observations on the Office of Constable*, 1754, p.12.
67. Anon, *Low-Life or one Half of the World knows not how the other half lives*, 3rd edn., 1764, p.18.
68. S. Welch, *Observations on the Office of Constable*, 1754, p.15.
69. OBSP, Trial of Mary Rosum, 29th Jun 1743.
70. W. Sheppard, *The Court-Keepers Guide*, 4th edn., 1656, p.50.

determined by the Lord Mayor (sitting on his own) or by two aldermen.[71] Outside the Square Mile, the Middlesex and Westminster justices were frequently involved in investigating allegations against, and punishing the failures of, their local officers. By a statute from Queen Anne's reign (12 Q. Anne, Cap. xxii. Sect. 24), constables were supposed to be fined 10 shillings each time they failed to remove loose, idle and disorderly people who were begging in the streets, after receiving a complaint from a local resident (this was often tacitly ignored).[72] In theory, a parish constable who failed to arrest those who cursed in public could also be punished at Quarter Sessions.[73] In reality, this very rarely happened, although, in 1701, the Grand Jury for Middlesex presented several men for neglecting this duty. This temporarily prompted officers in both the City and Westminster to give proof of their diligence by: "…taking up swearers in the streets and markets".[74] Such drastic action over minor matters was rare. More typically, the authorities, like the Lord Mayor and Court of Aldermen in 1720, would simply display notices reminding constables and other parish officers of their duty to enforce the laws against Sunday tippling, swearing and drunkenness.[75]

A failure to respond to a specific request for assistance was more serious, and formed the most common ground for investigating a constable. For example, in 1752, after two notorious pickpockets were caught stealing a silk handkerchief near Fetter Lane, they were held in a public house and a local constable was sent for. Unfortunately, this officer repeatedly ignored the summons, and insisted that they attend him at his own business premises. Even then, having quite improperly "sat as Magistrate in his own shop, to enquire into the merits" of the case, he refused to take charge of the pair, leaving the victim and those assisting him to make their own arrangements for the thieves to be taken to the Woodstreet Compter. Local justices later reprimanded the officer.[76]

71. J. Trusler, *The London adviser and guide*, 1786, p.59.
72. *Grub-street Journal*, 9 September 1731. The money raised was given to the poor of the parish.
73. J. Gonson, *The Charge of Sir John Gonson Knt. To the Grand Jury of the Royalty of the Tower of London, and Liberties and Precincts thereof*, 1728, p.10.
74. *Flying Post*, 8-10 July 1701.
75. *Weekly Journal or Saturday's Post*, 19 November 1720.
76. *General Advertiser*, 2 October 1752.

Similarly, in 1732, John Collins, a headborough from St. John's parish in Hackney, Middlesex, was produced before a local petty sessions, after a similar complaint. Collins had refused to get up during the night to secure two footpads. He was excused after persuading the JPs that he was sick in bed at the relevant time, and so unable to comply with the request. In 1736, a labourer complained to Hackney JPs that John Townsend, a constable from the same parish, had refused to help him arrest an army deserter (presumably he was after a reward). Townsend was initially bound over in the sum of 20 pounds to appear at the following Quarter Sessions, so that he could be prosecuted by the labourer.[77]

Constables and Corruption

Throughout the period, the position of constable, like that of watchman and beadle, afforded considerable scope for low-level corruption. In 1803, for example, John Newhouse, a City constable, was convicted and imprisoned for unlawfully imprisoning and extorting money from Jane Cracknel. He had stopped her in Giltspur Street, without any justification, around midnight and demanded seven shillings.[78] However, extortion was often much subtler. Although normally unpaid, officers were frequently "tipped" small sums for carrying out their duties. This could lead to improper pressure being placed on parties to "pay" for a constable's services, something that was technically an offence, although probably quite a common occurrence. Control of licensing regulations also furnished numerous opportunities for abuse. For example, in 1738, a Shoreditch constable was fined and sentenced to six months hard labour in the Bridewell for attempting to extort a guinea from a local victualler: "… on pretence of his retailing spirituous liquors contrary to law".[79]

77. R. Paley (Ed.), *Justice in 18th-Century Hackney*, 1991, p.87 and p.143.

78. *The Times*, Oct 25, 1803, p.3.

79. *Old Common Sense; Or, the Englishman's Journal*, 4 March 1738.

Reforming Constables

A few officers, often referred to as "reforming constables" in the early part of the century, belonged to, or were associated with, a moral campaigning group. They actively sought the office with a view to using it to promote their own moral agenda within the wider society. It was a matter of constant annoyance to such men that the theoretical obligations imposed by the constables' extensive oath, under which they were sworn to repress most forms of immorality, were simply ignored.[80] Many reformers such as John Disney urged constables to take their legal obligations more seriously.[81]

During the 1690s, one of the City's Societies for the Reformation of Manners was made up exclusively of constables from within the Square Mile, who were personally committed to its campaign. Its membership was reconstituted each year, as new men took on the office. They would meet periodically, to provide each other with mutual support and advice, and to divide the City into different areas of responsibility for inspecting disorderly houses and arresting drunkards, prostitutes, those who violated the Sabbath or used foul language in its streets and markets.[82] Such men were still active over 30 years later. Thus, in 1731, in the neighbouring city of Westminster, it was noted that several lewd women had been arrested by: "...constables belonging to the Reformation of Manners".[83]

The ill-fated John Dent, who was murdered in 1709, was typical of the most active type of reforming constable. He had been linked to the Society for the Reformation of Manners for almost 18 years at the time of his death, and it was claimed that he had been involved in apprehending or prosecuting several thousand "lewd and profligate" persons, including Sabbath breakers and drunkards, during this period. It was a dangerous life. Dent had been abused, beaten, mobbed, and wounded on several occasions during his career. Ironically, he had been one of the first to go to the assistance of another

80. J. Woodward, *An Account of the Societies for Reformation of Manners*, 1699, p.72.
81. J. Disney, *An Address to Grand-Juries, Constables and Church-Wardens*, 1786, p.10.
82. J. Woodward, *An Account of the Societies for Reformation of Manners*, 1699, pp.11-12.
83. *British Journal or the Traveller*, 6 March 1731.

reforming constable, John Cooper, who had been mortally wounded in a disturbance at Mayfair, seven years earlier, and who died in Dent's arms.[84]

Such formally organised reforming constables petered out with the decline to non-existence of the societies in the 1730s. However, several men still sought the position with a view to implementing a personal moral agenda. Later in the century, some members of the (re-founded) society would petition to be sworn in as "extra" constables. For example, in the early 1760s, a sympathetic Court of Aldermen in the City was annually approving the admission of its members as constables, on special terms. Instead of being given responsibility for a single parish, like ordinary constables, reforming constables were encouraged to act anywhere in the Square Mile.[85] Reforming constables attracted considerable, and not entirely deserved, popular cynicism.

It was frequently claimed that such men benefited financially from their work and were driven to it because they had no choice: "...but *Pimp* like, to Live upon other Peoples *Debaucheries*".[86] However, many appear to have been sincere in their commitment to the cause. As a result, there were regular complaints from "gentlemen" about the abuse they suffered at the hands of "insolent" reforming constables, who appear to have been less intimidated by social status than some of their colleagues. Libertines felt that preserving law and order amongst the masses did not entitle them: "... to break into private companies, and hurry gentlemen before a magistrate on a bare suspicion of being criminal".[87] Well-born "rakes" seeking prostitutes were particularly resentful about being treated as if they were thieves.[88] An example of this occurred in April 1730, and eventually resulted in four constables being tried and acquitted for assault at the Guildhall the following year. The officers' victim was one Charles Gery who had been accosted in Fleet Street by two women and returned to their room. The four "informing consta-

84. T. Bray, *Sermon Preach'd at the Parish-Church of St. Clements Danes, Westminster on the 24th of March 1709 at the Funeral of Mr. John Dent*, 1709, pp.15-16. *Post-Man* 8-10 July 1703, *Post-Man* 10-12 August 1703, and *Post Boy*, March 22 1709.

85. J. Innes, *William Payne of Bell Yard, Carpenter c1718-1782*, nd, p.19.

86. *The London Spy*, January 1700, p. 13.

87. *The Gentleman's Magazine*, 1732, vol. 2, p.1029.

88. *Spectator*, 11 September, 1728.

bles" sought entry some minutes later. Gery opened the door to them, was seized and, allegedly, beaten. Clearly, the constables were not on normal duty that night, as they refused to comply when he: "...begg'd to be carried before the Constable of the Night".[89] Additionally, when they dragged him to Woodstreet Compter they were careful to avoid local watch-houses and watchmen on the way. Gery claimed that the constables' subsequent acquittals were based on a legal technicality.[90]

Powers of Arrest

The general duty of constables was to keep the King's peace in their own districts, and for that purpose they were equipped with "very large powers, of arresting".[91] Under English common law, constables, like sheriffs, beadles and active watchmen, were authorised to arrest felons and those reasonably suspected of being felons. However, although a constable could, in theory, arrest on suspicion, without a warrant, doing so was fraught with danger as, to make it legal, it was essential that a felony had actually been committed. Otherwise, the arrest could constitute a false imprisonment that might form the basis of a civil suit and legally justify physical resistance. As a result, it was normally necessary that a victim had been present when an offence was committed and was absolutely sure in his identification of the alleged felon before constables would become involved, unless they had a warrant.[92]

Constables, beadles and watchmen also had the authority to arrest anyone committing a breach of the peace in their presence, if it could not be dealt with in a less drastic manner. However, it was generally thought to be: "...extremely dangerous to intermeddle after the affray or assault is over".[93] Any departure from the letter of the law might result in a civil action. It was

89. *The Gentleman's Magazine*, 1731, vol. 1, pp.538-539.

90. C. Gery, *Mr. Gery's Case With the Reforming Constables*, 1750, p.1.

91. W. Blackstone, *Commentaries on the Laws of England*, 1765-1769, vol. 1, p.344.

92. J. Fielding, *Extracts from such of the Penal Laws as particularly relate to the Peace and Good Order of this Metropolis*, 1768, p.336.

93. S. Welch, *Observation on the Office of constable, with cautions for the more safe execution of that duty, etc.*, 1754, p.7.

much easier, and safer, to wait for crime victims to seek a JP's warrant and then ask for the constable's assistance in enforcing it. For the same reason, constables always had to comply with an arrest warrant's precise terms if they were not to risk losing their legal protection. (They would be excused if they enforced an illegal arrest warrant, though the magistrate who issued it would be liable).[94]

The courts could be very strict about procedural niceties. In 1789, for example, John Wilkinson fetched an Aldgate headborough to arrest an intoxicated man who had earlier threatened him with a knife. This officer, although not a witness to the offence, failed to secure a justice's warrant. When the two men attempted to detain him, the drunkard produced a blade and killed Wilkinson. However, at trial, the judges presiding over the hearing swiftly concluded that the absence of a warrant made it an unlawful arrest, and thus essentially an assault on the defendant. Despite the horror of the crime, the court was adamant that where a man was illegally deprived of his liberty and then: "...causes the death of the assailant, in any manner whatever, certainly by law it reduces the offence to manslaughter". The jury were directed to acquit of murder and convict of the lesser offence. The defendant escaped execution due to the: "...mistake of the officer alone, who should first have obtained a warrant before he arrested you for the breach of the peace".[95]

Professional Knowledge

The professional ability of constables, whether serving in person or deputising for others, was very mixed. In the 1750s, John Fielding felt able to refer in moderately appreciative terms to the "general good Behaviour, Diligence, and Activity" of the constables of Middlesex and Westminster. However, they were often fairly ignorant of the duties attendant on their office. This produced two specific problems. Occasionally, officers would act "too confidently", exceeding their legal authority by, for example, arresting people without warrants where such authority was needed. They could even become tyrannical,

94. W. Lambarde, *The Duties of Constables*, 1640, pp.19-20.
95. OBSP, Trial of William Power, 9 September 1789.

especially in the comparative anonymity of London. Some lacked a sense of proportion. Saunders Welch was concerned that Metropolitan constables were too easily provoked by abusive bystanders, who called them names such as "fool" and "puppy". In the process, they sometimes lost "real" criminals, who were already in custody, while they sought to uphold their authority.[96]

Much more frequently, however, constables' ignorance of their office led them to underestimate their powers and proceed too cautiously. For example, many appear to have been unclear about the circumstances under which they could arrest persons *ex officio*, especially in assault or affray cases. Henry Fielding complained that, because of this, they often refused to arrest known felons until they were specifically issued with a JP's warrant.[97] Their caution was encouraged by the inherent risks of their position: litigation and physical attack.

Fear of Litigation

As well as seeing their prosecutions fail as a result of legal deficiencies, officers who exceeded their powers might find themselves being sued in the civil courts. Indeed, Sir John Fielding felt that for most constables a fear of litigation was even worse than that of physical attacks.[98] These could come from the most unexpected situations. For example, in 1751, a mob of 15 young men tried to force entry into a house in Fetter Lane, while looking for a woman. The local constable and watch were summoned, and a street battle ensued, in which two of the men were arrested and bound over to the following sessions. Unfortunately, one of the pair was an attorney who: "… travers'd the indictment, and brought a Certiorari to harrass the Constable and Watchmen". Fortunately, their parish resolved to "stand by them" and fund their defences.[99] On a more general basis, in 1742, the government provided that the Treasury Solicitor would defend all actions brought against

96. S. Welch, *Observations on the Office of constable*, 1754, p.4.
97. H. Fielding, *An Enquiry into the causes of the Late Increase of Robbers*, 1751 p.79.
98. Sir J. Fielding, *Extracts from Such of the Penal Laws, as Particularly relate to the Peace and Good Order of the Metropolis*, 1768, p. 322.
99. *Grub-street Journal*, 5 August 1731.

constables for acts committed in the "faithful Discharge of their Duty" at the Crown's expense.[100]

Fear of Physical Attack

As with the watchmen, a fear of the physical consequences of strict law enforcement was also conducive to caution. The work of a constable brought considerable risk of physical violence and intimidation, something that was often greater in London than in the provinces. For example, in 1744, a gang of robbers operating in Westminster became so audacious that they would visit local peace officers, at their homes, and: "...make them beg pardon for endeavouring to do their duty, and promise not to molest them". Several constables had to seek shelter in the security of the Bridewell Prison to escape the gang, and one was severely wounded in the street.[101] During the same decade, Richard Harper's gang attempted, unsuccessfully, to murder two Clerkenwell constables.[102]

Like watchmen, constables were often relatively isolated, not in the first flush of youth, and poorly armed. They were not ideally placed to defend themselves. As a result, in the area around Covent Garden, when fights broke out in the early hours of the morning, it was normal to see: "...frightened constables, whose staves are hardly of authority sufficient to prevent their being beaten".[103] Even intervening in a minor affray, or making a routine arrest, could be inherently hazardous. The detention of "lewd women" by active constables appears to have excited the ire of groups of soldiers on several occasions.[104] Similarly, mobs succeeded in rescuing several individuals arrested under the Gin Act 1736 from their custody. On one occasion, two men arrested in Southwark were rescued: "...out of the hands of the

100. *Gentleman's Magazine,* 1742, vol. 12, p.657.
101. *The Gentleman's Magazine,* 1744, vol.14, p.505.
102. *The Ordinary of Newgate, His Account of the Behaviour, Confession, and Dying words ... Who were executed at Tyburn, on Monday the 24th of December, 1744,* 1744, p.36.
103. Anon, *Low-Life or one Half of the World knows not how the other half lives,* 3rd. edn., 1764, p.9.
104. *Post Man,* 14-16 May 1702.

constable, who with his assistants narrowly escap'd the rough discipline of the rabble".[105]

Others were not so fortunate. Robert Rhodes, a headborough for St. Giles's Parish in 1740, was summoned from his shop one night in February and given a magistrate's warrant to arrest Thomas Robinson. He found him in a Drury Lane tavern but, when he sought to effect the arrest, Robinson resisted. A hostile crowd quickly gathered, armed with clubs, sticks and short swords, and swore they would "bail" Robinson, which they did by beating the hapless headborough and robbing him of his small change, pocket-knife and keys.[106] In 1715, two men were fined for viciously wounding a constable named Thomas Morton. They had been part of a mob that began smashing windows. This prompted Morton to ask them to be "peaceable and quiet". At this, the mob fell upon him, cutting his head open to the skull.[107] Some fared even worse. In 1738, Godfrey Walker, of St. Luke's parish in Middlesex, murdered a local headborough with an axe, while the latter was seeking to execute an arrest warrant at his house.[108] Breaking up heated domestic quarrels could be equally dangerous. In June 1732, James Martin, a Hackney headborough, attended a domestic disturbance and was immediately stabbed with a pitchfork.[109] Perhaps as a result of such incidents, Saunders Welch was adamant that force was very much a last resort, carrying many risks: "I advise never to strike, except it be absolutely in your own defence".[110]

Auxiliaries

A penumbra of fairly lowly men, drawn from, *inter alia*, bailiffs' followers, prison runners and other underlings also appear to have been involved in law enforcement. They played a significant, if often ignored, supporting role

105. J. Warner, "Damn you, you informing bitch. Vox Populi and the unmaking of the Gin Act of 1736", 1999, p.299.
106. OBSP, Trial of Richard Baker, 14 May 1741.
107. OBSP, Trial of Bolton Freeman and Thomas Page, 7 September 1715.
108. OBSP, Trial of Godfrey Walker, 28 June 1738.
109. R. Paley (Ed.), *Justice in 18th-Century Hackney*, 1991, p.12.
110. S. Welch, *Observations on the Office of Constable*, 1754, p.9.

in many aspects of policing, though they rarely held any official posts and were not usually entitled to a salary or even expenses. Instead, they operated as employees of those who were in official positions, or on the basis of what they could pick up through fees, rewards and even bribes.[111] Their names sometimes crop up in the *Sessions Papers* as prosecution witnesses and as the companions to constables, beadles, marshalmen and Bow Street Runners engaged on official business. Thus, when, in 1795, John Taplin, a constable in the City, saw a warehouseman named William Taylor run out of Seething-lane with a pack on his back, he quickly became suspicious. He followed and eventually stopped, questioned and arrested Taylor, before taking him to a nearby police-office. Throughout this incident, Taplin was accompanied by an ornament piercer named Charles Phillips. As a result of his acquaintanceship with Taplin, Phillips admitted that he had "left off piercing and turned thief-taker". Presumably, he assisted the constable in finding suspects in exchange for a share of the rewards.[112]

High Constables

Traditionally, one or more High Constables would be appointed to a hundred or lathe, the administrative district between county and parish. The large Hundred of Ossulstone encompassed most of the built up parts of the Metropolis north of the Thames that were outside the City, and several of the suburban villages immediately surrounding it. It included Westminster, High Holborn, Finchley, Islington, Hammersmith, Hackney, Stoke Newington, Bethnal Green, Fulham, Chelsea, Stepney, Poplar, Hoxton, Limehouse, Whitechapel and Shoreditch.[113] Ossultstone was split up into several further divisions for the purposes of appointing High Constables.[114] By the early seventeenth century it had four.

111. J. Innes, *William Payne of Bell Yard, Carpenter c1718–1782,* nd, p.27.
112. OBSP, Trial of William Taylor, 2 December 1795.
113. W. Hardy (Ed.), *Middlesex Sessions Records*, New Series, Volume III, 1615-1616, 1937, pp.57–60.
114. E. G. Dowdell, *A Hundred Years of Quarter Sessions,* 1932, p.17.

High Constables were usually appointed either by the sheriff or by JPs sitting at local Quarter Sessions.[115] In the eighteenth century, the latter was the "norm". They were also sworn into office by the justices.[116] However, in Westminster, the High Constable was chosen by the burgesses at their leet court.[117] A High Constable's term of office was normally for a maximum of three years. By the eighteenth century, it was a position that tended to attract prosperous members of the "middling" social orders; men of a somewhat higher social status than would normally be made petty constables. Some even went on to become JPs. For example, Saunders Welch had been a High Constable prior to becoming a magistrate at Bow Street.

High Constables often had some responsibility for maintaining the urban watch within their divisions and for organizing the removal of local vagrants. For example, they were frequently instructed to ensure that aggressive beggars in their areas were arrested.[118] Additionally, they investigated complaints made to JPs about their petty constables, assisted with the service of writs, and passed on directives issued by magistrates at Quarter Sessions.[119] They also provided liaison between local magistrates and petty constables, especially when large numbers of the latter were needed for specific operations. Very importantly, High Constables provided the legal authority for their accompanying petty constables to act outside their parishes without being *ultra vires*.[120]

Overnight Detention

If a suspect was arrested in the evening, whether by a watchman, constable or member of the public, it was often difficult to produce him before a magistrate until the following day. This would necessitate his being held

115. J. W. Willcock, *The Office of Constable*, 1827, p.1.
116. T. Barlow, *The Justice of Peace: A Treatise Containing the Power and Duty of that Magistrate*, 1745, p.139.
117. M. Gonzales, *London in 1731*, 1888, p.138.
118. *Grub-street Journal*, 9 September 1731.
119. Sir F. Bacon, *Cases of Treason*, 1641, p.25.
120. J. Ritson, *The Office of Constable*, 1791, p.2.

overnight. In built up areas, this would normally be in the cell of a watch-house or in a local prison, such as one of the City Compters. If an arrest had been effected in a rural part of Middlesex, detention could be in a constable's cellar, any other secure building, such as a public house, or a specially constructed "cage" specifically used for these purposes, provided the weather was not too severe. In 1718, Whitlocke Bulstrode encouraged members of the Middlesex Grand Jury to present parishes that did not have stocks, whipping posts and cages in them, and noted that a lack of the latter in the more rural parishes of the county (those "remote from hence") sometimes led to the escape of criminals who were under investigation.[121]

Being held overnight was an unpleasant experience, especially in the confined space of a watch-house. When General Clavering was held in the secure "dungeon" in the watch-house at Hanover Square, at the start of the nineteenth century, he found himself in a room that was 20 feet by 12 feet square, and only seven feet high. There was no fire or candle to light or warm it, no chair or bench to sit on, its floor was covered in vomit from other recent occupants and there was an overflowing privy in one corner. He was detained there, with several other suspects, for 12 hours before being produced before a magistrate.[122] Conditions for suspects detained overnight in one of the City Compters, rather than a watch-house, were equally atrocious.[123] However, as in prisons, financial resources, or the indulgence of officials, could produce better conditions for those accused of less serious offences. At St. Giles's Roundhouse, for example, William Davis "gave Sixpence for a Bed", so that he did not have to lie on the floor.[124] Nevertheless, poor detention conditions explain the determination of many suspects to go before a JP immediately, if at all possible, notwithstanding the late hour at which they had been arrested.

By law, constables had no authority to take bail from an overnight charge. However, in some situations, they might accept a suspect's word for their appearance before a magistrate the following morning, especially if they were

121. W. Bulstrode, *The Charge of Whitlocke Bulstrode Esq to the Grand-Jury, and other Juries, of the County of Middlesex*, 1718, p.38.
122. See for example "Law Report" in *The Times*, Dec. 19th, 1806, p.3.
123. E. Ward, *The London-Spy Compleat in Eighteen Parts*, 4th edn., 1709, p.91.
124. OBSP, Trial of Amy Armstrong, 15th Oct 1729.

able to leave a significant sum of money as security for attendance.[125] The granting of such informal liberty meant: "…taking the party's word [rather] than demanding bail, and in many cases might be convenient and proper".[126] It was normally only allowed in less serious or weak cases, or those involving well settled local men, and was often subject to criticism by magistrates and High Constables.

Quite frequently, overnight detention brought a change in attitude towards taking any further legal action by those at whose behest suspects had been arrested, whether they were watchmen or members of the public. This might be the result of second thoughts about the cost and trouble of prosecuting, or a feeling that a night in the cells was sufficient punishment by itself. As a result, some detainees would be quietly released when the constable of the night and the watch went off duty in the early morning. Strictly speaking, this was illegal. In 1759, for example, a constable from St Martin-in-the-Fields, who allowed a streetwalker who had been brought to his watch-house as a "lewd and disorderly person" to leave in the early morning, was convicted of a misdemeanour at Hick's Hall, which decision was upheld by the Court of King's Bench.[127] Even so, it seems to have been fairly common for a prostitute to be set free after a duty constable concluded that he might: "…not be able to bring any sufficient charge against her".[128] Strictly speaking, "night prisoners" were not supposed to be released until their prosecutors had sworn "to the nature of the offence" in front of a JP. Otherwise there was a risk of the prisoner bringing a successful action for false imprisonment.[129] However, with the more marginal members of Metropolitan society, this was a theoretical rather than real risk.

---

125. OBSP, Trial of Edmund Long and others, 17 Oct 1744.
126. *Murphy and Wedge* (1795) 1 Espinasse 294.
127. *Rex v Bootie* (1759) 2 Burrow 864.
128. Anon, *Thoughts on Means of Alleviating the Miseries attendant upon common Prostitution*, 1799, pp.20-21.
129. Sir T. Deveil, *Observations on the Practice of a Justice of the Peace*, 1747, p.16.

CHAPTER 9

THE WATCH

Introduction

Nocturnal policing in the Metropolis was conducted by parish and ward watchmen. They were a vital aspect of the capital's security. Given that night was the most common time for criminals to: "...put in practice their schemes of villainy, the consequences of an effectual watch must be immediately apparent".[1] In Middlesex, the parish was normally the crucial administrative unit for appointing the watch. In Westminster, they gradually acquired this position during the century. In the City, the Night Watch Act 1663, passed by the Square Mile's Common Council, had reorganised the Watch from local precincts into twenty-six ward watches with a constable assigned to supervise each one.[2] This Carolean Act also meant that watchmen were sometimes called "Charleys" in the Square Mile, the expression becoming more widely used throughout the Metropolis during the eighteenth century.

However, there were several special bodies, serving the same function, detailed to police particular institutions or areas within the Metropolis. For example, Inner Temple and Middle Temple, in the Inns of Court, had their own liveried watchmen, who would also shout out the hours at night and check on the security of barristers' chambers. Similarly, Chelsea Pensioners would patrol the area for a considerable distance around their Veterans' Hospital, armed with musket and bayonet. Additionally, private individuals and bodies could, and frequently did, fund their own watchmen, independent of, and additional to, the formal body. Thus, in 1767, shopkeepers in the

1. C. Whitworth, *The Draught of an Intended Act, For the better Regulation of the Nightly Watch and Beadles within the City and Liberty of Westminster, and Parts Adjacent*, 1773, p.1.
2. J. Paul, *The Compleat Constable*, 1785, p.6, and Anon, *The Complete Parish Officer*, 1772, p.11.

Fleet Market banded together to pay for and employ a private watchman "exclusive of the parish".[3] Nevertheless, these were localised exceptions to an otherwise clearly discernible general pattern.

Watchmen were parochial servants in every sense of the word. Each man normally received his pay, a caped greatcoat, a lantern, a wooden rattle to summon help after 1760, and a wooden staff, from the parish or ward that employed him. Some became familiar to local residents and, as a result, probably developed a sense of loyalty to their parish ratepayers. A few provided special services for local men without requiring extra payment, such as ensuring that the inebriated got back to their houses safely. For example, the Fleet Street area watchman John Sylvester, giving evidence in 1726, described a local barber as one of his "masters" and noted: "Now its always my way to take care of my Masters, and see them safe home, when ever I meet any of them as I go my Rounds".[4]

As will be seen, the Metropolis's watch attracted bad publicity throughout the eighteenth century. In 1793, when lauding the conduct of watchmen in Covent Garden, who attended a woman who had fainted in the street, *The Times* noted: "It is seldom that it is in the power of a Public Print to bestow praise on the conduct of watchmen and parish officers".[5] There were repeated claims that the watch needed greater regulation, more able-bodied and younger members, increased numbers, and a more effective command structure headed by improved constables.[6] Although much of this criticism was justified, it is possible to exaggerate the defects and low calibre of its members. The watch of 1800 was often very different to that of 1700. In many, but not all, London parishes there had been determined efforts over the intervening century to ensure that a competent and relatively able body of men was in place.[7] Such improvements required both a willingness and ability to raise and spend larger sums of money on the service.

3. *London Evening Post*, 6 October, 1767.
4. OBSP, Trial of Mary Blewit, 11 July 1726.
5. *The Times*, 2 November 1792, p.3.
6. Anon (A Citizen in London), *The Vices of the cities of London and Westminster trac'd from their original*, 1751, pp.30-31.
7. C. Emsley, *Crime and Society in England 1750-1900*, 1987, p.175.

Funding of the Watch

Historically, almost every adult male householder in a City ward had been liable to serve, by rotation, a turn in the watch. It was one of the duties of a constable to keep a register of the residents in his ward and order them for service.[8] A similar situation prevailed in the parishes of Westminster and urban Middlesex. This system survived intact for most of the seventeenth century, with the bulk of those who failed to perform their civic duty being subject to punishment. In 1680, for example, personal service was still sufficiently widespread that it could be noted that a group of five Metropolitan Quakers, who had refused to swear the oath required of a constable when appointed to that office, had earlier "watched according to their turns" to the full satisfaction of their neighbours.[9] As late as the 1710s, it seems that a tiny number of men were still performing this obligation in person, in a few Metropolitan locations.

However, even by the early decades of the seventeenth century, the use of substitutes had become fairly widespread amongst middle-ranking householders. There were frequent complaints that they would hire "aged and weake" men to take their places. Other expedients included asking their apprentices (if they had them) to stand-in for them, or paying the beadle small amounts of money to "exempt them from watching". He could then use this money to employ others to take their places.[10] During the second half of the seventeenth century, there was a decisive move towards the use of paid watchmen, who took the duty voluntarily as their primary (if not necessarily their only) source of income, and who served on a regular, if not nightly, basis. Personal service was increasingly commuted to paying a sum of money to the parish.[11] Over time, this pecuniary compound grew into a: "...kind of rate, and a sum demanded by the constable quarterly to defray

8. W. Sheppard, *The Whole Office of the Country Justice of Peace*, 1652, pp.41-42.
9. S. Dixon, "Quakers and the London Parish 1670-1720", 2007, p.237. It was taking an oath, not holding the office, which the men objected to.
10. P. Griffiths, *Lost Londons: Change, Crime and Control in the Capital City, 1550-1660*, 2008, pp.354-355.
11. W. Hardy, (Ed.), *Middlesex Sessions Records*, New Series, Volume III, 1615-1616, 1937, p.238.

the expense of paying his beadle and the watchmen he hires".[12] It was the usual practice for most City householders selected as watchmen by the 1670s, extremely widespread throughout the Metropolis by the 1690s, and almost universal early in the eighteenth century.

Nevertheless, because the change to commutation of personal service happened gradually, and without a statutory basis, there was, initially, little effective organisation behind the collection of monies. It was usually done on a local basis, in a process that was largely based on custom and precedent rather than clear regulation. There were repeated allegations of corruption, with claims that the money collected was being used for other purposes, or that those collecting it (usually constables or beadles), were pocketing part of the take.[13] Beadles were thought to be particularly bad when collecting these rates, giving the watchmen: "...what they pleased, and put[ting] the remainder in their Pockets".[14]

As a result, during the early 1700s, various attempts were made to regularise the practice. In the City, an Act of Common Council in 1705 expressly sanctioned the payment of money to a ward officer for the provision of a substitute. Additionally, the 1705 Act appointed special collectors rather than leaving the responsibility for gathering payments to constables. It led to the passing of general Watch Acts that formally replaced the householders' duty of personal service with a local rate, levied for the specific purpose of hiring full-time parish watchmen. By the 1720s, City housekeepers would pay about 10s a year (2s 6d a quarter) for their watch.[15]

Whether they got better value for their money was another matter. In 1727, Daniel Defoe claimed, albeit rather improbably, that almost £100 pounds was being raised via local rates to pay for each watchman, who received only 6d a night or £9 2s 6d a year, the balance being pocketed by the vestry.[16] Defoe suggested that watchmen be directly funded and appointed by

12. S. Welch, *A Proposal to render effectual a Plan to remove the nuisance of Common Prostitutes from the streets of this Metropolis*, 1758, p.66.
13. A. Moreton, *Second Thoughts are best: or, a Further Improvement of a Late Scheme to Prevent Street Robberies*, 1729, p.7.
14. Anon (Tom Tattle), *A Letter from Tom Tattle A Literate Watchman of Westminster to his Brother Jack Drydrub*, 1720, p.7.
15. D. Defoe, *Augusta Triumphans*, 1728, p.54.
16. A. Moreton (Daniel Defoe), *Parochial Tyranny*, 1727, p.13.

housekeepers, so preventing abuses and allowing them better wages. There were similar problems in Westminster.[17] Certainly, the sums raised by watch rates were very substantial. In 1785, the City of London collected £18,343.[18] By 1790, the total for "patroles", beadles and watchmen in the Square Mile was £24,453. This "immense sum" still raised questions about whether the City could not find a more cost effective way to secure its night streets.[19]

Supernumerary Watchmen

Along with their regular complement of watchmen, many parishes had "supernumerary"officers, who might be called upon when regular watchmen fell sick or went absent, or when it was felt that security needed to be enhanced in the short term. It is likely that many of these men would have been of a lower average standard than those entrusted with the task on a regular basis. They would often be paid by the night for their services. Thus, in 1782, Thomas Morgan, who answered a call for help after a domestic burglary in Great Queen-Street, noted at trial that he was a supernumerary. Another watchman, Francis Surgar, gave evidence about the condition of the house prior to the incident, on the basis that he was normally the officer belonging to that beat "but not on that night". Presumably, Morgan was filling in for him.[20]

Legal Powers

Watchmen temporarily acquired nearly all of their constables' legal powers and protections when on duty during the night, as they acted as their deputies, something that gave them: "...for the time being the authority of their

17. A. Moreton, *Second Thoughts are best: or, a Further Improvement of a Late Scheme to Prevent Street Robberies*, 1729, p.7.
18. *The Times*, 9 November 1785, p.2.
19. *The Times*, 17 November 1790, p.3.
20. OBSP, Trial of Charles Kelly and others, 11 September 1782.

principle".[21] For an example of its significance can be considered an incident from 1680, in which an affray developed between a fruiterer and his young friend and a pair of watchmen near Paternoster Row. During the disturbance the youth threw a watchman to the ground and struck him with his own staff. The injured watchman "languished" for three months before dying of his injuries. On his death, both men were accused of murder, convicted and sentenced to death, because the: "...Watchmen being upon their Duty, (as was proved by the Constable and Beadle, who that Night gave them their Charge and Stand) the court gave Directions, that it was Murder by Law in them both".[22] Similarly, in 1684, a watchman named Robert Teagle was murdered by a group of inebriated men who had refused to leave a public house. Although Teagle *may* have struck one of the defendants before he was stabbed, all three men were convicted of murder, whether as principals or accessories, and sentenced to death.[23] Both of these cases involved the sort of fracas in which, without the legal authority that the dead men's office attracted, the defendants would have been convicted of nothing more serious than (clergyable) manslaughter, and may have been acquitted altogether.

Supervision

Immediate supervision of the watch was in the hands of the "constable of the night", a man taking his place in a rota of local officers who were required to: "...attend the watch by turns, every night, and to go the rounds".[24] Ideally, such constables ensured that watchmen turned up for duty, and did not pass the allotted time "sotting in night cellars". It was felt that this was best achieved by regularly inspecting them at their posts when they were on duty.[25]

21. W. Blackstone, *Commentaries on the Laws of England*, 1765-1769, vol.1, p.345, and J. W. Willcock, *The Office of Constable*, 1827, p.121.
22. Anon, *The Narrative of the proceedings at the Session-house for London and Middlesex: giving an account of the tryals of...* 1680, pp.1-4.
23. OBSP, Trial of George Caskey et al, 3 September, 1684.
24. J. Paul (Barrister), *The Compleat Constable*, 1785, p.5.
25. S. Welch, *Observations on the Office of Constable*, 1754, Introduction p.12.

However, it was impossible for all members of the watch to be permanently under the constable's control. Sometimes, the allotted constables were not even present. This was a longstanding problem. In the previous century, night constables had often failed to appear, left early, or (more legitimately) been called away after the watch was set.[26] This remained an issue throughout the eighteenth century, and was often dealt with relatively benignly by the authorities. For example, in February 1732, at a petty sessions conducted at the Mermaid Tavern in Hackney, three JPs heard a complaint (one of many made to them over the years) that local constables had failed to attend watch-houses when they were supposed to be on duty. However, these officers: "... promising to attend constantly and carefully do their duties for the future the Justices excused them for what is past".[27]

Even if the constable of the night was on duty, watchmen were usually on their own, whether they were stationary at a stand or watch box, or walking their beats. This was especially likely after the practice developed, during the seventeenth century, of basing duty constables in watch-houses (see below). As a result, watchmen would often have to deal with urgent situations on their own. An Act of 1737 (10 Geo. II, c.22), regulating aspects of policing in the City (but not Middlesex), specifically declared that, in the immediate absence of a constable, watchmen were required to apprehend: "...suspected persons and to deliver them to the Constable of the night, who [the following morning] is to carry them before a Justice". However, if this individual could not be found, a watchman was allowed to commit them directly into custody, pending production the next day.[28]

Watch-houses

Significant numbers of watch-houses started appearing in the City after the middle of the seventeenth century. In 1705, the Act of Common Council mentioned above required that all wards provide them, to serve as an

26. W. Fenner, *The Compters Commonwealth*, 1617, pp.51-53
27. R. Paley (Ed.), *Justice in 18th-Century Hackney*, 1991, p.86.
28. J. W. Willcock, *The Office of Constable*, 1827, p.121.

assembly point for the watch before they went on duty, and as a place where those arrested during the night could be secured.[29] They gradually became more substantial buildings. In 1735, when Sir Francis Knight, the alderman for Farringdon, approved a plan for building a new watch-house near Fleet Bridge, it was claimed that it would be the most complete and commodious in London. It had a room for the duty constable, another for the watchmen, and a: "...prison room, to keep prisoners in till they can be carried before a Justice". This cell would prevent those arrested overnight from having to be sent to one of the Compters, something that would be more convenient and also save the prisoners themselves significant expense.[30]

The number and size of watch-houses also expanded in Westminster and urban parts of Middlesex, some acquiring the name "roundhouses" in the process. For example, in 1688, the Liberty of the Savoy erected a small (20 feet by 11 feet) building with a cellar. This was pulled down in December 1700, being replaced by another short-lived watch-house, which was, in turn, demolished to provide space for St. Mary-le-Strand. After a period in which constables of the night were based in the St Clement Danes church-house, another watch-house (and a set of stocks) was erected in 1739. This survived until 1780, when it was replaced by a building that matched the style of Sir William Chambers' Somerset House.[31]

As well as providing accommodation for the duty constable, parish beadle, and enough watchmen to secure suspects, watch-houses often sheltered men who were acting as a reserve, to deal with any nocturnal emergencies. For example, in an extreme (and highly unusual) case, in 1735, although one City ward was supposed to have 25 watchmen on nightly duty, only 12 of them would be at their stands at any one time. The remainder would be resting in their watch-house.[32]

29. J. M. Beattie, *Policing and Punishment in London, 1660–1750*, 2001, p.186.
30. *London Daily Post and General Advertiser,* 22 December, 1735.
31. R. Somerville, *The Savoy; Manor: Hospital: Chapel*, 1960, pp.182-183.
32. *London Daily Post and General Advertiser*, 22 December, 1735.

Organization of the Watch

There were major reorganisations to watch arrangements throughout the period, especially in the Square Mile and the more prosperous West End parishes. However, it should be remembered that for most of the eighteenth century critics of the watch were not campaigning for the move to central control that marked the advent of the Metropolitan Police in 1829. They wanted to see the existing system work more efficiently, with better-supervised watchmen of a higher standard, rather than an end to the role of the parish. Additionally, in all parts of the capital, whether the City, Westminster or urban Middlesex, there was a widespread feeling that more watchmen were needed than were actually serving. Typically, in 1728, Defoe asked that the watch be tripled in size so that there was a watchman to every 40 houses (20 on each side of a street) because it was apparent that a man could not: "... see distinctly beyond the extent of 20 houses in a row".[33]

The City

In the 1640s, the City's watch system had been reorganised from local precincts into twenty-six wards, with constables assigned to supervise each one. The number of watchmen son duty each night, in every ward throughout the city and its liberties, was fixed. These ranged from 130 for the largest ward, Farringdon Without, to only four for Bartholomew the Less. In theory, if followed to the letter, these reforms would have seen 1,095 nocturnal watchmen on duty each night. These manning levels were broadly reiterated in October 1663, when the Night Watch Act was passed by the Common Council which provided that 1,036 watchmen should be on duty in the City from Sunset to Sunrise each night. However, these targets were very rarely met, almost no ward being covered by its full quota of men. Under the 1663 Act, rates were supposed to be set by the court of Common Council, out of which the beadles' salaries would be paid.[34] Frequently, this did not happen,

33. D. Defoe, *Augusta Triumphans*, 1728, p.54

34. *An act of common counsel for the well-ordering and establishing of the watches within this city and*

and the beadles would make up their income by keeping money allotted to them for hiring watchmen. As a result, in 1700, Billingsgate, which was supposed to have 30 watchmen on duty each night, only averaged 14 men. Taken together, all 26 wards produced 469 watchmen, less than half their designated numbers. Accepting reality, the 1705 Act recommended a more modest complement of 551 men.[35]

In 1737, the nocturnal policing of the Square Mile was further defined by an Act (10 Geo II cap 22) for "better regulating the Night Watch and Beadles within the City of London and Liberties". This required the Court of Common Council to order and appoint whatever number of watchmen and Beadles for the Square Mile they thought necessary. It was a power they held for the rest of the century.[36] The Act also gave the wards power to levy rates to pay for their watch and specified how such men should be armed and the level of their pay. Additionally, it gave general guidance on their duties and, in particular, their obligation to "take up" suspicious and disorderly people. It also set out the number of constables who should be on duty every night in each ward. With some modification, this statute largely controlled the policing of the City for the following century.

Westminster and Middlesex

During the eighteenth century, there were major improvements in the organisation, supervision, financing and quality of the watch in several Westminster and Middlesex parishes. These were mainly, but not solely, in the more prosperous central areas and were usually brought about by private Acts of Parliament, instigated after petition from the parish concerned.

In the urbanised parts of Middlesex, the parishes had traditionally appointed watchmen. However, in Westminster, the early decades of the eighteenth century had seen a protracted three-way struggle between the city's Court of Burgesses, its parish vestries and local JPs (who had their

---

payment of the beadle's salary, 1643, pp.1-7.

35. J. M. Beattie, *Policing and Punishment in London, 1660-1750*, 2001, p.175.

36. Anon, *The Complete Parish Officer*, 1772, p.11.

own commission of the peace) for increased control of the watch. At the start of the century, all of these bodies had some input into the process of selecting, financing, or supervising watchmen. In several areas, they held an overlapping, or uncertain, jurisdiction. In the early years, the burgesses clearly held the upper hand, even though their performance was the subject of much criticism. There was an unavailing parliamentary attempt to reform the watch there between 1703 and 1705; the Bill failed repeatedly at its second reading, after opposition to the introduction of a new rate to support an enlarged watch. There was another, more concerted, but still unsuccessful, parliamentary attempt to introduce reform in 1720 in a Bill (defeated in the House of Lords) that gave the Westminster JPs "power to direct the watch".[37] Proponents of the 1720 Bill argued that JPs were likely to be more effective as they were drawn from higher social backgrounds than the burgesses, being "gentlemen of liberal education" rather than bakers, smiths and vintners. As the JPs lived in the Westminster parishes affected, they would be at least: "...as good judges of dividing and setting watchmen as burgesses".[38]

Much of the opposition to this proposal came not come from the burgesses, but from the "closed vestries" of the more prosperous West End parishes. Nevertheless, this did not mean that their members were satisfied with the policing status quo. Statutory reform, via a series of private Acts, ultimately enhanced the role of these vestries, rather than that of the area's magistrates.

The vestry was the controlling body for parochial administration. Closed or "select" vestries were undemocratic bodies, being the monopoly of a few dozen men who, as one of their number died or left the parish, voted amongst themselves to replace him. For example, in the 1730s, St. James, Westminster, had 34 men in its select vestry, while in St. George, Hanover Square, 101 men controlled the parish.[39] All nine Westminster parishes and liberties had closed vestries at this time. By contrast, in the "open" vestries

37. N. M., *A Letter to a Member of Parliament, Concerning the Bill for Regulating the Nightly Watch in the City of Westminster, and Liberties thereof*, 1720, p.2.

38. Anon, *A Letter from Tom Tattle A Literate Watchman of Westminster to his Brother Jack Drydrub*, 1720, p.20.

39. Anon, *Short Remarks Upon the Printed Case of the Burgesses and Inhabitants of Westminster against the Bill, &c. for the better regulating the nightly watch...*, 1735, p.2 and p.3.

that were still found in many Middlesex parishes, membership was elective, and any parishioner who paid "scot and lot" (a basic borough tax) could vote.

Closed vestries tended to contain wealthy, sometimes aristocratic and politically influential, men, a handful of whom were MPs. Inevitably, they were responsive to the concerns of their own social milieu and class, especially when it came to security. They were certainly not universally popular. It was frequently argued that they governed solely in their own interests: "…with no other intent, but to raise to themselves very unjustifiable advantages". It was also claimed, albeit rather optimistically, that open (or common) vestries were composed of the "most ancient and experience'd" parishioners.[40] It is, perhaps, slightly ironic that undemocratic select vestries initiated many of the policing innovations of the period, and that some ordinary (rather than wealthy) residents may have feared that any change would be "highly prejudicial to them".[41]

The Westminster Night Watch Act 1735 was the first of these private statutes to pass into law. It allowed St. George's, Hanover Square and St. James's, Piccadilly to impose an additional compulsory police rate on their householders and to raise their own watches from it. That these parishes took the lead is unsurprising. As a visiting German observed in 1725, they held a: "…very large share of the nobility and Gentry".[42] They also had select vestries whose members were acutely concerned about the threat that crime posed to their homes and persons. Prior to the 1735 statute, many streets in these two parishes had felt compelled to raise subscriptions to fund a private watch, independent of, and supplementary to, that of the parish, to promote their own security.

However, although they were socially unusual, it was always likely, and expressly recognised at the time, that the two parishes would provide a template for similar reforms in other, less august, localities.[43] This was borne out

40. Anon, *Parochial Tyranny, or, Select Vestries Become the Plague of the People*, 1719, p.2.
41. Anon, *The Case of the Burgesses and Inhabitants of Westminster, against the Bill for the better Regulating the Nightly Watch and Bedels within the two Parishes of St. James and St. George Hanover-Square*, 1720, p.3.
42. Anon (A German Gentleman), *A view of London and Westminster: or, the Town Spy*. 2nd. edn., 1725, p.5.
43. Anon, *Short Remarks Upon the Printed Case of the Burgesses and Inhabitants of Westminster against the Bill, &c. for the better regulating the nightly watch*, 1735, p.2 and p.3.

in subsequent years, although an attempt at introducing reform across the whole of Westminster failed in 1736. The reasons given to justify the new private Acts were usually very similar, stating in their preamble that no effectual provision was being made for the establishment and governance of a night watch, or for raising money to fund it.

Twenty local statutes followed the 1735 Act over the following 80 years, covering parishes in Westminster and Middlesex. Most of these were passed before 1786, such as that for St. Marylebone in 1756. Typically, the private Act for St. Clement Danes, in 1764, gave the parish power to raise a local rate of 4d. in the pound, as well as of appointing, paying, and disciplining its own watchmen. All but one of these statutes involved select vestries. Some suburban Surrey villages, lying close in to the Metropolis, also obtained legislation to put their watch on a proper footing. For example, the residents of Clapham sought an Act in 1785, on the grounds that their village had become large and populous, and, as a result of its vicinity to the Metropolis its inhabitants were experiencing high levels of crime.[44]

Collectively, all of the Acts that affected parishes in Westminster, like the original statute of 1735, strengthened the power of local vestries at the expense of the Court of Burgesses and their historic right to levy a watch rate and to appoint and regulate watchmen.[45] Unsurprisingly, this did not occur without resistance. Some local residents also complained that: "This innovation of an inhabitant Watch has been and is likely to be attended with many inconveniencies". It was suggested that watchmen would not be properly subject to the control of their supervising constables, who were still appointed by the burgesses, though this fear proved largely unfounded.[46]

The provision of extra financing permitted parishes to pay higher wages, attracting more, and better quality, recruits. It also allowed their watchmen to serve longer duties, and to specialise in patrolling and crime prevention, rather than having to "double up" in other roles, such as street cleaner. Many of these parishes also experimented with uniforms, hierarchical forms

44. P. Rawlings, *Policing: A Short History*, 2002, p.67.
45. E. Reynolds, *Before the Bobbies*, 1998, p.453.
46. Anon, *The Case of the Burgesses and Inhabitants of Westminster, against the Bill for the better Regulating the Nightly Watch and Bedels within the two Parishes of St. James and St. George Hanover-Square*, 1720, p.3.

of supervision, and other features that are traditionally associated with the post-1829 police. For a specific example, the reform of the St. Marylebone Watch in 1773 can be considered. A committee, chaired by the barrister Herbert Mackworth, devised a new "system" for policing the parish. It was divided into seven districts, which were further sub-divided into five beats. Each district was policed by six men, five of them patrolling the beats, with the sixth man functioning as their "Serjeant". The watchmen wore a basic uniform consisting of a brown coat marked with the parish initials, and the number of the beat they were patrolling, carried a lantern, a staff, and a rattle to sound the alarm. The sergeants had access to guns and cutlasses. Part of their duty was to check on the individual beats during the night (10 pm to 5 am in the winter and 11 pm to 5 am in the summer). The sergeants were supervised, in their turn, by a salaried beadle, and a traditional unpaid constable (the formal representative of the law).[47] These men were assigned to the watch-house, but would also patrol, checking up on the districts at least twice each night. The whole force was also inspected by the Parish Watch Committee two times a year.[48]

The Poorer Parishes

A major problem in leaving parish authorities to enhance their own policing was that London's social stratification meant that many vestries, in poorer areas, had neither the inclination nor the means to introduce the reforms pioneered by their richer neighbours. Selective improvement left marginal areas lagging behind. As the 1772 Select Committee on the Westminster night watch noted, parishes within the city that had not obtained special legislation, and could not, as a result, fund an efficient watch system, such as St. Giles-in-the-Fields and St George's Bloomsbury, were still largely regulated by the ancient Statute of Winchester of 1285. Attempts at extending their watches, such as they were, depended on voluntary contributions collected

47. J. Ritson, 1791, *The Office of Constable*, p.11.
48. E. Reynolds, *Before the Bobbies*, 1998, pp.453-456.

by the constables.[49] The "roughest" areas, those most in need of additional security, were the least able to afford them.

This was not an entirely new issue, even in the eighteenth century. For example, so many impoverished people had congregated in St. Katharine's by the Tower by 1690 that they petitioned at Quarter Sessions to be released from having to fund double watches, the: "...inhabitants of the said hamlets being generally very poor, and unable to sustain the charge".[50] However, increasing social segregation during the eighteenth century greatly compounded the problem. As a result, in 1758, Saunders Welch was convinced that although the "out-parishes" faced the greatest dangers from robbers and burglars, it was in just these parts that there were regular complaints about the lack of street lighting and the "insufficiency of the watch". Nevertheless, even rich people had to pass through them on their way to central areas. Given this situation, attention inevitably turned to making reform more widespread, if not universal. Welch, for example, felt that the answer was to introduce a "general law" that would provide for a competent night watch in all areas.[51]

The 1770 parliamentary Police Committee, the establishment of which had been prompted by a rash of 104 domestic burglaries in the Metropolis between Michaelmas 1769 and March 1770, gave a further impetus to such proposals when it identified widespread problems with the quality of the watch, including its lack of co-ordination and control. After hearing from several magistrates, including Sir John Fielding, it recommended improving the night watch of Westminster through enhanced supervision, by paid constables, who would report to salaried magistrates. Two years later, the 1772 parliamentary committee on the Westminster Night Watch reported in similar terms, though, unlike the 1770 Committee, it called in representatives of the parish rather than magistrates to give their opinions on how best to deal with the situation. One of its members was Sir Charles Whitworth, a strong advocate of reform. The Westminster Night Watch Act of 1774 (14 Geo. III c.90) effected some of its recommendations. This important statute produced a ban on watchmen visiting alehouses while on duty,

49. P. Rawlings, *Policing: A Short History*, 2002, p.71.

50. W. J. Hardy, *Calendar of the Sessions Books 1689 to 1709*, 1905, p.17.

51. S. Welch, *A Proposal to render effectual a Plan to remove the nuisance of Common Prostitutes from the streets of this Metropolis*, 1758, p.66.

provided them with a minimum wage, and better defined their duties (in broadly similar terms to the City of London's Act of 1737). It also obliged officers to come to each other's assistance without regard to parish boundaries. However, it was confined to Westminster, and did not extend to urban Middlesex. Additionally, it did not provide for any centralised, rather than parochial, form of control.

These sporadic reforms meant that, by the end of the eighteenth century, the quality of Metropolitan parish based policing was very varied. Many watchmen were still very poor (forming the basis for popular satire), some were competent, and, in several improved parishes, albeit usually not in the worst areas of the Metropolis, they were very good, being recruited from fit men of sound character.

Remuneration

Despite antisocial hours, a watchman's regular earnings were extremely small. In 1719, the ten watchmen employed by four of the wards in St. Clements Danes were only paid five shillings each a week (15 d. was also paid out for their drink each night).[52] This was by no means the lowest rate. In the 1720s, many earned around seven pounds a year from official payments for their duties. (To put some kind of value on these sums, in 1749 a pound of tea cost about 6s 7d and the same amount of tobacco about 10 1/2d).[53] At best, nightly payment was commensurate with or below that available for unskilled and relatively light diurnal labour, especially during the summer months, though the work was regular, and the parish usually supplied a coat along with other accoutrements. Even for single men, these sums were usually insufficient, and they were totally inadequate for those with families. In the 1720s, Daniel Defoe suggested that 20 pounds per annum was the minimum amount necessary to permit a poor, but frugal, watchman to live

52. J. Ritson, *A Digest of the Proceedings of the Court Leet of the Manor and Liberty of the Savoy*, 1769, pp.4-6.
53. Anon, *A Complete Guide to all persons who have any trade or concern with the city of London, and parts adjacent*...4th edn., 1749, p.159.

decently: "…allowing him to rest during the day instead of working, so that he was suitably vigilant to give vigilant attendance".[54]

Over the course of the eighteenth century, very modest improvements were made in levels of remuneration for watchmen in the City and the better Middlesex parishes. Thus, the Common Council Act of 1737 stipulated that each watchman in the Square Mile was to receive £13 a year. Nevertheless, in the early 1770s, even the best Westminster parishes still paid their watchmen only 10d a night in the summer and 1s 3d in the winter. The worst might pay as little as 8d for summer duty. An average over the entire city, and throughout the year, of 1s a night appears reasonable.[55] The variation in remuneration between parishes brought its own problems; bad paying parishes would lose their more able watchmen to better paying ones, leaving them undermanned or forced to depend on men of inferior quality. As Defoe's comment suggests, the low level of their pay also forced or encouraged many watchmen to have recourse to other sources of income. These were twofold: alternative payments connected to their policing duties, both legitimate and illegitimate, and second jobs that were pursued during the day.

Watchmen might be tipped for providing extra services to local residents, especially the more prosperous amongst them. For example, they might receive payment for lighting them home with their lanterns in the evening. Thus, in 1717, when a somewhat intoxicated man came out of a tavern his female companion persuaded him to: "…let the Watchman light him, to which he consented, saying he would give him something when he came to the Place where they were to go".[56] This could result in a payment of up to sixpence. (It might also explain why a forfeit of about the same amount was customary among some watchmen if "one comes into the other's Beat".)[57] This practice could have negative consequences. It might impinge on a watchman's ability to perform his duty elsewhere. Many poorer people also resented the way in which the prospect of tips encouraged watchmen to focus their energies on the well-to-do. In 1717, for example, when three

54. D. Defoe, *Augusta Triumphans,* 1728, p.54.

55. E. Reynolds, "Sir John Fielding, Sir Charles Whitworth, and the Westminster Night Watch Act, 1770-1775", 2002, p.6.

56. OBSP, Trial of Johnson Burdet and others, 11 January 1717.

57. OBSP, Trial of John Hewlet, 15 January 1725.

watchmen questioned a suspect in Drury Lane, he taunted them by saying: "You'll dance all Day long after a Gentleman to get a Pint of Drink of him".[58] For these reasons, it was often officially forbidden. In 1781, Edward Cox, a newly appointed Brompton watchman, was mortally wounded by a drunken chairman when he refused to light him on his way to London, saying: "I am on my duty and cannot do it".[59]

Displays of diligence by watchmen, when carrying out their normal duties, might also be rewarded by small payments from members of the public. For example, watchmen who detected that a door or window had been left unattended in a house at night, and alerted its occupants, were often tipped.[60] Watchmen would also wake up early workers and were, presumably, paid for this service.[61] If involved in arresting and prosecuting felons to conviction, they might also share in the substantial state and local rewards that were often available.

Despite such supplementary payments, many watchmen would work at other, usually low grade, employments, after they came off duty, as well as sleeping and enjoying recreation. Typically, their diurnal jobs included labouring, if they were fit enough, and working as porters. However, this inevitably compromised their nocturnal efficiency. Even in 1819, one reason that many Metropolitan watchmen were thought to be in a poor physical condition was that they were drawn from men who had: "...been at work all the preceding day, and whose families, possibly, compel them to earn an extra shilling at night".[62]

The low level of remuneration also encouraged corruption and greatly reduced the deterrent effect of dismissal from office. As one observer noted, watchmen usually had: "...nothing to apprehend from their neglect, but dismission from a troublesome employment". If the position had been more sought after, with provision for sick and retired watchmen, such a sanction would have been far more of a deterrent.[63]

58. OBSP, Trial of Johnson Burdet and others, 11 January 1717.
59. OBSP, Trial of Patrick Hoy, 22 Feb. 1781.
60. OBSP, Trial of Samuel Fuller, 5 December 1759.
61. M. Grosley, *A Tour to London,* vol.1, 1772, p.48.
62. W. Clowes, *Leigh's New Picture of London,* 1819, p.97.
63. Anon, *Outlines of a Plan for Patroling and Watching the City of London, Borough of Southwark,*

Operation of the Watch

Traditionally, the watch was supposed to operate from sunset to sunrise.[64] In reality, it often came on duty well after dusk. Sometimes, this might be as late as 10 pm in the summer. The watch would stand down in the early morning, usually between 5 am and 7 am. Starting and finishing hours were normally set at two different times, one for the late spring, summer and early autumn, and another for the rest of the year. Thus, in the City, it was ordered in 1643 that the watch be set from 9 pm until 6 am, between Michaelmas and Lady Day. For the rest of the year it would be operational between 10 pm and 4 am.[65] The fact that, during the 1770s, the Westminster parishes of St. Paul and St. James in Piccadilly paid their watchmen an intermediate rate in the Spring and Autumn suggests that some parishes experimented with three different lengths of duty. The "winter" duty was, of course, always the greater one.

Unfortunately, there appears to have been a tendency for watchmen to "trim" time off either end of their duty, wherever possible; for example, they would sometimes leave early, before daybreak. Even if the full time allotted was kept, the streets would often be dark or in half-light for a considerable period before and after they came on duty. Thus, one November evening in 1765, between seven and eight pm, Hardington Holdsworth detained a woman who had picked his pocket in a house near Church Lane, and dragged her to the local watch-house. He was disconcerted to find that there was no one there. (Ultimately, a friend of his approached the parish beadle for assistance). There were frequent complaints that watchmen were: "...too late before they are set upon duty, [and] leave it too early".[66] One answer to this problem was to extend their hours of duty. In November 1702, the Lord Mayor noted that many crimes were being committed in the City during the winter season after the "breaking up" of the watch, which was

and their Environs, 1786, p.8.

64. W. Sheppard, *The Whole Office*, 1652, pp.41-42.
65. *An Act of common counsel for the well-ordering and establishing of the watches within this city and payment of the beadle's salary*, London, 1643, printed by Richard Coles, p.7.
66. Anon (A Citizen of London), *The Vices of the cities of London and Westminster trac'd from their original*, 1751, pp.30-31.

commonly at about five in the morning. As a result, he ordered that from the First of November, to the First of February: "...good watch shall be kept from 10 at night, till 6 in the morning". Constables of the night were to be punished if they failed to enforce the change.[67] Another answer was to use a "double" watch during the winter months. This occasioned great expense and was usually unrealistic.

Going On Duty

The watch would normally be inspected by the parish beadle or (less commonly) the constable of the night prior to beginning their service, and dispersing to their stands, boxes and beats. When watchmen first went on duty, they would usually check that neighbourhood shops and houses were secure by ensuring that doors and windows had not been left open and alerting the owners of such premises to any lapses in security.[68] This was eventually reduced to a statutory responsibility in Westminster by an Act of 1802 that required every watchman to: "...carefully observe and try whether the houses, shops, warehouses or other buildings in his respective beat or walk, are safe and well secured".[69]

While on duty, most watchmen would, periodically, leave their designated position, whether it was a stand or watch-box, to walk a set path or "beat". For example, in 1740, when Henry Robinson was called upon to deal with a break-in at a small bookshop, he noted that at the time he had gone: "...to the upper End of my Walk, that I might beat down again, when the Clock struck".[70] The frequency with which such patrolling occurred varied from parish to parish, and over time. Much might depend on the energy of the watchmen involved. However, the 1802 Act in Westminster required that watchmen who were not on designated patrols go round their beats or

67. *English Post*, 6-9 November 1702.
68. M. V. Muyden (Ed.), *A foreign View of England in the reigns of George I and George II*, 1902, p.68.
69. 14 Geo.III Cap. 90 1802, "'An Act for the better regulation of the nightly watch and beadles within the City and Liberty of Westminster and parts adjacent".
70. OBSP, Trial of Robert Wilson and George Murray, 3 September 1740.

walks at least twice every hour. Beats were often relatively short by Victorian standards. The average was between 400 and 500 yards, and much of this was down small alleys and courts.[71] Even so, Sir John Fielding felt that they were still too extensive and, like Defoe many years earlier, suggested that they should not exceed 20 houses. Some watchmen might also accompany the duty constable as he made his rounds. This was normally done once or twice a night, so that at midnight observers could see: "Constables marching thro' their Liberties with long staves in their hands, attended by several watchmen, to see that the streets are free from House-Breakers and Night-Walkers".[72]

While walking, watchmen would usually cry the hour every time the clock struck and proclaim the state of the weather.[73] A typical post-midnight cry might be: "Past Twelve of the clock, and a cloudy morning".[74] Although some residents welcomed this highly audible assurance, others feared that, like watchmen beating the ground with their staffs as they patrolled, it merely alerted local criminals to their presence.

Whether patrolling or stationery, watchmen would investigate anything that appeared "untoward". For example, in September 1717, three men from Shoreditch were indicted for housebreaking after they were seen lurking outside Thomas Pate's home at two o'clock in the morning by watchmen "going their Rounds". Pate's door had been broken open, so the three men were arrested.[75] Similarly, when Alice Green, the mistress of an Irish "Captain", was thrown out of his rented apartment one evening, she initially sat on the man's doorstep, where she was duly found by the watchman "coming his rounds". She told him that she had quarrelled with her husband, who had shut her out of the building. The watchman was satisfied with this answer but, as he was leaving, the captain lent out of a window, told him that Green was a whore, and asked that she be removed. Green was arrested

71. A. Moreton (D. Defoe) *Parochial Tyranny*, 1727, p.13.
72. Anon, *Low-Life or one Half of the World knows not how the other half lives*, 3rd edn., 1764, p.3.
73. P. J. Grosley, *A Tour to London*, 1772, p.49.
74. *Tatler*, 15 February, 1711.
75. OBSP, Trial of Henry Floyd and others, 11 September. 1717. The prisoners had not been found with any of the victim's goods, having been interrupted in their work, and were able to secure an acquittal by giving "some trifling Excuses for their being there at that time".

and marched to the watch-house.[76] In like manner, late one night in 1745, a watchman in Drury Lane noticed a 14-year-old girl being manhandled by an older woman. The girl told him that the woman had beaten her and taken a silver medallion. The watchman conveyed both to the watch-house for investigation.[77]

In many street situations, allegation was met by counter-claim. In these circumstances, both parties might be arrested, with the magistrate having to decide on the merits of their respective cases the following morning. Thus, after William Davis accused Amy Armstrong of taking his money she claimed that he had attempted to blackmail her into sleeping with him, on pain of maliciously reporting her for theft, and "also charg'd the watchmen with him". They were both taken to the St. Giles's Roundhouse, and held overnight.[78]

Stop and Search

One of the principal tasks of the watch was to investigate people who were abroad after dark. The later they were out, the more likely this was to occur. At common law, watchmen, like constables and beadles, had authority to arrest any "nightwalkers" that they encountered. People who appeared dissolute, severely drunk, generally "suspicious" or worthy of further investigation for any other reason could be taken to a watch-house, presented to the duty constable and, if necessary, detained overnight. The following morning they would be produced for examination by a JP, after which they might be discharged, sent for trial, or committed to a bridewell or house of correction.

Investigating those found carrying suspicious packages after dark was especially important, as it might turn up recently stolen goods. Thus, in 1716, after Thomas Hyman broke into a house in the small hours and stole candlesticks and pewter plate, a watchman saw him carrying a large bundle, and asked him where he was going. His answers not proving satisfactory,

76. A. L. Hayward, *Lives Of The Most Remarkable Criminals*, 1927, pp.407-417.

77. OBSP, Trial of Mary Allen, 16 Oct 1745.

78. OBSP, Trial of Amy Armstrong, 15 Oct 1729. Davis was, presumably, discharged the next morning, while Armstrong was indicted and acquitted.

Hyman was detained, the immediate area searched, and the victim's door found open. He was roused and identified the stolen property as his own.[79] Similarly, in 1772, the burglars John Adshead and Benjamin Alsworth broke into the house of a widow living in Newman Street, and carried off silk, clothes, and other valuables. Having packed these goods into two parcels they walked towards Tottenham Court Road, where they were followed and arrested by local watchmen. At the watch-house, they were searched by the constable of the night, and the stolen items discovered.[80] At a more basic level, when a Clerkenwell watchman was going his rounds he came across a man carrying a large sack on his back. The man fled when stopped, abandoning the sack, which was subsequently found to contain a large amount of lead and iron.[81] Of course, investigating such men carried inherent risks. In 1737, for example, when an off duty guardsman was stopped by two watchmen, who asked to investigate a cask that he was carrying, a struggle ensued, in which one watchman was mortally wounded with a bayonet and the other stabbed in the arm.[82]

Even in the absence of obviously suspicious behaviour or packages, it was not difficult for watchmen to find a reason to make an arrest. As one observer candidly noted, "disorderly conduct" could mean almost anything that parish officers wanted. For example, in the summer of 1794, two men going home in the evening, talking loudly to each other, were told to shut up by a watchman. When they refused to do so, he arrested them. The pair subsequently sued for false imprisonment in the Court of Common Pleas. Lord Chief Justice Eyre held that, although talking loudly in the street might be disorderly behaviour, it was not something that would normally justify taking people into custody. Even so, the jury only awarded damages of a penny.[83] Nevertheless, using the power against the "well-to-do" could be very dangerous. In 1708, two constables from the City arrested a group of aristocrats and gentlemen for being disorderly. Showing considerable courage, if not prudence, they committed the men to the Poultry Compter. The tables

79. OBSP, Trial of Thomas Hyman alias Kettles, 11 April 1716.
80. OBSP, Trial of John Adshead and Benjamin Alsworth, 3 June 1772.
81. *Public Advertiser*, 16 March, 1767.
82. OBSP, Trial of William Maw, 16 February 1737.
83. *Hardy v Murphy and Wedge* (1795) 1 Espinasse 294.

were turned on them when the aristocrats sued. Fortunately, a settlement was reached. The two constables apologized and were forgiven for their "insolent" behaviour out of: "...compassion to them and their indigent families".[84]

Summoning Assistance from the Watch

Watchmen would actively respond to requests for assistance from the public. However, summoning help could be an uncertain business. When the Irish footpad James Carrick robbed a wealthy Frenchman of £230 near Covent Garden he escaped, although nearby chairmen: "...did all they could to raise the Watch in pursuit of us, and the French Gentleman cry'd out for that end".[85] In a delicious irony, when the notorious felon James Dalton became the victim of street robbers, he was unable to get help. Despite shouting so loud that he alerted all the watchmen between Newgate and Stocks-Market: "...not a man of them came to his assistance".[86] In 1790, in an incident resonant with modern concerns, Henry Burbage claimed that he had held a thief for over an hour before losing him, in the absence of help from local watchmen.[87]

However, on other occasions, the system worked well. For example, in the 1720s, when the burglar Martin Bellamy disturbed the occupant of a Holborn teashop in the middle of the night, several watchmen swiftly came running after the man jumped out of bed, and: "...bawl'd out, Thieves! Heigh! Watch! Watch!"[88] Similarly, when clothes were stolen from a washing line in 1740, and their owner pursued the thief shouting for help, a watchman ran into the middle of the street, intercepted, and knocked down the fleeing man.[89] It appears that there was a growing tendency for nocturnal

84. *Post Boy* 5-8 March 1709.
85. J. Carrick, *A compleat and True Account of all the Robberies Committed by James Carrick*, 1722, p.20.
86. J. Dalton, *A Genuine Narrative of all the Street Robberies Committed since October last, by James Dalton,* 1728, p.48.
87. Guildhall Justice Room Minute Book, CLA/005/01/045 19 August-14 September 1790, entry for 8 September.
88. M. Bellamy, *The Life of Martin Bellamy,* 1728, p.28.
89. OBSP, Trial of John Cane, 16 April 1740.

crime victims to seek official, rather than unofficial, help during the 1740s. More trial accounts than previously document shouts of "Watch!" rather than "Stop thief!" It is *possible* that this reflects an improvement in policing over the previous decade, in both Middlesex and the City of London.[90]

Proactive Watchmen

Even policing by the watch was never quite purely reactive and deterrent. In January 1715, for example, the career criminal John Smith (commonly known as "Half-hanged Smith" after surviving an execution earlier in his life) was accused of breaking into a residential building and the commercial warehouse that was situated on its lower floor. Unfortunately for him, the warehouse had been broken into on three earlier occasions, within a short period of time, so that two watchmen had been "put in to lie in wait for the Thieves if they came again". At about five o'clock one morning, the two men were alerted by a noise, saw the warehouse door being unlocked and its padlock wrenched off, after which Smith entered the building. As soon as he came in, one of the watchmen struck out, at which Smith ran away, closely pursued. He was captured at Rood Lane and, on being searched, was found in possession of several skeleton keys.[91]

Throughout the era, the surveillance of identified neighbourhood "suspects" was also an essential part of policing. Experienced parish officers, whether watchmen, constables or members of the various late century "patroles", would become familiar with local men and women with criminal associations or apparently dubious lifestyles. They would be subject to particular scrutiny if found in suspicious circumstances. For example, in February 1803, a City officer noticed two men of known previous bad character carrying a greatcoat of the sort worn by hackney coachmen, and he suspected they had come by it dishonestly. The officer approached a group

90. R. Shoemaker, *The London Mob: Violence and Disorder in Eighteenth-century England*, 2004, p.34.
91. OBSP, Trial of John Smith, 27 April 1715.

of coachmen standing nearby, one of whom it transpired was its owner. The two men were arrested.[92]

Inter-Watch Communication

Communication between watchmen, even those from the same parish, was not easy, except over the shortest distances. For this reason, in 1728, one observer suggested that they should always be equipped with a bugle with which to sound the alarm and alert their fellows to an emergency.[93] However, for much of the eighteenth century, shouting or banging their staffs on the ground was their primary means of attracting attention. The situation improved slightly after the rattle came into general service in the 1760s. They are first referred to in the *Sessions Papers* in 1765, when a Marylebone watchman mentions returning such an implement to his watch-house at the end of his duty.[94] It was still sufficiently novel and localised in its distribution that, towards the end of the same decade, a constable felt it necessary to explain its operation to an Old Bailey jury when telling them how he had heard an alarm given by a watchman: "…with his rattle (it is in the same form with a child's rattle, which they swing round, only it makes a greater noise.)"[95] It provided a loud and distinctive sound, although it did not carry very far when compared to the Victorian police whistle.

Weapons and the Watch

It was well established that although watchmen might be armed with staves and even halberds, they should not usually carry firearms.[96] The halberd, also known as the "Brown Bill", a cumbersome military weapon with limited non-lethal uses, was the most common watch-arm in the early seventeenth

92. *The Times*, 2 Feb 1803, p.3.
93. D. Defoe, *Augusta Triumphans*, 1728, p.54.
94. OBSP, Trial of Thomas Cross, 18 September 1765.
95. OBSP, Trial of Ruben Biggs, 28 June 1769.
96. *The Gentleman's Magazine*, 1737, vol. 7, p.806.

century.[97] However, even then, a wooden staff was often preferred.[98] After the Restoration of 1660, the halberd gradually went out of fashion. By the eighteenth century, watchmen almost invariably carried a "pole". This was frequently made of ash, was usually between five and six feet long, and was sometimes bound at each end with iron ferrules. Even this implement could be lethal, as a watchman from St. James, Westminster, found during a scuffle with a drunken man that he was conducting to the roundhouse. In the altercation, the drunkard was hit on the head and fatally wounded.[99] The parish "patroles" that became increasingly common in the latter part of the eighteenth century sometimes carried short swords or "hangers" but, again, were very unlikely to carry firearms. Similarly, after its formation in 1790, the Bow Street foot patrol was often issued with cutlasses.

However, as many Metropolitan criminals carried firearms, which were also more mechanically reliable than in the previous century, watchmen could be at a disadvantage. For example, one night in August 1720, the Hawkins gang robbed a coach in Lincoln's Inn Fields and, while escaping from the area, attacked the coach of Lord Westmoreland. By then, and alerted by the earlier crimes, the watch had arrived in numbers from surrounding areas: "...yet at the Fire of a Pistol over their Heads, they retired as fast, and gave us an opportunity of getting clear".[100] A few years later, John Dyer and a companion were cornered by up to 16 watchmen in the same location. After firing three pistol shots at them, all 16 officers fled.[101] At a more intimate level, when a watchman disturbed Martin Bellamy's gang as they broke into a teahouse in Thames Street, Bellamy held a loaded pistol to his head, and forced him to put out his candle and throw his staff and lantern into the Thames.[102]

Unsurprisingly, in these circumstances, there were periodic suggestions that the watch be allowed to carry pistols or even shoulder-arms, and that:

97. T. Dekker *The Gull's Hornbook*, 1609, pp.1-10.

98. W. Fenner, *The Compters Commonwealth*, 1617 p.51.

99. OBSP, Trial of William Harris, 16 January 1723.

100. R. Wilson, *A Full and Impartial Account of all the Robberies Committed by John Hawkins, George Sympson (lately Executed for Robbing the Bristol Mails) and their Companions*, 3rd edn., 1722, pp. 17–26.

101. J. Dyer, *A Genuine Narrative of the Memorable Life and Actions of John Dyer*, 1729, p.25.

102. M. Bellamy, *The Life of Martin Bellamy*, 1727, p.28.

"...every Watch-man be arm'd with fire-arms and sword".[103] One observer urged that each watch-house be provided with a reasonable number of "substantial short carbines of a large bore for slugs". In the inner parishes they would each be issued with six to eight of these weapons, for use in emergency. More would be held in the outer parishes, near to open country, to equip a road patrol.[104]

However, there were also strong reasons to resist such proposals. Most importantly, there was the potential for firearms to be abused by what was often a laxly disciplined body of men. They might encourage watchmen to commit crimes themselves or to insult gentlemen. Issuing them would be a: "...very dangerous way to cure the evil we are treating of, unless they were better regulated".[105] Even so, normal practice was occasionally ignored during the eighteenth century, and a few men were issued with small carbines while on duty. Additionally, it seems that firearms were sometimes to be found at the watch-house, for use in emergency by, or under the immediate supervision of, the constable of the night. Thus, in February 1781, John Wright mentioned at the Old Bailey that he had donated a blunderbuss to the Brompton watch-house.[106]

Effectiveness

By ignoring localised improvements to the watch, many writers (both contemporary and modern) have exaggerated their inefficiency, often taking the worst Metropolitan parishes as typical of the whole.[107] By 1800, a significant number of the more prosperous parishes had developed fairly sophisticated systems of local policing, something that, in part, explains their later resistance to the 1829 reforms. Indeed, it can even be argued that the eighteenth-century system had a few advantages over its successor. It

103. *The Weekly Journal; or, British Gazetteer*, 5 October 1728.
104. A. Moreton, *Second Thoughts are best: or, a Further Improvement of a Late Scheme to Prevent Street Robberies*, 1729, p.18.
105. D. Defoe, *Street Robberies Consider'd* ,1728, pp.1-10.
106. OBSP, Trial of Patrick Hoy, 22 February 1781.
107. C. Emsley, *Crime and Society in England 1750-1900*, 1987, p.175.

was answerable to the basic unit of London government (the parish) and so highly flexible and well equipped to respond to local anxieties. Because watchmen's beats were relatively short by later standards, most knew them intimately, in a way that could not be matched by many later police officers. Nevertheless, despite such local improvements, and the limited effects of wider schemes, it remains the case that the existing system was plagued with problems, even in the City.

Low Personal Quality of Watchmen

The quality of Metropolitan watchmen was a matter of permanent concern throughout the eighteenth century, though virtually all the criticisms that would be made about them had been made about their predecessors a century earlier.[108] One perennial complaint related to their age and physical condition. It was widely recognised that, ideally, watchmen would be between 20 and 35 years of age.[109] However, an open letter in the *British Gazetteer*, addressed to the Lord Mayor, suggested that the principal factor encouraging robbers in the Metropolitan area was the poor policing of its streets by watchmen who were: "...decrepid, superannuated Wretches, with one foot in the grave, and the t'other ready to follow; so feeble, that a puff of breath can blow 'em down".[110] Forty years later, a visiting Frenchman alleged that they were still: "...old men chosen from the dregs of the people".[111] Similarly, Martin Bellamy was to claim that he had been encouraged to offend by observing that many watchmen were: "...superannuated and decrepit old men".[112] At about the same time, it was claimed that it was rare for a Watchman to be under fifty (old given existing life expectancy).[113] This was a considerable exaggeration, but there are numerous well-documented cases

108. P. Griffiths, *Lost Londons: Change, Crime and Control in the Capital City, 1550-1660*, 2008, pp.354-355.
109. Anon, *Outlines of a Plan for Patroling and Watching the City of London, Borough of Southwark, and their Environs*, 1786, p.12.
110. *The Weekly Journal; or, British Gazetteer*, 5 October 1728.
111. P. Grosley, *A Tour to London*, 1772, vol.1, pp.48-49.
112. M. Bellamy, *The Life of Martin Bellamy*, 1728, p.34.
113. D. Defoe, *Street Robberies Consider'd* , 1728, p.60.

of elderly watchmen throughout the century. For example, in 1733, when a watchman named Green hanged himself while on duty in Red Lion Square, it was noted that he was aged "upwards of 60 years".[114] Over half a century later, in 1789, the arthritic Joshua Woodcock, then aged 76, who had served as a watchman in Bishopsgate Without for eighteen years, petitioned the Court of Common Council for a pension as he was no longer able to discharge his office. How effective he was in the latter years of his career must be a matter of conjecture.[115]

It was a particular complaint that many watchmen were charity cases, who were being employed by their parishes as a way of reducing local poor rates, and so explaining why some observers felt they were: "...fitter for an Alms-house than a Watch-house".[116] In 1816, Edward Sherrard, a sixty-three year old watchman from Bread Street ward, actually gave his residential address as the Bishopsgate workhouse.[117]

However, it was not purely a matter of age and infirmity. There were regular complaints that watchmen were "lazy, and inactive".[118] In 1776, there were claims that street robbers would often: "...take advantage of the watchman's absence, or sleep, or drunkenness, to knock down and plunder a single person".[119] On one occasion, when a toyshop was burgled, it was noted that the crime occurred even though a watch-stand was within three doors of the place.[120] In another case, it was claimed that thieves had stolen the iron rails from in front of a gentleman's house in Holborn: "...notwithstanding the watchman's box stood directly on the spot".[121]

114. *Parker's Penny Post*, 21 May, 1733.
115. A. Harris, *Policing the City: Crime and Legal Authority in London, 1780–1840*, 2004, p.22.
116. *The Weekly Journal; or, British Gazetteer*, 5 October 1728.
117. A. Harris, *Policing the City: Crime and Legal Authority in London, 1780–1840*, 2004, p.22.
118. Anon (A Citizen of London), *The Vices of the cities of London and Westminster trac'd from their original*, 1751, pp.30–31.
119. J. Fielding, *A Brief Description of the Cities of London and Westminster*, 1776, p.xxx.
120. *Penny London Post or The Morning Advertiser*, 15 September 1746.
121. *Public Advertiser*, 13 February 1767.

Corruption Amongst the Watch

Corruption and personal dishonesty amongst watchmen was another persistent problem throughout the period. Some of them even turned to straightforward crime. Thus, in 1725, a watchman was convicted of stealing smocks, a shirt and stockings while on duty.[122] Their constant presence on the streets allowed them to take advantage of lapses in security amongst local residents. For example, in 1738, a watchman in Coleman Street in the City noticed that a door had been left carelessly on the latch. He looked inside and saw a snuffbox and some garments on a table. He took these, and returned an hour later to warn the inhabitants that their door was unlocked, for which service he received a shilling. The residents subsequently realized that items had gone missing, and the family's maid immediately suspected the watchman. Her master visited the constable who had been on duty that night and, together, they searched watchman's lodgings, where they found several of the stolen items; the rest had already been pawned. The watchman was taken before the Lord Mayor and committed to the Wood Street Compter.[123] Similarly, in 1767, a watchman was arrested for stealing at the scene of a major fire in Rotherhithe.[124]

There were also periodic allegations of brutality amongst younger watchmen. In 1804, for example, two watchmen from St. Giles parish were sentenced to a year in prison for assaulting a baker, his wife, and another woman, in "circumstances of peculiar wantonness and atrocity".[125] Nevertheless, a search of the *Old Bailey Sessions Papers* suggests that it was fairly rare for watchmen to be prosecuted for personally committing criminal offences, though this may reflect processing rather than incidence.

Despite this, many observers complained that the large number of crimes in the Metropolitan area could not occur without the "connivance or negligence" of its watchmen.[126] The former was particularly troubling. Not a few were suspected of being: "...in league with, or intimidated by the Rogues

122. OBSP, Trial of Richard Brecknell, 27 August 1725.

123. *Old Common Sense; Or the Englishman's Journal*, 23 September 1738.

124. *Gazetteer and New Daily Advertiser*, 4 May 1767.

125. *The Times*, 14 January 1804, p. 3.

126. *London Daily Post and General Advertiser*, 22 December 1735.

that infest our Streets".[127] There were occasional complaints that they took payments from housebreakers for the freedom to commit their crimes unmolested.[128] Sir John Fielding was convinced that, in several cases of burglary that he had investigated, there had been good reason to suspect that the: "... night-officer himself has been the thief's accomplice".[129] The Home Office papers on the Ratcliffe Highway murders of 1811 contain a statement by a watchman named Thomas Hickey admitting that some watchmen were bribed to look the other way by felons.[130]

More insidious, and probably far more common, was endemic low-level corruption. Even in the 1600s, it was thought that watchmen would release drunk and disorderly people who were willing to pay a bribe.[131] Such claims continued on a regular basis until 1829. Thus, when a watchman arrested Alice Green, she bribed him with a shilling while they were on the way to the watch-house so that he gave a favourable report to the "constable of the night" as to how she came to be abroad.[132] By contrast, in the 1750s, an intoxicated man coming home from Hoxton, shortly after Christmas, was arrested and taken back to a watch-house, where he was held for two hours, which the watchmen spent "teizing him for drink". Unfortunately, he did not "bleed" enough, and, as a result, was sent to the bridewell.[133]

Watchmen might have recourse to other ruses to raise money. In 1757, it was claimed that they sometimes met in night cellars to plan quarrels with drunken gentlemen. They would then arrest and produce them before the magistrates, demanding compensation for broken lanterns, a large quantity of which they kept ready for that purpose.[134] However, the authorities were sometimes alert to such behaviour. In 1791, when a young woman was

127. Anon (A Citizen of London), *The Vices of the cities of London and Westminster trac'd from their original*, 1751, pp.30-31.

128. Anon, *Low-Life: or One Half of the World Knows not how the Other Half Live*, 2nd edn., 1755, p.2.

129. J. Fielding, *A Brief Description of the Cities of London and Westminster*, London, 1776, p.xxx

130. P. D. James, and T. A. Critchley, *The Maul and the Pear Tree*, 1971, p.6 & p.19.

131. W. Fenner, *The Compters Commonwealth*, 1617 p.50.

132. A. L. Hayward, *Lives Of The Most Remarkable Criminals*, 1927, pp.407-417.

133. J. Ilive, *A scheme for the employment of all persons sent as disorderly to the house of correction in Clerkenwell*, 1759, pp.5-7.

134. *The London Chronicle or Universal Evening Post*, Sept.1-3 1757.

brought before the magistrate Sir Lawrence Cox, charged with assaulting two Oxford Street watchmen: "This attempt to extort money was too palpable: she was discharged and ordered not to give the watchmen a farthing".[135]

Prostitution was a particularly fertile source of bribery. Extortion from streetwalkers by watchmen (and constables) was long-standing and widespread, and only rarely resulted in punishment.[136] Some parishes took steps to alleviate such corruption. Thus, several of them would rotate watchmen around different beats, stands and watch-boxes so that they did not become excessively intimate with neighbourhood prostitutes. In 1801, the parish of St. Paul, Covent Garden, even forbade watchmen from serving on the same beat for two successive nights, though this policy was later abandoned.[137]

Pusillanimous

Another constant complaint was that Metropolitan watchmen lacked courage, so that: "Their cowardice, too, as a body, was proverbial".[138] This allegation lasted throughout the eighteenth century. According to Martin Bellamy, in the 1720s, they would take any opportunity to avoid their duty: "...especially if the season is intemperate or they apprehend any danger".[139] It was even claimed that hardy thieves were so unafraid that they would force watchmen to light their activities.[140] Recorded examples of their timidity abound; for example, one night in 1766, a small gang robbed Thomas Porter near Blackboy Alley. Porter briefly detained one of the men and unavailingly begged a passing watchman to help him hold the robber. He refused: "... for if he did he should be murdered, there was such a gang of them".[141] Such allegations also became a staple of popular entertainment.[142]

135. *The Times*, 11 October 1791, p.3.
136. A. Moreton, *Parochial Tyranny*, 1727, p.20.
137. T. Henderson, *Disorderly-women in Eighteenth-century London, Prostitution and Control in the Metropolis, 1730-1830*, 1999, pp.113-116.
138. J. Grant, *Sketches in London*, 1838, p.386.
139. M. Bellamy, *The Life of Martin Bellamy*, London, 1727, p.34.
140. *The Weekly Journal; or, British Gazetteer*, 5 October 1728.
141. OBSP, Trial of John Wright and others, 16 January 1766.
142. See, for example, J. Gay, *The Mohocks*, 1712, Scene 1.

However, a degree of caution on the part of watchmen is not entirely surprising. Frequently alone, sometimes elderly, and usually armed only with a staff, facing even a single armed man could be hazardous; dealing with a group of criminals was exceptionally dangerous. It was the relative isolation of watchmen when faced with an emergency, as much as cowardice, which encouraged their caution. What could one man do when he was: "…in terror of his life, surrounded by a pack of ruffians, and no assistance near?"

The dangers were very real. For example, in August 1747, a watchman who had been savagely beaten by a group of men outside a tavern in Piccadilly died of his wounds.[143] The following year, a Covent Garden watchman, described as an "old man" of sixty, was knocked down by four youths who broke his thigh and then stamped on him.[144] Two men were subsequently fined and imprisoned for short periods for this assault.[145] A few months later, yet another Piccadilly watchman was "left for dead" after being attacked by three footpads.[146] There was also the possibility of reprisals after a successful arrest. Jonathan Dickenson, who had detained an armed thief, noted that the man had since threatened to get "even" with the watch.[147] The danger did not just come from the lower orders. In 1720, Maurice Fitzgerald, an Irish gentleman from the parish of St Martin-in-the-Fields was convicted and executed for murdering a watchman with his sword. The officer had gone to the assistance of a woman whom Fitzgerald and a group of drunken "libertines" were abusing.[148]

If a watchman (or anyone else) was killed while attempting to arrest a burglar or housebreaker, the dead man's executors were entitled to a payment of £40 under a statute from the reign of Queen Anne (5. Ann. c.3), on the issue of an appropriate certificate by two JPs.[149] However, his dependants had no entitlement to a pension. If watchmen were severely injured while on duty there was usually no one to assist them other than the parish, with

143. *Whitehall Evening Post or London Intelligencer*, August 15, 1747.

144. *London Evening Post*, 4 August, 1748.

145. *London Evening Post*, 8 October 1748.

146. *London Evening Post*, 7 January 1749.

147. OBSP, Trial of William Raven, 4 April 1733. Dickenson asked that the presiding Old Bailey judge protect them, which he did by sentencing the defendant to transportation.

148. OBSP, Trial of Maurice Fitzgerald, 12 July 1720.

149. *The Complete Parish Officer*, 1772, p.394.

its meagre level of relief. Although, from the late eighteenth century, some of the wealthier Metropolitan parishes introduced annuities for parish officers injured or worn out in the course of their duties, such maintenance was comparatively rare. This did not encourage risk-taking.

Discipline Amongst the Watch

Irrespective of corruption, discipline amongst watchmen could be very lax, and a better disciplined watch was widely viewed as a necessary prerequisite for awarding them strengthened legal powers, if serious, liberty-threatening, abuses were to be avoided. Alcohol was widely and, in the early part of the eighteenth century, often openly consumed, public houses were frequented and "visitors" entertained while watchmen were on duty. Thus, in January 1725, when John Hewlet, a watchman from St. Andrew's, Holborn, was convicted of murdering a colleague with his staff, another watchman testified that, shortly before midnight, Hewlet had come to his stand, very drunk, abusive and bellicose.[150] Some claimed that burglars would take advantage of this and divide themselves into two groups: "...some of whom go to the Watch House to make the Constable and Watchmen drunk, while the others break open houses".[151]

As the eighteenth century advanced, both Parliament and individual parishes attempted to prevent drinking on duty. Nevertheless, such initiatives met only limited success and abuses continued. Indicative of this, in November 1796, a watchman named Richard Croft was indicted for stealing a damask tablecloth from a public house in Red Lion Square, Holborn while ordering a pot of beer. The landlord, who suspected him of the crime, waited until he passed by on duty a few hours later, calling the hour of the night, then accused him of the theft, found the cloth on his person and left him in the custody of some customers while he went for the constable, who took him back to his own watch-house as a prisoner.[152]

150. OBSP, Trial of John Hewlet, 15 January 1725.

151. Anon, *Low-Life or one Half of the World knows not how the other half lives*, 3rd. edn., 1764, p.3.

152. OBSP, Trial of Richard Croft, 30 November 1796.

Alcohol was often linked to another major problem, that of watchmen sleeping on duty. Samuel McGall, a Westminster beadle, noted that when he had accompanied his constable on an inspection of watchmen in the upper division of their parish, shortly before midnight, they: "...found Ritchard Thorne in ye ale house & as I returned after one I found him asleep Resting on a cord hucked across his Box".[153] Given that many watchmen had worked the previous day, that their hours of duty were long, and some were elderly, it is not, perhaps, surprising that they were often: "...asleep or absent from their boxes when their presence is most desired".[154] As was noted in 1786, the: "...incessant fatigue of watching every night, must inevitably be productive of a languor little compatible with the vigilant exertion to be expected of a useful guard".[155]

Additionally, the minute books of parish vestries and wardmote courts contain numerous complaints about watchmen (and even constables) fraternising with prostitutes, such as that made against a supernumerary watchman for "harbouring loose women in and about his Box or stand".[156] It would appear that a pragmatic attitude was often the "norm". Producing streetwalkers before a justice was also a time-consuming business, taking place outside the normal hours of watch service.

Various attempts were made over the course of the century to enhance discipline and promote diligence amongst watchmen and, more particularly, to prevent them sleeping, drinking or gossiping with each other when on duty. Some suggestions were completely unrealistic. For example, in the late eighteenth century there were periodic and usually short-lived proposals by several parishes, including St. Marylebone, that all watchmen whose "walks" (or beats) saw a burglary should be dismissed. Such orders were normally revoked fairly quickly, as it was swiftly appreciated that crimes could be committed "without the possible knowledge of the watchmen". It was often impossible for them to keep their entire areas under effective

153. Westminster Archives, Piccadilly Beadles Reports, No D 2092.

154. W. Clowes, *Leigh's New Picture of London*, 1819, p.97.

155. Anon, *Outlines of a Plan for Patroling and Watching the City of London, Borough of Southwark, and their Environs*, 1786, p.7.

156. T. Henderson, *Disorderly-women in Eighteenth-century London, Prostitution and Control in the Metropolis*, 1730-1830, 1999, pp.110-111.

surveillance when on duty. If sanctions were ineffective, rewards might be used as incentives to good performance. For example, in 1791, St. James's Piccadilly put up notices in every street offering a parish reward of three guineas to any constable, "patrole" or watchman who arrested those stealing lead from buildings or attempting to break into them.[157]

Deterrent Value of Watchmen

Of course, timid or not, the very presence of watchmen in the night streets had some deterrent value. As one contemporary observer noted, if they were not asleep and came across criminals they might be of service simply by making a noise with their rattles.[158] Burglars would normally run if disturbed in this fashion.[159] When Martin Bellamy and his gang were confronted by a passing watchman while breaking into a shoemaker's shop in Eastcheap, they knocked him down but were: "...oblig'd to walk off without booty".[160] Similarly, after the notorious James Dalton and two armed colleagues stopped a coach in London, they initially let it drive on when they saw two watchmen coming by. It was only when they found that the watchmen had not noticed them that they renewed their robbery.[161]

The Patroles

As concern grew that the watch was excessively static and lacking in vigour, several Metropolitan parishes started to experiment with mobile "patroles". Unlike the watch, their members usually acted in small groups, or at least pairs, and were not confined to set beats, but operated over the entire parish.

157. E. Reynolds, *Before the Bobbies. The Night Watch and Police Reform in Metropolitan London, 1720–1830*, 1998, pp.81–82.
158. W. Clowes, *Leigh's New Picture of London*, 1819, p.97.
159. J. W. von Archenholz, *A picture of England: Containing a description of the laws, customs and manners of England*, 1790, p.184.
160. M. Bellamy, *The Life of Martin Bellamy*, 1727, p.27.
161. J. Dalton, *A Genuine Narrative of all the Street Robberies Committed since October last*, 1728, p.20.

They were often a little younger and fitter than watchmen, were constantly moving, and frequently had a degree of responsibility for supervising the watch with whom they worked closely.

The practice of appointing such men appears to have started amongst some suburban parishes in the 1750s and 1760s. For example, in the winter of 1766, the inhabitants of Kensington, still (if only just) a suburban area, engaged four extra men to "patrole between that place and London". They would set off every half-hour from Hyde Park Corner between 5 pm and 11 pm for the protection of travellers walking the same route.[162] Some individual Westminster parishes were also experimenting with small specialist "patroles" by the early 1770s. Thus, in St. Andrew's, Holborn, six men were engaged in patrolling, compared to a complement of 30 watchmen, and in the Liberty of Saffron Hill there were two men so engaged, compared to 13 watchmen.[163]

In 1783, a committee was set up by the parishes of St Margaret and St John the Evangelist in Westminster to raise money to keep armed patroles in their area. The second subscription alone amounted to over £271, this being donated by more than 300 people, who gave sums ranging from a shilling to three pounds or more. The following year, the committee observed that 12 men, armed with pistols and cutlasses, were "constantly moving" about during the same hours that the watch was on duty, under the supervision of a regulator. Most of the money raised was spent on wages with smaller amounts going on the cost of prosecuting those who assaulted the patroles, Christmas gratuities to the men, and extra payments for early attendance (prior to the watch going on duty) and giving evidence at the Quarter Sessions or Old Bailey.[164]

In 1784, a City Patrole, made up of day and night patrols, up to a dozen strong, under the direct supervision of the City marshals, were introduced in the Square Mile. This was an important, albeit small, step towards a police force under the direct control of the Corporation, rather than local (ward) authorities. The following year, William Blizard suggested that 150 fit, honest,

162. *The Whitehall Evening Post; or, London Intelligencer*, 23 September 1766.

163. Information contained in C. Whitworth, *The Draught of an Intended Act, For the better Regulation of the Nightly Watch and Beadles within the City and Liberty of Westminster*, 1773, p.1.

164. Anon, *St. Margaret and St. John the Evangelist, Westminster. State of the Second Voluntary Subscription for the Armed Patroles*, 1784, pp.1-6.

salaried men, would be enormously effective in the City if employed to: "... patrole the streets; [and] to keep constables and watchmen on their duty".[165] Although this proposal was not implemented, in 1791, the City Patrole was expanded and issued with blue uniforms and hats. Its officers patrolled designated beats, reporting to, and signing in at, existing watch-houses. The Square Mile was divided up into four policing divisions, with three diurnal and two nocturnal patrols assigned to each, tasked to remove nuisances, stop begging, and prevent all forms of theft.

165. W. Blizard, *Desultory Reflections on Police: with an essay on the means of preventing crimes and amending criminals*, 1785, pp. 80-83.

CHAPTER 10

BEADLES, CITY MARSHALS AND THE MILITARY

Beadles

Beadles were paid employees of the parish, appointed to act as their "messenger or servant". It was a full-time position, though some dabbled in other trades at the same time. In most of Middlesex, they were appointed and controlled by their parish vestry. However, in Westminster, many were appointed by the Court of Burgesses, while in the City, they were ward officers (Confusingly, men with the same title were also found in many eighteenth-century institutions, such as guilds and bridewells).

Beadles would normally wear a form of parish uniform. Typically, one was described as being attired in a comfortable broad-cloth horseman's coat, with a large velvet cape adorned with gold lace, and a hat that was ornamented in a similar manner.[1] This description conforms closely with Hogarth's portrayal in his "Industry and Idleness" series (see images depicting beadles in the plate section). Although Beadles were amongst the earliest paid, and so "professional", police officers, their remuneration was relatively modest. For example, the beadle of St. Clement's Danes was only paid £7 a quarter in 1719.[2] Despite this, the position was sufficiently attractive for some men to serve for several decades.

Historically, one of their major functions had been keeping order during divine service and on church premises. Additionally, they would give notice of vestry meetings, and assist the churchwardens, overseers of the poor, and parish constables in their respective duties.[3] Very importantly, beadles helped

1. Anon, *The Midnight Rambler or, New Nocturnal Spy*, 1770, pp.107-108.
2. J. Ritson, *A Digest of the Proceedings of the Court Leet of the Manor and Liberty of the Savoy*, 1769, pp.4-6.
3. J. Bird, *The laws respecting parish matters. Containing the several offices and duties of churchwardens*, 1799, p.91.

to supervise the watch, usually sharing this duty with the allotted constable of the night. For example, in Piccadilly, Samuel McGall, a local beadle, could note that on a typical night he had helped inspect the watch:

> Mr. Baxter [the] Constable he and I went ye lower Division at 12 & returned at one. I went the upper ditto at 2 and returned after 3 & ye lower a second time at 4 & returned Before 5, all was in good order.[4]

Similarly, in 1719, James Barber, a beadle from St Martin-in-the-Fields, noted that after several robberies had been committed in the parish it was feared that their watchmen did not do their duty properly: "...therefore he was ordered to walk from 11 to 4 to look after them".[5]

When their supervising constables were away, as was frequently the case, beadles were, effectively, the ranking officers in the nocturnal watch-house. As a result, it could be observed that:

> Beadles of Parishes and Precincts are very great men in the Constables absence, by sitting in their chairs, drinking their liquor, and deciding what squabbles are brought before them.[6]

They also had the huge advantage (over constables) of experience. This meant that they became familiar with neighbourhood criminals in a way that a temporarily appointed officer might not. Thus, the Covent Garden beadle arrested John Evans for stealing a large quantity of valuable clothes from a house in St Martin's Lane. He saw Evans carrying the garments and: "...knew him well enough to suspect him".[7] They also became experienced at identifying generally suspicious behaviour. For example, Anthony Rogers was arrested in St. Clement Danes by a local beadle for stealing a very large Cheshire cheese from a neighbourhood shop. The beadle had seen Rogers

4. Westminster City Archives, Piccadilly Beadles Reports D 2092.
5. OBSP, Trial of James Barber, 14 Oct 1719.
6. Anon, *Low-Life or one Half of the World knows not how the other half lives,* 3rd. edn., 1764, p.4.
7. OBSP, Trial of John Evans, 23 August 1676.

with the cheese, accompanied by several "'shifty men'" and " …seiz'd him upon Suspicion, and found it [the cheese] belong'd to Mr. Eaton".[8]

Sometimes, the beadle would be summoned to a crime scene, in the same manner as a constable. In April 1746, for example, Jane King, a housemaid, was suspected of stealing a pair of diamond earrings from her erstwhile employer, after she was summarily dismissed from his service. When King returned to recover her belongings, a local beadle was sent for. King eventually admitted the crime to him, was arrested and taken before Sir Thomas de Veil.[9]

Beadles provided a modicum of continuity in local policing and a pool of expertise for newly appointed and inexperienced constables to lean on. Thus, in 1744, when a beadle named Edmund Long was accused of murder, one of his character witnesses, John Hull, testified that he (Hull) had served as both headborough and constable in St. George's parish, Bloomsbury, and that Long was: "…with me for two years, almost every day". This experience and familiarity with procedures also gave them great influence over their nominal superiors, so that a factional watchman, writing to an associate in 1720, could counsel him to: "Obey your Master Sharp the Beadle, whom you know commands Tool the Constable".[10] In the Metropolitan area, especially the City, some beadles would also serve periodically as constables. This was usually as a paid substitute for the man actually allotted the office. There were some disadvantages to this practice. Obviously, one man could not perform two duties simultaneously.

Very importantly, beadles were one of the few, often the only, parish officers regularly involved in full-time diurnal policing prior to the advent of the New Police in 1829. As a result, they would deal with vagrants, prostitutes, beggars and those creating obstructions on the highway. This made them the: "…terror of boys, whores and dogs".[11] For example, in November 1700, numerous vagrant children were "taken up" by beadles in the City, and produced before the Court of Aldermen.[12] In the following year, bea-

8. OBSP, Trial of Anthony Rogers, 23 February 1715.
9. OBSP, Trial of Januarye King, 15 May 1746.
10. Anon (Tom Tattle), *A Letter from Tom Tattle A Literate Watchman of Westminster to his Brother Jack Drydrub*, 1720, p.6.
11. Anon, *The Midnight Rambler or, New nocturnal Spy*, 1770, pp.107-108.
12. *London Post*, 8-11 November 1700.

dles assisted constables and JPs in Westminster to detain almost 40 "lewd" women at the May Fair held near Hyde Park.[13]

This inevitably brought them into conflict with elements of the "lower orders", so that a typical beadle, although well thought of by influential men in his parish, was: "...disregarded among the inferior sort of people, because he is by his office employed to remove nuisances".[14] Such popular animosity was frequently exacerbated by their behaviour and social backgrounds. Although they were vested with significant powers of arrest, they were often fairly poor, and sometimes lazy, drunken and corrupt. They were also prone to ignoring misbehaviour by the upper classes and taking bribes from prostitutes.[15]

City Marshals and Marshalmen

The position of City marshal was established in the 1570s. Its holders were originally termed "provost marshals", their initial purpose being to deal with an apparent rise in vagrancy within the Square Mile. In 1603, the provost marshal's position became a permanent office, and was placed under the jurisdiction of the Court of Aldermen, the holder quickly becoming known as the "City marshal". In 1626, after the aldermen defined his duties more precisely, the Bridewell Prison's own private provost marshal (created in 1619) also came under his authority, henceforth being termed the "under marshal". During the seventeenth century the two men were the senior police officers for the Square Mile.[16] In due course, six, rising to twelve, extra "marshalmen" were appointed to assist them in carrying out their duties, and to execute warrants and summonses.

The City marshal received a salary of £100 a year at the end of the seventeenth century, along with a uniform and an allowance to maintain his horse.[17] He supplemented this with the considerable fees that were available

13. *English Post,* 12-14 May 1701.
14. OBSP, Trial of Edmund Long and others, 17 October 1744.
15. Anon, *The Midnight Rambler or, New nocturnal Spy*, 1770, pp.107-108.
16. G. Howson, *Thief-Taker General: The Rise and Fall of Jonathan Wild,* 1970, p.27.
17. J. M. Beattie, *Policing and Punishment in London, 1660-1750*, 2001, p.159.

for performing some of the specific duties attendant on his office. These made it a fairly profitable position. As a result, both the marshals' posts were routinely sold for significant amounts of money. Thus, the notoriously corrupt Charles Hitchen used an inheritance to pay £700 for the position of under marshal in 1712. Thomas Gates paid £800 for the position of marshal in 1764, while, in 1771, John Bradley spent £500. The fall in value is probably explained by a change in 1770, whereby the Common Council decided to award the marshal and under marshal larger salaries but at the same time to reduce their fee income. This was partly done because the office attracted regular allegations of corruption, even though the marshals' orders came directly from the Lord Mayor, and they could be disciplined by suspension or dismissal by the aldermen.[18]

The marshals and their men helped supervise the ward constables and watchmen, and recorded any untoward incidents in a daily book of occurrences. This was kept so that the Lord Mayor and Court of Aldermen could be informed about the state of the City. They were also required to give notice of any non-freemen exercising their trades within the Square Mile, put in force all orders of the Court of Aldermen and Common Council, attend and regulate public processions, and visit markets to ensure that they were kept in an orderly and proper manner. For example, in November 1737, the City marshal and his assistants detected that a butcher in the Square Mile was selling unwholesome meat. It was carried before the Lord Mayor, who ordered that it be burnt.[19] In 1763, gentlemen attending a procession from Holborn to Throgmorton Street were asked to put their carriages in rows so that they could: "...be placed by the City marshal in proper ranks".[20]

Like the beadles, the marshals and their men provided a rare source of permanent diurnal policing, albeit only in the City. In April 1787, for example, the Lord Mayor ordered the City marshals and marshalmen to visit public houses in the Square Mile on Sundays, and arrest those found tippling in them during divine service, along with anyone selling fruit in the streets. Publicans who allowed such practices were to be presented at

18. CLRO: Misc. ms 135,4.
19. *Country Journal or The Craftsman*, 12 November 1737.
20. *Public Advertiser*, 25 April 1763.

Quarter Sessions, so that they could lose their licences.[21] A few months later, the mayor reiterated that the marshals and their men should "patrole the streets every Sunday" so as to arrest drunks and those guilty of swearing in public or tippling in gin shops and public houses.[22]

The upper marshal also had a vague, and sometimes neglected, duty to supervise the City's nocturnal policing, a function which he usually discharged by periodically riding around the Square Mile, ensuring that the watches were set, the beadles were doing their duty, and that vagrants and prostitutes were being taken up. However, some would take a more active role in policing. Thus, in March 1701, the City marshal arrested Ann Williams, and three of her prostitute colleagues for being "lewd & idle persons". They were produced before Sir Thomas Abney, the Lord Mayor, and committed to bridewell.[23] Similarly, in September 1728, the marshals arrested nine "sodomites" in a gin shop near Whitechapel Church.[24] In 1785, the City marshal was also given leadership of the Square Mile's new day patrol. Some marshals and their men were clearly very dedicated. In 1744, when the deputy marshal was returning to the City from a liaison meeting with Sir Thomas de Veil, he recognised a well-known criminal, and attempted to arrest him. He was attacked, and slightly injured, by a large gang, before he managed to drive them off with a pocket blunderbuss loaded with duck-shot.[25]

The Military

The military was the only body above the constables and watch that could engage in policing. Soldiers were used to suppress major riots in the Metropolis throughout the century. For example, there were serious disturbances in 1765, 1768 and, of course, 1780, all of which required that the army be

21. *World and Fashionable Advertiser*, 7 April 1787.
22. *World and Fashionable Advertiser*, 30 June 1787.
23. Mansion House Justice Room Charge Book, 1699-1705, CLA/004/01/4 entry for 28 March 1701 p.98.
24. *London Evening Post*, Saturday, 28 September 1728.
25. *The Gentleman's Magazine*, 1744, vol. 14, p.505.

called out.[26] However, troops were also used to bolster "routine" policing by backing up, or acting as, ordinary law enforcement officers. At least a fifth of the army's time was devoted to some form of policing duty, and soldiers were always readily available in the London area. For example, they were regularly used to secure the Tyburn gallows, and provided prisoner escorts where necessary. Thus, when 20 felons were executed in March 1741, the notorious "Jenny Diver" among them, each of the seven carts making the journey to the gallows was guarded by four infantrymen and two cavalrymen, while Diver, travelling in her own mourning coach, was escorted by 20 soldiers.[27] They could also provide escorts in other situations. For example, in 1739, Colonel de Veil, having examined Mary Brown, a suspected shoplifter, late at night, was forced to send for a guard of soldiers to escort her to Newgate, because there was a large: "...gang of thieves waiting near the Justice's house to rescue her".[28] Additionally, soldiers were sometimes used to patrol the Metropolis's environs. Thus, in 1738, two 12-man troops of cavalry from the Light Horse were patrolling commons at Hounslow and Finchley each night during the winter to: "...prevent the great number of Robberies at those Places".[29]

Nevertheless, there was also a considerable, and growing, degree of concern about using soldiers for routine law enforcement. Professional standing armies were acutely unpopular in England, especially at the start of the era, when they were still a relatively new phenomenon. Many feared that it was: "...absolutely impossible, that any nation which keeps them amongst themselves, can long preserve their liberties".[30] Their use in the domestic sphere was often viewed as oppressive, unconstitutional, and "continental". Sir John Fielding never called for troops if he could possibly avoid it.[31] For this reason alone, it was argued that reform in Metropolitan law enforcement was vital, so that a fear of crime did not force the authorities to station troops throughout the capital, giving the appearance that everything was held by

26. A. J. Hayter, *The Army and the Crowd in Mid-Georgian England*, 1978, pp.128-129.
27. *Common Sense or The Englishman's Journal*, 21 March 1741.
28. *Read's Weekly Journal*, Saturday, 15 September 1739.
29. *Old Common Sense; Or, the Englishman's Journal*, 25 November 1738.
30. Anon (by Cato), *A Discourse of Standing Armies*, 2nd edn., 1722, p.25.
31. A. J. Hayter, *The Army and the Crowd in Mid-Georgian England*, 1978, p.18.

the "courtesy of a military power".[32] It was also one reason that private plans for reforming the existing militia regiments in London, so that they doubled as watchmen, were never effected, although occasional and limited use was made of part-time military volunteers in crime-fighting.

The presence of troops in the capital was a mixed blessing in other respects. There were permanent problems with the London garrison. The conduct of soldiers, and sometimes even their officers, could be very poor. Prior to his embarkation for Canada, General James Wolfe observed that in Portsmouth the garrison was made up of insolent, undisciplined and disorderly: "…vagabonds that stroll about in dirty red clothes from one gin-shop to another".[33] Those in London, if not usually in quite such a parlous condition, were often not much better behaved. Indeed, it was his experience of being robbed by soldiers from the foot guards that prompted Joseph Villers to begin a personal campaign against London crime in 1706. He obtained information implicating up to 90 guardsmen in various offences.[34] Daniel Defoe also felt that the military made a major contribution to Metropolitan offending levels.[35] Time and again, soldiers, especially the foot guards, appear in the *Old Bailey Sessions Papers*, accused of serious or violent crimes, while clerics frequently complained of their "wicked lives and manners" and their penchant for drinking, cursing and fighting.[36] To ameliorate such problems, it was proposed that those based in the capital be forbidden from wearing weapons except when on duty.[37]

This poor situation was compounded by the limited barrack accommodation available in the Metropolis. With the exception of those based in the Tower, most soldiers were billeted in twos and threes with private landlords

32. Anon (A Citizen of London), *The Vices of the cities of London and Westminster trac'd from their original …* , 1751, p.11.
33. J. Warner, "My Pappa is out, and my Mamma is asleep", 2003, pp.561-584.
34. J. Villers, *The Case of Joseph Villers, Citizen of London*, 1715, p.1.
35. D. Defoe, *Street-Robberies Considered: The reason of their being so frequent …*, 1728, p.49.
36. T. Bray, *Sermon Preach'd at the Parish-Church of St. Clements Danes, Westminster on the 24th of March 1709 at the Funeral of Mr. John Dent*, 1709, p.15-16.
37. C. Jones, *Some Methods Proposed Towards putting a Stop to the Flagrant Crimes of Murder, Robbery, and Perjury*, 1752, pp.5-6.

or in taverns, by legal order where necessary. As a result, they were usually beyond the immediate control of officers and senior NCOs.[38]

If only because of their social provenance, the commitment of many regular soldiers to the "establishment" was also sometimes suspect. According to Horace Walpole, those barracked in the capital had been unenthusiastic about their duties in suppressing the Gordon Riots in 1780 and were, apparently, "by no means active" in executing the commands of their officers. Harriet Frankland, visiting London from Wales, observed that some soldiers had refused to fire until threatened with execution, being "much on the side of the Populace".[39]

38. J. Childs, "War, crime waves and the English army in the late seventeenth century", 1997, p.16.
39. P. Rawlings, *Crime and Power,* 1999, p.36.

CHAPTER 11

POST-CRIME DETECTION

Introduction

During the eighteenth century, as in all previous eras, a high proportion of prosecuted felons were caught "red-handed", either while attempting to commit their offences or immediately after having done so. Unsurprisingly, victims would normally take the lead in this process, and much would depend on their presence of mind and speed of reaction. For example, the infamous pickpocket Mary Young ("Jenny Diver") was finally caught by one of her victims while conducting an ingenious criminal venture with other members of her gang. They would offer to help women across some wooden boards lying in the road, during which manoeuvre she stole from them. However, when Judith Gardner felt Young's hand in her pocket, she reacted immediately, and seized her by the wrist. Although Young struck her viciously in the face, she refused to let go: "I then took fast hold of her Cloak and never left her "till I got Assistance to take her from me". Passersby intervened, and a constable was summoned.[1] In another typical case, when a gentleman was attacked by a footpad, intent on seizing his gold watch, and not expecting any resistance, his victim: "...got fast hold of him, and secured him till others came to his assistance".[2]

As these incidents suggest, in an urban and suburban environment, a call for assistance was likely to attract support, especially if there was the possibility of a statutory reward. In all but the most nefarious areas, a cry of "stop thief" would be taken up by the surrounding populace and a fleeing man pursued. So effective could this be that, in 1766, when bailiffs chasing a poor debtor down Temple Lane (fraudulently) gave vent to the cry, their

1. OBSP, Trial of Mary Young, 16 January 1741.
2. *Weekly Journal or British Gazetteer*, 30 May 1724.

quarry was immediately seized by other pedestrians and "re-delivered to their custody". There was a considerable moral debate as to whether bailiffs should brand an innocent man with such a capital crime, damaging his reputation in the process, and also exposing him to bodily risk via the "casual resentment of the populace".[3] In appropriate circumstances, the cry could be altered to fit other crimes, with equally effective results. For example, John Lowther was pursued with the shout of "Stop, sodomite" after indecently assaulting an apprentice near Gracechurch Street. He, too, was swiftly apprehended.[4]

The frequent presence of passersby probably helps to explain why the proportion of those who were caught red-handed appears to have been higher in the capital and its environs than it was in the provinces. Immediate assistance was less likely to be available in rural areas, where there were fewer people close at hand. Reports from the Old Bailey would suggest that a majority of Metropolitan felons were caught in the act, by hot pursuit, or in the immediate aftermath of their crimes. By contrast, in Essex, it seems that only a little over a quarter of those who came before the courts had been apprehended in this manner.[5]

Even if they were not caught while committing their crimes, many Metropolitan felons were detained at other traditional "danger points" in the offending process. For example, a significant number were apprehended while trying to liquidate stolen goods. Despite the unenviable reputation of the city's pawnbrokers, many did involve the authorities when offered valuable items in suspicious circumstances. Thus, after Elizabeth Fowlis of St. Peters Cornhill stole clothes and other goods from her employer, she attempted to pawn them with Abraham Bibbin, but he became suspicious: "...examined her how she came by them and she confest they were her Master's, and where she lived; whereupon he secured her".[6]

Occasionally, arrests were initiated by ordinary members of the general public, rather than by victims. For example, when John Allen cut his sweet-heart's throat in Holloway Fields, her body was discovered almost

---

3. *The Whitehall Evening Post; or, London Intelligencer*, 20 September 1766.
4. Anon, *The Tryal of Mr. John Lowther, For an Assault on John Bushnell, with an intent to commit the Crime of Sodomy*, 1761, p.10.
5. P. King, *Crime, Justice and Discretion in England 1740-1820*, 2000, p.21.
6. OBSP, Trial of Elizabeth Fowlis, 12 October 1720.

immediately by a local man named Johnson, who also saw the defendant walking nearby in a somewhat "dejected" manner. This led him to suspect Allen. As a result, he followed him, and had him arrested for murder in Islington. Allen was then examined, in the presence of Johnson, by a local JP, and made a full confession to the killing.[7]

In other cases, the defendant had made no attempt to conceal his identity, and merely hoped that the victim would be reluctant to prosecute. Prostitutes, in particular, appear to have relied on embarrassment acting as a bar to prosecution, even though the victims of their thefts (usually their erstwhile clients) were often familiar with their haunts. Sometimes, however, victims swallowed their pride and went looking for them. Similarly, in a case of homosexual assault, where the victim had met his assailant during divine service at a nonconformist meeting house, the complainant merely had to get an arrest warrant from a JP and go with it, accompanied by a constable, to the same meeting house the following Sunday. Once there, the suspect, noticing their arrival, tried to escape, but they: "... soon overtook him and carried him before the Justice".[8]

Nevertheless, many Metropolitan felons were not caught *in flagrente delicto,* while attempting to pawn stolen goods, or at a well-known haunt, yet ended up before the courts. Until recently, the "orthodox" modern analysis was that eighteenth-century policing "experts" (or at least those men with a specialist interest in the subject) regarded crime prevention as being far more important than post-offence arrest, detention and prosecution.[9] Certainly, John Fielding had been sure it was: "...much better to prevent even one Man from being a Rogue, than from apprehending and bringing forty to justice". The "traditional", pre-modern, English system of parish constables and watchmen was expected to deter crime by surveillance of the urban environment. It was not normally thought to be part of the duties of even the best officers to actively seek out and prosecute those offenders who were

7. Anon, *The Whole Tryal, Examination, Confession, and Condemnation of Mr. John Allen, the Merchant's Son*, 1703, p.1. A letter was found in the dead woman's pocket which at trial was: "... proved to be Mr. Allen's own Hand writing by a whole Court of Witnesses".
8. OBSP, Trial of George Duffus, 6 December 1721.
9. L. Zedner, "Policing Before and After the Police", 2006, p.85.

not caught red-handed or delivered to them by members of the public who had made what would now be termed a "citizen's arrest".

However, this analysis is misleading. Post-crime detection played a vital role in eighteenth-century policing. Indeed, it lay behind many of the era's criminal justice initiatives, especially in the Metropolis. Unlike the police force established in London in 1829, which was (initially) committed to defeating crime by surveillance, the eighteenth-century "solution" to the capital's crime problem was substantially premised on detection and prosecution.[10] Serious crimes that did not result in their perpetrators being caught when they occurred were not simply ignored.

The murder of John Hayes by his wife and lodgers in 1726 provides an illustration of the sophisticated collective response that could go into investigating a particularly grave crime. John's body had been decapitated, dismembered and scattered to prevent identification. A Westminster watchman found his head near the Thames. It was taken to the nearby St Margaret's Church, where the churchwardens ordered that it be cleaned of blood and dirt, and the hair combed, so that it would appear as close to life as possible. The head was then set up on a post so that the public could view it and, hopefully, identify the dead man. After being on display for three days, the parish surgeon preserved it in spirits, so that it could be viewed to order without decaying. When the remainder of the body was, eventually, found buried under rubble in Marylebone (some distance away) it was married up with the skull, in the presence of several surgeons, and found to "correspond exactly". A witness then came forward to identify the head, as a result of which John's wife, Catherine and the male defendants were suspected, and questioned by a magistrate. One swiftly made full admissions.[11]

Traditionally, post-crime detection had been left to victims and concerned members of the public, supplemented in homicide cases by coroners and, in the case of serious felonies generally by the more energetic type of magistrate. However, from the late seventeenth century onwards, the successful detection and prosecution of felons came to be seen as an increasingly important

10. J. M. Beattie, "Garrow and the Detectives", pp.5-23.

11. Anon, *A Narrative of the Barbarous and unheard of murder of Mr. John Hayes, by Catherine his wife, Thomas Billings, and Thomas Wood, on the 1st of March at Night*, 1726, pp. 6-7.

aspect of crime fighting. This led to the active encouragement of detection via the introduction of statutory rewards for prosecuting to conviction those who had committed several (but not all) of the most serious types of offence. Additionally, it led to a great expansion in the use of accomplice information and evidence, to identify suspects and then to secure their convictions.

Taken together, these stratagems, victim initiative, rewards, and accomplice evidence, largely amounted to what might be termed the eighteenth-century "system" of detection. The highwayman James Carrick alluded to all of them in 1722. Carrick had left his native Ireland with some criminal colleagues because he feared that their gang was becoming dangerously well known. They naturally gravitated to London, and swiftly resumed their varied criminal careers. However, at one point, Carrick, becoming nervous about his group's long term prospects, unavailingly suggested a return to Ireland by dwelling on the risks that they faced in the Metropolis: "I backed this with Reasons deduced from the Greatness of the Reward, which was no less than 140L. for taking a single Highwayman, the Vigilance of such as were employed by the Government in such discovery, and the many examples that had been made, by putting to death such as had been taken either by Treachery, in being betrayed by their own comrades, or by force, in being over-powered by numerous pursuers, or by their own want of caution".[12]

Personal Detection

Many crime victims were prepared to carry out detective work on their own account. For example, in 1752, Gaspar Valle, a Haymarket milliner who had lost several hats over a relatively short period of time, decided to be proactive in finding the thief. He fastened a small bell inside the brim of an attractive headpiece then tied a string from the bell to a nail driven into a wooden chest. He secreted himself in his shop until he heard it ring, at which he leapt from his hiding place and seized a woman named Elizabeth Ainsworth, whom

12. J. Carrick, *A Compleat and True Account of all the Robberies Committed by James Carrick, John Malhoni, and their Accomplices*, 1722, p.10.

Valle immediately carried before Justice Fielding.[13] Similarly, John Godfrey had written off the loss of some small jewels from his house until learning that diamonds and a pearl matching their description had been offered to a goldsmith in Whitechapel. He then linked the crime to a "lying in" nurse from that area who had attended his wife. He "took her up" and carried her before a Justice in the Tower Liberty, where she swiftly confessed.[14] Nathaniel Lucas was tried at the Old Bailey in 1784, accused of stealing over two pounds worth of clothes belonging to Mary Davis from her parents' house in Red Lion Street, because her father had immediately suspected the prisoner, who lodged at a public house next-door. He fetched a constable and beadle, and accompanied them to Lucas's room with the publican. There, the three men carried out a search and discovered the missing items.[15]

Such personal detection was not confined to offences of dishonesty. In 1761, when a young apprentice was accosted by an older man named Lowther, but escaped his aggressive homosexual advances, he returned to the scene of the incident the following day, accompanied by a companion armed with a heavy stick, who secreted himself behind a cask. The apprentice then successfully sought to lure Lowther into repeating his previous behaviour. When Lowther (who lived nearby) had thoroughly incriminated himself the apprentice and his colleague seized him.[16]

Justices and Detection

Historically, some of the more energetic and committed English JPs had engaged in active detective work, rather than being the purely passive recipients of others' information who limited their work to examining suspects brought before them or issuing search and arrest warrants. A number of magistrates continued this tradition during the eighteenth century. For a

13. *The Covent Garden Journal*, 20 January 1752.
14. OBSP, Trial of Susanah Harvey, 7 December 1743,
15. After Lucas was convicted, he was held on a hulk at Woolwich before sailing with the first fleet for Australia in late 1787.
16. Anon, *The Tryal of Mr. John Lowther, For an Assault on John Bushnell, with an intent to commit the Crime of Sodomy*, 1761, pp.1-12.

provincial example can be considered Samuel Lister, a very conscientious Yorkshire JP of the 1750s and 1760s. Thus, when documents found in the possession of a man who had been arrested for failing to pay a tavern bill led Lister to suspect that he had been engaged in large-scale fraud in the West Country, the magistrate made numerous enquiries, advertising the man's description in a London newspaper, liaising with lawyers and communicating with the authorities in Gloucestershire. The suspect was identified and sent to that county for trial. Lister showed the same dedication in several other cases, including a major investigation into clipping and coining.[17]

Although few magistrates would go to quite such trouble to detect crime, there were instances of similar dedication in the Metropolitan area, and many magistrates were willing to take more modest steps. For example, in 1730, after several businessmen in the Strand received threatening letters demanding money, local justices "spent several hours" examining the documents and discussing stratagems to identify who had written them.[18] Similarly, in 1737, three men were convicted of a highway robbery near Hampstead after one of their number, Terence O'Bryan, had been arrested in the Tower Liberty by a local magistrate "on suspicion of being a naughty person". He was found in possession of a loaded pocket pistol and two coats, one worn on top of the other. Two justices then questioned him. Although the evidence was fairly nugatory, they threatened to commit him to prison and to advertise his appearance in the newspapers if he did not "discover his accomplices". Eventually, he cracked, provided information and offered to become a Crown witness.[19] In like manner, in 1798, Hannah Bromley, from the borough, was connected to a burglary because a woman who had learnt of the crime remembered hearing an "unusual noise and bustle" in the small hours of the morning on the night it occurred. Learning about this, the area's JPs sent their officers to search the courtyard where she lived where they discovered some of the stolen goods.[20]

---

17. See generally J. Styles, "An eighteenth-century magistrate as detective: Samuel Lister of Little Horton", 1982, pp.98-117.
18. *Read's Weekly Journal or British Gazetteer*, 14 November 1730.
19. OBSP, Trial of James Ryan et al, 4 January 1737.
20. Anon. *The Young and Thoughtless Criminal*, 1798, pp.4-5.

A new approach to magisterial detection in the capital was to be pioneered by Colonel de Veil, who, with the aid of government subventions, was particularly painstaking in his examination of suspects and in arranging follow up enquiries. De Veil was to solve several of the most notorious crimes of his era. On one occasion, a suspect was brought before him, on vague circumstantial evidence, accused of stealing a large quantity of plate from an eating-house near Chancery Lane. The colonel appreciated that this would "not justify a commitment". However, learning that a lock in the eatery had been picked, he suddenly asked the suspect to lend him his knife, and discovered that its point was missing. De Veil sent the arresting constable and the owner of the eating-house to search the crime scene, which duly produced the missing part of the blade. The suspect then made full admissions.[21] The Fielding brothers were to continue, and expand on, de Veil's legacy.

Rewards and Thief-Takers

Given that the formal agencies of the State were relatively weak and, after the Glorious Revolution, there was little political willingness to alter that situation, other means necessarily had to be developed to deal with crime in the years after 1688. One of them was to encourage the public to police itself via the use of rewards. In turn, the existence of such rewards, both state and (to a lesser extent) private, spawned the emergence of professional "thief-takers" who detected and convicted criminals for the bounties available.

The occasional presence of thief-takers in the London area had been noted in the late sixteenth century, and their numbers grew after 1660.[22] However, as Joseph Cox was to note in 1756, the level of thief-taking was in: "...proportion to the increase of the rewards designed for the suppression of robberies".[23] This meant that their heyday occurred after 1692, with

21. Sir T. Deveil, *Memoirs of the Life and Times of Sir Thomas Deveil, Knight*, 1748, p.55.
22. Anon, *News from Newgate Or, a true Relation of the manner of taking Seven persons, very notorious for Highway-men, In the Strand*, 1677, pp.4-5.
23. J. Cox, *A faithful Narrative of the most wicked and inhuman Transactions of that Bloody-Minded Gang of Thief-takers*, 1756, p.1.

the advent of large-scale government funded rewards.[24] Their expansion in the 1690s may also have been encouraged by the large number of coiners then at work, prior to a national re-issuing of the currency. Such criminals were inherently vulnerable to thief-takers. By the end of the seventeenth century, there appears to have been a hardcore of 11 Metropolitan men who were engaged in the trade on a professional footing, though there were others operating on a more occasional basis.[25] As well as arresting suspects, they would often take steps to ensure that the ensuing proceedings resulted in a conviction (and so a reward). In 1700, for example, Joseph Fisher was accused of housebreaking by a thief-taker named Anderson who "managed the prosecution" against him.[26]

Nevertheless, at the turn of the century, thief-takers were as likely to make their incomes through mediation between crime victims and criminals, as via rewards. Such men necessarily had to cultivate underworld contacts for information, and this encouraged them to negotiate the return of stolen property from thief to owner for payment, part of which they would receive. This was especially common where an item had little intrinsic value but was worth a great deal to its loser because it had sentimental value, was an important commercial document or some other form of record, or where, by its inherent nature, it would be hard to fence at a reasonable rate (such as a very distinctive timepiece).[27] Even for more conventional items, the loser was often prepared to pay rather more than a receiver, to secure its return.

As a result, most thief-takers made a mixed living by combining payments from negotiating the return of stolen goods with the rewards available for arresting and prosecuting felons to conviction. Unfortunately, from being directly involved in negotiations between criminals and victims it was often only a short step to becoming personally involved in organizing thefts and commercial receiving. In 1690, for example, the thief-taker John Whitwood was narrowly acquitted of perverting the course of justice. He had been

24. Parliament had experimented with a ten-pound reward for those who secured the conviction of felons in a temporary order made on 10 January 1650.
25. T. Wales, "Thief-Takers and their Clients in Later Stuart London", 2000, p.70.
26. Anon, *An Account of a new and strange discovery that was made by John Sheirly, alias Davis, & Joseph Fisher, the same day of their execution relating to the ordinary of Newgate*, 1700, pp.1-2.
27. B. De Mandeville, *An Enquiry into the Causes of the Frequent Executions at Tyburn*, 1725, p.10.

found with a thief named Taylor and another man named Eades, together with a valuable stolen silver tankard, in his own house. At trial, Whitwood called a witness: "...to prove that he chid his man for committing such a crime; and endeavoured to prosecute both Taylor and Eades". Why they should have been in his home in the first place was never fully explained.[28]

Whitwood set a pattern for subsequent decades, one that was followed by the most notorious thief-taker of the era, Jonathan. Wild used his early personal experience of custody to make extensive criminal contacts. He secured himself from most of the risks associated with negotiating the return of stolen items by avoiding physical possession of them. Many respectable crime victims, including Daniel Defoe, had recourse to his services. He continued operating from his office near Newgate, despite specific legislation being passed in 1718 that made accepting rewards for the return of stolen goods, without prosecuting, an offence. Eventually, however, he was prosecuted and convicted under the 1718 Act, being executed in 1725.

Wild's demise appears to have reduced (though it did not end) the involvement of thief-takers in mediation, and encouraged them to concentrate more of their efforts on seeking rewards for securing convictions. Although no single individual achieved Wild's dominance again, by the middle of the eighteenth century, there were between 30 and 40 active thief-takers in the London area, with a near full-time nucleus of 24 men working there. Much of their *modus operandi* had changed little from Wild's era, four decades earlier. Thus, the cultivation of criminal intelligence, stop and search of suspects, bullying, bribing, extracting confessions, and informing were all vital aspects of their work.[29] Some would resort to blackmail to make money. In 1700, Joseph Fisher offered a thief-taker named Anderson six guineas to make sure he was acquitted after he was accused of housebreaking. Unfortunately, Anderson insisted on twenty, which was beyond Fisher's means. He was capitally convicted.[30]

During the 1750s, two of the deputy turnkeys or gatekeepers at the Clerkenwell Gaol were prominent thief-takers (possibly working for Sir John

28. OBSP, Trial of John Whitwood, 15 January 1690.
29. J. L. McMullan, "The New Improved Monied Police", 1996, p.87.
30. Anon, *An Account of a new and strange discovery that was made by John Sheirly, alias Davis, & Joseph Fisher, the same day of their execution relating to the ordinary of Newgate,* 1700, pp.1-2.

Fielding). They would supplement their prison salaries with rewards, while using their occupation acquired criminal intelligence for their detective work. An inmate noted that they were: "...continually at the beck of certain persons, and go and take thieves at all times, and on all occasions". For example, one of them took a street robber, and received £15 as his share of the reward money.[31] Some private thief-takers became "attached" to one of the other justices' offices in the capital and performed many of the same tasks that the runners carried out.[32] Even as Fielding was establishing himself at Bow Street, a second group of magistrate based thief-takers was forming around Sir Samuel Gower, a leading JP in the Whitechapel area.

Thief-taking was not an employment for the weak or scrupulous. It carried considerable physical dangers. Wild suffered 17 wounds to his body during his career, and most thief-takers received scars in the course of their work. Even so, several men worked as thief-takers for over a quarter of a century, while the brothers Daniel and John Forrester operated for 40 years.[33] The "trade" did not attract men of good character. Their general conduct, irrespective of that pertaining to their professional activities, was often deplorable. Most of them, apart from Henry Fielding's handpicked men, appear to have had previous criminal records of their own. Some continued to offend despite their new careers. For example, in 1739, George Harris was committed to Newgate for rape.[34] In 1751, Gerard Bunn, another "noted Thief-Taker" of the period, whose evidence had hanged several men, was committed to the same prison for robbing a Dutch sailor.[35] The need for information also encouraged fraternisation between thief-takers and underworld elements. Significantly, many of the score or so of professional mid-eighteenth-century thief-takers lived in "thieves' sanctuaries", despite the perceived unpopularity and physical dangers of their calling.[36]

31. J. Ilive, *Reasons offered for the Reformation of the House of Correction in Clerkenwell*, 1757, p.37.
32. J. M. Beattie, "Sir John Fielding and Public Justice: The Bow Street Magistrates' Court, 1754–1780", 2007, p.73.
33. J. L. McMullan, "The New Improved Monied Police", 1996, pp.88-89.
34. *Daily Post*, 16 February 1739.
35. *General Evening Post*, 19 March 1751.
36. R. Paley, 1989, "Thief-takers in London in the age of the McDaniel gang c.1745-1754", 1989, p. 303.

Scandals

The whole thief-taking system was fraught with dangers. Even the availability of relatively small sums, such as those granted under the Gin Act of 1736 for reporting the unlicensed sale of spirits, bred numerous malicious and unfounded accusations. Although the Act required that those who gave information for reward should be "creditable" witnesses, many magistrates initially defined this as not being a (provably) convicted criminal. As a result, the most "destitute and dissolute" people sometimes convicted the eminently respectable on false evidence.[37] A few were eventually prosecuted for perjury. For example, in September 1738, a man and woman were convicted at the Middlesex Quarter Sessions and sentenced to a year's imprisonment for: "...swearing against several innocent persons for retailing spirituous liquors".[38] At the time of his death in 1739, the Middlesex Grand Jury had found several bills of indictment for perjury against the notorious informer Edward Parker (so hated he had to be buried in secret).[39] As a result of such cases, there was a growing distrust of informers on the part of many JPs, so that by the end of the 1730s it was increasingly difficult, if not impossible, to secure convictions solely on their testimony.[40]

Perhaps unsurprisingly, the huge sums available for the successful prosecution of felons had exactly the same results, with very much more serious consequences. They also produced similar popular and (eventually) judicial and jury reactions. There were numerous proven cases of professional thief-takers and ordinary members of the public committing perjury to secure rewards, while the former also had recourse to actively encouraging marginal individuals to commit crimes, with a view to claiming rewards for their prompt capture (entrapment). However, the sheer scale of the rewards available meant that even the well-to-do could find them enticing, so that perjury or exaggeration was committed not just: "...by the needy and unprincipled,

37. Anon, *A Short History of the Gin Act: Or, An Impartial Account of the Conduct of Some of those who have been intrusted with the Execution of it*, 1738, pp.1-18 and pp.26-27.
38. *Old Common Sense: Or, the Englishman's Journal*, 16 September 1738.
39. *Read's Weekly Journal, or, British-Gazetteer Saturday*, 6 January 1739.
40. J. Warner, F. Ivis and A. Demers, "A Predatory Social Structure: Informers in Westminster, 1737-1741", 2000, pp.619-620.

[but] even by the opulent". They encouraged ordinary prosecutors to "strain the circumstances" of an incident. As a result, what, in reality, were actually simple thefts (which did not carry a reward) sometimes became burglaries (which did) while private street quarrels might be turned into robberies.[41]

There were other problems with a reward-based system. It was widely believed to discourage many of London's police officers (of all types) from dealing with the capital's minor criminals, because of the paucity of remuneration available for convicting for lesser offences. Instead, they would sometimes be left to "mature" into more serious offenders. In 1785, Blizzard observed that several constables had told him: "...it is in our interest to let little fish go, that we may get great ones".[42] However, as the Police Committee of 1816 expressly noted, it was exactly at the early stage of a delinquent's career that his criminal progression might most readily be arrested.

Concern about Rewards

Almost from the beginning, it was appreciated that the reward system was likely to occasion injustice. For example, in 1696, only months after the advent of a £40 statutory reward for those who detected and prosecuted coiners to conviction, Sir Isaac Newton, the warden of the Mint, complained that the "reproach of prosecuting and swearing for money" had made it very difficult to secure convictions, because courts and jurors were averse to believing such potentially tainted evidence.[43]

Nevertheless, it was only in 1732 that the King became sufficiently concerned by reports of perjury and the "other ill consequences" resulting from large rewards to take action. He ordered that they be awarded at the discretion of the Lord Mayor and the judge who had presided over the relevant trial.[44] This proclamation did not come "out of the blue". It appears to have

41. Anon, *Directions for Prosecuting Thieves Without the Help of those False Guides, The Newgate Solicitor,* 1728, p.4.
42. W. Blizard, *Desultory Reflections on Police: with an essay on the means of preventing crimes and amending criminals*, 1785, p.18.
43. J. H. Langbein, *The Origins of Adversary Criminal Trial*, 2003, p.151.
44. *Gentleman's Magazine,* vol. 2, 1732, p.1029.

followed representations from Baron Thomson, the influential Recorder of London. Thomson had warned the King that the extra £100, over and above existing statutory schemes, being offered to those who convicted highwaymen and street robbers who committed their crimes in, or within, five miles of London, had acted as a temptation to wicked individuals to make a: "... trade of prosecutions for the sake of so large a reward, whereby it may be feared many perjuries will happen, and innocent lives be brought to destruction through this most infamous practice".[45]

Thomson's representations had been prompted by the exposure of John Waller, who had frequently prosecuted reward cases at the Old Bailey during the 1720s and early 1730s. He was finally caught when, under the name of John Trevor, he made a false allegation of highway robbery against John Edlin. When the matter came before a local JP for examination, the magistrate's instincts told him that something was amiss. He also felt that he had seen 'Trevor' on other occasions and, having made enquiries about Edlin, found him to be a man of good reputation. The JP committed Waller to Newgate to await trial at the Old Bailey, where he was duly convicted of perjury. Because this was only a misdemeanour, he was merely sentenced to imprisonment and the pillory.[46] However, while he was standing in the latter, at the Seven Dials, Edward Dalton, the brother of James Dalton, whom Waller had capitally convicted some 18 months earlier, took the opportunity to lead a crowd in beating him to death.[47] It seems that Waller had been exposed for less than five minutes before being mortally wounded by the "exasperated" mob.[48] James Dalton was a notorious career criminal who, at his trial, freely conceded that he had committed many capital offences, but who insisted that he was innocent of the crime for which he was eventually hanged. He described Waller as "common affidavit man" and former Newgate inmate. It is apparent that Waller had aroused considerable unease in several quarters before he was finally brought to justice.

However, James Dalton's selection as a "patsy" was not a coincidence. Waller, like other thief-takers, was well aware that prosecuting such a

45. *Read's Weekly Journal, or, British-Gazetteer*, 14 October 1732.
46. OBSP, Trial of John Waller, 25 May 1725.
47. OBSP, Trial of Edward Dalton and others, 6 September 1732.
48. *Grub-street Journal*, 15 June 1732.

notorious man would occasion little surprise. In a similar case involving an alleged housebreaker named Joseph Fisher, it was noted that the fact that he had previously been convicted of an almost identical offence, and pardoned on account of earlier military service to the King: "...induced his jury to believe what was sworn against him".[49] It was for the same reason that the MacDaniel gang, 20 years later, would prey on individuals who had already been tried and acquitted for small offences at the Old Bailey.[50]

With signal bad timing, but indicative of the scale of the problem, at the same sessions at which Edward Dalton was convicted of murdering Waller, an Irishman named Bartholomew Harnet attempted to prosecute William Holms for highway robbery, in similarly dubious circumstances. In this case, and influenced by the Waller incident, the jury acquitted without leaving court, and the presiding judge ordered that Harnet be detained for trial at the ensuing December sessions.[51] He was duly convicted of perjury and sentenced to transportation.[52] Despite this case, the following year, the Old Bailey Grand Jury presented four solicitors who had been: "...fomenting and carrying on prosecutions against innocent persons for the sake of rewards".[53]

Both Waller and Harnett had acted alone. However, the availability of rewards was to spawn much more extensive conspiracies. The most extreme of these involved a group of thief-takers led by Stephen McDaniel in the 1750s. Their modus operandi was rather more sophisticated than that used over two decades earlier. They would actively entice members of the Metropolitan underclass into committing crimes for which they would promptly be arrested. At least 10 were prosecuted, several to conviction and execution, by this group.[54] Eventually, McDaniel was caught after luring two youths into committing a "robbery" against one of his colleagues in Deptford, prompting public outrage when the plot was discovered.[55] Even so, Joseph Cox, the High

49. Anon, *An Account of a new and strange discovery that was made by John Sheirly, alias Davis, & Joseph Fisher, the same day of their execution relating to the ordinary of Newgate*, 1700, pp.1-2.
50. J. Cox, *A faithful Narrative of the most wicked and inhuman Transactions of that Bloody-Minded Gang of Thief-takers*, 1756, p.2.
51. OBSP, Trial of William Holms, 6 September 1732.
52. OBSP, Trial of Bartholomew Harnet, 6 December 1732.
53. *Gentleman's Magazine* vol. 3, 1733, p.493.
54. J. L. McMullan, "The New Improved Monied Police", 1996, p.91.
55. L. Radzinowicz, *A History of English Criminal Law and its Administration from 1750*, vol.2,

Constable of Blackheath, had had to go to almost heroic efforts to expose the gang.[56] This case was a major shock to the entire criminal justice system. It prompted the Fielding brothers to stress the integrity of their own runners.[57]

However, and as Isaac Newton's comment suggests, it would be a mistake to attribute the delay in reform until 60 years after large-scale rewards were first introduced, *purely* to a lack of awareness. In reality, although an increase in knowledge must have played *some* part in the process, a growing degree of sensitivity towards the injustice occasioned by such cases was almost as important. There appears to have been a reduction in previously "robust" attitudes towards the conviction of innocent, but socially marginal and sometimes even nefarious, individuals. Society became more nervous about treating them as unavoidable casualties of its war on crime.

Lawyers and Rewards

The availability of rewards provided a ready avenue for successful cross-examination of prosecution witnesses. This made it harder to secure convictions, especially after the major expansion in the use of defence counsel towards the end of the century. Witnesses were routinely asked how much they expected to earn from a conviction, and whether they were "straining" the evidence as a result.[58] For example, in 1787, William Garrow successfully defended two men accused of stealing a watch in a street robbery. The victim, John Harman, had been watching the Lord Mayor's procession and claimed that the pair had pushed him and snatched his watch while he was off balance. The defendants were clearly guilty of theft, but were they also guilty of robbery? It was a crucial issue for the prosecutor, because there was a statutory reward of £40 a head for the conviction of a robber, but no reward at all for men who stole without force. It was equally important to the defendants, as robbery was a capital offence. Garrow forced Harman to agree that it was part

1948-56, p.326.

56. J. Cox, *A faithful Narrative of the most wicked and inhuman Transactions of that Bloody-Minded Gang of Thief-takers*, 1756, pp. 1-25.

57. J. Fielding, *A Plan for Preventing Robberies Within Twenty Miles of London*, 1755, p.7.

58. A. N. May, *The Bar and the Old Bailey, 1750-1850*, 2003, p.113.

of the "fun of the day" for the crowd to push and shove, and that he lost his timepiece in the midst of this jostling. Garrow also pressured Harman into admitting that a constable had given instructions that the violence of the attack be emphasized, so that the offence could be charged as a robbery and Harman "get two forty's". The defendants were merely convicted of simple theft, and sentenced to transportation to Australia. No reward was paid.[59]

Members of the judiciary also expressed concern about the influence of rewards, even in the absence of defence counsel, and regularly questioned prosecutors about their motivation in bringing proceedings. For example, in 1786, after a Bow Street Runner gave evidence in a robbery case, the Recorder of London warned the jury to show the "strictest caution" before convicting on the testimony of witnesses who would receive a substantial payment. (They swiftly acquitted).[60] Similarly, when Hannah Lout and Mary Walker were accused of burglary, in 1790, on legally very dubious evidence, the presiding judge alerted the jury to the potential motivation behind the prosecution: "Gentlemen, you are trying these two prisoners for their lives; the consequence of which is, that if they are convicted there will be eighty pounds reward".[61]

Unsurprisingly, in these circumstances, by the second half of the eighteenth century juries were taking much greater care over potentially reward-driven evidence. Nevertheless, despite increased judicial caution and public concern, independent (of the Fielding brothers) thief-takers continued to operate after the 1750s. In the 1780s, William Blizzard could still note that victims of crime who were rich and vengeful might pay a "thief taker for the life of the robber".[62] Scandals based on the reward system also continued, albeit less dramatically. No amount of precautions could entirely eliminate the problems of a system premised on payment by results. Thus, the thief-taker Richard Swift was alleged to have personally run a Fagin-like school for criminals in London during the 1760s. As late as 1816, six constables, including a highly respected member of the Bow Street Patrol, were prosecuted for

59. J. H. Beattie, "Garrow for the Defence", 1991, pp. 49-53.

60. *The Times,* 29 April 1786, p.3.

61. OBSP, Trial of Mary Walker and Hannah Lout, 7 July 1790.

62. W. Blizard, *Desultory Reflections on Police: with an essay on the means of preventing crimes and amending criminals,* 1785, pp.34-35.

inciting the commission of crimes with a view to obtaining the attendant rewards for solving them. As a result, in 1818, most of the remaining fixed rewards for the conviction of offenders were ended by statute, being replaced by rewards granted at the court's discretion.[63]

Nevertheless, their use also attracted support until well into the century. For example, in 1744, the Middlesex Justices made representations to the Duke of Newcastle, the *Custos Rotulorum* of their county, asking that the rewards available for peace officers and members of the public who arrested felons be enhanced. They argued that it was very unlikely that, without a reward proportionate to the dangers: "...constables or others will hazard their lives and the ruin of their families".[64] In the 1750s, it was suggested that if the public carrying of unlicensed swords was fined, the money raised could be used for funding extra rewards.[65]

Accomplice Evidence

Accomplice evidence came in two forms. Felons who were still at liberty could, in theory, come forward to admit their crimes, impeach criminal colleagues, and claim a pardon as of legal right under a variety of old statutes. This practice had largely fallen into desuetude by the early eighteenth century. As was noted in 1781, although the system whereby a felon who admitted his guilt could become an "approver" against other felons, upon whose conviction he was entitled to a pardon, had never been formally abolished, it had been "gradually discouraged and disused".[66]

Much more commonly, an accomplice would attempt to make an informal (but almost always honoured) "deal" with the authorities. Unlike the situation with "approvers", such a pardon was not given as of right, but amounted to the promise of a recommendation for mercy, *if* the accomplice fulfilled his part of the agreement. This being done, the practice was to stop

63. D. Bentley, *English Criminal Justice in the Nineteenth Century*, 1998, p.8.
64. Anon, *The Constable's Assistant*, 2nd edn., 1808, p.14,
65. C. Jones, *Some Methods Proposed Towards putting a Stop to the Flagrant Crimes of Murder, Robbery, and Perjury*, 1752, pp.5-6.
66. W. Eden, *Principles of Penal Law*, 1781, p.170.

any prosecution and release the witness.[67] Such "evidences" would usually be detained in custody prior to trial, but, for obvious reasons, in a different prison to those they were going to incriminate. Normally, the evidence would be sent to the Marshalsea or the New Prison in Clerkenwell, while his accomplices would be committed to Newgate.[68]

In 1745, Joshua Brogden, the clerk to Sir Thomas de Veil, explained how such agreements might be effected. In one case, Henry Simms was brought before de Veil by a Covent Garden constable, accused of assault. However, on examination by Sir Thomas, it was established that the prisoner had recently broken out of the New Prison. Simms then asked to speak to the magistrate in private (to escape onlookers), claiming he could make "large discoveries". Sir Thomas agreed and took a statement from him implicating several other criminals.[69] More directly, in 1724, a footpad was so terrified at the sight of his examining magistrate preparing a *mittimus* to commit him to Newgate that he: "...instantly named a gang of five others, with whom he had been concern'd in many robberies".[70]

Some did not even have to be arrested. Mary Burton, one of a gang of shoplifters for whose prosecution the Crown had promised a substantial reward, surrendered herself to the authorities in order to be made an evidence against her confederates.[71] Similarly, after four men stole cloth from a shop in Wapping, a thief-taker identified a likely suspect, whose house was searched, revealing some of the stolen items. At this, one of the detained man's colleagues, although still at liberty, became fearful that his former accomplice would implicate him. He voluntarily went to the thief-taker's house and offered himself as an evidence. The thief-taker then went to a local JP and negotiated on this man's behalf, the magistrate agreeing to admit him as a Crown witness the following morning. The accomplice then implicated the other three other men involved in the crime, one of them his own brother,

67. Sir W. Holdsworth, *A History of English Law*, vol.xii, 1938, p.514.

68. J. Ilive, *Reasons offered for the reformation of the house of correction in Clerkenwell*, 1757, p.32.

69. OBSP, Trial of Henry Simms, 30 May 1745. Joshua Brogden was to be "inherited" by Henry Fielding, who unavailingly petitioned to have him appointed as an assistant magistrate at Bow Street.

70. *Weekly Journal or The British Gazetteer*, 30 May, 1724.

71. *Weekly Journal, or The British Gazetteer*, 9 July 1726.

and two of whom were still free. The thief-taker hired some assistance and arrested them.[72] Thomas Neaves, the leader of a gang of street robbers, and a prematurely returned transport, provides yet another illustration. Feeling insecure, he went voluntarily to a Southwark JP and gave information against his colleagues, who were immediately arrested and committed to Newgate, while Neaves was detained in the Compter prison. During his time in custody, he was very industrious about apprehending other former associates, who were tried at the May Sessions at the Old Bailey, where six were convicted and executed. At the following July Sessions, Neaves was produced before the court, formally: "...pleaded his Majesty's Pardon, and was discharged accordingly".[73]

The informality of this process could occasion problems. For example, when Stephen Dowdale, a habitual thief, became apprehensive that one of his companions was planning to impeach him, he decided to preempt this possibility, and gave as much information as he could against his erstwhile criminal colleagues. Unfortunately, most of them were alerted to what he was doing and escaped, while those who were prosecuted were acquitted. As a result, no convictions having been secured: "...some people thought proper to turn his own confession upon himself". He was capitally convicted in February 1730, largely on the strength of his earlier admissions. While under sentence of death (he died of disease before execution), Dowdale observed that he had been: "...hardly dealt with by those who had received his confession".[74] At his Old Bailey trial, a JP accepted that Dowdale had received a promise that the Justices would try to make him an evidence.[75] The Newgate ordinary was convinced that, had he lived, Dowdale would eventually have been pardoned.[76]

By the early 1700s, the growth of the press meant that it was sometimes possible for the authorities to actively encourage criminals to become evidences. Some foreign observers found this remarkable: "An announcement is published in the gazette and other public papers that those among the

72. OBSP, Trial of George Anderson and others, 9 Sept. 1742.
73. T. Neaves, *The Life of Thomas Neaves, The Noted Street-Robber*, London, 1729, pp.12-26.
74. A. L. Hayward, *Lives Of The Most Remarkable Criminals* ... 1927, p.524.
75. OBSP, Trial of Stephen Dowdle (sic). 28 Feb 1730.
76. Ordinary's Account, 17 April, 1730.

suspected who will deliver themselves up to justice, constitute themselves prisoners, denounce their accomplices and give evidence against them, will be pardoned". This appeared particularly strange when, as Cesar de Saussure noted, such felons might also receive a financial reward. However, even he acknowledged that many criminals who would otherwise escape were caught by this procedure.[77]

It was universally recognised that there was no merit in the individuals who gave accomplice evidence. In 1723, when William Duce faced execution at Tyburn for robbery, after being convicted on the evidence of John Dyer, his erstwhile gang leader, he left a letter pointing out that his own offences had been committed on Dyer's advice and urging.[78] In 1732, when Richard Marshall was convicted of burgling a JP's house in Islington, he complained that an evidence against him had been a thief for a quarter of a century, during which time he: "...brought so many People into trouble only to save himself".[79] Jack Hall and Richard Low, a pair of habitual housebreakers, escaped execution by hanging nine of their companions, but were ultimately executed after wounding a constable.[80] Early in his criminal career, the notorious Joseph Blake, known as "Bluebeard" after his swarthy countenance, had convicted four of his accomplices, who were then executed.[81]

Many, probably a majority, of accomplices who gave evidence subsequently re-offended.[82] Sometimes, this happened very quickly. Philip Lipscombe, who testified at the Old Bailey against an accomplice in February 1740, was back before that forum as a defendant in October of the same year.[83] Known as "puffs" in underworld cant, those who had given evidence to secure their own necks never fully regained the confidence of their erstwhile acquaintances, being looked upon with a: "...sort of shyness and

77. M. V. Muyden, (Ed.), *A foreign View of England in the reigns of George I and George II*, 1902, pp.116-117.
78. A. L. Hayward, *Lives Of The Most Remarkable Criminals*, 1927, pp.121-123.
79. OBSP, Trial of Richard Marshall and others, 11 Oct. 1732.
80. Anon, *A full and true account of the apprehending and taking of Jack Hall and Richard Low ...*, 1707, p.1.
81. J. Sheppard, *A Narrative of all the Robberies, Escapes, &c. of Jack Sheppard*, 2nd edn., 1724, pp.12-14.
82. J. Fielding, *A Plan for preventing Robberies Within twenty miles of London*, 1755, p.11.
83. OBSP, Trial of Philip Lipscombe, 15 October 1740.

Indifference, because they dare not trust him". Nevertheless, it appears to have been tacitly accepted, especially if it was done for immediate personal survival. This allowed many evidences, like Bluebeard, to make fresh criminal associates and continue their nefarious careers. The fact that legitimate employers who were aware of their pasts would be reluctant to hire them made this all the more likely.[84] It was for this reason that the footpad Thomas Neave found Metropolitan life very difficult after turning King's evidence. He reoffended within months of securing a pardon.[85]

Unsurprisingly, criminals were acutely aware of the risks that their colleagues posed. James Carrick fled immediately he received news that a fellow gang member had been captured, rightly assuming that he would be impeached.[86] In an attempt at reducing such dangers, some gangs entered into complicated agreements as to their obligations to each other if one of them was taken. According to Captain Alexander Smith, writing in 1719, a typical highwayman's oath would contain an undertaking to reveal nothing, if arrested, even if faced by execution: "And this oath, when I break in the least tittle may the greatest plagues and D—tion seize me here and hereafter".[87] It was a mark of "dying game" at the scaffold and so becoming the object of popular approval that a condemned man did not "whittle" on his comrades, refusing pressure from the ordinary and gallows' officials to impeach others.[88]

Nevertheless, such compacts notwithstanding, solidarity between criminals was usually minimal. As Carrick realistically accepted, although his colleague had sworn on the four evangelists not to betray them: "Fear of Death might in all probability, notwithstanding the Engagement of a solemn oath to the contrary, make him to impeach us".[89] Even strong bonds of personal affection could break down in these circumstances. Early in his career, the notorious highwayman John Everett reluctantly impeached his erstwhile

84. J. Fielding, *A Plan for Preventing Robberies Within Twenty miles of London*, 1755, pp.7-8.
85. T. Neaves, *The Life of Tho. Neaves, The Noted Street-Robber*, 1729, p. 24 and p.41.
86. J. Carrick, *A Compleat and True Account of all the Robberies Committed by James Carrick*, 1722, p.22.
87. A. Smith, *A Complete History of the Highwaymen*, A.L. Hayward (Ed.), 1926, pp.188-189.
88. A. McKenzie, "Martyrs in Low Life? Dying Game in Augustan", 2003, p.184.
89. J. Carrick, *A Compleat and True Account of all the Robberies Committed by James Carrick*, London, 1722, p.22.

friend, Richard Bird, after deciding that: "I had better hang twenty, than be squeez'd myself". Bird was duly executed, though Everett later reproached himself for his conduct.[90] Even family members might implicate each other. The brother of a burglar named Romsey "turn'd evidence" against his sibling after being captured in 1741.[91]

The circle of criminals associated with Jack Sheppard, a serial prison escapee in the early 1720s, is particularly illustrative of this phenomenon. Jack had committed several robberies in and around Clare Market with his brother William and girlfriend Elizabeth Lyon. However, on being apprehended, William immediately impeached his sibling. Before he could be held pursuant to his brother's evidence, Jack met an old companion for a pre-arranged game of skittles. This man, quite independently, brought along a constable and sought to have him arrested. Subsequently, after he had escaped from this imbroglio, Elizabeth Lyon betrayed Sheppard to the notorious thief-taker Jonathan Wild.

As these examples suggest, in some respects, the accomplice system worked very well. The use of such evidence against highwaymen: "...inspires them with distrust and prevents from uniting in associations".[92] Quite frequently, the arrest of one gang member might produce snowballing chains of mutual incrimination, allowing examining magistrates to select their evidence from several equally well-qualified candidates. However, the system was necessarily susceptible to abuse, as desperate individuals of little probity sought to save themselves at the expense of others. The more information they could provide, the more likely it was that they would warrant immunity, encouraging fabrication.

Concern about the accomplice system

Because of its inherent dangers, both the judiciary and juries became increasingly nervous about receiving and convicting on accomplice evidence. Indeed, the practice occasioned wider concerns about the justice provided by the

90. J. Everett, *A Genuine Narrative of the Memorable Life and Actions of John Everett*, 1730, p.34.
91. *The Gentleman's Magazine*, 1741, vol. 11, p.552.
92. J. W. von Archenholz, *A picture of England: containing a description of the laws, customs, and manners of England ...*, 1790, p.181.

whole criminal process.[93] The practical consequences of this anxiety can be seen in the robbery trial of Henry Fluellin and John Slade in 1738. This was largely based on the evidence of their accomplice, William Udal. The pressure on him to implicate others was readily apparent. It was only when other suspects, who had initially been implicated by Udal, could not be arrested that he had made the allegation against the two men. The victim was prepared to swear positively to Fluellin's identity, but was not sure about Slade. Fluellin was convicted but Slade was acquitted. The accomplice's evidence, on its own, was clearly not enough for the jury.[94]

Even more significantly, after the middle of the eighteenth century, the uncorroborated testimony of an accomplice, "alone and unsupported", was *legally* not deemed to be enough to secure a conviction.[95] It seems that this rule first emerged in December 1744, though its operation was initially uncertain. In that month, the *Sessions Papers* record three acquittals in which the grounds for returning a "not guilty" verdict appear to have been a simple want of corroboration. Although the "rule" does not *always* seem to have been observed, there were numerous similar cases after 1744 in which a lack of corroboration was the only ground for an acquittal. Thus, in 1761, Thomas Taylor and John Russell were acquitted of stealing 12 cod fish after one of their accomplices, Stephen Boon testified against them; as there was: "... no other evidence of credit to confirm Boon, who owned himself to be a guilty person, they were acquitted".[96] By contrast, at the trial of several men convicted in 1786, prosecuting counsel stressed that the main Crown witness, although an accomplice, was "corroborated in many circumstances" by other witnesses.[97]

Many Metropolitan law enforcement officers and magistrates, including Henry Fielding, deprecated the existence of this new corroboration rule, feeling that it made convicting the guilty excessively difficult. Perhaps as a consequence of such criticism, it was watered down in 1787 to being merely

93. L. Radzinowicz, *A History of English Criminal Law and its Administration from 1750*, vol.2, 1956, p.54.
94. OBSP, Trial of John Slade and Henry Fluellin, 6 September 1738.
95. A. N. May, *The Bar and the Old Bailey, 1750–1850*, 2003, p.113.
96. OBSP, Trial of Thomas Taylor and John Russell, 16 January 1761.
97. OBSP, Trial of William Oliver and others, 31 May 1786.

advisory, requiring a mandatory judicial warning to the jury on the dangers of convicting on unsupported accomplice testimony, rather than a firm direction to acquit in its absence.[98] (The need for such a warning survived in England until 1994). Although accomplice evidence gradually declined in importance after the 1750s, it remained a vital part of the prosecution armoury until the end of the period.

The Coroner's Investigation

The coroner's most important duty was to investigate suspicious or sudden deaths, especially those that might have been occasioned by murder or suicide. Additionally, they examined all deaths, however caused, that occurred in prison.[99] Their function was vital in homicide investigations, as a system in which victims played a primary role in bringing prosecutions was necessarily unviable in such cases, the victim, of course, being dead. The coroner could ensure that a prosecution for murder ensued even where the: "...relations of the deceased or others refuse [to prosecute], or are slack in so doing".[100]

Coroners' inquests that resulted in verdicts of murder or manslaughter, as opposed to "natural death", death caused "accidentally, casually, and by misfortune", suicide, or the era's equivalent of an open verdict ("but how... no evidence doth appear to the said jurors"), and which named likely perpetrators, would be used to found homicide (usually murder) indictments at the Old Bailey or provincial Assizes. A coroner had the power to indict directly to the higher courts (as they would until 1977), without needing the agreement of those forums' own grand juries before a trial could take place. Of course, this required that their inquisition positively identify a suspect. At the Old Bailey murder trial of Edward Dalton, the coroner who had initially investigated the victim's death testified that he had not been able to

98. J. H. Langbein, *The Origins of Adversary Criminal Trial*, 2003, pp.205-210.

99. For example, in 1788, when John Morris died in Newgate prison, the City of London Coroner concluded that he died a "natural death" after ailing for five months, and was "not misused at all". The prison apothecary gave evidence that he had attended him in a professional capacity: LMCLIC650010013 document at www.londonlives.org Last accessed 17 January 2011.

100. H. Care, *English Liberties: or, the Free-Born Subject's Inheritance*, 1703, p.179.

commit anyone for trial, as the jury had not been satisfied as to the identity of the killers. He even admitted that, as there was then no obvious suspect, he had not been very: "...curious in examining the witnesses, and therefore no indictment could be grounded on my Inquisition".[101]

If a suspect was identified by an inquest, not only could they be sent for trial, but a constable could be required to enforce a coroner's warrant to arrest them, if they were not already in custody.[102] Additionally, a coroner could commit a suspect directly to prison, pending trial. Thus, in 1741, John King, the Middlesex coroner, sent Hannah Biggs to Newgate for murdering her illegitimate child.[103] Normally, in such cases, any ensuing trial would be held on both the Grand Jury's indictment and that from the Coroner's inquest. Coroners' juries were normally more, rather than less, willing to commit homicide suspects for trial than were Grand Juries; they did not usually require so strong a *prima facie* case.[104] As a result, albeit very rarely, a homicide case would proceed to trial even where the grand jury had found the bill of indictment "ignoramus". This meant that the trial was heard solely on the coroner's inquisition (a standard, signed, parchment document). Such cases were very unlikely to produce a conviction, the Grand Jury's assessment normally proving correct.

By contrast, if a coroner's court found that someone had died of natural causes, any subsequent prosecution for murder was highly unlikely to be successful, and was often not even attempted. For example, when Mary Pritchard died in January 1740, her husband claimed that it was the result of a beating she had received a few weeks earlier from John Pateman. Pateman was committed to Newgate by a magistrate to await trial. However, a coroner's inquisition subsequently found that Mary had died of natural causes. There was no attempt even to indict Pateman, and he was discharged at the following gaol delivery.[105]

---

101. OBSP, Trial of Edward Dalton, 6 Sept 1732.
102. S. Welch, *A Proposal to render effectual a Plan to remove the nuisance of Common Prostitutes from the streets of this Metropolis*, 1758, pp.27-28.
103. *Common Sense or The Englishman's Journal*, 21 March, 1741.
104. R. Baldwin, *Considerations on some laws relating to the office of Coroner*, 1776, p.63.
105. R. Paley (Ed.), *Justice in 18th-Century Hackney*, 1991, pp.56-57.

Effectiveness

The effectiveness of the coroner's investigation was limited by the relatively low prestige accorded to both his office and inquest, the lack of regular expert medical evidence at such hearings in the early decades of the century, and the inherent limitations of the era's medical knowledge, even when it was called. The position did not necessarily attract the highest quality men, at least in urban Middlesex. Until 1751, much of its remuneration was still regulated by an Act dating from 1487, and was woefully inadequate. In 1751, it was placed on a new statutory basis, which provided a modest fee of 20s and travel expenses for each inquest held.[106] Additionally, the training for those appointed was almost non-existent. This sometimes led to a lack of care and diligence. Their effectiveness was further limited by a widespread belief, at the start of the period, that only sudden deaths, with clear evidence of violence, should be the subject of inquiry. This discouraged the use of medical evidence as, where the cause of death was obvious, there was little perceived need for such assistance.[107]

Some coroners' inquisitions were lamentable in their inefficiency. For example, in 1764, a respectable North Country surgeon was forced into print, when he and his wife were blamed for the murder of one of their female servants, who appears to have committed suicide by drowning herself after being accused of theft. The inquest jury, infected by local gossip and anger, with no apparent discouragement from the coroner, and without the surgeon and his spouse being given an opportunity to put their case, returned a verdict accusing them of murdering the dead girl. The coroner then issued a warrant for their arrest and they were indicted at the Durham Assizes. Both defendants were swiftly acquitted.[108]

Nevertheless, despite such cases, it seems that many coroners were at least competent and some were very good. For example, those involved in examining suspected homicides in the North, at the start of the nineteenth century, manifested a considerable degree of determination when carrying out their investigations, usually acting swiftly after being summoned

106. P. Knapman, "The Crowner's Quest", 1993, p.719.

107. M. Jackson, *New Born Child Murder*, 1997, pp.85-86.

108. J. Oliphant, *The Case of Mr James Oliphant, Surgeon,* 1768, pp.1-60.

by a local JP and enquiring thoroughly into the matters that came before them.[109] Much the same could be said of many, though certainly not all, of their eighteenth-century Metropolitan counterparts. As a result, one modern medical observer, reviewing the documentary evidence of inquests into 377 suspicious deaths in eighteenth-century Middlesex, concluded that they ranged from perfunctory to penetrating, depending on the personal ability and energy of the coroner involved and the concern that individual cases had aroused.[110] For example, in 1727, after Widdington Darby was shot in the head and killed in his apartment within the Inns of Court, a coroner supervised an exceptionally thorough autopsy, conducted by an eminent London surgeon. During it, Darby's brain was removed and the fatal bullet recovered. This was then compared with other bullets, and the calibres of various pistols, found in a suspect's lodgings. They produced a positive match. (The suspect escaped from Newgate prior to trial and was never seen again).[111]

A general increase in professionalism can also be discerned during the course of the 1700s. For example, in earlier periods, there had been considerable cultural resistance to, and religious concern about, the forensic dissection of corpses. However, the late seventeenth and early eighteenth centuries saw a marked growth in the willingness of coroners to order full examinations. In 1729, 40 per cent of all suspected homicide cases resulted in judicially ordered autopsies.[112] By the mid-century, it had long ceased to be an exceptional source of information at London inquests, and it became even more common in ensuing decades, being present in the great majority of cases by the end of the period. It was gradually accepted that the medical cause, as opposed to merely the circumstances, of violent or suspicious deaths should usually be reported at an inquest, and that this required a proper postmortem examination.[113] In the 1780s, Samuel Farr could claim that a dissection was "almost always necessary" when examining a dead body.[114]

109. R. W England, "Investigating Homicides in Northern England, 1800-1824", 1985, p.120.
110. T. R. Forbes, "Inquests into London and Middlesex Homicides, 1673-1782", 1977, pp.219-220.
111. A. L. Hayward, *Lives Of The Most Remarkable Criminals*, 1927, pp.417-420.
112. V. McMahon, "Reading the Body: Dissection and the 'Murder' of Sarah Stout, Hertfordshire, 1699", 2006, p.1 and p.24.
113. T. R. Forbes, "Inquests into London and Middlesex Homicides, 1673-1782", 1977, pp.219-220.
114. S. Farr, *Elements of Medical Jurisprudence*, 1788, p.74.

If a coroner decided that he needed a medical opinion he would normally summon the doctor who had attended the dead man prior to his demise, especially early in the century. However, if no one had treated the deceased person, the nearest medical man was often selected, irrespective of his specific qualifications and area of expertise. During the eighteenth century, this would frequently be the local parish surgeon. In one case, Alexander Reed, the surgeon to the Chelsea Hospital, even carried out an autopsy on the body of a man for whose murder two of the hospital's pensioners were standing trial. (He also gave the defendants a good character and a partial alibi).[115] Little was to change in this respect until the 1800s and, in particular, the advent of the Medical Witnesses Act of 1836, which also provided a statutory basis for their remuneration. The first lectureship in forensic medicine, at Guy's Hospital, was not established until 1831.[116]

England lagged behind much of Europe in this regard. As Farr observed, in foreign countries, forensic medicine had even been: "...dignified with a peculiar name, as the medicine of the courts, legal medicine, or medical jurisprudence". Nevertheless, knowledge of "best practice" was readily available, because many continental works on the subject had been imported. Furthermore, in 1788, and concerned at the lowly status of forensic medicine in England, Farr adapted a Swiss textbook to produce his own work on the subject. In it, he urged that all the body's cavities should be opened and that an examination be conducted with surgical instruments rather than "coarse and rude" knives that might mutilate the corpse without establishing the cause of death.[117] Of course, it is at least questionable as to whether some of the era's autopsies were tremendously helpful, anywhere in Europe, given the rudimentary state of much medical knowledge, even where they followed best practice. For example, there were no reliable tests for even the most common poisons until the 1800s.[118]

115. OBSP, Trial of Joseph Gould and Jonathan Stevens, 18 September 1765.
116. K. D. Watson, "Medical and Chemical Expertise in English Trials for Criminal Poisoning", 2006, pp.378-379.
117. S. Farr, *Elements of Medical Jurisprudence*, 1788, p.1 and p.74.
118. K. Kesselring, "Detecting 'Death Disguised'", 2006, p.26.

Reporting Suspicious Deaths

No matter how good a coroner's inquest might be, the proper medico-legal investigation of suspicious deaths requires that there is an effective method for bringing them to his attention.[119] In the eighteenth-century Metropolis, the coroner would usually be summoned by a constable or JP from the parish or precinct where a suspicious death had occurred, and a body been found. For example, in 1759, when Susannah Walker was murdered by her niece Mary Edmondson, while at home in Rotherhithe, neighbours detained Edmondson at the crime scene, after becoming suspicious of the younger woman's claim that the killing was committed by a gang of burglars. They then notified the Churchwardens and officers of the parish who, in turn, sent an account of the matter to the Surrey Coroner.[120]

Unfortunately, in Middlesex, during the middle of the century, there were claims that some coroners were forced to take more active steps to ensure that suspicious deaths came to their attention. In 1761, for example, one of the county's coroners was concerned that, instead of receiving notice of a violent death from a peace officer, as should happen, a coroner was often forced: "...meanly by himself or emissaries, to run or hunt after the dead".[121] Numerous cases of sudden death, in strange circumstances, probably slipped through the net as a result, and went entirely unexamined.

Many Metropolitan parishes employed "searchers" to decide whether sudden deaths were worthy of investigation. These were usually elderly local women who would examine a corpse after an unexpected death, such as that of a young person, and then report their findings to the parish clerk. If the searcher voiced concern, the clerk might inform the coroner.[122] For example, in 1735, Margaret Hambleton and two of her daughters were accused of murdering another daughter, Catherine, when the landlady in their rooming house became suspicious after seeing a coffin arrive at her premises. The landlady told her neighbours, who immediately sent for the local searchers.

---

119. J. Havard, *The Detection of Secret Homicide*, 1960, pp.77-78.
120. Anon, *A Genuine Narrative of the Trial and Condemnation of Mary Edmondson, for the Murder of Mrs. Susannah Walker, her Aunt*, 2nd edn., 1759, pp.9-10 and p.16.
121. Anon, *A Treatise of Distresses, Replevins, and Avowries*, 1761, p.280.
122. T. R. Forbes, "Inquests into London and Middlesex Homicides, 1673-1782", 1977, pp.219-220.

These women arrived promptly and carried out an initial investigation by candlelight. They made a second visit to inspect the corpse the following morning, when the light was better, and had then noticed bruises around the dead woman's neck. This led them to suspect that she had been strangled, rather than dying of convulsions, as the defendants claimed, especially as the body evinced no signs of having had a fit. A surgeon was sent for and confirmed their diagnosis; the coroner was then informed.[123]

To take another example, in 1773, Elizabeth Hanson, an apprentice silk winder of about sixteen years of age, died after a prolonged course of mistreatment during which she had been regularly beaten, chained to a wall and denied food by her master and his wife (Mr and Mrs Morgan), to the latter of whom she was apprenticed. The searcher saw bruises on her dead body and signs of emaciation. Mrs Morgan offered her bread and cheese, along with a pot of beer, and begged her to say that the girl had died of a fever, and to ignore what she had seen, as otherwise the couple "would be ruined". In this case, the searcher did report on what she had observed and an inquest and trial ensued.[124] However, as this example suggests, a searcher could easily be subject to illicit pressure or low-level bribery. It is impossible to say how many succumbed to such blandishments.

The Coroner's Jury

Having decided to hold an investigation, the coroner would instruct a local constable to summon jurors from the parish in which the death had occurred, or those immediately adjacent to it. The requirement that jurors be local was still thought to be important, as the dead man's: "...neighbours are supposed to be the best judges of the fact". Unlike trial juries, where there was no expectation that jurors would have personal knowledge of the matters on which they passed judgment, early modern coroners' juries often relied on personal knowledge to help identify secret homicide. They might know, for example, whether there were obvious reasons for suspicion: had a failed

123. OBSP, Trial of Margaret Hambleton and others, 15 October 1735.
124. T. R. Forbes, "Inquests into London and Middlesex Homicides, 1673-1782", 1977, p.219.

business transaction led to recriminations and anger between the parties; was there a history of abuse between spouses?[125] Although strained in eighteenth-century London, some such awareness was probably often still present.

Usually, 24 jurors would be called, although some might fail to attend. Inquests could not sit with less than 12 men, and it was rare to find fewer than 18. In theory, they were normally drawn from the same "middling" social groups that provided the trial juries found at Metropolitan Quarter Sessions and the Old Bailey. However, although coroner's jurors were supposed to be "good and sufficient men", if Saunders Welch is to be believed, it was a singularly unpopular form of jury service. As a result, constables would often be forced to summon: "...very indifferent people, both of character and worth". Frequently, they were people with whom the constables had had a personal disagreement. As Welch acknowledged, this was unfortunate, as the coroner's role in identifying murder meant that his inquest was of the "highest consequence to society".[126]

The Inquest

The speed with which coroners sat following a death, especially in an urban environment, can be astonishing to modern eyes. In 1728, for example, after an elderly Frenchman shot himself in Charles Street, the inquest met on the evening of the day he killed himself, received evidence from the dead man's friends as to his mental state, and returned a verdict of "lunacy" that same night.[127] This did, at least, mean that memories were fresh and trails less likely to have run cold.

Jurors would normally be sworn in at the start of the procedure and then informed by the coroner of their duties. Typically, this was: "...to inquire, on behalf of the King, how and by what means Richard Fenn [illustrative example] came to his death". Once this was done, both the coroner and all members of his jury would physically inspect the body of the dead man.

125. K. Kesselring, "Detecting 'Death Disguised'", 2006, p.23.

126. S. Welch, *A Proposal to render effectual a Plan to remove the nuisance of Common Prostitutes from the streets of this Metropolis*, 1758, pp.27-28.

127. *Daily Post*, 12 August 1728.

This was vital. Indeed, they did not have the authority to return a verdict on a suspicious death in which the corpse was not available. As a result, they also had the power to: "…take up a dead body out of the grave, in order to view it".[128] Where necessary, they had no hesitation about doing so.

The body would normally be laid out, usually on a table, in a building near where it had been found or in which the coroner sat. As a matter of law this had to be located in the same parish as that in which the corpse had been discovered. Typically, the building might be an inn or tavern. More rarely, a workhouse might be employed, as could any other building that was large enough to hold 30 or more people.[129] For example, the coroner's jury that sat on the death of Edward Luttrell, having viewed the body: "…adjourn'd to the Sun Ale-house, over against Norfolk-Street, there to receive depositions".[130] Similarly, in 1792, when Thomas Shelton, the City of London Coroner, instructed the beadles and constables of St. Dunstan's to summon 24 men from their parish to sit on an inquest on the death of William Jackson, they were told to meet two days later at 10 am at the Sign of the Cock in Fleet Street.[131]

Coroners' juries decided by a simple majority, unlike those found in a criminal trial. Where there had been a murder they would, if possible, identify its likely perpetrator, as with Mary Edmondson. However, this was often not possible, in which case, as the coroner who presided over the inquest into the murder of the Marr family in 1811 noted, their verdict would have to be: "Wilful Murder against some person or persons unknown".[132] Even if no suspects had initially been found, the coroner's involvement seems to have encouraged the supply of information as to possible perpetrators. For example, in a notorious murder case from 1699, a member of the public had been alerted to the killers' identity by an anonymous letter, which she then passed on to a local constable, who arranged to have the suspects arrested

128. J. Impey, *The Office and Duty of Coroners*, 1800, p.17.
129. T. R. Forbes, "Inquests into London and Middlesex Homicides, 1673-1782", 1977, pp.207-220.
130. Anon (By a Gentleman of the Inner Temple), *The Widow Lutterel's Cry for Justice for the Blood of her Murthered Husband*, 1722, p.17.
131. LMCLIC650050009 document at www.londonlives.org Last accessed 17 February 2011.
132. Anon, *Fairburn's Account of the Dreadful Murder of Mr. Marr and Family, … Including the Whole Investigation Before The Coroner's Inquest*, 2nd edn., 1812, p.18.

in the middle of the night at their lodgings in the Strand. The following morning, they were both produced before the coroner, who had already sat on the dead woman's body. He examined the two men separately, so that they "confused each other with their answers" and revealed their guilt.[133]

As well as committing suspects to prison pending trial, and issuing warrants for their arrest if they were still at liberty, the coroner would also bind: "...all proper persons over in a recognizance, to prosecute, and give evidence".[134] This might require witnesses to give evidence twice, once at the inquest and once at trial. As a result, Rebecca Holder, testifying at the Old Bailey in a murder case, could observe: "I was last Monday before the Coroner".[135] Occasionally, discrepancies in their evidence to the two forums would be identified. However, although a coroner was required to return the recognisances of witnesses who had given evidence at his inquest to the criminal courts, he was not responsible for their subsequent appearance at trial, let alone for finding further evidence to bolster the prosecution case.[136] Sometimes, a coroner might also be called to give evidence about his investigation at the ensuing trial on indictment.

An assortment of witnesses would normally testify at the coroner's inquest, responding to a call for anyone to come forward who could give evidence as to: "...when, how, and by what means [victim's name] came to his death". Thus, constables who had been summoned to a suspicious death would give evidence of the body's discovery; surgeons would give any conclusions reached in an autopsy, if one was conducted; neighbours would testify about anything that they were aware of that appeared suspicious. Witness evidence would be taken down as depositions, which their makers would then sign, though coroners' jurors would normally be given an opportunity to question them about their testimony before they did so. These depositions could be adduced at a subsequent trial on indictment *if* their makers were, by then,

133. Anon, *An Account of the apprehending & taking of Mr. John Robinson and William Criss for the murther of Mrs. Mary Robinson*, 1699, pp.1-2.

134. J. Impey, *The Office and Duty of Coroners*, 1800, pp.56-66.

135. OBSP, Trial of Mary Terry, 14 July 1742.

136. J. Oliphant, *The Case of Mr James Oliphant, Surgeon*, 1768, pp.1-60.

dead, unable to travel through illness, or had been abducted at the behest of the defendant.[137]

The inquisitorial process that coroners' inquests employed was very different to the procedures used in common law courts. Unlike a criminal trial jury, the coroner's jury was not confined to a specific time or place to produce its verdict. The coroner could adjourn the jury to another day and/or place if necessary, to get further evidence that would be helpful in reaching a decision. Additionally, coroners' jurors appear to have taken a highly active role in proceedings, being much more involved in the investigation than their Old Bailey counterparts, frequently making suggestions for further enquiries. Occasionally, coroners would also work closely with JPs to investigate obvious and sophisticated murders, as with Catherine Hayes' killing of her husband.

Operation

Examining a selection of inquests shows how the system worked in practice. For example, the morning after receiving reports of the suspicious death of Susannah Walker, the Surrey coroner summoned a jury from Rotherhithe and neighbouring parishes, who sat at the Noah's Ark public house, within a few doors of the dead woman's home. Having been sworn in, the jury inspected the corpse, apparently without medical assistance, noting that Walker's throat was cut but that no other part of her body was injured. In conjunction with the coroner, they then examined the neighbours who had first come across the crime scene. Next, Edmondson (the main suspect) was produced from custody and questioned. The coroner then directed the jury as to the law, and allowed them to withdraw to consider the evidence. They returned a verdict: "That Mary Edmondson was guilty of murdering Mrs. Susannah Walker, widow, by cutting of her throat with a case-knife, in a most barbarous, cruel and inhuman manner". On receiving this, the coroner made out a warrant committing Mary to the county gaol in Southwark, pending her trial at Kingston Assizes. At that trial, it also emerged that the

137. *Lord Morley's Case* (1666) 6 How. St. Tr. 769.

coroner had personally conducted a thorough search of the dead woman's house, to look for evidence, prior to sitting with his jury.[138]

Similarly, when Mary Terry was accused of murder at the Old Bailey, William Wintx, a coroner's deputy, gave evidence about the steps that had been taken to examine the place where the body had been discovered. He observed that he had gone with the jury to the room where the corpse was found, and noted that, although its head was almost cut off, he could find no blood on the floor, even after he had examined it with a candle. This led him to conclude that the murder was not committed there. The whole house was then carefully, if unsuccessfully, searched for blood.[139]

The inquest into the death of Ann Sharp, conducted in Marylebone in October 1760 is particularly revealing, as the author of a detailed tract on the inquest was one of the 24 local men summoned for jury service (in his case one of eight called by their parish constable), of whom 23 eventually sat. The hearing took place in the King's Head tavern. Sharp, who seems to have dabbled in prostitution, had apparently died of the combined effects of venereal disease and alcoholism before being buried in a local churchyard. However, on her death bed she attributed her illness to wounds inflicted with a blade by three wealthy local "rakes", one of them a titled man, who had been her patrons.

In advance of the inquest, the coroner requested in writing that Sharp's body be exhumed. This was done the evening before the hearing. The sexton and an assistant were then given a rusty sword and old firearm and paid to guard the corpse overnight in a shed in the churchyard, while a watchman was instructed to visit regularly, as there were fears that the rakes might try to recover it to prevent inspection. Two local surgeons were summoned by messenger, but were out when he arrived. Instead, two other surgeons, attracted by the crowd, were pressed into service and inspected the body with the coroner and his jury, while it lay on a table in the shed. All then repaired to the tavern and listened to a number of witnesses describing the life and final illness of the dead woman. A lawyer was present to take a note

138. Anon, *A Genuine Narrative of the Trial and Condemnation of Mary Edmondson, for the Murder of Mrs. Susannah Walker, her Aunt.* London, 1759, 2nd edn. pp.9-10 and p.16.

139. OBSP, Trial of Mary Terry, 14 July 1742.

of proceedings for the (wealthy) potential suspects. The medical evidence was, apparently, overwhelming. Although Sharp had been very badly treated by the three men, this was not the cause of her death. The jurors asked several questions of the witnesses on their own initiative.[140] (Not everyone accepted this conclusion, some arguing that the dead woman's injuries must have been subtly linked to the ensuing death).[141]

Mr Fielding's Men

Sir Thomas de Veil had provided the public access to a magistrate on a regular basis, at fairly reliable times, in his house in Bow Street. However, although he had personally investigated serious crimes with considerable thoroughness, his work was primarily, and necessarily, magisterial. He was not supported by a force of detectives and there were time constraints on what a single man could do. The advent of quasi-state detectives would wait until the appointment of Henry Fielding, de Veil's lineal successor (there was a two year gap between their tenure of the house in Bow Street).

In November 1749, Fielding, who was already a JP for Westminster (appointed in 1748) and Middlesex (early in 1749), began using the Bow Street police office as his own headquarters. Initially, he worked with his blind half brother, John Fielding (also a magistrate) and Saunders Welch, the High Constable of Holborn, as his assistants. After Henry's death in 1754, John became the "chief Magistrate" at Bow Street with Saunders Welch as his assistant JP Sir John (he was knighted in 1761), though blind, was to be a major figure in Metropolitan police reform until his own death in 1780. However, to a significant degree, he carried on the work initiated by his older half-brother.

In 1749, the Duke of Newcastle had summoned Henry Fielding to a meeting with his representative to discuss various proposals that could be put to the Privy Council for bringing an end to the apparent spate of Metropolitan

140. Anon (By one of the Jury), *The True and Whole Proceedings of the Coroner's Inquest at St. Mary-Le-Bonne; On Saturday, October the 11th, 1760. Touching the Death of Ann Sharp*, 1760, pp.3-24.

141. Anon (By a Lover of Justice), *An Answer to the Pamphlet wrote by the Juryman Touching the Death of Ann Sharp*, 1760, pp.3-21.

murders and robberies in the aftermath of the Seven Years War. Fielding spent four days drawing up a plan of action, that was then agreed and funded by the government, which deposited six hundred pounds into his bank account. He undertook to destroy several large Metropolitan gangs with this money, and used some of it to pay an informer to: "...betray them into the hands of a set of thief-takers whom I had enlisted into the service". The notion of government financial support for an individual magistrate in the Metropolitan area was not unprecedented. However, his grant included an allowance for officers as well, which was novel, although relatively informal groups of constables had already been established to deal with specific Metropolitan crime problems.

The first operations of Henry Fielding's "people", essentially a body of retained thief-takers who were later to become popularly known as the "Bow Street Runners" (the title is sometimes mistakenly ascribed to members of the later patrols which operated out of that location), and more correctly as Principal Officers, took place in 1750. Like any other individuals, these men were eligible for the rewards available for convicting criminals. However, although the runners would often follow their former trades and occupations while employed by the Fieldings, unless actively engaged in responding to a summons, they also received a small weekly stipend. Additionally, and unlike many "private" thief-takers, who could be highly corrupt, Fielding's men were dismissed if it was suspected that they were operating improperly. Indeed, they were quite frequently recruited from parish constables who had finished their year in office. All but one of the original batch had this qualification, and the only exception was a former court-officer for the marshalsea prison (and so familiar with arresting debtors). As a result, not only were they usually respectable householders but they had normally acquired some policing expertise before appointment. Some of the more important members of this group, those who had secured crime-fighting successes, were also rewarded with a minor public appointment. Thus, one was made deputy-governor of the Tothill Fields Bridewell. This was a position in which he could also secure valuable criminal intelligence from the many minor, often female, prisoners committed there for short periods, some of whom consorted with highwaymen.

Although the runners never numbered more than twelve men at any one time during the eighteenth century, they accumulated considerable experience and expertise in basic detective techniques, whether these were developed in the field or passed from officer to officer over the generations. As a result, they were the most competent crime investigators ever to have worked in the London area prior to this era. Significantly, in the immediate aftermath of the Gordon Riots, the runners provided a valuable service accompanying and directing the military (many of whom were totally unacquainted with the London area) in searching the haunts of the "incorrigible criminals" who had escaped from the Metropolitan gaols during the disturbances.[142] The names of some runners, such as that of Charles Jealous, who was active in the 1780s and 1790s, crop up regularly in the *Sessions Papers* for years at a stretch. Most acquired basic skills in crime scene investigation and the questioning of witnesses, while some developed specialist knowledge about specific forms of crime, such as coining. Many of them would also have become familiar with giving evidence at Metropolitan courts, especially the Old Bailey, making them more persuasive, less likely to be unsettled by defence counsel, and more aware of the sort of evidence that appealed to jurors.[143]

Where a crime was extremely serious, especially if it involved the victimisation of members of the upper social orders, the steps taken by Sir John Fielding's men could be exceptionally thorough and painstaking. Thus, when Lord Harrington's house was burgled in December 1763, and more than three thousand pounds worth of silver, gold and jewels were taken, Fielding investigated the theft personally, spending a whole day and much of the night examining and questioning suspects and witnesses. (His suspicions eventually fell on a servant, who later confessed to the crime). A stolen £30 bank note was traced back through numerous intermediaries, and a man was sent to Ireland to conduct investigations.[144] The sophistication of the runners' detective techniques can also be seen in the trial of Francis Lewis in 1778. Lewis was the butler to Thomas Edmonds. He staged a fake break-in, having hidden or taken jewellery, silver, plate and other valuable items.

142. *The Gentleman's Magazine*, 1780, vol.50, p.368.

143. J. M. Beattie, "Early Detection: The Bow Street Runners in Late Eighteenth- century London", 2006, pp.28-29.

144. J. Bevell, *An Authentic Narrative of the Methods by which the Robber ...*, 1764, pp.1-15

In the process, he discharged a pistol, cut himself, damaged a door and tied himself up, claiming to have been the victim of three violent intruders. John Clarke, a runner, investigated the crime. Becoming suspicious about the defendant's account, he examined the window near the door that had been forced and noticed that a pane of glass had been broken from the inside, as a spider's web was intact that would necessarily have been destroyed if it had been forced from outside. The door had also been damaged from inside, and there was no sign of the ball from the fired pistol. Clarke immediately appreciated that it was an "inside job" and, on learning that the butler had visited his spouse that night was sure "the things are at his wife's". He proved to be correct, and Lewis was convicted and executed.[145]

Although, in many ways, detectives, the runners also operated as a fast reaction force, on the basis of "quick notice and sudden pursuit". As intelligence came in of a major Metropolitan crime, they would be sent out by the Bow Street magistrates to arrest the culprits.[146] For example. in 1773, after notice of a robbery reached Sir John Fielding's office, men were sent out to patrol several of the roads in its immediate vicinity, and the notorious William Field was seen and arrested.[147] This method of operating meant that the runners were especially successful in breaking up the larger Metropolitan gangs or criminal groupings, which could not easily conceal themselves after an attack, such as a band of 13 Irishmen who operated together in the early 1750s. Sometimes, the runners were even pro-active, operating from the cover of a "decoy" coach. These were filled with armed thief-takers and would patrol the city's outskirts, firing immediately if attacked by highwaymen.[148]

The runners' work could be dangerous, as it made them "obnoxious" to many poor people. Early on, one man was killed on duty, while others, including Charles Jealous, were shot at. This meant that John Dickson, one of the "thief-takers" at the Rotation Office in 1790, and a man of: "...gigantic stature and great strength, was extremely well qualified for his office".

145. OBSP, Trial of Francis Lewis, 29 April, 1778.

146. J. Fielding, *A Plan for Preventing Robberies Within 20 miles of London*, 1755, pp.7-8.

147. J. L. Rayner and G. T. Crook (Eds.) *The Complete Newgate Calendar*, vol. IV, 1926, pp.95-96.

148. J. W. von Archenholz, *A picture of England: Containing a description of the laws, customs and manners of England*, 1790, p.181.

(Unfortunately, he was also willing to pick fights and then prosecute his victims).[149] Nevertheless, by 1780, the Bow Street Office and its runners were considered the main national resource for police expertise, becoming the model for the seven new police offices established by the Middlesex Justices Act of 1792.

Conclusion

As the eighteenth century moved to its close, the proper role of detection within Metropolitan policing was a matter of debate. Many proposals for reform envisaged a combination of detection and preventative patrolling. William Blizzard firmly believed in a "combined" approach. He felt that one of the inherent problems in "thief-taking", that officers would wait for crimes to be committed that were sufficiently serious to warrant a reward, before apprehending criminals, could be solved by the simple expedient of granting "handsome rewards" for arresting petty offenders. Blizzard was also keen that prison turnkeys should be trained to act as detectives and obtain criminal intelligence from their charges.[150] A few years later, Patrick Colquhoun stressed that the aim of any police force was both the "Prevention and Detection of Crimes".[151] Similarly, Jonas Hanway's "system", though partly preventative, would only have produced the very modest total of one professional constable for each 6,000 Londoners. It was still heavily based on private initiatives supported by financial payments. He was keen that a proper sum should be raised by the authorities to reward those who caught criminals, though he preferred to call them "pursuers" rather than thief-catchers, that name being "rather contemptible".[152] Even the 1812 Committee, which came down heavily in favour of emphasising prevention rather than post-crime detection, noted that it was wrong to believe that the "two systems", preventative patrol and detection, were not compatible. They complimented and afforded "mutual

149. *The Times*, 22 October 1790, p.4.

150. W. Blizard, *Desultory Reflections on Police: with an essay on the means of preventing crimes and amending criminals*, 1785, pp. 80-83.

151. "Preface" to P. Colquhoun, *A Treatise on the Police of the Metropolis*, 1800, 6th edn.

152. J. Hanway, *The Defects of Police*, 1785, p.238.

aid and assistance" to each other. The initial marginalisation of detection, in the years after 1829, could not have been anticipated in 1800.

CHAPTER 12

THE METROPOLITAN MAGISTRACY

Introduction

The justice of the peace was a key figure, of ubiquitous importance, within the eighteenth-century criminal justice system. Arguably, his role was even more important in the capital than it was in the provinces because, as contemporary observers noted, cities needed magistrates of higher professional abilities and in greater numbers than rural areas.[1] The incidence and consistency of urban crime meant that a "loose and unsettled" magistracy was particularly inappropriate.[2]

Frequently, a justice of the peace was referred to simply as a "justice" or even by the abbreviation "JP" The title "magistrate", though found throughout the period, was comparatively rarely used until the later decades of the century, but will be employed here as a generic term, not least because those found in the Square Mile were City aldermen, who became JPs *ex officio* (though without normally being referred to by the title).

Originally, only those aldermen who had served, or were serving, as Lord Mayor, or who had been in office for a lengthy period—by a Charter of 1638, the three most senior aldermen who had not previously served as Mayor—were automatically made magistrates. However, their number was expanded considerably in 1692, after the mayor and aldermen petitioned William and Mary for an increase, arguing that without more men justice could not be administered as expeditiously within the City as was desirable. As a result, a further six aldermen were authorised to sit as magistrates. This was still not enough, given the advent of a rota system at the Guildhall (see below) and

1. *The Ordinary of Newgate, His Account of the Behaviour, Confession, and Dying Words of the Malefactors who were executed at Tyburn on Tuesday the 9th of July, 1745*, 1745, p.16.
2. E. Sayer, *Observations on the Police or Civil Government of Westminster, with a Proposal for a Reform*, 1784, p.17.

that their legal duties had been greatly increased by statute. This prompted a further petition to George II, as a result of which, after 1741, all aldermen became magistrates as soon as they were elected.[3] Aldermen were usually drawn from the wealthy merchants and financiers who made up the City's elite. They were elected to office for life, one man being chosen by each of the Square Mile's 26 wards.

Elsewhere in the Metropolis, JPs had to have been appointed to the Middlesex, Westminster or Tower Liberty Commissions of the Peace. Such commissions were the formal documents that named and authorised certain prominent men in a county or borough to act as justices, and which defined, in broad terms, their powers and duties. New commissions, issued at irregular intervals, changed the names of the JPs appointed, by adding some and "dropping" others.[4] For example, in June 1721, 37 new men were added to the Middlesex Commission, and the names of 11 existing men were left off.[5] The number of justices who were on the Middlesex Commission, even if they were not active magistrates, grew as rapidly as the area's population during the first half of the century, going from 212 in 1702 to 499 in 1761.[6]

The Westminster jurisdiction had been made independent of its parent county in the seventeenth century (it was reabsorbed in 1844), supporting its own Commission of the Peace from 1618 onwards. However, there was a considerable overlap in both personnel and responsibility, as Westminster was still part of Middlesex. Many JPs were simultaneously enrolled on both the Middlesex and Westminster Commissions of the Peace, membership of the former carrying slightly more social status than the latter.

The Tower Liberty was by far the smallest of the Metropolitan Commissions of the Peace. It covered the Tower of London and its immediate surrounding area, including Tower Hill and the Little Minories, though much of the locality outside the walls of the fortress had only been added to the Liberty in 1678. Despite its diminutive size, it was independent of both the City and Middlesex, its administration being headed by the Constable

3. *The King v The Mayor and Aldermen of London, on the Prosecution of Thomas Wooldridge* (1785) 4 Douglas 360.
4. L. Glassey, *Politics and Justices of the Peace, 1675-1720*, 1979, pp.2-3.
5. *London Journal*, 17 June 1721.
6. N. Landau, *The Justices of the Peace 1679-1760*, 1984, p.369.

of the Tower. It also had its own gaol in Wellclose Square, and conducted its own Quarter Sessions in a courthouse situated on Tower Hill. However, like the other parts of the Metropolis, it fed its serious cases into the Old Bailey system and its Quarter Sessions were timed, like those for London and Middlesex, to facilitate this. For example, in the Autumn of 1744, its Grand Jury sat as part of a Quarter Sessions held on Tuesday the 16th October, allowing the area's felons to be committed for trial to the Old Bailey Sessions that began on Wednesday the 17th October. The Tower area's small size and population necessarily meant that only a handful of men were indicted to the Old Bailey from the Liberty each year.

Selection and Service

Justices held their positions for life, or until removed for bad behaviour, sickness, or as a result of political infighting. The last of these was important in the early decades of the century, as the role of "party" allegiance, whether Whig or Tory, in appointment and retention was at its peak during the period of acute political strife between 1689 and 1721.[7] For example, in July 1715, 68 JPs were removed from the Middlesex Commission of the Peace, and 44 were added. A large number of those excluded appear to have been Tories, some of whom were believed to harbour sympathies for the Jacobite cause and its recent rising.[8]

Such political considerations appear to have waned swiftly after this time. Lord Hardwicke, appointed Lord Chancellor in 1737, does not appear to have removed a single justice for reasons of political allegiance, largely separating the office from politics.[9] Many justices served for long periods. Thomas Railton, for example, spent half a century as an active magistrate in the Westminster Commission during the late seventeenth and early eighteenth centuries.[10]

7. P. Langford, *Public Life and the Propertied Englishman: 1689-1798*, 1991, p.420.
8. L. Glassey, *Politics and Justices of the Peace, 1675-1720*, 1979, p.248.
9. N. Landau, *The Justices of the Peace 1679-1760*, 1984, pp.126-127.
10. *The London Journal*, 24 April 1731.

Ostensibly, JPs were appointed by the Lord Chancellor, though this was usually on the basis of advice to the Crown from various local sources, particularly that of the Lord Lieutenant of the relevant county. The Lord Lieutenant was, himself, normally influenced by the views of existing magistrates, who might petition for certain individuals to be appointed to their ranks. In the first half of the eighteenth century, recommendations had also come from other local dignitaries, such as the diocesan bishop.

The Amateur Tradition

Unlike their state-funded counterparts at the bottom of the judicial pyramid in continental countries, English magistrates were, historically, unsalaried, legally unqualified, part-time amateurs, rather than paid, legally trained, professional judges. However, they (or their clerks) were entitled to modest fees for some individual pieces of judicial work. In the 1760s, at least 34 of these could be identified, ranging from 6d. to three shillings. For example, issuing an arrest warrant attracted a fee of one shilling, while a recognisance cost 2s 4d. Examining a woman with regard to bastardy and swearing in a constable cost (the relevant parish) a shilling, the same amount as the fee for discharging anyone brought before a magistrate by warrant for committing a misdemeanour.[11] The better sort of magistrate was not concerned about such paltry (to a gentleman) sums, and would often remit or reduce his entitlements for those who were in great financial distress.[12] Nevertheless, this right to court fees was to have very significant consequences in eighteenth-century Middlesex and Westminster.

JPs usually had little or no formal legal training, unless they had earlier sought qualification as barristers or attorneys, though the latter could not practice as such while in office and, for much of the period, were not supposed to be appointed to the position. Even informal preparation prior to becoming a justice was rare. The influential Middlesex JP, Sir Thomas de

11. E. Silverthorne (Ed.) *Deposition Book of Richard Wyatt*, 1978, p.1 and p.51.

12. T. Gisborne, *An Enquiry into the Duties of men in the Higher and Middle Classes of Society in Great Britain, London*, 1794, p.290.

Veil, was considered unusual in making a close study of the office before being appointed in 1729.[13] Historically, in an attempt to remedy this lack of legal knowledge, commissions of the peace had been bifurcated into ordinary justices and a special group, known as the "quorum", of proven competence and experience. Such magistrates had enhanced legal powers and had to be represented on the bench at Quarter Sessions and in a few other situations. However, by the eighteenth century, it was normal practice to advance almost all JPs to that status as soon as they were appointed.[14] As a result, membership of the quorum did not serve as an effective form of quality control.

When it came to legal knowledge, magistrates were largely dependant on the numerous legal handbooks and justices' *vade mecums* of the era, such as the regularly re-editioned works of Edmund Bohun, Richard Burn, Samuel Blackerby, Joseph Keble and John Bond. In the Square Mile, during the latter part of the century, sitting aldermen could also take advantage of the advice provided by the City Solicitor. All magistrates could draw on the support of their clerks, if they had them (as most did), and that of more experienced colleagues, if they were to hand. The former were a particularly important source of information, so that it was sometimes said that the: "...old well-season'd clerk is his worship's director".[15]

Justices' Clerks

Most magistrates' clerks were attorneys or solicitors by training, though there was no legal requirement that this be the case. They usually continued to practice as lawyers after their appointment. As a result of their experience, they often had significant expertise in the technical aspects of the law, even if they were not the cream of their professions. Justices' clerks would also act as the "eyes and ears" of their masters; for example, they could note the number of people who had been held overnight for production before the

13. T. Deveil, *Memoirs of the Life and Times of Sir Thomas Deveil*, 1748, p.16.
14. W. Blackstone, *Commentaries on the Laws of England*, Oxford, Clarendon Press, 1765-9, vol. I, p.340.
15. Anon ("Tom Tattle"), *A Letter from Tom Tattle A Literate Watchman of Westminster to his Brother Jack Drydrub*, 1720, p.19.

magistrate the following morning.[16] Additionally, they might become aware of potentially important matters that had been "noised abroad" in their localities, such as suspicious deaths, and draw them to their master's attention. It is indicative of the public perception of their power and influence that David Hamilton was committed to the Gatehouse Prison for impersonating justice de Veil's clerk and extorting money from suspects, under the pretence of: "...suppressing informations that would be given against them before Justice Deveil for several offences".[17]

Clerks were remunerated via the receipt of specific fees for different pieces of work, rather than by being paid salaries, until well into the nineteenth century. However, those appointed in the Metropolis pursuant to the Middlesex Justices Act of 1792 were exceptions to this general position, being salaried men (and not entitled to fees).

Inevitably, and despite the availability of various forms of assistance, the English tradition of magisterial amateurism had very significant implications for the way in which JPs carried out their work. Nevertheless, ignorance did not prevent increased legal standardisation in practice during the 1700s, this being the continuation of an already established process. This development was greatly facilitated by the growing use of printed forms for commonly recurring types of work. For example, pro-forma settlement certificates, removal orders, search and arrest warrants could be purchased in bulk from legal stationers, such as John Cole in Chancery Lane. These documents had blank spaces for personalised details — name, place etc.—to be filled in by the magistrate.[18]

The Magistrates' Work

The justice's office could trace its history back to the late twelfth century, and its title to 1361. However, its responsibilities had changed considerably over

16. Anon, *Low-Life: or One Half of the World Knows not how the Other Half Live*, 2nd edn., 1755, p.36.
17. *Read's Weekly Journal or British Gazetteer*, 14 November 1730.
18. J. Kent, "The Centre and the Localities: State formation and Parish government in England, Circa 1640-1740", 1995, p.391.

time. In the eighteenth century, the justice's role in both the Metropolis's criminal and civil administration was paramount (In continental Europe, the two functions were often given to different officials). The former included the preparation of felony cases and punishing less serious matters. The latter, matters as diverse as poor relief and the maintenance of local highways and orphans.

The focus of this chapter is the justices' criminal rather than their extensive civil jurisdiction, but it should be noted that, in a few situations, there was not a clear dividing line between the two types of work. For example, it was an important part of the JP's role to "reconcile differences" between masters and apprentices. Some of these "differences" might have amounted to criminal allegations had they been heard in another context, while others were treated as quasi-criminal matters even though they would have been quite legal for most people. If a master was to blame for a serious problem in the working relationship, his apprentice could be discharged from his articles. If the apprentice was at fault, he could be punished by committal to a house of correction or bridewell.[19] Thus, in 1790, the sitting alderman committed John Tash to The Bridewell for a month, as an "idle and disorderly apprentice", following a complaint from his master. Tash had had a number of previous appearances for the same "offence".[20]

In the City, an apprentice could also make a formal complaint about the treatment he received under his articles to the Chamberlain's Court. Such complaints could include allegations of excessive violence (essentially assault) on the part of their masters, although it was accepted that an employer could use moderate "correction" on an apprentice. This forum was usually reluctant to find for an apprentice. Nevertheless, in extremely grave cases, the court did intervene, usually by granting a discharge from the apprenticeship and ordering a master to repay an apprenticeship fee (normally to the youth's father). For example, Peter Kearnan, a 12-year-old who had been apprenticed to a stationer, received such a disposal after claiming that his master and his master's wife frequently beat him without any cause, whipping him with a

19. T. Pearce, *The compleat justice of the peace, and parish officer*, 1756, p.21.

20. Guildhall Justice Room Minute Book, CLA/005/01/045 19 Aug-14 September 1790, entry for 8 September.

thick rope, striking him with a brass ruler and, on one occasion, trying to spear him with a red hot poker when intoxicated.[21]

Conversely, and much more commonly, a master could take action against his apprentice in such a forum, and apprentices who had assaulted their masters, been disobedient, run away from their articles or stayed out at night made up a major component of The Bridewell's inmates until late in the century. Indeed, these institutions normally had an apprentices' wing specifically to cater for the large number of young people committed for short periods.[22] After release, they would often resume their apprenticeships, if their masters were willing to take them back.

In urban Middlesex, such matters would often be determined by JPs sitting at Quarter Sessions, as in provincial England. A standard precedent book for the era suggests that a typical apprentice allegation might be that his master had failed to teach him his trade and, instead:

> ...swears and curses at, and damns your petitioner, and often kicks and beats your petitioner in a barbarous manner without any just provocation.[23]

Ubiquity of JPs

When it comes to criminal matters, it must be remembered that, although they were the most visible of its components, the Old Bailey Court and the Tyburn gallows stood at the apex of a justice system that had a huge base, one in which the only judicial figure that most offenders encountered was a magistrate. While graphic accounts of the "London hanged" provide dramatic stories, the drudgery of most of the work considered by magistrates, with its endless succession of minor assaults interspersed with the occasional allegation of criminal damage or petty theft, is easily ignored, if only because of its innate tedium and poorer documentation. It is indicative that the law

21. G. T. Smith, "Expanding the Compass of domestic violence in the Hanoverian Metropolis", 2007, pp.42-43.
22. W. Fuller, *Mr William Fuller's Trip to Bridewell*, 1703, pp.10-14.
23. Anon, *A compendious library of the law, necessary for persons of all degrees and professions. In two parts...*,1740, p.177.

governing late night drinking and insulting behaviour was normally: "…so familiar to his worship, that he had it at his fingers end, without consulting Keble".[24] By contrast, most magistrates would not investigate a case of murder during their careers.

In theory, a crime victim could, sometimes, circumvent the need for a justice of the peace altogether. In serious cases, he could go directly to a sitting Grand Jury, with his witnesses, and ask for a suspect to be indicted. In these circumstances, the accused man would know nothing of the forthcoming proceedings against him until arrested under a court issued warrant, granted to secure his attendance at trial. In 1787, for example, the Middlesex Grand Jury found a true bill against a solicitor for perjury in these circumstances. Two days later, the lawyer was arrested on a judge's warrant.[25] However, this very rarely happened in practice.

At the opposite end of the prosecution spectrum of gravity, constables, apprentice masters, and even parents in the City of London had the power to commit those guilty of disorder direct to the Bridewell Prison, without recourse to a magistrate, for most of the eighteenth century. This practice, though long in decline, was only formally ended in 1785, when it was ordered that all committals be made by aldermen.[26] Such a power never existed in Westminster or Middlesex, where a constable could not commit to a house of correction without a magistrate's warrant: "…and so make himself a Judge".[27]

With these small qualifications, magistrates were the first judicial figures that the vast majority of people who were accused of crimes, or who wished to report crimes, whether grave or minor, encountered. They acted as gatekeepers to the wider criminal justice system and constituted the interface between defendants, law enforcement agencies and the courts.

In the modern era, the separation of police and judicial functions is taken for granted, at least in common law countries. It is more than 180 years since Metropolitan magistrates lost any vestigial responsibility for supervising policing in their immediate areas and concentrated their efforts purely on their judicial function. However, in the eighteenth century, justices had an

24. E. Ward, *The London-Spy Compleat in Eighteen Parts*, 4th edn., 1709, p.91.
25. *The Times*, 27 Feb 1787, p.3.
26. F. Dabhoiwala, "Summary Justice in Early Modern London", 2006, p.799.
27. Holt CJ in *The Case of the Reforming Constables* (1709) Holt, KB, 485.

important investigative as well as interlocutory and adjudicative function. Thus, magistrates would issue search and arrest warrants, examine and take depositions from suspects and other potential witnesses, commit suspects to trial in the higher courts (subject to Grand Jury determinations), grant or refuse bail when they did so, and even exercise a summary jurisdiction to dispose of many of the less serious matters that came before them. Sometimes, in major policing operations, JPs might even accompany officers in the field. For example, in 1723, three justices went with a High Constable and several of his petty constables when they raided Fryer's Gaming House in the Haymarket, and made several arrests.[28]

The importance of the justice's office, and its versatility, meant that some very high-ranking officials sought the position for specific purposes. Thus, during the 1690s, Sir Isaac Newton, who, as well as being an eminent scientist, was the warden of the Mint between 1696 and 1699, had himself added to the Commission of the Peace in seven counties so that he could personally supervise coining prosecutions.[29] A selection of the cases that might be heard by the same magistrate, on a typical day, is illustrative of the breadth of their workload when "out of sessions". For example, when Alderman Townsend was sitting at the Justice Room in April 1787, Mary Jones was brought before him by Alice Inglis, accused of stealing a cloak in Long Lane, Smithfield. After examining them, he committed Jones for trial, sending her to Newgate in the meantime. On the same day, Townsend committed four disorderly prostitutes to the Bridewell Prison, while discharging several others on: "... promise of quitting their abandoned course of life".[30] Neophyte prostitutes, who had not previously come before the magistrates, would often receive such a benign disposal.

28. *London Journal*, 23 November 1723.
29. N. Tosney, "Women and 'False Coining' in Early Modern London", 2007, p.107.
30. *World and Fashionable Advertiser*, 17 April 1787.

The Men Appointed as Justices

In theory, only men of the highest calibre, educationally, intellectually, and socially should have been selected as JPs. The personal qualifications deemed vital to a magistrate in the discharge of his duties were demanding, and included a: "...calm attention and unwearied diligence in investigating the cases brought before him, and perfect integrity in deciding them".[31] The reality had never entirely matched this ideal. However, in the years after 1660, a marked and general decline in willingness on the part of "upper class" men to accept the loss of time and personal inconvenience that was required to serve as an active magistrate led to significant changes in the profile of appointments.

By the late seventeenth century, many gentlemen preferred to live in "perfect idleness, and luxury" rather than mete out justice.[32] Some observers claimed that this was not purely the result of indolence, but was linked to the ever-greater demands that were being made on active justices by a proliferation of statutes and the growth in their legal responsibilities. As a result, those who served would find their: "...whole time must necessarily be spent in this occupation and business if followed as the laws require". Far from abating during the eighteenth century, this process continued relentlessly, with more work being "heaped" on magistrates, so that the law governing the office was ever more intricate.[33]

William Blackstone thought that upper class reluctance to serve was particularly connected to the expansion of summary jurisdiction, and the attendant increase in a magistrate's workload that this occasioned. This discouraged many of "rank and character" from acting in the commission.[34] It also meant that there were periodic attempts at identifying "core responsibilities" that competent justices should fulfil, so that other duties might be

31. T. Gisborne, *An Enquiry into the Duties of men in the Higher and Middle Classes of Society in Great Britain*, 1794, p.279.
32. E. Bohun, *The Justice of Peace His Calling and Qualifications*, 1693, pp.18-19.
33. T. Woodford, *A Discourse Concerning Some of the most important Branches, and Parts, of the Office of the Justices of the Peace*, 1749, p.ii.
34. W. Blackstone, *Commentaries on the Laws of England,* Oxford, Clarendon Press, 1765-9, vol. 4, p.279.

marginalised.[35] Nevertheless, the decline in elite participation also reflected much broader social changes, whereby members of the political nation found other, more amenable or personally beneficial, ways to spend their free time, not least by enjoying the London season. Gentlemen were increasingly reluctant to carry out the office: "...through a false delicacy and dissipation".[36]

However, as eighteenth-century Lord Chancellors were well aware, the justices' work had to be done, so that sufficient numbers of *active* magistrates necessarily had to be found. If the bar was set too high, and too few men were recruited, it would have to be lowered or tacitly ignored. As a result, and as Edmund Bohun had anticipated in the 1690s, it became necessary to recruit "minor" but industrious gentlemen to the bench as active magistrates, and even those who, with the best will in the world, could not qualify for such a modest title. Another option was to recruit clergymen.

Clerical Magistrates

As the eighteenth century advanced, clerical magistrates, who had been a rarity for much of the previous century, became vital "workhorses" in many local commissions of the peace, providing some of the most diligent and educated magistrates in rural areas.[37] There had only been about 50 justices in Holy Orders, nationwide, in 1700. By 1761, there were over a thousand, attracted by both the status of the office and the practical power that went with the position (potentially important in disputes over tithes). Of the 26 Buckinghamshire magistrates who regularly attended Quarter Sessions in the 1770s, 12 were clerics, even though clergymen were often only selected when other, more traditional, sources of recruitment had failed.[38] Similarly, in County Durham there had only been a couple of clergymen on the county bench in the 1720s, but by the 1750s there were ten, and twenty

35. Anon, *Certaine Statutes Especially Selected, and Commanded by his Majestie to be Carefully Put in Execution by all Justices*, 1730, pp.6-7.
36. *Gazetteer and New Daily Advertiser*, 18 May 1774.
37. G. Morgan and P. Rushton, "The magistrate, the community and the maintenance of an orderly society in eighteenth-century England", 2003, p.59.
38. P. Langford, *Public Life and the Propertied Englishman: 1689-1798*, 1991, pp.411-420.

at the end of the century. Clerics also served in numbers in the developing urban industrial areas of the midlands and the north, such as parts of Staffordshire.[39] For a notable example of such men, can be considered the Reverend Richard Burn, who became the vicar of Orton in 1736. Burn was the author of a leading justices' *vade mecum* of the period, and a very active JP in Westmorland and Cumberland.

Recourse to minor gentlemen and clergymen meant the traditional JP system remained just about viable in most of England. In 1792, Charles James Fox was exaggerating, for argument's sake, when he claimed that outside London English justice was:

> ...well administered in the ordinary mode by gentlemen who undertook to discharge the duty without deriving any emolument from it.[40]

There were problems in most counties. Nevertheless, these were generally manageable, with a degree of administrative flexibility and imagination when it came to appointments. However, London and its immediate environs were a major exception to this general situation.

In the Metropolitan area, including urban Surrey and even parts of Kent, such as Blackheath, there was an especially marked increase in reluctance amongst the social elite to take on the particularly onerous, and often singularly unpleasant, duties attendant on being an active urban magistrate. This had become evident well before the end of the seventeenth century. By 1725, even a foreign visitor could express sympathy for magistrates in the crime-prone parish of St. Giles-in-the-Fields who were: "...worn out in determining and healing the Breaches as continually happen among these various species of people".[41] Seven years later, another Metropolitan observer was more brutal, claiming that in areas inhabited by the "scum and dregs" of society it was a simple fact that gentlemen of: "...any great figure or fortune,

---

39. G. Morgan and P. Rushton, "The Magistrate, the community and the maintenance of an orderly society in eighteenth-century England", 2003, p.59.
40. W. Cobbett, *The Parliamentary History of England From the Earliest Period to the Year 1803*, vol. xxix, 1817, p.1464.
41. Anon (A German Gentleman), *A view of London and Westminster: or, the Town Spy*, 2nd edn., 1725, p.12.

will not take such a drudgery upon them".[42] As a result, many men declined to act as justices who had the: "...Inclination and Capacity to render great Service to the Public".[43] Greatly aggravating this situation, suitable men of the cloth who were ready, willing and able to become JPs were usually totally absent in the capital, where tithes were not a significant issue.

The City of London

The City of London was a special case within the Metropolis, as serving in a magisterial capacity there was incidental to being appointed to the prestigious position of alderman. Even so, a reluctance to carry out this sort of work increased rapidly during the first three decades of the century, many men avoiding such time consuming and tedious work which was at the expense of their increasingly pressured professional lives as merchants and financiers. By the end of the 1720s, only three aldermen were regularly involved in magisterial work, a figure that was set to decline further. This process of withdrawal led to a near crisis in November 1737, when Sir Richard Brocas, the last man with any great enthusiasm for carrying out criminal duties died.[44] (He had been appointed alderman after winning a bye-election in 1719).[45] As contemporaries noted after his passing, Brocas had been an "able magistrate".[46]

In response to his death, an element of compulsion had to be introduced by the Square Mile's authorities to ensure that the burden of magisterial duties was shared out amongst those who were technically qualified to sit.[47] Ultimately, on 6th December 1737, the Lord Mayor and Court of Aldermen resolved that all aldermen qualified to act as justices would group together in a rota system, taking turns to sit at the Justice Room of the Guildhall on

42. *Gentleman's Magazine*, vol. 2, 1732, p. 911.
43. N. Blackerby, *The Speech of Nathaniel Blackerby Esq; At A General Meeting of his Majesty's Justices of the Peace for the City and Liberty of Westminster*, 1738, p.9.
44. J. M. Beattie, *Policing and Punishment in London, 1660–1750*, 2001, p.99.
45. *Evening Post*, 8 January 1719.
46. *Country Journal or The Craftsman*, 12 November 1737.
47. J. M. Beattie, *Policing and Punishment in London, 1660–1750*, 2001, p.107.

each weekday from 11.00 am to 2.00 pm to deal with judicial business. The scheme came into force six days later, on the 12th of December.[48] It swiftly became an integral part of the office, and operated for the remainder of the century, so that, in 1785, the Westminster judges, describing the duty of a City alderman, could note that: "...one part of it is to sit by rotation as justice of the peace".[49]

By the 1750s, the "rota of justices" was planned in advance on an annual basis, with the agreement of the aldermen affected. In 1781, for example, it involved 23 aldermen (but not the Lord Mayor), who were scheduled to sit about once each month, though sometimes one man would deputize for another who unexpectedly could not meet his commitment.[50] The pattern of attendance can be extrapolated from litigation connected to the dismissal from office of Alderman Thomas Woodridge. Woodridge had been put down to sit as a justice at the Guildhall on a rota covering the period from the 1st of October 1781 to the 24th of October 1782. During this time he was required to serve once each month, but on radically differing days, ranging from the 26th of December to the 4th of March.[51]

This fragmentation of effort presented some problems. No alderman could hope to achieve the expertise and experience of a dedicated quasi-"professional" justice of the peace like, for example, the Fielding brothers in neighbouring Middlesex. Additionally, a multiplicity of aldermen might deal with the same case, something that encouraged the use of Minute Books explaining what had happened on any given day, earlier in the proceedings. Even this was not always enough. In 1790, for example, the sitting alderman at Guildhall, John Boydell, was forced to discharge Thomas Bellers, who had been produced on an arrest warrant: "...of which I can't make head or tail for my life".[52] It probably led aldermen to rely heavily on their immediate

48. *The Gentleman's Magazine*, 1737, vol.7, p.763.
49. *The King v The Mayor and Aldermen of London, on the Prosecution of Thomas Wooldridge* (1785) 4 Douglas 360.
50. J. H. Langbein, "Shaping the Eighteenth-century Criminal Trial: A View from the Ryder Sources", 1983, p.80.
51. *The King v The Mayor and Aldermen of London, on the Prosecution of Thomas Wooldridge* (1785) 4 Douglas 360.
52. Guildhall Justice Room Minute Book, CLA/005/01/045 19 August-14 September 1790, entry for 8 September.

clerical support. It also helps to explain a move, late in the century, to a rota under which the aldermen would spend a week at a time on duty, rather than a single day, though the usual hours of attendance remained from 11 am to 2 pm. Sitting less frequently, but for a longer period, allowed some continuity in the repeat examinations of suspects. By the latter part of the century, the mayor and aldermen never conducted judicial business, of any sort, in their own homes (something that had been quite common at the start of the period). However, this also meant that a suspect taken at 3 pm in the City would not normally be examined until 11 am the next day (usually two days later if it occurred on a Saturday evening), something that could slow down the investigation of serious crime.[53]

In 1737, the City authorities created what was, effectively, the first "rotation office" in the Metropolis. Initially, it also seems to have absorbed the sittings of the Lord Mayor who, in the late seventeenth and early eighteenth centuries, had been required to be particularly active as a magistrate, sometimes hearing cases on an almost daily basis during his year in office.[54] Eventually, however, pressure of work meant that the City required two such offices. As a result, after 1753, the Lord Mayor began sitting on his own again, at 11 am every morning, in the Justice Room of the newly built Mansion House. He conducted most of the criminal work carried out there, his attendance supplementing the legal work conducted by the aldermen at the Guildhall.[55] Thus, and typically, Richard Alford was brought before the Lord Mayor at the Mansion House when accused of stealing a silk handkerchief, and committed for trial.[56] A large amount of the Mayor's work came from the eastern half of the Square Mile. Occasionally, another alderman would assist him, especially when it was legally necessary for a second magistrate to be present.

However, although he accepted a heavy duty during his period of service, much of the Mayor's legal business at the Mansion House was not criminal work, his time also being taken up with many administrative matters that

53. Anon, *The Report of the Select Committee Appointed by the House of Commons, Relative to the Establishment of a New Police in the Metropolis, &c.*, 1799, pp.73-74.

54. F. Dabhoiwala, "Summary Justice in Early Modern London", 2006, p.799.

55. *The Times*, 16 November 1796, p.1.

56. *The Times*, 2 February 1803, p.3.

were: "...irrelevant to the great features of police". Perhaps, in part, because of this, by the end of the century many observers felt that the provision of magisterial services in the Square Mile was inadequate, and that the City would benefit from introducing stipendiary Justices like those established in the neighbouring jurisdiction by the Middlesex Justices Act of 1792.[57]

As well as sharing the burden more equably, a rotation system ensured that members of the public and the City's constables could always be sure of finding a magistrate at a set time and in a fixed location, something that was extremely valuable when it came to encouraging recourse to the law. Although there were fairly large numbers of Metropolitan justices, and they lived quite close together (unlike those in rural areas), under the traditional system it could still take much time and labour to find them, especially as: "...oftentimes they are not at home, or [are] at leisure".[58] Additionally, the new system allowed a healthy degree of public scrutiny of decisions. As a result, shortly after its introduction, a Middlesex JP publicly observed that he hoped to see the day when justice in his own county would be administered in a similarly open manner, following the: "... laudable example of the present Lord Mayor of London, and the rest of the worthy Magistrates of that great and opulent City".[59] Despite such aspirations, Westminster and Metropolitan Middlesex had to resolve the reluctance of members of the "political nation" to serve as magistrates in a slightly different fashion.

Middlesex and Westminster

In the City, the position of alderman was sufficiently prestigious and sought after that being forced to take a turn in handling the Square Mile's criminal business, though unwelcome, was not enough of a disincentive to prevent rich, able and politically well connected men from seeking the office. The

57. Anon, *The Report of the Select Committee Appointed by the House of Commons, Relative to the Establishment of a New Police in the Metropolis, &c.*, 1799, p.73.
58. J. Dunton, *The Shortest-Way with Whores and Rogues*, 1703, p.47.
59. N. Blackerby, *The Speech of Nathaniel Blackerby Esq; At A General Meeting of his Majesty's Justices of the Peace for the City and Liberty of Westminster*, 1738, p.10.

same could not be said of those who were willing to become a JP in Westminster and Middlesex.

There were, realistically, two possible solutions to this problem. One was to make prominent local political leaders *ex officio* magistrates, as occurred with the City aldermen, and then to require them to set up rotation offices like those found in the Square Mile. This was considered in Westminster, where it was suggested that the city's problems would be greatly reduced if its dozen burgesses were: "...cloathed with the Powers of justices of the peace, in the same manner as the aldermen of London; and that they should sit daily by Turns, for the Dispatch of business".[60]

However, comparing the burgesses to the aldermen in this context was misleading. They were drawn from very much more modest social and educational backgrounds and occupations; some were even artisans. The prestige of their positions was not remotely comparable. Unlike the aldermen, who were elected by their wards, and so had some political legitimacy, burgesses were nominated to their office by the Dean and High Steward of Westminster.[61]

In any event, in *theory*, the high steward and burgesses *could* determine many minor offences that occurred within the city and liberties of Westminster, when sitting together as a Leet Court. Significantly, by the 1730s, this forum largely confined itself to offences relating to weights, measures, and public nuisances, though on rare occasions brothels and gaming houses might also be prosecuted. The absence of more serious matters was indicative of the way in which the burgesses were viewed. The Westminster JPs had largely taken their place in respect of any other type of offence, so that it was by virtue of justices' warrants that: "...all petty offenders almost are apprehended and sent to Tothill Fields Bridewell".[62] The burgesses did not offer a credible alternative. Additionally, of course, making them JPs would not have solved the problem in other parts of urban Middlesex, the Metropolis's so-called "out parishes".

60. Anon (A Citizen of London), *The Vices of the Cities of London and Westminster. Trac'd from their Original*, 1751, p.16.
61. N. M, *A Letter to a Member of Parliament, Concerning the Bill for Regulating the Nightly Watch in the City of Westminster, and Liberties thereof*, 1720, p.15.
62. M. Gonzales, *London in 1731*, 1888, p.139.

Alternatively, and much more realistically, a "decent salary" could be offered to recruit professional men, of good character, as permanent active magistrates. Such men would take the position as a career opportunity. Their remuneration would also mean that they were not tempted to do: "...low and mean things, for the necessary support of their families".[63] Instead, it was hoped that the presence of attractive salaries would ensure the disinterested performance of the duties of the office.[64] Proponents of such a solution pointed out that no one cavilled about the substantial sums paid to members of the higher judiciary, and suggested that similarly attractive stipends would draw "intelligent and uncorrupted" men to the position. They were also careful to reduce potential opposition by confining such a proposal to the Metropolis, where: "...crimes are so frequent, and consequently the office of a magistrate is so very laborious".[65]

It was this solution that was ultimately (if belatedly) to prevail, effectively being trialled at the Bow Street Office by the Fielding brothers and then formalised and extended in the Middlesex Justices Act 1792 to most of the Metropolis outside the City. This was some 31 years after John Fielding had first proposed the creation of paid magistrates as part of the "police plan" he put to George Grenville, the then prime minister, under which magistrates would be free to devote themselves full-time to their work.[66]

The 1792 Act marked an acceptance of the impossibility of finding men of substance and ability who were willing to perform the office on a regular basis in Middlesex, Westminster and urban Surrey. Such a stratagem had been "tried, and had failed". Even so, proponents of the Bill expressed the hope that it would not prevent suitably qualified gentlemen serving on a supplementary basis, where they were still available.[67] Unfortunately, such men did not come forward very often, even where lay magistrates were still recruited in numbers. In 1815, an observer could still lament that Justices

63. Anon (A Citizen of London), *The Vices of the Cities of London and Westminster, Trac'd from their Original*, 1751, p.16.
64. J. Dornford, *Seven Letters to the Lords of the Privy Council, on the Police*, 1785, p.xii.
65. Anon (A Gentleman of Lincoln's Inn), *A Letter to Archibald MacDonald, Esq. on the Intended Plan for Reform in what is called the Police of Westminster*, 2nd edn., 1786, p.40.
66. J. M. Beattie, "Sir John Fielding and Public Justice: The Bow Street Magistrates' Court, 1754–1780", 2007, p.73.
67. *The Calcutta Gazette*, 13 December 1792.

from counties that did not border the Metropolis were usually respectable, while those found in those parts of Middlesex and Surrey outside the remit of the 1792 Act were often woefully deficient.[68]

Prior to reform in 1792, the capital's magisterial work had to be carried out and, in such circumstances, it was inevitable that the: "...book of numbers must eventually prevail".[69] Men who were less than ideal would have to be selected. East London's Justices, for example, often had a poor reputation precisely because they tended to be drawn, and so indistinguishable, from the wider community that they served. Thus, Clifford William Phillips, a distiller who served in the Tower Hamlets area, was eventually removed from office for intervening on behalf of a woman who had been convicted by a fellow magistrate of selling spirits outside the terms of the Gin Act of 1736. It was alleged that Phillips had frequently encouraged breaches of the same Act on earlier occasions.[70] One way in which the shortage of appropriate justices could be addressed was via a heavy recourse in Westminster, urban Middlesex, and some locations south of the river, to "trading justices".

Trading Justices

Trading justices were men of relatively low social status who took the office for largely mercenary reasons. Such magistrates made most of their incomes from the court fees that they collected for providing judicial services.[71] Although, individually, these were quite modest, in an urban or suburban area with a high local population a JP who sat regularly, and enforced his entitlements rigidly, could secure a: "...bare subsistence upon the perquisites

68. Anon, *An Address to the Magistracy of the City of Middlesex and of the City and Liberties of Westminster*, 1815, p.5.
69. Anon, *An Address to the Magistracy of the City of Middlesex and of the City and Liberties of Westminster*, 1815, p.6.
70. J. Warner and F. Ivis, "Informers and Their Social Networks in Eighteenth-century London", 2001, p.568.
71. J. Davis, "A Poor Man's System of Justice: The London Police Courts in the Second Half of the Nineteenth Century", 1984, p.311.

of office".[72] Indeed, most could make a reasonable income, at least for a person of their station in life.

Such magistrates were not an entirely new phenomenon in the eighteenth century, as many contemporary observers appreciated.[73] However, the problem became much more acute during the late 1600s and early 1700s, particularly in the Metropolitan area, because of the lack of ready alternatives. One modern observer has described trading justices as being members of the "lower middle" class, while a contemporary critic claimed that they were often former pawnbrokers, tailors or even bricklayers.[74] One of their number, Justice Hyde, was originally a carpenter and, it was claimed, from the: "...nature of his trade, and the manner of his education, he could not have any great knowledge of the law".[75] One or two of them appear to have seen previous service as parish constables.

Nevertheless, not all trading justices were impecunious. Minimum property requirements for those appointed to the Middlesex commission, like those of other counties, were in force throughout the century. These included an Act of 1732 for the "Better Qualification of Justices" which decreed that, after the 25th March 1733, no county JP should have an estate worth less than £100 a year, nor should any of them be taken from the inferior branches of the legal profession (solicitors, attorneys or proctors).[76] This was a modest requirement for the London area, as £100 a year was only a "small estate to live upon in Town". It was easily met given the value of property in the Metropolis.[77] Most Middlesex justices, even if fairly marginally, could fulfil its requirements.[78] More ambitious parliamentary Bills, aimed at setting the bar rather higher, such as that of 1742, were usually unsuccessful, giving way to practical considerations. It was widely thought that JPs had to be local to be effective, and the increasing social segregation of the Metropolitan area

72. E. Sayer, *Observations on the Police or Civil Government of Westminster, with a Proposal for a Reform*, 1784, p.18.
73. *The Gentleman's Magazine*, 1732, vol. 2, p.892.
74. Anon, *A Letter to his Grace the Duke of Northumberland; on the Intended Meeting of the Justices of Middlesex*, 1777, p.22.
75. *The Times*, 14 February 1791, pg. 3.
76. Anon, *Abstract of Several Acts*, 1733, p.2.
77. *Gentleman's Magazine*, vol. 2, 1732, p.892.
78. N. Landau, *The Justices of the Peace 1679-1760*, 1984, p.162.

placed limits on how high a property qualification could be set. If the poor were to have access to local men, the £100 qualification was: "...sufficiently high; for if it were higher, proper persons would not be found in such places for the Commission".[79]

The 1732 legislation only affected county justices. Those from towns or cities, such as Westminster (a separate commission to Middlesex), and a place with many trading justices, were exempt. Nevertheless, it was not entirely without effect. In the late 1740s, Henry Fielding's difficulties in meeting the £100 property requirement for membership of the Middlesex Commission appears to have delayed his appointment, leading him to seek assistance from the Duke of Bedford.[80] For all their faults, trading justices were appointed in the same way as other magistrates.

As they made money from the fees attendant on criminal prosecutions, it was widely thought that trading justices actively encouraged recourse to the law, so that their offices inevitably became: "...shop[s] of litigation, where the poor people are encouraged to harass one another to increase his worship's income".[81] This was significant, as traditionally one of a justice's most important roles had been to settle many of the allegations that came before him informally (see below). Such settlements did not result in court fees, and so had few attractions for mercenary magistrates. It was sometimes alleged that trading justices deliberately inflamed quarrels between neighbours with a view to binding them over to keep the peace, and then releasing the disputants from their bonds, for both of which services they were entitled to a fee.[82] So many people were bound over as a result of drink-induced disturbances during the festive season in December 1727 that justices and their clerks were able to enjoy a "good" Christmas on the proceeds.[83] One observer claimed that he had even seen a magistrate allow a poor man to take his shirt off his back and pawn it, so as to pay the fee to discharge an arrest warrant.[84] A decent justice would have remitted it. It was also claimed

79. *Gentleman's Magazine* vol. 2, 1732, p.911.
80. W. B. Coley, "Fielding's Two Appointments to the Magistracy", 1965, p.145.
81. *Gentleman's Magazine* vol. 2, 1732 p.893.
82. N. Landau, *The Justices of the Peace 1679-1760*, 1984, p.185.
83. *Original Weekly Journal*, 3 January 1728.
84. *Gazetteer and New Daily Advertiser*, 17 January 1772.

that some Westminster trading justices organized large-scale arrests of local prostitutes with a view to extorting bail-money from them.[85]

Even worse than their alleged rapaciousness in taking (legitimate) fees, was a fear that trading justices were always alert to finding other, more ethically dubious, ways to make a profit.[86] Like King Midas, they would: "… turn everything they touch to gold".[87] For example, it was widely suspected that they augmented their "legal" payments by taking bribes to overlook the transgressions of their local bawdy and gaming houses, and split rewards with the informers on whose evidence they convicted those accused of regulatory offences. In a parliamentary debate after the first reading of the Middlesex Justices Bill of 1792, the Chancellor of the Exchequer claimed that much of the trading justices' income was taken from fees that had been "obtained illegally".[88]

There were more general concerns about the quality of many men attracted to the Metropolitan bench. In the early 1700s, for example, Daniel Defoe complained that many used profane language and were themselves habitual drunkards.[89] There were also regular fears that such justices could abuse their extensive powers for reasons of "personal resentment".[90] For example, in one case a prosecution for rape only occurred because there had been an altercation between a JP named Powys and another man, after they had fallen out during a heavy drinking session at the Bedford Head Tavern.[91]

The behaviour of Metropolitan trading justices was sufficiently notorious that it became the butt of contemporary satire in the work of men like Fielding, Gray and Smollett. To Robert Holloway, writing in 1773, the Middlesex Commission of the Peace contained the: "…most wicked, illiterate, avaricious, and rapacious men in the kingdom". He claimed that: "Middlesex Justice and scoundrel are synonymous terms".[92] Their conduct was also increasingly seen to be at variance to the relatively corruption-free senior

85. B. Simpson, "The Mouth of Strange Women is a Deep Pit", 1996, p.59.
86. Anon, *The Means of Effectually Preventing Theft and Robbery*, 1778, pp.7-8.
87. *World*, 5 December 1787.
88. *World*, 18 April 1792.
89. D. Defoe, *The Poor Man's Plea*, 1927, pp.6-7.
90. W. Blackstone, *Commentaries on the Laws of England*, 1765-9, vol. 4, p.279.
91. OBSP, Trial of unidentified man, 1 March 1721. Unsurprisingly, a "not guilty" verdict ensued.
92. R. Galloway, *The Rat-Trap*, 1773, p.v and p.10.

judiciary that emerged in the decades after the Glorious Revolution.[93] It was also argued that, because of their venality, trading justices were unlikely to inspire popular respect and would, as a result, be more likely to find it necessary to call out the army to enforce their decisions.[94]

However, criticism of the trading justices was almost certainly exaggerated, and partly based on social antagonism amongst the "political nation" towards the magistrates' lowly origins. Members of the upper social orders were happy to deplore the presence of such men on the bench, but were singularly unwilling to take on the office themselves. Some contemporary observers recognised the importance of trading justices to the Metropolis, even at the time, and appreciated that their existence reflected a popular demand for legal services that would not otherwise have been met. In February 1776, when the Society for Free Debate, one of the many London debating societies of the era, discussed whether they were hurtful or beneficial to the country, a: "...great majority appeared in their favour".[95] Even critics could accept that they were a necessary evil, as: "...if there were not such little magistrates, the laws could not be well put in execution".[96] Although despised by their superiors and hated by their inferiors, their work was vital to keeping the: "...common people within due bounds, as well in regard to their superiors as to one another".[97] Even William Mainwaring, the chairman of the Middlesex Commission, could observe that for all their faults they did some good.[98]

More constructively, trading justices were likely to gain a detailed knowledge of legal procedures through constant exposure, and thus a degree of personal expertise. For example, towards the end of the century, it was felt that Hyde's misconduct in office had been particularly reprehensible because, although ill-educated, he had considerable experience of the law.[99] More gentlemanly magistrates were prone to being "guided", and so dominated,

93. W. Prest, "Judicial Corruption in Early Modern England", 1991, p.68.
94. *Gentleman's Magazine*, vol. 8, 1738, p.513.
95. D. T. Andrew (Ed.), *London Debating Societies, 1776–1799*, 1994, p.5.
96. T. Deveil, *Observations on the Practice of a Justice of the Peace*, 1747, p.18.
97. *The Gentleman's Magazine*, 1747, vol. 17, p.562.
98. W. Cobbett, *The Parliamentary History of England From the Earliest Period to the Year 1803*, 1817, vol. xxix, p.1179.
99. *The Times*, Monday, 14 February 1791, p. 3.

by their clerks.[100] There were advantages to having knowledgeable JPs, even if Holloway was convinced that it was hard to find a Middlesex justice who could read a passage in Burn's *vade mecum* for magistrates.

It is also possible that both the authorities and the general public overestimated the income made by urban JPs. Henry Fielding complained that the yearly pension he received from the government out of the public service money would have been larger had his patron, the Duke of Newcastle, not been convinced (mistakenly) that acting as the principal JP in Westminster was a very lucrative office, although: "The truth is, the fees are so very low, when any are due, and so much is done for nothing".[101] Arguably, his view is borne out by the fact that the post-1792 stipendiary magistrates and their offices cost about £16,000 a year to run, yet took in only £2,605 a year in fees, though the former sum also covered the funding of a small number of constables, while few fees remained payable after that year.[102] The trading justices probably provided the state with reasonable value for money, if nothing else.

Furthermore, the definition of "trading justice" was itself ambiguous. Did it refer to any magistrate who took and relied upon his court fees, or merely to those who did so in inappropriate circumstances or who actively encouraged litigation? If the former definition were used, Sir Thomas de Veil, who was appointed a JP for Middlesex and Westminster in 1729, would certainly qualify. Despite enjoying significant treasury grants and a sinecure from the government he made much of his living from fees, albeit that it was claimed that he: "...did not consider justice merely as a commodity which he was to vend for money".[103] De Veil himself advised JPs to follow the letter of the law when receiving remuneration for legal services, and suggested that payment was best done through the magistrate's clerk, as it was undignified to take money in person. His lineal successors, Henry and John Fielding, also received court fees for providing legal services, and so might qualify as trading justices, though Henry insisted (perhaps more convincingly than de Veil)

100. Anon ("Tom Tattle"), *A Letter from Tom Tattle A Literate Watchman of Westminster to his Brother Jack Drydrub*, 1720, p.19.
101. H. Fielding, *Journal of a Voyage to Lisbon*, 1755, p.26.
102. L. Norma "The Trading Justice's Trade", 2002, p.65.
103. *Gentlemen's Magazine*, 1747, vol.17, p.562.

that he always showed great restraint in what he took.[104] There appears to be no evidence that the Fieldings took a bribe or illegal payment while in office.

Of course, it is hard to argue with contemporary claims that there could not be so many allegations about the misconduct of trading justices without some basis in reality. As a result, several observers lamented the lack of effective punishment for errant JPs (and High Constables), contrasting the situation unfavourably with that found in France.[105] Nevertheless, in *theory*, there was little leniency shown towards transgressing magistrates: "If a Justice offend, let any Man complain to the Lord Chancellor, he is turned out with Infamy".[106] Although this was an exaggeration, Metropolitan JPs who blatantly and repeatedly broke the law would usually find themselves reported to the Lord Chancellor fairly swiftly and, eventually, removed from office.

Control of Justices

If a justice's misconduct was venial or occasional, his name could simply be left off the relevant Commission of the Peace when it was next reissued. In 1738, for example, when a new commission for Middlesex was produced, 75 men were left off the list (and 98 added). Contemporary observers felt that many of them had been considered unsatisfactory in some way or other, some even being labelled "trading harpies".[107]

If a justice's transgressions were so grave that he had to be removed immediately, the Lord Chancellor might issue a writ of *supersedeas*, ordering him to stop executing his office.[108] Some argued that this power meant that trading justices were much less dangerous than would otherwise be the case, as their conduct was regularly "inspected by superior authority".[109] It was a drastic remedy, and it seems that only a dozen magistrates were

104. H. Fielding, *Journal of a Voyage to Lisbon*, 1755, p.26.
105. *Review of the State of the British Nation*, 15 October 1709.
106. Anon (Tom Tattle), *A Letter from Tom Tattle A Literate Watchman of Westminster to his Brother Jack Drydrub*, 1720, p.19.
107. *Gentleman's Magazine*, 1738, vol. 8, p.435.
108. N. Landau, *The Justices of the Peace 1679-1760*, 1984, p.128.
109. *The Gentleman's Magazine*, 1747, vol. 17, p. 562.

A parish watchman arrives to deal with a disturbance in a gaming house (Hogarth).

Elizabeth Brownrigg beating her domestic servant Mary Clifford who died from cumulative injuries. Mrs Brownrigg was hanged at Tyburn in 1767.

A satirical portrayal of the magistrate Sir Thomas de Veil accompanied by a constable (Hogarth).

The body of an executed murderer is dissected at Surgeon's Hall pursuant to the Murder Act 1752 (Hogarth).

A beadle breaks up a group of youths who are gaming in a churchyard during Divine Service. Note his parish issued uniform (Hogarth).

A constable and his watchmen arrive at a murder scene (Hogarth).

Bow Street Office.
From Ackerman's Microcosm of London (1808).
The architectural drawings are by Augustus Pugin and the figures by Thomas Rowlandson.

An unsatisfactory apprentice is discharged from his articles and sent to sea. Recruitment to the army and navy coincided with a reduction in indictment levels, discharge with an expansion (Hogarth).

A convict arrives at Tyburn (Hogarth).

An accomplice gives a deposition implicating another felon during an examination in front of a City alderman. The magistrate is sitting in the Justice Room of the Guildhall (Hogarth).

Detail from the drawing on the left — the condemned man being ministered to by a Methodist clergyman, while the Ordinary rides to the gallows in a carriage.

Water Engine, Cold Bath Fields Prison.
From Ackerman's Microcosm of London (1808). The architectural drawings are by Augustus Pugin and the figures by Thomas Rowlandson.

dismissed from the Middlesex Commission in these circumstances during the years between 1716 and 1792. Amongst them was William Booth, who was removed in 1719 for extorting totally exorbitant court fees from those who appeared before him; in one case he demanded four times the normal rate.[110] (It appears that he was reinstated to the Commission the following year)[111] Similarly, Justice Charles Whinyates was removed in the 1720s after he used his position to extort complementary sexual services from prostitutes, and ordered his local watchmen to arrest law-abiding pedestrians. In 1731, the King dismissed William Pulteney and John Webster from all commissions of the peace.[112] In Webster's case, this was for stabbing his fellow magistrate Sir Thomas de Veil during a heated altercation (see below). Much later in the century, Justice Hyde, a particularly notorious magistrate, came before the Court of King's Bench. Hyde had already been warned by the Lord Chancellor that any further complaints about his conduct would lead to the removal of his *dedimus*, and so his ability to sit.[113]

However, trading justices were more typically associated with behaviour that while technically legal was considered to be "unseemly" for some reason, and so not approximating to the gentlemanly ideal of a magistrate's conduct. Most commonly, this would be for some form of improper "touting" for legal work, especially where it impinged on the rights, or intruded on the work, of a fellow justice. For example, William Blackborow was alleged to have granted arrest warrants on credit (without first receiving the appropriate fee), to encourage "business", while it was claimed that Charles Triquet had employed a clerk to stand outside his office, publicly advertising his legal services. Others might intervene in cases that had been initiated by fellow justices.[114] It was this that prompted Webster's violence towards de Veil. Even parish officers who facilitated such behaviour might be punished. Thus, a constable who was given a *mittimus* by a justice to carry a suspect to the Gatehouse Prison, but took the man before another magistrate who

110. N. Landau, "The Trading Justice's Trade", 2002, pp.49-52.
111. *The London Journal,* 5 August, 1721.
112. *The Gentleman's Magazine*, 1731, vol.1, p.307.
113. *The Times*, 14 February 1791, p. 3.
114. N. Landau, "The Trading Justice's Trade", 2002, p.48.

then bailed him, was bound over to appear at the next Westminster Sessions for the "offence".[115]

This type of misbehaviour could result in the erring magistrate being formally invited to dine with his colleagues on "county day", the day during each Middlesex Quarter Sessions when the bench dealt with the county's administrative business. After dinner, the justice would be asked to explain the actions that had formed the basis of the complaint. Frequently, if he could not do so satisfactorily, he would apologise, and the matter would go no further. Occasionally, it would lead to more investigations and, ultimately, even to a representation to the Lord Chancellor that the offending justice be removed from the commission.[116]

It must also be remembered that trading justices were never the *only* active magistrates to be found in the Metropolis outside the Square Mile, even if they were the most visible and the busiest. Upwards of a hundred men were on the commissions for Middlesex and Westminster at any one time.

Non-Trading Justices

A significant number of magistrates were largely inactive, if not purely honorary. Throughout the century, in both rural and urban areas, most of the judicial work of a magistrate was carried out by less than 20 per cent of those who were formally appointed to a commission.[117] Reflecting this, it was sometimes claimed that the Westminster Commission was bifurcated into two "species" of JP One was alleged to be the trading justice, men who carried out all the "active parts" of that office. The other type (numerically the most common), were men who sought the office "merely for the sake of placing a feather in their cap". Such men simply wished to enhance their social status. Because they rarely acted in a magisterial capacity, they were considered to be "neutral, insipid, and inoffensive" Justices, doing neither good nor harm.[118] Certainly, many Metropolitan justices were drawn from

115. *Weekly Journal or British Gazetteer*, 10 March 1722.
116. N. Landau, "The Trading Justice's Trade", 2002, p.48.
117. P. Langford, *Public Life and the Propertied Englishman: 1689-1798*, 1991, pp.411-420.
118. Anon, *The Means of Effectually Preventing Theft and Robbery*, 1778, pp.7-8.

the sort of man who, having enjoyed a "rapid acquirement of property in trade", decided that being appointed to the bench would confer on him an: "...elevation much beyond his former situation".[119] Many did not even bother to take out their *dedimus potestatem*, the formal document that authorised them to serve as acting justices.[120]

However, this distinction between quasi-honorary JPs and active trading justices is too simplistic, especially for the first half of the eighteenth century. Although it appears that at least four of the seven most active JPs at the Middlesex Quarter Sessions in 1737 were trading justices, such men did not make up the entirety of the working members of the Middlesex Commission, even then.[121] Until well into the eighteenth century, there were many respectable and prosperous local men on the Middlesex bench, who sat regularly, if less frequently than their more mercenary colleagues, apparently acting out of traditional notions of social responsibility and prestige, rather than avarice, even if they were not quite as genteel as some of their provincial counterparts.

Henry Norris, a very active Hackney JP during the 1730s and 1740s, was an example of this type of magistrate. Norris was an upwardly mobile local merchant who was also a member of the Hackney select vestry, although it took him several years to be accorded the courtesy title "esquire" rather than "Mr" by that body.[122] He was certainly not an "ornamental" magistrate, as his detailed *Justicing Notebook* makes clear, nor does he appear to have been attracted to the office by pecuniary gain, as he was a comparatively wealthy man. Most of the local magistrates that he associated and worked with had similar backgrounds. In 1773, even the cynical Robert Holloway accepted that there were still working magistrates in Middlesex who were not trading justices.[123] Indeed, in the early 1780s, some observers felt that the Middlesex justices were more respectable than they had been for several years. This

119. Anon (By a Barrister), *A Letter to a Member of Parliament, on the Police of the Metropolis*, London, 1821, p.4.
120. D. Phillips, "A 'Weak' State? The English State, the Magistracy and the Reform of Policing in the 1830s", 2004, p.883.
121. N. Landau, *The Justices of the Peace 1679-1760*, 1984, p.185.
122. R. Paley (Ed.), *Justice in 18th-Century Hackney*, 1991, pp.xii-xiv.
123. R. Galloway, *The Rat-Trap*, 1773, p.15.

probably reflected the determined work of the Duke of Northumberland, the then Lord Lieutenant of Middlesex and Westminster, who tried to prevent improper people from being appointed to the two Commissions of the Peace.[124] There were also several attempts by "respectable" Metropolitan magistrates in the late eighteenth century to establish rotation offices of their own to rival those of their colleagues who were trading justices.[125]

Continuing Problems

Nevertheless, even allowing for reservations about both the ubiquity and malignancy of the trading justices, the situation was increasingly deemed to be unsatisfactory by both local and national authorities. After his death, it was observed that even the Duke of Northumberland had been largely unsuccessful in his attempts at enhancing the composition of the Middlesex and Westminster benches, at least in the long run. It was impossible to find significant numbers of respectable men willing to take on the office without a view to its remuneration.[126] Even where good men were recruited to the bench, the demands of their ordinary lives, and their lack of legal knowledge, meant that their attendance would not normally be maintained.[127]

Rightly or wrongly, the provision of magistrates' services in Middlesex and Westminster was perceived to be corrupt, inadequate, and inferior to that found in the Square Mile. In 1785, *The Times* observed that, given the apparent crime rate in the capital: "...the inefficacy of the present administration of justice, by trading magistrates, is palpable".[128] However, by then, there had been one localised, government supported, initiative in the capital for almost half a century. This was the court justice.

124. E. Sayer, *Observations on the Police or Civil Government of Westminster, with a Proposal for a Reform*, 1784, p.iv.
125. Anon (By a Barrister), *A Letter to a Member of Parliament, on the Police of the Metropolis*, 1821, p.6.
126. *The Calcutta Gazette*, 13 December 1792.
127. Anon (By a Barrister), *A Letter to a Member of Parliament, on the Police of the Metropolis*, 1821, p.6.
128. *The Times*, 25 June 1785, p.4.

The Court Justice

To address some of the problems occasioned by defects in the eighteenth-century Metropolitan magistracy, the government had built on the existing, and very informal, "office" of the court justice. This rather nebulous, unofficial, and often (by both modern historians and contemporary observers) exaggerated position, dated back to the previous century, if not before, though its precise history, in so far as it existed, is uncertain.[129]

Nevertheless, it seems that, by the Restoration period, the Crown, anxious about the proximity of its palaces and government to a rapidly growing urban area, had sought close links with a prominent Middlesex JP who could be relied upon to carry out difficult, sensitive and important policing duties in a manner that was beyond the abilities and inclinations of ordinary magistrates. Thus, in the late seventeenth century, Sir John Reresby had been appointed to the Middlesex Commission and taken an active role in sensitive investigations at the Crown's behest.[130] Similarly, in 1726, the very active Middlesex JP Thomas Robe was granted the office of Clerk of the Market of the Royal Household, a position that appears to have been a Crown sinecure. This seems to have been as a reward for his dedicated work as a magistrate, although his career ended in scandal.[131] At about the same time, Nathaniel Blackerby also received some government support.

However, until the 1730s, the position of court justice appears to have provided little more than enhanced lines of communication between the government and their chosen magistrate, along with occasional financial subventions. The situation began to change in 1729, with the appointment of Thomas de Veil, a former soldier and largely self-made man, to the Middlesex Commission. He set up an office in Thrift Street the following year. In 1739, he moved to Bow Street (next to Covent Garden) and set up his own "rotation office", mimicking that already established in the City's Guildhall Justice Room. There, along with other magistrates under his immediate supervision, he took turns to be on duty and hear complaints. Bow Street's

129. De Veil's biographer was one of those who stressed, if not exaggerated, its history.

130. Sir J. Reresby, *The Memoirs of Sir John Reresby*, 1734, pp.78-79.

131. *London Journal*, 30 July 1726.

central location made it convenient for both Westminster and nearby parts of urban Middlesex, such as Holborn. De Veil was highly professional in his work, showing great competence and efficiency in keeping the affairs and records of his office in order. This distinguished him from many other fee-orientated magistrates, and made him popular with both the authorities and the general public. Unfortunately, as he took business away from trading justices, it made him acutely unpopular with many of his colleagues.[132] In 1731, one of them, an Irish Justice named Webster, struck and stabbed de Veil during an argument over arrest warrants in a coffeehouse. De Veil suffered a five-inch wound to his stomach.[133]

To allow him to concentrate his energies on administering justice, and as a reward for his magisterial work, Thomas de Veil was granted a substantial sinecure as Inspector General of Exports and Imports. This came with minimal duties and a salary of £600 a year.[134] More directly, in 1740, he received a grant of £100 simply for his diligence as a JP, and was frequently given other sums of money to cover his expenses in office.[135] In further recognition of his work, he was knighted in 1744. Reflecting his government responsibilities and connections, de Veil appears to have been far more willing than most of his fellow Metropolitan justices to enforce the ill-conceived Gin Acts of 1729 and 1736. He was in regular contact with the Duke of Newcastle in the difficult days after the 1736 Act came into force, though he was to be critical of the statute in his memoirs. He also suppressed attacks on informers, something that prompted riots outside his house in Westminster.

De Veil's death in 1746 left a void in the Metropolitan criminal justice system. It was, eventually, to be filled by Henry Fielding, who moved into the same house (number four) in Bow Street, shortly after taking the oath of appointment as a justice of the peace for Westminster in October 1748. Fielding greatly enhanced the position that de Veil had developed, prior to his own death in 1754, and received a significant, if not publicly revealed, salary from the secret service fund. His half-brother, John Fielding, was made a justice for Westminster in 1751 and for Middlesex in 1754, becoming the

132. T. de Veil, *Memoirs of the Life and Times of Sir Thomas Deveil, Knight,* 1748, p.18.

133. *The Gentleman's Magazine*, 1731, vol. 1, p.125 and p.307.

134. *Old Common Sense: Or, the Englishman's Journal,* 11 February, 1738.

135. A. Babbington, *A House in Bow Street,* 2nd edn., 1999, p.52.

'court justice' in succession to Henry, the same year, and moving into the house in Bow Street. In many respects, he built on the work of his sibling, eventually producing the general preventative plan of 1772, which aimed at deterring potential offenders by speedy detection. This would be achieved, in part, by collating intelligence about felonies and maintaining a correspondence with other active magistrates. He continued Henry's practice of using a small group of thief-takers to pursue serious offenders in London and beyond.

The original government grant to Henry Fielding had allowed: "...one or more magistrates in this great Metropolis to give up their whole Time to the Public".[136] John Fielding wished to increase cover in the central Metropolitan area, and sought the assistance of associate justices. These included Saunders Welch, a former friend of his brother, who had been High Constable of Holborn, and who was appointed to the Westminster bench in 1755. Unfortunately, Welch was not treated as an equal by John Fielding, and was disappointed to receive only a quarter of the government's £400 annual payment. After a couple of years, he set up his own magistrates' office in Litchfield Street, for which he was granted a small stipend from the Crown.

John Fielding then recruited other Westminster magistrates to assist him. For example, during the 1750s, John Spinnage occasionally covered for him while he attended the Westminster Sessions or was engaged in conducting enquiries. By 1765, Spinnage was relieving him on at least one day a week, and shortly afterwards was himself in receipt of a government stipend. As a result, in the early 1760s, John Fielding occasionally called his office "The Felony Rotation". A more thorough rotation of magistrates was in place by 1768, when Fielding persuaded the Grafton administration to provide stipends to William Kelynge and Thomas Kynaston, magistrates who had acted on an occasional basis earlier in the decade. Together, their presence meant that the Bow Street office was open every day from, ten to two and five to nine in the evening.[137] Additionally, three or more JPs would sit each

136. J. Fielding, *Extracts from Such of the Penal Laws, As Particularly relate to the Peace and Good Order of this Metropolis*, 1768, p.4 and p.7.

137. J. M. Beattie, "Sir John Fielding and Public Justice: The Bow Street Magistrates' Court, 1754–1780", 2007, p.84.

Wednesday to re-examine prisoners and to exercise those powers that required more than one magistrate; effectively, these were regular petty sessions.[138]

Their presence made it easier for crime victims outside the Square Mile to locate a magistrate, lay charges, get assistance in finding their attackers, and uncover the evidence that would lead to a conviction and the possible return of stolen goods.[139] Typically, when a party of Runners captured the notorious highwayman William Hawke and his two associates in 1773, they were immediately taken to the Bow Street Office for a preliminary examination. From there, notice was sent to members of the public who were suspected of being Hawke's victims, and who had recently informed the office of his robberies, so that they, too, could attend his examination the following day and positively identify their attackers. After this was done, the whole gang was remanded in custody, being re-examined the following week in the presence of further witnesses, who also identified them, and who were then bound over to prosecute the highwaymen.[140]

The efficiency and effectiveness of Sir John's Bow Street Office made it very popular with victims/complainants from the entire (and very considerable) Middlesex area, many of whom eschewed more local justices to have recourse to it, even if it necessitated a long journey. By the late-1750s, half of all the felony cases arising in the Middlesex area were being dealt with by the Bow Street Office.[141] Between 1767 and 1773, almost fifty per cent of all Middlesex felony commitments still originated there, though the proportion waned slightly thereafter.[142] Its jurisdiction was even extended to Surrey after 1802 (42 Geo III c.76). The Bow Street Police Office also became the centre of police administration for the wider nation. Information about serious crimes might be sent there by magistrates throughout the country, and

---

138. J. Fielding, *Extracts from Such of the Penal Laws, As Particularly relate to the Peace and Good Order of this Metropolis*, 1768, pp.4 and 7.
139. J. M. Beattie, "Sir John Fielding and Public Justice: The Bow Street Magistrates' Court, 1754–1780", 2007, pp.77-78.
140. J. Villette, *A genuine Account of the Life, Robberies, Trial and Execution, of William Hawke*, 1774, pp.10-11.
141. J. H. Langbein, "Shaping the Eighteenth-century Criminal Trial: A View from the Ryder Sources", 1983, p.77.
142. J. M. Beattie, "Sir John Fielding and Public Justice: The Bow Street Magistrates' Court", 2007, p.76.

then disseminated on a national basis in the *Hue & Cry*, published in Bow Street from 1786 (it eventually developed into the *Police Gazette*).

The Fielding brothers were not universally popular with Londoners. Many impugned their motives, denigrated their effectiveness, and expressed concern about their apparent "empire building". One complained about the skilful manoeuvres of that:

> ...wooden-headed justice, Sir John Fielding, who is continually making a vast parade of preserving the peace, and keeping up the police of this city, to increase the business of his office, without lessening the number of thieves.

In 1758, a shilling pamphlet even compared him to the notoriously corrupt thief-taker Jonathan Wild.[143] Fifteen years later, William Miles mocked him for trying to prevent productions of John Gay's 1729 play *The Beggar's Opera* (Sir John was one of a number of eighteenth-century observers who were alarmed at its potentially criminogenic effects). Miles claimed that it was yet another manifestation of his life-long "impertinent officiousness" and lack of awareness as to the limits of his powers. He also complained about the uninterrupted scenes of debauchery that, he claimed, continued without hindrance in the area immediately around Bow Street.[144] Others, too, remarked on the brothels that existed close to Fielding's office in Covent Garden, and observed that it was incredible that the: "...most active Justice in England would let any such houses remain under his very nose"[145] (Sir John was open about the need to be "realistic" about the presence of such establishments).[146]

Despite such criticism, the Bow Street experiment was widely seen as a success, one that eventually provided a model worth replicating. John Fielding actively encouraged other Westminster and Middlesex Justices to band together to create their own offices, in which, by taking turns, they could provide a reliable service to the public at fixed times. As a result, several

143. W. Irwin, "An Attack on John Fielding", 1941, pp.523-525.

144. W. A. Miles, *A Letter to Sir John Fielding, Knt. Occasioned by his Extraordinary Request to Mr. Garrick, for the Suppression of the Beggars Opera*, 1773, pp.11-12.

145. Anon, *A Congratulatory Epistle From a Reformed Rake*, 1758, p.15.

146. H. Fielding, *The Case of the Unfortunate Bosavern Penlez*, 1749, p.6.

Rotation Offices emerged in the decades after 1760. For example, in 1763, they were set up at St. Andrew's, Holborn and St. Giles-in-the-Fields. Some were short-lived, others became more established, though their activism varied with the energy and willingness to serve of their magistrates. Nevertheless, over the next three decades the public was able to find magistrates with some degree of consistency at a number of busy locations, such as Clerkenwell, to the North of the City, and Shoreditch, Whitechapel, and Shadwell, in the East End. On a more erratic basis, magistrates could also be found at offices in Bloomsbury and other parts of Westminster, as well as St Margaret's Hill in Southwark, across the River Thames.[147]

These offices were usually set up in public places, such as the Guildhall in Westminster or the vestry room of a parish church, rather than in the private houses in which most magistrates had previously worked. They, too, sometimes became known as "public offices". However, even the most stable of them remained in Bow Street's shadow, in large part because they lacked its great advantage, government funding and the quasi-professional magistrates that came with it. This was not matched until Parliament provided financial support for other offices in 1792. As a result, in 1791, newspaper reports might contrast the "Rotation Office" at Litchfield with the "Public Office" in Bow Street.[148]

The Middlesex Justices Act of 1792

The Middlesex Justices Act of 1792 established seven new police offices in Westminster, Middlesex and urban Surrey, each with three stipendiary magistrates and (initially) six attached constables. This legislation was, in the words of Lord Grenville, a final acceptance of the impossibility of finding enough fit men within the Metropolis who were willing to carry out the duty without proper remuneration.[149] The new offices were established at Great Marlborough Street; Hatton Garden; Worship Street in Shoreditch; Lambeth Street

147. J. M. Beattie, "Sir John Fielding and Public Justice: The Bow Street Magistrates' Court, 1754–1780", 2007, p. 73.

148. *Evening Mail*, 17 October 1791.

149. *The Calcutta Gazette*, 13 December 1792.

in Whitechapel; the High Street in Shadwell; Queen Square; and, across the Thames, at Union Street in Southwark. To these can, of course, be added the three magistrates at Bow Street acting under the historic jurisdiction established by the Fielding brothers and (eventually) the three magistrates at the Thames Police Office, which was established in 1800 and tasked with addressing riverine crime.

As a result, by the end of the eighteenth century, there were twenty-seven stipendiary magistrates working outside the Square Mile. These professional magistrates normally sat daily, from 10 am to 8 pm. When sitting alone, they possessed the powers and jurisdiction of a bench of two or more ordinary JPs, and so always had the criminal jurisdiction of petty sessions.[150] The quality of stipendiary magistrates also gradually improved in the decades after 1792, as salaries (initially quite low at £400 per annum) increased, and prior qualification as a barrister became a prerequisite for appointment. Most of the initial holders of these offices were not legally qualified, and several former JPs were simply re-appointed to the new positions. Some of those initially selected by Henry Dundas, the home secretary, were chosen without as much "delicate discrimination" as might have been desirable.[151] One immediate improvement brought about by the 1792 Act was that JPs within the area covered by the statute were prohibited from receiving fees, other than those paid out for licensing alehouses.[152]

These developments did not wholly bring an end to "traditional", part-time, amateur magistrates in the Middlesex area. They survived on the outskirts of the Metropolis, and in those parts of the county that were still largely rural, and so outside the territorial limits of the 1792 Act. Indeed, they did not entirely eradicate trading justices: some magistrates simply moved their business outside the statute's jurisdiction, to places such as Brent, specifically with a view to continuing their work. As late as 1827, there was concern that the "old race" of trading justices was not quite extinct in the "outlets of the Metropolis".[153] Nevertheless, the 1792 reforms went a huge way towards

150. D. Bentley, *English Criminal Justice in the Nineteenth Century*, 1998, p.21.
151. Anon (By a Barrister), *A Letter to a Member of Parliament, on the Police of the Metropolis*, 1821, p.9.
152. J. M. Beattie, "Garrow and the Detectives", 2007, p.6.
153. *The Times*, 5 February 1827, p.3.

ending their significance. By 1811, Francis Grose could note that they were "by no means so common as formerly".

From Houses to Courts

Traditionally, individual magistrates had conducted much legal business from their own homes. Many Middlesex JPs and several City aldermen still followed this practice at the start of the eighteenth century. Some even had a specific "justice room" for this purpose. Sometimes, they would use a parish vestry room to examine suspects and carry out other business, especially if a bench of justices was to be present.[154] In the early 1740s, de Veil appears to have been the first English magistrate to arrange the justice room in his house in Bow Street into a recognizably "modern" fashion for a summary court, with the magistrate sitting on a raised dais, with his clerk seated at a desk immediately below him, and a raised gallery for spectators.[155] In 1772, John Fielding rebuilt this courtroom on an even more formal basis. Other Metropolitan magistrates gradually followed their lead. As a result, by 1779, one observer could note that, in late years, it had become the: "...practice in this metropolis to convert the houses of justices of the peace into public offices".[156]

In the City, the Justice Room at the Guildhall was used for legal business throughout the century, being joined by the Mansion House after 1753. An alderman sitting at the Guildhall, in the early 1700s, was described as being seated on an elbow-chair, which was placed behind a bar to stop unruly defendants from getting too close and constables from stepping on his toes. At about the same time, William Hogarth provided a detailed portrayal of such a scene (see plate section).

154. *Weekly Journal, or the British Gazetteer*, 19 October 1728.
155. A. Babbington, *A House in Bow Street*, 2nd edn., 1999, p.51.
156. J. Hackman, *The Case and Memoirs of the Late Rev. Mr. James Hackman ... With an Appendix on the ill Effects Offices of Justices of the Peace*, 1779, p.i.

PART THREE: JUSTICE

CHAPTER 13

THE MAGISTRATES' WORK

Interlocutory Proceedings

The majority of an eighteenth-century magistrate's work, unlike that of their modern counterparts, was interlocutory rather than judicial. They spent far more time dealing with the pre-trial phase of proceedings and investigation than in presiding over hearings, whether summarily or at Quarter Sessions, though the importance of their summary jurisdiction increased steadily during the course of the century. Of course, the pre-trial phase had an enormous influence on the eventual trial process.

Arrest Warrants

If a suspect was not caught red-handed, a warrant for his arrest would normally have to be issued by a JP before he could be detained. Frequently, the victim would enforce this in person, albeit usually with the support of a parish officer. An arrest warrant had to be in writing; it could not be issued orally, and had to be properly specific as to the person to be detained, and the crime for which he was being held. This could create problems in an urban environment, where a person's proper name was not always known, or readily ascertainable, in the way that it might be in a village.[1]

Frequently, parish officers would also insist on having a justice's warrant if they were personally unsure of the legality of detaining someone on their own authority, as it provided protection against any ensuing civil suit for false arrest and imprisonment. As with many legal services provided by the justices, if a petitioner was unsuccessful with one magistrate, he could

1. J. Dunton, *The Shortest-Way with Whores and Rogues*, 1703, p.48.

renew his application before another. For example, when William Horne was belatedly accused of murder, decades after the offence occurred, his prosecutor had to approach several justices before finding one willing to entertain such an old complaint.[2] More typically, when Bartholomew Greenwood was robbed in 1740, and thought that he could identify one of his attackers, he initially sought a warrant for this man's arrest from a justice named Frazer. However, Frazer was unwilling to grant it, because he was concerned that the applicant could only identify the suspect by his voice, rather than his face. Instead, Greenwood was forced to apply to Colonel de Veil, who was it seems less fastidious in this respect.[3] The justice's clerk would normally draw up the warrant for a shilling.[4]

When issuing arrest warrants, magistrates would, of course, only hear the complainant's version of events. There was considerable scope for abuse, given that he would often enforce it in person. Warrants might be secured maliciously, without justification, and used to blackmail those named in them into paying money under threat of being arrested. The disastrous raid by reforming constables on the Rummer Tavern had been based on warrants issued by a magistrate five weeks earlier, and kept until the constables observed an apparently "lewd" woman entering the premises.[5] Nevertheless, many justices appear to have been aware of such possibilities.[6]

Search Warrants

A constable normally needed a magistrate's warrant to enter premises without invitation, whether it was to search for stolen goods or fugitives. Like an arrest warrant, this would usually be obtained by a complainant. For example, in 1752, Richard Goldsborough secured a search warrant at the

2. Anon, *A Genuine Account of the Life and Trial of William Andrew Horne*, Esq. 3rd edn. 1760, p.8.
3. Anon, *The Genuine and Authentic Trial of Mr. Bartholomew Greenwood, Charg'd with Robbing Mr. Roger Wheatly near Camberwell*, 3rd. edn., 1740, p.14 and p.24.
4. J. Dunton, *The Shortest-Way with Whores and Rogues: Or, A New Project for Reformation,* 1703, p.48.
5. *Leeman v Allen and Others* (1763) 2 Wilson K.B. 160.
6. N. B., *A Compleat Collection Of Remarkable Tryals Of the most Notorious Malefactors, at the Sessions-House in the Old Baily, for near Fifty Years past*, 1718, pp. 120-126.

Guildhall Justice Room, after he suspected that Sarah Broughton had stolen a silver teaspoon and two blankets from his house and concealed them in an associate's residence.[7] Similarly, in 1758, when a constable enforced a search warrant at the house of one Thomas Foley to look for stolen horseshoes, their erstwhile owner went with him and, when they found 24 metal shoes, positively identified them as his own. This prompted the arrest of Foley.[8]

In theory, search warrants had to be of named premises. General warrants, i.e. those that did not specify the premises to be searched, were forbidden. Nevertheless, there was considerable debate as to *how* precisely the locations that were to be investigated needed to be specified. In 1742, a handbook for justices and their clerks suggested that a post-burglary search warrant, issued to constables by a magistrate at the behest of a crime victim, might simply specify that they could enter and search any houses, outhouses and other places belonging to a named suspect that were within their precincts.[9] As this indicates, many requests for search warrants were granted despite being fairly vague about the properties that were to be entered. It also appears that the degree of evidence required to obtain a warrant was relatively small, as most searches do not seem to have produced any results at all, whether it was the discovery of stolen property or suspects.[10]

Legal Advice

An examining JP might also tender advice to a complainant about how to enhance the wider prosecution, though, by the end of the century, it seems that this was becoming slightly constrained by a previously absent need to show a modicum of impartiality. For example, in 1781, when the victim of a robbery who had been followed out of a pub and attacked went to a magistrate, the JP: "...with much propriety, hinted to the prosecutor to serve the

7. Minute Book of the Guildhall Justice Room 25 May to 19 June, 1752, LMA CLA 00501, entry for 5 June.
8. OBSP, Trial of Thomas Foley and Paul Neal, 6 Dec 1758.
9. J. Higgs, *A Guide to Justices or Modern English Precedents for the Direction of Justices of the Peace and their Clerks*, 2nd edn., 1742, pp.95-96.
10. J. M. Beattie, *Policing and Punishment in London, 1660-1750*, 2001, pp.24-33.

master of the public house with a subpoena, to appear and to give evidence against the prisoner at the Old Bailey".[11]

The Examination

Once a suspect was arrested for a felony or, sometimes, even a serious misdemeanour, he would be examined by a magistrate, whether this was an alderman or JP The procedure was conducted pursuant to important and technical Marian statutes from 1555 (1 & 2 Philip & Mary c. 13) and 1556 (2 & 3 Philip & Mary c. 10). Normally, only one justice would be present at this stage, and there was no legal requirement that more attend. However, in the Metropolis, several JPs might sit in on an examination in very serious cases, whether through personal interest or out of a desire to lend their expertise and authority to their colleagues. For example, in 1726, when Thomas Wood was examined about his role in the murder of John Hayes, three Middlesex JPs were present.[12] In Hackney, during the 1740s, examinations were occasionally conducted at petty sessions, in which case there would always be at least two magistrates present.

Sometimes, such examinations were held in private. Frequently, however, they were open to the general public, or at least interested parties. The move from magisterial business being carried out in a justice's parlour, to being conducted in what roughly approximated to a modern type of courtroom, inevitably encouraged more people, including the "idle or curious" and newspaper reporters, to attend.[13] As a result, Sir Thomas de Veil noted that there might be a 'crowd' of onlookers present at such hearings in the 1740s.[14] Sir John Fielding's office even made extensive seating available for observers. Examinations in the Guildhall Justice Room were also open to the public, as can be seen from Hogarth's portrayal of 1751. Indeed, on one day in July 1787, there were so many people present while the sitting alderman was examining suspects and taking witness depositions that he asked

11. *The Times*, 27 August 1789, p. 3.
12. Anon, *A Narrative of the Barbarous and unheard of Murder of Mr. John Hayes*, 1726, p.11.
13. J. Hackman, *The Case and Memoirs of the Late Rev. Mr. James Hackman*, 1779, p.iv.
14. Sir T. De Veil, *Observations on the Practice of a Justice of the Peace*, 1747, p.2.

for the room be cleared: "...on account of the heat arising from people who had no business [there]".[15]

Suspects could be searched as well as questioned by examining magistrates, and even stranger tests might be conducted. In 1702, for example, when Sarah Morduck, a Southwark woman accused of witchcraft, sought the protection of one of the City's aldermen after she was 'mobbed' while in the Square Mile, Alderman Sir Thomas Lane sent for Morduck's alleged victim and allowed the popular 'blood drawing' method for neutralising a witch's power to be applied in his presence. Morduck was scratched by her victim until she bled. Additionally, Lane had her intimately searched for the 'witch's teat' in a private room, and committed her to prison pending trial for the occult crime.[16] In 1786, when John Hogan was questioned by magistrates about the murder of Ann Hunt, he was taken to her body and told to touch it while being asked further questions about his relationship with the dead woman.[17] This had echoes of 'cruentation', the ancient belief that the corpse of a murder victim would bleed if touched by the killer.

The justice's clerk would normally keep a written note, or at least a summary, of the examination (occasionally the JP did this himself). This record was important, as any confession made by a suspect to a justice could be adduced against him at trial.[18]

Confessions

Successful prosecutions in the Metropolitan area were often founded on an effective initial examination, especially one that produced an admissible confession. For example, when Isaac Dennis was brought before Henry Norris, accused of taking a few pennies from a group of women during an

15. *The Times*, 2 November 1787, p.3.
16. R. Hathaway, *The Tryal of Richard Hathaway*, 1702, p.2 and p.5.
17. *The Times*, 14 January 1786, p.3.
18. As today, confessions made to people other than magistrates could also be adduced. As was noted in 1728, a confession, whether made to an examining justice: "...or spoken in private discourse, has always been allow'd to be given in evidence against the party". Thus, in 1716, Christopher Tedder was convicted: "...partly by his own confession to a watchman".

alleged highway robbery, he swiftly admitted the offence, albeit claiming that he was not acting alone and stressing that it was his first crime. This statement was to prove unfortunate at trial, where his defence was that his action had been nothing more than 'aggressive begging'.[19] Similarly, in 1718, Mary Lovelock, suspected on fairly weak circumstantial evidence of housebreaking, was convicted largely on the strength of a confession she subsequently sought to retract: "She confessed the Fact before the Justice: But upon her Tryal she denied the Fact".[20]

As Lovelock's case suggests, and as today, there was nothing to prevent a defendant who had made full out-of-court admissions, prior to trial, from going back on them and pleading 'not guilty', even if he had signed a written confession. This was a sufficiently common phenomenon for the magistrate Thomas Robe to warn a suspect, from whom he had earlier obtained a confession to murder, not to renege on his admissions:

> You may have been told, that when you verbally confess before a Justice, you may retract upon your Trial; but ... I advise you to sign the confession you have now made, and give the court no trouble upon your trial.[21]

In 1750, the celebrated highwayman James Maclaine attempted to go back on comprehensive admissions he had made to an examining justice. After his conviction, the Reverend Dr. Allen reproached Maclaine for the "evasive ways" in which he had tried to avoid his confession at trial. The highwayman claimed that it had been done on legal advice.[22]

In these situations, some would blame their initial confessions on a general sense of disorientation occasioned by arrest and interrogation. When Rebecca Jones's admission to theft was read out in court: "The prisoner in her defence said she did not know what she said before the Justice".[23] Sarah

19. R. Paley (Ed.), *Justice in 18th-Century Hackney*, 1991, p.29.
20. OBSP, Trial of Mary Lovelock, 27 February 1718.
21. Anon (Philo Patriae), *A Full and Genuine Account of the Murder of Mrs. Robinson, by Elton Lewis*, 1735, pp.4-18. The author claimed to have been present throughout the examination.
22. F. Allen, *An Account of the Behaviour of Mr. James Maclaine, from the time of his Condemnation to the Day of his Execution*, 1750, p.8.
23. OBSP, Trial of Rebecca Jones, 8 April 1719.

Carvel claimed that she was: "...frighten'd into the confession by the dread of going to Newgate, and that she knew nothing of the matter".[24] Others would attribute their admissions to alcohol or threats from their interrogators. For example, John Williams, accused of attempted sodomy, admitted his guilt when examined by Sir Richard Levet, but tried: "...to deny on his Tryal, all he had said before the Justice, and said the Prosecutors threatened him if he did not own it". After John Daley made full admissions to a burglary, while being examined by the Lord Mayor, he: "...deny'd his former confession, saying he was in drink".[25]

Any confession would have to be formally proved at the ensuing hearing by the magistrate to whom it had been made or, perhaps more commonly, by his clerk. For example, when Richard Sampson was accused of robbery in 1737, Colonel de Veil's clerk gave evidence at the Old Bailey, noted that he had been present at Sampson's examination, and stated that it was: "... taken from his own Mouth, 'twas read over to him, and he own'd it to be true, and sign'd it in my Presence". It was then read out in full to the jury.[26]

The thoroughness, skill and fairness with which suspects were examined varied greatly. Sir Thomas de Veil owed much of his considerable success against Metropolitan and suburban criminals to a mastery of the techniques of interrogation, being tireless in conducting "long and tedious examinations".[27] In 1732, he questioned an eighteen-year-old accused of sodomy for almost three hours, before the youth made admissions and impeached a group of men who had been involved in the incident.[28] Additionally, de Veil demonstrated great skill when cross-examining suspects, knowing how to disorientate them so that they spoke freely. His questioning of a burglar named Ogden as to how he had come by a large sum of money was typical. Ogden initially claimed that it had come from a bank note of 15 guineas. De Veil later pointed out that notes did not exist in that denomination, forcing him to change his story, claim that the money had

24. OBSP, Trial of Sarah Carvel, 6 December 1721.
25. OBSP, Trial of John Daley, 25 February 1713.
26. OBSP, Trial of Richard Sampson and John Nugent, 26 May 1737.
27. *The Gentleman's Magazine*, 1747, vol. 17, pp.562-565.
28. *The Universal Spy*, 5 August 1732.

been given to him by a friend, and that he had been: "...drunk, when he was first examined".[29]

De Veil's lineal successor, the magistrate Henry Fielding, also stressed the importance of a well-conducted examination. He had been willing to spend days, and even nights, questioning suspects and taking depositions from witnesses.[30] His half-brother (and successor), John Fielding, was also highly skilled in this art. For example, in 1763, his clerk, William Marsden, noted that a servant suspected of murdering and stealing from a colleague had been assiduously examined over a two-day period. He explained his new-found wealth by saying that he had received ten guineas from his brother the previous week. Marsden then visited the suspect's sibling and found this to be untrue. The servant made a full confession to the murder.[31] Similarly, in 1756, Sir John and Saunders Welch rigorously examined William Cannicott, who had strangled and stabbed his estranged wife. On the first day of his examination he admitted nothing. However, when he discovered that his (innocent) mistress had been arrested, and threatened with being implicated in the crime, he made full admissions, exonerating her in the process.[32] Even towards the end of his career, in 1775, a visiting American who watched the blind magistrate at work was struck by Sir John's "ready apprehension, and great penetration" when questioning suspects.[33]

Of course, de Veil and the Fielding brothers have a special place in the history of Metropolitan law enforcement; they were not 'typical' justices. Nevertheless, they were not unique. For example, Thomas Robe's examination of Elton Lewis, suspected of murdering his cousin in a fit of anger in 1735, and recorded by an eyewitness, shows how far other conscientious JPs would go to solve a very serious crime. Lewis was taken to Robe's house with his wife and a young servant girl. The justice ordered that they be searched, kept apart, and examined separately. Over five hours of questioning ensued, in which the magistrate used a number of ruses to extract a confession from an equally determined suspect. Fragments of the dead woman's shattered

29. OBSP, Trial of John Ogden, 27 February 1740.
30. H. Fielding, *Journal of A Voyage to Lisbon*, 1755, p.20.
31. OBSP, Trial of Daniel Blake, 23 February 1763.
32. W. Cannicott, *A Genuine Account of the Life and Actions of William Cannicott*, 1756, pp.9-10.
33. G. A. Ward (Ed.), *The Journal And Letters Of Samuel Curwen*, 1864, 4th edn, p.37.

skull were shown to Lewis to disorientate him. He was also warned that his wife might be accused of the crime if he did not make admissions. Eventually, after hairs from the dead woman were (allegedly) found sticking to some string in his pocket, he made a full confession.[34]

Nevertheless, many Metropolitan magistrates did not have the forensic ability, time or inclination to go to these lengths. In the case of trading justices, it would not have been cost-effective, as examinations carried no remuneration. Additionally, robust or devious questioning, the offer of inducements in exchange for admissions, or the use of threats, could occasion injustice. It was a regular criticism of de Veil that he assumed that all those brought before him must be guilty. Similarly, the barrister William Augustus Miles compared Sir John Fielding's conduct of examinations, especially his aggressive browbeating of witnesses, to the behaviour of a member of the Spanish Inquisition "rather than a British magistrate".[35] William Cannicott thought that the justices had been "cruel and uncharitable" in threatening to implicate his mistress.

Even so, there were always limits as to what was considered 'acceptable' magisterial conduct, and these gradually became stricter during the course of the century. Some seventeenth-century legal commentators had talked of confessions having to be 'wrung' out of suspects. By the end of the eighteenth century, there was a growing feeling that it was wrong for prisoners to be pressed excessively when questioned.[36] Several observers stressed that examinations should also be viewed as an opportunity for an innocent prisoner to clear himself, at an early stage in proceedings.

More specifically, certain safeguards were gradually introduced or enhanced. Thus, the general practice of magisterial cautioning of suspects has been traced back to 1730, and is probably even older, though it was not mandatory until the 1840s.[37] Similarly, the clear guidance on rejecting confessions obtained by threats or inducements, set down in *R v Warwickshall*

34. Anon (Philo Patriae), *A Full and Genuine Account of the Murder of Mrs. Robinson, by Elton Lewis*, 1735, pp.4-18. The author claimed to have been present throughout the examination.
35. W. A. Miles, *A Letter to Sir John Fielding*, 1773, p.19.
36. D. Bentley, *English Criminal Justice in the Nineteenth Century*, 1998, p.30.
37. W. Wesley Pue, "The Criminal Twilight Zone: Pre-Trial Procedures in the 1840s", 1983, pp.335-364.

(1783), and which was to last until well into the twentieth century, largely restated what had long been regarded as both correct practice and the law.[38] Decades before 1783, JPs (or their clerks) were stressing to juries that any admissions that they adduced at trial had not been obtained by a fear of prejudice or hope of advantage. To take an extreme example, in 1763, when Daniel Blake, a servant accused of murdering his master, pleaded 'not guilty' at trial, prosecuting counsel emphasised that he had made his written confession to Sir John Fielding after receiving: "…repeated warning to be cautious what he said, and after being told that all admissions might be used as evidence against his own life". Indeed, when giving evidence, Fielding's clerk claimed that the magistrate had gone so far as to advise the suspect that he would be putting a noose around his own neck, warned him about the consequences of signing such a confession, and asked whether it was being done voluntarily.[39]

Nevertheless, treatment of confessions obtained in dubious circumstances seems to have differed widely until the 1740s. At the start of the century, some Old Bailey judges did nothing about potentially tainted admissions. Others confined themselves to cautioning the jury about the inherent dangers of a confession that might have been obtained in such a manner, but left it to jurors to assess what, if any, weight to place on the confession. By contrast, several judges effectively excluded such confessions altogether. Thus, if a prosecutor had promised that he would not bring proceedings against a suspected thief if he made admissions and restored any stolen property – a common scenario, especially where the suspect was a domestic servant–they might not allow any ensuing confession to go to the jury.

A widespread change in forensic practice becomes discernible in about 1740, with judges becoming more uniformly willing to exclude improperly obtained confessions. For example, at the Kingston Assizes that year, James Tigwell was accused of housebreaking with a colleague, during which some clothes had been stolen. One of the missing garments had been found on his back. Tigwell was examined by a local magistrate, but when the resulting confession was read out at trial, the court: "…not being satisfy'd that

38. *R v Warwickshall* (1783) 1 Leach 263.

39. OBSP, Trial of Daniel Blake, 23 February 1763.

the said information was made voluntarily, and there being nothing else to affect the prisoner but his own confession, the jury acquitted him". His co-accused, Edward Waller, who had been implicated by Tigwell's confession, had had his case thrown out by the Grand Jury.[40] An out-of-court confession was only evidence against its maker, not anyone else implicated in it (still largely the case today).[41]

An initial exception was made over unsuccessful negotiations held between a suspect and a magistrate with a view to becoming a Crown witness against accomplices. In these situations, a suspect might reveal much incriminating information in an attempt to whet the authorities' appetite for granting him immunity. Nevertheless, if they subsequently decided not to make him a prosecution witness, his incriminating remarks could still usually be adduced against him at trial. Even here, however, the 1770s saw a change in direction, with such evidence no longer being adduced.[42]

The modern *voir dire* procedure, or 'trial within a trial', conducted in the absence of the jury to determine evidential admissibility, was absent at this time, and would not be used until the end of the following century.[43] Instead, the presiding judge might direct the jury to disregard what had proved to be an unsatisfactory confession, if it had already been adduced, discuss its admissibility in the presence of the jury, *before* it was adduced, or even interrupt its adduction if it appeared to have been obtained in improper circumstances. This occurred in 1809 in a case where the victim and prosecutor had pressured the defendant into making out-of-court admissions. At trial, he started to say that their conversation ended in a confession but the: "… judge prevented him from giving testimony of a mere verbal confession".[44]

Until 1848, suspects had no *entitlement* to legal representation at their pre-trial examination, though magistrates could allow it at their discretion. Many were reluctant to do so. Thomas de Veil warned them about the

40. Anon, *The proceedings at the Assizes of Peace, Oyer and Terminer, for the County of Surrey, held at the Town-Hall of Kingston upon Thames on Wednesday the 30th… Saturday the 2nd Day of August*, 1740, p.10.
41. Anon, *Directions for Prosecuting Thieves Without the Help of those False Guides, The Newgate Sollicitors*, 1728, p.20.
42. J. H. Langbein, *The Origins of Adversary Criminal Trial*, 2003, pp.225-226.
43. D. Bentley, *English Criminal Justice in the Nineteenth Century*, 1998, p.211.
44. *R v Richard Griffin* (1809) Russell and Ryan 151.

dangers posed by corrupt "Newgate solicitors" who would "skip into Justices' Houses with a crowd" while felons and witnesses were being examined, searching for a technical defect in proceedings.[45] However, a few suspects had both the means and permission to avail themselves of legal advice. In 1793, for example, James Remnant, a high-class professional thief arranged for a senior barrister to attend his examination at the Bow Street Office as "counsel for the prisoner".[46] Even so, the vast majority of defendants were not legally represented when questioned, either because their examining JP did not allow it, or because they could not afford it.

The presence of an admissible confession could be very significant. In 1715, it reduced the likelihood of acquittal in what was otherwise a purely circumstantial case from 37 per cent to 5 per cent; in 1780 the figures were 50 per cent compared to 20 per cent. The increase in acquittal rates amongst those confessing towards the end of the century probably reflects increased judicial suspicion about the manner in which confessions were being obtained, and a reduced willingness on the part of jurors to accept them.[47] Even statements that did not amount to full confessions could be highly damaging. For example, when a servant implicated in the murder of John Penny was questioned by de Veil and the dead man's nephew at Bow Street, the nephew got the servant to claim that he had seen the victim go out in an unseasonably thick woollen winter waistcoat that had subsequently been found wrapped around the dead man's corpse.[48]

Full confessions, when recorded, would typically begin with a phrase such as: "This examinant confesseth and saith …". Its maker would usually be asked to sign or mark (if illiterate) the clerk's account, to help authenticate it at trial, though this was not a prerequisite for admissibility. In the modern era, prior to the advent of tape-recorded police interviews in the 1980s, there were allegations that some unsigned interviews had been made up by investigating officers. It is possible that there were instances of this in the eighteenth century. One might, perhaps, wonder about Charles Rex's confession to theft, made before a Middlesex JP in June 1753, in which he

45. Sir T. Deveil, *Observations on the Practice of a Justice of the Peace*, 1747, p.2.
46. *The Times*, 2 July, 1793, p.3.
47. G. Fisher, "The Jury's Rise as Law Detector", 1997, p.644, note 323.
48. G. H., *Matchless Villany; or a full … narrative of the robbery and murder of J. Penny*, 1741, p.36.

allegedly "refused to sign" the document recording his extensive admissions.[49] However, and as is still the situation today, confessions had to be given in their entirety; they could not be edited and given "by parcels".[50]

Depositions

As part of the same procedure, magistrates would take depositions from the complainant (also normally the prosecutor) and any other potential prosecution witnesses. Unlike the suspect, they would be examined on oath.[51] In William Hogarth's print of such an examination, the duty alderman's clerk can be seen keeping a note of the testimony of the suspect's erstwhile accomplice, while seated at a side table to the magistrate. Normally, an examining magistrate would not take statements from defence witnesses other than the accused, though, even in this regard, he might listen to someone who could clearly exonerate a suspect.

Obtaining information from witnesses, like questioning suspects, required certain skills. For example, when Saunders Welch, a Westminster justice and the assistant to Sir John Fielding, examined a street boy in the presence of Samuel Johnson, Welch initially spoke in a manner that was utterly unintelligible to the boy, to impress the man of letters. Realising this, Johnson changed the magistrate's phraseology into colloquial English, so that it could be: "... understood by the vulgar, from whom information was to be obtained".[52]

Depositions would usually be taken down in outline or summary form, being written out in longhand. Their thoroughness varied, depending on the nature of the offence and the inclinations of the magistrate. Some contained considerable incidental detail, such as the verbal expressions used by perpetrators; others were more "bare bones". When Charles Proby was robbed

49. MSP 1753 Ju/36.
50. Anon, *Directions for Prosecuting Thieves Without the Help of those False Guides, The Newgate Solicitors*, 1728, p.3.
51. In 1661, the Westminster judges reiterated at the Old Bailey that, under the Marian statutes, justices of the peace should take examinations: "...both of the felons *without oath*, and the informers and witnesses against them upon oath in writing". *Directions for Justices of the Peace* (1661) Kelyng, J. 1.
52. J. Boswell, *Life of Samuel Johnson*, vol. 2, 1904, pp.1203-19.

by a highwayman in Berkeley Square he swore a deposition before a Middlesex JP in the presence of an arrested suspect. Proby, "being upon oath" (a formal part of all such affidavits), declared that he had been attacked by a man on a brown horse, who: "...very much resembles a person now present who calls himself John Parry". The time and place of the incident, and the amount taken, was also provided. A servant who was with him had his account recorded in slightly more graphic detail, recalling that their attacker had threatened to "blow [their] brains out" with his pistol.[53]

Depositions were produced at trial, where they could be used to inform the judge, refresh memories, and impeach hostile witnesses who deliberately failed to come up to proof.[54] Inconsistencies between the testimony given at trial, and that provided earlier to an examining magistrate, might also be stressed. For example, when John Lowther was arrested for attempted sodomy in 1761, he was initially examined by the Lord Mayor at the Guildhall, as were the two main prosecution witnesses. At the ensuing Quarter Sessions for the City, a friend of the defendant, who had evidently been present at the pre-trial examination, suggested that one of the key Crown witnesses had given a somewhat different version of events at trial to that which he had furnished in the Justice room. In rebuttal, the prosecution called John Gregg, described as the Lord Mayor's officer (presumably his clerk), to state that he had been present when the defendant was brought before the Mayor, that the witnesses were examined separately, and that: "...when Bowden was examined, he gave much the same account as he has now done".[55] By contrast, at a murder trial in 1796, the presiding judge noted in his summing-up that the jury had heard what a key witness had said:

> But she did not say so before the magistrate ... there is therefore a contradiction in her evidence.

53. MJ/SP/1754/04/122.
54. J. H. Langbein, "Shaping the Eighteenth-century Criminal Trial: A View from the Ryder Sources", 1983, p.83.
55. Anon, *The Tryal of Mr. John Lowther*, 1761, pp.1-12.

As a result, he suggested that her recollection of the incident might have been "wholly imperfect".[56]

Despite these forensic uses, the evidential value of pre-trial depositions made by prosecution witnesses was very limited, even though made on oath. If a prosecutor or crucial prosecution witness failed to testify at trial, an acquittal was almost certain to follow, even if they had earlier made a deposition strongly implicating the accused. Unlike suspects' confessions, witness depositions could only be received as evidence, in the absence of their makers, in exceptional situations. How far these extended was a matter of periodic debate at the Old Bailey and other criminal courts during the course of the eighteenth century. That they could be received at all appears to have been a result of the specific wording of the Marian statutes. For this reason, such affidavits could never be received in misdemeanour (rather than felony) hearings.[57]

Nevertheless, provided that the full technical prerequisites of the sixteenth-century Acts had been met, namely that the examination had been conducted by a justice, on oath, been written down, and that the maker of the statement had subsequently died or was physically unable to travel to court, whether through illness or having been kept away at the behest of the defendant, they could, sometimes, be received as evidence in felony cases. In these situations, the statement was: "...substituted in the room of that *viva voce* testimony which the deponent, if living, could alone have given".[58] As a result, in 1744, George Cooke, a Middlesex Justice was summoned by a surgeon to attend an apparently mortally wounded man, to: "...take what evidence he was capable of".[59] In 1722, two magistrates and a clergyman visited Edward Luttrel, a former guards officer, who was mortally wounded in his home during an argument with Middlesex bailiffs who were trying to arrest him for debt. The justices: "....administer'd the oath, in order to take the examination in form".[60] They then questioned him about his wounds.

56. Anon, *The Trial of Miss Jones, &c. For the Murder of Mr. Thomas Yates*, 1796, p.33.
57. S. Eure, *Trials per pais: or, the law of England concerning juries by nisi prius, & c.*, 7th edn., 1739, pp.380-381.
58. *King v Woodcock* (1789) 1 Leach 500.
59. OBSP, Trial of Robert Fuller, 10 May 1744.
60. Anon, *A Select Collection of Remarkable Trials in One Volume*, 1744, p.373.

The clergyman wrote down the deposition, acting as a clerk.[61] Unfortunately, at the subsequent trial at the Court of King's Bench (one of that forum's rare murder cases), technical problems in the taking of the deposition, along with the absence of the original document, meant that the statement was not admissible.[62] Even when they were admitted, case law suggested they would normally need to be: "...strongly corroborated by other testimony".[63]

Additionally, and much more seriously, as the century advanced the courts became increasingly insistent that such a statement had to have been made in the *presence* of the accused, so that they had an opportunity to cross-examine its maker when it was drawn up. This was stressed in the 1791 Old Bailey trial of George Dingler for murdering his wife, in which William Garrow successfully objected to a statement made by the mortally wounded woman to a magistrate when he visited her in the Westminster Infirmary.[64] By contrast, in 1787, while Hannah Morgan "languished" from fatal injuries inflicted by her maid, she was visited by James Crofts and Sir Robert Taylor, two Middlesex magistrates, and eventually carried to a public office, where Crofts took down her deposition. This was read over to her in the presence of the accused woman and all were signed in Taylor's presence. When Morgan died a few weeks after the examination, her deposition was held to be admissible at the ensuing murder trial, as it had: "...been given in the presence and hearing of the prisoner, upon an oath lawfully administered to Mrs. Morgan".[65]

In exceptional circumstances, such a pre-trial statement might be admissible in a murder trial, even if these prerequisites were not made out, provided it satisfied the separate requirements of a "dying declaration". This was a common law exception to the hearsay rule, whereby, the identification by a homicide victim of their attacker, made while under a publicly expressed expectation of imminent death from their wounds, and as a result of which

61. Anon (By a Gentleman of the Inner Temple), *The Widow Lutterel's Cry for Justice for the Blood of her Murthered Husband*, 1722, p.15. At the bailiffs' subsequent trial for murder at the Court of King's Bench the author of this pamphlet, which was freely aimed at securing their prosecution, was the subject of strong criticism.

62. Anon, *A Select Collection of Remarkable Trials in One Volume*, 1744, pp.374-376.

63. *King v Westbeen* (1739) 1 Leach 12.

64. *R v Dingler* (1791) 2 Leach 561.

65. *The King v Henrietta Radbourne* (1787) 1 Leach 457.

they subsequently died, was admissible at trial.[66] This applied as much to a statement made to a justice as one made to an ordinary member of the public, and was sometimes employed to circumvent the inadmissibility of fuller but defective depositions to justices. An example occurred when a mortally wounded wife spoke to a magistrate in the absence of her husband, the defendant.[67] Nevertheless, its strict prerequisites greatly limited its use.

Recognisances to Prosecute

At pre-trial hearings, JPs would also bind over prosecutors and other important Crown witnesses to appear at trial by entering them into recognisances. These would be forfeit if they did not attend to testify. This helped to prevent complainants who either lost interest in the proceedings, or who were bribed or threatened between arrest and trial, from going back on their allegations. For an example can be considered the case of Bezer Blundell, who had his watch stolen by Ann Connelly, a Drury Lane prostitute. He had her arrested, but subsequently negotiated the return of the valuable timepiece with Connelly's friends for £10. He freely admitted at trial that he had promised Connelly he would not proceed against her if he got his watch back, and that: "I should not have prosecuted, but that I found afterwards that I was bound in a recognizance of 40 l".[68] In 1789, the victim of a highway robbery, who had produced three of his assailants before a Bow Street magistrate, was warned by the justice that it was likely that he would be approached "to go out of the way" prior to trial, with a view to stifling the prosecution. The magistrate reminded him that, in these circumstances, he would forfeit his £40 recognisance, which, as he could not afford to pay it, would result in his being committed to prison.[69]

66. L. MacNally, *The rules of evidence on pleas of the Crown: illustrated from printed and manuscript trials and cases*, 1802, pp.283-305.

67. *The King v Reason* (1722) 16 How. St. Tr. (K.B.) and *The King v. Woodcock* (1789) 168 Eng. Rep. 352.

68. OBSP, 15 October 1740, Trial of Ann Connelly.

69. *The Times*, 27 August 1789, p.3. The judge also reminded him that he would be compounding a felony, for which offence he would be indicted. On a more encouraging note, he observed that, on conviction of the men, the complainant would receive a reward of £40.

Forty pounds was a fairly standard sum for much of the period, though it could be less or more. Thus, in 1790, the sitting alderman at Guildhall bound over the victim of a robbery, during which his watch had been taken, in a £20 recognisance for himself and for another prosecution witness.[70] In exceptional cases, where a magistrate was particularly keen that a prosecution proceed, and especially fearful that it might be settled out-of-court, much larger sums might be stipulated, especially if the witness was wealthy. For example, in 1777, the chief complainant in the notorious case involving Dr. Dodd, having appeared before the Lord Mayor, seen the pitiable condition that the clergyman was reduced to, and been assured of recovering his money, "shewed no forwardness" in prosecuting the matter. Unfortunately for Dodd, the Lord Mayor had a different view: "...he called upon Mr. Fletcher to prosecute, who was bound in a recognizance of 500 [pounds]".[71]

The document would set out the sum that would be forfeit for non-appearance and then stipulate that provided the person named in it personally appeared at the next General Gaol Delivery:

> ...and there prefer a bill of indictment against R.D. for (as the case is) and shall also then give evidence [to the Grand and Trial Juries] ... this recognisance shall be void.[72]

The use of recognisances to prosecute was largely confined to felonies. They could be issued for misdemeanour cases, but this was rare. During the first 60 years of the eighteenth century, for example, fewer than five percent of indictments for non-felonious offences against the person that were heard at the Middlesex Quarter Sessions were brought by prosecutors who were compelled to appear in this manner.[73] There was a large expansion in their use after the mid-century, something that may have been linked to

70. Guildhall Justice Room Minute Book, CLA/005/01/045 19 August-14 September 1790, entry for 8 September.
71. W. Dodd, *Authentic Memoirs of the Life of William Dodd, LL.D. who was executed at Tyburn, on Friday, June 27, 1777*, 3rd edn., 1777, p.17.
72. J. Higgs, *A Guide to Justices or Modern English Precedents for the Direction of Justices of the Peace and their Clerks*, 2nd edn., 1742, p.97.
73. N. Landau, "Indictment for Fun and Profit: A Prosecutor's Reward at Eighteenth-century Quarter Sessions", 1999, p.510.

their attractions to trading justices; issuing them involved payment of a fee. In turn, the Middlesex Justices Act 1792 (effectively abolishing the trading justices) led to a massive reduction in their use.

At the end of the examination process, the magistrate would have to make a decision as to whether to commit the suspect for trial on indictment and, if he did so, whether to grant him bail or to remand him in custody.

Committal

There was considerable debate as to the precise degree of persuasion needed to activate the criminal justice process. According to many "traditional" commentators, a magistrate had a very limited discretion when faced by an allegation of felony. He had to be satisfied that a crime had actually been committed, but it was then only necessary that there be a reasonable suspicion that the detained person was its perpetrator. In these circumstances, the suspect *had* to be committed for trial.[74] Sworn evidence directly implicating a suspect had a similar effect, irrespective of its provenance. The magistrate's personal view of the guilt or innocence of the accused person was supposed to be irrelevant. This approach to felony allegations appears to have been dominant in the final years of the seventeenth century, and the early years of the ensuing one. Absurd as it seemed even to contemporary observers, in theory, if a larceny had been committed, and a suspect implicated, but the examining JP thought the accused person was innocent, he could: "...not discharge him, but must commit [him to prison] or bail". As a result, a man accused of stealing a few pennies worth of goods, on fairly weak evidence, who could not provide sureties for bail, might languish in gaol for months, losing his business and reputation, until acquitted at trial.[75]

There were certainly cases of a strict, if legally correct, approach being taken in this regard. For example, in 1729, an experienced (but elderly) Westminster JP committed a Welsh maid to the Gatehouse Prison on suspicion of

74. Anon (By an Attorney at Law), *The Law of Arrests in Both Civil and Criminal Cases*, 1742, p.237.

75. *The Covent Garden Journal*, 25 February 1752.

committing a felony, after her mistress noticed that a very high denomination banknote was missing, and declared that she did not know who could have taken it apart from her servant (The magistrate's decision prompted surprise).[76] As late as the 1770s, there were complaints that JPs were too willing to commit people under the "pernicious pretext of suspicion". It was claimed that as many as 40 per cent of committals made by Middlesex magistrates were unjustified, and that both Hick's Hall and the Old Bailey were regularly: "...astonished how a magistrate could in the first instance, be invested with an idea of their guilt".[77]

In *practice*, however, and irrespective of the academic debate, some JPs had always been more robust about throwing out weak cases than traditional theory might suggest. In 1729, for example, when three women were carried before Sir William Billers, accused of knocking down and robbing a gentleman in a public street, the justice decided that they should only be committed for assault, proof of the more serious offence "being insufficient".[78] The traditional approach to such decisions was increasingly disregarded during the second quarter of the century, with a change in practice becoming particularly noticeable in the 1730s.[79] By then, it was often argued that if an allegation appeared to be: "...frivolous or ill-grounded, he [the JP] may discharge the person".[80] In the 1740s, Sir Thomas de Veil stressed that a magistrate should always make sure that he had sufficient "cause and circumstances" to justify committal before sending a suspect to prison.[81] Several other observers emphasised the consequences for those who were wrongly held in custody, and argued that a suspect should not be detained unless there was: "...such a probability of guilt as justly makes the complainant's suspicion that of the Justices".[82] Thus, in 1752, Henry Fielding discharged a

76. R. Whatley, *A Friendly Admonition to Gentlemen in the Commission of the Peace*, 2nd edn., 1729, pp.6-7.
77. R. Holloway, *The Rat-Trap, Dedicated to the Right Hon. Lord Mansfield, Chief Justice of England*, 1773, pp.20-23.
78. *Daily Post Boy*, 1 February 1729.
79. J. M. Beattie, "Sir John Fielding and Public Justice: The Bow Street Magistrates' Court", 1754–1780", 2007, p.67.
80. A. L. Hayward, *Lives Of The Most Remarkable Criminals*, 1927, p.239.
81. Sir T. Deveil, *Observations on the Practice of a Justice of the Peace*, 1747, p.8.
82. R. Galloway, *The Rat-Trap*, 1773, p.24.

mother of three small children, accused of stealing a cap worth three pence, because the evidence against her was not sufficiently "positive".[83] By the end of the period, even an allegation of serious felony might be dismissed if the evidence appeared vague.

Magistrates would also consider factors other than the available evidence when deciding whether to commit a matter for trial. Amongst them was the suspect's reputation. For example, in 1779, when William Cherry was arrested on suspicion of stealing a large quantity of clothes, he was discharged after several reputable people gave him an "excellent character".[84] Conversely, men of bad character could expect to be committed for trial on "slighter presumptions" than those of good repute, even if, by the end of the century, many thought that this did not justify the acceptance of weaker proof to found a conviction.[85] The complainant's character relative to that of the suspect could also be important. For example, when Jack Macdonald accused William Corn and others of stealing a saddle, in what Corn alleged was essentially a civil dispute, Norris dismissed the allegation after the local parish clerk swore that Corn was a man of very good character, while the complainant was of equally bad reputation.[86]

However, problems remained where there was unambiguous direct evidence, whatever its provenance, a magistrate who took a "traditional" approach to such matters, and a clear "Charge on Oath".[87] In 1772, for example, a well-dressed prostitute maliciously accused a respectable young man of robbery, in the most absurd circumstances, and without a scintilla of supporting evidence. The examining (trading) justice in Bethnal Green took the woman's deposition and: "…never suffered the young fellow to speak in his own defence". The youth was committed to prison to await trial.[88] Similarly, in 1790, a watchman who had made an unfounded allegation of assault against a member of the public had the matter committed

83. *The Covent Garden Journal*, 25 February 1752.
84. CLA/005/01'008, Guildhall Justice room Minute Book, 21 April 1779.
85. T. Gisborne, *An Enquiry into the Duties of men in the Higher and Middle Classes of Society in Great Britain*, 1794, p.280.
86. R. Paley (Ed.), *Justice in 18th-Century Hackney*, 1991, p.4.
87. H. Fielding, *of the Case of Elizabeth Canning*, 2nd edn., 1753, p.2.
88. *Gazetteer and New Daily Advertiser*, 17 January 1772.

by a magistrate without the defendant's witnesses being heard: "The Justice observing that his Office was no place for trying causes".[89]

In some cases, taking the decision not to commit a case for trial forced a magistrate to persuade or pressure a complainant into "voluntarily" withdrawing their allegations. In others, the justice appears to have simply refused to entertain the matter. In these situations, albeit only rarely, a complainant might have recourse to a second Justice, one who was more accommodating to his own view of the case, as occurred in the prosecution of William Horne for murder, in which several JPs were approached before one was found who was willing to commit the matter for trial.[90]

Re-examinations

In both Middlesex and the City it was quite common, after the early eighteenth century, for magistrates to re-examine already charged suspects in the light of new evidence, whether for the Crown or the accused. By the 1730s, important Justices like Sir Thomas de Veil were regularly holding second examinations and discharging previously detained felony suspects if the evidence against them then appeared weak.[91] In the 1760s, Sir John Fielding and other magistrates sat every Wednesday at Bow Street specifically to re-examine prisoners taken the previous week, in the light of any witnesses that they had been able to call, or who had come forward, in the ensuing period. This allowed them to: "...shew their innocence, and prevent their being unwarrantably precipitated into trials for fraud or felony".[92] For example, in September 1766, two Hackney coachmen who had been charged with driving away with a passenger's box of clothes were re-examined by

89. *The Times*, 8 January 1790, p.4.
90. Anon, *A Genuine Account of the Life and Trial of William Andrew Horne, Esq.* 3rd edn., 1760, p.8.
91. Sir T. Deveil, *Observations on the Practice of a Justice of the Peace*, 1747, p.8.
92. J. Fielding, *Extracts from Such of the Penal Laws, As Particularly relate to the Peace and Good Order of this Metropolis*, 1768, p.7.

the sitting alderman at the Guildhall: "...when several persons appearing to their character, they were discharged".[93]

At other times, the prosecution case was strengthened by re-examination. Thus, after two men found late at night, carrying apparently stolen goods, were carried before a justice they claimed that the property was their own, removed to prevent their landlord seizing it in lieu of rent. This story did not seem at all plausible, as they refused to give an address for their erstwhile residence. The magistrate detained them. By the time they were re-examined, the loser of the goods (an elderly widow) had come forward and recognised the stolen items.[94]

Occasionally, especially as the century advanced, there might be several re-examinations of individual suspects. However, some observers questioned the legality of this practice. According to William Augustus Miles, once a magistrate had committed a suspect to gaol for felony, he had "no kind of business with them".[95] Nevertheless, the increasing thoroughness of the justices' examination, and their greater willingness to exclude weak cases, probably contributed to the growing number of cases that survived Grand Jury scrutiny. By the mid-eighteenth century, 85 to 90 per cent of felony indictments were being returned as "true bills".[96]

If the next sessions were imminent, an examining JP might agree that a suspect's hearing would not be brought on until the sessions immediately after that, so allowing him more time to prepare for trial. For example, in early September 1726, a watchcase maker from Bishopsgate, accused of clipping coins, was committed for trial by Alderman Crosby with an order that this not be until October, after he begged the magistrate that he should not be tried at the September Sessions.[97] However, such delay was unusual, and most defendants were tried at the next sessions.

93. *The Whitehall Evening Post; or, London Intelligencer*, 13 September 1766.
94. OBSP, Trial of John Adshead and Benjamin Alsworth, 3 June 1772.
95. W. A. Miles, *A Letter to Sir John Fielding*, 1773, p.21.
96. T. A. Green, *Verdict According to Conscience*, 1985, p.272.
97. *Whitehall Evening Post*, 4 September 1766.

Bail

Even if an examining justice decided to commit a suspect for trial, he would have to make a decision as to whether he remained in custody, pending his hearing, or was granted bail. All misdemeanours were bailable, provided that appropriate recognisances were available to guarantee the suspect's appearance. By contrast, someone suspected of felony would find it much harder to obtain release pending trial. However, the law governing this topic was notoriously confused, and was sometimes tacitly ignored in practice. Although a few very serious felonies, such as murder, were not bailable *per se*, how far this list extended, and whether it applied where the evidence implicating a suspect was relatively nugatory, was not entirely clear.

Most crimes, including burglary, housebreaking and robbery, *could* be bailed in the right circumstances. Relevant factors in this regard included the gravity of the offence, the suspect's previous reputation and record, his state of health and his ability to arrange recognisances. The strength of the evidence against him was particularly important, as it was felt that bail should often: "...be allowed in such cases wherein it seems doubtful whether the person accused be guilty or not".[98] For example, early in his nefarious career, the notorious thief-taker Stephen McDaniel attempted to persuade Henry Fielding that two men he had detained had tried to rob him. Fielding formed so bad an impression of McDaniel that the prisoners: "...though charged with a capital offence, were both admitted to bail".[99] By the eighteenth century, it was generally thought that even a man taken on a "light suspicion of homicide" could be bailed.

By contrast, those caught red-handed committing even a minor felony could not normally expect to be released pending trial.[100] It was for this reason that there was so much controversy over the bailing of John Eyre, accused of stealing six shillings' worth of stationery in 1772. Eyre had been denied bail by both a City alderman and the Lord Mayor because he had been caught *in flagrente*, in possession of the stolen paper, and proffered no defence to the

98. A. Highmore, *A Digest of the Doctrine of Bail in Civil and Criminal Cases*, 1783, pp.152-155.
99. J. Fielding, *A Plan for Preventing Robberies Within Twenty Miles of London*, 1755, p.5.
100. A. Highmore, *A Digest of the Doctrine of Bail in Civil and Criminal Cases*, 1783, pp.152-155.

allegations made by several complainants. As the clerk to the Justice Room put it, in this situation, bail was: "...impossible, there never was an instance of it, when the stolen goods were found on the thief". Despite this, Lord Mansfield granted him bail in the Court of King's Bench.[101]

A great deal would depend on the suspect's ability to find suitable recognisances, people who were both willing and able to guarantee his future appearance, on pain of forfeiting a substantial sum of money if he failed to attend trial. They had to be men of some means, several observers feeling that for a potentially capital crime the required sum should never be set at less than £40, and often required very much more.[102] Thus, in 1786, two porters who had been committed to prison for stealing from their master were granted bail for £40 each, using four sureties of £20.[103] The wealthier the suspect, the greater the sums would normally be, as it was feared that otherwise he could reimburse any sureties whose recognisances were estreated for his non-appearance.

There were regular allegations that Metropolitan JPs and even judges were too lax in this regard, accepting inadequate recognisances from wholly inappropriate men. Several observers claimed that the sureties that Lord Mansfield had required for John Eyre's release — three Scotsmen who were bound over to the total value of £300 — were woefully deficient for such a prosperous man, who could easily have repaid them if he had decided to flee. Fortunately, having arranged his affairs, Eyre answered to his bail and pleaded guilty at the Old Bailey.[104]

Against this, others complained that it was a "great grievance" that magistrates set bail too high, making it almost impossible to fulfil.[105] In 1702, for example, a City alderman set the suspected witch Sarah Morduck's bail at the enormous sum of £500.[106] When an alderman was, himself, accused of

101. C. W. Everett (Ed.), *The Letters of Junius*, 1927, pp.272-288. Junius appears to have been Lord Shelburne.
102. Anon (By an Attorney at Law), *The Law of Arrests in Both Civil and Criminal Cases*, 1742, p.237.
103. *The Times*, 11 October 1786, p.3.
104. *London Evening Post*, 18 January 1772.
105. Anon (By an Attorney at Law), *The Law of Arrests in Both Civil and Criminal Cases*, 1742, p.238.
106. R. Hathaway, *The Tryal of Richard Hathaway*, 1702, p.5.

a serious crime in 1724, his bail was contingent on being personally bound in a recognisance of £2,000, while two sureties were pledged by his friends in the sum of £1,000 each.[107]

The substantial sums involved encouraged some defendants to pay relatively wealthy individuals, with whom they were personally unacquainted, to stand surety on their behalf. Sometimes, this illegal business was even negotiated by dubious members of the legal profession.[108] Such Newgate solicitors were able to provide: "Honest charitable housekeepers that for a valuable consideration will bail a man at any time". Unfortunately for the incarcerated person, this would usually be for an exorbitant fee.[109] In 1733, an elderly Irish attorney was convicted at Hick's Hall of extorting money on: "...pretence of procuring Bail for a person in Bridewell". He was sentenced to six months' hard labour in the Middlesex House of Correction.[110]

In 1730, the Middlesex Sessions even issued a warning list of men who had stood surety, whose recognisances had subsequently been estreated, and who were reputed to be "common bail", men providing sureties for money. There were over 180 of them. Their backgrounds varied; some were described as "gentlemen", only one or two were labourers. The great majority fell between these extremes, listing victuallers, distillers, bricklayers, plasterers, wigmakers, shoemakers, surgeons, carpenters and hatmakers amongst their number.[111] In 1733, it was noted that one "notorious common bail" had forfeited 20 recognisances to the Crown for non-appearance by his clients.[112]

Ostensibly, the power of a single JP to bail an accused felon, when outside sessions, was very limited and, even where it was *theoretically* permissible, they were encouraged to be very cautious about exercising it. In the 1660s, the Westminster judges had required that a magistrate who granted bail improperly should be reported to the Lord Chancellor, so that he might be "turned out of his Commission".[113] There were occasional cases of action being taken

107. *Daily Post*, 27 August 1724.
108. T. Deveil, *Observations on the Practice of a Justice of the Peace*, 1747, pp.4-5.
109. E. S. (gentleman in prison), *A companion for debtors and prisoners, and advice to creditors in ten letters*, 1699, p.34.
110. *Parker's Penny Post*, 21 May 1733.
111. Anon, *An Alphabetical List of Persons who are reputed to be common Bail*, 1730, p.1.
112. *Daily Journal*, 21 December 1733.
113. Sir John Kelyng, *A Report of Divers Cases In Pleas of the Crown, Adjudged and Determined; In*

against eighteenth-century magistrates for this reason. For example, in 1732, a Middlesex JP was presented at the Court of King's Bench for granting bail to a group of men who had been arrested for robbing Lady Crew. Both the accused and their bail had absconded.[114] However, despite such cases, bail was granted rather more frequently than strict legal theory might suggest, even by single magistrates. This was widely appreciated. In 1730, when two brothers, who had been active in suppressing disorderly houses, were accused of robbing the owner of such an establishment of a pair of valuable rings, they retorted that even if the allegation had involved the theft of a hundred pounds, their local JP would bail them.[115]

Even if not initially bailed by an examining magistrate, prisoners could still be granted bail at Quarter Sessions. A bench of two or more JPs had far greater theoretical powers in this respect. The higher courts, including the Old Bailey, also had a general power to allow bail in the cases that came before them. Additionally, and as with John Eyre, the Court of King's Bench could grant bail on a writ of *habeas corpus* if inferior courts had refused it improperly, though such an application would necessarily require considerable legal advice and resources, was not lightly granted, and normally required four sureties.[116]

Conditions on Remand

Despite these exceptions, most men accused of a serious felony supported by tangible evidence were remanded in custody prior to trial. In theory, because they were imprisoned purely to secure their appearance at court, and did not stand convicted of any offence, they were supposed to be treated with the "utmost humanity". For example, they were not to be fettered, unless they tried to escape or proved to be unruly. In reality, their treatment was usually little different to that of convicts, if only because gaolers were generally a

the Reign of the late King Charles II, 2nd edn., 1734, p.3.

114. *Grub Street Journal,* 29 June 1732.

115. OBSP, Trial of Thomas Willis and Michael Willis, 28 August 1730.

116. Anon (By an Attorney at Law), *The Law of Arrests in Both Civil and Criminal Cases*, 1742, p.237.

"merciless race of men".[117] Additionally, in the largely unsegregated prisons of the era it was often not practicable to differentiate between those awaiting trial, and those held post-conviction.

This had numerous ramifications for both the accused person and the trial process. A defendant who was in custody was likely to deteriorate physically and mentally. The harsh prison conditions of the era did not facilitate effective preparation for a 'life or death' felony trial, in which those who had their wits about them were much more likely to secure benign verdicts. They would also find it harder to obtain legal advice or to arrange the attendance of defence witnesses. All of these factors made it significantly less likely that they would be acquitted. Even if an unbailed defendant secured a 'not guilty' verdict, they were likely to be in bad health as a result of their incarceration, devoid of reputation and money, and so, ironically, sometimes forced to choose between extreme want and turning to crime.[118]

117. W. Blackstone, *Commentaries on the Laws of England*, 1769, vol. 4, p.297.
118. H. Zouch, *Hints Respecting the Public Police*, 1786, p.11.

CHAPTER 14

OPTIONS FOR PROSECUTION

Introduction

In strict legal theory, London magistrates had a simple choice after they had examined someone accused of a felony. They could commit the suspect to the Quarter Sessions or (much more commonly) the Old Bailey for trial on indictment in front of a jury. Alternatively, if there was little or no evidence to support the allegation for which a suspect had been arrested, the magistrate could discharge him altogether.

However, for less serious criminal matters, and even some that were not so minor, there was a much greater range of possibilities. These can be seen in the results of a localised campaign conducted in 1731 by a committee of Westminster JPs specially set up to deal with the city's night-cellars, disorderly houses and thieves' dens. This body met 42 times, and eventually reported on its endeavours. It employed just about every means of prosecution, *other* than indicting for felony, to address the area's problems. It bound over 58 people accused of keeping such establishments to appear at Quarter Sessions. Additionally, it committed 16 people to prison for the same offence; presumably, unlike the other 58, these had been unable to find bail while waiting to appear at the sessions. Another 14 men were bound over to the Quarter Sessions for assaulting constables who were executing search and arrest warrants. However, 24 people were formally indicted to stand trial before a jury for a misdemeanour (keeping a disorderly house). In this last situation, it was noted that the neighbours of the defendants had been bound in recognisance to prosecute, suggesting that the availability of evidence had been a crucial factor in the decision to indict. The same committee also committed 127 people found within these establishments (but not managing them), or who had been out at night in suspicious circumstances, to the house of correction as idle and disorderly persons, and summarily convicted and fined another 11 people for profane cursing and swearing.[1]

Thus, the committee had used four separate mechanisms to prosecute low-level crime: indicting for a misdemeanour; binding-over a suspect to appear at the next Quarter Sessions for committing a misdemeanour (whether on bail or not); committing "disorderly" people to a house of correction or bridewell, and summary conviction and punishment. These were the mainstays of non-felony prosecution during the eighteenth century, though their relative importance varied over time. Only one involved indictment. In other situations, an informal but magisterially supervised settlement with a complainant might have been added to them.

Misdemeanour Indictments

Many misdemeanours were indicted for trial in front of a jury, in which case, the matter would first be considered by the City Grand Jury, at the Guildhall, the Middlesex Grand Jury, at Hick's Hall, or, less commonly, the Westminster and Tower of London Grand Juries. Most misdemeanours would then be determined at the Quarter Sessions held in these locations, although, in theory, there was nothing to prevent them being tried at the Old Bailey, and a handful were heard at that forum.

Prosecution by Recognisance

Many misdemeanours were "prosecuted" by magistrates issuing recognisances against suspects binding them over to appear at the next Quarter Sessions, on pain of forfeiting a significant sum of money if they failed to do so. These were nearly always issued at the behest of their alleged victims. Thus, in a "factional" case from 1709, involving a man who had been held overnight by a constable for drinking after hours, insulting and assaulting (in a very minor way) the same officer, the suspect skilfully talked his way

1. *The London Journal*, 24 April 1731.

out of trouble in front of the alderman on duty at the Guildhall, and was discharged. However, he noted that: "Had it not been for the assistance of a few brains, and a little confidence, I had been bound over to the sessions".[2]

Because recognisances served multiple purposes both for justices of the peace and in the wider trial process it is easy to get their roles confused. In outline, wherever magistrates had the authority to make a person do something, they also had: "…in congruity power given them to bind the party by recognisance to do it". If the person refused to be bound over in this manner, a magistrate could commit them to gaol. As a result, recognisances could be issued to require individuals to: keep the peace; be of good behaviour; prosecute a felony or misdemeanour; give evidence in a felony or misdemeanour trial (i.e. attend as a witness), or answer to an indictment by attending for trial (if granted bail as a defendant).

However, a recognisance could also be issued that merely required a person suspected of committing a misdemeanour to attend the next Quarter Sessions. JPs could commit to gaol anyone who refused to be bound over in this manner or who were not able to provide sureties guaranteeing their attendance.[3] As a result, the procedure could not only be used as an appendage to the indictment process, one aimed at securing the attendance of the parties and prosecution witnesses, but could also be an alternative means of prosecuting a matter in its own right.[4]

The recognisance would contain the name, address and occupation of the person bound over (the principal) and also those of his sureties, the condition stated on the recognisance (to attend at the following sessions) and, perhaps, especially early in the century, a requirement to be of good behaviour and to keep the peace in the meantime. It would also specify the amount that would be forfeited to the Crown if the principal failed to meet that condition; this would usually be at least £20.[5]

Typically, those entering into recognisances would be named in the document and acknowledge owing the King the designated sum of money unless the named principal:

2. E. Ward, *The London-Spy Compleat in Eighteen Parts*, 4th edn., 1709, p.91.
3. W. Sheppard, *A Sure Guide for his Majesties Justices of Peace*, 2nd edn., 1669, p.197.
4. R. Shoemaker, *Prosecution and Punishment*, 1991, p.25.
5. R. Burn, *The Justice of the Peace and parish officer*, 1755, vol.1, p.538 and vol.2, pp.317-318.

> ...personally appear[ed] at the next General Quarter Sessions of the Peace, to be holden at *Hick's-Hall*, in St. John Street, for the said County, to answer to all such Matters of Misdemeanour, as on his Majesty's Behalf shall be then and there objected against him by H.M. [the victim] for [the crime].[6]

Under this process, once a magistrate was persuaded — usually by hearing evidence from the complainant — that there was a case to answer, the accused person was, effectively, required to promise to appear at the following Quarter Sessions. Two days before the ensuing sessions began, JPs would send their recognisances to the clerks of those courts, to be recorded in a ledger, so that, despite the enormous numbers that they would be asked to deal with, they could be processed effectively when the sessions began.[7]

Simply binding an accused person over to appear at the next sessions might appear a strange procedure for a crime victim to adopt. However, the alleged victim could also attend the ensuing Quarter Sessions, at the same time as the defendant, and ask for him/her to be indicted for the misdemeanour about which he had complained to the justice. The matter, including the complainant's evidence, could then be considered by the Quarter Sessions' Grand Jury with a view to going before a trial jury at the same sessions.

Nevertheless, although it secured the attendance of a suspect for trial on indictment, the complainant was not *required* to attend sessions and prosecute. He would not forfeit anything if he failed to appear and the matter was then dismissed. As a result, the procedure provided a "cooling off" period, giving the parties concerned a chance to reflect on what had occurred, to consider their options, to come to a personal settlement, or simply to avoid any repetition of previously objectionable behaviour.

A minority of complainants did choose to prosecute, either because they had tried and failed to reach an out-of-court accommodation with the suspect in the meantime, because the suspect had continued to act in what they considered to be a reprehensible manner during the interim period, or because, having reflected on the case, they had decided that it warranted

6. W. Stubbs, *The Crown Circuit Companion; containing the practice on the crown side, and of the Courts of general and general Quarter Sessions*, 1762, p.74.
7. N. Landau, "Appearance at the Quarter Sessions of Eighteenth-century Middlesex", 1998, p.41.

going before a jury. For example, in December 1735, Shadrack Huslett was arrested for assaulting and beating Delme Vanheythryson and bound over with sureties to appear at the Middlesex Quarter Sessions in January, where he was duly indicted and convicted.[8]

In *practice*, however, in most cases, the complainant would not attend court at the following sessions. Even in the late seventeenth and early eighteenth centuries only 19 per cent of defendants appearing at Middlesex and Westminster Quarter Sessions, as a result of a simple recognisance, were subsequently indicted for trial. At least 62 per cent were simply discharged.[9] If anything, this proportion seems to have increased during the early 1700s. The defendant would usually appear, pay a small fee to the Quarter Sessions' clerk and court crier (the combined cost would be about 2s 4d.), and the recognisance document, a small slip of parchment, would be marked *ven & exon*, signifying that they "came and were exonerated". They were then free to leave court, poorer only by time, a few shillings, some inconvenience and, perhaps, a modicum of embarrassing publicity.

Sometimes, even if a complainant did appear at Quarter Sessions, the threat that they would indict the matter could be used to force a settlement at court, without the matter going for trial. For example, at the Guildhall Sessions in 1724, a married chemist from Walbrook appeared pursuant to a recognisance issued at the behest of his spouse for wifebeating. On this occasion, his spouse also attended, and told the court that her husband had threatened to lock her up in a room for seven years, and to beat her on a daily basis. Even so, the chemist asked to be discharged from his recognisance. At first, this was rejected by the court, which clearly anticipated a trial on indictment for assault and battery taking place. However, his wife indicated that she would be satisfied if he granted her £12 a year as "separate maintenance". The court promised that if this was accepted, the defendant would be discharged from his recognisance and no trial would take place.[10]

The defendant would usually have to provide two sureties to guarantee his appearance at the Quarter Sessions. However, in almost two thirds of cases

8. R. Paley (Ed.), *Justice in 18th-Century Hackney*, 1991, p.140.
9. R. Shoemaker, *Prosecution and Punishment*, 1991, p.102.
10. *The London Journal*, 4 July 1724. She also promised that he would not be answerable for any debt she incurred, as would otherwise be the case under the doctrine of marital coverture.

in eighteenth-century Middlesex, one of these was the defendant himself, acting in his personal capacity. Nevertheless, others could stand surety on behalf of (and with) the principal. They would usually have to be reputable men of reasonable means, such as tradesmen or skilled artisans, prepared to pledge £20 or more.

Defendants were *normally* only inconvenienced by this part of the process, unless they were unable to find the necessary sureties, when they might be committed to a bridewell, house of correction or other prison pending their attendance at court (or their finding suitable sureties). In Middlesex, the New Prison and the Clerkenwell House of Correction were frequently used for holding people in this situation.[11] This was particularly likely to occur when poor people, without reputable connections, were involved. For example, low-grade prostitutes, and those who were far from home, such as recent arrivals from the provinces, might not be able to find appropriate people to stand surety or have the means to do so themselves.[12] In 1721, when constables raided an illegal gaming house in Westminster, they arrested nine men. Two "gentlemen" were released after being bound over in a recognisance: "...not to frequent or play at those gaming-houses for the future". However, the other seven men, including several servants, an apothecary, a law student and a watchmaker, were initially committed to Newgate or the Tuttlefields Bridewell "for want of sureties".[13]

Several contemporary observers condemned a situation in which people accused of minor assaults could end up in custody. Many of them, although drunk when these incidents occurred, were: "...otherwise honest and industrious people, and it is great pity they should be committed to prison, to lie there for want of sureties". They argued that poor people should be able to promise their own appearance, even if they could not produce recognisances, and that: "Their own undertakings to appear should be sufficient".[14] Incarceration in these circumstances could have grave consequences. For example,

11. N. Landau, "Appearance at the Quarter Sessions of Eighteenth-century Middlesex", 1998, p.41.
12. Anon (By a Lover of his Country), *The Thief-Catcher; or, Villainy Detected*, 1753, p.10. Prostitutes who were "managed" would often be bailed by their pimps.
13. Anon, *An Account of the Endeavours That have been used to suppress Gaming-Houses*, 1722, p.12.
14. J. Ilive, *Reasons offered for the reformation of the house of correction in Clerkenwell*, 1757, p.32.

Thomas Burgess and his wife were committed to prison in Oxfordshire after being maliciously accused of assault by a local attorney. Because they were "very poor" they could not secure or provide satisfactory recognisances to ensure their appearance at the following Quarter Sessions. As a result, they languished for some time in the county gaol, even though they had seven small children, left alone in their cottage, and were being imprisoned during harvest time, when labourers had a rare opportunity to make extra money.[15]

However, even after they were committed, misdemeanour suspects could still secure their release by finding suitable people to provide recognisances. In 1703, for example, William Fuller observed several fellow bridewell inmates, who had been arrested at Bartholomew Fair while intoxicated, bribe the gaolers to allow them to write messages to the outside and: "...beg for a pen and ink, and some body to go and fetch their friends to bail them".[16]

Those who could not find sureties after being committed would be produced from custody at the next Quarter Sessions. The majority, who had provided recognisances, would appear under their own steam. A failure to do so would result in the sureties having their recognisances estreated and so forfeit to the Crown. For example, in May 1732, Margaret Thomson failed to appear at the Middlesex Quarter Sessions, after being accused of assaulting a young girl. Her husband had entered into a recognisance for £40 and two other men for £20 each, to ensure her attendance and good behaviour in the meantime. The court ordered that these be estreated. This order was rescinded when Margaret persuaded the court that she had been ill on the day in question.[17] In practice, estreatment very rarely occurred, as the sessions' clerks were extremely efficient in "chasing" sureties, especially principals, and allowing them the opportunity to "respite" the estreatment for a larger (usually 14s. 8d), but still relatively modest amount, provided they responded swiftly and appeared at the following hearing.[18]

---

15. Anon, *The Case of William Aynsley, an Attorney at Law, in Oxford*, 1734, pp.6-7. Even the court hinted that the prosecutor might properly abandon the matter.
16. W. Fuller, *Mr. William Fuller's Trip to Bridewell*, 1703, p.23.
17. R. Paley (Ed.), *Justice in 18th-Century Hackney*, 1991, pp.10-11.
18. N. Landau, "Appearance at the Quarter Sessions of Eighteenth-century Middlesex", 1998, pp.34-35.

This method of "prosecution" was, statistically, very important in the first half of the century. In Middlesex, during the early 1700s, approaching two hundred people accused of misdemeanours would attend to answer to the recognisance procedure at each of the county's Quarter Sessions. As a result, when a previously adjourned sessions of the peace was eventually held at Hick's Hall, in September 1766, it was noted that the: "...great number of persons who were bound over in recognisances, appeared and discharged the same".[19] Because of the huge numbers of people appearing at Metropolitan Quarter Sessions for this reason, compared to the few dozen at their equivalents in the provinces, their clerks necessarily had to develop a well-oiled and efficient legal machine, in which records could be readily accessed and easily cross-referenced.[20]

A case from Westminster in 1692 is illustrative of the procedure's operation. Thomas Taylor reported Elizabeth Woosey to a magistrate for assaulting him with a pitchfork. He decided against prosecuting her on indictment because of the attendant expense, and merely asked that she be bound over. After deciding that Taylor's story warranted action, the JP had Woosey brought before him and told her to find two respectable people to stand surety for her appearance at the following Westminster Quarter Sessions, in the sum of £20 each, to "appear and answer" Thomas Taylor for beating him. After her name was called out at the Quarter Sessions (Taylor not attending) she presented herself to the clerk, paid her 2s 4d, and left court a free woman.[21]

As this case suggests, asking for a recognisance to be issued against a suspect was a much cheaper alternative to prosecuting by indictment, as it did not attract the latter's fees. Plaintiffs merely paid one or two shillings for the warrant that brought the suspect before the magistrate (still 10 or 20 per cent of the lowest paid journeyman's weekly income).[22] Furthermore, the procedure could not, *per se*, result in the defendant being fined or imprisoned,

19. *The Whitehall Evening Post; or, London Intelligencer*, 25 October 1766.
20. N. Landau, "Appearance at the Quarter Sessions of Eighteenth-century Middlesex", 1998, p.31.
21. J. Hurl-Eamon, *Gender and Petty Violence in London, 1680–1720*, 2005, p.1.
22. R. Shoemaker, *Prosecution and Punishment*, 1991, p.117.

something that might be socially disruptive, especially where complainant and accused would continue to live in close proximity in the future.

Such a procedure could only be employed for misdemeanours, not for felonies, which had to be prosecuted by indictment. Most commonly, it would be used for minor assaults, incidents of domestic violence and offences against the peace. More rarely, it would be employed to deal with allegations of gambling and, very exceptionally, even certain sexual offences, though prostitutes were usually committed to a bridewell or house of correction.

Interestingly, in Middlesex at least, the use of recognisances in this way appears to have been greatly reduced by the advent of stipendiary magistrates under the Middlesex Justices Act 1792, perhaps, in part, because the salaried justices who were appointed to these positions were not interested in the small fee that attached to them. Thus, in 1791, 7,322 recognisances were returned to the forthcoming sessions in Westminster and Middlesex; in 1793, the total had fallen to 2,752.[23] It continued to fall in ensuing years, though it was used into the nineteenth century.[24]

In many ways, such a procedure, effectively entailing a formal public warning about possible action, may have fulfilled a widespread need amongst those who lived in eighteenth-century cities. For example, for a small fee, eighteenth-century Parisians could make a written complaint about another person's objectionable behaviour to their police. In principle, these indicated an intention to have recourse to the courts. However, the vast majority were not pursued. They were public statements, intended to force a settlement or warn others that their behaviour was unacceptable.[25] It is probable that less formal warnings were often effective in rural areas, in both England and France, but not so viable in cities.

23. N. Landau, "The Trading Justice's Trade", 2002, p.68.
24. Anon, *The Crown Circuit Companion*, 8th edn., 1811, p.15.
25. D. Garrioch, "The People of Paris and their Police in the Eighteenth Century", 1994, p.521.

Summary Conviction

Although active eighteenth-century JPs might complain that they had been heavily engaged in indictment-related tasks, these were a relatively small part of their legal work. Far more time was spent disposing summarily of the matters that came before them. However, historically, magistrates had possessed almost no legal powers to determine a criminal allegation laid by "information". Summary jurisdiction was a stranger to common law, whether by magistrates sitting on their own or on a bench with one or more colleagues.[26]

During the early modern period, this situation changed, as a result of specific Acts of Parliament. Although the origins of these statutes are uncertain, it seems that there were occasional summary convictions for arcane offences, such as carrying short "daggs" (guns), from the reign of Henry VIII onwards. In the early seventeenth century, summary jurisdiction started to expand: "…as the nation became more familiarised to its use".[27] This process accelerated after the Restoration. By the eighteenth century, the "vast variety" of matters dealt with summarily, included, *inter alia*, public swearing, drunkenness and vagrancy.[28] Thus an arrested inebriate could note that he had been released by a magistrate: "…without paying for drunkenness, swearing, or the like, which are … commonly accumulated upon transgressors under our circumstances".[29]

By the middle of the period, William Blackstone was alarmed at the growth of such a jurisdiction, which was usually at the expense of jury trial. He was not alone. In 1786, the Yorkshire JP Henry Zouch was persuaded that trial on indictment, although a bulwark of the country's liberties, had: "… in many places been dispensed with, and a mode of summary proceedings substituted in the room of it". Zouch thought that the powers vested in English magistrates made them amongst the most potent judges in the world.[30]

26. M. Cottu, *On the administration of Criminal Justice in England*, 1822, p.25.
27. W. Paley, *The Law and Practice of Summary Convictions on Penal Statutes by Justices of the Peace*, 1814, p.1, p.7, p.xxvii and p.xxix.
28. W. Blackstone, *Commentaries on the Laws of England*, vol. 4, 1769, pp.277-279.
29. E. Ward, *The London-Spy Compleat in Eighteen Parts*, 4th edn., 1709, p.91.
30. H. Zouch, *Hints Respecting the Public Police*, 1786, p.1.

The expansion of summary jurisdiction was assisted by the void left by the decline in the Church Courts. Until the Civil War, some lesser offences — such as tippling on the Sabbath and swearing in public — had been punished in these forums. Although they survived, in theory, into the eighteenth century, prosecutions before them swiftly declined to near non-existence after 1660. Nowhere was this more apparent than in the Metropolitan area. As a result, by 1710, John Disney could observe that the:

> Discipline of the Church, and the Terror of Penance and Excommunication are (thro' some Body's fault or other) at a very low ebb, seldom exercised, and little fear'd.

This meant that such matters were necessarily left almost entirely to the secular courts.[31]

Despite the criticism of men like Blackstone and Zouch, many reformers wished to see JPs use their statutory powers to convict and punish more freely. For example, Whitlocke Bulstrode (1652-1724), a moralising Middlesex Justice and the eventual chairman of that county's Quarter Sessions, reminded the Middlesex Grand Jury that the statutes proscribing minor offences, such as public cursing, allowed the summary levying of small fines and urged them to: "...complain of these vile wretches to the magistrates".[32] Unusually, the level of the fine imposed on those convicted of swearing was contingent on their social status and any similar convictions that they had accrued on earlier occasions. It started at a shilling per incident for working men. Thus, in 1766, a City alderman fined an Irishman who had used foul language on 13 separate occasions as many shillings.[33] However, such cases were very rare, even though London was full of the "hellish noise" of people cursing in its streets.[34]

---

31. J. Disney, *An Essay Upon the Execution of the Laws Against Immorality and Prophaneness*, 2nd edn., 1710, pp.16-17.
32. W. Bulstrode, *The Charge of Whitlocke Bulstrode Esq to the Grand-Jury, and other Juries, of the County of Middlesex...*, 1718, pp.7-9.
33. *The Whitehall Evening Post; or, London Intelligencer*, 18 September 1766.
34. J. Gonson, *The Charge of Sir John Gonson Knt. To the Grand Jury of the Royalty of the Tower of London*, 1728, p.10.

Similarly, a single justice could convict those who: tippled on Sundays; allowed such drinking in their alehouses; sold ale without a licence; or who were drunk in a public place. Alcohol-related summary matters were a small but regular part of Henry Norris's duties as a Middlesex JP For example, in June 1732, Samuel Fenner was convicted on the evidence of a Hackney "gentleman" of being drunk and fined five shillings. In January of the following year, Anne Trott was convicted of the same offence on the evidence of a local Churchwarden.[35]

Nevertheless, drunkenness appears to have been even harder to prosecute than cursing. In the year from the 1st January 1717, the Societies for the Reformation of Manners in London and Westminster brought prosecutions against only 17 people accused of the former offence, compared to 202 individuals for the latter.[36] (In theory, it could also be prosecuted on indictment at Quarter Sessions, but this very rarely occurred "notwithstanding this offence is so common").[37] Many a man arrested for public drunkenness was simply held overnight, and discharged the following morning, by a magistrate who had first: "...reproved him for being out late and getting fuddled".[38]

Statutory authority also meant that single justices could summarily determine and punish specific forms of instrumental crime, such as the theft of timber from woods or fruit from orchards, along with a significant number of other minor offences, including, *inter alia*, people who secretly carried pistols about their person.[39] Penalties for these offences were usually mild, normally being relatively modest fines, the proceeds of which were used for local purposes, such as support for the poor, rather than being forfeit to the Crown. A period in the stocks or pillory, a whipping, or a short custodial sentence was often specified in lieu of payment, depending on the offence involved.[40]

35. R. Paley (Ed.), *Justice in 18th-Century Hackney*, 1991, p.12 and p.17.
36. *White-hall Evening-Post*, 13-15 January 1719.
37. J. Gonson, *The Charge of Sir John Gonson Knt. To the Grand Jury of the Royalty of the Tower of London*, 1728, p.15.
38. J. Ilive, *A scheme for the employment of all persons sent as disorderly to the house of correction in Clerkenwell*, 1759, pp.5-7.
39. J. W., *A Compleat Guide for Justices of the Peace*, 1707, pp.10-21.
40. S. Blackerby, *The Justice of Peace His Companion*, 3rd edn., 1715, p.3 and pp.2-5.

Of course, some summary offences, though very common amongst the workload of rural magistrates, were encountered less frequently in a built-up or suburban environment. For example, William Hunt, a Wiltshire JP of the 1740s, was regularly involved in summarily convicting and fining those accused of stealing wood. Typically, Betty Draper was fined a shilling in 1745, after being: "…convicted by one witness and her confession".[41] Such cases were necessarily less likely to occur in (largely deforested) Middlesex, though the county had many orchards, and thefts of fruit were a frequent source of work for the justices.

A modest degree of magisterial flexibility and ingenuity could greatly extend the circumstances in which summary jurisdiction might be employed, though this risked further undermining trial on indictment. For example, in rural North Lincolnshire, after about 1747, if a minor allegation of assault was made to a JP, the magistrate would often make a swift determination as to which of the men involved had been the aggressor, or at least most blameworthy, and then fine him a modest amount for the summary offence of swearing, before dismissing the matter. It was very rare that a fistfight did not involve raised voices and bad language. This appears to have largely replaced the more cumbersome recognisance procedure for such offences in the county, and, as each profane oath warranted a fine of a shilling, it allowed slightly more serious allegations to be dealt with on the basis that they had involved at least two or more oaths![42] Doubtless, similar cases and comparable flexibility sometimes occurred in the Metropolis.

Summary matters also included a significant number of regulatory and quasi-regulatory offences. For example, instances of "bullock hunting", a violent popular pastime in which an enraged beast was chased through the streets by young men, regularly came before the City's aldermen, as did cases in which hackney cabmen had charged their passengers extortionate fares for a journey. Such offences, if proved, usually attracted relatively small fines. Thus, William Hopkins, caught taking part in a bullock hunt, was fined a few shillings, while some of his associates, whose role was peripheral, were

41. E. Crittall (Ed.), *The Justicing Notebook of William Hunt, 1744–1749*, 1982, p.34.
42. B. J. Davey, *Rural Crime in the Eighteenth Century: North Lincolnshire 1740–80*, 1995, p.73.

merely warned about their future conduct.[43] Similarly, in September 1790, John Edwards, a hackney coachman, was fined 10 shillings for exacting the excessive amount of 3s 6d from William Ellis for a journey from Aldersgate to Rotherhithe.[44]

Evidential requirements

There were specific, statutory, evidential requirements for proving most summary offences. This was usually via one (or a combination) of three forms: "...either on view, confession of the party, or on the oath of one or more credible witness or witnesses".[45] For example, drunkenness could be established by a "view", that is, a situation in which a magistrate had personally seen the intoxicated man. Alternatively, it could be proved by the evidence of one reliable witness or via a confession by the suspect. Keeping an alehouse could be established in a similar fashion, but required the evidence of two witnesses, if this was the method of proof employed.[46] It was for this reason that informers were so important in summary matters. Very few of those accused of such crimes would confess to them, and justices were usually reluctant to "view" this type of offence.[47]

Fairness

Summary trials were swift and informal; the: "...justice convenes the delinquent before him, and proceeds to immediate tryal, conviction, or acquittal".[48] Perhaps, in part, because of this, the quality of summary justice had a bad reputation amongst many eighteenth-century observers. These included

43. Guildhall Justice Room Minute Book, CLA/005/01/045 19 August-14 September 1790, entry for 31 August 1790.
44. Guildhall Justice Room Minute Book, CLA/005/01/025, entry for 8 September 1790. He was convicted on Ellis's sworn testimony.
45. N. Blackerby, *The Speech of Nathaniel Blackerby Esq; At A General Meeting of his Majesty's Justices of the Peace for the City and Liberty of Westminster...*, 1738, p.9.
46. S. Blackerby, *The Justice of Peace His Companion*, 3rd edn., 1715, p.3.
47. N. Blackerby, *The Speech of Nathaniel Blackerby Esq... On Saturday, April 1. 1738, To the Justices, High Bailiff, High Constable, and Petty constables of the City and Liberty of Westminster*, 1738, p.3 and p.9.
48. Anon (A Middlesex Freeholder), *A Dialogue Between a Lawyer and a Country Gentleman, Upon the Subject of the Game Laws*, 1771, pp.6-7.

distinguished lawyers and judges such as William Blackstone.[49] Indicative of this poor reputation, when a defendant at the Middlesex Quarter Sessions complained that his jury trial had been particularly badly conducted, with the court initially forgetting even to swear the main prosecution witnesses, he resorted to comparing it to a:

> ...summary charge, [brought] by a confidential Beadle, against a known common rogue, [rather] than the tryal of a person of credit upon a plea of not guilty.[50]

Did summary justice deserve this poor standing? The answer would probably be a qualified "yes". Hearings were so quick and informal that they were sometimes almost extra-legal. Some crimes, such as poaching cases being heard under the Game Act 1671, pitted the powerful against the weak in an environment in which many justices would be intimidated by the status of the prosecutor. As was noted in Parliament, in 1792, it was usually the lower classes that were on the receiving end of summary justice.[51] The poor normally lacked the legal resources to challenge a decision, even though there might have been grounds to do so. As a result, legal theory and reality frequently parted company. The assessment of witness credibility was entirely a matter for the individual JP, as he was "placed in the situation of a jury", and could not normally be challenged in the Court of King's Bench.[52] This gave them enormous power. In 1790, for example, one trading justice, who had received two informations against a respectable tradesman for offences under the excise regulations had "so far previously decreed his doom" that he had already summoned a parish churchwarden to receive a moiety of the fine (the other half would usually go to the informer). Unfortunately for the justice, the tradesman had the wit to bring along counsel, who swiftly found serious legal flaws in the process.[53]

---

49. W. Blackstone, *Commentaries on the Laws of England*, 1765, vol.iv, p.277.
50. Anon, *Account of a tryal at Hick's Hall. Tuesday, April 25, 1786*, 1786, p.11.
51. W. Cobbett, *The Parliamentary History of England from the Earliest Period to the Year 1803*, 1817, vol. xxix, p.1465.
52. W. Paley, *The Law and Practice of Summary Convictions on Penal Statutes by Justices of the Peace*, 1814, p.28 and p.37.
53. *English Chronicle or Universal Evening Post*, 9 February 1790.

However, prosecutions for poaching were an extreme case, and of limited significance in an urban and suburban area. They were not necessarily typical of such hearings. The notebooks of contemporary magistrates suggest that many summary prosecutions *were* dismissed.[54] It would be wrong to imagine that such hearings were entirely devoid of legal niceties. It also seems that, during the eighteenth century, summary proceedings became more regulated than had previously been the case. It was increasingly recognised that, although designed to replace jury trial with a "more expeditious process", summary jurisdiction should be exercised in a legally just and proper manner. Evidence was supposed to be given on oath and delivered in the defendant's presence.[55] The latter rule was enforced quite strictly.[56]

The "Bloodless Code"

The summary offences created by statute during the seventeenth and early eighteenth centuries had largely been concerned with personal morality and misconduct, such as public drunkenness. Dealing with most offences involving the appropriation of property was seen as being legally outside a magistrate's remit, whatever might have been the practical reality when it came to informal settlements or the use of the Vagrancy Acts to deal with pilfering (see below).

However, after the middle of the eighteenth century, Parliament created a series of new summary-only misdemeanours to facilitate the conviction of those suspected of specific types of theft, committed in circumstances where proving essential legal elements of the full felony would otherwise be very difficult.[57] Many of these new offences were particularly relevant to the London area. Their introduction was often prompted by petitions from

54. J. Innes, "Statute Law and Summary Justice in Early Modern England", 1986, pp.3 and 34. I am very grateful to Joanna Innes for making this unpublished paper available to me.
55. W. Paley, *The Law and Practice of Summary Convictions on Penal Statutes by Justices of the Peace*, 1814, p.28 and p.37.
56. W. Blackstone, *Commentaries on the Laws of England*, 1765, vol.iv, p.280.
57. See generally B. P. Smith, "The Presumption of Innocence and the English Law of theft: 1750-1850", 2005, pp.133-173.

interested parties in the capital, who asked for new property offences that would make: "…conviction easy (in a summary way), and the punishment made more moderate".[58]

The motivation behind the creation of these offences has been the subject of considerable debate. The advent of lawyers to the trial process *may* have made proving simple larceny at trial on indictment much harder than had previously been the case. However, many had been criminalised in earlier eras by bodies, such as the manorial courts, that had become defunct by the eighteenth century. Additionally, it seems that much of the growth in summary offences occurred *before* the great expansion in the use of defence counsel during the 1780s.[59] Collectively, these statutory offences are sometimes known as the "Bloodless Code" by modern historians, in counterpoint to the era's better known "Bloody Code", whereby numerous arcane and, theoretically, capital felonies were created. Parish officers could often prosecute the new, minor, offences without the active assistance of a complainant/victim.

In a large conurbation it was frequently difficult to prove that goods found in suspicious circumstances had actually been stolen. For example, in conventional cases of theft it was normally essential that the loser of stolen items be found, identify his stolen goods, and then agree to prosecute the suspect, if a conviction (or even a prosecution) at the Old Bailey or Quarter Sessions was to be secured. Although, in theory, stolen goods could be charged on an indictment as the property of a "person or persons unknown", this found little favour with the higher courts and was only successful on rare occasions. If the loser could not be found, was unable to identify his goods–either because they were too nondescript or because he was reluctant to proceed further with the matter–or, alternatively, he simply refused to initiate proceedings (as often occurred), the felony process would usually be stillborn.

Even if such a case got to trial on indictment, there could be major problems in securing a conviction. The stolen items would have to be established as the victim's property to a high standard of proof, in a forensic environment.

58. Anon (by a Member of Parliament), *Further Observations on the Buyers or Receivers of Stolen Goods, particularly, of lead, iron, copper, brass, bell-metal, and solder*, 1756, p.22

59. N. Landau, "Summary Conviction and the Development of the Penal Law", 2005, p.176.

This might be difficult. For example, if a man was found in suspicious circumstances, late at night, carrying a large bag of sugar, which he then refused to account for, it might be impossible to prove that it was a particular complainant's sugar, rather than that of another merchant or importer, or even of the suspect himself. The same might be said about numerous other commodities, ranging from lead to tea.

Unsurprisingly, the theft of such items was a particularly serious problem in the Metropolitan area, because of their ready availability in the city's docks, warehouses and streets. For example, in 1733, a watchman who had arrested a thief who had removed an iron railing from a fence in Marlborough Street, noted that his area had been plagued by similar thefts and, as a result, had: "...lost a great deal of iron and lead".[60] Illustrative of the difficulties in prosecuting, late one evening in May 1727, Andrew Moodey was stopped by a watchman and found to be in possession of two large Cheshire cheeses and eight pounds of sugar. When questioned, he could not give a "good account" as to how he came by them. His eventual claim, that the dairy products came from a cheesemonger in Southwark, was carefully investigated by the watchmen. However, they could find no such person. Even so, the apparent absence of a proven loser was fatal to the prosecution; Moodey was acquitted, the "fact not appearing plain".[61]

Of course, where specific and identifiable goods were stolen, especially if they were distinctive, the authorities were much more likely to experience success in tracing their "losers" and in positively identifying items in court. It was for this reason that some highwaymen would not take watches.[62] One reason for the length and success of the habitual thief Charlotte Walker's criminal career was that she normally confined herself to stealing cash, rather than goods. Her luck only ran out when she took a timepiece.[63]

However, in low to medium value cases involving generic items, such as solder and lead, the ease with which the outward form of the material could be changed frequently rendered it almost impossible to prove their

60. OBSP, Trial of William Raven, 4 April 1733.
61. OBSP, Trial of Andrew Moodey, 17 May 1727.
62. J. W. von Archenholtz, *A picture of England*, 1791, p.182.
63. M. Clayton, "The Life and Crimes of Charlotte Walker, Prostitute and Pickpocket", 2008, pp.3-19.

origin. Defence lawyers (if present) would often vigorously cross-examine complainants about their ability to identify lost property, so raising a doubt in the mind of jurors.

Unsurprisingly, given the era's (ostensible) faith in trial by jury, these new summary offences carried relatively modest punishments, usually a small fine or a short custodial sentence. Anything more would have been unacceptable, especially as they normally operated by reversing the traditional common law burden of proof. Many of these statutes made it an offence to be found in possession of commonly stolen commodities, such as metal, wool, silk, wood and rope in "suspicious" circumstances, unless the defendant was able to give a satisfactory account as to how he came by them. Thus, if someone was found carrying lead late at night, with the metal concealed under his coat, and it was suspected that it had been stolen from a roof, he would have to satisfy the court that he had purchased the metal quite legitimately, perhaps by identifying or even calling the vendor, an independent and credible witness to the transaction, or producing a bill of sale.

Such statutes included the Stealing of Lead Act of 1756, which made unexplained possession of lead, iron, copper, brass, and solder punishable with a fine on summary conviction. Similarly, the Bumboat Act of 1762 made it an offence for those rowing the type of small boats ("bumboats") that sold wares to sailors stationed on vessels moored in the Thames to be found in possession of ships' stores and accoutrements (such as rope), unless they could produce positive evidence as to how they came by them. This particular misdemeanour was punishable by a forty-shilling fine, with a month's imprisonment in lieu of payment. For example, in 1798, John Saunders was brought before the Marine Office magistrates under the statute, after being found in possession of a large quantity of rum. The spirits were confiscated and he was fined 40 shillings with costs. Another man, who had been found in possession of a quantity of sugar, received a similar disposal.[64] In like manner, the Frauds by Workmen Act of 1749, and a successor Act of 1777, authorised summary conviction and punishment of men who were

64. *Oracle and Daily Advertiser*, 6 October 1798.

suspected of purloining materials such as cotton, iron, hemp, flax and silk from their places of work.[65]

An even more controversial power was given to Metropolitan magistrates by the Middlesex Justices Act of 1792, which contained a clause allowing JPs to summarily convict "reputed thieves", for which offence they could be sentenced to a maximum term of six months' hard labour. This provision was primarily intended to combat gangs of pickpockets and footpads. It was claimed that, without it, the latter would wait until the watch had "gone their rounds" before attacking passers-by.[66] However, it was bitterly opposed, particularly by the Foxite Whigs, whose leader, Charles James Fox, complained that it undermined fundamental principles of English common law. Even Lord North, although acknowledging that petty crime was a serious Metropolitan problem, felt that it was not so grave that it justified entrusting such a "dictatorial power" to the Bow Street Runners.[67] Illustrative of its use, in 1797, John Cole was arrested by a Runner as a "reputed thief" and, after being produced at Bow Street, was sent to the house of correction. The Runner had recognised Cole as a notorious pickpocket and then seen him acting suspiciously around theatres in Covent Garden, during a Royal performance.[68]

Nevertheless, it should also be noted that some of the new offences were only rarely prosecuted. Additionally, the authorities appear to have been reluctant to bring them if traditional (and more serious) offences could realistically be charged. For example, in 1796, James Wilkinson was arrested in the Square Mile and found to be in possession of a quantity of copper and not: "...able to account how he came in possession of the same". Even so, rather than see him prosecuted for a summary offence, the Lord Mayor, sitting at the Mansion House, committed him to Newgate pending further examination, and ordered that the discovery of the copper be advertised.[69]

---

65. B. P. Smith, "The Presumption of Innocence and the English Law of theft: 1750-1850", 2005, p.135.
66. *The Calcutta Gazette*, 13 December 1792.
67. J. M. Beattie, "Garrow and the Detectives", 2007, p.21.
68. *London Chronicle*, 7 February, 1797.
69. *The Morning Advertiser*, 20 August 1796.

In some cases, the authorities would use one of the new summary offences to deal with apparently habitual receivers of stolen goods, until such time as they were able to bring a more serious charge. For example, the Middlesex Sessions eventually convicted Benjamin Hill, a Limehouse metal-smith, and sentenced him to transportation, for receiving stolen nails from a group of children. He had regularly encouraged them to pilfer from their employer, the proprietor of a factory, and had earlier been summarily: "… convicted several times for having iron found in his possession, which he could not account for".[70]

Appeals from Summary Convictions

By the eighteenth century, it had long been possible to challenge a summary conviction in the Court of King's Bench, just as many other aspects of a justice's work could be reviewed in that forum, whether by writ of *habeas corpus*, if the subject was in custody, or by challenging the legality of a summary conviction by a writ of *certiorari* (issued to remove the record of an inferior court into the King's Bench for review).[71] Normally, such challenges had to be based on a legal flaw in the earlier proceedings in front of a justice, whether over jurisdiction or the technical requirements of proof. The court would not "second-guess" the magistrate's decision on the merits of the evidence unless, perhaps, it was manifestly absurd.

How effective was this procedure? Some contemporary observers thought that summary convictions for the notoriously complex offences created by the game laws were extremely difficult to sustain on review: "…very few of which are able to stand the test when removed into the King's Bench". The vast majority were quashed for a technical defect, such as the lack of competence of a prosecuting witness.[72] The ability of King's Bench to strike down magistrates' decisions also featured in several literary accounts from the era.

---

70. *The Times*, 2 November 1801, p.3.
71. W. Paley, *The Law and Practice of Summary Convictions on Penal Statutes by Justices of the Peace*, 1814, p.xxvii and p.xxix.
72. Anon (A Middlesex Freeholder), *A Dialogue Between a Lawyer and a Country Gentleman, Upon the Subject of the Game Laws*, 1771, p.8.

Nevertheless, in reality, the power to review decisions made by individual justices does not seem to have been exercised on a very regular basis. There were several reasons for this. Most potential litigants in these situations were poor, and the cost of seeking relief from King's Bench was very high. In 1792, Charles James Fox could warn that a new summary offence was particularly dangerous because those who were: "…likely to be the objects of it, the lower classes of the people, had seldom the means of applying for redress against abuse of power".[73] Additionally, King's Bench seems to have been mindful of the need not to discourage lay justices from serving, in an era when it was often hard to find high-quality men. It frequently took a relatively benign view of their mistakes, especially where they had been made in good faith.

As a result, whether because the costs of litigation were too great for the poor to bear, or because the King's Bench judges sympathised with magistrates of their own social background, *certiorari* does not appear to have had a huge effect in controlling erring *provincial* magistrates.[74] However, in London and Middlesex, things *may* have been slightly different. In 1694, a temporary statute, lasting just three years, had been passed to place restrictions on defendants who sought writs of *certiorari* to remove indictments for offences such as assault and battery from Quarter Sessions into the Court of King's Bench. This had, apparently, become such a regular practice that it was discouraging prosecutors and parish officers, who were put to the expense of pursuing matters in the higher forum.[75] In the 1750s, Jacob Ilive, then incarcerated in the Clerkenwell House of Correction, successfully threatened the prison's keeper with an action in King's Bench when he was warned that he would be put in the stocks if he were lax about doing his enforced work.[76] In the Metropolitan area, at least by the last quarter of the century, the ready presence of the court seems to have encouraged greater care on the part of magistrates when it came to legal niceties.

---

73. W. Cobbett, *The Parliamentary History of England From the Earliest Period to the Year 1803*, 1817, vol. xxix, p.1465.
74. D. Hay, "Dread of the Crown Office: the English Magistracy and King's Bench 1740-1800", 2002, pp.19-45.
75. O. Ruffhead, *Statutes at Large*, vol.2, 1763, p.555.
76. J. Ilive, *A scheme for the employment of all persons sent as disorderly to the house of correction in Clerkenwell*, 1759, p.48.

Slightly more realistically for most defendants, it was possible, and from the reign of Charles II fairly common, to appeal a summary conviction by a single justice to the next Quarter Sessions, where the case would be reconsidered on its merits, i.e. there would be a fresh hearing. However, the appeal would still be heard by the attendant justices sitting on their own: "...without the privilege of a trial by jury".[77] This meant that unless the earlier decision was manifestly wrong, collective solidarity between magistrates would make it difficult to achieve success. Unsurprisingly, the number of appeals that were successful was tiny in comparison to the total number of summary convictions.

Petty Sessions

Some summary matters and interlocutory procedures required the presence of more than one magistrate before they could be heard, though aldermen and (even more so) the Lord Mayor had greater powers when acting alone in the City of London than their Middlesex counterparts, as did the post-1792 stipendiary justices. Sometimes, these magistrates could deal unaided with minor offences that, elsewhere, required a bench of at least two Justices. Nevertheless, the existence of such legal requirements meant that two or more JPs would often sit together at what were termed "petty sessions". To circumvent these limitations, in a case from 1799, it emerged that search warrants (for vagrants) that required the support of two Justices were being signed blank, long in advance, by one magistrate and then filled in and second-signed by a colleague, as and when the need arose. This raised serious doubts about the legality of the orders, given that they required two magistrates "together at a meeting" to be valid.[78]

The origins of petty sessions can be found in the seventeenth century, with the 1630s being a formative period.[79] They became the forum of choice

77. W. Paley, *The Law and Practice of Summary Convictions on Penal Statutes by Justices of the Peace*, 1814, p.xxx.
78. OBSP, Trial of Timothy Brian and Others, 8 May 1799.
79. H. Langeluddecke, "'Patchy and Spasmodic'?: The Response of Justices of the Peace to Charles I's Book of Orders", 1998, p.1231.

for minor prosecutions conducted by the post-1690 campaigns for the reformation of manners, encouraging their expansion, though it was only in 1828 that they were formally established on a statutory basis.[80] Petty sessions gradually assumed responsibility for a variety of lesser offences, some of them quite arcane, such as breaking excise regulations, as well as some of the new eighteenth-century, statute-created, summary only misdemeanors.[81] They were also used to deal with much of the administrative work that was entrusted to Justices, such as conducting settlement and bastardy examinations. Many decisions and verdicts reached at petty sessions, like those taken by a single magistrate, could be appealed to the following Quarter Sessions, where they would be reheard (without a jury).

Although petty sessions would usually be held every month, they often met more frequently in urban areas, sometimes more than once a week, and were regularly convened on an *ad hoc* basis. For example, at the Bow Street Office, during the 1760s, petty sessions were, effectively, conducted every Wednesday. Arranging such sessions elsewhere in the Metropolitan area was also relatively easy, as JPs were likely to be living in much greater proximity than was the case in rural areas. In some Westminster parishes, petty sessions would take place at the same time as meetings of the local vestry.

The use of public houses or hotels was commonplace. In his populous part of Middlesex, during the 1730s, Henry Norris would regularly sit at The Mermaid or The Blue Posts, perhaps twice a month on average, with between one and three colleagues. Along with many administrative matters, such as making orders under the poor law, arranging apprenticeships for pauper children and supervising the maintenance of nearby highways, Norris and his fellow justices would determine minor criminal offences. Amongst them were Sabbath violations and the unlicensed sale of alcohol (especially spirits). Additionally, a considerable amount of criminal work that could have been conducted by a single magistrate, but which was not very urgent, such as the issuing of arrest warrants and even the examination of suspects, appears to have been carried out at such forums.

---

80. H. Langeluddecke, "Law and order in seventeenth-century England: the organisation of local administration during the personal rule of Charles I", 1997, pp.57-59.
81. E. Melling (Ed.), *Crime and Punishment, Kentish Sources VI*, 1969, p.44.

Committal to a Bridewell/House of Correction

When several MPs expressed outrage at the allegedly novel power contained in the Middlesex Justices Bill of 1792 (see above), allowing summary conviction and imprisonment of "reputed thieves", some of their colleagues pointed out that there was nothing new in giving justices the power to punish for such a vague offence. It was merely the mechanism (summary conviction) that was unprecedented. One MP even claimed that its antecedents could be traced back to the thirteenth century, and then regaled his colleagues with a selection of statutes that had allowed just such an eventuality in the ensuing 500 years. They included the considerably more draconian Vagrancy Acts passed over the previous 200 years, some of which were still in force, even if their use had declined by the early 1790s.[82] For decades before 1700, magistrates had had the power to punish "night-walkers", amongst others, for pursuing a generally "suspicious" lifestyle.[83]

One of the most important of these powers had originally been established by statute in 1610 (7 Jac. I c.4). This promoted the nationwide construction of bridewells and houses of correction, and authorised JPs to commit those who were "idle and disorderly" to them. Once incarcerated, such individuals would be set to work and could also be subject to a "moderate whipping"[84] (Early in the eighteenth century, this was often inflicted with a scourge made of holly fronds).[85] The most common form of work provided in such establishments was hemp beating and oakum picking. The former entailed using a heavy beetle to separate fibres from the core of the hemp plant. These could then be spun into rope. The latter required inmates to

82. W. Cobbett, *The Parliamentary History of England from the Earliest Period to the Year 1803*, 1817, vol. xxix, pp.1178-1179.

83. W. Sheppard, *The Court-Keepers Guide*, 4th edn., 1656, p.48. Later, the term was largely used for prostitutes.

84. O. Ruffhead, *The Statutes at Large*, vol. 3, 1763, p.76. Clause four of this statute had envisaged that many such commitments would be made at Quarter Sessions rather than out of sessions, as was often the case in practice.

85. R. Shoemaker, *Prosecution and Punishment*, 1991, pp.169-171. Anon, *Reports from Select Committees, Respecting The Arts-Masters and Apprentices of Bridewell Hospital*, 1799, p.8.

use their fingers to dig out the fibres from old, often tarred, ropes.[86] Inmates would work for their keep, unless sick or disabled.

The magistrates' power to commit "disorderly" people to such establishments was reiterated, in various forms, and using slightly different wording, by several subsequent statutes. Amongst them was the Vagrancy Act 1713 (12 Anne c.23), which was aimed at reducing the laws relating to rogues, vagabonds, sturdy beggars, and vagrants, to one statute. It provided, *inter alia*, that dangerous or incorrigible rogues, and those who refused to be examined by a magistrate (i.e. to answer his questions) after being arrested, might be sent to a house of correction until the following Quarter Sessions, which could then order that they be whipped or kept at hard labour.[87] Thirty years later, this statute was largely replaced, in its turn, by the Vagrancy Act of 1744 (17 George 2, c.5). This provided the legal framework for dealing with vagrants, with some amendments, until 1792, when it was replaced by yet another specialist statute. The 1744 Act also listed numerous employments that were indicative of vagrancy. These included beggars, unlicensed pedlars, jugglers and fortune-tellers.

Both genders were regularly imprisoned under these provisions during the eighteenth century, especially its first half. For example, in August 1748, it was reported that ten "loose and disorderly" men and women had been summarily committed to hard labour in the Tothill Fields Bridewell, after being arrested in St Martin's-in-the-Fields. At the same time, it was noted that, over the previous three months, another justice had committed 70 people, of both sexes, for: "...infesting the streets in the night".[88] As these cases suggest, the meaning of statutory phrases such as "idle and disorderly" came to be construed very broadly. Most obviously, they covered those who were drunk or occasioning public disturbances.

However, justices used these powers as a "catch all" to dispose of a huge range of criminal activity, disorder and generally nefarious behaviour.[89] For example, it was frequently used to deal with those who were engaged in beg-

86. W. G. Hindle, *A History of Bridewell Prison, 1553-1700*, 2006, pp.201-206.

87. O. Ruffhead, *The Statutes at Large*, vol. iv, 1763, p.602.

88. *General Advertiser* 16 August 1748 and 20 August 1748. Tothill Fields Bridewell later became the Westminster House of Correction.

89. J. Innes, *Statute Law and Summary Justice in Early Modern England*, 1986, p.11 and p.13.

ging and street prostitution or who were unemployed and sleeping rough. Bridewells and houses of correction always contained large numbers of streetwalkers who had been incarcerated in this fashion.[90] Any lower class women found wandering the streets late at night, who were unable to explain how they made a living, or why they were abroad at that hour, were potentially at risk. The majority of those sent to the Westminster Bridewell during the 1720s were imprisoned for particularly vague allegations, such as: "...raking up and down at unseasonable hours".[91] "Suspects" could also be detained if they could not maintain themselves, were not lawfully employed, and refused work. They might then be: "...deemed idle and disorderly persons, and be sent to the House of Correction to hard labour".[92] James Ross, an itinerant Scotsman, was committed to the Clerkenwell House of Correction after being found sleeping in a hayloft and: "...not giving a satisfactory account in what manner he maintained himself". He spent over two weeks there before the committing magistrate authorised his discharge.[93]

It could also be used to deal with individuals who had been found out late at night, in suspicious circumstances, where no specific offence could be laid to their account. As a result, magistrates had enormous powers to deal with people: "...even without any known crime actually [being] committed".[94] They would normally be produced before a magistrate the morning after their arrest, and required to explain themselves and their presence on the night streets. If they did this satisfactorily, they would be released; if not, they would be committed to a short period in custody. For example, in May 1752, a man and woman were committed to the bridewell and the penal wing of the London Workhouse respectively, as disorderly persons, having been found on the streets together, late on a Friday night, and been: "...unable to give a good account of themselves".[95] By contrast, when Thomas Hawkins was arrested in Chick Lane, as a suspicious person, one night in 1784, and

90. W. Fuller, *Mr William Fuller's Trip to Bridewell*, 1703, pp.10-14.

91. J. Innes, *Statute Law and Summary Justice in Early Modern England*, 1986, p.11 and p.13.

92. *The Times*, 14 October 1789, p.3.

93. J. Ilive, *A scheme for the employment of all persons sent as disorderly to the house of correction in Clerkenwell*, 1759, p.12.

94. *The Times*, 14 October 1789, p.3.

95. *The Covent Garden Journal*, 5 May 1752.

then produced before an alderman the following morning, he was discharged after calling two reputable people to speak to his character.[96]

A selection of cases is indicative of its versatility. For example, in February 1734, the Lord Mayor committed several women found carrying dice for use in rigged street games as "loose idle vagabonds" to the bridewell.[97] Five years later, when a Dutch Jew was arrested outside the door of Bow Church, during divine service, for selling little boxes with "filthy obscene figures" on them, he was carried to the Guildhall Justice Room, and committed to the bridewell for "hard labour as a common vagrant".[98] In 1766, the Cornishman John Crouch and his wife received the same disposal after they were arrested by beadles in the Royal Exchange for attempting to "sell" their 14-year-old niece to members of the public.[99] In 1787, Alderman Crosby committed two men to the bridewell as vagrants for (illegally) issuing lottery tickets.[100]

The power to incarcerate under this provision also allowed action to be taken against individuals who were suspected of being habitual criminals, where the evidence to prove a substantive offence against them was elusive. For example, in 1730, the suspected leader of a gang of pickpockets was committed to the Tothill Fields Bridewell by Sir John Gonson, after being found in possession of six handkerchiefs.[101] Similarly, in 1738, several members of another gang were arrested after complaints that they were infesting the piazza in Covent Garden and stealing from people attending nearby theatres. After being examined by Gonson, some of the "most notorious" were committed to the bridewell.

The procedure was also important because of the then rudimentary state of the common law governing inchoate offences, such as attempt. This often made securing convictions difficult where a substantive offence had not clearly been committed. For example, in a case from 1717, George Cole was indicted for burgling the house of Henry Willoughby. The prosecutor

96. CLA/005/01/025, Guildhall Justice Room Minute Book, entry for 12th May 1784. Two days later, Roberts was back before the same magistrate after arresting Henry Grey for "loitering" in the same place.

97. *Grub-street Journal*, 14 February 1734.

98. *Read's Weekly Journal*, 10 March 1739.

99. J. L. Rayner and G. T. Crook (Eds.), *The Complete Newgate Calendar*, vol. iv, 1926, pp.25-26.

100. *World and Fashionable Advertiser*, 17 April, 1787.

101. *London Journal*, 22 August 1730.

gave evidence that the outward shutter of his window had been bored full of holes with a gimlet and cut by a knife. A patrolling watchman had seen the prisoner skulking nearby and searched him, discovering a gimlet and knife in Cole's pocket. However, and influenced by the fact that the glass in the window had not been broken, the jury acquitted. When first brought before a justice, Cole could have been committed to the bridewell as a disorderly person, as an alternative to indictment.

The existence of a power that could summarily criminalise anyone who appeared undesirable or suspicious, had numerous advantages for the authorities, freeing them from the exigencies and expense of pre-trial procedure, offence definition, forensic proof and the vagaries of juries. Although used throughout England, it was especially favoured in the London area. Every year, several hundred people were imprisoned in this manner in the City, perhaps as many as nine or ten men and women for every thousand inhabitants in the Square Mile. This was about three times its per capita incidence in the provinces.[102] Its use in the City was matched in urban Middlesex and Westminster. Cases in which Henry Fielding dealt with people accused of being "idle and lewd", "idle and disorderly" or "idle & dissolute" (the phraseology varied) were so common that the details supplied by his clerk, Joshua Brogden, to the *Covent-Garden Journal,* would normally merely provide the number of those committed to the bridewell, rather than their names, leading to succinct reports such as: "Twenty to Bridewell, as idle and disorderly persons".[103]

As some of these cases suggest, during the eighteenth century, those who were arrested in the Square Mile would usually be sent to the Bridewell or, in the first half of the century, to the keeper's side of the London Workhouse. The (original) Bridewell, whence many other houses of correction acquired their names, was a former royal palace, situated on the west side of the Fleet Ditch. In the eighteenth century, it was based around two main courts, the larger of which was five stories high.[104] The London Workhouse was a 400-foot long brick edifice, situated on the edge of Bishopsgate. The keeper's

102. F. Dabhoiwala, "Summary Justice in Early Modern London", 2006, p.802.

103. L. Bertelsen, "Committed by Justice Fielding", 1997, p.340.

104. M. Gonzales, *London in 1731,* 1888, pp.89-90.

side of the institution opened in 1700, and fulfilled a broadly similar role to the bridewell. Unlike the steward's side of the workhouse, which had been founded in 1699 (along with the institution itself), that educated poor and orphaned children, and put them to work spinning and sewing, the keeper's side was clearly penal. Its inmates were usually employed in beating hemp and picking oakum, in the same manner as bridewell prisoners.[105]

The main distinction between the workhouse and the bridewell appears to have been geographic. The former catered primarily for those arrested in the parts of the City furthest from the bridewell. However, pressures on accommodation also played a role in allotting institutions. For example, in 1752, after two suspected pickpockets arrested in Fleet Street were examined at the Guildhall, one was committed to bridewell and the other to the London Workhouse.[106] The keeper's side of the workhouse was closed down during the 1750s, and turned into a debtors prison. As a result, the bridewell became, once again, the City's only house of correction. Although its penal regime was substantially revised in the 1790s, it lingered until 1855.[107]

The Tothill Fields Bridewell fulfilled a similar function for those arrested under the same power in Westminster, while the Middlesex House of Correction in Clerkenwell served the needs of the county in this respect. An inmate in the latter prison, observing that there were many rather dirty young women in the institution, found that: "...most of them, were sent thither by the Justices, as loose and disorderly persons".[108]

Use against felons

Even if the power to commit people summarily to these institutions had been confined to drunks, prostitutes, vagrants and generally "suspicious" individuals, it would have been enormously significant. However, it was also used to divert numerous petty thieves and other "mainstream" criminals from the trials at Quarter Sessions or the Old Bailey that their crimes theoretically warranted, especially in the first half of the century. Instead, they were committed to bridewells, houses of correction and the "penal" wings of

105. Anon, *An Account of the Work-houses in Great Britain in the year MDCC*, 3rd edn., 1786, p.3.
106. *General Advertiser*, 3 October 1752.
107. F. Dabhoiwala, "Summary Justice in Early Modern London", 2006, pp.803-804.
108. J. Ilive, *Reasons offered for the Reformation of the House of Correction in Clerkenwell*, 1757, p.11.

workhouses for being "idle and disorderly" rather than being indicted for the substantive offences for which they had initially been arrested. Thus, in 1732, the Bishopsgate workhouse was used to dispose of the City's: "Vagabonds, beggars, pilferers, lewd, idle and disorderly persons".[109] As this suggests, the inmates of these short-term prisons usually included significant numbers of petty thieves ("pilferers"), as well as those accused of offences of immorality or incontinence.[110] For example, in 1704, Philadelphia Hunt was committed to hard labour in this institution for being an "idle, pilfering & vagrant person".[111] In the year from 1691 to 1692, 307 men and women were committed to the bridewell for theft and fraud (45 per cent of the total).[112]

Such a disposal was especially common for women, particularly prostitutes who stole from their clients, even for comparatively serious thefts. However, it was also used to deal with men, especially those accused of stealing small value items. In 1732, for example, the Hackney magistrate Henry Norris committed Henry Tewson to hard labour in the Clerkenwell Bridewell after he admitted stealing small pieces of ironwork from a stable.[113] In 1741, Sir George Champion committed Christopher Peterson to the bridewell for "pilfering" a tart from a pastry cook's shop. At about the same time, Sir Robert Baylis sent William Clayton to the same prison for pilfering tobacco from a wharf. Similarly, William Cox was committed to the bridewell for "pilfering an old pail & shovel of small value".[114] A decade later, in 1751, the unemployed John Crosier was also sent to the bridewell as a loose and disorderly person for "pilfering" a small quantity of sugar from the Keys at Bottolph Wharf.[115]

As several of these cases suggest, the word "pilfering", rather than "theft", would often be employed in such cases, and it would frequently be stressed

---

109. Anon, *An Account of the Work-houses in Great Britain in the year MDCC*, 3rd edn., 1786, p.3
110. W. Fuller, *Mr William Fuller's Trip to Bridewell*, 1703, pp.10-14.
111. Mansion House Justice Room Charge Book, 1699-1705, CLA/004/01/4 Entry for 24 February 1704.
112. F. Dabhoiwala, "Summary Justice in Early Modern London", 2006, p.807.
113. R. Paley (Ed.), *Justice in 18th-Century Hackney*, 1991, p.15. Located just north of the City, it was superseded by the nearby Coldbath Fields Prison in 1794.
114. Bridewell Royal Hospital: Minutes of the Court of Governors, 18 June 1741, RMG202060131 document at www.londonlives.org (Last accessed 17 February 2011).
115. BBBRMG202060146 document at www.londonlives.org (Last accessed 17 February 2011).

that the stolen items were of "small value". Many would have constituted petty thefts (less than a shilling in value). However, serious felonies, crimes that *might* have been subject to a death sentence if proved and not clergyable, were also sometimes dealt with in this manner.[116] For example, when William Miller was arrested on suspicion of housebreaking, in 1704, he was simply charged as an "idle person", and committed by Sir John Parsons, the Lord Mayor, to hard labour in the workhouse, with a note that he was not to be discharged without Parson's knowledge.[117] In February 1752, Henry Fielding committed George Upton to Clerkenwell Bridewell for the theft of several pewter pots; taken together, these were undoubtedly worth more than a shilling.[118]

Sometimes, the committal document would even make the reality of the crime explicit in its terminology. In 1779, Catherine Webb was committed to the bridewell for "feloniously stealing" 11 yards of valuable silk ribbon.[119] In 1784, when John Roberts was produced before the sitting alderman at the Guildhall Justice Room, also accused of "feloniously stealing" two handkerchiefs (one of them silk), he, too, was merely committed to the bridewell for a month.[120] So ubiquitous was this disposal for lesser offences of dishonesty that, in the 1720s, a group of Metropolitan retailers complained that shoplifters were not being properly punished. Provided that stolen goods were recovered, and the crimes were not especially serious, they would: "...escape with a bridewell whipping, and soon return to their trade".[121]

At the bridewell, those inmates committed for pilfering would be dealt with in much the same manner as others accused of vagrancy or disorderly conduct, being made to beat hemp etc. (though this practice gradually declined amongst all prisoners). Normally, they would be held for a set

116. N. Rogers, "Policing the Poor in Eighteenth-century London", 1991, p.131.
117. Mansion House Justice Room Charge Book, 1699-1705, CLA/004/01/4 entry for 7 August 1704, p.213.
118. *The Covent Garden Journal*, 5 February 1752. By contrast, Richard Sneesby was committed to Newgate to await trial on indictment for stealing a coat and a: "...great quantity of iron, and other things".
119. CLA/005/01'008, Guildhall Justice Room Minute Book, 8 April 1779.
120. Guildhall Justice Room Minute Book, GJR/M 25 1784 30 April-21 May, Entry for 11 May 1784.
121. Anon, *The Great Grievance of Traders and Shopkeepers*, c.1720, p.1.

period or until the institution decided to release them. In the first half of the eighteenth century, this decision was usually made by the Bridewell Court, which met every two to three weeks. Later, it was taken by a special internal prison committee.[122]

Of course, such disposals deprived suspects of their right to a jury trial. However, they were not readily susceptible to judicial review, especially as the poor could not usually afford the cost. Additionally, in many situations, those arrested for felonies must have viewed it as a very satisfactory alternative to the grave risks of trial on indictment, and would have been unlikely to challenge them, even if they could.

Restraint in its use

Even in the Metropolis, the power to commit for vagrancy was usually exercised with considerable restraint, if only for practical reasons. If parish officers and local magistrates wished, they could have speedily arrested and imprisoned huge numbers of people. This sometimes happened. For example, one night in September 1718, 32 prostitutes were arrested in Drury Lane: "...most of whom were the next day sent to the House of Correction".[123] However, there were simply too many potential candidates for such a disposal for it to be applied without great discrimination. It would have been quite impossible to deal with every vagrant, drunkard and prostitute in this fashion without overwhelming the capital's bridewells and houses of correction. For example, although Mathew Martin estimated that there were 15,288 beggars on the streets of London (over 90 per cent of them women) in 1796, it is apparent that the great majority were able to operate without being incarcerated.[124] The same could be said of the capital's numerous prostitutes. As a result, Daniel Defoe could profess astonishment at how the capital's magistrates ignored them, despite having ample legal powers to "restrain this tide of

122. J. M. Beattie, *Policing and Punishment in London, 1660-1750*, 2001, pp.24-33, p.66 and pp.313-314.
123. *Original Weekly Journal,* 13 September 1718.
124. T. Hitchcock, "Begging on the Streets of Eighteenth-century London", 2005, p.481.

uncleanness".[125] Instead, a "winking indulgence" was often shown towards aggressively soliciting women in the centre of the Metropolis.[126]

Frequently, where several people had been arrested in this fashion, only the worst would be detained. For example, in February 1731, after Sir John Gonson examined a large number of "disorderly persons", several of them reputed pickpockets, only four of the "most notorious" were committed to hard labour in the Tothill Field's Bridewell. The rest were discharged.[127] The following month, after the same magistrate examined several "idle and disorderly" people who had been arrested overnight, only three were committed to the bridewell.[128] When it came to prostitutes, the authorities would often act only if the women had created some kind of disturbance. For example, in July 1741, Elizabeth Rolfe and two of her friends were committed to the bridewell after making a "great noise" in Fleet Street at 5 am.[129] In 1803, when a streetwalker named Mary Littlehall was produced before an alderman, the magistrate stressed that it was her aggressive and abusive behaviour in the street, not her trade, which led to a similar disposal.[130] Many aldermen actively discouraged City constables from arresting women who had solicited in a discreet manner.[131]

Legal concerns

The vagueness of the wording contained in the enabling statutes also occasioned a considerable degree of legal confusion. This could become a major problem on the rare occasions when those arrested gained access to legal advice. In 1730, for example, Mary Freeman, an alleged prostitute who had been committed to the Tothill Fields work-house for being "idle and disorderly", was brought before the Court of King's Bench in a *habeas corpus* action (funded anonymously). She had experienced counsel to plead for her. At the hearing, it was argued that the Jacobean statute of 1610, which used

125. D. Defoe, *Augusta Triumphans: Or, The Way to make London the most flourishing City in the Universe*, 1728, p.27.
126. D. Defoe, *Some considerations upon street-walkers*, 1726, p.2.
127. *Daily Journal*, 5 February 1731.
128. *Grub Street Journal*, 11 March, 1731.
129. BBBRMG202060136 document at www.londonlives.org Last accessed 17 February 2011.
130. *The Times*, 2 February 1803, p.3.
131. A. E. Simpson, "The Mouth Of Strange Women Is A Deep Pit", 1996, p.61.

the words "idle and disorderly" had been repealed, and that the wording of its replacement did not cover what had occurred in her case. Counsel for the Crown was forced to argue that even if Freeman's commitment could not be justified under the Jacobean Act, it might be valid under a more recent statutory provision, as a: "...woman, who is idle and disorderly, might well come under the description of a rogue".[132] Three years later, John Harper successfully brought an action for *habeas corpus* against the keeper of the Westminster House of Correction. A local JP had committed him for being a rogue and vagabond under the same statute (12 Ann 2. 23). Harper, who was legally represented by counsel, appears to have been a street musician. His barrister argued that he did not come within the words or intention of the Act as: "...it was not pretended he was a vagrant".[133]

There were also jurisprudential objections to its use. Even when first introduced, it had been the subject of fierce criticism. It was subsequently condemned as excessively draconian by several senior and distinguished judges. Thus, Sir John Holt (1642-1710), the Lord Chief Justice, repeatedly argued that it was contrary to the rights of even the poorest Englishman to be imprisoned purely at the discretion of a magistrate.[134] In 1709, Holt, and several of his fellow Westminster judges, questioned the legality of arresting street women who were merely suspected of being "lewd and disorderly" but had not been witnessed doing anything.[135]

As the century advanced, the numbers committed under this power declined as a result of increased legal scrutiny and recourse to more specific summary offences. Magistrates appear to have become particularly nervous about using it to deal with "mainstream" offenders, rather than streetwalkers, drunkards, the disorderly, and vagrants. As a result, Lord Russell was unaware that he was exaggerating the novelty of clause five of the Middlesex Justices Act of 1792, when he complained that it vested magistrates with a dangerous power that was previously: "...totally unknown to the constitution — that of apprehending and imprisoning suspected persons".[136]

132. *Anonymous* (1730) 1 Barnardiston K. B. 393.
133. *The King and Harper* (1733) 2 Barnardiston K. B. 349.
134. F. Dabhoiwala, "Summary Justice in Early Modern London", 2006, p.797.
135. *The Case of the Reforming Constables* (1709) Holt, K.B. 485.
136. *The Times*, 22 June 1793, p.1.

Enhanced concern about legal "niceties" may also explain why it had been thought necessary to introduce a series of new, summary only, misdemeanours, as the eighteenth century advanced. In the early 1700s, those found in possession of lead that they could not account for might simply have been committed to a house of correction as "disorderly". A few decades later this made magistrates uncomfortable.

Mediation and Arbitration

Conscientious English justices saw their primary function as ensuring neighbourhood peace, rather than enforcing the strict letter of the criminal law.[137] This meant that "victimless" crimes might be dealt with informally. For example, in 1798, a group of five young men who had been arrested overnight for firing off guns and pistols in the street were examined and then released by the Bow Street magistrate: "...on promising never to be guilty of the like offence in future".[138]

However, even where there was a "victim", many felt that a JP worked best when acting as a peacemaker between the parties, preventing future animosity and restoring concord by "private arbitration". Many minor and some middle-ranking cases were disposed of by magistrates, sitting alone, using the inherent authority of their office and employing their personal skills in conflict-resolution, rather than any firm legal power. A good magistrate would refrain from proceeding to a formal legal enquiry in, for example, an assault case for as long as: "...reasonable hopes remain that the aggressor might be induced, by the reiterated application of the person injured, to make satisfaction".[139] As a result, the great majority of conflicts that came before the Justices were resolved: "...as Mediators and Reconcilers of Differences, and not as Magistrates in which they can act by any authority of Law".[140]

137. G. Morgan and P. Rushton, "The Magistrate, the community and the maintenance of an orderly society in eighteenth-century England", 2003, p.56.

138. *Oracle and Daily Advertiser*, 6 October 1798.

139. T. Gisborne, *An Enquiry into the Duties of men in the Higher and Middle Classes of Society in Great Britain*, 1794, pp.282-283.

140. *The Gentleman's Magazine*, 1732, vol. 2, p.910.

One reason that trading justices were so disliked was that they were often unwilling to mediate, in situations where this should have been possible, and would, instead, encourage matters to proceed to formal litigation and its attendant charges.[141] A "sordid knave" who viewed his office as a commercial venture, would take special care that the parties were not given an opportunity to cool down. He might even inflame their disagreements, so that fees were accrued. By contrast, a good JP would never take advantage of angry complainants to instigate formal proceedings that might ultimately have disastrous financial consequences. Instead, they would work to: "…compromise differences, and heal the breaches of the peace by kind admonitions and advice".[142] Henry Fielding claimed that by composing the quarrels of porters and beggars he had reduced what had previously been an income of £500 a year of the "dirtiest money upon earth" to one of little more than £300 per annum.

A frequent feature of such informal determinations was the divorce between strict legal theory and practical reality, provided this was amenable to the parties concerned. As Thomas Gisborne observed, many magistrates would decide the matter in front of them: "…partly or entirely by their own unauthorised ideas of equity". Though their critics claimed this was motivated by laziness and reluctance to consult the relevant legal texts, in many cases it was prompted by their personal views of justice.[143] However, this view was not usually plucked from the air. It often appealed to a more widespread, even communal, set of social values and drew on a fairly widely shared sense of moral order.

As a result, magistrates would often discharge a matter on terms, having summarily arranged a compromise between the prosecutor and defendant. This could entail a small amount of money and an apology being given to the alleged victim, and/or a verbal warning being administered from the bench. This approach is particularly well evidenced in the City of London, where aldermen and the Lord Mayor sitting in the Justice Rooms at the Guildhall and Mansion House would record their decisions in Minute Books, many

141. *Gazetteer and New Daily Advertiser*, 17 January 1772.

142. *Gazetteer and New Daily Advertiser*, 18 May 1774.

143. T. Gisborne, *An Enquiry into the Duties of men in the Higher and Middle Classes of Society in Great Britain*, 1794, p.281.

of which still survive. Numerous apparently well-evidenced allegations that were brought before them in their magisterial capacity went no further.[144]

The vast majority of assaults, in particular, were disposed of summarily, without the alleged perpetrator even entering into a recognisance to appear at the next Quarter Sessions, let alone facing trial on indictment. In the latter years of the eighteenth century, it seems that between 10 and 20 times as many assault cases were resolved in the City by magistrates acting on their own as by the three higher forums (Quarter Sessions, King's Bench and the Old Bailey) combined. Taken together, aldermen dealt with between 800 and 1,000 assault cases each year at the Guildhall Justice Room and the Mansion House. Even late in the century, between 1784 and 1796, only about 14 per cent of defendants in these cases were bailed or remanded in custody (in the absence of sureties) to appear at Quarter Sessions or the Old Bailey. In the Metropolis, most allegations of assault would be dealt with by a magistrate dismissing the matter as unfounded or frivolous, reprimanding the accused person (and then dismissing the matter) or supervising a swift settlement between the parties, which might entail an apology by the accused person to his victim and/or the payment of a modest amount of compensation, if only to cover the victim's court fees and loss of time.[145] In other situations, the culprits were simply given an informal verbal reprimand and dismissed.

For example, in 1784, when two men were produced before an alderman accused of assaulting and beating William Trow and Samuel Roberts, the parties "withdrew and agreed" the matter, presumably by paying a small sum in compensation, so that it could immediately be discharged when they returned to the magistrate. Several other assault cases came before the same alderman on the same day, nearly all of which were recorded as "agreed and discharged".[146] A case from 1766, in which eight "young bloods" knocked down several porters in Fleet Street market, is also indicative of this process. When the local constable and watchmen came to the porters' assistance, a violent affray ensued. Two of the gentlemen involved were eventually arrested,

---

144. See, for example, Minute Book of the Guildhall Justice Room 25 May to 19 June, 1752, LMA CLA 00501, entry for 11 June.
145. D. Gray, "The Regulation of Violence in the Metropolis; the Prosecution of Assault in the Summary Courts, c.1780-1820", 2007, p.76 and p.82.
146. CLA/005/01/045, Guildhall Justice Room Minute Book, entry for 11 May 1784.

subsequently being produced before the sitting alderman at Guildhall, where the watchmen appeared to prosecute: "...some with broken heads, and others much bruised". Nevertheless, the offenders were discharged on paying the injured men sums of three or five shillings each.[147]

Given that many assaults that did reach trial on indictment at Quarter Sessions were treated as quasi-civil matters, until late in the century, and were, effectively, settled by agreement between the parties it is not, perhaps, surprising that this occurred.[148] This approach was not special to the London area. For example, the Reverend Edmund Tew, a County Durham magistrate in the mid eighteenth century, *personally* dealt with almost as many cases of assault, over the space of 14 years, as were determined at the county's Quarter Sessions. His primary aim was to negotiate peace between disputants, rather than to secure convictions. Formal prosecutions were rare.[149]

Nevertheless, such informal resolutions were not confined to offences of violence and disorder. JPs in Middlesex and Westminster also dealt with many minor offences of dishonesty in this fashion.[150] For example, in September 1740, Edward Dixon and a constable brought Sarah Chandler before Henry Norris, a Hackney justice. She had been caught red-handed in Dixon's garden, early in the morning, with her apron full of plums and apples. Chandler claimed that they were windfalls, rather than having been picked directly from the trees. Norris recorded in his notebook that: "On considering ye whole & ye prosecutors desiring it might be forgiven dismissed her with a reprimand".[151] It seems that a significant proportion of the 70 per cent of Metropolitan property crimes that were disposed of by magistrates were resolved informally. Of course, many of these involved cases of petty theft. Given its unique legal status as the only non-capital felony, it is, perhaps,

147. *The Whitehall Evening Post; or, London Intelligencer*, 20 September 1766.
148. See generally, N. Landau, "Indictment for Fun and Profit: A Prosecutor's Reward at Eighteenth-century Quarter Sessions", 1999, pp.507-536.
149. G. Morgan and P. Rushton, "The Magistrate, the community and the maintenance of an orderly society in eighteenth-century England", 2003, p.68.
150. D. Gray, "The People's Courts? Summary Justice and Social Relations in the City of London, c.1760-1800", 2008, pp.1-15.
151. R. Paley (Ed.), *Justice in 18th-Century Hackney*, 1991, p.59.

unsurprising that justices did not necessarily feel constrained to commit them for a trial on indictment.[152]

However, even cases of grand larceny would sometimes result in a supervised but informal settlement. There were a number of scenarios in which this was likely to occur; for example: where the victim indicated that he was reluctant to prosecute, provided his stolen goods were returned; where the allegation arose from a quasi-civil dispute, in which the suspect claimed to be legally entitled to dispose of another's goods, even where their case did not appear very strong; and where the "theft" could be dismissed as a "jape" or case of high spirits.

Some of the practical mechanics of this process can be seen in a case from 1791, in which there was an attempt to prosecute Justice Foster, in the Court of King's Bench, for compounding a felony. The Middlesex magistrate had dealt with a dispute between two women over a gold pin, one of whom eventually accused the other of stealing it. When the suspect was arrested, and brought before him, he advised her to "Go and make it up". Initially, she was adamant that she would not do so, at which point the magistrate pointed out that she was likely to be incarcerated pending trial, as the victim: "...swears positively [to the crime] and [so] you must be committed". The JP eventually persuaded her to pay the complainant 15 shillings to avoid such an outcome (it was this that formed the basis of the compounding allegation). He then endorsed the arrest warrant as: "Discharged for want of sufficient evidence".[153] Some other property crimes were resolved in equally informal, but rather different, ways. In 1790, for example, a youth named Thomas Whittington was produced before Alderman Combe for breaking open a shop, and taking a large sum of money, in a "shocking instance of early depravity". He was sent to the Philanthropic Society "out of humanity" rather than being prosecuted.[154]

Again, this approach to lesser property offences was not confined to the Metropolitan area. In eighteenth-century Wiltshire, for example, the magistrate William Hunt was regularly faced with allegations of minor theft, even

152. J. M. Beattie, *Policing and Punishment in London, 1660–1750*, 2001, p.26.

153. *Morning Post and Daily Advertiser*, 13 July 1791.

154. Guildhall Justice Room Minute Book, CLA/005/01/045 19 Aug-14 September 1790, entry for 27 Aug.

if the word itself was only rarely used. Instead, items would be "detained" or "taken". However, only a handful of the most serious matters would go for trial on indictment. As with the numerous assaults that came before him, Hunt would usually "reconcile" the parties, if he did not dismiss a matter as unfounded or frivolous. Thus, when David Batt stole eggs from under one of Alexander Gidding's hens: "The parties agreed upon hearing". As with assaults, the transgressing party might beg and receive forgiveness, receive a warning, or pay costs and damages in a supervised settlement.[155] Edmund Tew in Durham also dealt with a large number of minor property offences, most of which were recorded as being "made up" or "agreed". Only about one in eight appear to have led to a formal prosecution.[156]

As the Foster case suggests, magistrates would often initiate the idea of a settlement, and suggest to the suspect that they approach the complainant and make some satisfaction, perhaps telling them that many other people had done this in the past.[157] Sometimes, this could be difficult, as even the poor were often eager to have their "day in court". In 1816, a Metropolitan magistrate complained that he and his fellow justices had to use all their powers of persuasion to reconcile poor complainants and prevent matters going to the Quarter Sessions or petty sessions.[158]

However, where necessary, justices could use a degree of pressure to bring about such informal disposals. For example, in 1815, after Thomas Cobham, an inebriated Irishman, objected to being ejected by a pub landlord in West Smithfield, a fight ensued in which a large amount of glass was broken. The matter came before a magistrate, who warned the two men that, unless they could settle it between themselves, it would have to go for trial on indictment. This was not an attractive proposition for either party, and the matter was swiftly resolved. Cobham publicly apologised for his behaviour and payed compensation for the damage he had caused.[159] In many cases, however,

155. E. Crittall (Ed.), *The Justicing Notebook of William Hunt, 1744-1749*, 1982, p.13 and p.62.
156. G. Morgan and P. Rushton, "The Magistrate, the community and the maintenance of an orderly society in eighteenth-century England", 2003, p.74.
157. *The Times*, July 13 1791, p.3.
158. P. King, "The Summary Courts and Social Relations in Eighteenth-century England", 2004, p.146.
159. D. Gray, "The Regulation of Violence in the Metropolis; the Prosecution of Assault in the Summary Courts, c.1780-1820", 2007, p.75.

suspects actively encouraged such a disposal. For example, a thief who was carried before Colonel de Veil for stealing clothes from a washing line: "... offered to make Mr. Wren [his victim] full satisfaction for the Goods".[160]

The factors that prompted magistrates to decide that a case of, for example, assault or domestic violence was sufficiently trivial that it could be dismissed on terms or, alternatively, was serious enough to warrant a jury trial, were rarely clearly identified. However, it seems that these decisions were shaped by fairly well established criteria, some of which can be extrapolated from the records. An ability to pay compensation, and a willingness to receive it, was usually very important. Unsurprisingly, the inherent gravity of the allegation was also significant. Assault cases that went to trial would often emphasise that the victim's life had been feared of as a result of the injuries incurred. The "innocence" of the victim, and whether they had played any role in precipitating events, could also be important. For example, injured wives who had "provoked" their husbands were unlikely to receive much sympathy, unless their injuries were very grave. If a crime was relatively modest, and there was a suggestion that its perpetrator was suffering from some form of mental disturbance, even if it did not properly amount to insanity, a magistrate was also more likely to supervise a settlement or discharge the accused person with a verbal warning.[161]

Nevertheless, and inevitably, this degree of discretion sometimes produced radically different outcomes in almost identical cases, even from the same justice. Some suspects might be indicted or committed to a house of correction, while others, faced by similar allegations, were released with a warning or a supervised settlement.[162]

Of course, a justice's effectiveness as a conciliator, or when "imposing" solutions for which there was little firm legal justification, was largely contingent on the parties' willingness to accept his authority, and to acquiesce in his method of adjudication. This was, in turn, based on patterns of deference

160. OBSP, Trial of John Cane, 16 April 1740.
161. D. Rabin, "Searching for the Self in Eighteenth-century English Criminal Trials, 1730-1800", 2003, pp.85-106.
162. G. Smith, "Expanding the compass of domestic violence in the Hanoverian Metropolis", 2007, pp.35-36.

and a faith in the office's general legitimacy.[163] Edmund Bohun was not alone in believing that the era's culture of social respect meant that many Englishmen preferred to have their justice meted out by men of "quality".[164] Patrician aldermen in the City were, perhaps, inherently more likely to command such respect than were trading justices in Middlesex.

163. J. M. Rosenheim, "Documenting Authority: Texts and Magistracy in Restoration Society", 1993, p.594.
164. E. Bohun, *The Justice of Peace His Calling and Qualifications*, 1693, pp.15-16, and p. 19.

CHAPTER 15

A PRIVATE SYSTEM OF PROSECUTION?

Introduction

Although many eighteenth-century observers believed that English criminal law was defective, to some degree, it was its enforcement that was seen as the primary problem within the Metropolitan justice system. One reason for this was that eighteenth-century trials on indictment were largely founded upon charges and evidence brought by private individuals (usually victims), even though they were, theoretically, prosecuted in the name of the Crown. Private prosecutors often needed considerable persistence, time, and some money, to pursue matters to a conviction.[1] Many thought that such a system was inherently flawed, if only because: "...most men preferred their own interest, their ease and pleasure, to the public good".[2] However, any potential reform carried its own problems, discouraging radical change until the following century.

The Appeal of Murder

There was still one exception to this general position, whereby a criminal prosecution was not even theoretically conducted in the name of the monarch. This was the almost moribund appeal of death or murder, which was brought in the name of a private individual (It had nothing to do with taking an adjudicated matter to a higher court for reconsideration). It was the only significant survivor of the medieval appeal of felony, which had been a

1. G. Morgan and P. Rushton, "The Magistrate, the community and the maintenance of an orderly society in eighteenth-century England", 2003, p.58.
2. *British Journal* (1722), February 27 1725.

genuine private criminal prosecution in theory as well as practice. Although it was formally abolished in 1819, its very survival during the eighteenth century is indicative of the importance of private individuals to the wider system.

Even so, it was very little used, not least because the complicated technical prerequisites for bringing such an action greatly reduced its prospects of success. For example, the 'accusator' or 'appellant' (terminology varied) was necessarily drawn from the dead person's spouse or heir (usually siblings or children), and a woman lost the right to appeal her husband's death if she got remarried.[3] It also had to be brought within a year and a day of the victim's death, while the details of the offence, the victim's wounds, etc., had to be specified with the "utmost certainty".[4] Defendants could always be fully legally represented in such actions, unlike those who were tried on indictment, although there was no requirement for an appeal to be considered by a Grand Jury before going for trial.

In practice, the appeal of murder was almost invariably used to retry a homicide that had failed to produce a murder conviction after an earlier prosecution on indictment. This was because the action was not affected by the doctrine of *autrefois acquit*, which normally prevented re-prosecution on indictment. It could even be used to re-prosecute a murder conviction that had been followed by a reprieve. There was no royal power to reprieve those capitally convicted on appeal, unless the pardon was issued under the 1693 Act for Suppressing Highwaymen.[5] A rash of reprieves for cases involving murder that had been tried on indictment in the 1770s, prompted one observer to ask why no appeal had been prosecuted successfully for many years.[6] As a result, although the action had many detractors, who thought it "odious", it also had a few supporters, who felt that it sometimes safeguarded victims' rights.[7]

However, it seems that, by the late eighteenth century, if a killer had been convicted of manslaughter, rather than murder, and clergied for that

3. G. Jacob, *The Laws of Appeals and Murder*, 1719, p.4
4. *London Chronicle*, 3 March 1778.
5. See letter from 'Memmius' in the *Middlesex Journal or Chronicle of Liberty*, February 22 1772.
6. *Bingley's London Journal*, 5 September 1772.
7. W. Eden, *Principles of Penal Law*, 1781, p.166.

offence, he could not be appealed.[8] This had not always been the case. In 1709, for example, the widow of constable John Dent had the three soldiers who killed her husband arrested as they left the Court of Queen's Bench, after being told that a majority of the 12 Westminster judges had decided that they were only guilty of manslaughter, rather than murder, and ordered their release. She had lodged an appeal in anticipation of just such a verdict, though nothing seems to have come of it in the end.[9]

Even if they did not eventually bring an appeal, relatives could use the threat of such proceedings to pressure financial compensation from the erst-while defendant.[10] Thus, in 1770, the widow of John Bigby, a watchman, initiated an appeal against a pair of brothers who had killed her husband, after they had been reprieved following capital conviction. This (unusual) executive decision was the result of extra-judicial pressure from Lord Sandwich, whose mistress was the men's sister. Their reprieve had been on condition of transporting themselves for life, and one was already aboard an America bound vessel when they were detained pursuant to the appeal, which was set out on a large "skin" of parchment.[11] The widow was only persuaded not to appear in the Court of King's Bench, to pursue the matter, after receiving at least £350.[12] Other reports spoke of as much as 500 guineas being paid out, after Lord Sandwich advised that the men: "...count out the gold before her, throw it into her lap and see if she will refuse it".[13] If an appeal were brought before the court at which a defendant had been acquitted rose, the accused man would normally be remanded in custody to await a new trial.[14]

Very occasionally, in the early decades of the century, an appeal produced both a conviction and execution, especially if the initial trial on indictment

8. *London Chronicle*, 3 March 1778.
9. *Post Boy*, 26-29 November 1709.
10. For example, in the trial of Duncumb Abercony in 1683, for murdering William Godolphin, the jury convicted of manslaughter, but the: "Prosecutors telling the Court they would bring him in an Appeal, he was obliged to give Bail to answer the same next Sessions". OBSP, 17 January 1683.
11. *Lloyd's Evening Post*, 27 April 1770.
12. C. W. Everett, *The Letters of Junius*, 1927, p.174, n.1. Junius appears to have been Lord Shelburne.
13. W. R. Riddell, "Appeal of Death and Its Abolition", 1926, p.806.
14. *Grub Street Journal*, 27 January 1732.

had been conducted in a casual or incompetent manner. In 1709, for example, Christopher Slaughterford, acquitted at Kingston Assizes of murdering his fiancée "for want of positive witness", was appealed by the dead woman's brother and tried at the Court of Queen's Bench in a much more carefully prepared prosecution. On this, second, occasion, he was convicted, sentenced to death and, after much legal argument, executed at Guildford.[15]

In a more specifically Metropolitan context, Lovi Houssart (Lewis Hussar) was acquitted on indictment, and then convicted and executed on appeal, for murdering his wife in 1724.[16] To preclude any suggestion of hard usage, the "cause being uncommon", his execution was delayed a month, so that the conviction could be reviewed by the Westminster judges.[17] Similarly, in July 1729, James Cluff was tried at the Old Bailey on an appeal. This had been lodged after Cluff's acquittal for murdering a fellow domestic servant at the same forum, the previous April, following trial on indictment. It was brought by the brother (and heir) of the dead woman. On this occasion, the jury returned a guilty verdict. Cluff was sentenced to death and duly executed at Tyburn.[18] This was the last case at the Old Bailey to produce such a result, though the possibility of an appeal was threatened in that court, by the barrister William Garrow, as late as 1787.[19] Several Metropolitan appeals were heard at other forums, such as the Court of King's Bench. Thus, in 1729, the widow of Robert Castill, who had died of mistreatment while imprisoned in the Fleet for debt, appealed the acquittal of the prison's warden for his murder. The appeal was heard before Lord Chief Justice Raymond, sitting at the Guildhall, the following year. On this occasion, the warden, Thomas Bambridge, was acquitted again.[20]

---

15. Anon, *The Birth, Parentage, and Education, Life and Conversation of Mr. Christopher Slaughterford*, 1709, pp.1-8.
16. OBSP, Trial of Lewis Hussar, 14 October 1724.
17. *British Journal*, 24 October 1724.
18. OBSP, Trial of James Cluff, 16 April 1729 and, *The Ordinary of Newgate his Account, Of the Behaviour, Confession, and dying Words of James Cluff, who was executed at Tyburn, for the Murder of Mary Green, on Friday the 25th of this Instant July, 1729.*
19. OBSP, Trial of Griffin Thomas and William Roberts, 23 May 1787.
20. J. Hostettler, *A History of Criminal Justice in England and Wales*, 2009, pp.151-152, and *Country Journal or The Craftsman*, 13 September 1729.

Despite such cases, by the 1750s, Henry Fielding thought that the appeal of murder was: "...now obsolete, and where the proceedings are still [brought] more ceremonial and tedious".[21] In the following decade, William Blackstone also observed that the action had long fallen into desuetude. Although this was not quite true, only three cases are found in the law reports after 1730, though the last was in 1817, and others probably went unreported. The procedure was considered in Parliament in 1774, when several MPs, including Charles James Fox, suggested that it be formally abolished, albeit that nothing was done in this respect for another 45 years.[22]

Prosecution on Indictment

Unlike an appeal, prosecution on indictment, whether at the Old Bailey or one of the Metropolitan Quarter Sessions, at least took the 'form' of a public action. Nevertheless, this often meant little more than that criminal process against a suspected felon was brought in the name of the Monarch. It did not necessarily, or even normally, mean that the state became actively involved in preparing and presenting such prosecutions. Much of the practical reality of a private action, especially the victim's initiation of proceedings and gathering of evidence, remained.

Traditionally, the Crown had only taken an active role in cases that directly affected its own interests, such as high treason and piracy. As a result, and as William Blackstone noted, there was an important distinction between prosecutions in the name of the King, which were: "...truly and properly his own suits, and filed *ex officio* by his own immediate officer, the attorney general ... [and] those in which, though the king is the nominal prosecutor, yet it is at the relation of some private person or common informer".[23] This remained the situation throughout the 1700s. Indeed, even in the early decades of the following century, the visiting French lawyer, Charles Cottu, then engaged in researching the common law criminal justice system, noted

21. H. Fielding, *A Clear State of the Case of Elizabeth Canning*, 2nd edn., 1753, p.3.
22. W. R. Riddell, "Appeal of Death and Its Abolition", 1926, p.804.
23. W. Blackstone, *Commentaries on the Laws of England,* Oxford, Clarendon Press, vol.4, 1765-9, p.305.

that the victims of serious crimes were, effectively, the arbiters of a suspect's fate. They were able to follow any option from ignoring an offence, prosecuting for a less serious crime than that committed, to pursuing a matter to the utmost rigour of the law. Additionally, they would have to obtain much of the evidence that would be used at trial.[24] As a result, Cottu felt that it was the victim's desire for legally sanctioned revenge that was the primary determinant in the prosecution process, the wider nation appearing largely indifferent where people were too compassionate or indolent to prosecute.[25]

As will be seen, this was an exaggeration. However, private prosecutors *were* normally the key component in the system, and were often confined to the personal satisfaction of performing their civic duty as compensation for their labours. As a result, much could turn on chance factors. For example, in 1787, a servant who had provoked his master into striking him, prosecuted his erstwhile employer for assault at the Guildhall Quarter Sessions after receiving entirely unsolicited advice to do so from an attorney who had a deep personal dislike of the accused man.[26]

Not only did victims usually decide whether to bring a criminal action, they were often able to choose the offence charged. The *Old Bailey Sessions Papers* reveal cases where a non-clergyable offence *could* have been charged but, instead, simple grand larceny, or an even more minor crime, was indicted. An illustration of the consequences of such choices can be seen in the cases of two men accused of stealing metal from houses in the 1720s. In 1727, Simon Sherlock was prosecuted for felony after stealing the modest total of 30lb of lead and six iron bars from an empty house owned by the Corporation of London that was awaiting demolition. By contrast, the following year, Jonathon Dove and Joseph Monday were indicted for a misdemeanour when caught with the enormous quantity of 700lb of lead taken from Belsize House, the Metropolitan residence of the Earl of Chesterfield.[27]

24. C. Cottu, *On the administration of Criminal Justice in England*, 1822, p.38.
25. C. Cottu, *On the administration of the criminal code in England, and the spirit of the English government*, 1820, p.23.
26. *The Times*, 2 November 1787, p.3. Although the defendant admitted the incident, the Recorder fined him just a shilling, as he thought no encouragement should be given to such prosecutions.
27. OBSP, Trial of Simon Sherlock, 22 February 1727. OBSP, Trial of Jonathon Dove and Joseph Monday, 17 July 1728.

Similarly, in 1723, John Clifton was indicted for a misdemeanour, after entering a domestic residence, late at night, with intent to steal. He had been caught after ascending three flights of internal stairs. He could have been prosecuted for the capital felony of burglary, but his intended victim preferred a course of action that merely led to him being fined.[28]

In these situations, the prosecutor/victim normally made the initial decision not to bring proceedings for a more serious offence, though pressure from the examining magistrate as to the appropriate charge was also important. Some prosecutors would expressly tell the clerk of indictments at Hick's Hall or the Guildhall "not to lay it capital" when drawing up their charge. However, magistrates such as John Fielding, were aware of this, and would occasionally stipulate that prosecution must be for a capital offence, as a condition of the recognisance they placed a complainant under, forcing them to bring the more serious charge or lose a substantial sum of money.[29]

In most cases, it was the victim of a crime, or at least someone intimately connected with it, that brought a prosecution. However, this was not *necessarily* so. Anyone could, in theory, prosecute any crime in England and Wales. This is illustrated by the extraordinary 'cold case' trial at the Nottingham Assizes in 1759 of a septuagenarian man, William Horne, who had murdered his three-day-old baby, 35 years earlier. The whole affair, though widely rumoured, had then been hushed up for decades. However, Horne had fallen out with his brother (a witness) many years later, his sibling apparently experiencing pangs of conscience about what had happened to the baby. Even worse, Horne had successfully prosecuted a local man who had called him an "incestuous old dog" for slander in the Litchfield ecclesiastical court. When this individual and his brother came together, the information provided by the latter allowed the former to set about arranging a prosecution for murder, searching around for a justice willing to entertain such an old complaint, and assembling the evidence to be adduced at trial. William Horne was duly convicted and executed on his 74th birthday.[30]

28. OBSP, Trial of John Clifton, 30 May 1723.
29. J. H. Langbein, *The Origins of Adversary Criminal Trial*, 2003, p.344.
30. Anon, *A Genuine Account of the Life and Trial of William Andrew Horne, Esq.*, 3rd edn., 1760, p.8.

There was no legal obligation on victims who apprehended criminals to turn them over to a constable, let alone to prosecute them, for any offence at all, though many thought it was a civic duty. A magistrate also seems to have had a vague and very rarely exercised power at common law to bind a reluctant victim over to prosecute if he became aware of a crime and suspect. In any event, the victim's freedom to prosecute may not always have been appreciated. In 1733, for example, Joseph Fretwell, indicted for snatching a hat and wig from a child, claimed that his victim had been threatened into prosecuting, against his own wishes, by a nearby watchman. Even the watchman conceded that he had warned the child that Fretwell had:

> ...not stood in Defiance of your good Nature only, but in Defiance of Justice and Authority, and therefore if you don't prosecute him, I'll proceed against you in a Process of Justice.[31]

Although this was an empty threat, some observers wished to see such a possibility become law. In 1754, for example, it was suggested that those who refrained from prosecuting criminals who had victimised them should be fined.[32]

Whatever the strict legal position, in an urban setting the frequent presence of crowds, after a man had been caught red-handed, could lead to extrinsic pressure on victims of crime to prosecute (or not). Nevertheless, most victims were well aware that the 'ball' was firmly in their own courts. This could cause intense irritation amongst law enforcement agencies. The watchman in Fretwell's case freely admitted that he had used his staff to hit the defendant when the child made it clear that he did not wish to prosecute. This prompted the court to point out that he was placing himself at the risk of a civil action by the defendant, and to ask: "What right had you

31. OBSP, Trial of Joseph Fretwell, 12 January 1733. Despite the watchman's claim to have been acting in the public interest, the court suggested that he may have been influenced by the availability of a reward, and the jury acquitted.
32. Anon (C.D.), *A Letter To a Member of Parliament Upon the Subject of the present reigning Enormities of Murders and Robberies*, 1754, p.2.

to assault him after he had been discharged by the Prosecutor, and while he behaved himself peaceably?"[33]

Reluctance to Prosecute

Throughout the eighteenth century there were regular complaints about the reluctance of Londoners who had become crime victims to prosecute, even where a suspect had been identified and detained.[34] Dr. Johnson claimed that almost every Metropolitan thief had been held and released on more than one occasion.[35] More precisely, in 1785, it was alleged that only 10 per cent of criminal incidents in the capital were brought to trial (for all reasons).[36] Such claims also had the support of magistrates like Henry Fielding.[37] It was widely believed that this meant that the consequences of committing crime, even if they entailed death, were often too remote to outweigh the immediate attractions of offending.[38]

It is not difficult to find ready explanations as to *why* prosecutors were so reluctant to bring criminals to trial. There was considerable inconvenience and cost involved, with much time being wasted on attending an examining JP and subsequently in going to court. Significant expense would also be incurred via the payment of court fees. These would usually include a fee for the initial arrest warrant, those required for entering witness recognisances, that payable to the clerk of the court for drawing up the bill of indictment (normally two shillings), swearing to it (four pence), as well as those for the doorkeeper, the crier and the bailiff.[39] Although some JPs refused to accept fees from impoverished complainants, or at least reduced their entitlement,

33. OBSP, Trial of Joseph Fretwell, 12 January 1733.
34. Anon (A Citizen of London), *The Vices of the Cities of London and Westminster, Trac'd from their Original*, 1751, p.11.
35. S. Johnson, "Crime and Punishment", 23 April 1751, in *The Rambler*, 1953, p.186.
36. *The Times*, 5 December 1785, p.3.
37. H. Fielding, *An Enquiry into the causes of Late Increase of Robbers*, 1751, p.72.
38. Anon, *A Method whereby Criminals liable to Transportation may be render'd not only useful but honest Members of the Publick*, 1727, pp.3-4.
39. Anon, *Directions for Prosecuting Thieves Without the Help of those False Guides, The Newgate Solicitors*, 1728, p.6.

others insisted on full payment and claimed that to do otherwise merely encouraged excessive litigiousness amongst the lower orders.[40]

In the mid-eighteenth century, personally pursuing an indictment for petty larceny at the Quarter Sessions could cost 15s.[41] If a solicitor was employed to organize the prosecution, as became increasingly common, considerable further expense might be incurred. As early as 1728 a tract complained of the extortionate amounts that 'Newgate solicitors' charged crime victims.[42] In 1720, the prosecution of an indictment at Middlesex Quarter Sessions by a solicitor would cost about £2. The expense could be much greater if a barrister was involved. A manual published in the late eighteenth century, reproducing bills presented to clients by the attorneys who had managed their cases, included one of £14 13s. 8d. for prosecuting a special indictment for assault at the Westminster Quarter Sessions using counsel (this was an extreme case).[43] Perhaps unsurprisingly, in these circumstances, a popular reluctance to pay for a criminal prosecution to be conducted by counsel was one reason given for experienced, and legally represented, criminals escaping conviction towards the end of the eighteenth century.[44]

The often slipshod scheduling of trials at court further aggravated the situation. In 1787, for example, a Metropolitan magistrate claimed that a Middlesex prosecutor at the Old Bailey had travelled to that court from the "extremity of the county" with three other prosecution witnesses, and been detained in London for a week while waiting for his trial to come on, at a personal expense of over £20 when his solicitors' fees were also taken into consideration. Despite this, the defendant was acquitted.[45] In these

40. T. Gisborne, *An Enquiry into the Duties of men in the Higher and Middle Classes of Society in Great Britain*, 1794, p.290.

41. N. Landau, "Indictment for Fun and Profit: A Prosecutor's Reward at Eighteenth-century Quarter Sessions", 1999, p.534.

42. Anon, *Directions for Prosecuting Thieves Without the Help of those False Guides, The Newgate Sollicitors*, 1728, pp.3-8.

43. N. Landau, "Indictment for Fun and Profit: A Prosecutor's Reward at Eighteenth-century Quarter Sessions", 1999, p.534. If the prosecutor had had no recourse to lawyers, his fees would still have been £3 15s. 10d. as the case was unusually complex.

44. Anon, *The Report of the Select Committee Appointed by the House of Commons, Relative to the Establishment of a New Police in the Metropolis, &c.*, 1799, pp.745-777.

45. Anon (By a Magistrate), *Some Hints Towards A Revival of the Penal Laws*, 1787, p.11.

circumstances, it was, inevitably, a common complaint that the prosecution of theft on indictment often cost more than the value of the goods stolen.[46]

Automatic provision for reimbursing some of these costs was delayed until 1752, and then was confined, for many years, to poor and successful prosecutors. However, it was regularly urged that this indulgence should not be "limited to paupers only". Extending it would dissuade ordinary (rather than impoverished) crime victims from: "…keeping out of the way, and never appearing".[47] These arguments bore fruit in 1778, when all successful prosecutors were allowed costs, even if they had means. Nevertheless, this still left many who failed to secure a guilty verdict having to fund their own actions. Even though the strict letter of the law was not always followed, and expenses were sometimes awarded to those who failed to secure convictions, the situation was far from being satisfactory. The alternative was obvious to contemporary observers, some of whom urged that: "All prosecutions for felony should be carried on at the Expense of the Public".[48] However, this was likely to be both extremely expensive and bureaucratically quite difficult to implement, without radical change to the entire process.

There were other factors discouraging prosecution, not least of which was compassion. The potentially serious punishments available for many property crimes, including the possibility (sometimes even likelihood) of execution, appear to have deterred many victims from taking action. As William Smith noted in 1777: "From the severity of our punishments many decline to prosecute, and suffer criminals to go unpunished". Numerous ordinary people agreed with widely circulated tracts that argued that imposing the death penalty for simple theft was excessive.[49] The knowledge that, by the: "…laws of God, theft was not punishable with death, occasion many when robb'd (scrupulous of prosecuting) to sit down quietly with their loss". As a result,

46. Anon, *Directions for Prosecuting Thieves Without the Help of those False Guides, The Newgate Solicitors*, 1728, p.1.
47. Anon (By a Magistrate), *Some Hints Towards A Revival of the Penal Laws*, 1787, p.11.
48. C. Jones, *Some Methods Proposed Towards putting a Stop to the Flagrant Crimes of Murder, Robbery, and Perjury*, 1752, p.14.
49. W. Smith, *Mild Punishments Sound Policy*, 1785, p.6.

some argued that if most serious property crimes were punished by hard labour, such as sawing rough stone, indictment rates would greatly increase.[50]

The hearts of crime victims might also be moved by pity at the captured man or woman's plight and pleas, especially if he or she was young and had small children. Such entreaties against prosecution were regularly made. Of course, many failed, even when supported by the return of stolen goods. In 1717, for example, John Hall stole three wigs from the shop of Benjamin Smith. Hall later admitted the crime to Smith: "…telling him his Life was in his Power, and if he would be favourable to him he should have his Goods again, giving him the Key of his Lodging, where the Wiggs were found". Even so, he was prosecuted to conviction.[51] Similarly, when George Duffus was detained, after homosexually assaulting a youth, he unavailingly: "… cry'd, entreated for mercy, and begg'd they would not expose him to open shame".[52] Nevertheless, there must have been numerous successful appeals, even if they have left few records.

Unlike compounding, simply importuning a prosecutor to abandon, or not bring, felony proceedings was legal, though it carried some attendant risks. For example, when a group of men who had conspired to accuse Edward Walpole of sodomy were held in custody they wrote the "most penitential letters" begging him to drop his prosecution. Walpole refused, preferring the "welfare of the public to the weakness of pity". The letters were later adduced as evidence at the defendants' trials in the Court of King's Bench and, unsurprisingly, the jury took just two minutes to convict them.[53]

Alternatively, rather than openly forgiving offenders, crime victims might accept absurdly implausible explanations for highly incriminating circumstances, so avoiding the responsibility either for prosecuting a suspect or openly letting him go. For example, in the early 1770s, when the youthful William Cox stole a watch from a house in Islington, and was caught red-handed by the occupiers, who threatened to take him before a JP, he burst

50. Anon, *A Method whereby Criminals liable to Transportation may be render'd not only useful but honest members of the publick*, 1727, p.3 and pp.4-5.
51. OBSP, Trial of John Hall, 17 July 1717.
52. OBSP, Trial of George Duffus, 6 December 1721.
53. Anon, *A Full and genuine Narrative of the Confederacy Carried on by Cather, Cane, Alexander … Against the Hon. Edward Walpole, Esq.*, 2nd edn., 1751, pp.20-21.

into tears and, claiming that he only took it to see whether it was time to go school, his: "...counterfeit simplicity so wrought on their credulity, that they let him go without any further examination".[54]

Crime victims and bystanders might also prefer the immediate, and cheap, satisfaction of inflicting summary punishment on offenders, via a beating or ducking in a pond. This would allow them to avoid the trouble and expense of formal legal proceedings. It was especially common when pickpockets "working" crowds were caught and there were many hands available to assist in the process. For example, when, during a particularly well-attended execution at Tyburn, a thief was caught trying to pick the pocket of one of the spectators (a common occurrence on hanging days), he was immediately: "...hurried to a pond, where he underwent the usual discipline of the mob".[55]

Sometimes, this could have fatal consequences. In December 1729, a Westminster beggar who had pretended that a kitten hidden under a blanket was a baby, to make her mendicancy more lucrative, was ducked so often in a horse pond that she died from the effects of her exposure.[56] In 1785, John Fray was convicted of manslaughter (but acquitted of murder) after Thomas Waking drowned in a pond. Waking, a "boy", had been caught picking gentlemen's pockets in Tottenham Court Road, taken to a nearby pond, and thrown in. When he attempted to get out, Fray pushed him back in; out of his depth, Waking got into difficulties and died.[57] That Fray was tried for murder is, perhaps, itself suggestive of lower tolerance thresholds for interpersonal violence in these situations towards the end of the eighteenth century. This may have made recourse to summary chastisement more dangerous for its perpetrators, perhaps reducing its incidence, as members of the public faced the possibility of prosecution for assault.

Fear also played a role in popular reluctance to prosecute. If criminal proceedings failed to secure a conviction, a prosecutor might find himself at the end of a costly civil action for malicious prosecution. Sometimes, those who had accused neighbours of felonies were forced to make public recantations

54. Anon, *A Genuine Account of the Life Robberies, Trial and Execution of William Cox*, 1773, p.17
55. *Old Whig*, 12 June 1735.
56. *London Journal*, 27 December 1729.
57. *The Times*, 17 September 1785, p. 3.

in the press to avoid such an outcome.[58] To reduce the widespread concern engendered by this risk, a group of senior judges sitting at the Old Bailey during the Restoration period had ordered that copies of their indictment should not be given to acquitted defendants without the permission of the court, as this was often a prerequisite for actions for malicious prosecution, a fear of which: "...deterreth People from Prosecuting for the King upon Just Occasions".[59] Although defendants in treason cases had an automatic right to this document, as a result of a statute from 1696, those in misdemeanour cases would wait until 1819, and those accused of felonies until 1915, before they were legally entitled to them (by the nineteenth century, the rule was frequently being evaded in practice).[60]

During the 'long' eighteenth century, copies of the indictment were usually only furnished by the courts where the presiding judge or jury thought that the proceedings were malicious. They were quite discriminating about this. An acquittal was not sufficient, on its own, to secure the document; there had to be tangible evidence of malice. For example, in 1730, when a lawyer named Tempest, who had been acquitted of robbery, asked for a copy of his indictment, the application was refused.[61] However, when Thomas Stevenson was indicted for arson at the Old Bailey: "It appear'd by the Course of the Evidence to be a malicious prosecution, the Jury acquitted the Prisoner, and granted him a Copy of his Indictment".[62]

Quite significant sums could be awarded in civil actions for malicious prosecution, even to ordinary people. Thus, in 1720, a woman who had been servant to a man who attempted to "debauch" her, and who had been accused of stealing the presents that he gave her after she resisted his advances, was granted a copy of her indictment, following acquittal at the Old Bailey. She then sued her former employer in the Court of King's Bench and secured fifty pounds in damages.[63] Others were less successful. Elizabeth Barker also

58. P. King, *Crime, Justice, and Discretion in England 1740–1820*, 2000, p.31.
59. Sir J. Kelyng, *A Report of Divers Cases In Pleas of the Crown, Adjudged and Determined; In the Reign of the late King Charles II.* 2nd edn., 1734, p.3.
60. D. Bentley, *English Criminal Justice in the Nineteenth Century*, 1998, pp.39-40.
61. *Fog's Weekly Journal*, 4 July 1730.
62. OBSP, Trial of Thomas Stevenson, 2 March 1709.
63. *Applebee's Original Weekly Journal*, 3 December 1720.

'won' her case, but was only awarded five shillings by the trial jury.[64] In particularly flagrant cases, the criminal court might urge, or even "direct", the acquitted defendant to bring a criminal prosecution against the complainant, for perjury, as well as a civil action.

However, although it was usually a crime victim's decision to involve the authorities, this choice was not open-ended. Once a JP had been involved, it became much harder to back-out of a prosecution, as magistrates would usually bind-over felony complainants to prosecute on pain of losing a substantial financial recognisance. Nevertheless, even this was not always enough, with some crime victims forfeiting the sum involved rather than continuing with a prosecution, having changed their minds about proceeding. As a result, there were periodic suggestions that those who failed to appear to give evidence should face additional court-administered punishments as well as having their recognisances estreated.[65]

Public Prosecution

One answer to the problems inherent in private prosecution would have been to follow continental practice and develop a system of public prosecutors, funded by the state, to identify, prepare and bring criminal matters to trial. For example, in serious criminal cases in eighteenth-century Madrid, a judge would supervise constables and notaries while they accumulated evidence, before presenting the results of his investigations in *sumaria* to a panel of three to five of his peers.[66]

However, this did not occur in England. It was well into the Victorian period before any public prosecuting officials — the Director of Public Prosecution's office was set up in 1879 — were established, and then only to deal with the most serious crimes.[67] Many modern observers have attributed

64. *London Daily Post and General Advertiser*, 11 June 1736.
65. Anon. (C. D.), *A Letter To a Member of Parliament Upon the Subject of the present reigning Enormities of Murders and Robberies*, 1754, p.2.
66. F. López-Lázaro, '"No Deceit Safe in Its Hiding Place": The Criminal Trial in Eighteenth-century Spain", 2002, p.449.
67. D. Hay and F. Snyder (eds.), *Policy and Prosecution in Britain, 1750–1850*, 1989, pp. 23-4.

this to an exceptional national commitment to civil liberties, especially the freedoms that had been guaranteed by the 1689 settlement, and a fear of adding to the Crown's power and patronage. Certainly, there was a strong desire not to be seen to emulate continental systems, with their large investment in public prosecutors, though a similar political culture to that found in England did not preclude a much earlier public involvement in criminal prosecution in America.[68] As a French observer noted, Englishmen entertained the: "... idea that, to continue to be free, they must continue in danger of being robbed and murdered".[69]

Another reason for their general aversion to the civil law tradition was that, until the early eighteenth century (and in some places rather later) European legal systems had regular recourse to judicial torture. This had always been absent in English common law, and produced a deeply entrenched suspicion towards all continental legal practices.[70] Additionally, constant warfare with France did not encourage the emulation of 'French' procedures.

It should, perhaps, also be noted that English observers (then and now) sometimes exaggerated the degree of state involvement in the prosecution of felons in continental Europe. Magistrates in eighteenth-century Madrid, for example, were regularly accused of being excessively lenient in criminal cases where no offended party filed charges. The Spanish state often appears to have been reluctant to pursue matters without active private support, and frequently acted almost as an accessory to private prosecution.[71] Similarly, in France, the government only funded prosecutions in *grand criminel* cases, leaving those defined as *petit criminel* to the parties themselves. In many cases, it was only if a private complainant failed to come forward that the Royal Prosecutor would consider initiating a criminal action at the Crown's expense. In some areas, this meant that only about a quarter of cases were prosecuted by the state.[72]

---

68. B. P. Smith, "The Emergence of Public Prosecution in London, 1790-1850", p.29.
69. M. De Calonne, *A Proposal for Preventing Highway Robberies in the Environs of London; or, an Account of the Marechaussee in France*, 1801, p.7.
70. J. H. Langbein, *The Origins of Adversary Criminal Trial*, 2003, pp.338-342.
71. F. López-Lázaro, ""No Deceit Safe in Its Hiding Place": The Criminal Trial in Eighteenth-century Spain", 2002, p.449.
72. S. G. Reinhardt, "The Selective Prosecution of Crime in Ancien Régime France: Theft in the Senechaussee of Sarlat", 1986, pp.4-6.

Even so, the merits of the continental system were not entirely lost on eighteenth-century Englishmen. In 1751, for example, one observer argued that the only answer to the public's aversion to undertaking the expense and trouble involved in a criminal prosecution was to appoint a: "...proper officer to carry out all criminal prosecutions at the public expense, in the name, and under the inspection of the attorney-general". This would also have the effect of preventing compromises, or "underhand dealings", between criminals and their victims.[73] In 1754, another proposed that local boards of worthies should be established to investigate and prosecute "suspicious"people on their own initiative.[74] Patrick Colquhoun, while a magistrate at the Thames Police Office, proposed the creation of an office of Crown Prosecutor when giving evidence to the 1798 Finance Committee on Police, although his suggestion was not followed.[75] The following year, it was suggested by the Select Committee on Police that a body of "Prosecutors for the Crown" should be established to conduct all criminal prosecutions. Such counsel would be appointed by the Attorney General and so avoid the problems occasioned by the "carelessness and inattention" of private individuals, and their frequent reluctance to pay for legal representation, even where an accused person had a barrister to conduct his defence and raise legal technicalities. Additionally, it was recognised that such a system would require a force of solicitors to support the Crown's new prosecutors, prepare their briefs and gather evidence.[76]

Exceptions to the Private Prosecution Model

The prevalence, and degree, of the 'typical' model of victim prosecution during the 1700s can also be exaggerated, both nationally and, more specifically, in the Metropolis. Government, whether national or local, became more

73. J. Fitzsimmonds, *Free and Candid Disquisitions on the Nature and Execution of the Laws of England, Both in Civil and Criminal Affairs*, 1751, p.52.
74. Anon., *A Letter To a Member of Parliament Upon the Subject of the present reigning Enormities of Murders and Robberies*, 1754, p.2.
75. *Twenty-eighth Report from the Select Committee on Finance: Police, including Convict Establishments*, June 1798, p. 355.
76. *The Report of the Select Committee Appointed by the House of Commons, Relative to the Establishment of a New Police in the Metropolis, &c.*, London, 1799, pp.745-777.

actively involved in the process than the traditional interpretation might suggest. For example, the late seventeenth and early eighteenth centuries saw the emergence of several important quasi-government institutions that were prepared to pay their own solicitors to handle prosecutions by conducting pre-trial investigations, including the gathering of evidence, advising on the most appropriate indictment and other relevant aspects of the law, briefing counsel where necessary, and generally instituting and supervising proceedings. Amongst them were the Post Office, the Mint, the Bank of England and the Treasury.

There were obvious reasons for these bodies to become involved. The Mint needed to combat clipping and coining, which had reached endemic levels towards the end of the seventeenth century. The Bank of England had to deal with those who forged its increasingly-widely-used banknotes. The Post Office wished to prosecute those of its employees who pilfered letters or parcels, and the many highwaymen who intercepted and robbed its mail coaches. Many of these cases could not be left to citizen victims to prosecute because there were none. Clipping gold coins, for example, affected the whole community by undermining the currency, rather than any single individual. Additionally, such prosecutions, if they were to be successful, often required considerable resources and legal skill.[77]

To take a late example, during the war against France at the end of the century, the Bank of England suspended payment in specie from 1797 until 1821; instead, it produced low denomination notes of an inferior quality, that were correspondingly easy to forge. To deal with this problem, the Bank employed its own solicitors and investigators, briefed counsel, and built up links with various public officials. Unlike private prosecutors, the Bank's officials were not influenced by sympathy with a suspect or concerned about the potential cost and loss of time attendant on pursuing a case through the courts. They dropped weak or trivial cases and vigorously prosecuted those that appeared serious and well-founded.[78]

77. J. H. Langbein, "The Prosecutorial Origins of Defence Counsel in the Eighteenth Century: The Appearance of Solicitors", 1999, pp.325-327.
78. R. McGowen, "The Bank of England and the Policing of Forgery, 1797-1821", 2005, pp.86-92.

Local authorities could also become actively involved in prosecuting both serious and minor offences. Typically, in cases of infanticide, the parish where a dead baby's body had been discovered, and a suspect identified, would instruct and fund its beadle to initiate and conduct the ensuing prosecution. This involvement could extend to other domestic crimes. When Anna Maria Thorn was accused of murdering her fifteen-year-old daughter by prolonged neglect and starvation, the parish appears to have funded the ensuing prosecution after being alerted by the searchers who had examined the child's body.[79] Most parishes also felt that they had a responsibility to prosecute cases involving victimised apprentices that they had bound out. In 1803, for example, when Ann Brown was indicted at the Guildhall Sessions on 23 counts of assault, the prosecution was paid for by the City's Bishopsgate ward. The victim, an eleven-year-old girl who subsequently died, had been apprenticed to Brown by the ward, which: "…deemed it their duty to exert the utmost rigour of the law against her". They even paid for two distinguished barristers to conduct the case.[80]

Similarly, parish officers who were assaulted in the course of their duties would usually attract local funding and support when prosecuting their assailants. Thus, in April 1732, two Middlesex JPs, sitting at the Mermaid Tavern in Hackney, approved a request from a headborough called James Martin that St. John's parish pay for the cost of prosecuting a man who had wounded him when he attended a disturbance at a neighbourhood house.[81] In 1748, the parishioners of St. Paul's, Covent Garden, resolved to prosecute "with the utmost rigour and severity" anyone who interfered with their constables and watchmen while they were carrying out their duties.[82] Conversely, local authorities might accept responsibility for dealing with criminal activity by their own agents. In 1803, for example, when a constable in the Square Mile attempted to extort money from a woman going about her (entirely) lawful business, the sitting alderman, Sir William Curtis: "…gave orders for prosecuting the prisoner at the expense of the City".[83] A parish might

79. OBSP, Trial of Anna Maria Thorn, 10 December 1735.
80. *The Times*, 15 February 1803, p.3.
81. R. Paley (Ed.), *Justice in 18th-Century Hackney*, 1991, p.96.
82. *London Evening Post*, 8 October 1748.
83. *The Times*, 25 October, 1803, p.3.

even fund the prosecution of an ordinary crime victim who lived within its bounds, if their case was thought sufficiently deserving. Thus, in 1737, Hackney paid the £1 4s 4d prosecution costs of Margaret Parker, after two men were detained for stealing shirts from her washing line. Their justification for this expenditure was that she was "very poor". Ultimately, Parker even used a solicitor to pursue her case at the Old Bailey.[84]

Additionally, from early in the century, especially after 1714, the Monarch would sometimes order the funding of prosecutions in ordinary cases of great gravity, such as murder. For example, when copies of the confessions made by the two men who had assisted Catherine Hayes in the notorious murder of her husband were shown to King George I he ordered that they be prosecuted by the Attorney General, at the Crown's expense.[85]

At the opposite end of the penal spectrum, prosecution of lesser crimes, especially those determined summarily, was, *de facto*, often in the hands of a local official. For example, constables necessarily played a crucial role in prosecuting minor offences that were: "...hurtful only to the community in general, and from which no person in particular suffers any harm". These included many misdemeanours, such as public drunkenness and vagrancy.[86] Parishes might also pay for the prosecution of local nuisances. In August 1731, for example, the vestry of St. Dunstan in the West resolved that all houses of ill fame, gin shops and night-houses within their borders be prosecuted at the parish expense.[87] Indeed, the Disorderly Houses Act of 1752 (25 Geo. 2, c.36) required that parishes fund the prosecution of any brothel found within their boundaries, provided that two householders paying "scot and lot" attested to its existence.[88] Furthermore, under the "Bloodless Code", a range of statutory, summary only, offences were created that were frequently prosecuted by parish officers without the assistance of a complainant/victim.

A number of non-government initiatives also meant that, on some occasions at least, a private organization might become involved in prosecuting both minor and serious crimes. For example, in 1718, the Societies for the

84. R. Paley (Ed.), *Justice in 18th-Century Hackney*, 1991, p.44.
85. Anon, *A Narrative of the Barbarous and unheard of Murder of Mr. John Hayes*, 1726, p.14.
86. Anon (The Society for the Suppression of Vice), *The Constable's Assistant*, 2nd edn., 1808, p.10.
87. *Grub-street Journal*, 5 August 1731.
88. Anon, *The Complete Parish Officer*, 1772, p.38.

Reformation of Manners in London and Westminster prosecuted about 2,000 people for petty crimes involving morality.[89] "Private" prosecutions for more serious matters might also attract the support of a prosecution association. Membership of such a body helped defray the considerable costs involved, while also providing a public indication of a willingness to prosecute if victimised. These associations normally consisted of up to 100 members, living in roughly the same locality, whether borough or county, or engaged in the same trade. They would usually elect a treasurer and secretary, and hold regular meetings. Each member contributed a fixed payment, normally between 5s and a guinea per year, to a common fund. This money was then made available to pay the costs of prosecuting crimes committed against any individual member.

Hundreds of prosecution associations were established in the eighteenth century, most after the middle of the period, and especially during the 1780s. Potential criminals would often be made aware of who was in the association, as lists of members were often published in local newspapers or periodicals. This might, in turn, discourage them from stealing from such individuals. The great majority of societies did not fund prosecutions by non-members, even if from the same area or trade, though there were a few exceptions. Most commonly, their members would be shopkeepers and those with industrial premises. Typically, such associations would also pay private rewards, the cost of solicitors to manage a prosecution, and the court fees of any action. In 1797, for example, the Chiswick Association for the Prosecution of Thieves and Felons advertised a reward of three pounds in the *True Briton* for the arrest of an apprentice named Thomas Gardner. Gardner, a "very audacious fellow", had previously resided in an unprepossessing location named "Slut's Hole" in the same parish, before burgling the premises of a nearby butcher and association member.[90] Some London merchants formed associations to deal with thefts from the docks. However, such associations were found far more frequently in the provinces than in the Metropolitan area, perhaps because of the presence of thief-takers in the capital.

89. *White-hall Evening-Post*, 13-15 January 1719.

90. L. James, *The Middle Class: A History*, 2006, p.201.

Nevertheless, despite these qualifications to the general picture, private prosecution remained the bedrock of the English system, and occasioned many problems. Along with a simple reluctance to prosecute on the part of the public, it gave rise to a number of more specific ills that are considered below.

Private Arrangements between Felon and Victim

Private arrangements between criminals and victims for the return of stolen items were, inevitably, fairly common in a system of private prosecution. The satisfaction of recovering stolen items, at substantially less than replacement cost, could outweigh any desire for retribution. The growth of both newspapers and mass literacy, after the late seventeenth century, which allowed communication via published notices and private letters, facilitated this process. Thus, in the 1720s, after the highwayman John Everett and a companion robbed two military officers on Hounslow Heath, taking their money and watches, they left the timepieces at a coffeehouse near Charing Cross, by prior agreement, and received twenty guineas for restoring them.[91] Similarly, when James Carrick's gang robbed a man of a valuable silver watch in Marylebone, they saw an:

> Advertisement, in one of the News-Papers, offering a greater reward for it than it could be sold for, viz. Six Guineas, [so] we left it where it was appointed to be delivered, and received the premium.[92]

Such agreements normally seem to have been honoured, although, if the correspondence between Horace Walpole and the highwaymen James Maclaine and William Plunket was typical, they might be accompanied by threats as to the consequences of bad faith. Walpole was told that he would get his stolen items back, for a price, if he sent a servant to the Tyburn

91. J. Everett, *A Genuine Narrative of the Memorable Life and Actions of John Everett*, 1730, p.6.
92. J. Carrick, *A compleat and True Account of all the Robberies Committed by James Carrick*, 1722, pp.19-20.

gallows one evening, but warned that if he attempted to involve the authorities the two men had made an agreement with associates to ensure his total destruction.[93]

So common were these arrangements by the early years of the eighteenth century, that the authorities became alarmed at their potential impact on crime rates, and sought to prevent them, and to punish intermediaries like Jonathan Wild who facilitated such transactions. A clause in the Transportation Act 1718 made it a felony to accept a reward for recovering stolen goods without attempting to prosecute the thief. Many have seen this legislation as aimed at Wild's brokering of deals between felons (who often worked at his behest) and their victims, and it is sometimes termed 'Wild's Act' as a result.[94] Several accounts even claimed that the City's recorder, Sir William Thomson, the principal architect of the Act, took Wild aside to warn him that the newly created offence was capital.[95] Far from heeding this, Wild continued in his trade with more "shameless boldness than ever" until his arrest and execution in 1725.[96] Although the new statute may have encouraged an increased degree of discretion, and reduced the role of go-betweens, it certainly did not prevent dealings between thieves and their victims. As late as 1824, there were complaints that they were widespread in the Metropolitan area, even though the 1718 Act was still in force.[97]

Compounding

Even if caught, an apprehended felon might be allowed to 'buy' his way out of trouble. As Henry Fielding observed, any system of criminal justice that was reliant on individual initiative was inherently open to the illegal bribing of prosecutors and prosecution witnesses. Compounding, that is accepting payment for not prosecuting crimes, was illegal for felonies, being

93. P. Toynbee (Ed.), *Supplement to the Letters of Horace Walpole*, vol. III, 1925, pp.132-135.
94. Anon, *The History of the Lives and Actions of Jonathan Wild, Thief-Taker*, 1725, p.A3.
95. A. L. Hayward, *Lives Of The Most Remarkable Criminals* ... 1927, p.46.
96. D. Defoe, *The True and Genuine Account of the Life and Actions of the late Jonathan Wild*, 1725, p.251.
97. *The Times*, 29 November 1824, p.3.

a misdemeanour at common law. Nevertheless, it seems to have occurred on a frequent basis. In the early decades of the century, there were even regular complaints about solicitors becoming involved in negotiating such transactions.[98] Indeed, as contemporary observers noted, some of the settlements that were summarily negotiated in front of magistrates could, technically, amount to compounding.[99]

Such arrangements were most common before formal law enforcement agencies had become involved. Nevertheless, some occurred afterwards, though they were then likely to command larger payments, especially if recognisances had been entered into. Thomas Neaves, for example, enjoyed a narrow escape early in his criminal career, when his victim, a mercer, compounded the theft of a large piece of fine silk while he was in prison. A female associate approached the mercer who, after he had recovered his material and been paid generously, ensured that, when the bill of indictment was preferred against Neaves at Hick's Hall, it was returned "ignoramus" by the Grand Jury.[100] Similarly, in 1773, it was noted that after the highwayman William Cox was captured, a man and woman who had: "...positively sworn against Cox before a justice of peace, swore as positively in his favour at the Old Bailey, for the consideration of three guineas".[101] Of course, in both these cases, the witnesses, by appearing (whether before Grand Jury or trial jury), but reneging on their earlier testimony, avoided having their recognisances estreated. Many such cases must have gone completely undetected.

That compounding was a (relatively minor) crime seems to have had little effect in preventing the practice, though there were occasional cases in which it does appear to have operated as a deterrent. For example, when John Edwards accused a drinking companion of picking his pocket, the suspect was unable to settle the matter for this reason; when he asked: "... me to take half a guinea; I said I dare not, it was compounding felony".[102] Some suspects were mindful of this when making offers and tried to make

98. Anon, *Directions for Prosecuting Thieves Without the Help of those False Guides, The Newgate Sollicitor ...*, 1728, pp.3-8.

99. *Morning Post and Daily Advertiser*, 13 July 1791.

100. T. Neaves, *The Life of Tho. Neaves, The Noted Street-Robber*, 1729, p.27.

101. Anon, *A Genuine Account of the Life Robberies, Trial and Execution of William Cox*, 1773, p.18.

102. OBSP, Trial of William Singleton, 15 May 1782.

the process easier for their victims. Thus, when William Morgan was accused of stealing expensive buttons in a shop, and sought to buy his way out of the situation, he offered the shopkeeper his silver watch (rather than cash) to: "...indemnify him, that he should not be prosecuted for compounding a felony, if he would let them go".[103]

It seems that only in the most blatant cases would formal action be taken, though it made a valuable threat. In 1762, for example, a well-to-do lady was caught shoplifting two yards of silk by a mercer. The mercer agreed not to prosecute her in exchange for a large sum of money. Getting greedy, he then sought more, while reminding her that she was "still open to the law". The lady sought advice from a lawyer relative, who pointed out that though she: "...once was in the mercer's power, but that now he was at hers, since no crime is more severely punished by the law, than that of compounding felony". She then prosecuted the mercer for compounding, who offered her double the sum that she had initially paid to stop the prosecution (as it was a misdemeanour this action could be compounded).[104] Crime victims were best advised to insist on a prompt payment in cash when compounding. In one pickpocketing case, in which rings had been taken, the prosecutor agreed to compound the matter with the suspect's spouse. However, he took a "note of 16s" for the rings, rather than money; when this was not paid he arrested the prisoner's husband. In response, he (the husband): "...indicted the Prosecutor in the Crown Office [of the Court of King's Bench] for compounding Felony". The pickpocket was acquitted at the Old Bailey.[105]

A relatively rare example of a successful prosecution occurred after John Thomas, from Stepney, was accused of stealing 2s.6d. from the shop of John Smith. Evidence was called to show that the defendant was a simpleton. As a result, Thomas was acquitted. However, other witnesses gave evidence that Smith would have taken money to compound the alleged felony, but insisted upon being paid at least £12 to do so. On hearing this, the Court ordered that he be bound over to appear at the following sessions, along with the witnesses who had implicated him, so that he might be prosecuted

103. OBSP, Trial of William Morgan and John Forrester, 6 July 1763.

104. *London Chronicle* (Semi-Annual), 13 July 1762.

105. OBSP, Trial of Barbara Adams, 8 July 1724.

for the misdemeanour.[106] A few weeks later, Smith was duly convicted. At his hearing, evidence was called to show that he had already accepted four guineas from relatives of the youth not to prosecute. Additionally, the original prosecution appears to have been influenced by the fact that Thomas was obviously an "idiot", suggesting that it may always have been aimed at exacting money rather than retribution.[107]

Nevertheless, penalties for compounding were modest; even Smith was only sentenced to a relatively small fine. By contrast, the sums exacted by crime victims could be very substantial, as the prospect of imprisonment, transportation, and even death were powerful bargaining chips. Indeed, the possibility of having to make such payments must have acted as a deterrent to committing crime in many cases.

For misdemeanours, compounding was both entirely legal and often actively encouraged by magistrates. The justification for this distinction was not obvious to everyone, one observer noting that he could not easily: "...discern, however different they are in degree, where, as to complexion, the compromising of misdemeanors differs from compounding a felony".[108] Even so, the practice was extremely widespread. For example, when a headborough named John Pike was attacked with a hatchet, while attempting to enforce a magistrate's warrant, and his wound did not initially appear mortal, both assailant and victim seem to have entertained the possibility of a composition.[109]

Even where a prosecution by indictment had been started for a misdemeanour, it was often done as a way of increasing pressure on the defendant to come to a financial arrangement with the complainant, rather than to secure his punishment. Once this had occurred, the court would be made aware that an accommodation had been reached and a nominal penalty would be imposed on the defendant after a guilty plea.[110] For an example, can be considered a *cause célèbre* from 1731, in which a trading justice named

106. OBSP, Trial of John Thomas, 27 Feb 1723.
107. OBSP, Trial of John Smith, 30 May 1723.
108. *North Briton*, 4 December 1762.
109. OBSP, Trial of Godfrey Walker, 28 June 1738.
110. N. Landau, "Indictment for Fun and Profit: A Prosecutor's Reward at Eighteenth-century Quarter Sessions", 1999, p. 533.

Webster stabbed Thomas de Veil with a sword during a quarrel, inflicting a severe wound. At the ensuing Quarter Sessions, it was noted that Webster: "...having compounded the affair, was fin'd only 1s. for wounding Justice De Veil".[111] Towards the end of the century, it was not always even necessary for a defendant to appear and plead guilty at trial, where an allegation of common assault had been indicted but the parties had agreed a settlement. The "usual course" in these situations at the Middlesex Sessions was for the prosecutor to give a written acknowledgement that he was satisfied and the court would discharge the recognisance requiring the defendant to appear.[112]

Revenge, Blackmail and Extortion

Conversely, the importance of private action to the system meant that unjustified proceedings could also be threatened or initiated with a view to revenge or personal gain and advantage. For example, in 1750, a woman was pilloried for perjury after taking out 400 warrants against her neighbours over the course of a single year.[113] Potentially more serious, at one point in his criminal career, the highwayman John Everett had developed an implacable hatred for a cooper named Picket, maliciously implicated him in a non-existent crime, and then given evidence against him at the Old Bailey (Fortunately, he was acquitted).[114] Civil disputes, such as that between a landlord and his (shut out) lodger, could sometimes be presented as crimes. In one case, watchmen were summoned, the lodger identified to them as a housebreaker, arrested and held with common felons in the Clerkenwell Bridewell.

Such allegations were unlikely to result in a conviction, usually being discharged by an examining JP, dismissed by a Grand Jury, or, if they got to trial, producing an acquittal. However, this did not prevent them from having appalling consequences. In 1727, for example, a man named Merry, who had been falsely accused of a burglary was released from custody before trial but after spending four months in Newgate. As a result of his confinement,

111. *The Gentleman's Magazine*, 1731, vol. 1, p.307.
112. Anon, *The Crown Court Circuit Companion*, 8th edn., 1811, p.21.
113. *Whitehall Evening Post or London Intelligencer*, 20 February 1750.
114. J. Everett, *A Genuine Narrative of the Memorable Life and Actions of John Everett*, 1730, p.34.

his wife and children were reduced to the "utmost want", so that they were forced to sleep in a single bed. Even worse, Merry contracted "gaol fever" (typhoid) while in custody, which promptly claimed his own life and that of several members of his family.[115]

However, most threats of malicious prosecution were aimed at financial gain rather than revenge. Allegations could easily be fabricated and money obtained in lieu of bringing proceedings. Even the post-1690 Societies for the Reformation of Manners accepted that there were people who extorted money via the threat of prosecution from "honest men".[116] This was particularly common where the accusation was simultaneously highly embarrassing, a serious crime, and hard to disprove. As a result, malicious allegations of sodomy were particularly common, especially when made against confirmed bachelors.

The trials of Thomas Vaughan and Thomas Davis at Hick's Hall, in 1707, for attempting to extort money from an apothecary and a tallow-chandler, provide an obvious example. The hearing revealed the existence of a fairly large-scale blackmail operation aimed at individuals who appeared vulnerable. Two men accused of a similar crime at the Guildhall Sessions, fifty years later, observed that: "...gentlemen, who are tender of their reputation, are the fittest persons to work upon".[117] The Vaughan gang would go before a JP, make a statement implicating such a man in a homosexual offence, and obtain a warrant to arrest him. However, before they served it, Vaughan would go to their chosen target and offer not to enforce the warrant if he paid over a large sum of money. Eventually, one of their marks had the courage to inform a magistrate about what had occurred.[118] In like manner, in 1730, John Lewis and John Jones successfully extracted ten guineas from John Battle, who was terrified that the accusation of homosexuality would "blast

115. *The Weekly Journal; or, British Gazetteer*, 22 April 1727.

116. Anon, *The Three and Thirtieth account of the progress made in the Cities of London and Westminster*, 1727, pp.39-40.

117. S. Scrimshaw, *The Trial of Samuel Scrimshaw and John Ross, For A Conspiracy*, 1759, p.241.

118. N. B., *A Compleat Collection Of Remarkable Tryals Of the most Notorious Malefactors, at the Sessions-House in the Old Baily, for near Fifty Years past*, 1718, vol. 2, pp.120-126.

my Reputation". In the end, Battle obtained an arrest warrant against them from Sir Richard Brocas, which he enforced with the aid of a constable.[119]

Because it was only a misdemeanour, such extortion was punished quite mildly. In 1727, Joseph Lee was sentenced at the Guildhall Sessions to six months in Newgate, fined and ordered to stand in the pillory for: "...threatening to swear Sodomy against a Person, in order to extort Money from him".[120] However, widespread fear of spurious allegations meant that men like Lewis and Jones were "severely handled" by the mob when pilloried at the Royal Exchange.[121] Malicious allegations were sometimes made for offences other than sodomy. For example, in 1721, an attorney and a prostitute were prosecuted at Hick's Hall for conspiring "falsely and maliciously" to accuse a man of rape, with a view to extorting money from him. Both were convicted and sentenced to six months in Newgate and a public whipping.[122]

Rewards and Accomplice Evidence

It has been suggested that the problems raised by the traditional system *might* have forced the authorities to face up to the need for radically new police and prosecuting institutions in the London area.[123] Whether this was ever a real possibility, the opportunity was not taken at the end of the seventeenth century. Instead, Parliament had recourse to a number of shorter-term stratagems and palliatives, to avoid recourse to drastic change. The 1692 Act for Suppressing Highwaymen (4 William and Mary cap. 8) was candid about the need to introduce reform to the country's criminal justice system. The nation's roads were, apparently, infested with robbers, something that was attributed to the lack of: "...sufficient encouragement given and means used for the discovery and apprehension of offenders".

119. Anon, *Select Trials, for Murders, Robberies, Rapes, Sodomy, Coining, Frauds, And other Offences*, 1735, vol. 2, pp.396–8.
120. *The London Journal*, 2 September 1727.
121. *The Grub-street Journal*, 24 December 1730.
122. *Weekly Journal or Saturday's Post*, 29 April 1721.
123. J. H. Langbein, *The Origins of Adversary Criminal Trial*, 2003, p.158.

The Act dealt with this problem in two ways. On the one hand, it offered a reward of £40 and the defendant's goods (provided they were not the proceeds of theft) to those who apprehended and prosecuted a highwayman to conviction. This would be paid over by the county sheriff within a month of the highwayman being found guilty. The streets of London and Westminster were deemed to be highways for the purposes of such rewards.[124] However, the Act also provided an alternative means for dealing with the problem. Anyone who had committed a robbery and who was still "out of prison" (i.e. was still at large) could claim a royal pardon as of right if they came forward and identified two or more other robbers, whom they then prosecuted to conviction.[125] The policing of serious crimes over the next half-century would be dominated by rewards and accomplice evidence, while the fifty years after that would see the flaws of such a system gradually exposed and witness a slow retreat from their use.

Rewards

A series of statutes, introduced over the half century after 1692, offered major rewards to the successful prosecutors of a growing number of grave felonies, so encouraging them to invest their time and money in such actions. This did not occur entirely without antecedents. As early as the sixteenth century, statute had decreed that a victim's prosecution of a thief was a sufficient step to warrant recovery of the lost item if it had been found on the defendant, although, as late as 1701, there were complaints that a:

> ...man's own goods or money taken from him by violence, are not easily (if at all) to be recovered, even though the thief be apprehended and convicted.[126]

In any event, on its own, the prospect of such restitution was not enough, especially as many felons were caught red-handed, so that goods or cash were automatically recovered or, if this was not the case, had long since been

124. J. Higgs, *A Guide to Justices or Modern English Precedents for the Direction of Justices of the Peace and their Clerks*, 2nd edn., 1742, p.98.
125. A. Browning, *English Historical Documents, 1660–1714*, vol. viii, 1957, p.478.
126. Anon, *Hanging, not Punishment Enough*, 1701, pp.11–13.

disposed of or spent by the time a suspect was finally apprehended. There had to be a more effective inducement.

Rewards had been central to many Metropolitan prosecutions for well over a hundred years prior to the late seventeenth century. However, they had traditionally been employed to deal with minor, victimless, regulatory offences. Their use for this purpose continued during the eighteenth century. For example, in 1701, Usher Eastwick was convicted by the Lord Mayor, on the sworn evidence of Edward Newport, for selling 34 undersize lobsters, contrary to a statute aimed at preserving fish stocks. He was fined 34 shillings (one for each crustacean), of which half went to the informer (Newport) and the remainder to the poor.[127] Similarly, within weeks of Sir Robert Walpole's poorly conceived Gin Act of 1736 becoming law it was claimed that there were 20 quasi-professional informers operating with a view to obtaining the relatively small sums available for securing the conviction of those selling spirits without proper authorisation.[128] Such inducements entered the popular consciousness. In 1703, John Dunton even suggested that those caught masturbating be forced to pay 10s to the informer who had given evidence of their Onanistic behaviour.[129]

However, traditionally, rewards had not been used to encourage prosecutions in serious felony cases, except on an *ad hoc* basis after a particularly heinous crime had been committed. This changed in 1692. The aim of these new rewards was to:

> ...prompt men to do publick service, not thro' Sentiments of Duty, and the Dictates of publick spirit, but from the infinitely more sordid principle of private interest.[130]

Obviously, in serious cases, the level of reward available would have to be commensurately larger than it was for regulatory offences, as prosecuting felons was a time-consuming and expensive business and carried serious

127. Mansion House Justice Room Charge Book, 1699-1705, CLA/004/01/4 entry for 28 March 1701 p.97. This was a fairly common division for such summary fines.
128. Anon, *A Short History of the Gin Act*, 1738, pp.1-18 and pp.26-27.
129. J. Dunton, *The Shortest Way With Whores and Rogues: Or a New Project for Reformation*, 1703, p.34. He also felt that they should be made to publish details of their 'crime' in a newspaper.
130. Anon, *An Enquiry into the Causes of the and Miseries of the Poor of England*, 1738, p.49.

inherent risks. Further statutes (to that of 1692) were passed in 1699, 1706, and ensuing years, covering an extensive range of grave offences. Under them, forty pounds was made available to those who convicted burglars and housebreakers, while twenty pounds was to be awarded to those who prosecuted to conviction men who returned prematurely from transportation. Forty pounds, and a pardon for all felonies previously committed (apart from murder and treason) was even offered to burglars and house-breakers who, while at liberty, discovered and convicted two or more of their colleagues (5 Anne, ch.31, s2).[131] All of these sums were to be paid within a month of conviction.[132] (There were periodic complaints that the Treasury was late in making payment). To put such sums into perspective, it seems that a 'common' or unskilled labourer in the Metropolitan area received about 1s 8d a day for his work for much of the century.[133]

Exemption from being required to undertake parish and ward duties, such as serving as a constable, via a so-called "Tyburn Ticket", a certificate signed by the judge of a convicting court, was also awarded to those who prosecuted some types of less serious felony to conviction. These included "privately" stealing goods to the value of five or more shillings from a shop, warehouse or stable, and stealing a horse.[134] Tyburn tickets were negotiable, but could only be sold on once, by the original recipient. In 1756, the Court of King's Bench quashed the conviction and fine of a man named Davies, who had refused to take on the office of collector of rates, as he was in possession of a Tyburn ticket. Davies was the assignee of the certificate, which had, apparently, been obtained at the Old Bailey in 1724, by a man named Hickman, for securing the conviction of a horse thief, and sold on to Davies a month later.[135] If the original recipient was from a fairly humble background, one that was unlikely to lead to parish office, sale of the ticket made a great deal of sense.

---

131. T. Dogherty, *The Crown Assistant: Being a Collection of Precedents of Indictments*, 1787, pp.549-551.
132. Sir J. Fielding, *Extracts from such of the Penal Laws, As particularly relate to the Peace and Good Order of this Metropolis*, 1762, p.305.
133. E. W. Gilboy, *Wages in 18th -Century England*, 1934, pp.8-9.
134. Sir J. Fielding, *Extracts from such of the Penal Laws, As particularly relate to the Peace and Good Order of this Metropolis*, 1762, p.306.
135. *The King v Davies* (1756) 1 Kenyon 329.

Perhaps because they were mindful of the enormous sums that were being distributed, and their potential to have a malign impact on the criminal justice system, the courts appear, where possible, to have spread reward money around as widely as possible, rather than concentrating it on individuals. Inevitably, there was frequent criticism as to how such apportionments were made. For example, in 1719, when the statutory reward for apprehending a group of highwaymen at the One Tun Tavern in The Strand was divided up, "only £10" went to the tavern drawer who had first identified the robbers, while the same amount was given to the owner of the public house. Others, including two JPs involved in the arrest, received five pounds each.[136]

Additionally, special rewards were sometimes offered on top of the statutory scheme, whether locally, nationally, or for a specific offence. For example, in 1707, the inhabitants of Hackney offered a reward of £20 to anyone arresting and convicting burglars in their parish, with £10 being given for robbers and £5 for housebreakers. Three men even agreed to advertise the fact that they had received such a reward for apprehending Philip Levy.[137] Similarly, in 1749, St. Paul's Covent Garden offered twenty guineas to anyone apprehending and convicting a robber in their parish.[138] Most importantly, a royal proclamation of 1727 added £100 to existing (nationwide) statutory rewards for robbers taken in, or within a five-mile radius of, the Cities of London and Westminster. It was introduced to deal with an apparent crime wave in and around the capital.[139] As a result, between 1727 and 1745, and again between 1750 and 1752, the reward for the arrest and prosecution to conviction of a Metropolitan robber was, when the local and statutory rewards were taken together, at least £140. This was not far short of three years' income for a relatively skilled workman in London.[140] Such rewards were regularly paid out. In August 1731, for example, £600 was paid to a number of people who

136. *Original Weekly Journal,* 14 February 1719.
137. *Daily Courant,* 14 November 1707.
138. *The Gentleman's Magazine,* 1749, vol. 19, p.522.
139. Proclamation of 1st March 1727, reproduced in M. Bellamy, *The Life of Martin Bellamy,* 1727, p.7.
140. J. M. Beattie, "Early Detection: The Bow Street Runners in Late Eighteenth- century London", 2006, p.16.

had been involved in apprehending and prosecuting five highwaymen to conviction at the Old Bailey.[141]

These inducements certainly 'worked', if at a cost (both financial and social). For an obvious example can be considered a crime that occurred on a winter evening in 1732, in which Edward Dell broke the window of a shop belonging to John Davis, near the Tower, reached inside and helped himself to a silk handkerchief worth three shillings. Because this involved breaking 'into' premises, albeit to the most modest degree, and was conducted after dark, it was, technically, burglary (rather than housebreaking or theft). The noise caught the attention of the occupants, who were sitting in a back room, and, more pertinently, a local waterman, who pursued Dell and brought him down, detaining him and recovering the (rather dirtied) handkerchief. Dell was convicted at the Old Bailey and sentenced to death, although: "The prosecutor would have discharg'd me, but the waterman said, he should get 40l. for hanging a house-breaker".[142] Even after an arrest, there might be scope for members of the public to claim a small share of the reward by rendering assistance. After Thomas Gordon was held overnight in a watch-house in Kensington he was escorted to Newgate by a group of eight men the following morning, all of them, presumably, hoping to secure a small portion of the available bounty.[143]

For a more detailed illustration as to how the system worked in practice can be considered a case from 1732, involving two Hackney footpads, Thomas Foxton and Thomas Smith. After robbing a traveller at knifepoint and taking 3s. 9d. and a hat they were apprehended by a swiftly organized search. Largely as a result of the singular nature of the hat, combined with Faxton's ill-considered attempt at turning King's evidence, they were convicted and sentenced to death.[144] Because the royal proclamation of 1727 was then in force, £280 was available for distribution. The apportionment of this money required an assessment of the respective importance of everyone involved in the arrest and subsequent prosecution. William Davis, the victim, and chief prosecution witness, received the modest amount of £16. The bulk of

141. *The Gentleman's Magazine*, 1731, vol. 1, p.351.
142. OBSP, 23 February 1732, Trial of Edward Dell.
143. *Parker's Penny Post,* 2 March, 1733.
144. OBSP, Trial of Thomas Faxton and Thomas Smith, 23 February 1732.

the money, £70 each, deservedly went to two local men, Brian Oram and Richard Wingfield, who had pursued and arrested the two robbers. Smaller sums, all under ten pounds, were paid to a variety of minor actors in the drama; for example, eight pounds was given to the prosecutor's father, who was in the group that accompanied the prisoners to the JP, and who gave evidence of an incriminating remark made by one of them that led to the recovery of the stolen money. Similar amounts appear to have been given to men who assisted with detaining the felons overnight in the nearby Buffalo's Head public house in Hackney, prior to their being produced before the magistrate.[145]

Doubtless, Oram and Wingfield were greatly influenced in their willingness to go after the robbers — a highly dangerous task — by the availability of a substantial reward. However, it was still an enormous amount of money to pay for solving a rather amateurish robbery, in which the victim had even been given one of the robbers' hats in lieu of his own stolen headwear.

Influence of rewards

Historically, the English system of prosecution had been premised on legally unaided individuals personally bringing their cases to court. It was axiomatic that: "Every prosecutor, who appears in a court of justice, is not expected to be a lawyer".[146] However, there was nothing to prevent prosecutors seeking legal advice and, unlike defendants in felony cases prior to the 1730s, there was never a formal embargo on having prosecutions presented by counsel. In England generally, and the Metropolis in particular, the late seventeenth and early eighteenth centuries saw increased legal involvement in private prosecutions, both prior to, and during, the trial. There were several reasons for this. Most importantly, it seems that the possibility of securing a significant reward if a conviction was secured (a prerequisite for payment) made it appear a good investment.

This process was encouraged because many magistrates' clerks were attorneys or solicitors and, rather strangely to modern eyes, a considerable

145. R. Paley (Ed.), *Justice in 18th-Century Hackney*, 1991, p.9.
146. Anon, *Directions for Prosecuting Thieves Without the Help of those False Guides, The Newgate Solicitors...*, 1728, p.12.

number appear to have gained paid legal work preparing the prosecutions of complainants they met via their official position.[147] Other lawyers also congregated around active justices, hoping to secure such work. Later in the century, William Garrow complained bitterly of the solicitors who attended Metropolitan magistrates: "...for the purpose of being employed in criminal prosecutions".[148]

As well as advising on charges, legal technicalities and procedures, prosecuting solicitors would often attempt to secure extra evidence, where it was either necessary or readily available. Indicative of this, when a coroner went "hunting" extra prosecution witnesses *after* his inquest had been held, not normally part of his duty, it was observed that: "It appear'd that he had become as a solicitor in this prosecution".[149] In 1728, there were also complaints that prosecution solicitors were 'coaching' their witnesses to increase their persuasiveness at trial.[150]

Criticism of rewards

Perhaps unsurprisingly, the apparent illogicality of statutory rewards being generally available for robbery, however small the sum taken, but not for murder, however brutal its circumstances, was heavily criticised.[151] Of course, rewards *could* be offered for specific murders, as they might for any other crime. Thus, in 1703, the Crown offered 50 pounds for the capture of Thomas Cooke, who had killed a reforming constable.[152] Nevertheless, such rewards were certainly not universal. Where they were offered, they were also sometimes quite modest, such as the five pounds offered for information on the killing of James Knight in 1765.[153]

Equally unsurprisingly, the rapidly increasing scale of these inducements in the first decades of the eighteenth century, especially in and about the London area, produced a series of scandals that encouraged much greater

147. J. H. Langbein, *The Origins of Adversary Criminal Trial*, 2003, p.127.
148. *London Chronicle*, 7 February 1797.
149. J. Oliphant, *The Case of Mr James Oliphant, Surgeon*, 1768, pp.1-60.
150. Anon, *Directions for Prosecuting Thieves Without the Help of those False Guides, The Newgate Solicitors*, 1728, pp.3-8.
151. Anon (By a Magistrate), *Some Hints Towards A Revival of the Penal Laws*, 1787, pp.12-13.
152. *Post-Man* 8-10 July 1703 and *Post-Man* 10-12 August 1703.
153. OBSP, Trial of Joseph Gould and Jonathan Stevens, 18 September 1765.

caution on the part of both judges and juries towards evidence that may have been reward-driven. By the end of the century, it was almost universally accepted that the presence of rewards made: "…some men look rather too sharp to criminal prosecutions".[154] This issue is considered more fully in chapter eleven.

154. *The Times*, Thursday, 27 August 1789, p.3.

CHAPTER 16

TRIAL ON INDICTMENT

Introduction

Unlike the subjects of most other *ancien régime* societies, nearly all Englishmen, apart from a tiny number of aristocrats, who were entitled to trial by their peers and a few other legal privileges, were, in theory, subject to the same criminal process, whether pre-trial or at Quarter Sessions and the Old Bailey/Assizes. In reality, the system could be tinkered with to accommodate high status but non-noble defendants, who might, for example, have jurors who were of a somewhat higher class than normal determining their cases, and whose trials would also last rather longer than the very short average. Nevertheless, English procedure was fairly uniform and universal.

Eighteenth-century criminal justice was swift and cheap, unlike its slow and expensive civil counterpart. The sheer speed of the process, even in serious cases, is astonishing to modern observers. As late as 1812, for example, after John Bellingham assassinated the Prime Minister, Spencer Perceval, he was arrested at the scene of the crime, examined by Michael Angelo Taylor, a Middlesex magistrate, on the same day, transferred to Newgate Prison and tried for murder four days later, when he was duly convicted and sentenced to hang. Defence requests that more time be allowed to bring potential witnesses to Bellingham's mental condition from Liverpool were rejected.[1] Elements of theatre permeated the era's felony trial, which was, to an extent, a social morality play. This was necessary in a system that dealt in selective example. Trials for misdemeanours, usually held at Quarter Sessions, were slightly different, occasionally having similarities with civil proceedings.

1. K. S. Goddard, "A Case of Injustice? The Trial of John Bellingham", 2004, p.2.

Fairness

Many modern notions of what constitutes a "fair" trial in serious criminal matters were notably absent during the 1700s. For example, the accused's right to legal advice and representation at all stages of proceedings, in even the most serious cases, publicly funded if necessary, did not exist. Additionally, he or she had: no entitlement to advance notice of the prosecution case prior to trial; little protection against prejudicial pre-trial publicity; no right to give sworn evidence and (usually) no entitlement to an appeal against conviction if an error was made at his hearing. Furthermore, there was often no lengthy jury-direction by the trial judge on the law and evidence that was relevant to the case.[2] Throughout the eighteenth century, the accused was also denied a copy of his indictment as a matter of right, though he could insist that it be read over to him in the vernacular at a measured pace.

Nevertheless, to associate the absence of many modern rights with unfairness is, perhaps, to introduce anachronistic concepts of justice to the 1700s. Many Englishmen of the time were impressed with their trial process and did not see it as unfair. Henry Fielding, for example, felt that in most countries the niceties of an English criminal trial were not observed and, as a result, foreign criminals were often: "…hurried to execution, with rather less ceremony than is required".[3] Another contemporary observer even thought, albeit rather optimistically, that: "…as to any Danger of an unfair Trial at the Old Bailey, no Body in his right wits, who knows any thing of that court, ever feared it".[4] Although hearings at the Bailey, conducted by a collegiate bench and under more intense general scrutiny, were probably slightly fairer than those conducted on the Crown side of many provincial Assizes, most modern observers have not shared this confidence.

Even so, some recent portrayals of the workings, and deficiencies, of the eighteenth-century criminal trial process have clearly been exaggerated. For example, it is not entirely true that: "…verdicts of not guilty were rare; there was nothing approaching the modern presumption of innocence; and most

2. D. Bentley, *English Criminal Justice in the Nineteenth Century*, 1998, p.xiv.
3. H. Fielding, *A Clear State of the Case of Elizabeth Canning*, 2nd edn., 1753, pp.1-2.
4. M. Squires, *The Controverted Hard Case: Or Mary Squires's Magazine of Facts Re-examin'd*, 1753, p.8.

of the argument concerned factors which should mitigate the full rigour of the penal law".[5] As will be seen, many defendants were acquitted, the onus of proof was (roughly) on the prosecution throughout the period, and significant doubt was normally interpreted in the defendant's favour.

In the Metropolis, at least, it is also an exaggeration to say that criminal trials in the higher forums were as much about an individual as they were about his actions and even, in some cases, whether he had committed the alleged crime at all.[6] This *may*, sometimes, have been the case in rural areas, where prosecution was often used as a last resort, after a series of criminal acts had initially been dealt with informally, and where the parties were already well acquainted with each other. However, in the Metropolitan area, they were often total strangers. As a result, and as has already been noted, the area posed special problems when it came to an excessive exercise of discretion.

Old Bailey hearings were so brief, and urban society so transient, that jurors had very little opportunity to make a fully informed decision about the personal merits of the individual men and women who appeared before them. Obviously, they could seek visual and aural cues, and ask themselves how "respectable" the defendant appeared to be; for example, whether he was in regular employment and had reputable people who were prepared to speak for him. However, most Metropolitan jurors would have appreciated that these were not infallible indicators. It was much harder to establish a man's general character to any degree of precision than in more stable rural areas.

In the relatively anonymous environment of the Metropolis, it was notorious that people claimed reputations, occupations and social status to which they were not entitled. Criminals who were gang members, who had connections or money, could, and frequently did, arrange for bogus witnesses to testify to their reputations. Thus, in 1738, when Mary Young (or "Jenny Diver"), one of the century's most notorious pickpockets, was tried under the name of Jane Webb, she called six people who "gave the Prisoner the Character of an honest Woman". The jury was not impressed and swiftly convicted her.[7]

---

5. N. Lacey, "In Search of the Responsible Subject: History, Philosophy and Social Sciences in Criminal Law Theory", 2001, p.361.
6. J. M. Beattie, *Crime and the Courts in England 1660–1800*, 1986, p.436.
7. OBSP, Trial of Januarye Webb, 12 April 1738.

By contrast, those who were newly arrived in London from distant parts, as was the case with many defendants, were not able to call character references or, if they did, were required to have recourse to marginal individuals. Interestingly, even Henry Fielding was well aware of the difficulties in assessing character reliably in such an environment. In *Jonathan Wild,* a good but mistaken magistrate convicts "Heartfree" on false evidence. In another of his papers, Fielding expressly noted that: "Actions of the worst nature have, by the assistance of false glosses, been accompanied with honour".[8] As a result, forensic argument was not largely confined to factors that might mitigate the full rigour of the law rather than determining innocence or guilt. Eighteenth-century juries in the Metropolis normally had to be firmly persuaded that a defendant had committed the criminal act of which he was accused before considering discretionary mitigation.

The Standard of Proof

It has been argued that a standard of proof that was "beyond reasonable doubt" was not formally enunciated until 1777, when Lord Mansfield directed that the evidence should irresistibly prove the crime, and that if a jury was not "perfectly convinced" it was required to find the accused not guilty.[9] It is certainly true that the phrase "reasonable doubt" is not employed at the Old Bailey until the early 1780s, after which time it is regularly encountered for the rest of the century.[10] However, this is slightly misleading.

Throughout the period, there was a general recognition that, in "run of the mill" criminal cases at least, the prosecution had to prove the defendant's guilt to a high degree of certainty. This was something that always struck foreign observers, most of whom had watched trials at the Old Bailey. In the early 1700s, for example, Cesar de Saussure was fully persuaded that England had a higher standard of proof than that found in most continental jurisdictions, and operated on the basis that it was: "...better that

8. A. F. Wilner, "Henry Fielding and the Knowledge of Character", 1988, p.181.
9. B. J. Shapiro, "To a Moral Certainty: Theories of Knowledge and Anglo-American Juries 1600-1850", 1986, p.156.
10. OBSP, Trial of John Higginson, 30 April 1783.

twelve culprits should escape human justice rather than that one innocent man should perish".[11] Even more generously, in the 1760s, the French magistrate Pierre-Jean Grosley was convinced that this approach was rooted in the maxim that it was better that 20 guilty people escaped, rather than that an innocent man be convicted, and that in England: "...every circumstance tends to the acquittal of the prisoner".[12] These observations are particularly significant because, contrary to some modern perceptions, many civil law criminal justice systems put the onus of proof fairly firmly on the prosecution as well. The Madrid *Sala*, for example, held that it was "incumbent on the accuser in criminal cases to prove the delictive nature" of any alleged offence.[13]

Such notions also entered the English popular consciousness. Thus, in the 1790s, a domestic observer, Rhynwick Williams, the alleged "London Monster", felt that a high onus of proof had always been axiomatic in English law: "I have always heard it maintained, that any man or woman at a Bar of Justice, should be presumed innocent".[14]

Juries were often highly discriminating in their verdicts where there were multiple allegations, something that is often taken by modern appellate courts to be indicative of a degree of care in the original decisions. In 1715, for example, Henry Cockale was capitally convicted on two counts of burglary, but acquitted on a third, the: "...jury not being satisfied with the evidence".[15] The prevalence of the death penalty in England, when compared to some European jurisdictions, may have led jurors to be more cautious before convicting. Judges sometimes encouraged this, by expressly reminding jurors that an offence on which they were to return a verdict would be capital if proved.

Contemporary observers were also well aware that there had been cases in which mistaken capital convictions had led to tragedy, and several popular tracts and books publicised such errors. Amongst them was the well-known

11. M. V. Muyden (Ed.), *A foreign View of England in the reigns of George I and George II*, 1902, p.119.
12. P. J. Grosley, *A Tour to London: or, New Observations on England, and its Inhabitants*, vol. 3, 1772, p.36.
13. F. López-Lázaro, "'No Deceit Safe in Its Hiding Place": The Criminal Trial in Eighteenth-century Spain", 2002, p.449.
14. R. Williams, *An Appeal to the Public, by Rhynwick Williams*, 1790, p.20.
15. OBSP, Trial of Henry Cockale, 2 June 1715.

trial and execution of James Crow for a burglary of which he was "entirely innocent", that took place at York in 1727.[16] Similarly, in 1749, Richard Coleman was convicted at the Surrey Assizes in Kingston, and executed on Kennington Common, for a murder that was subsequently admitted by two other men.[17] In 1797, Martin Clench and James Mackley were convicted of murdering a man during a botched robbery, and executed. Strong doubts were subsequently raised about the safety of their convictions, after other prisoners made admissions to the crimes.[18] Cases like these led some to fear that there was: "...nothing more frequent than persons confessing the crimes that others had suffer'd for before".[19] Several prominent jurists, including Mathew Hale and William Blackstone, shared some of these concerns.[20]

Of course, that the burden and standard of proof was not as clearly enunciated to the jury as it is in the modern era, until the very end of the period, must have reduced its impact. For example, at a robbery trial held at Kingston Assizes in 1740, Mr Baron Carter summed up to the jury by directing them in the following terms: "Gentlemen, if you believe Mr. Wheatley you will find the prisoner guilty, if [you] do not believe Mr. Wheatley you'll acquit him".[21] There was no mention of any quantum of proof that might be required to convict the accused. Anecdotal evidence suggests that, nowadays, Crown Court judges very rarely feel, post-trial, that jurors have convicted innocent defendants. By contrast, during the eighteenth century, doubts about the safety of a conviction were regularly cited as a reason for recommending a post-conviction reprieve. Thus, in 1751, one judge supported the commutation of a death sentence to transportation for 14 years, the whole case: "...depending upon one single witness".[22] Nevertheless, such recommendations were still extremely small as a proportion of total convictions.

16. Anon, *The Cries of Blood, or Juryman's Monitor*, 1767, p.31.
17. J. L. Rayner and G. T. Crook, *The Complete Newgate Calendar*, 1926, vol. III, pp.167-169.
18. J. L. Rayner and G. T. Crook, *The Complete Newgate Calendar*, 1926, vol. IV, pp.223-224.
19. M. Blandy, *Genuine letters that pass'd between Miss Blandy and Miss Jeffries, before and after conviction*, 1752, p.23.
20. See generally Bruce P. Smith, "The History of Wrongful Execution", pp.1185–1233, and A. McKenzie, "God's Tribunal: Guilt, Innocence, and Execution in England, 1675–1775", pp.121–144.
21. Anon, *The Genuine and Authentic Trial of Mr. Bartholomew Greenwood*, 3rd. edn., 1740, p.24.
22. T. A. Green, *Verdict According to Conscience*, 1985, p.281.

Perhaps most pertinently, for the bulk of the period, although a trial jury had to be firmly persuaded that the accused person was guilty, the defendant was expected to assist them in reaching this decision. To some extent, once a clear *prima facie* case had been set out, defendants had to establish their innocence. For most of the period, the felony trial was premised on using the accused as an informational resource.[23] For example, when John Mills was accused of wounding, the court (i.e. the presiding judge) asked him: "Can you give the jury any satisfactory account of yourself, that may induce them to believe that you are not a man that would commit such an offence".[24] This approach waned after the advent of counsel, a phenomenon that made it possible to mount an effective defence without the accused first having to testify.

Additionally, there were a few situations in which it was clear that an accused person *did* have the legal onus of proving his defence. For example, by the eighteenth century, it was established that insanity placed a legal burden on the defendant.[25] A few other defences that, today, merely place an evidential burden on the accused, were thought to place a legal onus on him during the 1700s. A raft of new summary misdemeanours, enacted during the course of the century, also placed a legal burden on the defences in respect of key aspects of the offences.

Conviction Rates

Throughout the eighteenth century, large numbers of criminal defendants on trial at the higher courts received outright acquittals. Conviction rates at the Old Bailey, even if for a lesser offence than that charged, fluctuated, but only averaged about 62 per cent during the whole of the century.[26] More specifically, of 967 property offences tried at that forum between 1690 and

23. J. H. Langbein, *The Origins of Adversary Criminal Trial*, 2003, p. 20.
24. OBSP, Trial of John Mills, 30 April 1783.
25. *Arnold's Case* (1724) 16 St Tr 694.
26. A. L. Cross, "The English Criminal Law and Benefit of Clergy during the Eighteenth and Early Nineteenth Century", 1917, p.560.

1713, 283, or 31 per cent, resulted in an acquittal.[27] Similarly, of 204 defendants (of all types) who were tried at the same forum at the four sessions presided over by Sir Dudley Ryder in the 1750s, 84 (more than 40 per cent) were acquitted.[28]

These verdicts are particularly significant, given that nearly all crimes that came for trial had survived an initial, if sometimes rather cursory, examination by a JP, and subsequent scrutiny by a Grand Jury. Of course, in some of these cases, a key prosecution witness had failed to appear, forcing a "not guilty" verdict. Against this, however, if the number of genuinely "contested" trials is considered, and those in which token defences leading to swift convictions are excluded (a consequence of the eighteenth-century judiciary's reluctance to accept guilty pleas), the proportion of acquittals "on the evidence" becomes higher than these figures suggest. Intelligent criminals, who were fast on their feet, and aware of basic forensic procedures, were particularly likely to escape. In 1764, for example, it was claimed that Dick Swift had faced a felony trial 13 times, yet only been convicted on one occasion.[29] Acquittal rates were markedly higher during the eighteenth century than they were to be in the Victorian period, when little more than a fifth of defendants received such verdicts.

Although, by modern standards, the speed with which life-threatening decisions were reached, and the general atmosphere in which criminal trials were held, is acutely distasteful, this should not be taken to suggest that judges and jurors were unconcerned about rectitude in decision-making and correctness in adjudication. There were regular instances in which the trial jury at the Old Bailey, though persuaded of the defendant's guilt, acquitted because they could not find evidence that would positively link the accused person to the crime with which they were charged. For example, when Christopher Matthews was accused of stealing a valuable wig in 1716, there was, apparently "no doubt" that he was guilty. However, he had, by some means, spirited away the chief prosecution witness, as a result of which the

27. J. M. Beattie, *Policing and Punishment in London, 1660–1750*, 2001, p.340.
28. J. H. Langbein, "Shaping the Eighteenth-century Criminal Trial: A View from the Ryder Sources", 1983, p.43.
29. *London Chronicle*, 24 May 1764.

jury were "oblig'd to acquit him".[30] Many defendants, like the soldier and four women accused of committing a murder in Leadenhall Street, experienced benign outcomes and: "...for want of due proof were all acquitted".[31] Some defendants were simply lucky with their juries. In 1763, when John Moody was caught in possession of a stolen horse, he was found "not guilty"at trial. His examining justice, Richard Wyatt, claimed that he had been: "Acquitted by an ignorant jury at Kingston Assizes, not one circumstance appearing in his favour".[32]

Contrary to some modern suggestions, it seems that, by the eighteenth century, criminal juries usually had to be fairly firmly persuaded that an offence had been committed, and that the defendant had committed it, before any question of "pious perjury", as opposed to outright acquittal, arose. By then, jurors were more reluctant than previously to engage in a "balancing act", in which a serious, but not overwhelming, doubt about whether a defendant had committed the crime charged was factored into their deliberations to produce a conviction for a lesser offence. Late seventeenth-century courts had sometimes been quite open about this, so that a minor but niggling doubt about whether the accused had actually committed the offence charged might lead to a grand larceny indictment producing a conviction for petty theft.[33]

It appears that this waned during the course of the eighteenth century. Of course, although no longer explicit, it probably still went on, albeit without express acknowledgement. Thus, when Josiah Brooks was indicted for stealing 34lb. of beef from the stall of Hugh Gilbert, in Leadenhall Market, he was charged with grand larceny, but merely convicted of petty theft, though such a quantity of meat was inherently valuable. After Gilbert was told that a man carrying a similar amount of beef had been seen going into a nearby alehouse he confronted Brooks, who claimed he had bought it from some men he had earlier met in Wapping. This: "...not being prov'd, nor believ'd by the Jury, and the Butcher being positive it was his Beef, the Jury found

30. OBSP, Trial of Christopher Matthews, 22 February 1716.
31. *The Original Weekly Journal,* 20-26 April, 1718.
32. E. Silverthorne (Ed.), *Deposition Book of Richard Wyatt*, 1978, p.3.
33. *The Ordinary of Newgate's Account ... Wednesday the 24th of January 1694.*

him guilty to the Value of 10 d".[34] It is impossible to establish precisely what motivated the jury to reach their verdict in this case. They may well have thought that Gilbert had been crassly negligent, perhaps leaving his stall enticingly unattended (a factor that influenced jurors in other cases). However, it is also possible that, when it came to such non-descript goods, in the environs of a market in which meat was regularly traded, with no confession or direct evidence of appropriation, they had minor reservations about the safety of their verdict.

Where pious perjury was not legally possible other steps might be taken to allow for a doubt. Thus, can be considered a case from 1744, in which the victim of a highwayman was the key identification witness in his trial. The victim was of very good character, the defendant of poor reputation. The former was adamant as to the reliability of his observation. Nevertheless, during the hearing it transpired that the victim had already positively identified another man as his assailant, but not appeared against him at trial, so that he was acquitted. In light of this, the jury in the instant case still convicted of the capital offence, but recommended the defendant for a pardon![35] Obviously, they harboured a doubt; the pardon was duly granted.

Directed Acquittals

Where a trial judge or Quarter Sessions chairman concluded that the evidence, taken at its highest, did not *legally* support an allegation, he could direct the jury to return a "not guilty" verdict. For example, in a pick-pocketing case under the Elizabethan Act, in which it transpired from the prosecution evidence that the victim had grabbed the defendant's hand *before* his handkerchief had been entirely removed: "…the court directed the jury to acquit him, which they did".[36] In 1803, problems arose at the Middlesex Quarter Sessions, when the chairman directed a jury to acquit a male defendant of assaulting a woman because she had first seized him

34. OBSP, Trial of Josiah Brooks, 16 April 1729.
35. OBSP, Trial of Robert Fuller, 10 May 1744.
36. OBSP, Trial of Robert Colthorp, 4 April 1722.

by the hand and attempted to prevent his departure. Despite this, the jury, shocked by the accused's ungentlemanly conduct, initially returned a guilty verdict. The chairman then reminded them of his direction, and sent them out again to reconsider, after which they acquitted.[37]

Although the presence of several judges on the bench, combined with journalistic interest, probably meant that such directed acquittals occurred more frequently at the Old Bailey than they did at provincial Assizes, they were still very rare. There were only about 25 of them at the Old Bailey during the course of the century. The vast majority of verdicts were left to the active consideration of jurors.

Jury Acquittals

Certain, fairly consistent, principles were applied by eighteenth-century juries when reaching decisions. Most would be regarded as entirely proper today. For example, any doubt about the accuracy of the identification of a defendant was likely to be fatal to a prosecution. As the Newgate ordinary warned, it was necessary for: "...all persons to be extremely cautious how they swear to the identity of a person in the case of life and death".[38] In pursuit cases, in which a suspect had been chased through the streets and then captured, the court (i.e. the judge) was usually careful to ensure that the defendant had been kept under continuous view, during the chase, or was highly distinctive in appearance, to ensure that an innocent passer-by had not been caught up in the general melee. This was something that many victims would also stress without prompting.

Similarly, in purported recognition cases, where a suspect had been taken long after the incident for which he was accused, the quality of the initial identification would be carefully tested. Given the poor street lighting of the era, it was particularly easy to make a mistake at night. Thus, in a nocturnal highway robbery case from 1774, the court repeatedly asked a key prosecution witness: "Are you sure the prisoner at the bar is one of the persons that

37. *The Times*, 13 September 1803.

38. *The Ordinary of Newgate's Account...Friday the 5th of October, 1744.*

robbed you? … Are you certain as to the identity of the prisoner? … what kind of light had you?"[39]

Anything that smacked of a quasi-civil matter was also likely to result in an acquittal, as it usually does today. Indeed, to pre-empt such situations, Sir Thomas de Veil had been careful to warn magistrates not to allow petitioners to turn what were essentially civil disputes about, for example, the respective rights of landlords and tenants, into criminal allegations, which they: "…endeavour (very often) to disguise under the colour of felonies, force or assault".[40] This was an important factor behind the acquittal of Henry Burrows, an apprentice clog-maker from St Giles-in-the-Fields, who was prosecuted for stealing seven pairs of his master's shoes. He had pawned them for half a guinea with his employer's regular broker, albeit that, on this occasion, they were not taken there on his master's orders. Burrows claimed that he did so "for want of victuals", as his employer wouldn't give him any food, forcing him to eke out a penny loaf and a halfpenny worth of cheese over several meals.[41] Apprentices were usually treated sympathetically with regard to the use of work materials with which they had been entrusted, and many argued that such materials could not be the subject of a felony indictment if misappropriated.

Any suggestion that a prosecution had been driven by a desire to extort money from the defendant was likely to result in a "not guilty" verdict, even if the accused appeared guilty. Another reason for Burrows' acquittal was that his mother had given the prosecutor a crown after he told her that if she gave him a guinea he would clear her son, but if she failed to do so, he would "either hang or transport him". Even a plausible suggestion that the prosecutor had offered to compound a matter, or seriously entertained such a possibility, was often fatal to an ensuing prosecution. Juries would also look askance at any suggestion that a prosecutor had gone back on his word when questioning a suspect, or was personally unconcerned about securing a conviction. In 1753, for example, Charles Rex was acquitted of stealing 14lb of sewing thread from a warehouse, after questioning by the presiding judge

39. OBSP, Trial of William Royle, 6 July 1774.

40. Sir T. Deveil, *Observations on the Practice of a Justice of the Peace,* London, Edward Withers, 1747, p.8.

41. OBSP, Trial of Henry Burrows, 15 October 1740.

elicited that the prosecutor had promised that he "would not hurt him" if he confessed, and candidly admitted that he would not have prosecuted at all if he had not been bound over to do so by an examining JP[42]

In a system in which the individual complainant played a vital role, there was, inevitably, considerable scope for malicious and unfounded prosecutions, and both judges and jurors appear to have been alert to this possibility. For example, after Eleanor Quinby quarrelled with her neighbour Edmund Dawson he claimed that she had stolen some of his possessions. These were duly found in Quinby's apartment, but in circumstances that suggested that he might have planted them there. Quinby was acquitted, as the prosecution "carried in it a flagrant suspicion of being malicious".[43]

Insanity

In theory, insanity was the only exculpatory mental state allowed at law.[44] In 1726, for example, Rebecca Gardner was accused of housebreaking but: "In consideration of her lunacy, the jury acquitted her".[45] Although the legal definition of insanity was not very precise during the eighteenth century, the ability to distinguish between right and wrong, good and evil, appears to have been crucial. The consequences of acquittal on this ground could be very benign, even for those accused of the most serious offences. It was only after the case of *R v Hadfield* (1800), in which a brain damaged former soldier who had attempted to murder George III was found "not guilty" by reason of insanity, that the Criminal Lunatics Act from the same year formally gave the courts the power to keep those acquitted for this reason in custody, if they constituted a danger to the public. Prior to this date, they would normally be released to their families, unless incarcerated in a house of correction as vagrants under the 1744 Act, or sent via a civil commitment to

42. OBSP, Trial of Charles Rex, 7 June 1753.
43. OBSP, Trial of Eleanor Quiby, November 1716.
44. See generally, J. Brydall, *Non compos mentis: or, The law relating to natural fools, mad-folks, and lunatick persons*, 1700.
45. OBSP, Trial of Rebecca Gardner, 7 December 1726.

a private mad hospital.[46] In the Metropolitan area, some were also committed to the Bethlem Hospital for the Insane "Bedlam"), the only institution of its type in England. It was alleged that three out of every seven inmates there from Middlesex were a "hazard" to the lives of their neighbours, or likely to commit some other form of serious mischief.[47] In 1739, the hospital's managing committee was expressly encouraged not to take in: "...ideots [mental defectives], or mopes [depressives], but such as were mischievous, or might be troublesome to their friends or the publick".[48]

Pleas of insanity appear to have been quite rare *nationally* until about 1740, after which they expanded significantly.[49] However, at the Old Bailey, claims and acquittals on this ground were fairly well spread throughout the century. There were less than 50 of them in total. A proven history of strange behaviour, prior to the incident that brought the defendant to court, was often very helpful, if not vital, in such cases.

Popular Notions of Responsibility

Despite the firm theoretical preconditions placed on the insanity defence, some eighteenth-century defendants argued that they should not be held responsible for acts committed while they were not insane, but were severely intoxicated, in a passion, suffering from a head injury, or acting under the pressure of extreme necessity. The large measure of discretion accorded to juries meant that popular conceptions of criminal responsibility had the potential to affect verdicts, even where they departed from strict legal theory.

It has been suggested that, during the 1700s, some of the previous century's emphasis on crime as the product of sin was replaced by a novel emphasis on a language of the mind. This amplified the "vocabulary of excuse" by explaining crime as the product of forces that had temporarily overwhelmed

46. K. S. Goddard, "A Case of Injustice? The Trial of John Bellingham", 2004, p.2.
47. A. Suzuki, "Lunacy in seventeenth-and eighteenth-century England: analysis of Quarter Sessions Records", 1992, p.31.
48. *Read's Weekly Journal, or, British-Gazetteer,* 3 November 1739.
49. R. D. Moran, "The Origin of Insanity as a Special Verdict: The Trial For Treason of James Hadfield (1800)", 1985, pp. 601-633.

the defendant's normal self, and so propelled him into offending.[50] For example, when tried for attempted sodomy in 1749, Richard Spencer unavailingly sought to explain his behaviour with a young apprentice by making a: "... long and artful defence, to prove himself out of his senses at times". He claimed that he had received treatment from a doctor, at a guinea a time, who had found him incurable, but who was (conveniently) not called to give evidence on Spencer's behalf.[51] Similarly, when James Askoe stole a horse in 1787, he attributed it to an: "...unhappy imbecility of mind occasioned by a violent fever".

Sometimes, if only very rarely, these arguments were accepted by juries. For example, when John Thomas was indicted for stealing 2s. 6d. from a Stepney shop there was no medical evidence, or even formal claim, of insanity. Nevertheless, he was acquitted after several laymen gave evidence that he was: "...so silly, that he had rather have a Half-penny than a Shilling; and gave several Instances of his want of Reason".[52]

Similarly, in theory, intoxication did not provide a defence in English law, though laymen did not always appreciate this. Richard Frost felt that it was very common for people to apologise for offending and say: "...I was drunk, otherwise I should never have acted at so foolish a rate".[53] After Thomas Douglas was found guilty of a tavern murder in 1714, it was, apparently, difficult to make him appreciate the enormity of his crime, because he thought that as he was: "...drunk when he perpetrated the fact, he ought to be considered in the same light as a man who was a lunatic".[54] Nevertheless, most legal observers subscribed to the view that such "voluntarily contracted madness" was, if anything, an aggravation, rather than an excuse, for criminal misbehaviour.[55] (Some felt that this might not be the case if a man had unwittingly had his drinks "spiked").[56]

---

50. See generally, D. Rabin, *Identity, Crime, and Legal Responsibility in Eighteenth-century England*, 2004.
51. OBSP, Trial of Richard Spencer, 5 July 1749.
52. OBSP, Trial of John Thomas, 27 February 1723.
53. R. Frost, *The Folly and Danger of Drunkenness*, 1729, p.13.
54. A. Knapp And W. Baldwin, *Newgate Calendar Comprising Interesting Memoirs Of The Most Notorious Characters*, vol. 1, 1824, p.97-98.
55. W. Blackstone, *Commentaries on the Laws of England*, 1765-9, vol. 4, pp.25-26.
56. M. Hale (updated by G. Wilson and S. Emlyn), *The History of the Pleas of the Crown*, vol.1,

However, in *practice*, attitudes towards the effect of drunkenness on criminal responsibility were slightly more nuanced and indulgent than such comments would suggest, so that some defendants secured favourable results after attributing their offending to intoxication.[57] Occasionally, for example, juries were willing to distinguish between a drunken intent and defendants who were so drunk that no conscious intent could have been formed. Thus, Thomas Bradmore, found in an unoccupied house, with pieces of lead gutter removed from the same building lying nearby, merely claimed that he was intoxicated at the time: "I did not know what I did". On producing witnesses to his good character, he was acquitted.[58]

Nevertheless, judges would normally discourage jurors from being influenced by such extra-legal considerations. For example, in 1754, Sir Dudley Ryder recorded in his judicial notebook that he had urged a jury at the Old Bailey, which had heard that a defendant committed an offence out of pressing necessity, to ignore this when determining guilt as: "...compassion could not justify finding contrary to truth". Such mitigating factors were for the post-conviction reprieve process.[59]

Dislike of Circumstantial Evidence

Certain types of evidence were viewed as inherently suspect by eighteenth-century judges and jurors, and prosecutions that were heavily reliant on them were more likely to fail. Both the *Old Bailey Sessions Papers* and Metropolitan Quarter Sessions reports reveal a decided preference for what is termed "direct" evidence in the modern era, and which was often called "positive" evidence during the 1700s. This was evidence directly implicating a defendant in a crime. There was a corresponding reluctance to accept

---

1800, p.31.

57. D. Rabin, "Drunkenness and Responsibility for Crime in the Eighteenth Century", 2005, p.474.
58. OBSP, Trial of Thomas Bradmore, 15 October 1740.
59. D. Rabin, *Identity, Crime, and Legal Responsibility in Eighteenth-century England*, 2004, p.59, p.126 and p.132. One major limitation on this analysis is the shortage of full trial records for earlier periods.

cases that were built on a purely "circumstantial" basis. The former encompassed the testimony of eyewitnesses, the latter covered things like motive and opportunity. Thus, a female defendant accused of participating with a male accomplice in a burglary, and then disposing of the proceeds of the crime, was found not guilty even though it appeared that she was: "...likely enough to be guilty of such a crime, yet no direct evidence coming against her, she was acquitted".[60]

This was not a legal rule, and guilty verdicts could be, and occasionally were, secured purely on strong circumstantial evidence. In 1759, for example, Mary Edmondson was convicted of murder entirely on such evidence, although the trial judge felt obliged to remind the jury that there was nothing "positively proving" the defendant's guilt, the prosecution case depending entirely upon "circumstances".[61] Although William Cox was a habitual criminal, his biographer was acutely concerned about the manner in which he had been capitally convicted of a robbery. Despite accepting that Cox was guilty, he was alarmed that the prosecution case had been based "only on *circumstances*". He thought that it was highly questionable whether any man, however bad his character, should be found guilty and executed: "...in consequence of circumstantial evidence, though that evidence be as strong as in its nature it can be".[62]

In 1715, it seems that an accused person facing a purely circumstantial case was more than twice as likely to be acquitted as one who was confronted by a sworn eyewitness (39 per cent compared to 16 per cent). In 1780, the proportions were similar (50 per cent compared to 26 per cent).[63] Inconclusive circumstantial evidence that was otherwise unsupported by either eyewitness testimony or a confession was highly unlikely to produce a conviction. This probably reflected a widespread recognition that there was simply not enough forensic time available to explore other, legitimate, explanations for

60. Anon, *A True and Perfect Account of the Proceedings at the General Sessions of the Peace, holden for London and Middlesex, upon the 15 and 16 of January. Instant*, 1674, p.5.
61. Anon, *A Genuine Narrative of the Trial and Condemnation of Mary Edmondson, for the Murder of Mrs. Susannah Walker, her Aunt*, 2nd edn., 1759, p.19.
62. Anon, *The Genuine Life of William Cox, Who is now under Sentence of Death in Newgate*, 5th edn., 1773, pp.22-23.
63. G. Fisher, "The Jury's Rise as Law Detector", 1997, pp.643-645.

the existence of apparently incriminating circumstances, in the very swift criminal trials of the era. The limited provision made for pre-trial crime investigation was also unlikely to exclude such possibilities.

As a result, if the accused was of good character, even vaguely plausible explanations for highly suspicious circumstances might be accepted. For example, in 1691, an acquittal followed an apparently powerful prosecution case for murder by stabbing, which included the discovery of a bloodied sword in the defendant's possession. He initially explained its condition by saying that it had been employed to kill a stray dog, and then by claiming that it had been used in a sea battle and not cleaned! Even so, the evidence against him was not deemed to be "positive in all its circumstances".[64]

Hostility towards circumstantial evidence appears to have declined slightly during the latter part of the century, when several judicial and academic commentators began to argue that it had some advantages over direct evidence. For example, William Paley asserted that as "circumstances cannot lie", such evidence might be stronger than: "...positive testimony, unconfirmed by circumstances". Lord Justice Buller also stressed its importance in *R v Donellan,* a case tried at the Warwick Assizes in 1781. The judge suggested that, in some situations at least, a chain of circumstantial evidence could be "more convincing than positive evidence".[65] In some types of case, of course, it was all that was likely to be available. As prosecuting counsel was to note in a Yorkshire murder trial from 1775, in many situations it could only be: "...circumstances both before, and after, relating to the person deceased, and the prisoner at the bar, that constitute the crime, and can confirm the evidence".[66]

64. OBSP, Trial of Lewis Rantzau and another, 15 January 1691.
65. A. Welsh, "Burke and Bentham on the Narrative Potential of Circumstantial Evidence", 1990, p.615.
66. S. Williamson, *The Trial at Large of John Bolton, Gent. Of Bulmer, near Castle-Howard, for the wilful Murder of Elizabeth Rainbow*, 1775, p.3.

Jury Deliberations

Juries had to be unanimous when returning a verdict. This seems to have occasioned very few problems in practice. Certain fairly consistent legal "rules of thumb" appear to have dominated jury deliberations, over long periods of time, if only because every jury contained what were still sometimes termed, at the start of the period, "ancient jurymen". These were men with significant previous experience of service in this capacity. For example, in the first half of the eighteenth century, London juries at the Old Bailey normally contained up to three very experienced men, and slightly more with *some* experience of previous sessions, albeit that at least half of their members would usually be neophytes. There was even more "strength in depth" in the Middlesex jury. Many of that county's jurors were enormously experienced, serving repeatedly, sometimes more than a dozen times over the course of their careers. It seems that they were largely recruited from a tiny proportion of the Middlesex population, often being taken from urban and suburban parts that were close in to the City.

It is likely that such men transmitted informal, flexible, but well established rules of adjudication to their less experienced colleagues. Indeed, some even argued that experienced jurors with academic ability should consciously study the law. They thought that active, spirited jurors, men who had a "stock of knowledge" about jury matters, were likely to be thanked and encouraged by the court and judiciary, rather than subject to criticism.[67]

The medieval notion that jurors should bring personal knowledge of a criminal allegation as a result of coming from the immediate vicinity of the crime ("vicinage") was long dead by the eighteenth century. Nevertheless, in a relatively confined urban area there was always the possibility that some jurors would possess information about the matters that came before them. In 1754, for example, Hannah Scelley was tried for murder after two watchmen in St. George's Hanover Square detained her in the early hours of the morning, and found that a bundle that she was carrying contained a man's skull, testicles and an arm. However, she was acquitted on the basis that this

67. Anon, *Directions for Prosecuting Thieves Without the Help of those False Guides, The Newgate Sollicitors,* 1728, p.22.

was a case of "body-snatching", the removal of an already dead and buried corpse for medical purposes. The foreman of the trial jury informed the court that: "Some of my brother jurymen were upon that vestry, and they were very well satisfied the head was taken out of a church-yard".[68]

Jury Independence

The principle of jury independence established by *Bushel's Case* in 1670 meant that juries that resisted judicial pressure to return a certain verdict (usually guilty) could not be punished for their recalcitrance. However, such cases had always been very rare. The decision did nothing to prevent or discourage presiding judges from making their views as to the merits of a case abundantly clear. Judicial dominance could even extend to refusing to accept a jury's decision when it was first given. Only four years after *Bushel's* case, when a man was acquitted of burglary in legally debateable circumstances, the judge: "...not being satisfied with that Verdict they [the jurors] went out again and brought in a special verdict, which is to be argued at another time".[69] In some cases, juries even reversed their initial decision altogether, convicting where they had previously acquitted.

By the middle of the eighteenth century, this practice was very much more rare than it had been at its start and, by the era's close, it was being argued that excessively firm judicial guidance on the merits of a case risked usurping the jury's function.[70] This did not prevent judges giving their views in strong terms, as they would until well into the nineteenth century. However, they normally appear to have accepted jury decisions with reasonable grace, though there were periodic reports of judges castigating jurors who returned the "wrong" verdict.[71]

68. OBSP, Trial of Hannah Scelley and James Scelley, 30 May 1754.
69. Anon, *A True and Perfect Account of the Procedings at the General Sessions of the Peace, holden for London and Middlesex, upon the 15 and 16 of January Instant*, 1674, p.5. The facts established by the special verdict would be considered by the 12 Westminster judges.
70. *The Times*, Thursday, 18 September 1788, p. 2.
71. D. Bentley, *English Criminal Justice in the Nineteenth Century*, 1998, p.68.

Although they were greatly influenced by firm indications from the bench, jurors were rarely just ciphers for judicial views on the merits of a case. For example, they refused to convict any of the prisoners charged with the capital offence of uttering forged notes at the December 1818 Sessions at the Old Bailey, even though the presiding judge had pressed for a guilty verdict. The jurors were concerned at the failure of Bank of England Inspectors to explain why they were sure certain notes were forged.[72] Nevertheless, dwelling on such incidents can be misleading. In the great majority of cases, it seems that judge and jury worked in harmony, something that was necessary given the huge workload that had to be accommodated within a relatively short time. Juries normally deferred to judicial guidance, and judges respected the realm of jury discretion, leaving key issues to their determination.

In the early eighteenth century, it was not uncommon for jurors to pursue a line of questioning of their own. For example, in 1744, when a witness from an accused man's locality gave helpful evidence on his behalf, it was the jury that asked him whether he was related to the defendant (he was, by marriage).[73] By the latter decades of the century, this sort of juror participation had become more rare. Nevertheless, it still occurred, although by then it was normal to wait until counsel (if present) had finished their own examinations before posing such questions. Even late in the century, a jury could openly criticise the barrister William Garrow for wasting court time with his excessive prolixity.[74]

Evidential Rules

Evidential rules, although often present in proto-form, were fairly flexible at the start of the eighteenth century. The first major text on the subject, by William Nelson, only appeared in 1717, and much of this book focussed on procedural matters.[75] However, several new rules gradually emerged, or,

72. J. Oldham, "The Limits of Discretion: Forgery and the Jury at the Old Bailey, 1818-1821", 2002, p.160.
73. OBSP, Trial of Robert Fuller, 10 May 1744.
74. P. King, *Crime, Justice, and Discretion in England 1740-1820*, 2000, p.229.
75. J. H. Langbein, "Historical Foundations of the Law of Evidence: A View From the Ryder

if already present, were applied much more strictly than had hitherto been the case, in a process that accelerated rapidly in the final decades of the era. There are several explanations for this development.

During the second half of the century, members of the judiciary appear to have become seriously concerned about the reliability of certain types of evidence. For example, there was acute judicial anxiety about the extensive use of accomplice testimony. As a result, the judges devised or promoted rules that precluded some problematic types of evidence, or only permitted their adduction if certain prerequisites were satisfied.[76] The presence of laymen on the jury may have encouraged this process, even if it was not directly its cause, as fears grew that they were unable to properly assess the weight of certain types of information.[77] There was also a newly perceived need, at a time when there were few, if any, ways of appealing a jury's decision, and many potentially capital crimes, to provide extra procedural safeguards for a defendant.

Although the initial development of the law of criminal evidence was largely the work of the bench, its expansion was greatly assisted by the presence of lawyers, who swiftly appreciated that the exclusionary rules enhanced their ability to influence the outcome of a trial. This process was particularly marked during the 1780s, when an influx of able criminal barristers was accompanied by an increase in their willingness to take issue with evidence that they felt was flawed.[78] Such attitudes swiftly spread to less distinguished counsel.[79]

The most important of these evidential rules governed: the need for accomplice testimony to be corroborated; restrictions on evidence of a defendant's previous bad character; the admissibility of confessions obtained by duress or inducements; stricter controls on the reception of hearsay; and an increased reluctance to accept non-expert opinion evidence. Of these, confession evidence is dealt with in *Chapter 13*, while that relating to accomplices is considered in *Chapter 11*.

Sources", 1996, p.1172.

76. J. H. Langbein, *The Origins of Adversary Trial*, 2003, pp.178-179.
77. J. M. Beattie, *Crime and the Courts in England 1660-1800*, 1986, p.147.
78. J. M. Beattie, *Scales of Justice*, 1991, p.239.
79. T. P. Gallanis, "The Rise of Modern Evidence Law", 1999, p. 499.

Hearsay

Even at the start of the century, hearsay had sometimes been excluded, witnesses being told to testify as to: "...what you know and saw, but not what others said, for that is no evidence".[80] Nevertheless, the application of the rule was often lax and haphazard. Many witnesses were allowed to testify about what they had learnt from others. Only occasionally, did judges show major concern about the admissibility of such evidence.[81] However, as the century advanced, the exclusionary rule was enforced increasingly strictly, and it was fairly rigid by its end. The *Old Bailey Sessions Papers* use the word "hearsay", in an at least vaguely evidential context, 48 times during the 1700s.[82] Of these, only nine occur between 1700 and 1749; in the final 50 years of the century it is used 39 times, with 27 uses coming in the last two decades of the era. In 1766, it could be firmly asserted of potential forensic information that: "...it was only hearsay, and not evidence".[83] By the end of the century, hearsay was normally only allowed if it came in the form of an admissible confession or other recognised exception to the general exclusionary rule.

Bad character evidence

For much of the eighteenth century, the prosecution in a criminal case could adduce evidence of a defendant's previous bad character as part of its case. This might include any previous convictions he had accrued. Indeed, in theory, until 1779, those who had been convicted, clergied, branded and discharged carried the sign of their earlier conviction indelibly on their bodies, even if, in practice, this was often not the case. In the 1720s, the visiting Frenchman Cesar de Saussure noted that if a witness was called to give evidence that an Old Bailey defendant was a person of bad antecedents, he would be "listened to with attention". The *Sessions Papers* routinely record that the jury's appreciation that a defendant was an "old offender" had contributed to their decision to convict. This was especially likely if the earlier crimes were of the same type as those presently charged, as with Jane

80. Anon, *Directions for Prosecuting Thieves Without the Help of those False Guides, The Newgate Sollicitors...*, 1728, p.6.
81. T. P. Gallanis, "The Rise of Modern Evidence Law", 1999, p.503.
82. It was also a not uncommon attributed surname, and even an occasional first name.
83. OBSP, Trial of William Wyatt, 19 February 1766.

Housden, who was convicted of coining offences in 1702.[84] Similarly, when John Hall, Richard Low and Stephen Bunch were tried for burglary, in 1707, their convictions were the result of the: "...evidence being very clear, and the Prisoners Old Offenders".[85] This applied to Quarter Sessions as well as to hearings in the higher courts. For example, when a woman was tried at the Guildhall for keeping a notorious bawdy-house she was convicted: "... after a short hearing (it being proved that she was an old offender)".[86]

Sometimes, it was not even readily practical to conceal a defendant's history from the court. William Cox suspected that the reason he was convicted on an almost purely circumstantial case in 1773 was that the court and jury had been aware of his general reputation as a notorious thief; the presiding judge, Mr. Baron Eyre, had sat on several of his earlier trials when he had been Recorder of London.[87] Nevertheless, that this could be the subject of adverse comment is itself indicative of a change in attitudes at this time.

The latter decades of the century witnessed the gradual emergence of a rule preventing the adduction of a defendant's previous "bad character", exceptional cases apart, though this did not become rigid until the early 1800s. Sir Michael Foster first hinted at such a rule in his treatise on *Crown Law* in 1762. As a result, although the expression "old offender" occurs 116 times in the *Old Bailey Sessions Papers* during the eighteenth century, 84 of these are in the first fifty years of the period, and only 15 in its last quarter ("Old offenders" occurs 13 times during the century, but with over half occurring before 1724).

By 1786, it was a matter of bitter complaint by a defendant in an assault case, tried at the Middlesex Quarter Sessions, that the prosecutor had been allowed on several occasions to attack his: "...general character, by charging him with crimes and disorderly behaviour entirely foreign to the subject of the indictment".[88] In 1792, an MP could observe, albeit with slight exaggeration, that the courts: "...never heard evidence of the badness of a prisoner's

84. OBSP, Trial of Januarye Housden, 14 October 1702.
85. OBSP, Trial of John Hall and others, 10 December 1707.
86. *General Advertiser*, 25 September 1752.
87. Anon, *The Genuine Life of William Cox, Who is now under Sentence of Death in Newgate*, 5th edn., 1773, pp.22-23.
88. Anon, *Account of a tryal at Hick's Hall. Tuesday, 25 Apri, 1786*, London, 1786, p.3.

character".[89] In the same decade, Thomas Gisborne warned magistrates that, when determining summary matters, a defendant's previous bad character, even the commission of the very same offences as that with which he was presently charged, was not a valid reason for convicting him: "...on weaker proofs than would have been deemed satisfactory had his integrity been unsullied".[90]

It has been suggested that the emergence of this general exclusionary rule may help to explain why some habitual thieves, such as Charlotte Walker, escaped conviction for so long in the final decades of the century, even though the Home Department's Criminal Register was established in 1791 and increased the authorities' ability to distinguish between "old and new offenders".[91]

Expert opinion evidence

By the eighteenth century, ordinary witnesses were being discouraged from providing the court with opinion, as opposed to evidence of facts. They were told to state what they had heard or seen, "not what they believe".[92] Nevertheless, such opinion was not (usually) firmly excluded until after the mid-century.

In any event, expert evidence was a well-recognised exception to this general situation. As Lord Mansfield observed in 1782, when it came to technical and scientific matters, about which a court could not, on its own, form an informed opinion: "...special study, skill or experience being required for the purpose, "expert" witnesses may give evidence of their opinion".[93] However, the use of experts in criminal trials remained rare to the end of the period, if only because of the attendant expense. Even at the Old Bailey, only slightly

---

89. W. Cobbett, *The Parliamentary History of England from the Earliest Period to the Year 1803*, London, 1817, vol. xxix, p.1170.
90. T. Gisborne, *An Enquiry into the Duties of men in the Higher and Middle Classes of Society in Great Britain*, 1794, p.280.
91. M. Clayton, "The Life and Crimes of Charlotte Walker, Prostitute and Pickpocket", at p.14. The Register would usually record offence, age, height, complexion, hair and eye colour, occupation, place of origin, date, location, and sentence passed by the convicting court, for those convicted of serious felonies.
92. W. Nelson, *The Law of evidence*, 1717, p.7.
93. *Folkes v Chadd* (1782) 3 Doug KB 157.

over a dozen cases a year on average involved the use of experts during the eighteenth century. Where they did appear, it was far more often for the prosecution than for defendants, who were often too poor to afford experts, even if they had been minded to instruct and call such evidence.

Although a diverse range of experts testified, on many different subjects, by far the most important general area related to medical matters. This was provided by surgeons, midwives, and physicians. Three quarters of all medical experts heard at the Old Bailey were called in murder and infanticide cases. For example, when the Marquis of Palleotti killed his Italian servant in the Metropolis, in 1718, the surgeon John Stevens gave evidence at his trial, telling the Bailey that the stab wound on the dead man's body was not inflicted by a: "...hollow Blade, but with such a sword as produced in Court, and Sworn to be the Prisoners".[94] The remaining cases involving expert medical evidence were divided between rapes and those involving non-lethal violence.[95]

Forensic Atmosphere

Criminal courts in the Metropolis often had a raucous and unruly atmosphere. Modern levels of forensic decorum were notably absent. They were also low by the standards of much of continental Europe. A German visiting the Old Bailey in 1710 was "greatly disgusted" at the throngs of people who often made it impossible for him to hear the judges. Spectators would crowd the public gallery, though they had to pay a shilling if they wished to have a chair.[96] Quarter Sessions could be equally boisterous. In January 1779, it was noted by another (English) visitor that, at the Surrey Sessions held at the Town Hall in Southwark, the people in court made so much noise that: "Silence being called for, without effect, the writer could not hear a single

94. F. Palleotti, *The Life, Actions, and Amours, of Ferdinando, Marquis of Palleotti, Lately Executed at Tyburn, for the Murther of his Servant*, 1718, p.31

95. S. Landsman, "One Hundred Years of Rectitude: Medical Witnesses at the Old Bailey, 1717-1817", 1998, p.445.

96. H. Quarrell and M. More (Trans and Eds.), *London in 1710 From the Travels of Zacharias Conrad Von Offenbach*, 1934, p.124.

sentence".[97] This lack of decorum was not special to the Metropolitan area; a similar situation frequently prevailed at the Assizes and provincial Quarter Sessions.

The defendants at felony trials, usually taken direct from custody, would often be in a squalid condition. Some would even be suffering from "gaol fever", a form of typhus brought about by overcrowding combined with poor hygiene, sanitation and nutrition. This could also pose hazards for court personnel, producing multiple deaths on the bench and among lawyers, all of whom were thought to have "caught some infection", at the Old Bailey sessions of May 1750.[98] The poor physical condition of many of those accused of felonies undoubtedly compromised their ability to make effective defences during hurried trials.

Courts and Procedure

The sheer size and population of the London area, its crime rate, the diversity of its legal jurisdictions, the number of its prisons, and the quantity of its defendants, meant that processing suspects through the Metropolitan criminal justice system posed problems that were not encountered elsewhere. This was certainly not a new phenomenon in the eighteenth century. In an attempt at remedying some of these difficulties, several senior Westminster judges sitting at the Old Bailey in the 1660s had issued firm guidance to Metropolitan JPs and gaolers on various aspects of their work. They hoped that these would make the process more efficient and ensure that such key men could not "pretend ignorance of their duty". The judges also required that accurate gaol calendars be produced.[99]

Court officers could play an important role, not least because of their familiarity with interlocutory and trial procedures, both of which could be highly technical. For example, during the trial of Dr. Dodd at the Old Bailey, in 1777, Mr. Deacon, the clerk of the arraigns, was called upon in

97. H. Finnimore, *The Trial of Humphry Finnimore, Esq*, 1779, p.27.
98. *Whitehall Evening Post or London Intelligencer*, 19 May 1750.
99. Sir J. Kelyng, *A Report of Divers Cases In Pleas of the Crown, Adjudged and Determined; In the Reign of the late King Charles II*, 2nd edn., 1734, pp.1-3.

"very severe terms" to justify an order that he had issued requiring Dodd's co-defendant, against whom prosecution witnesses were already bound over to give evidence, to be taken before the Grand Jury at Hick's Hall to give evidence against Dodd. This was highly unusual, and possibly irregular. However, while considering this matter, the Old Bailey court was, itself, forced to seek the opinion of a Mr. Reynolds on the same issue. Reynolds was an "old officer of the court".[100]

Quarter Sessions

Lesser crimes, such as minor felonies and misdemeanours, which had to be tried on indictment (before a jury), would usually be heard at one of the Metropolitan Quarter Sessions. In the City, these were conducted at the Guildhall, while, for much of the century, those held for Middlesex were tried at Hick's Hall in Clerkenwell. Built in 1611, and funded by Sir Baptist Hicks, for which act of generosity the Middlesex Justices named the building after him, this court replaced the Windmill Tavern as a venue for the county's Quarter Sessions. It was described in 1827 as having been a large, square, brick edifice, containing a "great warehouse" at its centre for the oval shaped courtroom, with smaller rooms for its officers connected to it.[101] Hick's Hall was in use until 1782 when, after considerable debate, it was replaced by the nearby, and newly built, Middlesex Sessions House, the construction of which had started in 1779. Westminster had its own Quarter Sessions, separate from those for the rest of Middlesex. These were conducted in a tavern near Westminster Hall prior to the eighteenth century, when a purpose-built court was constructed. The tiny Tower Liberty also had dedicated Quarter Sessions, held in its own Court House, which was situated on Tower Hill.

The City and Middlesex Quarter Sessions were usually held eight times a year, twice as frequently as their provincial equivalents, because of the "multiplicity of business" that they faced, and on account of their administrative

100. W. Dodd, *Authentic Memoirs of the Life of William Dodd, LL.D. who was executed at Tyburn, on Friday, 27 June, 1777*, 1777, pp.19-20.

101. J. Jeaffreson (Ed.) *Middlesex County Records*, vol. iv, 1667-1689, 1892, p.345.

links to the Old Bailey (which also sat eight times a year after 1669).[102] Nevertheless, they were broadly similar to the Quarter Sessions found elsewhere in England.[103] (Technically, four of the eight were "special" rather than "quarter" sessions, the two types alternating). Westminster's Quarter Sessions were held on the normal four occasions (Epiphany, Easter, Midsummer and Michaelmas), like those conducted outside the Metropolis. Despite its availability, many offences committed in Westminster were tried at Hick's Hall, as the city remained part of the wider county, which still had jurisdiction to hear its cases. Indeed, it was often argued that it was "much better" to prefer indictments for misdemeanours committed within Westminster at the county sessions, rather than to prosecute them at the city's sessions, if only because they would be heard much faster (Middlesex holding twice as many of them).[104] As a result, the work of the Westminster Sessions was largely made up of lesser assaults and minor frauds.

Trials at Metropolitan Quarter Sessions were presided over by a bench of magistrates made up of aldermen or JPs acting under their commission of oyer and terminer. Outside the City, the hearings were, effectively, conducted by the chairman of the relevant commission, whether it was Westminster, the Tower Liberty, or Middlesex. This magistrate would control the trial and formally pass sentence if a guilty verdict was returned. For example, during the 1740s, Sir John Gonson normally presided over the Westminster Sessions, while William Mainwaring was chairman of the Middlesex Sessions at the end of the eighteenth century. It was not until 1844 that it was made obligatory for the chairman of the Middlesex Quarter Sessions to be a barrister or serjeant-at-law of at least ten years standing.[105] In the chairman's absence, any other senior JP could be temporarily appointed to this role. For example, at a sessions held in 1752: "Mr. Justice Lediard [was] in the Chair, at the Desire of the Bench".[106]

How effectively magistrates conducted such proceedings depended on their ability and experience. One unsatisfied defendant complained that

102. Anon, *The Crown Circuit Companion*, 8th edn., 1811, p.14.
103. E. D. Mercer and K. Goodacre, *Guide to the Middlesex sessions Records, 1549-1884*, 1965, p.14.
104. Anon, *The Crown Circuit Companion*, 8th edn., 1811, p.14.
105. D. Bentley, *English Criminal Justice in the Nineteenth Century*, 1998, p.77.
106. Anon, *The Life of the Famous William Stroud*, 1752, pp.17-18.

when he stood trial at Hick's Hall, in 1786, the five justices, including the chairman, had appeared totally disinterested in his case, several whispering amongst themselves as it progressed.[107]

By contrast, in the City, the Recorder of London (a professional lawyer and judge) usually presided over the Guildhall Sessions, accompanied by the Lord Mayor and a bench of aldermen, although, again, alternatives could be employed if the Recorder was absent. Thus, when John and James Brownrigg were tried for assaulting their maid in 1767, the notorious case was heard in front of James Eyre, the City's Recorder and Robert Kite, the Lord Mayor, as well as several aldermen.[108] Perhaps, in part, because their function was often fairly ornamental in these situations, there were periodic complaints that aldermen failed to attend the Guildhall Quarter Sessions, according to the "established rotation" of the City, without having a proper excuse (such as sickness).[109] Many Middlesex JPs also missed their county's Quarter Sessions.

However, in all of these cases, the tribunal of fact (as opposed to law) was a petty (trial) jury, which body decided all questions of innocence or guilt. Additionally, all cases heard at Quarter Sessions would first have been filtered through a Grand Jury hearing, which would determine whether there was a case to answer at trial or whether to return the bill of indictment ignoramus/"no true bill".

In strict legal theory, Quarter Sessions had the power to determine all felonies, however serious, until the nineteenth century. Nevertheless, by 1700, such courts normally confined themselves to hearing misdemeanours and lesser felonies. Sir Clifford Phillips, the chairman of the Tower Liberty's Quarter Sessions felt that it was not even worth directing their Grand Jury on potentially capital felonies, as they were: "...seldom or never brought before this court".[110] Similarly, Sir John Gonson observed to the same body that although all crimes could be presented by their Grand Jury, those that

107. Anon, *Account of a tryal at Hick's Hall. Tuesday, 25 April 1786*, 1786, p.4.
108. Anon, *The Trials of James Brownrigg, and John Brownrigg, his Son, for Confining and inhumanly Scourging Mary Mitchel*, 1767, p.3.
109. *Morning Chronicle and London Advertiser*, October 16, 1775,
110. C. W. Philipps, *The Charge of Sir Clifford Wm. Philipps, Knt. To the Grand Jury of the Royalty of the Tower of London, Liberties, and Precincts thereof*, 1745, p.9.

were "both enquirable and punishable" by the Quarter Sessions tended to involve drunkenness, blasphemy, public gaming, petty larceny, assaults and riots.[111] As Gonson's comment suggests, the main form of theft heard at this forum was: "... what comes under the denomination of petit larceny".[112] Thus, at the Westminster Quarter Sessions held in January 1792, a number of petty thefts were tried, few of which were of "any consequence".[113]

English Quarter Sessions might also hear minor felonies that, although in *theory* subject to a death penalty, were automatically clergyable, such as simple grand larceny. These could be tried safe in the knowledge that a finding of guilt would not attract a capital sentence. However, as these forums almost never determined cases that might lead to an execution it was thought "advisible" for justices only to bind-over smaller matters to them.[114] A selection of cases is indicative. In 1766, Henry Seamburgh was convicted at Hick's Hall, and sentenced to transportation, for stealing several geese. At the same sessions, Samuel Pock received an identical disposal for stealing 20 lb of lead, as did Michael Robinson, for the theft of two coats.[115] In 1779, at the Surrey Quarter Sessions held at Southwark, a defendant was tried for stealing five turkeys valued at 15 shillings on the indictment, and half a guinea by the jury.[116] At the Middlesex Quarter Sessions held in December 1790, William Gordon was convicted of stealing a handkerchief from Francis Davis's pocket. He was sentenced to seven years' transportation. This was the most serious penalty that was normally handed down at Quarter Sessions. Gordon's sentence reflected his membership of a notorious gang of thieves and that he had used violence when trying to escape from custody.[117]

111. J. Gonson, *The Charge of Sir John Gonson Knt. To the Grand Jury of the Royalty of the Tower of London, and Liberties and Precincts thereof*, 1728, p.10.

112. G. Jacob, *An Appendix to the modern Justice: Containing the particular Business of the Quarter Sessions*, 1718, p.4.

113. *The Times*, 6 January 1792, p.3.

114. W. D. Rastall, *A Practical Guide, to the Quarter and other, Sessions of the Peace*, 1815, p.105. A tiny number of special Quarter Sessions, outside the Metropolitan area, continued to pass death sentences in exceptional cases during the eighteenth century.

115. *The Whitehall Evening Post; Or, London Intelligencer*, 28 October 1766.

116. H. Finnimore, *The Trial of Humphry Finnimore, Esq*, 1779, p.2.

117. *World*, 11 December 1790.

However, although such lesser (but not "petty") thefts were a staple part of the caseload of many Quarter Sessions in the provinces, those in the Metropolis were often reluctant to hear them in the first half of the century. There are several explanations for this phenomenon. It is likely that it was influenced by constraints of time; the Metropolitan Quarter Sessions were already fully employed with misdemeanours and, in particular, a heavy caseload of assaults and offences of public disorder. Additionally, in the City, there were limitations on the time that busy aldermen could spend on criminal administration.

However, it was not because such lesser crimes of dishonesty were going, instead, to the Old Bailey. That forum also evinced a notable reluctance to try minor property offences on a regular basis. In the first decade of the eighteenth century, less than five per cent of the property offences that were indicted at the Old Bailey from the City of London were below five shillings in value, and only 13 per cent were worth less than ten shillings. Instead, their absence reflects the diversion of many minor offences of dishonesty to the bridewell or a house of correction as examples of disorderly behaviour, rather than their being tried on indictment.[118]

By far the most common "mainstream" criminal offences prosecuted at the three Metropolitan Quarter Sessions were various forms of assault, battery, affray, riot and unlawful assembly.[119] As was noted in 1718: "...this Court takes Cognizance chiefly of Trespasses against the public Peace".[120] If proved, these offences usually resulted in fiscal penalties. For example, at the Quarter Sessions held at the Guildhall on the 13th September 1722, John Crady was fined five pounds for assaulting a constable in the execution of his duty. At the same sessions, another man was fined £50 and sentenced to six months imprisonment in Newgate for assaulting a total stranger in the street.[121] Sometimes, this was the only type of offence indicted. At the Middlesex Quarter Sessions held in December 1790, it could be noted that:

---

118. J. M. Beattie, *Policing and Punishment in London, 1660-1750*, 2001, pp.20-25 and p.31.

119. C. W. Philipps, *The Charge of Sir Clifford Wm. Philipps, Knt. To the Grand Jury of the Royalty of the Tower of London, Liberties, and Precincts thereof*, 1745, p.10.

120. G. Jacob, *An Appendix to the Modern Justice: Containing the particular Business of the Quarter Sessions*, 1718, p.2.

121. *London Journal*, 22 September, 1722.

"Nothing more material took up the time of the court … than trials for common assaults".[122] Nevertheless, along with a large number of "frivolous" offences, more serious crimes of violence were also dealt with at such forums, reflecting the relatively low importance ascribed to non-lethal violence. For example, in 1792, Mary Butler was convicted of a dangerous assault on a six-year-old boy and fined £10.[123] Cases of domestic violence, if they came to court, were also likely to be heard in these forums.

The low importance placed on inchoate offences by common law, at this time, meant that attempts to commit even serious crimes, for example, assault with intent to commit rape (i.e. attempted rape), were usually only misdemeanours, and so normally dealt with at Quarter Sessions rather than the Old Bailey. Defendants were well aware of this vital distinction. In 1707, one of a group of men convicted at the Guildhall of assault with sodomitical intent stressed that he had not planned to engage in anything more than mutual masturbation, and had never had any intention of proceeding to the: "…wicked act of Sodomy as the Indictment seem'd to set forth, but only used a Foolish Custom as he had got, of handling Young Men's Flesh".[124]

As with offences of violence, the relatively mild punishments imposed on those found guilty of attempting crimes reflected this low legal status. For example, at a General Sessions of the Peace held at the Guildhall, a woollen draper convicted of attempted sodomy was sentenced to stand in the pillory near his house in Cornhill, pay a fine of twenty pounds and serve three months in Newgate.[125] Similarly, in 1757, Thomas Crossley, convicted at Hick's Hall of attempting to rape a girl of less than ten years of age, and giving her venereal disease in the process, was sentenced to six months imprisonment and to be pilloried twice.[126] When John McGuire was convicted of an almost identical crime, at the same forum, he was sentenced to a fine of 13s.

122. *World*, 9 December 1790.

123. *Diary or Woodfalls Register*, 29 March 1792.

124. Anon, *Tryal Examination And Conviction Of several Notorious Persons call'd Sodomites, At Guild-Hall on Monday the 20th of October, 1707*, 1707, p.1.

125. Anon, *The Tryal of Mr. John Lowther, For an Assault on John Bushnell, with an intent to commit the Crime of Sodomy*, 1761, p.12.

126. *Lloyds Evening Post and British Chronicle*, 18 January 1758.

4d. (one mark) and two years' custody in Newgate, even though his victim was less than five years old.[127]

Lesser forms of fraud were also frequently determined at the various sessions of the peace, as were allegations of receiving stolen goods, both of which were often defined as misdemeanours. For example, Lavinia Whitney and a male associate were prosecuted at the Guildhall Sessions in 1730 after arranging for a man to go through a sham marriage to her, while pretending to be Samuel Brooks, a wealthy grocer. Their plan was to make the real Brooks responsible for Whitney's debts under the doctrine of *feme covert*. The couple were sentenced to six months imprisonment.[128] At the bottom of the scale of gravity, William Huff was convicted at the Middlesex Sessions in Clerkenwell of forging admission tickets to the Covent Garden theatre and sentenced to 14 days' custody.[129] More seriously, the habitual and notorious confidence-trickster William Stroud was sentenced to six months in the bridewell and to be publicly whipped half a dozen times, at the Westminster Quarter Sessions.[130] Local officials might also be prosecuted at Quarter Sessions for abuse in office. For example, in 1717, some of the overseers of St. Andrew's, Holborn, were indicted at Hick's Hall for conspiring to: "…lay a bastard to a person of good character".[131]

Even if a misdemeanour was indicted at the Quarter Sessions there was no guarantee that it would come to trial, especially if it involved an assault. In many situations, a prosecutor would receive satisfaction in the form of a public apology, sometimes in a newspaper such as the *Daily Advertiser* (the most common organ for such matters) or financial compensation and would then sign a "general release". This document released the person specified in it from any quarrels, controversies, and all manner of legal actions. Originally confined to civil matters, it was invented to give legal status to the settlement of disputes. However, by the start of the eighteenth century it was being used for cases that were due to be heard at Quarter Sessions. Where such

127. *The Whitehall Evening Post; Or, London Intelligencer*, 23 October, 1766.

128. Anon, *The Tryal of Thomas Thomson and Lavinia Whitney, On an indictment for a Conspiracy*, 1730, p.15.

129. *The Times*, 17 January 1803, p.3.

130. Anon, *The Life of the Famous William Stroud*, 1752, pp.17-18.

131. *Weekly Journal or British Gazetteer*, 14 September 1717.

an agreement had been reached, the defendant would normally appear in court and plead guilty to the indictment. He would then be sentenced to a nominal fine of a shilling or so and discharged.[132]

The Court of King's Bench

The Crown side of the Court of King's Bench was the only Metropolitan forum with the power to determine serious crimes apart from the Old Bailey. It was the sole Westminster court to have a criminal as well as civil jurisdiction. Customarily, many cases of sedition and other "high" misdemeanours were prosecuted there. Additionally, indictments in normal misdemeanour cases could be transferred to the court from other forums. As a result, it was used to determine a significant number of lesser criminal matters, such as assault, riot and various highway offences, especially early on in the century. There were, perhaps, 300 such cases a year at the start of the 1720s.[133]

Occasionally, however, high-profile treason and felony cases were also prosecuted at King's Bench, being tried before three judges and a jury.[134] Indeed, actions for seditious libel and, in more serious cases, high treason, were usually heard in this forum. For example, prior to the French Revolution, the court witnessed an average of just over two prosecutions a year for political beliefs, while between 1789 and 1810 there were 103.[135] Similarly, the trial of James Hadfield for committing high treason by shooting at King George III in Drury Lane was held at King's Bench in 1800.[136]

However, the jurisdiction of King's Bench also included a local power to hear all offences committed in Middlesex and Westminster.[137] This was very rarely exercised for serious but "conventional" criminal matters that might otherwise have gone to the Old Bailey. When it was, they were usually crimes

132. N. Landau, "Indictment for Fun and Profit", 1999, p.515.

133. R. Shoemaker, *Prosecution and Punishment*, 1991, p.22.

134. D. Bentley, *English Criminal Justice in the Nineteenth Century*, 1998, pp.58-59.

135. M. Lobban, "From Seditious Libel to Unlawful Assembly: Peterloo and the Changing Face of Political Crime c1770-1820", 1990, p.309.

136. *General Evening Post*, 26 June–28 June 1800.

137. E. D. Mercer and K. Goodacre, *Guide to the Middlesex sessions Records, 1549-1884*, 1965, p.14.

that had an unusual, political or aristocratic connection, or which were, in some other way, *causes célèbres*. For example, the trial of two Middlesex bailiffs accused of murdering a gentleman named Edward Luttrell in his home, while seeking to arrest him over a petty debt, was determined at this forum in 1722. Perhaps because there was much less pressure of work there, criminal business was usually conducted at a more leisurely rate than at the Bailey, even for less serious matters. Thus, when a woman was indicted by her landlord for keeping a disorderly house in the Haymarket, her hearing, presided over by Lord Chief Justice Raymond, lasted four hours and the jury considered the case for half an hour more before acquitting.[138]

Drawing Up Indictments

Although the more serious Metropolitan crimes, and all potentially capital felonies, would be sent to the Sessions House at the Old Bailey, located just inside the City's boundaries, the clerks of both the City and Middlesex Quarter Sessions served a vital function in drawing up the indictments on which the prisoners from their respective areas would be tried at the higher tribunal. Because of this, their Quarter Sessions would normally be heard at about the same time, starting just before, and usually overlapping with, or being followed immediately by, the Old Bailey Sessions. As a result, and typically, in February 1733, a journal could note that: "On Monday next begins the General Quarter Sessions of the Peace for the County of Middlesex at Hicks-Hall, and on Wednesday next the Sessions of Oyer and Terminer at the Old Baily".[139]

When the clerks of these lower courts drew up indictments for the Old Bailey they used set formulas. These were based on information about the nature of the crime and the identity of the accused person provided in the lists of prisoners supplied by the keepers of Newgate Prison (in the City), New Prison (for Middlesex) or the Gatehouse Prison (for Westminster) and in the recognisances of those who had been bound over to appear at trial.

138. *London Journal*, 21 February 1730.
139. *Parker's Penny Post*, 16 February 1733.

They could also make use of written informations taken from the parties concerned by JPs and, it seems, were frequently consulted by complainants in person. Thus, in 1728, it was urged that prosecutors make the clerks' lives easier by producing a full written statement of the details of the offence, along with their own address. They were then urged to: "...deliver it to the person appointed to draw up the Bills". This individual was also to be provided with a fee of two shillings and the names of the prosecution witnesses.[140]

Decisions taken at this stage of the legal process were very important, as the manner in which the offence was defined would determine the punishment the defendant would receive if convicted and, in particular, whether or not they might be subject to a death sentence.[141] For this reason, those instructing the clerks engaged in drawing up indictments were also urged to be precise about providing relevant details, such as: the name of the prisoner and the nature and value of any items stolen; the hour at which an alleged burglary had occurred, in so far as it could be determined; whether a weapon was used in a robbery, or a pickpocket was seen *before* removing stolen items.[142] Sometimes, at this stage, complainants would ask the clerk not to draw up a capital indictment, if they did not wish to see their prosecution end in an execution, though a recognisance might specify that a capital prosecution be brought.

The Grand Jury

Once drawn up, an indictment would have to be considered by the Grand Jury for Middlesex (sitting at Hick's Hall), the City (at Guildhall), Westminster or the Tower. The last two were of limited significance, as, in the case of Westminster, the County Grand Jury had an overlapping jurisdiction, and was often preferred by complainants dealing with serious offences, while the Tower's jurisdiction was exceptionally small.

140. Anon, *Directions for Prosecuting Thieves Without the Help of those False Guides, The Newgate Sollicitors,* 1728, p.6.
141. A. Babbington, *A House in Bow Street,* 2nd edn., 1999, p.51.
142. Anon, *Directions for Prosecuting Thieves Without the Help of those False Guides, The Newgate Sollicitors,* 1728, pp.3-8.

Grand Juries would decide whether there was a case to answer, one that warranted going before the trial or petty jury (also known as the "jury of life and death"). In theory, a Grand Jury could indict on its own initiative, without complaint from a private individual, having become aware of a transgression. This had been an important part of its work during the medieval period, but had declined rapidly in significance in the early modern era. Nevertheless, there were occasional instances of it happening during the eighteenth century. For example, in 1723, the Middlesex Grand Jury presented the publisher of the third edition of Bernard Mandeville's *Fable of the Bees* for prosecution in the Court of King's Bench, on the grounds that the tract was likely to: "...run down Religion and Virtue as prejudicial to Society".[143] However, such cases were statistically insignificant; the eighteenth-century Grand Jury was overwhelmingly a scrutinising body, considering bills of indictment that had been brought before it by members of the general public.

The Grand Jury could not sit with less than 13 men and, in London, normally numbered 17 jurors. This was fewer than was usually found in the provinces, where as many as 23 men was common. An uneven number was favoured because it decided by a simple majority, albeit one that had to be made up of at least 12 jurors (i.e. in a jury of 13, 12 men had to find a "true bill", while in one of 23, the same number could reach that conclusion). In the provinces, there was usually a clear social distinction between the Assizes Grand Jury, which was often gentry and JP dominated, and the trial jury, which was typically drawn from the "middling" orders.[144] In London, however, this distinction was very much more modest. The same men often served on both tribunals, though there was a tendency for the latter body to number slightly more prosperous individuals amongst its members than the former.[145]

Unlike the provincial Assizes, the Old Bailey did not have its own Grand Jury. There was a single Grand Jury for all indictments, great or small, from Middlesex, and another for all those from the City (as well as less pressured bodies for Westminster and the Tower); both of these met at their

143. W. A. Speck, "Bernard Mandeville and the Middlesex Grand Jury", 1978, pp.362-363.
144. C. Fiennes, *Through England on a Side Saddle in the Time of William and Mary*, 1888, p.277.
145. J. S. Cockburn and T. A. Green (Eds.), *Twelve Good Men and True*, 1985, p.235.

jurisdictions' respective Quarter Sessions. The same Grand Juries that determined whether there was a case to answer for the misdemeanours and very minor felonies normally tried at the inferior sessions would also decide whether there was a case to answer for the more serious matters that would be sent to the Old Bailey.

It was the duty of the respective clerks of the peace for the various Metropolitan Quarter Sessions to ensure that indictments approved by Grand Juries for Old Bailey matters were safely transmitted to that court.[146] Thus, in Middlesex, the Grand Jury sat at Hick's Hall and, if dealing with an indictment that had to be heard at the higher forum, sent their decision on to the Old Bailey together with its attendant documents. As a result, in 1785, after the Grand Jury found Mary Doran's bills of indictment to be "true bills", the: "…indictment for the felony was transmitted as usual, from Hick's Hall to the Old Bailey, to be tried".[147] In the City, the Grand Jury sat at the Guildhall, also sending its decisions on to the Bailey. However, this forum (unlike its equivalent for Middlesex) would often adjourn its work after the Old Bailey Sessions started, and physically move to the higher forum, to continue considering bills of indictment from the Square Mile within the same building as the Old Bailey court.

The normal bifurcation of location between trial and Grand Jury venue could result in inconvenience for prosecutors, as they might have to attend two different forums, which were some distance apart, to have their cases processed and determined. By contrast, at provincial Assizes, they could usually walk a few yards from the closed room in which the Grand Jury sat to the courtroom, where any *billa verra* or (after 1733) "true bill" would then be tried.

In theory, the Grand Jury's duty was: "To screen innocence from the blush and hazard of public trial, and, to deliver real guilt over to it".[148] As a result, applications were made privately, to prevent malicious but embarrassing prosecutions — in a system where there was enormous scope for such actions — from being aired in public. In the 1660s, the "normal" provision

146. Anon, *The Crown Court Circuit Companion*, 8th edn., 1811, p.14.
147. *The King v Mary Doran* (1790) 1 Leach 538.
148. Anon, *The Coroner's Guide: or, the Office and Duty of a Coroner*, 2nd edn., 1756, p.xix.

for the Middlesex Grand Jury, when sitting at Hick's Hall, had been for it to be secreted in a special room by themselves with a: "...door-keeper, and witnesses to call and examine them, as they themselves pleased".[149] Little had changed a century later.

Applications were almost invariably made *ex parte*, that is, in the absence of representations by, or evidence from, the defendant. However, there was some doubt about whether this reflected substantive law or was merely normal practice. Several observers complained that it was inherently unsatisfactory that Grand Jurors could only hear prosecution evidence which might, on closer examination, prove to be perjured.[150] In quite exceptional circumstances, usually involving people of note, the Grand Jury does appear to have received defence testimony. For example, in 1723, a Mr. Edmondson, a former director of the then liquidated South Sea Company, who had been accused of concealing his assets from creditors (a potentially capital offence), escaped trial when the Grand Jury at the Old Bailey returned the bill of indictment "ignoramus", after his mother appeared before them: "... swearing positively that the money in question was hers".[151]

The precise rules as to what evidence could be adduced before a Grand Jury were also uncertain for much of the century, as became apparent when Dr. Dodd was prosecuted for fraud in 1777. To bolster what appeared to be a somewhat weak case, the decision was taken to offer Lewis Robinson, the cleric's co-accused, the chance to be a Crown witness against Dodd, *after* he had been committed to Newgate to await trial. Robinson was then called to give oral evidence to the Middlesex Grand Jury. There was some doubt as to whether this was legally permissible, although, ultimately, the 12 Westminster judges were to conclude that the court was right to allow it. At trial, prosecuting counsel observed that it was the:

> ...first time he ever recollected an enquiry to be seriously made of the evidence requisite and competent to be produced before a Grand Jury.

149. Anon, *The cry of the innocent & oppressed for justice*, 1664, p.4.
150. W. Hutton, *A Dissertation on Juries; With a Description of the Hundred Court*, 1784, p.27.
151. *British Journal*, 31 August 1723.

Another prosecution barrister contended that a Grand Jury was obliged to receive all evidence that was offered.[152]

Oral evidence was an essential part of the Grand Jury's deliberations, particularly where it came from the prosecutor/complainant or other key witnesses. Indeed, Metropolitan prosecutors in felony cases were urged to take their most material witnesses to the Grand Jury, whether at the Guildhall or Hick's Hall, after which: "…you relate upon Oath the Circumstances, and what reason you have to charge the Prisoner".[153] Typically, in 1785, when Thomas Wilkinson was accused of assaulting Richard Harrow, the City Grand Jury, on finding a "true bill", endorsed the slim document accordingly on its back. Next to this, it was noted that "Richard Harrow [was] sworn", i.e. had given testimony to them.[154]

In the 1660s, it was a major criticism of the Middlesex Justices that they had tried to force the Grand Jury at Hicks Hall to find "true bills" against Quakers accused of holding illegal meetings, purely on the basis of written accounts and "without witnesses to testifie the fact". Although the justices of the peace claimed that their written records were sufficient for this purpose, they had, eventually, been forced to allow several live witnesses to give evidence.[155] It seems that Grand Jurors for the Old Bailey did not normally receive witness depositions until 1838.[156]

This reliance on oral testimony meant that attempts to deter witnesses from giving evidence were as likely to occur before the Grand Jury hearing as they were prior to trial. Indeed, in some situations, it might be done more easily at this stage of proceedings. Thus, when the notorious Mary Young ("Jenny Diver") was tried in 1738, under an alibi, one of the chief prosecution witnesses, the man who had arrested her, noted that: "Her Janizaries have been with me since she was taken up, and offer'd me Money to keep out of the Way, that the Thing might be dropp'd before the Grand Jury".[157] As

152. W. Dodd, *Authentic Memoirs of the Life of William Dodd, LL.D. who was executed at Tyburn, on Friday, 27 June 1777*, 3rd edn., 1777, pp.21-22.

153. Anon, *Directions for Prosecuting Thieves Without the Help of those False Guides, The Newgate Solicitors*, 1728, p.7.

154. CLA/047/CJ/03/002, Wood Street Compter Calendar.

155. Anon, *The cry of the innocent & oppressed for justice*, 1664, p.4.

156. D. Bentley, *English Criminal Justice in the Nineteenth Century*, 1998, p.133.

157. OBSP, Trial of Jane Webb, 12 April 1738.

the Grand Jury was concerned only to establish a *prima facie* case, it would normally confine itself to hearing a selection of prosecution witnesses, unless the case appeared weak. Towards the end of the period, this sometimes led to criticism that it was "second guessing" the decision of the committing magistrate, who had normally seen all of the available evidence, if it decided to discharge a matter.

Cases were considered very rapidly, a process that became more marked as the century advanced and legal business increased. By the 1820s, the Middlesex Grand Jury could scrutinise 600 bills of indictment in only six days.[158] Perhaps unsurprisingly, it seems that the pressure of such hearings sometimes led to a lack of thoroughness. For example, at the September Sessions in 1790, the Middlesex Grand Jury, sitting at Hick's Hall, found two alternative indictments against Mary Doran for arson. One was a felony and the other a misdemeanour. However, at the Old Bailey, counsel for the Crown, perusing the depositions taken before the examining magistrate swiftly appreciated that there was not sufficient evidence to sustain the felony charge, and declined to prosecute it.[159]

Although jurors merely had to decide whether there was sufficient cause to call upon a party to answer the allegation made against him, there was, historically, considerable dispute as to the precise level of persuasion that was required before this occurred. This debate had attained political connotations and lingered into the eighteenth century. Some late-seventeenth century commentators had thought it important to increase the number of indictments going for trial, and emphasized that the Grand Jury was merely an accusing, not a convicting, body. By contrast, others stressed the need to prevent people from facing the risk and unpleasantness of a public criminal trial on vague or even fabricated grounds. They complained that a dangerous opinion had gained ground to the effect that Grand Juries might find bills of indictment "upon slight or probable evidence". Instead, they should have been protecting innocent people and their reputations from false accusations by insisting on a very firm *prima facie* case.[160]

---

158. P. Laurie, *An Inquiry into the Use and Abuse of Grand Juries*, 1832, pp.13-14.
159. *The King v Mary Doran* (1790) 1 Leach 538.
160. J. Oliphant, *The Case of Mr James Oliphant, Surgeon,* 1768, pp.60-61.

Even so, it was generally agreed that Grand Jurors were not required to "rest satisfied merely with remote probabilities" of conviction before committing a matter for trial. At the very least, it was their duty to ensure that the evidence was "fully to the point" in the case under consideration; that is, that the essential elements of any offence were made out and that the prosecution witnesses had not colluded.[161] Similarly, William Blackstone thought that to avoid oppressive prosecutions a grand jury ought to be: "...thoroughly persuaded of the truth of an indictment, so far as their evidence goes".[162]

Despite the limitations placed on their enquiries, a significant proportion of bills of indictment were rejected by Grand Juries throughout the eighteenth century. However, the number of these gradually declined, so that, by the middle of the era, it seems that (nationally) 85-90 per cent of felony indictments were being returned as "true bills".[163] The general decline in findings of "ignoramus/no true bill" is partly explained by the manner in which the examining justice's committal proceedings became more thorough during this period, and magistrates became increasingly willing to throw out weak cases, without allowing them to enter the system.

Nevertheless, the habitual thief Charlotte Walker's good fortune in front of this body indicates that the process was certainly not a formality, even late in the century, and especially in the Metropolitan area. Walker was discharged by the Middlesex Grand Jury on at least a dozen occasions, and probably considerably more. She was not alone. During the 1780s, an average of eight women accused of felony, many of them prostitutes, were discharged before each Old Bailey sessions. In some, a complainant simply did not appear, perhaps having reached an accommodation with the defendant, or decided that the matter was too embarrassing to pursue. In others, it seems that the Grand Jury decided that the victim was obviously inebriated during the incident, and blaming whoever came most readily to hand.[164]

161. Anon (By a Friend to the Constitution), *Observations on the Duty and Power of Juries, as established by the Laws of England*, 3rd edn., 1796, p.22 and 5th edn., 1800, p.30.

162. W. Blackstone, *Commentaries on the Laws of England*, 1765-9, vol. 4, p.300.

163. T. A. Green, *Verdict According to Conscience*, 1985, p.272.

164. M. Clayton, "The Life and Crimes of Charlotte Walker, Prostitute and Pickpocket", 2008, pp.4-9.

Female suspects were not the only people to experience success at this stage of proceedings. In 1764, after the notorious Dick Swift was sentenced to transportation for receiving stolen goods, it was noted that the Newgate Record Books indicated that he had been in custody in that prison on 18 occasions, over the previous 25 years, yet had only been tried on 13 times, suggesting that five cases had not reached or survived a Grand Jury hearing.[165] As late as the 1820s, it seems that Metropolitan Grand Juries threw out about 10 per cent of the cases that came before them, something that sometimes led to them being termed "The Hope of London Thieves".[166]

If the Grand Jury returned a finding of "ignoramus" or "no true bill" there was, in theory, nothing to prevent the application being renewed on a future occasion, particularly if fresh evidence became available. The finding did not constitute an acquittal, anymore than a modern magistrate's refusal to commit a matter for trial to the Crown Court.[167] Although this was very rare in practice, after the Grand Jury "threw out" the bill of indictment against Elizabeth Canning at the April Sessions in 1753, it was successfully renewed at the following sessions held in June of the same year.[168]

Production from Prison

All defendants, who were not on bail, being tried at the Old Bailey during the eighteenth century, whether they were from the City or Middlesex, would have to be produced from Newgate Prison for their hearings. In the 1660s, senior judges had ordered that felons awaiting trial should always go to that gaol, and not to the New Prison: "It being found by Experience that they are often set at Liberty there without Tryal".[169] In 1777, considerable legal problems were caused when the notorious Dr. Dodd was left in

165. *London Chronicle*, 24 May 1764.
166. D. Bentley, *English Criminal Justice in the Nineteenth Century*, 1998, p.132.
167. W. Blackstone, *Commentaries on the Laws of England*, 1765-9, vol. iv, p.302.
168. M. Squires, *The Controverted Hard Case: or Mary Squires's Magazine of Facts Re-Examin'd*, 1753, p.3.
169. Sir J. Kelyng, *A Report of Divers Cases In Pleas of the Crown, Adjudged and Determined; In the Reign of the late King Charles II*, 2nd edn., 1734, pp.1-2.

Wood Street Compter, as a special indulgence, until the start of the sessions at which he was tried for forgery.

However, after their initial justices' examinations, a few of those from the City, and rather more of those from the neighbouring county, were held in other prisons, such as the two compters (the sheriff's prisons in the City), the Clerkenwell House of Correction or the Tothill Fields Bridewell (in Middlesex), pending their trials coming on. This was largely for reasons of space. Newgate had limited accommodation. However, the financial opportunities provided by holding suspected felons were also to blame. The keeper of the Clerkenwell Gaol even purchased a large set of fetters and actively petitioned for the right to hold felons alongside his traditional short-term inmates.[170] Some contemporary observers felt that the use of bridewells and houses of correction for this purpose was very unsatisfactory, as they were not designed to provide a high level of security; felons held in them pending trial regularly threatened to escape.[171]

As a result of the requirement that all defendants be produced from Newgate, a day or two before the Old Bailey Sessions began, a considerable number of prisoners would have to be moved across the Metropolis from outlying gaols. For example, in January 1738, it was noted that 30 defendants were taken from the: "...several Gaols in the county of Middlesex and Liberty of Westminster, to Newgate, in order to take their Trials the next Sessions at the Old Baily".[172] This also meant that, immediately before the sessions started, Newgate was often very overcrowded.

The Old Bailey Sessions

The Old Bailey sessions were somewhat different to their provincial counterparts, the Assizes, though conducted under the same commission of gaol delivery. Because they followed immediately after the City and Middlesex Quarter Sessions, and determined indictments drawn up in these lower

170. J. Ilive, *Reasons offered for the Reformation of the House of Correction in Clerkenwell*, 1757, p.32.

171. J. Ilive, *A scheme for the employment of all persons sent as disorderly to the house of correction in Clerkenwell*, 1759, p.46.

172. *Old Common Sense: Or, the Englishman's Journal*, 7 January 1738.

courts, they necessarily met eight times a year (four times more frequently than the bi-annual Assizes).[173] This was also vital for practical reasons, as they had to meet the heavy pressure of criminal business found in the capital. Indeed, it was periodically urged that Metropolitan criminal courts be in permanent session, so that prisoners were not held on remand for long periods prior to trial, and so exposed to the numerous corrupting factors found in gaol.[174] In 1792, for example, it was unsuccessfully proposed in Parliament that the Old Bailey's sittings be increased significantly, with the extra sessions being judged by temporarily appointed barristers of 20 years' standing (though this also prompted concern that the reputation of the court's judiciary would be undermined by such part-timers). Nevertheless, the frequency of sittings at the Old Bailey, when compared to provincial Assizes, meant that most witnesses at that court normally only had to remember back an average of 25 days, when giving evidence, rather than the three months that was normal outside London. By 1800, each Old Bailey sessions would last for four or five days, compared to about three at the start of the century.

Although the Old Bailey was a joint court, serving both the City of London and the county of Middlesex, its two jurisdictions were kept quite distinct, each having its own clerical staff and records, and returning separate juries to conduct the trials emanating from each location. Inevitably, this meant that as the population of the City declined relative to that of the rest of the Metropolis, so did its share of the court's trials. Indeed, pressure of work meant that an extra jury had to be added for Middlesex, long before it became necessary for the City, to cater for the county's increased number of criminal defendants. Even so, there were fewer than 500 trials each year at the Old Bailey for most of the first two thirds of the century. Thereafter, numbers increased, slowly and unevenly, reaching 1,011 in 1784.[175] Throughout the century (and until 1824), all had to share a single courtroom.[176]

Despite covering two (main) jurisdictions, the Old Bailey was dominated by officials from the City, which paid for its upkeep and provided the court's recorder, its most important permanent judicial figure. Additionally,

173. A. Babbington, *A House in Bow Street*, 2nd edn., 1999, p.51.
174. *The Times*, 6 October 1789, p.3.
175. T. P. Gallanis, "The Mystery Of Old Bailey Counsel", 2000, pp.160-164.
176. D. Bentley, *English Criminal Justice in the Nineteenth Century*, 1998, p.55.

the City's common serjeant, the legal adviser to the Court of Common Council, was, *ex officio*, one of the court's judges. However, in strict order of precedence, the Lord Mayor was the Chief Judge of the Old Bailey Court; he had even held the power to reprieve capital convicts during the Interregnum.[177] In practice, a lack of legal training meant that he would frequently sit next to a professional judge on the bench, leaving the trained lawyer to preside over the trial, simple cases apart.

Although the recorder, sheriff and (occasionally) the Lord Mayor conducted many of the Old Bailey trials, in others, the presiding judge would be one of the 12 senior judges who normally sat at the Westminster courts, whether King's Bench, Common Pleas, or Exchequer, to hear important civil, and some criminal, matters (King's Bench was the only one to have a criminal jurisdiction). Several (usually two) of these were seconded on a very temporary basis, often for only a couple of days, to the Old Bailey, just as Westminster judges conducted the bi-annual Assizes while on circuit in the provinces. Typically, they might preside over the most serious or difficult trials. To facilitate this, the sessions (like provincial Assizes) were arranged so that they did not normally clash with the law terms kept by the Westminster courts.

Although there would often be several judges on the "collegiate" bench that was usually found at the Old Bailey, unlike the Crown Side of Assizes (which usually had just a single judge), only one of them would actively preside over a trial, though he could, if necessary, consult his colleagues. As a result, one contemporary observer, after listing the names of several Westminster judges, the Recorder of London and the Lord Mayor as being present at Charles Bradbury's trial for sodomy, could asterisk one name as: "The judge who tried the prisoner".[178] This judge would normally (though not invariably) be referred to in the reports as the "court" when it came to reporting questions from the bench, whereas questions or submissions on the law from any other judge present would normally identify him by name.[179]

177. J. Howel, *Londinopolis*, 1657, p.392.

178. Anon, *The Tryal of Charles Bradbury, for the Detestable Crime of Sodomy*, 1755, p.3.

179. See, for example, questions from Mr. Justice Gould and Mr. Baron Perryn in a case over which Mr. Justice Buller presided: OBSP, Trial of Thomas Turner, 25 February 1784.

A set number of aldermen were also supposed to sit on the bench during the Old Bailey Sessions, though their position was even more ornamental than it was at the Guildhall Sessions, which might explain periodic concern about their failure to attend in adequate numbers.[180] The Middlesex JPs, although they were the legal representatives of the adjacent county, had very much a secondary role in proceedings. The City, concerned about their sometimes lowly social provenance, long refused even to allow them to sit flanking judges on the bench, unlike their own aldermen, although it permitted them to attend court as part of the gaol delivery commission.[181]

There was nothing to prevent the Old Bailey from trying misdemeanours. However, in practice, only a small number of the more serious forms of these lesser offences, such as crimes like perjury, were normally heard at that forum, and these were often heard towards the end of proceedings and linked to cases that had earlier been determined at the same court. For example, they might include prosecutions for the misdemeanour of attempted sodomy or rape, where an apparent lack of penetration had produced an acquittal in an otherwise strong case at an earlier trial for the substantive felony, or for perjury committed at an Old Bailey hearing. Nevertheless, pressure of time precluded trying too many offences that could properly be heard at Quarter Sessions.

Trial Listing

All prosecutors were supposed to attend court, with their witnesses, at the start of each sessions and, until their cases were called on for trial, at the beginning of each subsequent day's proceedings. The inevitable delays that this entailed, with some witnesses waiting several days to testify, occasioned many problems. For example, one key witness in the Elizabeth Canning case in 1753 explained his failure to give evidence at the first trial by saying that he had, initially, been in court but, as butler of the Goldsmiths Company, he was in charge of a great deal of plate that had required his attendance

180. *Morning Chronicle and London Advertiser*, 16 October 1775.
181. J. M. Beattie, *Policing and Punishment in London, 1660–1750*, 2001, pp.13–14.

elsewhere before the case came on.[182] The inconvenience that this occasioned meant that there were regular calls that trials be: "…fix'd to respective days, that prosecutors may not lose so much time".[183]

Additionally, in the confusion that often surrounded the Old Bailey court, with its pressured caseload, rather *ad hoc* listing, swift hearings and ability to produce prisoners from the adjacent prison with relatively little notice, prosecution witnesses would sometimes fail to be in court without being entirely at fault. For example, in 1755, John Moore, from St Martin-in-the-Fields, accused Joseph Smith of stealing five two-shilling corkscrews. He attended Hick's Hall to secure a bill of indictment from that court's Grand Jury and then, as advised by that forum, attended the Old Bailey the following morning at 10 am. However, on that day, an administrative error meant that the defendant's name was not listed for trial. Moore was told to come back the following morning. Assuming that the court's hours of business would not alter much, he attended at 9.45 am, only to find that Smith had been called on for trial some time earlier, but that: "…the prosecutor not appearing, he was acquitted". Moore also discovered that his recognisance had been forfeited for his failure to attend at the appropriate time.[184] Fortunately, after swearing a deposition to this effect at the Old Bailey, and stressing that he had always intended to prosecute the matter, and had simply been ignorant of the correct time to appear on the second day of the sessions, the court discharged his recognisance.[185] (Smith, of course, was covered by the doctrine of *autrefois acquit*, and so could not be re-tried for the theft).

On another occasion, in about 1720, Jonathan Wild used the uncertainty of Old Bailey listing to his own advantage when he wanted one of his highwayman associates to escape. He offered to "manage the prosecution" on behalf of the highwayman's victims who, knowing of his skill in such matters, were: "…glad to have part of the trouble taken off their hands". At his suggestion, they met up at a public house near the Old Bailey the following day, when the matter was due to be heard. However, Wild told them that

182. M. Madan, *Thoughts On Executive Justice*, 2nd edn., 1785, p.7.

183. A. Moreton, *Second Thoughts are best: or, a Further Improvement of a Late Scheme to Prevent Street Robberies*, 1729, p.24.

184. OBSP, Trial of Joseph Smith, 5 December 1755.

185. MJ/SP/1755/12/010.

the courthouse was packed, and advised them to stay in the tavern until the matter was called for trial, which, he claimed, was due at about 3 pm. The gentlemen became tipsy, with Wild's assistance, and lost track of the time. When they finally attended the Bailey to investigate what had happened to their case, it was to find that the: "...court was broke up, and the two highwaymen discharg'd, because no evidence appear'd against them".[186]

It was not just prosecutors who were prejudiced. Ann Connelly, an Old Bailey defendant, complained at her trial that she had had friends "ready" at court to testify on her behalf for four or five days, but that they had gone by the time her trial was called on, late in the sessions.[187] Similarly, in 1782, two women accused of murder at the Old Bailey claimed that defence witnesses would have been present but for their being called on suddenly: "I expected people here, I was told my trial would not come on till about two o'clock, we were told so".[188]

Arraignment and Plea

Once the defendant or "prisoner" had been brought into court he would be arraigned. He was usually ordered to hold up his hand when his name was called out, so that he could be identified, though, in practice, he sometimes merely acknowledged his presence verbally. A court officer would then read out the indictment in English (even prior to 1733), and the defendant would enter a plea of "guilty" or "not guilty". The indictment could be a long and complicated document, and some observers feared that this meant that it was often read in a "very indistinct manner", making it difficult to spot legal flaws, even though these were potentially fatal to prosecutions.[189]

During this part of the proceedings, any shackles with which the defendant was secured would normally be removed. The widespread practice of fettering prisoners while they were in the dock had been ended by Sir John Holt at the start of the period, unless security considerations, such as the

186. Anon, *The History of the Lives and Actions of Jonathan Wild, Thief-Taker*, 1725, pp.25-26.

187. OBSP, Trial of Ann Connelly, 15 October 1740.

188. OBSP, Trial of Januarye Sweatman and Mary Humphries, 20 February 1782.

189. *World and Fashionable Advertiser*, 1 February 1787.

presence of an unruly prisoner, meant that the gaoler was forced to have: "... recourse to them by the actual necessity of safe custody".[190] A German visitor in the early years of the century was alarmed to find that prisoners were not shackled, though the presence of six pike-men provided some security.[191]

Assuming that he pleaded "not guilty", the clerk of the arraigns would then ask the defendant how he would be tried, to which the customary answer was: "By God and my Country". If an accused person failed to enter a plea, a jury of 12 men would have to determine whether he was "mute of malice", that is deliberately remaining silent, or was simply unable to speak as a result of infirmity. In the latter case, a "not guilty" plea would be entered on his behalf. In the former situation, in a felony case, a refusal to plead would (theoretically) result in the imposition of the *peine forte et dure* until 1772, when it was abolished by statute, and remaining mute of malice was made tantamount to pleading guilty. In treason and misdemeanour cases a refusal to plead was deemed to be the equivalent of a guilty plea throughout the eighteenth century.

The *Peine Forte et Dure*

The *peine,* which had its origins in the medieval period, entailed being gradually pressed to death under a board holding progressively larger weights, unless and until a plea (either way) was forthcoming, which could then be accepted with permission of the court.[192] It was ordered on a handful of occasions at the Old Bailey in the late seventeenth century and, very occasionally, even applied. More commonly, the threat of such punishment was enough to persuade the defendant to enter a plea. By the early 1700s, the courts were increasingly reluctant to resort to this draconian provision, which was starting to offend the sensitivities of the era. It does not appear to have been employed at all in the 30 years after 1742, the last confirmed

190. W. Eden, *Principles of Penal Law*, London, 1781, p.168.

191. H. Quarrell and M. More (Trans and Eds.), *London in 1710 From the Travels of Zacharias Conrad Von Offenbach*, 1934, p.124.

192. W. Blackstone, *Commentaries on the Laws of England,* 1765-9, vol. 4, p.320. See also J. H. Baker, "Criminal Justice at Newgate 1616-1627", 1973, p.316.

case apparently occurring at the Cambridge Assizes of that year. Nevertheless, as late as 1770, Mr. Baron Smythe, the presiding judge at the Kingston Assizes, used the threat of its imposition to persuade an initially recalcitrant George Allen to enter a plea. He claimed that during his own legal career he had been aware of it being used on two occasions, but in both of them the men involved had been unable to tolerate the growing pressure of the weights on their bodies and, after a short time, had changed their minds and asked to enter a plea.[193]

Where it was likely to be ordered during the early decades of the eighteenth century, the public executioner was normally called in first to bind the defendant's thumbs with whipcord, to see if this might force them to enter a plea without requiring recourse to the full procedure. This worked in 1695, with the highwayman Luke Page, who, after he refused to plead, had his thumbs: "...tyed very hard together with a cord, to make him sensible of pain". Chastened by this, Page pleaded "not guilty".[194] Even if this initial procedure was not effective, the mere sight of the board and weights in the Newgate Press Room might force a change of heart, as was the case with the highwayman Thomas Phillips in 1721. Nevertheless, Phillips's colleague, William Spigget, was made of sterner stuff, and only changed his mind 30 minutes into the procedure, after having 400lb placed on his chest. Both men were subsequently convicted and executed.[195] In the same year, Nathaniel Hawes managed only 250 pounds, for seven minutes, before asking (and being allowed) to enter a plea. The bruises he received from this experience were so severe that he was hardly able to perform his religious devotions prior to execution, following conviction at trial.[196]

Traditionally, the main reason for refusing to enter a plea, and accepting such a painful death, was that the accused person, though dead, was not formally *convicted* of a felony. This was important as, theoretically, all the property of a felon was forfeit to the Crown until 1814 (Thereafter, only

---

193. Anon, *An authentic Account of the Trials, Behaviour, and Dying declaration, of the Five Malefactors, Who were executed at Kennington-Common, on Monday the 23rd April, 1770*, 1770, p.5.
194. OBSP, Trial of Luke Page, 14 October 1695.
195. A. McKenzie, "'This Death Some Strong and Stout Hearted Man Doth Choose'", 2005, pp.279-280.
196. A. L. Hayward, *Lives Of The Most Remarkable Criminals*, 1927, p.62.

those guilty of murder, treason, or petty treason stood to lose real estate, though forfeiture of goods and chattels remained the law until 1870). An accusation that someone had committed such a crime was not enough. A conviction was a prerequisite for confiscation, and this could only occur if there was a plea and trial.

Nevertheless, several men who underwent the *peine* were of very modest wealth, and may well have done so for other reasons, especially as it seems that by the early eighteenth-century forfeiture was only being erratically enforced. The jury that found a felon guilty would be asked whether he had any goods or chattels, but would often return a negative answer, as a matter of course: "Juries agree to answer, none that they know of; nor do they take care to know of any".[197] This comment is slightly misleading. sheriffs, bailiffs, and constables often collected offenders' possessions, regardless of the jurors' response to this question, and efforts were made to enforce the rule almost up to abolition in 1870. Nevertheless, it seems that the great majority of felons forfeited little or nothing after conviction. For example, the Crown's agents appear not to have sought to profit from the sizeable estate left by Lord Ferrers after his execution for murder in 1760. Those accused of felony could, in any event, arrange their affairs so that property was conveyed to relatives prior to conviction (Ferrers distributed £4,500 to his illegitimate children).[198] Where forfeiture did occur, receipts suggest that many individuals lost only what was on their person (such as a watch or penknife), though in a few cases constables visited a convict's lodgings to gather other items.[199] It is possible that some defendants viewed the *peine* as preferable to the disgrace of a felony conviction, even where they thought that forfeiture was not a major risk. Others may have wished to avoid the humiliation of a public trial and execution.

197. A. Moreton, *Second Thoughts are best: or, a Further Improvement of a Late Scheme to Prevent Street Robberies*, 1729, p.12.

198. K. J. Kesselring, "Felony Forfeiture in England, *c.* 1170-1870", 2009, p.218.

199. K. J. Kesselring, "Felons' Effects and the Effects of Felony in Nineteenth-Century England", 2010, p.123.

Rarity of Guilty Pleas

The vast majority of felony defendants pleaded "not guilty". Judges were often reluctant to accept guilty pleas, especially if the offence was unclergyable, even though they would have speeded up highly pressured hearings. (By contrast, they were relatively common for misdemeanours). Some judges actively discouraged them. For example, when the child-killer, Mary Price, pleaded guilty in 1718, the court was "surprised" at her decision and reminded her that if she pleaded "not guilty" the crime might not be proved.[200] If there was any doubt about a defendant's understanding of his plea, the matter might be set back so that he could reconsider. In 1730, when Peter Block tried to plead guilty to the murder of his infant daughter at the Old Bailey, the court: "...did not think fit to take his plea, supposing him to be lunatick". The following day, he pleaded "not guilty" and was tried and acquitted.[201]

There were several reasons for this judicial nervousness over guilty pleas. If the accused person testified, they might reveal information that would encourage a judicial recommendation for reprieve, or even pious perjury on the part of the jury. Additionally, there was always the possibility that a prosecutor would not appear to give evidence, or that an accused person, devoid of legal advice (as so many were), did not appreciate the technical legal prerequisites that were necessary for their offence to be made out or that a potential line of defence was open to them.

As a result, little more than one per cent of all cases tried at the Old Bailey during the eighteenth century produced pleas of guilty. Interestingly, and perhaps surprisingly, they were slightly less, rather than more, common in the second half of the century than they had been during its first fifty years. Where such pleas were forthcoming, they were often tendered in non-capital cases, and related to counts that were: "...within the benefit of Clergy, a knack of Law which the Newgate-students are generally well vers'd in".[202]

However, many of those accused of felony, facing strong prosecution cases, made only the most perfunctory defences after pleading "not guilty". For

200. OBSP, Trial of Mary Price, 9 July 1718.
201. *Fog's Weekly Journal*, 4 July 1730.
202. OBSP, Trial of two unnamed defendants for grand larceny, 11 October 1676.

example, Joseph Hughes, accused of stealing a 20lb lead pipe by wrenching it from a building in Stepney, put up almost no defence at all to the allegations against him, telling the court: "I have no witnesses, nor anything to say".[203] Similarly, when Robert Adams was accused of theft in 1719, he did not deny the matter at trial, despite his "not guilty" plea. Robert Lockey went even further, when accused of shoplifting in 1721: "His confession was read in court and he also owned it on his Tryal".[204] Unsurprisingly, convictions swiftly ensued in these situations.

Witnesses

Witnesses could be subpoenaed for both the prosecution and defence. In 1770, for example, Robert Lee appeared as a defence witness on behalf of Mathew Martin and noted that he had been: "...served with a subpoena to come here".[205] However, as with so many other legal procedures, this would normally require the payment of a fee. This could be beyond the means of very poor litigants, and the number of witnesses who were brought to court by this mechanism was, proportionately, extremely small. For example, when the mother of a child who had been raped tried to secure the attendance of the surgeon who had physically examined her daughter, she noted that he: "...would not come to give evidence without I subpoena'd him, and it was not in my power to subpoena him. I am a very poor woman".[206]

As in the modern era, it was customary for the victim/complainant to give his evidence first, being followed by any other witnesses that could support the prosecution case. Where a solicitor or attorney had become involved in the prosecution process, the lawyer might arrange a pre-trial conference, calling all of the potential Crown witnesses together and even (perhaps unethically) "coaching" them as to their evidence, directing: "...who shall speak first, and how they shall deliver themselves to the judge and jury".[207]

203. OBSP, Trial of Joseph Hughes. 15 October 1740.
204. OBSP, Trial of Robert Lockey, 30 August 1721.
205. OBSP, Trial of Matthew Martin, 21 February 1770.
206. OBSP, Trial of Charles Earle, 5 December 1770.
207. Anon, *Directions for Prosecuting Thieves Without the Help of those False Guides, The Newgate*

Unlike modern criminal practice, it was normal for witnesses to wait in court until called upon to give evidence, if only for reasons of convenience, in what was a hurried process. However, both prosecutor and defendant could ask that the opposing side's witnesses testify without other witnesses being present. This would mean that they could not tailor their own evidence to fit that already given. Such applications were normally acceded to in the eighteenth century, and witnesses would be required to wait outside court until the time came for them to testify. It seems that this had not always happened during the seventeenth century. For example, while awaiting execution at Tyburn in 1684, Edward Jackson complained that if the: "...witnesses against him might have been examined apart, they would have been intrapped".

At the Old Bailey, over 700 such applications are recorded during the course of the eighteenth century (there were probably considerably more), the vast majority being made by defendants. However, although found throughout the century, over half were made in the final two decades of the era, something that probably reflects the increase in defence counsel during this period. In case after case during the 1790s, it was recorded that: "The witnesses were examined apart, at the request of the prisoner". This was not invariably beneficial. When John Hawkins was tried for robbery, and successfully made such a request, the prosecution witnesses noted that it denied him an opportunity to explain why their evidence concurred in every detail. Had they been allowed to stay in the court: "...Hawkins might afterwards have well urged that it was no wonder there was such a chain in our evidence, when we had heard what one another said".[208]

Brevity of Trials

The eighteenth-century criminal trial was very short. During the early 1700s, up to 20 cases might be heard at the Old Bailey in the course of a typical

---

Sollicitors, 1728, p.3.

208. R. Wilson, *A Full and Impartial Account of all the Robberies Committed by John Hawkins*, 3rd edn., 1722, p.25.

day, and considerably over a dozen was normal. As a result, hearings rarely lasted much over half an hour, and sometimes took less than 15 minutes, with 30 minutes, perhaps, being the average. Such brevity remained common throughout the century, and beyond. As late as December 1838, a newspaper criticised the common serjeant for presiding over the trial of a sixteen-year-old for theft that had, apparently, lasted only six minutes.[209]

However, although the power to adjourn a normal felony trial overnight was only recognised in 1794, cases that were both very serious and legally complicated, or which involved important people, might last several hours. For example, in 1697, the murder trial of the French woman Margaret Martell, which involved telling circumstantial evidence that she sought to explain away, lasted four hours.[210] That of the poet Richard Savage, in 1727, lasted eight hours. It should also be remembered that the reluctance of judges to accept guilty pleas meant that the average trial length was brought down by cases in which there was little real challenge to the prosecution evidence. Vigorously challenged cases would last longer than the average might suggest.

Ironically, trials on indictment at Metropolitan Quarter Sessions (normally for misdemeanours) tended to be less pressured, and so last significantly longer, even though they usually involved very much less serious matters. For example, in 1738, Catherine Buckle's hearing at Hick's Hall, for defrauding a maid by pretending to be a fortune-teller, lasted fully three hours.[211] Quite exceptionally, even for these forums, the trial of Rhynwick Williams (the "London Monster") for assault, prosecuted by four distinguished barristers, lasted sixteen hours, with the jury returning a guilty verdict at 2.30 am.[212]

Despite the speed of individual proceedings at the Old Bailey, a combination of pressure of work and the limited numbers of sitting days available meant that the court could still be required to sit for very long hours, starting relatively early in the morning and going on extremely late into the evening. For example, even in 1800, sitting hours were normally 9 am until 9 pm or even later.[213] As a result, on one occasion in 1784, the barrister William

209. *The Times*, 25 December 1838.

210. OBSP, Trial of Margaret Martell, 7 July 1697.

211. *Old Common Sense: Or, the Englishman's Journal*, 8 July 1738.

212. *The Times*, 15 December 1790.

213. D. Bentley, *English Criminal Justice in the Nineteenth Century*, 1998, p.55.

Garrow, when prosecuting a woman for pickpocketing, felt compelled to open his case by reassuring the jury that he would not detain them "at this hour of the night" with a long opening speech.[214] The pressure that this placed on juries, which were required to produce unanimous verdicts in large numbers of trials, in a relatively short period of time, should not be underestimated. It helps to explain why they were willing to use fairly consistent principles when processing the cases that came before them. There was simply not enough time for a wildly varying exercise of discretion.

Eventually, there would come a point when proceedings had to be brought to a close, even if some defendants had not been tried. In these situations, they would be returned to Newgate to await the next sessions. Thus, late one Saturday night in April 1770, with the start of the Easter Law Term imminent, something that would require the attendance of the Westminster judges seconded to the Old Bailey, several defendants were remanded to the following sessions.

Orality

English criminal trials were held in public, and stressed the primacy of oral evidence. As a visiting French magistrate could note in 1765, the only written instrument normally used was the indictment. The: "...rest of the process is conducted by word of mouth, between the culprit, the judge, and the jury".[215] By contrast, the procedure found in many French royal courts was based on a fairly cumbersome and lengthy written process, one that was both complex and expensive for the authorities to administer.[216] The openness, and peer participation, of the English system was traditionally, and unfavourably, contrasted by native observers with the "slight, rigorous and summary methods" found in the inquisitorial systems of continental

214. OBSP, Trial of Drummond Clark, 21 April, 1784.

215. P. J. Grosley, *A Tour to London: or, New Observations on England, and its Inhabitants*, vol.3, 1772, p.34.

216. S. G. Reinhardt, "The Selective Prosecution of Crime in Ancien Regime France: Theft in the Senechaussee of Sarlat", 1986, p.5.

Europe.[217] Some visiting foreigners also thought it indicative of the "superiority of the laws of England".[218]

Whatever its merits, the emphasis on "live" testimony meant that if nobody appeared in person at trial, to give evidence against a defendant, he would normally be discharged: "...notwithstanding the strongest presumptions of his guilt".[219] By way of illustration, in 1740, Sarah Butcher, a Whitechapel woman accused of stealing pewter, pans, and a blanket belonging to John Parker, was fortunate: "The Prosecutor not appearing when called, the Prisoner was acquitted".[220] Of course, in such situations, the court would usually order that the prosecutor's recognisance be estreated for his non-attendance. At the Old Bailey, there were over a thousand acquittals due to the non-appearance of prosecutors during the course of the century. A myriad of reasons probably lay behind such cases: private compositions, compassion, laziness, poor personal organization, etc.

Confessions were the only form of extrinsically gathered evidence regularly admitted in English trials. Thus, at Sarah Darrent's hearing for theft her confession before Justice Perry was "read in court".[221] If a defendant disputed whether a confession had been made, or challenged the circumstances in which it had been obtained, it would have to be proved by the examining magistrate who had received it or his clerk who (normally) would have recorded it. Nevertheless, the courts appear to have been fairly reluctant to convict where the *only* evidence against an accused person was their own confession, unsupported by any other material. For example, at the trial for bigamy of Francis Leatherwood, there was no proof of his second marriage, apart from his admissions to a justice, after his first wife failed to appear against him: "...so there not being sufficient evidence, he was acquitted".[222]

In quite exceptional situations, other (i.e. non-confession) out-of -court depositions might be adduced at trial (see above). Exhibits were also

217. A. L. Hayward, *Lives Of The Most Remarkable Criminals*, 1927, p.240.
218. J. W. von Archenholz, *A picture of England: Containing a description of the laws, customs and manners of England*, 1790, pp.12-13.
219. M. Grosley, *A Tour to London: or, New Observations on England, and its Inhabitants*, vol.3, Dublin, 1772, p.33.
220. OBSP, Trial of Sarah Butcher, 15 October 1740.
221. OBSP, Trial of Sarah Darrent, 28 February 1722.
222. OBSP, Trial of Francis Leatherwood, 27 February 1717.

sometimes produced, where they were relevant to a case. For example, in 1691, when two foreigners were accused of murdering and robbing a Swiss man near Chelsea, the still bloody sword of one of the defendants was: "... produced in court as a further testimony against them".[223]

Credibility

As trials for even the most serious criminal matters were exceptionally brief, jurors were required to make an assessment of the relative credibility of the prosecution and defence cases in very pressured circumstances. Unlike most civil law systems, felony convictions could be founded on the evidence of a single witness, cases of high treason apart. The eighteenth-century process inherited two, linked, devices to assist truth-telling in a forensic environment: the use of an oath and a ban on sworn "party" witnesses.

The Oath

Evidence normally had to be given on oath. This could preclude Quakers from testifying. Although, from the end of the seventeenth century, a solemn affirmation from members of this group was acceptable in civil forums, witnesses in criminal trials had to swear on the bible to tell the: "...truth, the whole truth, and nothing but the truth".[224] As a result, Rebecca Sparrow, a Quaker who refused to be sworn when called to give evidence in a murder trial was not allowed to testify. (This situation would not be remedied until 1833). In theory, atheists were also unable to testify (until 1869) as they would not be able to take an oath, or fear its religious sanction if they did: "An infidel, also, that is one who believes neither the Old nor New Testament, cannot be a witness".[225] Very few would openly admit to such a status at this time.

---

223. OBSP, Trial of Lewis Rantzau and another, 15 January 1691.

224. Anon, *A Genuine Narrative of the Trial and Condemnation of Mary Edmondson, for the Murder of Mrs. Susannah Walker, her Aunt*, 2nd edn., 1759, p.17.

225. A. L. Hayward, *Lives Of The Most Remarkable Criminals*, 1927, p.240.

Strictly speaking, witnesses who were not able to understand the religious sanction imposed by taking the oath were also barred from giving evidence, even if willing to be sworn. However, minors and mental defectives apart, competence was normally taken as read, and, unless a prospective witness made a remark or comment that called such a matter into issue, they would usually be sworn without further investigation. Nevertheless, in an exceptional case from 1786, a prosecution witness named Thomas Atkins appears to have alerted the court to his lack of religious instruction when questioned by the celebrated barrister William Garrow. Garrow pointed out that as it was the:

> ...perception of moral good and evil that makes him a competent witness; he must be able to know what the solemnity of a Christian oath is.

Atkins was temporarily put aside as a witness, and not, it seems, called again.[226]

Because witnesses could take the oath on the Torah, without the New Testament, Jews were able to give sworn evidence.[227] As the eighteenth century advanced, members of some other non-Christian faiths were, in theory, allowed to testify with oaths that were appropriate to their religion. Lord Chief Justice Willes noted that taking an oath, unlike baptism, was not specific to Christian countries, so that sworn evidence might be received from: "...infidels who believe in a god and that he will punish them if they swear falsely".[228] However, such cases were almost unheard of in criminal matters. Provided they were Christians, the evidence of "blacks", such as Robert Wadeson, seems to have been received on exactly the same terms, and given much the same weight, as that of their white social counterparts, even though their ethnic status, and the time they had spent in England, was noted in the *Sessions Papers*.[229]

---

226. OBSP, Trial of William White, 25 October 1786.
227. G. D., *Tryals Per Pais: or, the Law of England concerning Juries, By nisi prius, &c.*, 3rd. edn., 1695, p.159.
228. *Omychund v Barker* (1745) 1 Atk. 21.
229. OBSP, Trial of Antonio da Silva, 6 May 1761.

At the start of the century, defence witnesses in felony cases, like defendants, could not give evidence on oath. As Celia Fiennes observed in the 1690s, witnesses: "...for the prisoners are not sworn but only examined to tell the truth".[230] This changed in 1702, when they were allowed and required to give sworn evidence, in the same manner as those testifying for the Crown.

Throughout the period, defendants (like the parties to civil cases) could not testify on oath, and would not do so, in most situations, until the end of the nineteenth century. This reflected a pervasive fear that they would otherwise be encouraged to manufacture evidence to support their cases. As Sir Geoffrey Gilbert noted, the: "...Law removes them from Testimony, to prevent their sliding into Perjury". Because the victim of a crime did not stand to benefit directly from any fine (or other penalty) enforced on the defendant by the Crown, he was not considered a party to criminal proceedings and could give sworn evidence as a prosecution witness.[231] This rationale, of course, conveniently ignored the fact that in many serious cases they stood to gain from the very substantial rewards available on conviction.

How much effect the absence of an oath had on the weight placed on a defendant's account of events by a trial jury is a matter of debate. Some modern academics have stressed the theoretical superiority of sworn testimony. However, in the eyes of the average juryman, it may not have been very significant. In practice, most contemporary observers had a fairly realistic, if not downright cynical, assessment of the: "...small regard which is now paid to an oath, the only barrier by them [defendants] between life and death". Many appreciated that deliberate perjury in criminal cases, both for the Crown and defendants, was widespread, whether it was motivated by malice, affection, self-interest, or some other cause. Not all perjury was for malign reasons. When, at the start of the eighteenth century, the Reverend George Stanhope reflected on why witnesses lied on oath, he specifically identified compassion in potentially capital cases as being in a class on its own, though the cleric thought this was a dangerous manifestation of the "most misplaced pity".[232]

230. C. Fiennes, *Through England on a Side Saddle in the Time of William and Mary*, 1888, p.278.

231. Sir G. Gilbert, *The Law of Evidence*, 2nd. edn., 1760, p.122 and p.126.

232. G. Stanhope, *The Duty of Witnesses. A Sermon Preached at the Summer Assizes Holden at Maidstone in Kent...August the 5th*, 1701, pp.12-13.

It seems that prosecutions for perjury were of little value in deterring false testimony. Technically, the crime was only a misdemeanour, and so the consequences of being convicted were usually limited to being placed in the pillory and fined. For this reason, in 1786, a newspaper reported, perhaps on rather dubious authority, that the Westminster judges had met at Lord Mansfield's chambers and considered making perjury a capital crime.[233] In any event, establishing the offence was legally quite difficult. The prosecution had to prove that the witness had given sworn testimony and that it was deliberately untruthful. This would require calling someone who had been in court and who could give a reliable account of what had been said. Given the passage of time in many cases, this was inherently difficult, though, at the Old Bailey, the shorthand writer, preparing a record for the *Sessions Papers*, could sometimes testify to these issues. Thus, in the prosecution of Elizabeth Canning for perjury, Thomas Gurney was called, and: "...deposed from his minutes to the contents of Canning's evidence given in court".[234]

As a result of these factors, it is likely that a defendant's account was not *normally* viewed as being enormously inferior to that of other (sworn) witnesses, simply because it was not delivered on oath. Nevertheless, there were occasional instances of sworn evidence being given preternatural significance by magistrates or the judiciary, though they sometimes attracted indignation. For example, a defendant at Hick's Hall in 1768 deplored the fact that, at his trial, the court had appeared to proceed on the supposition that he could not advance any circumstantial evidence, such as the light and distance in which a crucial observation was made, to undermine the sworn evidence of a watchman, the main prosecution witness in his case. He felt that this was treating the trial process as being akin to a Grand Jury hearing.[235]

Most defendants did not call supporting witnesses at the Old Bailey, other than those willing to speak to their general good character. However, the number of defence witnesses who "spoke to an issue" at trial rose during the course of the century, from at least seven per cent at the Old Bailey

233. J. Oldham, "Truth Telling in the Eighteenth-century English Courtroom", 1984, p.99.
234. OBSP, Trial of Elizabeth Canning, 24 April 1754.
235. Anon. *Account of a tryal at Hick's Hall. Tuesday, April 25, 1786*, 1786, p.11.

in 1715, to a minimum of 18 per cent in 1780[236] (Limitations on reporting might make these figures underestimates).

Despite this, the authorities were acutely concerned about the possibility of manufactured defence evidence. In the swift trials of the era it was often not possible to investigate or question dubious defence witnesses sufficiently to prevent them raising a doubt in the minds of a trial jury. Thomas Carr, for example, had made a living by "managing business" at the Old Bailey. While doing this, he became acquainted with a group of people who were involved in: "...procuring evidence on particular causes, when, and wherever such assistance was necessary". This had eventually incurred the hostility of the recorder. Nevertheless, it had initially produced results; Carr had enjoyed a: "...great share in the success which for some time that practice met with".[237] It was frequently claimed that dishonest "petty-fogging" attorneys and solicitors provided corrupt defence "witnesses", as part of their service, finding people who would "swear any thing" to secure an acquittal.[238]

The most common form of manufactured evidence was an alibi. As Henry Fielding was to note, it was also the most frequent defence for thieves, and: "...to prove this by perjury is a common act of Newgate friendship". Many contemporary legal observers were very cynical about their value as a result. In 1762, for example, Sir Michael Foster argued that an alibi should be viewed with great caution unless disclosed at the very first opportunity by the accused person, so that it could be investigated prior to trial.[239]

There were several well-documented examples of lawyers manufacturing alibis for their clients. Some appear to have done this in person. In 1741, for example, it was noted that several Newgate solicitors had travelled to the Northampton Assizes, with a view to giving evidence on behalf of the murderer Bryan Connell, offering to: "...swear him elsewhere at the time of

236. G. Fisher, "The Jury's Rise as Law Detector", 1997, pp.649-650.

237. OBSP, Trial of Thomas Car and Elizabeth Adams, 12 October 1737. *The Ordinary Of Newgate, His Account Of The Behaviour, Confession, And Dying Words, Of The Malefactors, Who Were Executed At Tyburn On Wednesday The 18th Of January* 1738.

238. C. Jones, *Some Methods Proposed Towards putting a Stop to the Flagrant Crimes of Murder, Robbery, and Perjury*, 1752, p.6.

239. Sir M. Foster, *A Report of some proceedings on the Commission of Oyer and Terminer and Goal [sic] Delivery for the trial of the Rebels in the year 1746 in the County of Surry, and of other Crown Cases*, 1762, p.368.

the murder, and to give him a good character". However, Colonel de Veil, becoming aware of this, and being familiar with the men concerned, also travelled to the Assizes, deterring them from giving evidence.[240] Interestingly, one contemporary observer felt that highwaymen usually made a "very poor and weak defence" when prosecuted, because they normally did not have readily accessible money or criminal associates to assist them in this regard.[241]

However, case-hardened jurors — and many eighteenth-century jurors served on numerous occasions — were also likely to become aware of the problems attendant on such evidence. Indeed, so common were alibi defences, and so notorious was it that they were often false, that counsel for a defendant accused of a robbery near Camberwell Green felt obliged to stress that, in his case, all of the alibi witnesses were of proven integrity and had also provided details of the alibi to an examining justice, long before the trial:

> This method has been abused, I acknowledge, to screen the guilty, but you will make a distinction, gentlemen, where a set of people are got together and tutor'd and instructed what to swear, and where several honest housekeepers, and persons of undeniable reputation, come and say, that this man was in their company.[242]

Inevitably, some defendants were disappointed in their attempts to obtain false evidence and alibis. For example, when Sarah Malcolm was found in possession of a stolen tankard that would firmly link her to a robbery and murder, a contact in the Compter Prison, where she was being held, told her that if she gave him some money he would find: "…people that would swear that the tankard was my mother's according as I would direct". In the end, Malcolm negotiated multiple alibis, covering the time of the murder, at a cost of 12 guineas paid in advance. However, the hired witnesses failed to materialise and she was committed to Newgate. While there, she was robbed of the rest of her money by another prisoner, who was confident, in his turn, that he could use it to secure an alibi defence and so be "cleared".[243]

240. *Universal Spectator and Weekly Journal*, 21 March 1741.

241. Anon (By a Lover of his Country), *The Thief-Catcher; or, Villainy Detected*, 1753, p.3.

242. Anon, *The Genuine and Authentic Trial of Mr. Bartholomew Greenwood, Charg'd with Robbing Mr. Roger Wheatly near Camberwell*, 3rd edn., 1740, p.17.

243. S. Malcolm, *A True Copy of the Paper Delivered the Night Before Her Execution by Sarah*

Character Witnesses

Perhaps because hearings were so brief, and so much turned on witness credibility, calling witnesses to speak to the good character of an accused person was a vital part of the trial process. Far more defendants adduced such testimony than called witnesses to speak to matters of fact. Indeed, although it was, theoretically, not allowed — rape complainants apart — even prosecutors sometimes called them. For example, on one occasion, the victim in a hotly contested robbery called several reputable witnesses to his character: "...who said, that he was a man that would not forswear himself on any account".[244] Similarly, in a case from 1744, Alexander Forfar, the chief prosecution witness, was allowed to call a man who had known him for almost eight years to say that he was a man of "veracity and truth" who would not lie on oath.[245]

For defendants, the calling of character witnesses was both permissible and actively encouraged. A judge might openly ask an accused person: "Can you show the jury that you are an honest man, that you live in a habit of honesty and sobriety?"[246] Although there was little attempt to annunciate the precise reasons for calling character witnesses until the nineteenth century, it seems that they served three purposes. As in the modern era, of course, their testimony could boost the credibility of a defendant giving (unsworn) evidence; was he likely to be telling the truth? To an extent, they were (very roughly) analogous to "oath helpers" in early modern ecclesiastical cases, and important in a trial process marked by extreme brevity, one that was unlikely to afford a huge opportunity to test a witness's veracity. Additionally, and as today, their evidence went to the issue of propensity; was it likely that a man of previous good character would suddenly have offended in the manner alleged? This could be crucial in cases that were evenly poised, and was something that judges expressly alluded to when directing juries. Thus, in a case from 1796, the presiding judge, noting that a defendant was of previous good character, also stressed that: "...in a doubtful case the character of a

Malcolm, 1732, pp.11-12.

244. Anon, *The Genuine and Authentic Trial of Mr. Bartholomew Greenwood, Charg'd with Robbing Mr. Roger Wheatly near Camberwell*, 3rd edn., 1740, p.24.

245. OBSP, Trial of Ann Collier, 5 December 1744.

246. OBSP, Trial of John Mills, 30 April 1783.

man is always taken into the scale".[247] More specifically, character witnesses in a murder case might be asked about the defendant's response to relevant stimuli, such as his normal reluctance to react violently to provocation.[248]

However, in the eighteenth century, character witnesses served a third purpose. Even if the jury were persuaded that the defendant had committed the offence with which he was charged their evidence might encourage "pious perjury" on the basis that the accused man had hitherto been a worthwhile member of the community, one who did not deserve execution or transportation (depending on the allegation). It might also encourage the recorder to recommend a post-conviction reprieve in his report, in a capital case.

Unsurprisingly, in a hierarchical society that prized status, the more prominent the position in life of the character witness, the better they would be for the accused man or woman. Nevertheless, most defendants would have to call witnesses from roughly the same social milieu as themselves, albeit its upper echelons. Some could not even do this. In an extreme case, when asked whether she had anyone to speak to her reputation, Elizabeth Harrison, accused of picking pockets in 1722, was forced to propose her co-defendant![249] Much more typically, Robert Hutchinson, being tried for burglary, called four witnesses to testify to his honesty. Amongst them was a coachman who noted that the defendant had worked for him and that he had "never heard any harm of him". Another witness observed that he ran a public house in Highgate and had always trusted the accused man, even when valuable pewter plate had been: "...lying about, and he never wronged me of a farthing".[250]

Such evidence could also be called in serious cases of misdemeanour heard at Quarter Sessions. Thus, when John Lowther was accused of attempted sodomy at the Guildhall Sessions, in 1761, he called well over 20 men to testify to his good character, one of them being a knight of the realm and others men with whom he had shared a bed on various occasions when travelling (as was common in the era), but who had survived the night unmolested. Unfortunately, the prosecution, conducted, like Lowther's defence,

247. Anon, *The Trial of Miss Jones, &c. For the Murder of Mr. Thomas Yates*, 1796, p.34.
248. OBSP, Trial of Antonio da Silva, 6 May 1761.
249. OBSP, Trial of Elizabeth Harrison, 28 February 1722.
250. OBSP, Trial of Robert Hutchinson et al, 15 October 1740.

by counsel, was prepared for this, and called rebutting evidence from local men who had "despised and hissed at the prisoner" because of his reputation for homosexuality. He was convicted.[251] As this case suggests, very exceptionally, the prosecution was in a position to counter false claims. Thus, when William Bird stood trial for murder in 1742, and adduced such evidence, prosecuting counsel pounced: "As you have led us into it, we shall call some Persons to your Character".[252]

Returning Verdicts

Throughout the seventeenth century, juries at the Old Bailey, like those at provincial Assizes, had been asked to consider their verdicts on batches of up to a dozen or more defendants, from as many trials, at the same time, although special or complex cases might be determined alone. The "modern" practice of discussing each case after it had been heard, and then returning a verdict on it before the next case was called on, was introduced at the Old Bailey in 1738. As a result, the jurors' seats were moved so that they could easily: "...consult one another and give in their verdict immediately, or in case of any Difficulty, withdraw for Consideration".[253]

As this suggests, in straightforward cases they would simply put their heads together and produce a decision without leaving their seats. For example, the jury capitally convicted Edward Lowe of arson "without going out of court".[254] More complex cases might require them to retire to the jury room, under the supervision of the court bailiff. In very rare cases, this could be for a prolonged period. At the trial of Henry Simons, at the Essex Assizes in Chelmsford, the: "...Jury was enclosed about nine at night, and did not agree till two the next morning".[255] However, this was exceptionally rare, particularly at the Old Bailey. Normally, a few minutes were quite sufficient.

251. Anon, *The Tryal of Mr. John Lowther, For an Assault on John Bushnell, with an intent to commit the Crime of Sodomy*, 1761, pp.10-12.

252. OBSP, Trial of William Bird, 13 October 1742.

253. *The Gentleman's Magazine*, 1738, vol. 8, p.659.

254. OBSP, Trial of Edward Lowe and William Jobbins, 27 October 1790.

255. Anon, *The authentick trylas [sic] at large of John Swan and Elizabeth Jeffryes, for the murder of the*

Special verdicts

In unusual situations, where jurors could not apply the substantive law to the facts of a particular case, they might return a "special" verdict. This would often be at the direction of a trial judge who was personally uncertain as to the correct legal position, though they differed greatly in their willingness to do this. In this situation, the jury made a finding of the relevant facts, which were then recorded and the matter reserved for the consideration of the 12 judges of the Westminster courts (i.e. the most senior judicial figures in the country). They sat, periodically, at Serjeants' Inn for this specific purpose. The judges would return a verdict, deciding by a simple majority if there was disagreement, having considered the facts found to be proved, and then debated the relevant law. At least fifty such cases were recorded at the Old Bailey between 1700 and 1799. For example, in 1721, when George Duffus was accused of sodomy, a special verdict was returned because the complainant's evidence indicated that there had been penetration of not more than an inch, and no emission of semen during the incident (the defendant subsequently masturbating and ejaculating in his own hand).[256]

Sentencing

Once a guilty verdict had been returned, sentencing would usually be deferred to the end of the Old Bailey sessions, this function normally being carried out by the recorder, even if he had not presided over the original trial. However, after 1752, statute required that the sentence of death and anatomisation for murder be passed immediately after a conviction for that crime, usually by the judge who had presided over the hearing. Acquitted defendants were released by proclamation, at the end of the sessions, as were those who had received a sentence, such as branding (after being clergied) that warranted immediate discharge.

late Mr. Joseph Jeffryes, of Walthamstow, 1752, pp.16-20.

256. OBSP, Trial of George Duffus, 6 December 1721.

Pleading the Belly

A woman found guilty of an unclergyable felony, and so sentenced to death, could postpone her execution if found to be pregnant. It was for this reason that Elizabeth Hughes, capitally convicted for horse-theft at the Oxford Assizes in 1726, was viewed as having had a great misfortune when she miscarried, just after the jury found her guilty, and: "...thereby lost the benefit of pleading her belly".[257] Once a woman made such a claim, the sheriff would have to return a jury of "matrons" to determine whether she was quick with child.[258] Although this issue was normally determined immediately prior to the death sentence being passed, there were occasional late applications. In 1787, for example, Sophia Pringle unavailingly claimed that she was pregnant two days before she was due to be hanged and was brought back to the bar of the Old Bailey to make her plea, albeit that it was not one that a specially empanelled jury of matrons was willing to accept.[259]

The matrons were usually midwives or women with extensive personal experience of pregnancy. Many were the wives of court personnel. Although termed a jury, they often numbered as few as three women, apparently deciding by a majority in the very rare situations where they could not reach a unanimous decision. They received their evidence in private, normally conducting an intimate physical inspection of the convicted woman in a closed room. If the jury decided that a convict was quick with child (i.e. several months pregnant), execution would be delayed until after the baby's delivery, or until it became apparent that the woman was not with child. In theory, the very early stages of pregnancy, prior to the foetus "quickening" did not qualify. However, in practice, even this requirement was sometimes overlooked. In September 1788, for example, when Christian Murphy, sentenced to be burnt for high treason for counterfeiting silver coins, pleaded her belly, the matrons concluded that she was: "...not quick with child, but it was their opinion that she was with child, and had been so a short time".[260] Strictly speaking, this was not enough; nevertheless, her sentence appears

257. *Mist's Weekly Journal*, 30 July 1726.

258. W. Blackstone, *Commentaries on the Laws of England*, 1765-9, vol. 4, p.388.

259. *Whitehall Evening Post*, 27 February 1787.

260. *London Chronicle*, 18 September 1788.

to have been suspended, as she was not ordered for execution until March 1789, being put to death a few days later.[261]

As Murphy's case suggests, in *theory*, being found to be pregnant merely delayed execution until after the birth, or the woman proving not to be with child. It was not until 1848 that all reprieves of execution for pregnancy were made permanent. Thus, in 1694, the burglar Jane Croucher, who had been respited from execution: "...as being with Child, yet now her time in that case being fulfilled, she was called to her former judgment". Two other women in exactly the same position were also executed at Tyburn on the same day.[262]

Such an outcome was particularly likely where the woman turned out not to be pregnant. At the start of July 1741, for example, Katherine Lineham, who had been capitally convicted at the Old Bailey in January, and pleaded her belly, was: "...called to her former judgment and receiv'd sentence of death".[263] The recorder later noted in his report that she had obtained her: "...long respite, under colour of a pretended pregnancy". Lineham was executed at the end of July.[264] However, in many cases during the eighteenth century, after a baby was born and, sometimes, even if the woman proved not to be pregnant, she would spend a few months in gaol and then be permanently reprieved and released, albeit often on condition of transportation to America.

Given its obvious benefits, it is unsurprising that many capitally convicted women should have claimed pregnancy, even when they knew they could not possibly have conceived. For example, Sarah Metyard, convicted with her mother of murdering their maid, unsuccessfully pleaded her belly, despite subsequently telling the ordinary that she had never had sexual intercourse with a man. She claimed that she had been: "...advised to use this plea, tho' without foundation, to gain a respite". Sarah also pointed out that, as she, like other defendants, was not on oath, she had not had to commit perjury when doing so. Unfortunately, her plea was made without knowing about

261. *World*, 16 March 1789, and *World*, 19 March 1789.

262. S. Smith, *A True Account Of The Behaviour, Confession, And Last Dying Speeches, Of The Criminals That Were Executed At Tyburn, On Wednesday The 24th of January 1694*, 1694.

263. *London Evening Post*, 4 July 1741.

264. *Daily Post*, 22 July 1741 and *Daily Post*, 1 August 1741.

the examination conducted by the jury of matrons, who swiftly produced a negative finding.[265]

As this case suggests, during the eighteenth century the matrons were usually highly discriminating about such claims. Only a relatively small and decreasing number of women were successful. There were just over a hundred findings of pregnancy during the century, but only three after 1758. In passing, it can be noted that such a bar to execution was not unique to England, or even Europe, at this time; it was also found in Japan.[266]

Benefit of Clergy

Benefit of clergy would be pleaded before sentence was passed, effectively making many offences non-capital. This vital privilege is dealt with in *Chapter 3*.

Appeals Against Conviction

There was almost no provision for a defendant to appeal a guilty verdict during the eighteenth century, unless the original trial was declared null and void for a serious technical fault "on the record", via a writ of error. In criminal matters, use of this writ was normally confined to flaws in the indictment or selection of the jury. There could not be an appeal based on the nature of a judge's summing up or his general conduct of the hearing. Additionally, the procedure did not cover convictions from Quarter Sessions (rather than the Old Bailey or Assizes). It was also expensive to bring, fairly slow, and required that the Attorney General's fiat be obtained first. Thus, when Colonel Francis Chartres petitioned the Monarch for leave to bring such a writ after his conviction for rape, the King referred the matter to both the

265. Anon, *God's Revenge against Murder*, 1762, p.24.
266. D. E. Wright, "Female crime and state punishment in Early Modern Japan", 2004, p.21.

Attorney General and Solicitor General for their consideration.[267] It was very rarely used successfully in criminal cases.

When it came to appeals, Londoners were at a disadvantage compared to their Parisian counterparts, who could usually refer their convictions for further consideration by a higher forum. For example, when Marie-Jeanne Bartonnet was convicted of infanticide in 1742, after giving birth in a privy, she was initially sentenced to death. However, a mandatory review of the case (effectively an appeal), which involved a further interrogation of the defendant, before the Parlement of Paris, the highest court in northern France, raised doubts about the evidence. The judges voted to commute her sentence to a public whipping and banishment.[268] There would have been no rehearing after an Old Bailey conviction for the same offence.

Nevertheless, even in England, if there were serious doubts about the safety of a conviction, representations could be made to the authorities prior to any capital sentence being imposed. These might result in the convict being reprieved by the Crown, often unconditionally. This procedure was sufficiently well-known that convicts occasionally tried to manufacture evidence, casting doubt on their guilt, to support a petition for clemency.[269] Sometimes, albeit very rarely, fresh investigations might also be conducted *after* conviction. An example of this occurred when Peter Piercey was found guilty of murder in 1726. Piercey was one of a group of off-duty soldiers involved in an altercation during which a man had been fatally stabbed with a bayonet. He maintained that he had not struck the fatal blow, or even been close to the dead man at the relevant time. Even so, at his trial at the Old Bailey he was convicted as a principal in the killing, while a co-defendant was acquitted of being an accessory.[270] However, there was a degree of concern about the verdicts. Thomas Robe, a very active Middlesex JP, investigated the matter and ordered several of the witnesses who had given evidence at trial to be produced before him for further examination. He focused on two of

267. *London Evening Post*, 4 June 1730.

268. B. Levack *et al, The West: Encounters & Transformations*, 2007, p.390.

269. J. H. Langbein, "Shaping the Eighteenth-century Criminal Trial: A View from the Ryder Sources", 1983, pp.29-30. These decisions raise intriguing questions about the standard of proof applied by trial juries and the directions presiding judges gave them on this subject.

270. OBSP, Trial of Peter Peircey, 11 July 1726.

the children who had identified Peircey as the killer. On being questioned by the JP they: "...varied very much from the evidence as to what they said at the Old-Bailey". Additionally, Robe received the evidence of a child who had not testified at trial but who suggested that it was the acquitted co-defendant who had struck the fatal blow.[271] In light of this, Piercey, who had consistently maintained his innocence to the ordinary, was reprieved.

Similarly, in 1769, two men were convicted of murder, after striking a young man at a Middlesex election in Brentford. The prosecution case had included the evidence of a surgeon. However, after a vigorous campaign against the verdict, the Secretary of State ordered that a group of ten eminent men from the Surgeons Company review the medical evidence that had been adduced at the court hearing. In the light of this, both of the convicts were granted a free pardon.[272]

Even more famously, in 1753, Sir Crisp Gascoyne, the Lord Mayor of London, became concerned at the capital conviction of the gypsy Mary Squires in the notorious Canning case, after serving on the bench at her trial (he had not presided over the hearing). Gascoyne established his own enquiry, which discovered several alibi witnesses for Squires, as a result of which he appealed to King George II, and Squires was reprieved.

In some respects, the "prosecution" (broadly conceived) were slightly better off with regard to appealing jury acquittals in murder cases, than defendants, because of the existence of the "appeal of felony", though this was very rarely employed. Additionally, the doctrine of *autrefois acquit* did not apply to allegedly felonious conduct that was re-prosecuted as a misdemeanour. For example, in 1766, James Coin and Peter Monks, who had earlier been acquitted at the Old Bailey of robbing William Norwell, were prosecuted purely for the assault stemming from the incident, at the ensuing Guildhall Sessions, convicted, and sentenced to six months in Newgate.[273]

271. *Weekly Journal or British Gazetteer*, 13 August 1726.

272. J. Foot, *An Appeal to the Public, Touching the Death of Mr. George Clarke*, 2nd edn., 1769, pp.1-51.

273. *The Whitehall Evening Post; or, London Intelligencer*, 18 September 1766.

Change during the Course of the Century

It has been argued that the English criminal trial, especially that for felony, underwent little significant change between *Bushel's Case* (1671) and the late eighteenth century. Instead, it experienced a series of less dramatic alterations.[274] However, this is to understate the totality of what occurred. Taken together, the mass of incremental changes produced a transformation in the nature of the forensic hearing.

At the start of the era, the largely unmediated, relatively informal, confrontation between prosecutor and defendant that had been inherited from the early modern period still prevailed, even if it was already in decline. In the absence of counsel for either the prosecution and defence — the situation in the great majority of felony trials before the final decades of the eighteenth century — it was largely for the presiding judge or, at Quarter Sessions, the chairman or recorder, to elicit and probe evidence from witnesses, though he shared this role with the parties themselves and, to a smaller extent, the jury.[275]

By contrast, the criminal trial on indictment of the 1790s was far more like its modern counterpart than its predecessor of a century before. Major rules of evidence had either emerged or, if already present, become much more rigid and universally applied. Additionally, trial procedure was far more precise, and less informal, than had been the situation at the start of the century, and both judges and, even more so, juries, were more "passive" than had previously been the case.

Of course, there were still many differences between the modern trial and that of 1800. The latter remained exceptionally brief, and judges and (to a lesser extent) juries were still very active by today's standards, if not those of 1700. For example, in a murder case from 1782, in which the alleged victim had, apparently, been strangled, an expert medical witness was questioned by both the judge and jury, as well as by counsel. The jury asked the doctor whether it was possible for a man to be strangled with a silk handkerchief

274. T. A. Green, *Verdict According to Conscience*, 1985, p.267.

275. S. Landsman, "The rise of the contentious spirit: Adversary procedure in Eighteenth-Century England", 1990, pp.505-506; J. Hawles, *The Englishman's Right*, 1680, p.4.

without there being marks of violence on his body. The trial judge then asked whether it would affect the dead man's countenance.[276]

Many of the era's changes were the continuation of trends that had already been underway for more than a hundred years before 1700. For example, the felony hearing in the early eighteenth century was already considerably more formal than its Tudor predecessor. By then, the parties to the trial would normally (though not invariably) put their questions to each other through the presiding judge, rather than directly, as they had usually done in the 1500s. If they tried to do otherwise, the judge might intervene, remind them that they should first put their question to the court, and, if the: "...question is proper, the court will require the witness to answer it". Even so, what has been termed an "unstructured bicker" still characterised many criminal trials in 1700. This gradually disappeared during the second quarter of the eighteenth century, so that, by the 1750s, there was a fairly crisp division along partisan lines.[277] This was partly a result of the advent of lawyers to the felony trial process, which encouraged a rigid separation of cross-examination from examination-in-chief.

Additionally, by the 1760s, the notion of there being a legal burden on the prosecution was more clearly enunciated, so that, if the Crown's case was very weak, an accused person could challenge the adequacy of the evidence brought against him, and exercise the right not to testify. In an exceptional case, it was noted that: "The evidence did not sufficiently affect the prisoner Adams to put him upon his defence".[278] Such changes were not necessarily entirely beneficial to defendants. A more structured trial meant that a damaging allegation made by a prosecution witness was less likely to be answered immediately, and might even be overlooked.[279]

---

276. OBSP, Trial of Januarye Sweatman and Mary Humphries, 20 February 1782.

277. J. H. Langbein, *The Origins of Adversary Criminal Trial*, 2003, p.16 and p.260.

278. *Leeman v Allen and Others* (1763) 2 Wilson K.B. 160.

279. T. A. Green, *Verdict According to Conscience*, 1985, p.272.

Juries

The two sheriffs of "London and Middlesex" (the county did not have its own High Sheriff until 1889) were responsible for returning juries in the Metropolitan area. In practice, most of the work was carried out by their officers, rather than in person. In London, these men were known as the "sergeants of the mace". Almost a week's notice was supposed to be given to potential jurors, a formal summons being served six days before they were due to attend court. If they were away, written notice was left at their homes.[280] Service on trial juries was often unpopular, as it involved an interruption of several days to the juror's own business. This was potentially expensive, as jurors were unpaid. As a result, some asked to be excused, on grounds of health, disability, or for some other reason. Others resorted to bribery, so that they were not selected in the first place. In the 1730s, it was claimed that the well-to-do could usually avoid service by: "...giving a Shilling or Half a Crown to the Sheriff's Officer".[281] So common was this that fraudsters in Middlesex would sometimes pretend to be that functionary to solicit bribes from people eager to avoid serving. Attempts to "crack down" on such practices produced periodic statutes designed to punish corruption in jury appointment.[282] Others would simply fail to answer to their summons, even though they could be fined for failing to appear or for leaving court before they were sworn. There was a set fine of between 20s and 40s for failing to attend any court of record in the City of London after being summoned to jury service.[283]

Nevertheless, it seems that the great majority of those called for potential service at Metropolitan Quarter Sessions and the Old Bailey appeared. At the start of the eighteenth century, a panel of 50 to 60 men from which to select the London jury at the Bailey was typical, and was probably matched by that for Middlesex. After 12 men had been chosen for this body, and another 17 or so for the Grand Jury, the remainder would be allowed to go

280. J. Trusler, *The London adviser and guide*, 1786, p.60.
281. *The Gentleman's Magazine*, 1737, vol. 7, p.808.
282. J. Oldham, "The Origins of the Special Jury", 1983, pp.142-144.
283. J. Trusler, *The London adviser and guide*, 1786, p.60.

home.[284] This "over-recruitment" was necessary, because several of the 60 might avoid the duty, or simply accept the fine for non-attendance. Others might be successfully challenged, whether peremptorily, without any grounds having to be given (20 such challenges being allowed for felony), or for cause, such as known personal animosity towards the accused man.[285] In practice, however, challenges of either type were very rare.[286]

After 1520, the various wards of the City would take turns in providing jurors for the eight sittings of the Quarter Sessions at the Guildhall and the London jury at the Old Bailey, a system that continued, in various forms, throughout the eighteenth century. As a result, jurors were not taken from all parts of the Square Mile for any single sessions, and those repeating service might find themselves next to men with whom they had previously sat. Those for Middlesex juries were disproportionately drawn from a penumbra of suburban villages, relatively close to the court.

In theory, there were personal and economic preconditions for jury service; some of these were special to the Metropolitan area, others reflected the general (national) position. The only geographic prerequisite for Old Bailey service during the 1700s was that those on the London jury came from the Square Mile (even this was only expressly spelt out in 1730) while those on the Middlesex jury came from the county. Jurors would have to be legally adult (over 21) but under the age of 70. It was unusual to summon jurors in their 60s who were decrepit, and in 1825 the maximum age was reduced to 60 by statute. Those who were sick, surgeons, clergymen, apothecaries, dissenting teachers and Quakers, military or government officers, along with several other groups and professions, were either exempt or disqualified from serving.[287] Jurors were supposed to be men of good character, without convictions for "notorious" crimes.[288] What this meant, in practice, was that a juror could be challenged if he had previously been found guilty of treason,

284. J. M. Beattie, "London Juries in the 1690s", 1988, pp.226-227.

285. M. Hale, *The History of the Common Law of England*, 1713, p.253.

286. M. V. Muyden (Ed.), *A foreign View of England in the reigns of George I and George II*, 1902, p.118.

287. J. Trusler, *The London adviser and guide*, 1786, p.59.

288. M. Hale, *The History of the Common Law of England*, 1713, p.254.

felony, returning a false verdict or perjury. Most defendants would have been unaware of such matters.

The original property requirement for London jurors, set in Henry VIII's reign, had been possession of lands, goods or tenements worth 100 marks (just under 67 pounds) in value. This had been amended by statute in the 1730s (3 Geo. 2. C.25), so that:

> In the courts of London and City of Westminster, jurors shall be householders within the city, and have lands, tenements, or personal estates, to the value of 100 l.

In Middlesex, leaseholders of appropriate wealth could also serve.[289] The reduced emphasis on freehold land, compared to the general (national) situation, made allowances for the realities of urban wealth. The property requirement meant that jurors in the Metropolis were drawn from the "middling" social orders. They usually consisted of tradesmen, merchants, shopkeepers or skilled artisans (such as clock and watch-makers).[290]

In the provinces there was often a modest social difference between those who sat as trial jurors at Quarter Sessions and those summoned for the more exalted Assizes, and a major one between all trial jurors and Grand Jurors. However, in the Metropolitan area, and especially the Square Mile, such differences were much more modest. Interestingly, service on the trial jury that determined misdemeanours at Quarter Sessions appears to have attracted men of a slightly higher social status than those who heard life or death matters at the Old Bailey, perhaps, in part, because they escaped the smell and general unpleasantness associated with trying prisoners fresh from Newgate.

However, none of these three bodies was hermetically distinct, some jurors seeing service on all three of them over the years. For an example can be considered the jurors who sat on the trials of John and James Brownrigg for assaulting their maid, conducted at the City Quarter Sessions held at the Guildhall in 1767. It seems that at least a third, possibly more, of the men in this case never sat at the Old Bailey. Nevertheless, a majority of them had sat, or would sit, to determine cases at the higher forum. Thus, Jeremiah Garrard

---

289. J. Trusler, *The London adviser and guide*, 1786, p.59.

290. M. Misson, *Memoirs and Observations in his Travels over England,* 1719, p.161.

seems to have attended sessions in 1749 and (more certainly) in 1764. John Cancellor had also sat in 1764. One or two men may have been extremely experienced, although, as they have common names, such as Joseph Brown and William Wright, it is hard to be absolutely certain.[291]

The eighteenth century appears to have seen some increase in the incidence of repeat attendance amongst jurors. This built on an already established trend. For example, of the 1,350 men who were sworn on a London jury, whether Grand or trial, for both Quarter Sessions and the Old Bailey, between 1692 and 1699, 744 made only one appearance. Another 268 men made just two. However, 173 men appeared between three and eight times, making a total of 830 appearances. The average was about two.[292] Some Old Bailey jurors would also have examined suspicious deaths as part of a coroner's jury. For example, in 1763, Benjamin Cotes and John Warton, who had sat on an inquest that committed a suspected murderer for trial at the Old Bailey, and were then called to sit on the same man's petty jury, asked to be excused for this reason. Two men were sworn in their stead.[293]

The Presence of Lawyers

In both misdemeanour and treason cases defendants had been entitled to full legal representation prior to 1700. It had always been allowed for those accused of misdemeanours, though many did not avail themselves of the right, if only for reasons of cost. Typically, in 1787, a servant who prosecuted his erstwhile employer for assault at Quarter Sessions was personally "cross-examined by his master".[294] In these situations, a few defendants might have advice from legally knowledgeable acquaintances. For example, though unrepresented at this forum, Rhynwick Williams had the assistance of a retired barrister as "next friend".[295] Nevertheless, the use of counsel was not

291. Anon., *The Trials of James Brownrigg, and John Brownrigg, his Son, for Confining and inhumanly Scourging Mary Mitchel,* 1767, p.3.

292. J. M. Beattie, "London Juries in the 1690s", 1988, p.236.

293. OBSP, Trial of Daniel Blake, 23 February 1763.

294. *The Times*, 2 November 1787, p.3.

295. *The Times*, 15 December 1790, p.3.

uncommon, even for such lesser criminal matters. Legal representation for those accused of treason was still quite novel at the start of the eighteenth century. The Treason Trials Act of 1696 had allowed an accused person to use counsel to mount a "full defence". This statute appears to have been introduced as a response to the treason trials of the late Stuart period, which had often been politically motivated and prosecuted by senior counsel at the Crown's expense. Those prosecuted under the very rare "appeal of murder" were also entitled to full legal representation.

By contrast, English felony trials were largely lawyer-free before the eighteenth century. In 1700, the prosecuting victim of a felony only rarely employed counsel, and the defendant was legally not entitled to representation, except to argue issues of pure law. When doing this, counsel was expressly forbidden to: "...enter into any discussion of the fact; his business is only to speak to the point of law".[296] The defendant would have to personally raise the legal issue, before the court made a decision as to whether or not it would hear counsel. Even this power could be very significant, in a system that was highly technical. For example, when two men who were accused of theft took issue with the indictment "by the advice of their counsel", they pleaded *autrefois acquit,* on the basis that they had previously been found "not guilty" for much the same offence. The judge presiding over the trial decided that the matter was so complex that it needed detailed legal argument before the 12 Westminster judges.[297] Had these two men been unrepresented it is unlikely that such a complicated legal point would have been taken.

Nevertheless, at the start of the century, defence counsel could not question witnesses or address the jury on the facts of a case via a closing speech. This greatly limited their value and use. The traditional justification for denying defendants' counsel on these matters was based on a belief in the value of their unmediated responses to potentially incriminating evidence.[298] Additionally, in common law theory, if not necessarily reality, it was supposed to be one of a trial judge's duties to represent a defendant, making

296. M. Grosley, *A Tour to London: or, New Observations on England, and its Inhabitants*, vol.3, 1772, p.33.

297. OBSP, Trial of James Vandercom and James Abbot, 13 January 1796.

298. J. H. Langbein, "The historical origins of the privilege against self-incrimination at Common Law", 1994, p.1053.

defence counsel unnecessary. England differed from many continental countries in this regard. For example, the *Sala,* eighteenth-century Madrid's most important criminal court, had an integral defence lawyer, the *abogado de pobres*, for the poor.[299]

This situation changed in the early 1730s, when defence counsel was first allowed to examine and cross-examine witnesses, though not to directly address juries. Exactly why this occurred, without any statutory authority, has been a matter of some debate. Two plausible explanations have been advanced by scholars of the period. As has been noted, because rewards were paid on conviction, not on arrest, both thief-takers and informed members of the public who had detained suspected felons had a strong incentive to avoid having their work undone by a "sloppy" prosecution, in which a legal flaw or an absent witness produced an acquittal. This prompted greater numbers to use lawyers, and even prosecuting counsel (as they were entitled to do), to prepare and present their cases. As a result, members of the judiciary *may* have become keen to level the forensic "playing field" by allowing defence representation. The second explanation focuses on a change in 1729, when Parliament reclassified forgery from a misdemeanour to a felony, hoping to improve the crime's deterrent value by allowing the death penalty to be imposed on those found guilty. Forgery tended to be a crime of the better off, and reclassifying it deprived such people of the defence counsel to which they had previously been entitled.

The advent of lawyers to the felony trial process was to be a huge catalyst for change, explaining or contributing to many of the era's forensic developments.[300] Initially, however, the number of lawyers employed at the Old Bailey was very modest. Out of a total of 422 trials heard in 1740, for example, there may have been as few as 13 cases with prosecuting counsel, and just two with defence representation (an absence of complete records mean that these figures are very likely to be underestimates). The number of cases with defence representation increased thereafter, significantly outnumbering those with prosecuting counsel by 1745, but still not exceeding 20 a year

299. F. López-Lázaro, ""No Deceit Safe in Its Hiding Place": The Criminal Trial in Eighteenth-century Spain", 2002, p.449.

300. D. Lemmings, "Criminal trial procedure in eighteenth-century England: The impact of lawyers", 2005, pp.73-82.

until after 1775. During this period, defence counsel tended to appear for very serious cases, which would be capital if proved, or on behalf of wealthy defendants. An exchange of letters between two well-to-do female murderers, simultaneously awaiting trial in an unconnected pair of *causes célèbres*, indicates the degree to which legal representation had entered public consciousness by the 1750s. One urged her correspondent to: "...have good council, for which I conjure you to spare no cost".[301]

However, in the last quarter of the century, the number of defence barristers at the Old Bailey increased suddenly and swiftly, being followed, albeit to a much more modest extent, by increased prosecution representation. By 1784, at least 178 trials had defence counsel (17.6 per cent of the total) and 80 prosecutors were also represented (7.9 percent). Exactly why the number of barristers should expand so quickly after 1775 has never been fully explained. Undoubtedly, it was a multi-causal phenomenon.

One plausible, if partial, explanation lies in changes to penal practice. Prior to the American War, many convicts were being transported across the Atlantic. After this became impossible, they were being held in the hulks or sent on a much longer, and far more unpleasant, journey around the world to Australia, a land, unlike the American colonies, that was almost devoid of European inhabitants and infrastructure. It may be that because the consequences of being convicted had become so much harsher than previously defendants were keener to arrange for counsel, however expensive.[302] Another possible cause can be found in changes to the amount of work available at the bar. There was a major decline in civil litigation during the first half of the eighteenth century. This *may* have encouraged a move into criminal practice.[303] Political developments in the wider society, and the individual fame achieved by some prominent Old Bailey practitioners, may also have contributed to the change.[304]

It was not just the number of defence lawyers that grew. They also became increasingly aggressive when challenging prosecution evidence. By the 1780s,

301. M. Blandy, *Genuine letters that pass'd between Miss Blandy and Miss Jeffries, before and after conviction*, 1752, p.23.
302. T. P. Gallanis, "The Mystery Of Old Bailey Counsel", 2006, pp.160-164.
303. D. Lemmings, "Blackstone and Law Reform by Education", 1998, p.222.
304. T. P. Gallanis, "The Mystery Of Old Bailey Counsel", 2006, pp.160-164.

foreign observers could note that they would defend the accused: "... with zeal, and the witnesses against him are questioned with much strictness, and sometimes with much severity".[305] This may have made them appear "better value" to defendants, further encouraging their use.

Towards the end of the century, cross-examination was made a highly effective forensic tool by a circle of talented Metropolitan lawyers. Foremost amongst them were barristers such as William Garrow, Edward Bearcroft, Thomas Erskine and James Adair.[306] In his first year in practice, Garrow appeared in almost 100 cases at the Old Bailey, over 80 per cent of them for the defence. He achieved immediate success, with considerably more than half his clients being acquitted.[307] His courtroom manner was often aggressive and sarcastic. At the trial of John Taylor for forgery, at the Essex Assizes in 1800, he openly boasted that he was "not afraid of giving offence to any judge".[308] A month later, he secured the acquittal of two alleged street robbers by a skilful and occasionally brutal cross-examination of the prosecutor, questioning her motives and the accuracy of her identification of the accused, and suggesting that it may have been influenced by drunkenness.[309]

As a result of these cumulative developments, by the end of the period, defence counsel could argue points of law, advise on the accused's defence, cross-examine prosecution witnesses, and examine-in-chief witnesses called by the defendant.[310] Nevertheless, they still could not directly address the jury via an opening or closing speech, a situation that would persist until 1836. Thus, in 1790, an Old Bailey judge warned a defendant: "...if you have any thing to observe on the evidence, you must do it yourself".[311] This meant that Rhynwick Williams, accused at the Bailey of being the "London Monster" on fairly tenuous evidence, had to open his case to the jury in person, although represented by counsel. Unfortunately, his performance was poor. Initially,

305. J. W. von Archenholz, *A picture of England: Containing a description of the laws, customs and manners of England*, 1790, p.12.

306. J. M. Beattie, "Scales of Justice", 1991, p.237.

307. T. P. Gallanis, "The Rise of Modern Evidence Law", 1999, p.545.

308. P. King, *Crime, Justice, and Discretion in England 1740–1820*, 2001, p.229.

309. J. H. Beattie, "Garrow for the Defence", 1991, pp.49-53.

310. B. Field, *A Vindication of the Practice of Not Allowing the counsel for Prisoners Accused of felony to make Speeches for Them*, 1828, p.5

311. OBSP, Trial of Thomas Newton and others, 13 January 1790.

he attempted to speak from memory, but became hopelessly confused. His high-pitched and faint voice did not carry across the courtroom.[312] Astute defendants could improve their closing addresses by having them written by counsel. Thomas Erskine, for example, wrote the speeches for several high profile defendants. Sometimes, if they were illiterate, defendants could even ask that a court officer read them out.

Despite this limitation, defence counsel became adept at stretching, and so circumventing, the law/fact divide, enabling them to provide a fuller service to their clients. Using submissions on points of law, and the cross-examination of prosecution witnesses, barristers were able to present the defence case and their views on that of the Crown without formally addressing the jury. As one observed in a theft trial at the Surrey Quarter Sessions, because the law and facts of the case were blended together, he was forced to take:

> ...some notice of the evidence that has been produced, and I shall avail myself of this opportunity, because I have a right so to do, that otherwise I could not have in a case of felony.[313]

Similarly, at an Old Bailey felony trial in the 1770s, the defendant's counsel deprecated the law that forbade him from commenting on the evidence, but then observed that he *could* comment on the Crown's evidence where it was inextricably intertwined with a point of law that he wished to make. He cleverly used this as a vehicle to criticise defects in the prosecution case, until opposing counsel complained that he was "observing on the evidence".

The advent of lawyers was not universally welcome. Their effect on forensic practice was deprecated in many quarters, while there was a widespread appreciation that there was little historic basis for the legal culture that began to develop in the later decades of the century. Many contemporary observers claimed that barristers would advance palpable untruths, and: "... browbeat, perplex, and confound the witnesses".[314] By the end of the 1780s, it was even feared that punishments like death and transportation were losing

312. J. Bondeson, *The London Monster*, 2000, pp.104-105.

313. H. Finninmore, *The Trial of Humphry Finnimore, Esq*, 1779, p.9.

314. Anon (By a Friend to the Constitution), *Observations on the Duty and Power of Juries, as established by the Laws of England*, 3rd edn., 1796, p.8.

their deterrent effect as a result of the various legal stratagems that the: "… ingenuity of Council has adopted to save a culprit from conviction".[315] In the same decade, Sir John Hawkins, a prominent London magistrate, expressed concern that a fear of abusive cross-examination had become a deterrent to potential prosecutors, worried that they might be "made to contradict themselves".[316] The Old Bailey Bar gained a particularly poor reputation, being associated with the bullying of witnesses and general rudeness.[317] At the start of the following century, there were further complaints about "railing abusive advocates" and their dishonest ingenuity, prolixity, ribaldry and willingness to twist the truth when questioning witnesses.[318]

It has been argued that felony trials had, to a considerable extent, become lawyer-dominated by the end of the century. This is a slight exaggeration. The majority of Old Bailey cases were still being heard without legal representation on either side, and judges were yet to become largely passive judicial umpires. It is probably even an exaggeration to say that they were "visibly uncomfortable" about being involved in fact-adducing.[319] Indeed, it has been argued that the common law system of criminal trial only adopted an aggressively adversarial process in the years *after* 1800, with the Prisoners' Counsel Act of 1836, and the intellectual rationalisation of vigorous advocacy that this produced.[320]

Nevertheless, by the end of the eighteenth century, nearly all very serious cases, and many that were much less grave, involved legal representation. Judges would often "assign" counsel in court to represent (for free) those who were too poor to afford the fees of barristers but who faced a potential death sentence.[321] The effects of this on the prevailing legal and forensic culture also affected those trials that were entirely devoid of legal representation. It is impossible to have a totally different set of rules that are applied

315. *The Times*, 6 October 1789, p.3.
316. J. H. Langbein, *The Origins of Adversary Criminal Trial*, 2003, pp.246–247.
317. D. Bentley, *English Criminal Justice in the Nineteenth Century*, 1998, p.100.
318. T. Hague, *A Letter to William Garrow, Esq.*, 1807, pp.4-20.
319. J. H. Langbein, *The Origins of Adversary Criminal Trial*, 2003, p. 312.
320. See D. J. A. Cairns, *Advocacy and the Making of the Adversarial Criminal Trial, 1800-1865*, 1998, p.3, and (for a strongly contrasting view) review of same, by A.N. May, in *Law and History Review*, 2001, vol. 19, p. 677.
321. D. Bentley, *English Criminal Justice in the Nineteenth Century*, 1998, p.110.

only when lawyers are present, even if their absence may have encouraged judges to "cut corners" on some occasions.

Pious Perjury

There was a well-documented willingness on the part of eighteenth-century felony juries to convict for lesser offences, rather than the more serious crimes initially indicted, with a view to mitigating the consequences of a defendant being fund guilty. This was usually tacitly accepted, and sometimes even actively encouraged, by the judiciary. Undervaluation as a way of softening the effects of conviction was medieval in origin and had become fairly common by Tudor and Stuart times. However, it reached its peak during the eighteenth century.[322]

Such down-charging was termed "pious perjury" by William Blackstone, as it was motivated by good intentions. There were cases in which jurors would be so blatant about it that they would value stolen coins or banknotes at less than their nominal worth. Thus, in 1730, Sarah Broomhall was indicted for stealing three and a half guineas from one of her clients but only convicted of stealing 10d. despite "the fact being plain".[323] Nevertheless, not all jurors were prepared to do this, even where they wished to save an accused man or woman from the gallows or transportation. For example, in one case involving the theft of almost seven guineas from a dwelling house, the defendant was capitally convicted by a Middlesex jury, which expressly refused to down-value, even though they recommended that he be reprieved: "The jury said, that as the evidence was positive as to the specific money in the purse, they could not lessen the value".[324]

Of course, not all cases in which partial verdicts were returned were instances of this phenomenon. Many reflected the evidence. Some prosecutors were excessively optimistic about the real value of their stolen items (as they often are today) or the circumstances in which a crime had occurred,

322. T.A. Green, *Verdict According to Conscience*, 1985, p.276.
323. OBSP, Trial of Sarah Broomhall, 28 August 1730.
324. OBSP, Trial of Christopher Smith, 12 October 1743.

especially if this raised the possibility of a reward being paid on conviction. Even so, a high proportion of cases in which a lesser verdict was returned involved a deliberate and, on the evidence, legally unwarranted underestimate of the gravity of the offence charged. Certain forms of pious perjury were almost institutionalised, with the same partial verdicts being reached, in similar circumstances, on a routine basis. Thus, Old Bailey juries frequently down-valued stolen goods taken by domestic staff below the strategic levels at which such offences ceased to be petty thefts (a shilling) or, alternatively, became unclergyable, and thus capital, felonies (40 shillings). Only cases with aggravating features would normally result in a conviction for the full offence.[325] Similarly, jurors would usually show little sympathy towards the many, frequently inebriated, men who were robbed by prostitutes. As Sarah Broomhall's case suggests, they would often return a set verdict of guilty to the non-capital value of ten pence (i.e. petty theft), whatever the worth of the items stolen, if they convicted at all.

A number of other, more general, factors appear to have encouraged pious perjury, a few of which were sometimes expressly alluded to in contemporary trial reports or by legal authors. For example, it was thought that jurors were more likely to down-value stolen goods where they thought the offence was a defendant's first crime.[326] Obvious remorse also helped; the jury in the trial of Hannah Ratford appears to have valued clothes that she stole at ten pence, because she seemed "very penitent and dejected".[327] It seems that John Taylor, accused of stealing and pawning goods worth six pounds from his employer, was convicted of a non-capital amount because they had been recovered: "The Jury considering the Master had all his goods again, found him guilty to the value of 39s".[328] George Twelves may well have been found guilty only of petty theft, after being convicted of stealing 96 straw hats valued at £9, because the hats had not been properly secured by their owner, so providing a tempting target.[329]

325. P. Humfrey, "Female Servants and Women's Criminality in Early Eighteenth- century London", 1998, pp.74-75.
326. G. Jacob, *Everyman His own Lawyer*, 4th edn., 1750, p.435.
327. OBSP, Trial of Hannah Ratford, 22 February 1716.
328. OBSP, Trial of John Taylor, 8 July 1719.
329. OBSP, Trial of Georges Twelves, 25 Feb 1713.

CHAPTER 17

THE METROPOLITAN PENAL REGIME

Introduction

This chapter will consider the capital's penal regime and, in particular, how it changed over the course of the eighteenth century. Some of its aspects, such as the Metropolitan execution ritual, the era's more gruesome non-capital penalties, and its generally appalling prison conditions, have been well documented in recent years.[1] Others, such as its use of transportation, corporal and fiscal punishments have received less attention, even though the great majority of those found guilty received such disposals.

Many features of the period's penal system present a litany of horror to modern observers. However, it should always be remembered that for many contemporary Englishmen, living in a much more brutal, less squeamish, society, they did not seem quite so shocking. This was a theme that William Hogarth was to explore in his "Four Stages of Cruelty", with its illustration of the hardening process occasioned by public viciousness.

Although there was a multitude of offenders in the capital, comparatively few were convicted, and so available to be punished, given the vagaries of the Metropolitan policing and justice system. As one career felon noted, the prospects of being caught, prosecuted and found guilty of a capital crime were so low that he had felt offending to be: "...very safe, with at least twenty to one in my favour".[2] This made a system premised on selective but draconian example attractive. If the *relatively* small number who were caught and convicted suffered a terrible and very public fate, even for comparatively minor offences, it might frighten others into leading law-abiding lives. However, as will be seen, such an approach to penal policy, already less marked in 1688

1. A. McKenzie, *Tyburn's Martyrs*, 2007, p.12.
2. M. Madan, *Thoughts On Executive Justice*, 2nd edn., 1785, p.39.

than it had been a century earlier, continued to decline during the 1700s, as more emphasis was placed on effective prevention and prosecution, less on fear and the public spectacle of punishment.

There were other important changes during the course of the century. For much of its first half, continental visitors were struck by the country's relative paucity of punishments, and the lack of fine gradations within its penal repertoire. At its start, in particular, there was an acute lack of secondary punishments to accommodate middle ranking offenders who escaped death. However, the modern notion of a "just" punishment, requiring gradations of sentence, calibrated to the gravity of the offence committed, and consistently, indifferently, and uniformly administered, slowly gained ground, as more observers asked that the: "...modes of punishment [be] more equally proportioned to the malignity of the offence".[3] By 1815, the Earl of Lauderdale could observe, during a debate in the House of Lords, that: "No principle in criminal law was better established than this, that the punishment ought to be commensurate to the offence".[4] This was not entirely true even then, and the very idea was far more recent than he appreciated. Nevertheless, the allocation of punishment in 1800 was significantly less arbitrary and more "proportionate" than had been the case a century earlier.

Rationale for Punishment

Throughout the era, there was surprisingly widespread agreement, among most interested observers, that punishment, especially the death penalty, served the primary function of deterrence rather than retribution or (in the case of non-capital sanctions) reform. Utilitarian notions dominated the debate on penal policy. Even at the start of the century, an observer could note that the country's sanguinary laws were: "...not chiefly intended to punish the present criminal, but to hinder others from being so".[5] More than 50 years later, Henry Fielding believed that: "Example alone is the

3. Anon (By a Magistrate), *Some Hints Towards A Revival of the Penal Laws*, 1787, p.6.
4. *Caledonian Mercury*, 10 July 1815.
5. Anon, *Hanging Not Punishment Enough*, 1701, p.5.

end of all public punishments and rewards".[6] Thirty years further on again, Martin Madan declared that: "The prevention of crimes is the great end of all legal severity".[7]

That such a view should be prevalent is, perhaps, not surprising. Judicial violence may have been necessary to suppress criminal violence, but the great majority of those who were executed died for property crimes, some of them relatively minor to modern and (more significantly) even contemporary eyes. This meant that they could not properly be said to have received their "just deserts", as a retributive approach would require. There was "no proportion" between many crimes and their punishment. Sentencing those who committed routine thefts to death was: "...rather intended to terrify, than punish".[8] Even Martin Madan thought that much English punishment would be straightforwardly cruel unless it acted as a deterrent.[9]

The primacy of deterrence over retribution surprised some foreign visitors. As late as 1802, a visiting Spaniard thought that it explained the traditional lack of fine gradation in English punishments (even though the situation had improved over the previous century). As they were inflicted to prevent further offences, not to reflect moral blame, crimes that were socially damaging and easy to commit, but not especially blameworthy, such as forgery, received the most condign punishment.[10]

Very few contemporary observers felt that much, if any, rehabilitation took place within their society's non-capital penal process. It was widely known that, in classical times at least: "...reformation of the offender was an aim of punishment".[11] However, it was also generally accepted that Newgate, like other English prisons and bridewells, would find it difficult to produce: "...twenty instances of persons reform'd by their having been there imprison'd". Indeed, it was almost taken for granted that most inmates became more hardened and vicious as a result of their incarceration.[12] They

6. H. Fielding, *Journal of a Voyage to Lisbon*, 1755, p.29.
7. M. Madan, *Thoughts On Executive Justice*, 2nd edn., 1785, p.11.
8. G. Ollyffe, *An Essay Humbly offer'd, for An Act of Parliament to prevent Capital Crimes*, 1731, p.1.
9. M. Madan, *Thoughts On Executive Justice*, 2nd edn., 1785, p.11.
10. M. A. Espriella, *Letters from England*, vol.1, 3rd edn., 1814, p.254.
11. J. Fitzsimmonds, *Free and Candid Disquisitions on the Nature and Execution of the Laws of England, Both in Civil and Criminal Affairs*, 1751, p.41.
12. L. Braddon, *The miseries of the poor are a national sin*, 1717, p.11.

contracted bad habits from exposure to experienced felons. Many who were neophytes in crime when first sent to prison mastered their nefarious trades there.[13] Indeed, some were not even criminals when first admitted. The footpad William Duce's entry into a life of crime was attributed to the bad associations he made during 15 months in Newgate, after being imprisoned for debt. It was not until the Penitentiary Act of 1779 that serious thought would be given to producing a regime that might reform inmates.

Decline in Draconian Example

By the early 1700s, a system of criminal justice premised on "deterrence by terror" was occasioning concern. Although this was a national phenomenon, it seems that it was particularly acute in London. This concern was to be a constant, and growing, factor throughout the remainder of the century. Although relatively few in number, there were still too many convicts, many of the wrong age and gender, found guilty of excessively petty crimes, for most eighteenth-century observers to feel entirely "comfortable" about large numbers of them being executed. In 1792, when an MP rhetorically asked the House of Commons why pickpockets were (by then) almost never hanged, he provided a ready answer. The crime was only a minor offence and: "...men's feelings would not bear such unmerciful and disproportionate punishment".[14] Others thought that the apparent humanity of the country's judges and juries, manifest in their frequent unwillingness to convict, despite strong evidence of guilt, combined with the "reluctance" of the King to sign death warrants, was also indicative of the country's laws being too severe.[15]

There were also serious and mounting doubts about the very effectiveness of such a regime. A system premised on deterrence assumes that a fear of sanctions is invariably a primary motivation in human behaviour, and so likely to secure an avoidance of rule-breaking. Some modern research has

13. S. Russell, *The Prisoner's Director*, 1742, p.87 and p.97.
14. W. Cobbett, *The Parliamentary History of England from the Earliest Period to the Year 1803*. London, 1817, vol. xxix, p.1170.
15. W. Smith, *Mild Punishments Sound Policy: Or Observations on the Laws Relative to Debtors and Felons*, 1777, p.18.

questioned the universality of such an assumption. Even at the time, many observers thought that savage punishments merely brutalised or, at the least, rendered the public apathetic, rather than actively deterring offenders. In some cases, as Cesare Beccaria suggested in the 1760s, it was feared that it made felons more, rather than less, ferocious.[16]

More generally, attitudes towards state-inflicted violence changed during the course of the eighteenth century. This was partly as a result of the influence of enlightenment thought, especially in the years after 1760. Cruelty, which had once been thought to enhance the deterrent effect of correction, was increasingly viewed as unseemly, especially when conducted in public, and so unlikely to promote individual reform.[17] Men like Joseph Bramah, a pioneer in the production of improved locks during the late 1700s, stressed the superiority of crime prevention via "target hardening" and denying easy access to "objects of temptation" over deterrence. The former removed the enticements that gradually led the weak-minded into crime, while the latter produced a grisly litany of executions that did not appear to have any impact on offending rates.[18] Additionally, highly public punishments, like the proceedings at Tyburn, the pillory, and public whippings, although necessarily central to a regime premised on deterrence, had to be controlled in an increasingly well-informed (via newspapers), huge and growing city, so creating major policing problems for the authorities and a vehicle for popular unrest.

This "gentling" process occurred very gradually, and was certainly not universally popular. Throughout the eighteenth century, a considerable, if steadily declining, number of interested observers argued for a ratcheting-up of penal sanctions, via more frequent recourse to the death penalty and the introduction of continental-style forms of aggravated execution, rather than a reduction. For example, one anonymous pamphleteer, writing in 1701, demanded that starving and whipping felons to death, or breaking them on the wheel, should be introduced for grave crimes.[19] A few observers did not even confine such savage regimes to the most serious offences.

16. J. S. Cockburn, *Punishment and Brutalization in the English enlightenment*, 1994, p.155.
17. G. T. Smith, "Civilized People Don't Want to See That Kind of Thing", 1996, pp.21-51.
18. J. Bramah, *A Dissertation on the Construction of Locks*, 1785, pp.2-6.
19. Anon, *Hanging, not Punishment Enough,* 1701, p.A2 and pp.1-5.

Only two years later, John Dunton (admittedly a penal extremist) suggested that capitally convicted thieves should be put to death by appointing skilled anatomists as executioners, and having them remove non-essential parts of the condemned man's body each day, so that his pain and terror, along with the attendant deterrent example, progressively increased. Dunton was convinced that this apparently: "...inhumane butchery wou'd restrain a great number from turning thieves". He felt that even petty thieves should spend four years in custody, on a bread and water diet, and then be sold as slaves or transported to the colonies.[20]

In 1731, Dunton's views were echoed by George Ollyffe, albeit for more serious crimes. Ollyffe proposed twisting cords around a convict's arms and legs to "produce the keenest anguish" prior to death, with those executed being positioned just far enough from passers by for their cries not to be annoying, yet close enough for them still to be clearly audible, and so of deterrent value![21] Four years later, another observer suggested that criminals who perpetrated non-lethal assaults should have the same degree of violence visited on their own bodies, then be tended until they had recovered from their injuries, after which time they would be hanged. Murderers would be tied up and fed alive to the lions and tigers kept in the Tower of London.[22] In 1752, another commentator proposed that, in appropriate cases, pre-execution whippings or disembowelling could be added to hanging. This would be far more effective than simply displaying an executed felon's body in chains, which: "As it gives no pain, it gives but very little concern".[23] Nevertheless, such views, though regularly reiterated, were increasingly in a minority as the era advanced.

---

20. J. Dunton, *The Shortest Way With Whores and Rogues: Or a New Project for Reformation*, 1703, pp.23-24.
21. G. Ollyffe, *An Essay Humbly offer'd, for An Act of Parliament to prevent Capital Crimes*, 1731, pp.8-9.
22. Anon (Philo Patriae), *A Full and Genuine Account of the Murder of Mrs. Robinson, by Elton Lewis*, 1735, pp.24-25.
23. C. Jones, *Some Methods Proposed Towards putting a Stop to the Flagrant Crimes of Murder, Robbery, and Perjury*, 1752, pp.8-12.

Capital Punishment

The eighteenth century opened with the English, and particularly the Metropolitan, penal regime revolving around the death penalty, as it had for centuries. Even so, it was not quite as sanguinary as sometimes suggested by historians in the early twentieth century. For example, the "Bloody Code", whereby numerous arcane and, theoretically, capital, felonies were created — on one count there were over 240 of them, though contemporaries frequently cited a figure of 160 — has long been recognised as being 'more bark than bite'. Many of the statutes that made up the code were poorly drafted and had not been fully considered or properly scrutinised before being rushed into law. Their enactment was often the work of small political pressure groups, both inside and outside Parliament. Most had been drawn up to meet a perceived need that had been occasioned by a particular, often localised, social problem or *cause célèbre*, with little thought as to the consequences of systematic enforcement. Unsurprisingly, they were only rarely implemented after being enacted. As William Blackstone observed, although this *ad hoc* passing of capital offences might appear ridiculous, they were largely empty statutes, such: "…outrageous penalties, being seldom or never inflicted".[24] Other contemporary observers freely noted that although most Englishmen would be astonished to know that a man could be executed for cutting down a cherry tree in an orchard or breaking down the wall of a fishpond, the reason they were oblivious to the existence of such offences was because they were so rarely enforced.[25] It may have been an unclergyable capital offence to damage various, named, Metropolitan bridges, but no one was hanged for doing so. Indeed, some observers argued that the deterrent value of the Bloody Code was limited precisely because it was so recondite and most of its capital offences: "…hardly known to be law by the public".[26] Not one person in five thousand read the statutes that extended the death penalty to such arcane crimes.[27]

24. W. Blackstone, *Commentaries on the Laws of England*, 1765-9, vol. iv, p.4.
25. Anon (A Middlesex Freeholder), *A Dialogue Between a Lawyer and a Country Gentleman, Upon the Subject of the Game Laws*, 1771, p.vi.
26. W. Blackstone, *Commentaries on the Laws of England*, 1765-9, vol. iv, p.4.
27. Anon (By a hearty lover of his country), *Solon secundus: or, Some defects in the English laws:*

The vast majority of executions during the eighteenth century were for "traditional" common law offences, such as robbery, burglary and housebreaking, with very much smaller, but not insignificant, numbers being hanged for murder, forgery, rape, coining, uttering (forged money) and theft in a dwelling house. For example, of the 179 confirmed Metropolitan executions in the decade from January 1705 to December 1714, 36 were for burglary, the same number for housebreaking, 31 were for highway robbery, and nine each for horse theft and stealing in a dwelling house. Only 22 were for murder or (in four cases) infanticide.[28]

The *per capita* level of execution had been higher *before* the advent of the "Bloody Code". It declined particularly sharply in the decades after 1650. Nationally, the number of executions appears to have fallen from about 800 per year in 1600, to between 80 and 100 a year in 1750, despite a large increase in England's population. Even as the growth in capital offences got underway, the use of execution was slowly, and unevenly, declining, especially outside the London area. Increasingly, it was being commuted or replaced by secondary punishments. All of those transported for 14 or more years after 1718 were sent to America as a condition of reprieve, after being capitally convicted. Most would have been executed if their crimes had been committed a century earlier.[29]

Nevertheless, despite these qualifications, England executed more people than any other major European country during the eighteenth century, and London had the highest rate of execution in the land, both on an absolute and per capita basis. This had always been the case. However, establishing the precise number of hangings during this period can be difficult. Records are sometimes poor or lost, especially early in the century, particularly for convicts who were initially sentenced to death but ultimately reprieved. Furthermore, not quite everyone who was executed had been sentenced at the Old Bailey; a tiny number came from the Court of King's Bench. Additionally, several convicts were executed near the scene of their crimes, for exemplary effect. Metropolitan assessments are also contingent on whether

with their proper remedies. 1695, p.6.

28. http://www.capitalpunishmentuk.org/tyburn1695.html. This site is largely based on the work of Mr David Mossop. Last Accessed 9/1/11.

29. P. Jenkins, "From Gallows to Prison?", 1986, pp.51-60 and p.66.

the urban parishes of Surrey, lying south of the river (whose executions were held in that county) are included in the total.

On one estimate, based on the work of the 1819 Police Committee, a total of 1,644 people were put to death in the Metropolitan area between 1701 and 1800, with the 1780s being the peak decade for executions (though not on a per capita basis).[30] Other contemporary estimates are more localised, whether chronologically or geographically, and place the rate of executions at slightly higher or lower levels. According to the Reverend Paul Lorrain, during his 18 years' service as Newgate ordinary, from 1701 to 1718, 494 malefactors from the City and Middlesex were put to death, an average of more than 25 a year. In the 20 years from 1729 to 1749, a period for which there is fairly complete data, it seems that 622 of those condemned at the Old Bailey were executed, an average of over 30 a year.[31] These numbers are a little higher than those identified for these periods by the 1819 Committee.

According to the best modern assessment of Metropolitan execution rates, during the 69 years from 1715 to 1783, some 2,168 people were put to death at Tyburn, producing an average of over 31 a year from Middlesex and the City of London. They were the unlucky "survivors" of a group of 4,240 people who had initially been sentenced to death. The six decades between 1715 and 1775 produce figures of 351, 344, 302, 366, 190 and 294 executions respectively. Whatever the average rate for decades, annual rates varied considerably. For example, 63 people were hanged in 1751, a figure that was not exceeded until 1785, when 97 were executed (the highest figure for the century). Against this, only six people were executed in 1759 (the lowest number for the period), and only seven people were hanged in 1794.[32] By the early 1800s, there was an average of eleven executions a year in the same area.[33]

Although these figures must be treated with some caution, taken together, their broad thrust appears to be clear. Given substantial population increases, it seems that there was, on a per capita basis, a very significant, but not spectacular, and regularly interrupted, downward trend in Metropolitan

30. V. A. C. Gatrell, *The Hanging Tree: Execution and the English People 1770-1868*, 1996, p.616.

31. A. McKenzie, *Tyburn's Martyrs,* 2007, p.5.

32. http://www.capitalpunishmentuk.org/tyburn1695.html. This site is largely based on the work of Mr David Mossop. Last Accessed 9/1/11.

33. J. Neild, *State of the Prisons in England, Scotland, and Wales*..., 1812, p.635.

execution rates during the course of the eighteenth century, even allowing for the spike in the 1780s (which prompted acute concern even at the time).

Many contemporary English observers were well aware of their country's unusual incidence of execution compared to continental practice. In 1735, for example, one claimed (a little improbably) that as many people were hanged each year in England as in the entire of the rest of Europe. A few Englishmen even had a fairly shrewd inkling that it was the country's reliance on deterrent savagery, combined with its longstanding lack of secondary punishments, which had brought this situation about. However, the second of these factors was ameliorated by the advent of large-scale organized transportation in the years after 1718.

Proto-abolitionism

Throughout the era, there was a debate about the efficacy and morality of capital punishment, and acute concern about the number of men and women who were hanged after each Old Bailey Sessions. Many observers yearned for a more constructive and less sanguinary penal regime. As a result, there always existed what might, very loosely, be termed a proto-abolitionist movement, which argued that capital punishment should be confined to the most serious crimes of violence. Its supporters felt that it would be better if sentences of imprisonment and hard labour were imposed for most non-lethal offences.[34] Thus, the Reverend Gillespy, who had buried some of the felons executed in London while working as a curate early in his career, sympathised with popular claims that many of them had been hanged for trivial matters. Like other observers of a clerical background, he also claimed that imposing the death penalty for theft was contrary to the Mosaic Law, which set out non-capital punishments for property crimes.[35] Others were concerned that executing convicts prevented them from having an opportunity for proper repentance, and made the rendering of reparations to their victims impossible.

34. Anon (By a hearty lover of his country), *Solon secundus: or, Some defects in the English laws: with their proper remedies*, 1695, p.13.

35. E. Gillespy, *A Disquisition upon the Criminal Laws; Shewing the Necessity of Altering and Amending them*, 1793, pp.13, 15, 18 and 19.

At the same time, it was claimed that capital punishment reduced the population, and so the potential strength, of the commonwealth.[36] Given the dominance of mercantilist economic theory, for much of the century, it is, perhaps, unsurprising that some were appalled at the waste of potential workers.[37] Yet others stressed the apparent inefficacy of the death penalty as a deterrent. Despite the large number of street robbers who were hanged after each Old Bailey Sessions, their numbers appeared to be increasing rather than diminishing.[38]

Against such views, many public officials and independent observers continued to believe that the death penalty was the most effective deterrent available, as well as being the cheapest. Sir Daniel Dolins, for example, was adamant that he had not come across prisoners who would exchange transportation for execution. If they existed, they were exceptionally rare, and certainly: "...not sufficient to contradict the assertion, that death is a more terrible punishment than Transportation, or the like".[39]

There was also a widespread fear that any amelioration in the nation's punishments would further reduce their already limited deterrent value. If the threat of public execution was not enough to deter those who committed property crimes, it was absurd to imagine that making a fourfold restitution of what had been taken, as some biblical precepts suggested, or being committed to a workhouse, would have the least effect. Additionally, it was argued that criminals were a "clog to society" rather than productive members, so that claims that capital punishment deprived the commonwealth of valuable workers were spurious.[40] Even in 1808, when Samuel Romilly began the political debate on the "Bloody Code" by advocating the abolition of the (theoretically available) death penalty for picking pockets it was met with vigorous objections from men like Thomas Plumer, the Solicitor General.[41]

36. H. Dagge, *Considerations on criminal law*, 1722, pp.272-273.
37. Anon (By a hearty lover of his country), *Solon secundus: or, Some defects in the English laws: with their proper remedies,* 1695, p.6.
38. D. Defoe, *Street-Robberies, Considered*, 1728, p.49.
39. D. Dolins, *The Third Charge of Sir Daniel Dolins, Kt to the Grand-Jury, and other Juries of the County of Middlesex*, 1726, p.13.
40. *Gentleman's Magazine*, vol. 8, 1738, p.179.
41. R. McGowen, "The Image of Justice and Reform of the Criminal Law in Early Nineteenth-Century England", 1983, pp.99-101.

Most eighteenth-century Londoners probably belonged to neither "camp". They would have viewed the notion of limiting the death penalty to murder as unrealistic. Nevertheless, they were also concerned about the high incidence of execution in their society, especially for non-violent property crimes.

The mechanics of execution

During the eighteenth century, there were usually eight "hanging days" a year at Tyburn, to correspond with the eight sessions at the Old Bailey. Sometimes, however, for a variety of reasons, there might be slightly more (up to ten) or, much more commonly, slightly less, with prisoners being held over to the next appointed day. Thus, those due to be executed in January 1741 were kept until March of the same year. The vast majority of executed convicts in the Metropolitan area were hanged on the historic fixed gallows, the "Triple Tree" at Tyburn, until 1759, when it was replaced by a moveable apparatus at the same location. In late 1783, the normal place for executions was moved to a space just outside the debtors' door at Newgate, where they were conducted on a temporary scaffold, set up for each hanging day. These new gallows were raised, so as to make them more readily viewable. They were also shrouded in black, to add to the gravity and decorum of the occasion.

This change in location was largely prompted by concern at the unruly scenes of public debauchery and disorder that attended both the traditional procession from Newgate to Tyburn, a distance of some three miles, and the ensuing execution. It was feared that these undermined the punishment's deterrent value, while also providing a vehicle for urban disturbances, so producing major public order problems for the authorities. Additionally, there was concern about the lack of prisoner security at Tyburn itself, and the inability of many of those assembled near its gallows to see the hangings.[42]

During the 1600s, several women being executed for treason (both petty and high) had been burnt at Smithfield. However, early in the following century, probably in 1721, the decision was taken to carry out such immolations next to the Tyburn (and later the Newgate) gallows.[43] The execution

42. S. Devereaux, "Recasting the Theatre of Execution: The Abolition of the Tyburn Ritual", 2009, pp.129-130.
43. *Evening Post,* 1 July 1721.

of those who were capitally convicted at the Surrey Assizes would normally take place in Kennington, close to home for those from the built up areas south of the river.

Occasionally, however, throughout the century, a capitally convicted felon, who had committed a particularly heinous offence, would be executed near to the scene of his crime, for exemplary effect. Thus, Herman Bryan, a Swiss manservant who, after being dismissed from his employment in 1707, returned to his former master's residence, burgled it, and then set the building on fire, was hanged in St. James's Street, near where the house was situated.[44] Similarly, in 1746, Matthew Henderson was executed in Oxford Street for murdering Lady Dalrymple, his master's wife, nearby. In these situations, as with provincial hangings, the convict would be "turned off" a ladder. Such *ad hoc* executions could create logistical problems and prompt local objections. In 1728, James Cluff would have been executed near to the door of the Green Lettuce tavern in Holborn, where he had murdered Mary Green, but local residents petitioned against it, so that he was hanged in the usual fashion at Tyburn.[45]

Those convicts under sentence of death would be returned to Newgate from the Old Bailey pending execution or reprieve. Sometimes, they would be held in the prison's condemned holds, one for each gender, while awaiting their trip to Tyburn. Most would attend chapel twice a day, where they would receive the sacrament from the ordinary, along with: "...such admonitions as are necessary to prepare them for future Happiness". However, both Newgate and the gallows officials appear to have been fairly tolerant of alternative (to the ordinary) sources of religious support, especially after 1735. Non-conformist ministers, and even Catholic priests, usually had access to inmates in the prison, on their way to Tyburn, and at the scaffold, though their ministrations were sometimes discouraged.[46] Thus, in 1786, a Catholic priest visited the murderer John Hogan the evening before he was hanged, so that he could make his confession.[47] Similarly, Margaret Sullivan was

44. P. Lorrain, *The Ordinary's Account of the Life and conversation, Birth, Parentage and Education of John Herman Bryan, The Switzer...*, 1707, pp.1-8.

45. *London Journal*, 26 July 1729.

46. A. McKenzie, *Tyburn's Martyrs: Execution in England 1675-1775*, 2007, pp.176-177.

47. *The Times*, 14 January 1786, p.3.

attended by a "priest of the Romish persuasion" on her way to Tyburn in 1788. Methodist-inspired preachers made frequent visits to the gaol, while rabbis or synagogue elders might attend Jews awaiting execution.

However, it seems that many inmates, especially those who were urban-reared, had little connection to any type of formal worship or religion. The "begging necessitous poor" were often unaware of the finer points of Christian doctrine.[48] Typically, in 1726, the Reverend James Guthrie observed that of a group of four condemned men who regularly came to Chapel while awaiting execution, three were: "...grossly ignorant of the Christian Religion". Such convicts would normally be dependant on the ordinary for their spiritual support, Guthrie noting that he had sought to instruct this trio in the essentials of the faith in a "familiar and easy manner".[49]

Despite this, the ordinary was not universally popular. If the founding Methodist Charles Wesley is to be believed, on one occasion, after he (Wesley) mounted the cart from which the prisoners were to be "turned off" to minister to them, the ordinary tried to follow, but the: "...poor prisoners begged he might not come; and the mob kept him down".[50] In the case of the Reverend Paul Lorrain, the ordinary between 1698 and 1719, it was claimed that even the: "...criminals whom he attended to execution, were wont to make wry faces at him at the tree".[51] In plate 11 of Hogarth's "Idle Apprentice" series of 1751, the prison ordinary can be seen arriving at the gallows in a carriage, while it is a Methodist cleric who ministers to the condemned in the prisoners' cart (see plate section).

Condemned prisoners posed special security problems, as they had very little to lose, especially once there was no chance of a reprieve. In 1728, for example, a group of street robbers, coming from chapel, threatened to murder prison officials before they were executed, so that they might be publicly displayed in chains after execution (the only way in which their sentences

48. J. Bellers, *An Abstract of George Fox's Advice and Warning, To The Magistrates of London, in the Year 1657*, 1724, p.10.

49. *The Ordinary of Newgate his Account, Of the Behaviour, Confession, and dying Words of the Malefactors, who were Executed on Wednesday the 3rd of this Instant August, 1726, at Tyburn.*

50. T. Jackson (Ed.), *The Journal of Charles Wesley*, vol. 1, 1849, pp.122-123.

51. Anon (By a German Gentleman), *A View of London and Westminster: or, the Town Spy, etc.*, 1725, p.37. Lorrain had been the secretary to Samuel Pepys and, as ordinary, played a major role in standardising the format of the prisoners' confessions.

might be enhanced). The keepers were obliged to chain them down to the ground.[52] Even if not recalcitrant, the condemned would usually remain in irons until their execution day, when these would be removed and a hemp rope placed around their necks shortly before they were taken out of the prison to a waiting cart or carriage (depending on their social status) and, amid some ceremony and popular clamour, transported across London to the gallows.

In July 1738, Charles Wesley attended several convicts on the day they were to hang, subsequently recording the events in his diary. He rose at six in the morning, before receiving the sacrament with the condemned men. It only took an hour for the execution procession to reach Tyburn (it could take much longer) though, as was normal, the convicts were not hanged until more than another hour after arrival there.[53] Occasionally, this was just as well. There were cases of reprieves reaching the gallows just prior to execution. Others still arrived too late. For example, George Jennings, executed for housebreaking, was: "…much pity'd, as a reprieve to stop [his] execution, thro' some mistake, came too late, it being the next morning before it arriv'd".[54] As a result, it was eventually decided that last minute reprieves, given within two hours of execution, would normally only be granted where there was new evidence from which a convict's innocence might be extrapolated.[55]

As the population of London grew, and publicity got better, the crowds attracted to Tyburn or to line the route taken by the execution procession inevitably got larger. Even before the century opened, there were complaints that hanging days had become undignified holidays, accompanied by "shouting and hallowing" which did not deter people from crime.[56] Execution day was frequently referred to as "Tyburn Fair", the name being indicative of the atmosphere around the gallows. It was even seen as a tourist attraction,

52. *The Flying-Post*, 9 November 1728.
53. T. Jackson (Ed.), *The Journal of Charles Wesley*, vol. 1, 1849, pp.122-123.
54. *General Advertiser*, Friday, 21 August 1752.
55. A. L. Cross, "The English Criminal Law and Benefit of Clergy during the Eighteenth and Early Nineteenth Century", 1917, p.558.
56. Anon (By a hearty lover of his country), *Solon secundus: or, Some defects in the English laws: with their proper remedies*, 1695, p.6.

foreign visitors being warned to be on their guard if they went there. The tight packed crowds meant that pickpocketing was a permanent danger, something that continued after their location was moved to Newgate.[57] At Tyburn, stalls and vendors selling refreshments and popular tracts were also widespread. Additionally, there were grandstands from which those who could afford a ticket might get a superior view of the proceedings, in relative comfort, though there were also numerous collapses in the years immediately prior to 1783, producing several deaths and many injuries. Unfortunately, the move to Newgate did not prevent 30 or more people being crushed to death in a crowd surge, while watching a triple execution there in 1803.

Samuel Richardson, writing in 1741, captured some of the atmosphere and characteristics of a hanging day, after following the procession of five convicts. The men exhibited a range of emotions. Some seemed unconcerned at their impending deaths, while others were clearly in despair. Three of them started to behave in an outrageous manner: "They swore, laughed, and talked obscenely, and wished their wicked companions good luck". The crowds were so large that the traditional exhortation by a bellman, spoken from the wall of St. Sepulchre's churchyard, urging repentance, was totally drowned out by the ambient noise. Indeed, there were so many spectators in the early stages of the journey that they obstructed the execution party's way every twenty or thirty yards.[58] Although the ancient custom of allowing convicts "going west" to Tyburn to stop for alcoholic refreshment at designated taverns, such as the Crown Inn in St. Giles, had been abolished by the Court of Aldermen in 1735, there were periodic breaches of this ruling in ensuing years.[59] Wine was still frequently offered to the condemned en route. Nevertheless, the change reduced the number of convicts who were heavily inebriated when they were executed.

The social profile of the dead after the disaster in 1803 was overwhelmingly young and male, although their number included four females and a man of 67. Most were drawn from the "lower" social orders, many being apprentices or day labourers. It is likely that it was very similar to that of the bulk

57. *Morning Chronicle and London Advertiser*, 29 April 1785.

58. S. Richardson, *Familiar letters on the most important occasions*, 1741, pp.239-241.

59. A. McKenzie, *Tyburn's Martyrs*, 2007, p.12.

of spectators found at Tyburn in the years before the move in 1783, though many of the capital's "well-to-do" also made regular visits to the gallows.

At the scaffold

In theory, the "triple tree", as the fixed Tyburn scaffold was known after its three spans, could accommodate 24 felons at a time, eight on each beam. On one occasion, in 1649, it had even been used to its full capacity, while on 18th March 1741, 20 malefactors had been executed there, with three carts moving away simultaneously to "turn them off". However, this was an extreme case. In the years between 1700 and 1749 an average of 3.4 to 3.8 convicts were executed on each hanging day.[60] Frequently, only one cart was required to carry the condemned, although, when coffins had been added, more might be necessary. In December 1750, for example, the 15 convicts being executed at Tyburn were carried in five carts and a coach, this last vehicle being used for the one "genteel" man amongst their number, though he mounted a cart for execution.[61]

After they arrived, the hangman would climb to the top of the gallows to connect the loose ends of each noose (already placed around the convicts' necks) to one of its crosspieces. He would then descend and wait for the sheriff or another official to give an indication that the cart should move away, so forcing the prisoners off the back of the vehicle to their deaths. Before this, however, the convicts would receive further religious ministrations and blindfolds would be pulled over their faces.[62]

According to Richardson, the attendant clergyman was largely ignored or ridiculed after he arrived at the place of execution. However, he managed to get a psalm sung before the convicts were "turned off", amidst the curses and quarrelling of hundreds of mirthful spectators, whose faces suggested that the: "…spectacle they had beheld had afforded pleasure instead of pain".[63] The hostility manifest towards the ordinary was partly the inevitable result of the demands of his office, which extended beyond providing

60. A. McKenzie, *Tyburn's Martyrs*, 2007, p.5.
61. *Old England*, 5 January 1751.
62. Anon (By a German Gentleman), *A View of London and Westminster: or, the Town Spy, etc.*, 2nd edn., 1725, p.37.
63. S. Richardson, *Familiar letters on the most important occasions*, 1741, pp.240–242.

spiritual sustenance, and included gaining criminal intelligence, public displays of repentance, and even moral exhortation to the spectators from the condemned.

For example, while the highwayman William Hawke was awaiting execution, the Reverend John Villette attempted to establish whether he had committed an unsolved robbery in Epping Forest, in which a woman and child had been cruelly treated (Hawke assured him that he never robbed on that road).[64] The Reverend Paul Lorrain's account of the last moments of a pair of convicts that he accompanied to Tyburn was typical of the ordinary's role in such proceedings. He made a final attempt to gain admissions and information from the men at the scaffold and:

> ...(as usually) exhorted them to clear their Consciences, and to leave nothing undiscover'd that they knew the World might be benefited by the knowledge of.

He then prayed with them, made the pair recite the Apostles' Creed, and got them to sing some penitential psalms. Lorrain also: "...advis'd them to speak to the Spectators that they might follow better Courses than themselves had done". This being done, they were given some time to make their private devotions and, while they were doing so, the cart drew away.[65] As this suggests, select convicts were encouraged to make a "dying speech" acknowledging their guilt and warning their audience to take heed from their fates, though constraints of time and articulacy meant that this was normally only possible for one or two of them.

Those being hanged would usually be strangled, as eighteenth-century gallows lacked a "drop" to break their necks until well after the move from Tyburn. The execution attended by Wesley apparently went off seamlessly: "...not one stirred, or struggled for life, but meekly gave up their spirits".[66] However, if he gave an accurate account, their deaths were exceptional. In 1777, Dr. Dodd was felt to have had a relatively benign end but, even so, did

64. Rev J. Villette, *A Genuine Account of the Behaviour, confession, and Dying-Words of William Hawke and William Jones*, 1774, p.18.
65. P. Lorrain, *The Ordinary of Newgate his Account of The Behaviour, Confessions, and Last Speeches of the Malefactors that were Executed at Tyburn, on Tuesday the 23d Day of December, 1712.*
66. T. Jackson, (Ed.), *The Journal of Charles Wesley*, vol. 1, 1849, pp.122-123.

not die instantly: "He appeared not to suffer much in dying, though it was near two minutes before all motion ceased".[67] Others struggled violently, for considerably longer. John Austin, a highwayman, and the last convict to be executed at Tyburn, writhed for at least ten minutes because the noose had slipped to the back of his head, so preventing a tight ligature from being formed. Several, such as William Duell, actually survived their hangings and were cut down from the gallows while still alive. Duell came round on a table at Surgeons' Hall, where his body had been taken for dissection. He was subsequently reprieved and transported to America. Duell later recalled that, upon the cart driving away, the sudden jerk as he fell caused "agony, confusion and uproar" in his senses.[68]

Frequently, the executioner would try to expedite the process, if death was particularly slow in arriving. Lord Ferrers, for example, struggled until the hangman pulled on his legs, mercifully speeding up the process of strangulation.[69] Occasionally, even members of the public would join him in trying to hasten deaths in this manner or by administering blows to the convicts' chests. Thus, in 1746, the light bodied, but bull-necked, Mathew Henderson struggled a great deal, so that after he had: "...hung a while, having still life in him, his legs were pulled, and some blows were given him upon the breast to put him out of his misery".[70]

After execution, bodies would be allowed to dangle for at least 30 minutes, and would then be cut down. Those who had friends or relations might have their corpses reclaimed for burial. For the rest, and as Duell's experience suggests, it was: "...customary to dispose of the dead Bodies by way of sale to surgeons for Anatomies". This could be for anything from half-a-crown to ten shillings.[71] The Surgeons' Company's accounts for this time regularly

67. W. Dodd, *Authentic Memoirs of the Life of William Dodd, LL.D. who was executed at Tyburn, on Friday, June 27, 1777*. 3rd edn., 1777, p.45.
68. Anon, *News from the Dead, or a faithful and Genuine Narrative of an extraordinary combat between life and death, exemplified in the case of William Duell*, 1740, p.11.
69. L. Shirley, *An Account of the Execution of the Late Laurence Earl Ferrers, Viscount Tamworth*, 1760, p.10.
70. J. Guthrie, *The Ordinary Of Newgate His Account Of The Behaviour, Confession, And Dying Words Of Matthew Henderson, Who Was Executed On Friday The 25th Of April, 1746*.
71. B. L., *An Accurate Description of Newgate*, 1724, pp.47-49.

include the cost of obtaining corpses directly from Tyburn.[72] They would normally be dissected at Surgeons' Hall. However, if there was more than one cadaver available, the surgeons might allow some of them to be anatomised at a Metropolitan hospital. Thus, in March 1741, when two bodies were obtained from the Tyburn gallows, that of Elizabeth Fox was dissected at St. Thomas's Hospital.[73]

There was often popular hostility to such disposals, and active resistance to attempts at recovering bodies for dissection, something that could even produce major riots.[74] Relatives of the dead might struggle with men sent by the surgeons to obtain corpses.[75] For example, in 1721, when rumours circulated that both the College of Physicians and the Company of Surgeons had obtained warrants for the bodies of those to be executed at Tyburn, the comrades of a soldier who was due to be hanged there marched to the gallows to guard his corpse.[76] In 1723, several members of a "mob" which had attempted to rescue the body of a felon from the Surgeons Company were committed to the bridewell.[77]

By then, the existing statutory allowance of felons' corpses was felt to be: "...insufficient for the expensive practice of anatomy". This resulted in the widespread digging up of corpses, or "bodysnatching", for commercial sale. However, this was both a crime (albeit of uncertain legal status) and spread diseases. As a result, it was suggested that any private doctor should be able to buy an executed corpse for 20s, as of right, unless relatives of the dead man paid five pounds to recover it.[78] Although this proposal was not followed, in 1752, dissection was made a mandatory part of the sentence for those executed for murder, so that even Lord Ferrers was anatomised before his remains were released for burial. Some observers subsequently suggested that using convicts' bodies for this purpose be expanded to other

72. A. Guerrini, "Anatomists and Entrepreneurs in Early Eighteenth-century London", 2004, pp.219-39.
73. *Universal Spectator and Weekly Journal,* 21 March 1741.
74. P. Linebaugh, "The Tyburn Riot Against the Surgeons", 1975, p.69.
75. S. Richardson, *Familiar letters on important occasions*, 1741, pp.240-242.
76. *London Journal*, 8 April 1721.
77. *London Journal*, 12 January 1723.
78. Anon, *A Method whereby Criminals liable to Transportation may be render'd not only useful but honest members of the publick*, 1727, p.10.

crimes, to enhance the fear of execution, while also satisfying the medical profession's needs.

Occasionally, the bodies of particularly heinous felons would be publicly displayed in chains after execution, until they decayed, for extra deterrent effect. For example, in July 1700, when two Dutch publicans were executed for murder, their corpses were hung on a gibbet set up near Mile End. This attracted numerous visitors, many of whom were so terrified by the "dismal sight" that they had to restore themselves at a nearby public house.[79] The monarch had traditionally held the power to order such a disposal, and this was extended to trial judges and put on a statutory basis in the eighteenth century (25 Geo. II. c.37 s.5). As a result, James Hall, the notorious murderer of John Penny (his master) was hung in chains at Shepherd's Bush, the offence being "extremely atrocious" and the dead man's brother, the Dean of Litchfield, having petitioned for such an outcome.[80] By the end of the century, this practice was in decline, with bodies hung to the west of London being taken down after a period of time, and the large number that had been simultaneously exposed 25 years earlier, emitting a "pestilential odour", a thing of the past.[81]

In 1735, it was noted that all three forms of post-mortem disposal had been used for the corpses of four men executed at Tyburn, so that, as soon as they were dead: "...the bodies of Sutton and Lewis were delivered to their friends, that of Gregory sent to Edgeware to be hung in chains with his companions, and Hughes to be dissected in Surgeons Hall".[82]

Reprieves

Many of those who were sentenced to death at the Old Bailey or Assizes were not executed, even though, throughout the century, numerous felonies were unclergyable. It was widely appreciated that if all capital sentences were carried out the law would lose legitimacy. However, in England, unlike

79. *London Post*, 19–22 July 1700.
80. *R v James Hall* (1741) 1 Leach 21.
81. M. A. Esprilla, *Letters from England*, vol.1, 3rd edn., 1814, p.62.
82. *The Old Whig*, 2 June 1735.

some continental countries, major reform of the criminal code, legally withdrawing some crimes from the shadow of the gallows, would wait until the nineteenth century. Instead, as the 1700s advanced, and attitudes towards capital punishment slowly changed, the Crown and members of the judiciary sought to moderate the indiscriminate and sanguinary nature of the "death for (unclergyable) felony" rule by the greater use of reprieves.[83]

All capitally convicted felons could be reprieved during the interval between sentence of death being passed and execution taking place. This was usually several weeks, unless the accused person was convicted of murder after 1752, when, by the Murder Act of that year, it had to take place within a matter of days. As a result, in a handful of exceptional cases, where the possibility of a reprieve was seriously considered for those convicted of murder, a temporary respite would have to be issued to avoid the statute's time constraints. For example, in 1761, Thomas Daniels secured a respite for a week from Metropolitan justices, a day after he was found guilty of murder, to allow time for the King to be petitioned.[84]

In the Restoration period, the Westminster judges, sitting at the Old Bailey, had insisted that those convicted of unclergyable felonies in the Metropolis should not be pardoned by members of the judiciary without the King's express warrant, granted in open court.[85] This practice had been put on a structured basis in the years after 1689, in a system that would continue until the end of the reign of William IV in 1837, when a reduction in the number of capital convicts as a result of penal reform, combined with the presence of a woman as the reigning monarch (considered to be of the wrong gender to consider such harrowing matters), brought it to a close.

Under this procedure, the Recorder or, in his absence, the Deputy Recorder of London's report on the Sessions' capital convictions, prepared immediately after the trials had been heard, would be submitted to the King, his Secretary of State and the Privy Council. It would recommend that some convicts be spared and others "left for execution", and was highly influential

83. Sir S. Romilly, *Observations on a Late Publication, Intituled, Thoughts on Executive Justice*, 1786, p.2.
84. T. Daniels, *The Affecting Case of the Unfortunate Thomas Daniels*, 1761, p.21.
85. Sir J. Kelyng, *A Report of Divers Cases in Pleas of the Crown, Adjudged and Determined; in the Reign of the Late King Charles II*, 2nd edn., 1739, p.4.

on subsequent decisions. At the end of the seventeenth century, this new process had occasioned some administrative problems. In the City, the Court of Aldermen, which had elected Sir Salathiel Lovell to the recordership in 1692, objected to his failure to consult them before making recommendations. In 1693, they insisted that he do this and obtain their views on the merits of individual convicts and how these should be presented to the Crown. (Sir Lovell's decisions were widely viewed as harsh and idiosyncratic). This was subsequently modified on Lovell's suggestion, and for administrative convenience, to consulting those aldermen who had attended the relevant sessions, according to the City's rota. These administrative problems had been resolved by the early part of the eighteenth century.

Until a report had been received, execution could not proceed. Thus, in February 1719, the hanging of the condemned prisoners from Newgate was delayed pending the completion of this process: "The Deputy-Recorder hath not yet made his report; but, 'tis expected he will do it to-morrow, and the execution be some day next week".[86] Although the final decision was always for the Crown, the recorder's advice was normally followed, especially where a reprieve was recommended. Indeed, in the provinces, judges on circuit would sometimes openly announce their decisions on this issue at the end of an Assizes hearing, before moving on to the next town, in anticipation that this would be the case.

In making his initial recommendation, the recorder would be influenced by a number of considerations. These appear to have been almost universal amongst members of the judiciary, and seem to have been taken into account throughout the century. They would also be influential if the Crown was asked to grant a reprieve after petition, where it had not initially been recommended. Most are still considered relevant today, even if issues of life and death no longer turn on them.

Foremost amongst them were any mitigating or aggravating features in the commission of the offences or in the convicts themselves. These included the: gravity of the crime; age of the convict and his offending history; whether his involvement was peripheral or central to the offence; his motivation; his submissiveness when arrested; whether he had shown evidence of contrition

86. *Original Weekly Journal*, 7 February 1719.

and remorse; whether he had been open with the authorities when questioned, or evasive and dissembling; whether he had been co-operative after arrest, for example, by helping the authorities recover stolen goods. His or her gender and familial circumstances might also come into the equation.

The decision would also consider whether there was a pressing need to make a deterrent example of a crime that had increased in prevalence at any particular time. In 1750, for example, the fairly well-born highwayman James Maclean realistically appreciated that his chances of a reprieve were very slim, and that the: "...great number of robberies committed by persons of genteel appearance rendered it very improbable that he should be spared".[87]

Additionally, Sir Dudley Ryder seems to have been typical of many judges in recommending reprieves where he felt the evidence against a convict was weak or defective in some manner. Thus, he reprieved a horse-thief "because the evidence [appeared] doubtful".[88] In the notorious Elizabeth Canning case, Sir Crisp Gascoyne, the Lord Mayor, who had been present (though not presiding) at the initial trial, and who had entertained serious doubts about the whole prosecution, ensured a reprieve was granted to Susannah Wells and her gipsy attendant, Mary Squires, after their capital convictions.[89]

The significance of these factors was also widely recognised by contemporary observers. For example, although legal commentators were clear that necessity was never a defence to theft, even of food, they sometimes followed this observation by expressly noting that the courts had the power to reprieve from execution any who were capitally convicted for stealing in such circumstances.[90] Similarly, the importance placed on previous character meant that, in 1751, one observer was convinced (albeit mistakenly) that there had been almost no cases for several years in which anyone had been executed at Tyburn for a first offence other than murder. Most of those hanged were

87. Anon., *Execution of Maclean Commonly Known by the name of the Gentleman Highwayman*, 1795, p.9.

88. J. H. Langbein, "Shaping the Eighteenth-century Criminal Trial: A View from the Ryder Sources", 1983, pp.29-30. These decisions raise intriguing questions about the standard of proof applied by trial juries and the directions presiding judges gave them on this subject.

89. B. Hillier, "The Mysterious Case of Elizabeth Canning", 2003, pp.47-53.

90. Sir M. Hale, *The History of the Pleas of the Crown*, updated by G. Wilson and S. Emlyn, vol.1, 1800, p.54.

"long hardened and experienced in the ways of vice". Although this was a wild exaggeration, first offenders were particularly likely to secure reprieves.

Petitions for reprieve

Several monarchs, including George III, took a keen personal interest in the decisions on execution and sometimes granted a reprieve after being petitioned on behalf of a convict, even if it had not, initially, been recommended by the recorder. The delay between conviction and execution gave those with friends and contacts, especially influential ones, the opportunity to seek clemency. Nationally, judges' letters in support of pardons often cited petitions from the convict's more prominent neighbours.[91] For example, Lord Sandwich's mistress used his high level influence to secure a reprieve for her brothers after they were convicted of an "atrocious murder". The two men were transported instead.[92]

As a result, there were periodic claims that individuals with connections, whether real or imaginary, were offering to intercede with the authorities on behalf of capitally convicted prisoners, in exchange for cash. At the start of the century, for example, there were ugly allegations that the Reverend Allen, the Newgate ordinary, had extorted two guineas from the wife of a felon awaiting execution by claiming that he could intercede with the King on her husband's behalf. These claims appear to have prompted a small protest petition to the monarch from other Newgate inmates.[93] Similarly, in 1785, a solicitor found that one of his female clients, temporarily respited from execution for a week, but with an express warning not to think that this would necessarily result in a pardon, was in exceptionally high spirits. When questioned about this, the prisoner told him that she had given eight guineas to a man who "did business" for the inmates, and who had promised to have her omitted from the death warrant.[94] At the start of the period, the very worst sort of solicitors would congregate around the condemned prisoners held in Newgate pending execution, inveigling themselves into their

91. T. A. Green, *Verdict According to Conscience*, 1985, Chicago University Press, Chicago, p.281.
92. *London Evening Post*, 18 January 1772.
93. Anon., *An Account of a new and strange discovery that was made by John Sheirly, alias Davis, & Joseph Fisher, the same day of their execution relating to the ordinary of Newgate*, 1700, pp.1-2.
94. *The Times*, Friday, 1 July 1785, p.2.

circle of family and friends, and promising that, for a considerable fee, they could use their: "...interest at court to get their friend a pardon or at least a reprieve sine die".[95]

Sometimes, ordinary people, without high-level influence, would petition for a reprieve, hoping to make up in numbers what they lacked in status. Major John Oneby, for example, was unable to use the direct influence of "people of quality", due to his lack of connections, so the: "...Method us'd by the common Malefactors was to be thought of, [namely] an humble Petition".[96] Such popular pleading might be done in a highly ritualised manner. Thus, on several occasions in the first half of the century, a petition was presented to the Crown by a party of white-robed women, carrying white wands, one of whom might offer to marry the convict under the gallows, if a reprieve was granted.[97] In 1721, the King received a group of 12 women attired in this fashion, who sought to intercede for the life of the burglar Thomas Knight. One of the women also offered to wed Knight.[98] Occasionally, this process was successful; at other times, it signally failed, even where a member of the royal family had initially expressed sympathy.

A few convicts even sought to bolster their petitions by attaching fresh evidence suggesting that they were innocent. For example, when John Pagon was awaiting execution he sought to avoid his fate by getting a woman to impersonate a key prosecution witness, and to swear an affidavit in front of a JP withdrawing "her" testimony at trial. His supporters then attached it to a petition pleading for clemency, and had it put before the King in Council. When it was read out, and questions were raised about Pagon's guilt, he was respited and avoided being hanged with others from the same sessions. However, his trickery was swiftly exposed, and he was executed on the next hanging day.[99]

---

95. E. S. (Gentleman in prison), *A companion for debtors and prisoners, and advice to creditors in ten letters*, 1699, London, p.37.
96. Anon, *A True and Faithful Narrative of the Life and Actions of John Oneby, commonly called Major Oneby Esq.*, 1727, pp.23-24. His attempts at securing a reprieve were unsuccessful.
97. *Weekly Journal, or British Gazetteer*, 10 April 1725.
98. *Applebee's Original Weekly Journal*, 21 January 1721.
99. *The Ordinary of Newgate's Account* ... 17 June 1747.

Both high-level intercession and mass petitions were used in the exceptional attempts taken to secure a reprieve for the well-known Dr. Dodd, capitally convicted of forgery in 1777. Noblemen and members of the clergy approached the King and Queen on his behalf, and the Court of Common Council, in the City of London, sent a petition to the Monarch. Nevertheless, the King insisted that the matter be dealt with in the normal manner. As a result, in due course, the Privy Council met to consider the recorder's report on Dodd and two capitally convicted highwaymen from the same sessions, along with the attendant petitions for clemency. The meeting was unusually well attended and prolonged, because it was dealing with a *cause célèbre*, and both the Lord Chancellor and Lord Mansfield spoke for almost half an hour each, on the relative benefits and disadvantages of reprieving Dodd. This boiled down to weighing the importance of deterrence against his previous good character and value to society as a clergyman. At the end of the meeting, a decision was taken to reprieve one of the highwaymen, and to execute the remaining two men, including the unfortunate Dodd.[100] As this case indicates, petitions for clemency were not indulged lightly. In a letter written in 1776, King George expressly noted that he was always pleased if he could spare the life of a "miserable wretch", but that high crime levels normally called for a rigid application of the law.[101]

A few very grave offences were inherently unlikely to result in a reprieve. Nevertheless, no class of crime was entirely excluded; the death sentences passed in 11 per cent of murder cases and 30 per cent of highway robberies committed between 1749 and 1771 were commuted.[102] For example, in 1769, two men were convicted of murder, after striking a young man at a Middlesex election in Brentford (notoriously rough affairs), from the effects of which he died a few days later. However, and perhaps as a result of political influence, there was immediate pressure to secure a reprieve, which was eventually granted.[103] Similarly, in 1761, Thomas Daniels was given an unconditional

100. W. Dodd, *Authentic Memoirs of the Life of William Dodd, LL.D. who was executed at Tyburn, on Friday, 27 June 1777*. 3rd edn. 1777, p.38.

101. A. L. Cross, "The English Criminal Law and Benefit of Clergy during the Eighteenth and Early Nineteenth Century", 1917, p.558.

102. A. R. Ekirch, *Bound for America*, 1987, p.35 at n 14.

103. J. Foot, *An Appeal to the Public, Touching the Death of Mr. George Clarke*, 2nd edn., 1769, pp.1-51.

pardon after being convicted of murdering his wife by throwing her out of a window during a heated domestic argument. There appears to have been grave concern about the safety of his conviction. Although the defendant's story that his wife had leapt out of the first-floor window during their argument seemed unlikely, she was a large and powerful woman and her body was, apparently, unmarked, while there were few signs of a struggle to force the defenestration. Additionally, the dead woman had been openly unfaithful to her spouse.[104]

In 1754, Thomas Rolf was also reprieved from execution, even though he had been convicted of highway robbery at the Old Bailey. He had behaved with extreme politeness towards his female victim, and informed her that he had been driven to crime by his inability to find work when his wife was about to give birth to their third child. Although the trial jury acceded to the presiding judge's direction that they should not let compassion cloud their judgment, they urged clemency, a position that was also subsequently supported by the recorder.[105]

Conditional reprieves

Entirely free pardons were comparatively rare, except where there was a doubt about the safety of a conviction. Most commonly, pardons would be issued on condition of transportation, usually for 14 or more years. However, as Lord Justice Gould observed in 1785, the King could grant a pardon "upon any condition he pleases".[106] Thus, in 1760, several men who had been pardoned by the King "on condition of serving as soldiers in the plantations" were put on ship with other (volunteer) recruits destined for the 49th Regiment in Jamaica.[107]

Technically, until 1797, convicts would have to be brought back to the Old Bailey to "plead their pardon", that is to be formally notified of it and to accept the condition on which it was granted, before they could escape death. Until at least the 1690s, and probably somewhat later, this had to be

104. T. Daniels, *The Affecting Case of the Unfortunate Thomas Daniels*, 1761, p.21.
105. J. H. Langbein, "Shaping the Eighteenth-century Criminal Trial: A View from the Ryder Sources", 1983, pp.20–21.
106. *The King v Aickles* (1785) 1 Leach 390.
107. *London Evening Post*, 30 December 1760.

done while kneeling. Unsurprisingly, this was usually a formality. Prisoners like Susannah Brammah and Arthur Bethell "thankfully accepted" transportation in exchange for their lives in 1740. However, there were a tiny number of cases in which convicts hesitated or refused to accept this condition. For example, in September 1789, William Davis initially declared that: "Death is more welcoming to me than this pardon". He was returned to the condemned cell in Newgate. Seven other men followed his lead. All were eventually pressured into accepting transportation.[108] The convicts in this case appear to have been well aware of popular anxiety about high execution rates in the 1780s, almost "daring" the authorities to hang them.

Indicative of the types of offence for which reprieves were granted, and the conditions imposed, can be considered a single day in August 1715, when 60 men and 25 women pleaded the King's pardon at the Old Bailey. Of these, 16 men and four women received a free pardon, which would allow their immediate release. The rest were granted on condition of transportation to the plantations. The offences pardoned were overwhelmingly property crimes, such as shoplifting, picking pockets, burglary, housebreaking and grand larceny. However, the politically well-connected Hugh Leeson received a free pardon for rape, as did his female accessory. Very few robbers were numbered amongst the 85, though the footpad John Dixon also received a free pardon, while Richard Shornbury and Thomas Smith were sent to the plantations for the same offence.[109]

A close examination of the offences committed by the convicts reprieved in 1715 indicates some of the more esoteric and specific factors that could influence both the recorder and the Crown when reaching a decision. For example, Edward Alcock received a free pardon after being convicted of stealing a silver tankard from a public house. He claimed that he had been so drunk when he committed the offence that he had no idea where he was at the relevant time. His crime had been carried out in an amateurish fashion and the tankard recovered. He also called several witnesses to his previous

108. S. Devereaux, "Imposing the Royal Pardon: Execution, Transportation, and Convict Resistance in London, 1789", 2007, p.102.

109. Anon, *A True and Exact List of all the Malefactors, Both men and women, Who pleaded to His Majesty's most Gracious Pardon, at the Sessions-House in the Old-Baily, On Saturday the 6th of August, 1715*, 1715, pp.1-6.

good character.[110] William Holyoak was slightly less fortunate when convicted of an almost identical offence; his pardon was on condition of transportation to the plantations. This may have been because Holyoak admitted that the stolen silver tankard had been sold on to a woman in Holborn for more than five pounds. It was not recovered.[111] In both situations, it is clear that theft of a drinking utensil from a public house, however valuable, was not viewed in quite the same way as theft from other domestic premises.

The reprieve process enhanced the role of discretion in the criminal justice system during the eighteenth century, though it was applied with some degree of consistency. Nevertheless, in exceptional cases, even those guilty of relatively minor crimes could be left for execution. As late as 1771, Mary Jones, a young mother of two small children, was prosecuted to conviction under the Shoplifting Act 1699 and executed for stealing muslin worth £5 10s from a shop in Ludgate Street. This was considered remarkable, even at the time, and was subsequently referred to in Parliament by Sir William Meredith, when he campaigned (unavailingly) against the Bloody Code. By this time, convictions under the 1699 Act were rare, and, where they did occur, usually resulted in reprieves (albeit normally on condition of transportation). As a young, single, mother, whose husband had been pressed for the navy, and a woman of previous good character, Jones was exactly the sort of defendant who normally attracted jury, judicial and executive sympathy. However, she was convicted of the full offence (rather than simple grand larceny), not recommended for a reprieve by the Recorder of London in his report, and a subsequent petition on her behalf, by neighbours in Whitechapel, was also rejected by the Crown.

There appear to have been several reasons for this draconian decision. On the evidence, Jones seems to have been one of a group of five women who had been seen hovering around shops for several hours before she was arrested, suggesting a degree of professionalism in her crime. Perhaps most significantly, she had been impertinent and abusive in court, calling the presiding

110. OBSP, Trial of Edward Alcock, 14 January 1715.
111. OBSP, Trial of William Holyoak, 30 June 1714.

judge and trial jury a lot of "old fogrum" after she was found guilty. Had she adopted a more supplicant posture, she may well have been spared.[112]

Incidence of reprieves

Throughout the period, the use of reprieves was statistically common. To take a very specific illustration, half of the 18 convicts sentenced to death at the April 1715 sessions escaped death.[113] On a more general basis, during the 20-year period from December 1729 to October 1749, 962 people, 832 men and 132 women, were condemned to death, for all types of offence, at the Old Bailey (91 per cent of them for property crimes). Of these, just over a third (35 per cent) received full or conditional pardons, the remainder being executed. Condemned men were twice as likely as women to be executed (69 per cent compared to 34 per cent), females being especially favoured when it came to being reprieved for property offences.[114]

As the use of transportation for 14 or more years as a condition of reprieve increased after 1718, the proportion of death sentences that were commuted also grew. About half of those capitally convicted in London in the second half of the century escaped execution in this manner.[115] By the last quarter of the period, reprieves were granted much more willingly than had been the case in its first 25 years. Thus, and typically, at the sessions held at the Old Bailey in May 1774, eight defendants were convicted of capital offences and sentenced to death. None were found guilty of murder, which would have required prompt execution, so all waited for just over a month for a decision on their fates. The day after the sessions finished, the recorder made his recommendations to the King, leading to five of the eight being reprieved. For the remaining three individuals, execution was appointed for the 1st July, some six weeks after their convictions. However, one of the three received a temporary respite on the 29th June, allowing the Crown more time to make

112. OBSP, Trial of Mary Jones, 11 Sept 1771. A. Marks, *Tyburn Tree its History and Annals*, 1908, pp.255-257.

113. P. Lorrain, *The Ordinary of Newgate, His Account of the Behaviour, Confession, and Last Speech of Thomas Douglas, that was Executed at Tyburn, on Wednesday the 27th October, 1714*, pp.1-4.

114. A. McKenzie, *Tyburn's Martyrs*, 2007, p.270.

115. L. Radzinowicz, *A History of English Criminal Law and* its Administration from 1750, vol. 1, 1948, pp.147-151.

a final decision on his case. The other two men, one of whom was the highwayman William Hawke, were executed at the appointed time.[116]

On a less particular basis, during the decade between the start of 1765 and the end of 1774, 686 death sentences were passed in the Metropolis, of which only 294 were carried out. Reprieves were granted to just over 57 per cent of the convicts (and three quarters of females), a few dying before either execution or a reprieve could intervene.[117] Not everyone was enthusiastic about such changes. By 1785, Martin Madan had become alarmed that the "uncertainty of punishment" occasioned by the very high number receiving clemency was undermining the deterrent value of capital punishment, especially in London.[118] Nevertheless, the scene had been set for the end of the Bloody Code in the following century.

Transportation

After execution, transportation was the most severe punishment dealt out in the Metropolis. It was also one of the most notable features of English penal practice during the century, and something that distinguished it from most other European countries. Indeed, many continental observers regarded it as a national curiosity.[119] However, forced exile was found in several other, more distant, eighteenth-century societies. In Edo, for example, the most severe punishment after the death sentence was *ento* (extreme exile), which normally meant being sent to one of the remote Izu Islands.[120]

Given the number of times that transportation was imposed in England when compared to the death penalty, and its effect on the wider society, it

116. Rev J. Villette, *A Genuine Account of the Behaviour, confession, and Dying-Words of William Hawke and William Jones*, 1774, pp.2-4.
117. Figures from David Mossop's work published at www.capitalpunishmentuk.org/tyburn65.html. Last accessed 15 January 2011.
118. M. Madan, *Thoughts On Executive Justice*, 2nd edn., 1785, p.91.
119. P. Rushton and G. Morgan, "Running Away And Returning Home: The Fate Of English Convicts In The American Colonies", 2003, p.61.
120. D. E. Wright, "Female Crime And State Punishment In Early Modern Japan", 2004, p.12. As with returning from Transportation in England, escape from these islands was punishable by death.

was arguably the country's most important punishment for the great majority of the century.[121] However, it only properly achieved this status after 1718, although it had been in the penal repertoire for decades before the so-called "Transportation Act" (also known as the "Piracy Act") of that year (4 Geo. I cap. 11) greatly expanded its use. This statute had been introduced, in part, to reduce the high incidence of execution, especially in the Metropolis.[122] Not everyone approved of its impact as a result, one journal even blaming it for an alleged increase in serious offences, and lamenting that it demonstrated that any: "...abatement of the rigour of the laws, begets new criminals".[123]

Despite such criticism, after 1718, transportation provided a much-needed intermediate punishment between death and (almost) immediate release, without occasioning the considerable public costs entailed in long-term penal imprisonment, the only realistic alternative, and its eventual replacement in the nineteenth century.

Origins of penal transportation

After the Restoration of 1660, recourse to the already established practice of reprieving prisoners from execution on condition that they agreed to transport themselves to the Americas increased significantly.[124] In 1661, the Westminster judges refined the punishment by stipulating that reprieved prisoners from Newgate should not be sent away as perpetual slaves, but under: "...indentures betwixt them and particular masters, to serve in our English plantations for seven years".[125] Nevertheless, prior to 1718, transportation was largely limited to reprieved convicts who had, initially, been sentenced to death, though fairly large numbers of them were sent across the Atlantic during the early years of the century. Additionally, it was plagued with problems of enforcement. For this reason, one observer in 1695 declared that he was "utterly and absolutely against transportation of felons". He feared that many

121. J. Willis, "Transportation versus Imprisonment in Eighteenth-and Nineteenth-Century Britain", 2005, p.174.

122. G. Ollyffe, *An Essay Humbly offer'd, for An Act of Parliament to prevent Capital Crimes*, 1731, p.2

123. *The Country Gentleman*, 11 March 1726.

124. J. A. Sharpe, *Crime in Seventeenth-Century England*, 1987, p.147.

125. *Directions for Justices of the Peace* (1661) Kelyng, J. 1.

of those who did go to America -and some did not even get there- swiftly returned, while others were further corrupted in the course of their travels.[126]

Even more significantly, convicts who received benefit of clergy, such as those convicted of simple grand larceny, could not be transported. As a result, they received the fairly nugatory punishment of branding (often not very thoroughly) and discharge or, occasionally, after the advent of the 1706 Hard Labour Act, a short custodial sentence.

The Transportation Act 1718

The situation was transformed by the advent of the Transportation Act 1718, which provided that those found guilty of clergyable offences could be sentenced to transportation for seven years. This became the most common disposal for offences of dishonesty, though not for manslaughter (where branding and release remained the standard sentence). Additionally, the Act allowed those convicted of petty theft (not punishable by death), to be sentenced to transportation rather than the customary whipping or bridewell incarceration that their crimes traditionally attracted. This disposal was comparatively rare in the Metropolitan area for those who were *indicted* for petty theft *ab initio* and, where it was imposed, was not always carried out. Some successfully petitioned for corporal punishment in lieu, citing a variety of mitigating factors.[127] However, transportation was frequently (though not invariably) imposed on those who received such a finding as a "partial" verdict, perhaps as a result of "pious perjury" on a more serious indictment.

The Act also placed the existing process by which those convicted of non-clergyable felonies could be reprieved from execution on condition of transportation on a sound statutory basis. After 1718, most such pardons were granted on condition of transportation for 14 years or, in a handful of cases, life. The new statute also made effective provision for forcibly removing convicts from the country after they had received their sentences, significantly reducing levels of absconding and re-offending prior to departure. Most importantly, the government did not attempt to charge merchants for

---

126. Anon (By a hearty lover of his country), *Solon secundus: or, Some defects in the English laws: with their proper remedies*, 1695, p.6.

127. K. Morgan, "Petitions against Convict Transportation, 1725-1735", 1989, p.113.

the privilege of transporting convicted felons, as had sometimes occurred in earlier periods. Instead, under an Act of 1720, they were offered a subsidy of several pounds for each convict they carried, so that it became profitable to take feeble prisoners who would not raise a decent price in America.

Convicted felons would remain in prison (usually Newgate) until their transportation date, when they were handed over to merchant agents who would march them to their vessels, ship them across the Atlantic, and then sell them on to planters and other Americans on arrival in the New World (wealthy convicts might "buy" themselves and walk free but could not return to England). Thus, in 1718, Jonathan Forward was awarded a contract to take London convicts to Maryland for five pounds a head, the fee to include both guards and leg irons to secure them while making the crossing.[128]

The most plausible estimate suggests that 36,000 convicts were transported from England between the advent of the 1718 Act and the Revolution of 1776, though some other assessments have produced a rather higher total. Whatever the precise figure, the number coming from London or its immediate environs, even if not originally born there, was disproportionately high. This is not surprising. The City and its aldermen had been a motive force behind the new statute's introduction and naturally encouraged recourse to it.[129] One assessment suggests that those from the Metropolis and the South Eastern counties made up half the total English figure. Between 1766 and 1776, London and Middlesex alone sent 3,100 felons across the Atlantic.[130]

As a result, Metropolitan penal practise was transformed after 1718. Between that year and 1776, approaching 14,000 such sentences were handed down at the Old Bailey alone. Additionally, of course, the Quarter Sessions for Middlesex, Westminster and the City of London all passed numerous sentences of transportation, if not so many as the Bailey. For example, in 1757, even a septuagenarian who had been tried and convicted of "robbery" (probably simple grand larceny) at the Middlesex Sessions at Hick's Hall was sentenced to seven years' transportation.[131] Additionally, hundreds of other

128. J. M. Beattie, *Policing and Punishment in London: 1660–1750*, 2001, p.430.
129. J. M. Beattie, *Policing and Punishment in London: 1660–1750*, 2001, p.429.
130. *The Gentleman's Magazine*, 1786, vol. 56, pp.263-264.
131. *Lloydes Evening Post and British Chronicle*, 2 November 1757.

convicts who had been sentenced to death at the Old Bailey were transported for 14 years or life as a condition of their executions being commuted.

Nevertheless, even after the mid-century, transportation continued to have its critics. There was still a widespread belief that many convicts swiftly ran away from their new masters and came home. As a result, in 1751, a journal correspondent was keen to explore the possibility of introducing penal galleys on the continental model, feeling that this would have both deterrent advantages over transportation, and naval benefits for coastal defence.[132] Similarly, in 1752, a parliamentary Bill suggested hard labour in dockyards as an alternative because, it was claimed, the punishment set out under the Transportation Act had: "...frequently been evaded, by the Offenders returning from thence before the Expiration of the Terms for which they have been transported".[133]

There were certainly *some* cases of transports making multiple returns. For example, Mary Young had been transported, returned illegally, and caught while re-offending in 1738. She then simply gave the false name of Jane Webb to the authorities, and was convicted and transported to America again.[134] Young returned from America once more, within a year of her arrival there, before being caught and capitally convicted in 1741. She may have been transported on other occasions, because, as the Newgate ordinary noted, it was: "...usual for such persons to change their names upon every occasion".[135] Richard Kibble, executed at Tyburn in 1743 for returning from America, had probably been transported at least five times.

However, information from both sides of the Atlantic suggests that, in reality, relatively few returned successfully before their designated time was up, a small number of skilled and well-connected professional criminals apart. The system of surveillance and pursuit found in the various American colonies was fairly effective at recapturing escaped convicts, while the

132. *Royal Magazine; or, Quarterly Bee*, January/March 1751.

133. P. Rushton and G. Morgan, "Running Away And Returning Home: The Fate Of English Convicts In The American Colonies", 2003, p.61.

134. OBSP, Trial of Jane Webb, 12 April 1738.

135. *The Ordinary Of Newgate, His Account Of The Behaviour, Confession, And Dying Words, Of The Malefactors, Who Were Executed At Tyburn, On Wednesday The 18th Of March, 1740.*

difficulties they faced when trying to get back to England were often almost insuperable, especially if they were women.[136]

Australia

Before the American Revolution broke out in 1775, almost a thousand convicts were being sent across the Atlantic every year, although this was already a reduction from its peak in the early 1760s. This immediately became impossible, although the courts, including the Old Bailey, continued to pass sentences of transportation that stipulated the American colonies until well into the 1780s, and there was one partially successful, but wholly uneconomic, attempt to "smuggle" convicts into America in 1783. The inability to transport convicts occasioned by the outbreak of the war, and the delay in finding an acceptable alternative, meant that the hulls of old dismasted warships, known as 'hulks', had to be used to hold many of those who received such a disposal. By a statute from 1776 (19 Geo 3 c 74), any convict who was liable to be transported could be sent to a hulk instead. These were moored in the Thames and other harbours. Frequently, their inmates would spend their days ashore, employed in guarded working parties engaged in manual tasks such as embanking and dredging, returning to the vessels at night. John Howard counted at least 1,937 convicts being held on hulks in 1788. Their living conditions were appalling. In 1779, it was claimed that a quarter died within 20 months of arrival.[137] Typhus exacted a particularly heavy toll, though a hospital ship was opened that year. Conditions improved slightly during the 1780s, but the vessels remained schools of vice.[138]

By 1785, the overcrowding on the hulks in Woolwich, where there were between 700 and 800 convicts, the shortage of work available for their inmates, and the fact that there were yet more men being held in Newgate pending transportation, was occasioning acute judicial concern.[139] As the country's fortunes waned in the American war, it became obvious that the

136. P. Rushton and G. Morgan, "Running Away And Returning Home: The Fate Of English Convicts In The American Colonies", 2003, p.61.
137. H. Zouch, *Observations upon a Bill Now Depending in Parliament*, 1779, p.ix and p.29.
138. J. Howard, *An Account of the Principal Lazarettos in Europe*, 1789, p.216.
139. *The Times, 8* November 1785, p.3.

hulks would not be a temporary measure. The loss of transportation was also blamed for an apparent upsurge in Metropolitan crime.[140]

Despite the efforts of prison reformers, seminal prison legislation, and a considerable increase in custodial sentences, attempts were swiftly made to find a substitute destination for transportation. The 1776 Act had expressly provided that convicts liable to be sent to America could be transported to "any parts beyond the sea". Jamaica, Nova Scotia, and British Honduras were all considered as potential destinations, while in 1784, William Hussy suggested New Zealand to the House of Commons. The West Coast of Africa, especially the area around the Gambia River, initially appeared the most promising possibility. Several judges sitting at the Old Bailey passed sentences during the 1780s that stipulated Africa as the prisoner's allotted destination.[141] About 200 convicts were even sent there from the Hulks and various metropolitan prisons in 1782, as members of two independent military companies, tasked to guard British trade on the coast and capture Dutch forts. Unfortunately, this badly organized expedition met with disaster, most dying of disease or deserting within a few months. Despite this setback, another, smaller, group of convicts was sent out, even though, as Edmund Burke pointed out, this was usually tantamount to executing them (via disease or the natives) in rather more brutal circumstances than were found at Tyburn. West Africa could not be a solution to the problem.

As early as 1779, Sir Charles Bunbury, the Chairman of a Commons Select Committee looking into alternatives to the Hulks, suggested Botany Bay, with its Mediterranean climate, good pasturage, absence of dangerous animals and abundance of fish, freshwater, and timber, as a solution.[142] Eventually, for want of anywhere else, and as the pressure to deal with mounting numbers of convicts became intolerable, Australia was selected, and the "first fleet" carrying over 700 convicts left England in May 1787, arriving at Sydney Cove in January 1788. A steady stream of prisoner-laden vessels followed. However, Botany Bay took only a selection of convicts, chosen by reference to age, health, work skills, gender and sentence, so that the Hulks

140. *The Gentleman's Magazine*, 1786, vol. 56, pp.263-264.

141. See, for example, OBSP, Trial of Patrick Madan, 10 April 1782.

142. M. Gillen, "The Botany Bay Decision, 1786: convicts, not empire", 1982, p.743.

necessarily remained in existence for decades after 1788.[143] Their continued presence appears to have provided an impetus to the development of shore-based custodial institutions.

Transportation, even across the Atlantic, was widely considered to be a harsh punishment, if preferable to execution. In 1750, when Samuel Jarret was caught pilfering nine shillings worth of stockings from his master's shop, even his employer sought to mitigate the consequences of conviction, begging the court that he be given: "…some corporal punishment, and not be sent abroad".[144] Convicts sentenced to transportation to America for relatively minor property offences during the 1720s and 1730s regularly petitioned for corporal punishment in lieu of expulsion. When doing so, they stressed much the same considerations as those who actively sought transportation in lieu of execution. These included their youth, as in the case of a 12 year old girl, gender, old age, as in the case of a man in his sixties, that a crime was not serious, that the convict had juvenile dependants, that the stolen goods had been recovered, previous commendable active military service for the Crown, especially if wounded, the commission of a first offence, and friends willing to stand surety for subsequent good behaviour.[145] In the decade from 1761 to 1770, 284 such petitions, from all parts of the country, were successful.[146] Transportation to Australia, much further away and far less settled, was to raise even greater anxieties.

Corporal and Shaming Punishments

The production of shame, via public exposure, was an essential component to many secondary (to execution) punishments. Indeed, transportation, fines and incarceration apart, it could be present in all of them, and, for some, it was their most important facet. In face-to-face communities, it was

143. See generally G. Durston, "Magwitch's Forbears: Returning from Transportation in Eighteenth-century London", 2005.
144. OBSP, Trial of Samuel Jarret, 25 April 1750.
145. K. Morgan, "Petitions against Convict Transportation, 1725-1735", 1989, pp.112-113.
146. A. R. Ekirch, *Bound for America,* 1987, p.40.

thought to promote deterrence and alerted others to the dangers posed by specific individuals.

However, during the course of the eighteenth century, judges and magistrates became increasingly reluctant to impose penalties involving physical chastisement that would be carried out in public, especially where women were involved. This process reflected a wider change in social attitudes as well as concern about the difficulties occasioned by policing such procedures.

The pillory and stocks

The most obviously shaming punishments were the pillory and stocks. The former held people by the wrists and neck, the latter by their ankles. The pillory was used to punish, *inter alia*, impostors, those who libelled the Crown, gave false testimony, attempted sodomy or rape, blasphemed in the streets (usually as repeat offenders), committed some types of fraud, or who could not pay minor fines. The stocks were normally employed for drunkards, though both devices could be used for some offences.[147] For example, in 1701 Alexander Turner, summarily convicted by the Lord Mayor of "prophane swearing", was set in the stocks for two hours.[148] Both punishments were frequently added to other (usually fiscal or custodial) penalties. They normally involved detention in a busy public place, such as the Royal Exchange, Charing Cross and Cheapside or a location close to where their crime had been committed.[149] Many pillories could revolve, so that all spectators were likely to get a good view at some point in the proceedings. The normal sentence involved spending an hour at a time in the apparatus, though, sometimes, two hours would be stipulated. Frequently, it would order that the procedure be carried out on several separate occasions. For example, in 1738, when Catherine Buckle defrauded a maid of her clothes and some money, she was sentenced at Hick's Hall to be pilloried on four occasions in Brentford (and a year in the New Prison).[150] Sometimes, where this occurred, the sentence

147. J. Seller, *A booke of the punishments of the common laws of England*, 1671, p.2.
148. Mansion House Justice Room Charge Book, 1699-1705, CLA/004/01/4 entry for 28 March 1701 p.97.
149. M. Misson, *Memoirs and Observations of his Travels*, 1719, p.218.
150. *Old Common Sense: Or, the Englishman's Journal*, 8 July 1738.

would also stipulate that different places be used on each occasion. Thus, in 1703, William Fuller was pilloried at three separate Metropolitan locations.[151]

Popular hostility was an implicit part of the punishment. Although the pillory was usually guarded by a considerable force of watchmen and constables, under the supervision of the sheriff, it was widely thought that the authorities "winked at" much of the abusive treatment that was meted out to those being punished, whether it involved being pelted with vegetables, offal, or even stones.[152] However, this was also a major criticism. After two homosexuals were fatally wounded while being pilloried, Edmund Burke demanded (unavailingly) that the punishment be abolished.[153] He felt it wrong that a sanction meant to shame could be made capital by "an enraged mob, or negligent officers". Burke was supported by Sir Charles Bunbury, who noted that those pilloried for less serious offences could also be killed.[154] In 1731, for example, the notorious "Mother Needham", pilloried for keeping a disorderly house, had died of her injuries. In 1815, during a debate in the House of Lords over its abolition, the Earl of Lauderdale reiterated Burke's criticism, noting that if the mob looked with favour on an accused person, it was extremely lenient. If they detested the crime or the individual who had committed it, their treatment was far worse than the law could ever have intended.[155] To encourage a benign response, some of those being pilloried would distribute favourable written accounts of their crimes in advance.

Nevertheless, on some counts, fewer than a dozen people a year were pilloried in London. Thus, a perusal of contemporary newspapers suggests that during the first six months of 1750 seven men and two women were pilloried in the Metropolitan area. Four were pilloried with a fellow convict, rather than on their own, making a total of seven occasions in total. Two of the men were pilloried for defrauding a pair of publicans, the remainder for attempted sodomy or attempted rape involving infant victims. The two women were pilloried together for running a bawdy house and debauching

151. W. Fuller, *Mr. William Fuller's Trip to Bridewell*, 1703, p.2.
152. M. Gonzales, *London in 1731*, 1888, pp.156-157.
153. *Public Advertiser*, Wednesday 12 April 1780.
154. *Adams's Weekly Courant*, 18 April 1780.
155. *Caledonian Mercury*, 10 July 1815.

young girls.[156] Whatever the total figure, the number of people being pilloried fell swiftly in the last quarter of the century, though it was only formally abolished in 1837, and cases occurred until (and beyond) 1800. For example, in 1793, an attorney named Lloyd was sentenced by the Court of King's Bench to spend an hour in the pillory at the Royal Exchange for sticking up "inflammatory bills" in The Fleet Prison.[157]

The authorities became particularly squeamish about pillorying women. No woman received such a disposal in London after 1798.[158] Even early in the century, when a woman was heavily pregnant, as with a Mrs Hayward, sentenced to the pillory for keeping a "lewd and disorderly house", the punishment would be postponed until after she had given birth.[159] Indeed, for one reason or another, it seems that a significant number of sentences were not, eventually, carried out at all, or were at least abbreviated.

Flogging

Public flogging was the traditional punishment imposed for offences against morality, some other misdemeanours, and petty theft of items worth less than a shilling in value. As with the stocks, it could also be imposed in lieu of payment of a fine. In some situations, a set corporal punishment was even specified, should payment not be made, when the original fiscal penalty was imposed.

Historically, whipping was carried out by the public hangman, with the convict either tied to a cart's "tail" (rear) and paraded through the streets while being beaten or, alternatively, attached to a stationary post. Vagrants were most commonly flogged at a post, while those guilty of petty larceny were often beaten at the cart's tail.[160] Thus, in 1734, John King, described as a "boy", was convicted at the Quarter Sessions held at Hick's Hall on five counts of stealing window curtains from hackney chairs. He was publicly

156. *General Advertiser*, 11 June 1750.
157. *Royal Gazette*, 6 April 1793.
158. R. Shoemaker, *The London Mob*, 2004, p.93.
159. *The London Journal*, 18 February 1720.
160. J. Seller, *A booke of the punishments of the common laws of England*, 1671, pp.5-6

whipped behind a cart on five occasions, once for each offence, in and around Hanover Square, Grosvenor Square, Bond Street and Brook Street.[161]

Even at the start of the period there had been observers who disliked this punishment, and who felt that being beaten: "...with a dog-whip, through the streets is barbarous and beastlike, and no where practise'd but in England".[162] This form of flogging was the first to decline during the 1700s. As the century advanced, the profile of those being beaten also changed. As with the pillory, both judges and magistrates became increasingly reluctant to pass such sentences on women, especially if they were to be imposed in public. Instead, where women were flogged, the order would often specify that it be done in private, as was the case with Isabella Philpot, convicted in 1762 of stealing a pair of worsted stockings.[163] The whipping of female vagrants was formally ended in 1792, and all flogging of women was abolished in 1817, a couple of decades before it ended for men (other than those being disciplined in prison). No woman was publicly whipped in London after 1798.[164] However, gender was not the only reason for permitting a private flogging. In 1752, for example, the young James Blond was convicted at the Westminster Quarter Sessions of stealing brass fixtures from a coach. By the: "...mercy of the court, in regard to his youth, [he was] ordered to be privately whipped".[165]

It also seems that floggings were being carried out with less savagery by the end of the century. In 1786, a newspaper correspondent could even claim that some public beatings, by then often conducted close to Newgate prison, bordered on the ridiculous. In one case, it was so "trifling" that it was a matter of general merriment to watching mechanics rather than an effective deterrent.[166] Floggings were increasingly replaced by fiscal penalties or short periods of imprisonment. Even so, corporal punishment remained a significant tool in the penal repertoire until the very end of the period.

161. *Penny London Post*, 11 March 1734.

162. Anon (By a hearty lover of his country), *Solon secundus: or, Some defects in the English laws: with their proper remedies*, 1695, p.8.

163. *London Evening Post*, 22 April 1762.

164. R. Shoemaker, *The London Mob*, 2004, p.93.

165. *London Evening Post*, 22 April 1762.

166. *The Times*, 7 June 1786, p.2.

Thus, after the Old Bailey sessions in December 1799, the court ordered that 14 convicts be whipped, eight in public and six privately.[167]

Fiscal Penalties

Fining convicts held enormous attractions for the authorities. Far from costing them money, like imprisonment and transportation, it actually raised revenue, though if fines were imposed summarily they might be used to reward informers and to fund local parish causes. Additionally, they were flexible and naturally susceptible to gradation, according to the gravity of an offence and a defendant's means. Fines were frequently imposed as a sole punishment in very minor, especially summary matters, and were often ordered as part of a sentence in middle-ranking cases, being combined with another corporal or custodial penalty. However, until the last two decades of the century, their use was largely confined to misdemeanours.

The sums imposed varied enormously, being limited only by statutory maximums (where they existed) and a realistic assessment of the convict's ability to pay. For example, in 1731, at the Middlesex Quarter Sessions in Hick's Hall, a shoemaker was fined a shilling, as well as being pilloried and imprisoned for six months, for attempting to extort money by threatening to make a false allegation of homosexuality. On the same day, at the same forum, a poulterer was fined 50 pounds for attempting to rape a woman, with no other penalty being imposed. Presumably, he had considerable means, and this had allowed the court to punish him in his pocket, rather than his person, something that the convict might have actively encouraged.[168] However, at the start of the century, 84 per cent of fines were for less than 13s 4d (one mark) and the most common fiscal penalty was 3s 4d (a quarter of a mark).[169] An alternative punishment might be specified when a fine was imposed, to be enforced if the convict failed to pay up. Thus, a man who had

167. *Morning Chronicle*, 10 December 1799.
168. *Daily Post*, 18 October 1731.
169. R. Shoemaker, *Prosecution and Punishment*, 1991, p.156.

been fined by a City alderman for using foul language in public received ten days' hard labour in the bridewell, when he was unable to find the money.[170]

Imprisonment

The City, Middlesex and Westminster had numerous gaols, ranging from private sponging houses, for the initial detention of civil debtors, to Newgate, which was, essentially, the county prison for London and Middlesex. There were still 20 prisons of various types during John Howard's era, towards the end of the century. Some, like The Fleet, specialised in debtors. Others only took in those who were suspected of committing a criminal offence. Many, including Newgate, were "mixed", being used for both purposes, even though this might mean unsuccessful businessmen or profligate youths having close contact with hard-core felons.

Eighteenth-century prisons served three functions: to hold those who were awaiting trial; to detain those awaiting penal disposal after conviction; and to punish those who had been found guilty. However, confinement was *primarily* a means of securing those awaiting trial or, after conviction, holding those awaiting execution or transportation. It was only rarely used as a punishment in its own right, especially at the start of the period, and long sentences of imprisonment were very unusual throughout the century. As late as 1819, over 60 per cent of criminals incarcerated at Newgate were awaiting trial at the ensuing sessions or being held prior to disposal.[171]

Nevertheless, sentences of imprisonment were passed throughout the eighteenth century. Traditionally, they were usually relatively short, rarely more than a few months or a year or two. For example, in 1752, a man who had been convicted at Hick's Hall of recruiting Middlesex men into foreign military service was sentenced to two years' custody in Newgate.[172] However, after 1771, but before the advent of the American Revolution, there appears to have been a slight shift towards the use of imprisonment, especially with

170. *The Whitehall Evening Post; or, London Intelligencer*, 18 September 1766.
171. *The Times*, 28 Oct. 28, 1819, p.3.
172. *The Covent Garden Journal*, 18 April 1752.

regard to those who were convicted of non-capital crimes against property.[173] Judges became significantly more willing to impose custodial sentences in ensuing decades. The loss of transportation to America, in particular, led to a very marked increase in sentences of imprisonment. Thus, in 1786, William Haslam, found guilty at the Guildhall Quarter Sessions of receiving stolen property (a misdemeanour in his case) was sentenced to four years in Newgate.[174]

Both imprisonment and fining, the essence of modern penal regimes, were increasingly seen as valid alternatives to more violent, physical and public forms of punishment. By the end of the century, they were more palatable to the "spirit of the age", and easier to administer, occasioning less disruption to the wider society.[175] As a result of this change in attitudes, the late eighteenth century is often considered to have been the formative period for the "modern" type of prison.[176] Certainly, there was a wave of prison building in England after 1775, something that was, in part, linked to the temporary ending of transportation.[177] Even more significantly, the Penitentiary Act of 1779, drafted by John Howard and influenced by William Blackstone, introduced the concept of state (rather than local magistrate) controlled prisons for the first time, and recommended imprisonment as an alternative sentence to death or transportation in some cases. One aim of the Act was to create a network of government prisons that would punish criminals with longer sentences, spent in a more strictly controlled environment.[178] These institutions would have an avowedly reformist ethos, and the lives of their inmates would be closely monitored, with an emphasis on work, solitude and religious instruction as aids to repentance.

However, the 1779 Act's results were initially very modest in the Metropolitan area. There was serious disagreement as to where the new prisons should be built. None were constructed there before the end of the century.

---

173. S. Devereaux, "The Making of the Penitentiary Act, 1775-1779", 1999, p.409.
174. *The King v William Haslam* (1786) 1 Leach 418.
175. G. T. Smith, "Civilized People Don't Want to See That Kind of Thing", 1996, p.45.
176. J. J. Willis, "Punishment and the cultural limits to state power in late 18th-century Britain", 2008, pp.401-43.
177. G. Fisher, "The Birth of the Prison Retold", 1995, pp.1267-1269.
178. J. J. Willis, "Transportation versus Imprisonment in Eighteenth-and Nineteenth-Century Britain", 2005, p.175 and p.177.

Nevertheless, Coldbath Fields Prison in Middlesex was rebuilt in 1794, providing solitary confinement for a majority of its inmates in 232 single cells, along with work and religious instruction. Even so, severe doubt was cast on whether any prisoners in the new gaol had properly experienced solitude accompanied by hard labour and religious instruction during the late 1790s. Instead, it was claimed that they spent their time in "unrestrained intercourse" with each other. It was also alleged that there was no more religious ministration there than in traditional prisons.[179] The Giltspur Street Compter, which opened in 1791 and had a small section for felons, was also influenced by the statute, but with equally disappointing results. The lack of centralisation in the British state was to limit the growth of penitentiaries until the nineteenth century (Millbank Prison opened in 1816), while the justices' high degree of autonomy and reluctance to take on extra duties meant that government legislation to regulate prisons was often not properly enforced. This was compounded by wider objections to custodial sentences, which seemed to impinge on the rights of "freeborn" Englishmen to an even greater extent than did transportation.[180]

Bridewells and houses of correction

Unlike the Metropolis's prisons, the capital's various bridewells and houses of correction had, originally, been specifically designed as short-term carceral institutions for minor offenders. Although they were often pressed into other uses during the course of the eighteenth century, such as holding felons awaiting trial, the great majority of inmates were imprisoned for less than six months, most for just a few days or weeks. For example, the Committee of Governors established in 1798 to investigate The Bridewell noted that, over the previous four years, it had held an average of 40 occupants (a majority of them women), either serving seven day sentences for vagrancy or a month for being disorderly.[181]

179. *Porcupine*, 29 December 1800.

180. J. J. Willis, "Transportation versus Imprisonment in Eighteenth-and Nineteenth-Century Britain", 2005, p.175 and p.194.

181. Anon, *Reports from Select Committees, Respecting The Arts-Masters and Apprentices of Bridewell Hospital*, 1799, p.8.

The inmates of such institutions would be put to work. In the Clerkenwell House of Correction, during the 1750s, women and older men were expected to beat eight "punnies" of hemp a day, each of two to three pounds, with 12 punnies being set for younger males. A failure to reach the requisite amount could result in punishment, such as being placed in the prison's stocks. Beatings had also been an inherent part of the punishment meted out in such institutions during the first half of the century, as well as being used to enforce internal discipline. At the start of the century, William Fuller's experience suggests that this was a very painful experience. By the 1750s, however, it seems that it was sometimes being done on a rather more ritualised basis, especially if a bribe had been paid, and was sometimes a: "... mere ceremony, according to the disposition or temper the whipper is in".[182]

Although bridewells and houses of correction had originally been intended to reform their inmates, by the eighteenth century they were similar in many respects to other Metropolitan prisons.[183] Nevertheless, conditions in the City Bridewell, at least, appear to have improved considerably during the second half of the period, so that it won approval from John Howard for providing straw bedding to inmates. Additionally, it was noted for its medical facilities, which included physicians and infirmaries. Other Metropolitan houses of correction were also improved in the final decades of the century, and a statute from 1782 authorised the raising of money to rebuild those that were decayed.

Prison conditions

Eighteenth-century penal conditions have been the subject of extensive work in recent decades, and will only be dealt with in outline. Although John Howard was to make the woeful state of the nation's prisons well-known towards the end of the century, he was merely the best known in a long line of eighteenth-century reformers and publicists who had sought to improve the country's gaols, especially those found in the Metropolis. Thus, the Society for the Promotion of Christian Knowledge (SPCK) had worked

---

182. J. Ilive, *Reasons offered for the Reformation of the House of Correction in Clerkenwell*, 1757, pp.37-38.
183. N. Morris and D. J. Rothman (Eds.), *The Oxford History of the Prison*, 1995, p.329.

for prison reform from its foundation in 1699. One of its members, the Reverend Thomas Bray, produced a report on the subject in 1702, though he focused on the moral corruption found in Metropolitan prisons, rather than their physical state.[184] Just before the start of the eighteenth century, a "gentleman" inmate in Newgate filled this gap by publishing a tract on the atrocious conditions found there.[185] Subsequently, James Edward Oglethorpe persuaded the House of Commons to establish a Gaols Committee and to hold a series of inquiries into prison conditions during the 1720s and 1730s. Four decades later, in the 1770s, William Smith, a medical doctor, developed an intimate knowledge of specifically Metropolitan prisons, while making charitable visits to provide medical assistance to their inmates, and produced an important study of their conditions.

It was not simple ignorance that prevented change. Oglethorpe's exposure of the brutality of London's prison officials temporarily increased public sympathy for incarcerated debtors, but his work did not give rise to substantive prison reform, and ultimately left England's penal system intact. Arguably, prison investigations had little effect because, for much of the eighteenth century, few Englishmen were sufficiently concerned about the state of the country's prisons to act on their findings. Although their appalling conditions and the widespread corruption found in them were common knowledge, they were usually viewed as unpleasant but unavoidable facts of life, conditions that gave prisoners the draconian treatment they deserved at a reasonable cost to the wider society. This meant that the political will to tackle abuses was absent, while the financial implications of taking control of the prisons from their entrepreneurial wardens, and introducing a new system of prison management, were all too apparent.[186]

---

184. T. Bray, *An Essay Towards the Reformation of Newgate and Other Prisons in and About London*, 1702.
185. E. S. (a gentleman in prison), *Companion for debtors and prisoners, and advice to creditors in ten letters*, 1699, p.16.
186. A. Pitofsky, "The Warden's Court Martial: James Oglethorpe and the Politics of Eighteenth-century Prison Reform", 2000, p.88 and p.102.

Dangers of prison life

The findings of all enquiries into prison conditions were uniformly depressing. Throughout the eighteenth century, prisons in the Metropolis, like those in other parts of the country, were squalid and dangerous. According to William Smith, visiting them was inherently risky because of "gaol fever", a form of typhus. Even in the 1770s, considerably more prisoners died from disease than were executed.[187] The prisoners were often crawling with lice and even the turnkeys were made nauseous by the sights and smells that they encountered in their work and the inmates' frequently bestial behaviour.[188] This was not confined to males; many thought female prisoners were "worse than the worst of the men".[189]

Gaols in and about London were particularly bad, so that in 1804, an observer describing the atrocious conditions of the country's gaols could note that: "In the metropolis the evil appears in its greatest magnitude".[190] Many of the changes associated with what Whig historians would later term the triumph of "humanitarian idealism" would wait until well into the nineteenth century. Newgate Prison was by far the most important of the Metropolis's numerous gaols and many of its characteristics can be considered as "typical" of other Metropolitan prisons.

Lack of segregation

Newgate had grown out of one of the city's medieval gatehouses, being gradually expanded over the ensuing centuries. Unfortunately, this growth was unplanned, and pressure of numbers meant that an excessive number of inmates were usually held in the institution. Although there were different wards and areas for debtors and felons, and males and females, segregation was extremely loose for much of the period. However, when Newgate was rebuilt after its destruction during the Gordon Riots in 1780, the prison was designed so that the "several grades of criminals might be kept separate". This process was supported by an Act of 1784 (Geo III chap 54), and reiterated in another statute from 1791, requiring the separation of those convicted or

187. J. Howard, *The State of the Prisons in England and Wales*, 1929, p.2.
188. W. Smith, *State of the Gaols in London, Westminster, and Borough of Southwark*, 1776, pp.9-10.
189. B. L., *An Accurate Description of Newgate*, 1724, p.45
190. W. M. Pitt, *A Plan for the Improvement of the Internal Police of Prisons*, 1804, pp.1-8.

accused of misdemeanours from felons, and both of these categories from debtors. Nevertheless, the 1791 statute was widely ignored, and it was alleged that the Newgate gaoler had "contrived to frustrate" its purpose, although, by then, the prison was at least relatively successful in keeping men and women apart.[191]

This was not the case in many Metropolitan gaols, for much of the century. For example, in the Clerkenwell House of Correction there was almost no effective segregation between the genders in the 1750s. Incarcerated females, especially the establishment's many prostitutes, engaged in sexual activity with turnkeys, other inmates and even visiting outsiders, on an almost routine basis, whether to secure an essential income, gain personal favours, out of affection or to avoid mistreatment. An educated man, committed to Clerkenwell for a lengthy period during the 1750s, could note that the intermixing of genders made the prison a "scene of debauchery". Almost every man had his favourite woman or "wife".[192] Similarly, in 1776, it was claimed that in the City's Poultry Compter men and women, whether felons or those arrested simply for being disorderly, were crammed together in one ward during the day, and at night would lie on dirty boards in "filthy holes almost unfit for swine". The prison was characterised by riot, debauchery, sickness and misery.[193] Little had changed a few years later, when Josiah Dornford visited.

Conditions were especially bad for those who did not have financial resources and outside friends or associates to support them. Those with a reason to visit prisoners could bring in provisions. Thus, at one point in her career, the notorious pickpocket Mary Young (Jenny Diver) had passed as the wife of a Newgate inmate, visiting him daily, supplying him with: "… victuals, and likewise gave Charity to the other Prisoners under Sentence, and to some on the Common Side".[194] Large amounts of ready cash were even better.

191. T. Lloyd, *To The Grand Juries of the City of London and County of Middlesex*, 1794, pp.1-2.
192. J. Ilive, *Reasons offered for the Reformation of the House of Correction in Clerkenwell*, 1757, p. 11. and p.15.
193. W. Smith, *State of the Gaols in London, Westminster, and Borough of Southwark*, 1776, p.33.
194. *The Ordinary Of Newgate, His Account Of The Behaviour, Confession, And Dying Words, Of The Malefactors, Who Were Executed At Tyburn, On Wednesday The 18th Of March, 1740.*

Rich inmates

In the entrepreneurial prisons of the era, superior accommodation, the removal, or at least a reduction in the size, of an inmate's iron fetters, clean bedding, good food, tobacco and alcohol could all be obtained, at a price, by those with money. As a result, prisoners who were very wealthy could avoid much of the unpleasantness associated with incarceration. Even in the 1790s, after limited reforms were supposed to have been introduced, an American inmate in Newgate could note that: "…money is the passe-partout, the master key".[195] Rich felons there, like those in other Metropolitan prisons, could purchase superior accommodation in the prison's Press Yard or the Master Felons' side, along with beer and spirits in the prison tap. The Master Felons' side had a large fireplace, three wards (one for women), wine at 2s a bottle and brandy at 8d a quarter. There were also "good flock beds" for hire at 3s 6d a week.

So lucrative were prisons for their directors that, in 1696, the head keeper of Newgate paid £3,500 for his office. By 1732, it was estimated to be worth between £5,000 and £6,000.[196] Perhaps appropriately, if keepers were incompetent, they were usually punished in their pockets, rather than with dismissal. In 1724, for example, the justices at Hicks's Hall fined the keeper of Newgate £50 for allowing Thomas Fox to escape.[197] This encouraged them to take active steps to recover escapees. In 1754, Thomas Stanley, who had escaped from Newgate, was recaptured by the keeper in a house in Smithfield, and returned to the prison.[198] Some even pursued escaped convicts outside London. However, the system of paying fees for almost every kind of privilege meant that there was a constant danger that gaols would degenerate into exploitative hostels.

Poor inmates

Prisoners without an abundance of private resources or friends, that is, in practice, the great majority of people accused of serious crimes, faired badly.

195. T. Lloyd, *To The Grand Juries of the City of London and County of Middlesex*, 1794, p.3.
196. *Grub-street Journal,* 25 May 1732. The money would be divided between the Lord Mayor, the two sheriffs, and the City.
197. *The Daily Journal,* 13 July 1724.
198. *Whitehall Evening Post or London Intelligencer*, 9 April 1754.

Many were dependant on the felon's basic allowance of a penny loaf a day. This bread was the only food supplied to the prisoners at public expense, though debtors, and inmates of the Houses of Correction, who were supposed to work for their livings, did not even receive this as of right, unless infirm.[199] During the 1780s, Josiah Dornford attempted to persuade the Corporation of London to provide inmates with more bread. He also argued that giving them only water to drink, and not providing them with a fire or beds, was both "impolitic, and disgraceful". Nevertheless, his considerable efforts merely resulted in them being issued with a rug, in which to wrap up at night.[200]

The Common Felons' side of Newgate catered for the poorer inmates and for much of the period consisted of five 30-man communal wards (two of them for females). These meant that its conditions could be further subdivided. The "Stone Hold", for felons who could not even pay the normal entrance dues, was (unsurprisingly) paved with stone, on which the inmates had to sleep without any form of bed. It had no natural light, was largely subterranean, and was a "most terrible stinking, dark and dismal place". The Middle Ward was fractionally better, and was open to inmates who could at least pay their entrance fees. It was warmer than the Stone Hold and had an oak plank floor, which was obviously more comfortable for sleeping on, though beds were still not provided.[201]

Unsurprisingly, in these general circumstances, mortality rates were also high, as many a wretch, clothed in rags, covered with:

> ...vermin, tortured with scorbutic, rheumatic, and, for the most part, venereal pains, his body full of sores, and loaded with fetters ... falls a victim to cold, hunger, and disease.[202]

Newgate's overcrowded and squalid conditions led to periodic outbreaks of "gaol fever" (typhus), such as the one in 1726 that killed 83 inmates. Another appears to have infected the sessions held in April 1750, leading

199. J. Howard, *The State of the Prisons*, 1929, pp.2-3.
200. J. Dornford, *Seven Letters to the Lords of the Privy Council, on the Police*, 1785, p.ix.
201. B. L., *An Accurate Description of Newgate*, 1724, pp.43-44.
202. W. Smith, *State of the Gaols in London, Westminster, and Borough of Southwark*, 1776, p.12.

to the deaths of up to 60 people, including the Lord Mayor, Sir Samuel Pennant, two senior judges, and assorted court officials, barristers and jurymen.[203] As a result of this contagion, a doctor urged that all prisons be kept as "airy and clean" as possible. Newgate was washed with vinegar, as were its inmates, while the numbers being sent for trial were temporarily limited to 15 at any one time.[204]

However, the outbreak of disease in 1750 also sparked a search for a longer-lasting improvement. George Dance, the Clerk of the City Works, was authorised to investigate the construction of an entirely new building. Even so, nothing was done until Parliament granted £50,000 for reconstruction in 1767. Unfortunately, this was only finally completed in 1780, just in time for the new prison to be burnt down by the Gordon rioters, necessitating a fresh reconstruction lasting until 1785.[205]

Despite such rebuilding, conditions remained very harsh even in the 1790s. One inmate noted that the windows of the felons' side were still unglazed, and that the gaol shop sold shoddy goods, in short measure, at extortionate prices. Vinegar was not distributed for sprinkling on the floor of the prison, as it was supposed to be, to guard against infection. Tubs of urine were left standing for long periods in the prison yard, until they found a buyer wishing to use them for industrial purposes. The practice of loading new prisoners with heavy fetters and irons, on the grounds of prison security, and then removing them on payment of substantial sums of money, was still prevalent.[206]

Physical brutality was also fairly widespread in the Metropolitan prison system, even at the end of the period, though fellow inmates were probably more of a threat than the turnkeys, as prisoners were still largely left to regulate themselves. Nevertheless, in 1798, an inmate at Coldbath Fields Prison, mistakenly accused of making a noise, was beaten ferociously with a set of keys by a turnkey, with the prison Governor joining in the attack, and breaking his stick over the man.[207]

---

203. *Whitehall Evening Post or London Intelligencer*, 19 May 1750.
204. *The Gentleman's Magazine*, 1750, vol. 20, p.235.
205. H. D. Kalman, "Newgate Prison", 1969, pp.50-53.
206. T. Lloyd, *To The Grand Juries of the City of London and County of Middlesex*, 1794, p.4 and p.5.
207. Sir F. Burdett, *An Impartial Statement of the Inhuman Cruelties Discovered! In the*

Eighteenth-century incarceration was not unremittingly bad. Even for poor prisoners, it had its lighter moments. For example, inmates in both Newgate and The Bridewell would sometimes pass their time playing Hunt the Slipper and Blind Man's Buff.[208] Unlike some of the later penitentiaries, there was little danger of loneliness.

Structural determinants

The pressures imposed by the need to imprison large numbers of people, in correspondingly big gaols, within major urban areas, were not unique to London, and often produced similar problems and responses elsewhere in the eighteenth-century world. For example, there are some remarkable parallels with conditions in Spanish gaols, even though John Howard commended them as being superior to the European average after a visit in 1783. Squalor and corruption amongst wardens and turnkeys was endemic in Madrid's prisons and those in other Iberian cities. Although there was effective segregation of the sexes, debtors mixed freely with felons, while all inmates, regardless of age or offence, were kept together indiscriminately. As in England, the keepers purchased their positions from local or national government, and ran them as businesses, securing fees from inmates and payments for services. As in the Metropolis, these included superior food, bedding and accommodation. Until 1788, discharge fees were paid, even by acquitted prisoners, as occurred in England until 1774. Remarkably, new inmates even had to pay "garnish" to other prisoners, when first admitted to the gaols, as was the custom in England. As with those admitted to Newgate, prisoners who could not pay were liable to have their clothes stripped from their backs in lieu.[209]

Indeed, structural determinants meant there were even parallels with urban prisons in very different societies. In eighteenth-century Peking (Beijing), for example, conditions for most prisoners were appallingly harsh and unhygienic, with disease being rife. However, those who could afford it could pay for better terms and to have their fetters removed. Even corporal

---

Coldbath-Fields Prison, 1800, p.9. This and other incidents did lead to an enquiry.

208. Anon, *Low-Life: or One Half of the World Knows not how the Other Half Live*, 2nd edn., 1755, p.83.

209. R. Pike, *Penal Servitude in Early Modern Spain*, 1983, p.58.

punishment could be ameliorated, by making payments to those required to carry it out, as occurred with wealthy bridewell inmates.[210] Similarly, although about three hundred people held in Edo's Kodenmacho Jail (the Japanese capital's equivalent of Newgate) received a death sentence each year, over a thousand died from "natural circumstances". Several hundred more died violently, in conflicts with other inmates or the authorities, something that was much less common in London's prisons.[211]

---

210. D. Bodde, "Prison Life in Eighteenth-Century Peking", 1969, pp.319-320.
211. D. E. Wright, "Female Crime And State Punishment In Early Modern Japan", 2004, p.14.

CHAPTER 18

CONCLUSION

Crime

The eighteenth-century Metropolis had a "crime problem", in that it experienced considerable and growing anxiety about crime. This concern was especially marked amongst its rapidly expanding, and increasingly wealthy, but also vulnerable, middle class. It was largely occasioned by a decline in tolerance for offending and disorder, something that was fanned by the new forms of mass print media, rather than any major growth in crime rates.

Despite the era's more alarmist publications, with their sensationalist accounts of Metropolitan felonies, and the campaigning work of moral and policing reformers, with their (frequently) exaggerated and (sometimes) self-interested reports on urban security, the capital was not as crime-prone as was (and is) sometimes suggested. Although no one could pretend that it was a "low-offending" environment, for those who were well-established in the city, and aware of its dangers, the risks were normally manageable. For the rich, they were often relatively small. Basic precautions in personal and residential security greatly reduced, though it could not eliminate, the danger of victimisation.

Moreover, overall security in the capital was not getting worse during much of the eighteenth century. Indeed, in some respects, it was clearly improving. As the per capita murder rate for the Metropolitan area suggests, the threat of serious violence was on a firmly downward trend. Rates of property crime are harder to ascertain. They probably did not fall, and may well have grown to some degree, especially towards the end of the century. However, they do not appear to have increased enormously, though the huge commercial developments of the era did provide an opportunity for some new forms of crime to take root. What would now be termed "white collar" crime, in particular, appears to have reached unprecedentedly high levels. The large stream of commodities of all types passing through, or to, the Metropolis were also highly vulnerable to theft, while the acquisition of valuables by the "middling" social orders meant that far more homes provided lucrative targets for burglars and housebreakers.

Nevertheless, the underlying reality, that taken as a whole there was no major deterioration in security, may, in part, explain why change in the capital's criminal justice system was relatively slow in coming. A significant number of informed Londoners appreciated that they were not living in the worst of times. It has also led some modern commentators to argue that eighteenth-century crime was given an importance that was disproportionate to its real significance.[1]

The Criminal Justice System

The Metropolitan criminal justice system of the eighteenth century has not received a good press from modern academics. Many have criticised it on moral grounds, and such antagonism has extended far beyond Marxist historians, or those writing from a broadly similar perspective. For example, a book on the capital's death penalty was main-titled *Tyburn's Martyrs*, although a martyr is usually someone who suffers undeservedly in order to advance a cause or principle. Another work on the role of gender in its criminal justice system expressed the view that: "The state was the main murderer in late eighteenth-century London".[2] By definition, legal execution cannot be murder, even if it is considered barbaric. Others have dwelt on the criminal justice system's seeming inefficiency and ineffectualness, arguing that, despite its frequently draconian nature, and apparent cruelty, it did not "work".

Is such hostility justified? Was the Metropolis's criminal justice system as inherently flawed as is sometime suggested? The answer to this question would probably be "yes", in some respects, but with major qualifications, especially when it is considered in a historical context. As has been seen, occasional (if still all too frequent) mistakes apart, the great majority of those

1. V.A.C. Gatrell, *The Hanging Tree: Execution and the English People 1770–1868*, 1990, p.244.
2. P. King, "Making Crime News", 2009, p.113.

executed at Tyburn were guilty as charged. Most had, at the least, committed "middle-ranking" property crimes, rather than the more trivial types of offence, though many who committed the latter were transported. Frequently, those who *were* hanged for relatively minor crimes had offended on an earlier occasion, committed multiple offences, or had done so in aggravated circumstances. It is true that levels of execution were significantly higher in London than in most other Western European cities, but, against this, the trend was gradually, if not uninterruptedly, downwards during the century, while the Metropolis had almost no aggravated form of capital punishment (treason apart), such as breaking on the wheel, to enhance deterrence, unlike many other *ancien régime* cities. Furthermore, some of the alternatives to execution that were found in continental Europe in the first half of the era, such as forced galley-service, would not be considered very enlightened today.

Many aspects of the era's criminal justice system can only be understood against its backdrop of harsh living conditions. The eighteenth century, like the eras that had gone immediately before it, was full of suffering for ordinary people. The individual was not protected against disaster and their (resigned) acceptance of inhumane treatment was probably much higher than it would be today. Indeed, in some contexts, suffering was even seen as redemptive, at least before the enlightenment took root in the final third of the period.[3] Much of life in London was lived close to the margins of survival, in an environment in which most people could not afford to be excessively squeamish. This produced a corresponding "robustness" amongst many of the city's inhabitants, especially in the early part of the period. To modern eyes, this frequently appears as callousness. For example, the impoverished parents of Mary Price, executed in 1718 for the murder of a child, raised a considerable sum of money by allowing curious members of the public to view her body, for a penny apiece, in their house near Long Acre, after it was cut down from the gallows. Some of the money was used to pay for her funeral; the rest went into their pockets.[4] It is a truism that the wider social and political culture of a society and its criminal justice system are closely

3. A. McKenzie, *Tyburn's Martyrs*, 2007, p.238.
4. *Original Weekly Journal*, 2-8 August 1718.

linked. To expect eighteenth-century English society to be highly sensitive to its era's legal cruelties might be slightly optimistic.

Nevertheless, both society and its criminal justice system became "gentler", or at least "politer" and more refined, during the course of the century, in a process that was accelerated by the spread of enlightenment ideas in its latter stages. This was reflected in a "softening" of manners and the end of certain historic practices that no longer corresponded to new notions of gentility and sensibility. Thus, in a minor but telling example, after 1770, Bethlehem Royal Hospital ("Bedlam"), in Finsbury Square, closed its doors to the general public, which had previously been admitted to gawp at its lunatic inmates on payment of a fee. This process also affected the country's criminal justice system. Some of its more glaring barbarities were abolished at about the same time. For example, the *peine forte et dure*, "becoming barbarous to Englishmen", was formally ended in 1772, after falling into desuetude for a generation. Branding of clergied convicts was abolished in 1779, having long been neglected. Execution at Tyburn, and its attendant raucous procession, came to an end in 1783. The burning of women convicted of (petty or high) treason was ended in 1790. The use of public flogging and the pillory declined. The continued existence of the "Bloody Code" was also being challenged long before the close of the century, though formal reform would only start in 1808.

Inevitably, this was a slow process. Many relics of the past, even if medieval in their origins, survived to the end of the era, and sometimes well beyond. For example, in a case from 1792, a carpenter cut his wife's throat and then killed himself. After the coroner's jury returned a finding of *felo de se* on the dead man, his corpse was buried in the traditional (if waning) fashion for suicides, especially murder/suicides, being interred at the crossroads between Bishopsgate and Sun Street, with a "stake drove through his body".[5] This practice persisted until at least 1811. Much more importantly, conditions in both the prisons and hulks remained appalling, even in 1800, though by then reform was "in the air".

It should also be noted that there was more logic to some of the apparent "irrationality" found within the eighteenth-century criminal justice system,

5. *The Times*, 23 July 1792, p.3.

than might at first appear, even if it requires some thought to ascertain, and is often not remotely attractive to modern observers. This is, perhaps, captured in the widely repeated (even in the eighteenth century) story of a capitally convicted horse thief who, when he complained that it was hard that he was to be hanged for taking a beast, was told by his sentencing judge: "You are not to be hanged for stealing a horse, but in order that horses may not be stolen". The high level of attrition between offending and punishment can also be misleading. That all apprehended felons were not convicted, or even prosecuted, did not necessarily mean that they experienced no adverse consequences from their actions. Those who compounded their crimes might be put to considerable expense, others were held in custody for some time before being released, while many received various forms of summary retribution. More generally, the English criminal justice system of the era had several inherent strengths. It was flexible, swift, and relatively cheap to administer.

Additionally, it should be remembered that many aspects of the system were influenced by the era's structural determinants, some of which were almost completely beyond its control. The eighteenth-century Metropolis was the first modern Western conurbation to rival ancient Rome in size, yet it was possessed of technology that was little different to that found in the Imperial City 1500 years earlier and had poorer lines of communication. These factors affected what was possible and practical. For example, although the Metropolis was an unprecedentedly mobile society, it existed in an era that still lacked a reliable system of personal identification (such as fingerprints and photographs) and significant bureaucratic capacity. This created numerous problems, though, by the end of the period, some attempts had been made to improve on this state of affairs, such as the establishment of the Home Department's Criminal Register in 1791. Nevertheless, the situation remained highly unsatisfactory.

Similarly, long-term mass imprisonment in an urban environment posed acute problems for eighteenth-century societies throughout the world. It had the potential to be very expensive, and was bureaucratically difficult to administer, encouraging the widespread sub-contracting of responsibility to entrepreneurial keepers. The era's understanding of hygiene meant that it was hard to hold large numbers of men in confined and crowded circumstances without a high mortality rate, whether in London or Peking.

Criticism also, perhaps, presupposes an ability to suggest a realistic alternative to the existing regime. These did not readily present themselves to contemporary observers. The obvious alternative model for London was Paris, with its quasi-military police and professional magistracy. However, although some well-travelled Englishmen were inclined to believe that the state ordered these things better in France, they tended to dwell on the theory, rather than reality, of French practice, to focus on the treatment of exceptional offences (such as murder) rather than routine theft and assault, and to exaggerate the differences in security and efficiency between the two cities. It is also easy for modern commentators to describe the trial process found at the Old Bailey at this time as being severely flawed. Certainly, it was appallingly hurried, while common law tradition and the growth of adversariality combined with legal representation meant that it was increasingly dominated by "technicality". However, although this had enormous implications for the future, at the time, the inquisitorial system found in most of continental Europe does not appear to have been vastly better or more efficient, very serious cases apart.

For all its defects, the Metropolitan criminal justice system maintained at least a modicum of popular legitimacy throughout the eighteenth century. There were several reasons for this. A wide range of people, from very different social backgrounds, used the criminal courts. One magistrate could even claim that the: "...lower orders of the people will actually pawn their clothes to take out warrants".[6] All but the most destitute were found amongst the ranks of prosecutors, although, inevitably, they often had a middle and upper class complexion. The criminal law was not just an instrument of the wealthy. Although the justice system was vulnerable to the influence of powerful people, it also placed constraints on their behaviour. As a result, while the criminal courts did not reflect the values and concerns of those on the margins of Metropolitan society, they did not necessarily mirror those of the social elite either.

Most importantly, members of the "middling" orders made many of the most important decisions. These were men with a stake in society, and

6. P. King, "The Summary Courts and Social Relations in Eighteenth-century England", 2004, p.146.

correspondingly conventional views, but who were not divorced from the realities of daily life for the average person in their city, or immune to the vicissitudes of that life, and its sudden reversals of fortune. They were well aware of the practical limitations placed on state power, often pragmatic and worldly in their outlook, capable of compassion where they believed it was deserved, and ruthlessness where they felt it was necessary. They did not necessarily make decisions solely on the basis of their immediate interests. For example, they might be reluctant to convict forgery defendants, even though the Bank of England would not pay out on such notes, and their recipients, often exactly the same sort of tradesmen and shopkeepers who served on juries, could not get rid of them without themselves committing a serious criminal offence.[7]

Furthermore, the wider policing system was dependant on men who were far below even members of the middling social orders in status. Indeed, it was claimed that the authorities' inability to control the Gordon Riots of 1780 had been exacerbated by their lack of confidence in elements of London's police system, because they were: "…so intimately intermixed in their connection with the people, as scarce to be considered as a distinct body".[8] This, too, placed constraints on what could be done by the political nation via the justice system.

Metropolitan authorities were also usually highly realistic about what could be achieved using the criminal process. In the seventeenth century, it had been impossible to suppress disorder and immorality in rural areas via its exercise, even during the Cromwellian Interregnum. By the eighteenth century, there was widespread acceptance that there was no possibility of such an approach working in the Metropolitan area. Instead, the authorities, at all levels, attempted to deal with very serious offences, such as murder and high-value robbery, and to contain lower-level crime and disorder. Parish watchmen and constables, JPs and City aldermen, were primarily concerned with placing limits on minor offending, whether it was manifest in prostitution, public indecency, gambling, the use of profane language, petty

7. J. Oldham, "The Limits of Discretion: Forgery and the Jury at the Old Bailey, 1818-1821", 2002, p.160.
8. *The Gentleman's Magazine*, 1780, vol.50, pp.314-316.

pilfering from market stalls, drunkenness, cock-fighting or public violence. They would attempt to ensure that it did not reach excessive levels, was geographically and chronologically confined to certain streets, areas, and hours of the day or, where appropriate, was conducted in a restrained and reasonably discreet manner. Typically, Henry Fielding freely accepted that, when it came to brothels, no one who made a realistic allowance for the frailties and temptations of human nature would ever support a: "…strict execution of the laws, especially in this great and populous city". It was keeping them away from major thoroughfares, and respectable women and children, that was important.[9]

This realism on the part of the authorities occasioned regular irritation amongst many Metropolitan observers who felt that an ever more efficient application of the criminal justice system would pay dividends. However, it greatly reduced conflict between bourgeois laws and proletarian norms in the capital's streets and courtrooms. More generally, although many twentieth-century historians were tempted to view criminal courts as agents of social control, recent years have seen an increased appreciation of the way in which such forums drew upon widely (though not universally) diffused communal values when making decisions.

Of course, popular recourse to the courts and an ability to manipulate the legal system does not necessarily mean that there was widespread confidence in the law that they meted out. The speed with which the Gordon Riots ran out of control in 1780, and the manner in which rioters evinced hostility to senior legal figures and institutions, would suggest that many marginal members of London society were severely alienated from their justice system. This was also manifest in the popular aggression shown towards informers in many summary matters.[10] Nevertheless, such feelings were very far from being universal amongst non-elite Londoners.

9. H. Fielding, *The Case of the Unfortunate Bosavern Penlez*, 1749, p.6.
10. N. Blackerby, *The Speech of Nathaniel Blackerby Esq … On Saturday, April 1. 1738, To the Justices, High Bailiff, High Constable, and Petty constables of the City and Liberty of Westminster*, 1738, p.3, p.8 and p.10.

Change

Increasing concern about crime and higher expectations for urban security, combined with a progressive withdrawal of popular willingness, at all social levels, to participate in communal policing, encouraged change in the criminal justice system, throughout the century. Many Londoners were keen to see an improvement in the efficiency of their neighbourhood law-enforcement agencies, *provided* it did not cost too much money, interfere excessively with the power and patronage exercised by local elites or enhance that of the Crown, and did not produce parish officials who would exercise their authority against the well-to-do in a bumptious manner. Unfortunately, this was a difficult circle to square. For example, at no point before 1785 was radical policing change of the type eventually seen in 1829 seriously mooted, and then it was swiftly abandoned. It was widely appreciated that any urban change would provide a precedent for the rest of the country, where strains on the traditional system were much smaller; this discouraged drastic reform until all other possibilities had been exhausted. Instead, it tempted the authorities to tinker with the capital's traditional legal structures, producing a series of incremental changes.[11] In a very "English" process, many of the city's criminal justice bodies and institutions slowly mutated, gradually changing to deal with new circumstances and demands, while retaining much of their outward form.

However, certain general trends can be identified during the century. For example, from the 1690s onwards, there was a gradual, if slow, infusion of public money into the system, aimed at making it more effective. This initially came in the form of government rewards for the prosecution of (some) felons to conviction. This process accelerated after the accession of George I in 1714. Both the King and his ministers were worried about the stability of the new regime and unlike most previous governments they regarded violent crime in and around the London area as a serious matter.[12]

11. E. Sayer, *Observations on the Police or Civil Government of Westminster, with a Proposal for a Reform*, 1784, p.13.
12. J. M. Beattie, "Sir John Fielding and Public Justice: The Bow Street Magistrates' Court, 1754–1780", 2007, pp.63-64.

It increased further with government support for the Fielding brothers and its funding of the post-1792 stipendiary magistrates.

The Metropolitan criminal justice system, like that of the wider country, also became significantly more "rational" to modern eyes during the century. The substantive criminal law, offence parameters and distinctions, and their requisite degree of premeditation, were much clearer and more refined in 1800 than they had been a century earlier. More generally, the system had become much more concerned about legal niceties and correct procedure than previously. The penal system was also far more graduated and proportionate than had been the case in 1700.

Just as significantly, there had been enormous developments in policing. In the modern era, it has sometimes been argued that the creation of a "policed" society was one of the major developments of the nineteenth century. In reality, it is clear that this development had its roots deep in the previous century, and that change in 1829, though radical, built on a hundred years of gradual reform. However, change in the eighteenth century, unlike its successor, was largely premised on localism rather than centralisation, and authorisation rather than compulsion.

Last Words

In theory, one answer to the "crime problem" in modern western cities would be to rediscover the "robustness" of the late medieval period towards offending and disorder, especially that involving inter-personal violence. However, this is highly unlikely to happen, and would be equally undesirable. Very few people today, of whatever political complexion, would feel remotely comfortable living in such an environment, with its attendant dangers and insecurities. That being the case, the effective imposition of the criminal law in urban areas has long assumed paramount importance. This is largely *faute de mieux*, as other, more efficient, forms of social control become attenuated in large cities that are faced by rapid, unmediated, social change. Unfortunately, there are inherent limitations as to what can be achieved by the criminal justice system on its own, as the Metropolitan authorities discovered during the eighteenth century.

A more realistic solution to the urban crime and order problem is to return to fundamentals. Although the work of the celebrated "Chicago School" of criminology in the 1930s was largely premised on the presence of rapid and unregulated change in big cities, this is not *necessarily* the "natural state" for such areas. Even London has experienced periods of relative stability over the past 400 years. Although major conurbations will always be at the forefront of national developments, these can often be controlled and modified, and the notion that cities are infinitely malleable abandoned. For example, the speed of inward migration and alterations to the built environment can be managed, amenities provided, and community and cultural cohesion and stability encouraged, at least to some extent. Whether it is wise to raise so much more in taxation from the Metropolitan area than is spent there, as is currently the case, is also questionable. A reduction in urban stress and the normlessness that comes with it, *combined* with an effective criminal justice system, is far more likely to reap dividends than a system based solely on criminal law enforcement.

BIBLIOGRAPHY

Allen, F. (1750) *An Account of the Behaviour of Mr. James Maclaine, from the time of his condemnation to the Day of his Execution, October 3rd, 1750*, London.

Andrew, D. T. (1994) *London Debating Societies, 1776-1799*, London: London Record Society.

Andrew, D. T. (2002) "The press and public apologies in eighteenth-century England", in Landau, N. (Ed.), *Law, Crime and English Society 1660-1830*, Cambridge: CUP, pp. 208-229.

Andrews, R. (1994) *Law, Magistracy and Crime in Old Regime Paris, 1735-1789*, Cambridge: CUP.

Anon (1811) *The Crown Circuit Companion* (8th edn.), London.

Anon (A Citizen of London), (1751) *The Vices of the Cities of London and Westminster trac'd from their original...*, Dublin: G. Faulkner.

Anon (By a Friend to the Constitution), (1796) *Observations on the Duty and Power of Juries, as established by the Laws of England* (3rd edn.), London.

Anon (By a German Gentleman), (1725) *A view of London and Westminster: or, the Town Spy* (2nd edn.), London.

Anon (By a hearty lover of his country), (1695) *Solon secundus: or, Some defects in the English laws: with their proper remedies*, London.

Anon (By a Jobber), (1719) *The Anatomy of Exchange-Alley: Or, a System of Stock-Jobbing* (2nd edn.), London.

Anon (By a Magistrate), (1787) *Some Hints towards a Revival of the Penal Laws, the better regulating the Police, and the Necessity of enforcing the Execution of Justice*, London.

Anon (Cato), (1722) *A Discourse of Standing Armies* (2nd edn.), London.

Anon (Philo Patriae), (1735) *A full and genuine Account of the Murder of Mrs. Robinson by Elton Lewis*, London.

Anon (1664) *The cry of the innocent & oppressed for justice: or, A brief relation of the late proceedings against the prisoners called Quakers, at the sessions holden at Hick's hall and Old Bailey, 14, 15, 17 Oct. 1664*, London.

Anon (1674) *A True and Perfect Account of the Procedings at the General Sessions of the Peace, holden for London and Middlesex, upon the 15 and 16 of January Instant*, London.

Anon (1674) *The Counterfeit Constable and the Wicked Watch*, London.

Anon (1677) *News from Newgate Or, a true Relation of the Manner of taking Seven persons, very notorious for Highway-men, In the Strand*, London.

Anon (1680) *The Narrative of the proceedings at the Session-house for London and Middlesex: giving an account of the tryals of divers traitors, clippers, coyners, highway-men, and other notorious offenders: the number condemned to die, to be whipt &c.*, London.

Anon (1681) *Seasonable cautions for juries, solicitors and witnesses, to deterre from man-catching*, London

Anon (1684) *The Proceedings of His Majesties justices of peace, at the sessions of Oyer and Terminer: held at Hick's-Hall, September the 6th, 1684, for the tryal of the constables, &c. of the hamlets of Spittle-fields, and Bethnal-Green*, London: Printed by R.R.

Anon (1692) *A Full and True Account of the Apprehending James Whitney, the Notorious Highway-man, near Bishopsgate with his Examination and confession before Sir Thomas Cook, Sheriff and the Recorder of the City of London*, London: Printed for Randal Taylor.

Anon (1699) *An Account of the apprehending & taking of Mr. John Robinson and William Criss for the murther of Mrs. Mary Robinson particularly how they were discovered by a letter, from an unknown hand*, London.

Anon (1700) *An Account of a new and strange discovery that was made by John Sheirly, alias Davis, & Joseph Fisher, the same day of their execution relating to the ordinary of Newgate: with a true copy of the petition, that was presented to the Lord Mayor, by the pris.*, London.

Anon (1701) *Hanging, not Punishment Enough, for Murtherers, High-way Men, and House-Breakers*, London: A. Baldwin.

Anon (1702) *An Essay Towards the Reformation of Newgate and Other Prisons in and About London*, London.

Anon (1703) *An Alphabetical List of Persons who are reputed to be common Bail, whose Recognizances (by suffering the same to be forfeited) have been divers times estreated in the court of exchequer*, London.

Anon (1703) *Hell Upon Earth: Or the most Pleasant and Deluctable History of Whittington's College otherwise (vulgarly) called Newgate*, London.

Anon (1703) *The Whole Tryal, Examination, Confession, and Condemnation of Mr. John Allen, the Merchant's Son*, London.

Anon (1707) *A full and true account of the apprehending and taking of Jack Hall … and Richard Low, for shooting a constable near Grays-Inn-Lane*, London.

Anon (1707) *Tryal Examination And Conviction Of several Notorious Persons call'd Sodomites, At Guild-Hall on Monday the 20th of October, 1707. With a List of the Names of those that were Try'd & Convicted*, London.

Anon (1709) *Reasons for suppressing the yearly fair in Brook-field, Westminster; commonly called Mayfair*, London.

Anon (1711) *An account of the life, birth, death, parentage, and conversation, of Mr. John Addison, a most notorious highwayman*, London.

Anon (1715) *A True and Exact List of all the Malefactors, Both men and women, Who pleaded to His Majesty's most Gracious Pardon, at the Sessions-House in the Old-Baily, On Saturday the 6th of August, 1715*, London.

Anon (1719) *Parochial Tyranny, or, Select Vestries Become the Plague of the People*, London.

Anon (1722) *An Account of the Endeavours That have been used to suppress Gaming-Houses, And of the Discouragements That have been met with*, London.

Anon (1722) *The Tryal and Condemnation of Arundel Coke alias Cooke Esq; and of John Woodburne Labourer, for Felony, In Slitting the Nose of Edward Crispe Gent*, London.

Anon (1722) *The Widow Lutterel's Cry for Justice for the Blood of her Murthered Husband*, London.

Anon (1723) *The Life of Mr. John Stanley*, London.

Anon (1725) *The History of the Lives and Actions of Jonathan Wild, Thief-Taker*, London: Printed for Edward Midwinter.

Anon (1725) *The Life and Glorious Actions of the most heroic and Magnanimous Jonathan Wilde*, London.

Anon (1726) *A Narrative of the Barbarous and unheard of murder of Mr. John Hayes, by Catherine his wife, Thomas Billings, and Thomas Wood, on the 1st March at Night*, London.

Anon (1727) *A Method whereby Criminals liable to Transportation may be render'd not only useful but honest members of the publick*, London

Anon (1727) *A True and Faithful Narrative of the Life and Actions of John Oneby, commonly called Major Oneby Esq*, London.

Anon (1727) *The Three and Thirtieth account of the progress made in the Cities of London and Westminster*, London.

Anon (1728) *Directions for Prosecuting Thieves Without the Help of those False Guides, The Newgate Sollicitors…*, London.

Anon (1729) *Hell Upon Earth: Or the Town in an Uproar*, London.

Anon (1730) *Certaine Statutes Especially Selected, and Commanded by his Majestie to be Carefully Put in Execution by all Justices, and other Officers of the Peace throughout the Realme*, London.

Anon (1730) *The Tryal of Thomas Thomson and Lavinia Whitney, On an indictment for a Conspiracy…*, London.

Anon (1733) *Abstract of Several Acts*, London.

Anon (1734) *The Case of William Aynsley, an Attorney at Law, in Oxford*, Reading.

Anon (1735) *A Trip Through the Town. Containing Observations on the Humours and Manners of the Age* (5th edn.), London.

Anon (1735) *Select Trials, for Murders, Robberies, Rapes, Sodomy, Coining, Frauds, And other Offences*, London: Printed for J. Wilford.

Anon (1735) *Short Remarks Upon the Printed Case of the Burgesses and Inhabitants of Westminster against the Bill, &c. for the better regulating the nightly watch*, London.

Anon (1737) *Some Observations on the Trial of Mr. Thomas Carr, Who was Executed at Tyburn, January 18. 1737*, London.

Anon (1737) *The Man of Manners: Or, Plebeian Polish'd* (2nd edn.), London.

Anon (1738) *A Short History of the Gin Act: Or, An impartial Account of the Conduct of Some of those who have been intrusted with the Execution of it*, London.

Anon (1738) *An Enquiry into the Causes of the Increase and Miseries of the Poor in England*, London: A. Bettesworth.

Anon (1740) *A compendious library of the law, necessary for persons of all degrees and professions. In two parts...*, London.

Anon (1740) *News from the Dead, or a faithful and Genuine Narrative of an extraordinary combat between life and death, exemplified in the case of William Duell*, London.

Anon (1740) *The Cruel Mistress; Being, The Genuine Trial of Elizabeth Branch, and Her own Daughter; For the Murder of Jane Buttersworth, Their Servant Maid*, London.

Anon (1740) *The Foreigner's Guide to London*, London.

Anon (1740) *The Genuine and Authentic Trial of Mr. Bartholomew Greenwood, Charg'd with Robing Mr. Roger Wheatly near Camberwell* (3rd edn.), London.

Anon (1740) *The proceedings at the Assizes of Peace, Oyer and Terminer, for the County of Surrey, held at the Town-Hall of Kingston upon Thames on Wednesday the 30th... Saturday the 2nd Day of August*, London.

Anon (1742) *The Law of Arrests in Both Civil and Criminal Cases*, London.

Anon (1744) *A Select Collection of Remarkable Trials in One Volume*, London.

Anon (1744) *His Account of the Behaviour, Confession, and Dying words... Who were executed at Tyburn on Monday the 24th December, 1744*, London.

Anon (1745) *A Plain Answer to a late Pamphlet, intitled, the Business of Pawnbroking stated and defended*, London.

Anon (1749) *A Complete Guide to all persons who have any trade or concern with the city of London, and parts adjacent...* (4th edn.), London: J. Osborn.

Anon (1751) *A Full and genuine Narrative of the Confederacy Carried on by Cather, Cane, Alexander ... Against the Hon. Edward Walpole* (2nd edn.), London.

Anon (1752) *A Method Proposed to prevent the many Robberies and Villainies Committed in and about the City of London*, London.

Anon (1752) *A Warning Piece Against the Crime of Murder*, London.

Anon (1752) *The authentick trylas [sic] at large of John Swan and Elizabeth Jeffryes, for the murder of the late Mr. Joseph Jeffryes, of Walthamstow, and of Henry Simons, a Polish Jew, ...Both try'd at the Lent Assizes at Chelmsford*, London.

Anon (1752) *The Life of the Famous William Stroud*, London.

Anon (1753) *The Genuine Lives of Christopher Johnson, John Stockdale, and William Peers, John Stockdale, and William Peers*, London.

Anon (1753) *The Thief-Catcher; or, Villainy Detected*, London.

Anon (1754) *A Letter To a Member of Parliament Upon the Subject of the present reigning Enormities of Murders and Robberies*, London.

Anon (1755) *Low-Life: or One Half of the World Knows not how the Other Half Live* (2nd edn.), London.

Anon (1755) *The Tryal of Charles Bradbury, for the Detestable Crime of Sodomy*, London.

Anon (1756) *Further Observations on the Buyers or Receivers of Stolen Goods, particularly, of lead, iron, copper, brass, bell-metal, and solder*, London.

Anon (1756) *The Coroner's Guide: or, the Office and Duty of a Coroner* (2nd edn.), London.

Anon (1756) *The Remarkable Life of James Smith, A Famous Young Highwayman*, London.

Anon (1758) *A Congratulatory Epistle from a Reformed Rake*, London.

Anon (1758) *An Essay on the Office of Constable* (2nd edn.), London.

Anon (1759) *A Genuine Narrative of the Trial and Condemnation of Mary Edmondson, for the Murder of Mrs. Susannah Walker, her Aunt* (2nd edn.), London.

Anon (1760) *A Genuine Account of the Life and Trial of William Andrew Horne, Esq* (3rd edn.), London.

Anon (1760) *An Answer to the Pamphlet wrote by the Juryman Touching the Death of Ann Sharp*, London.

Anon (1760) *Orders, resolutions, report and proposals for, and relating to, the passing vagrants in the County of Surrey, Quarter Sessions*, Surrey.

Anon (1760) *The True and Whole Proceedings of the Coroner's Inquest at St. Mary-le-Bonne; On Saturday, October the 11th, 1760*, London.

Anon (1761) *A Treatise of Distresses, Replevins and Avowries... Containing the common and statute law for securing the payment of rents ... also divers statutes touching the office of Sheriffs...* (4th edn.), London: J. Worrall.

Anon (1761) *The Tryal of Mr. John Lowther, For an Assault on John Bushnell, with an intent to commit the Crime of Sodomy*, London.

Anon (1762) *God's Revenge against Murder; Or, the Genuine History of the Life, Trial, and last Dying Words of Sarah Metyard, Widow, and Sarah Morgan Metyard, Spinster, for the Wilful Murder of Ann Nailor,* London.

Anon (1764) *Low-life or one Half of the World knows not how the other Lives* (3rd edn.), London.

Anon (1767) *The Cries of Blood, or Juryman's Monitor*, London.

Anon (1767) *The Trials of James Brownrigg, and John Brownrigg, his Son, for Confining and inhumanly Scourging Mary Mitchel, Spinster…*, London.

Anon (1768) *The Case of Mr James Oliphant, Surgeon, Respecting a Prosecution which He, together with his wife and maid servant, underwent in the Year 1764*, Newcastle upon Tyne.

Anon (1770) *An authentic Account of the Trials, Behaviour, and Dying declaration, of the Five Malefactors, Who were executed at Kennington-Common, on Monday the 23rd April, 1770*, London.

Anon (1770) *The Midnight Rambler or, New Nocturnal Spy,* London: J. Coule.

Anon (1771) *A Dialogue Between a Lawyer and a Country Gentlemen, Upon the Subject of the Game Laws,* London.

Anon (1772) *The Complete Parish-Officer, together with the new statutes relating to Hackney Coaches, etc.,* London.

Anon (1773) *A Genuine Account of the Life Robberies, Trial and Execution of William Cox,* London.

Anon (1773) *The Genuine Life of William Cox, Who is now under Sentence of Death in Newgate* (5th edn.), London.

Anon (1774) *A Genuine Account of the Life of John Rann, alias Sixteen-String Jack,* London.

Anon (1774) *A Genuine Account of the Life, Robberies, Trial and Execution, of William Hawke,* London.

Anon (1775) *A Description of the County of Middlesex, etc.,* London: R. Snagg.

Anon (1777) *A letter to his Grace the Duke of Northumberland; on the Intended meeting of the Justices of Middlesex,* London.

Anon (1778) *The Means of Effectually Preventing Theft and Robbery,* London.

Anon (1780) *The Trials at Large of W. Henry Turton, and Luke West, for the Murder of Charles Gutherson, in the Parish of Chatham,* Rochester.

Anon (1784) *St. Margaret and St. John the Evangelist, Westminster. State of the Second Voluntary Subscription for the Armed Patroles*, London.

Anon (1785) *Internal Police of the Kingdom Very Much Neglected.* London

Anon (1786) *A letter to Archibald Macdonald, Esq. on the Intended Plan for Reform in what is called the Police of Westminster* (2nd edn.), London.

Anon (1786) *Account of a tryal at Hick's Hall. Tuesday, April 25, 1786*, London.

Anon (1786) *An Account of the Work-Houses in Great Britain in the Year M,DCC,*XXXII [1732] (3rd edn.), London: W. Brown.

Anon (1786) *Defence of the Police Bill, in Answer to a Charge Deliverd by W. Mainwaring Esq.*, London.

Anon (1786) *Outlines of a Plan for Patroling and Watching the City of London, Borough of Southwark, and their Environs*, London.

Anon (1787) *A Candid Enquiry into the Right of Jurisdiction in the City of London over the Borough of Southwark*, London.

Anon (1787) *Some Hints Towards A Revival of the Penal Laws, the better regulating the Police, and the Necessity of enforcing the Execution of Justice*, London.

Anon (1795) *Execution of Maclean Commonly Known by the name of the Gentleman Highwayman*, Bath.

Anon (1796) *The Trial of Miss Jones, &c For the Murder of Mr. Thomas Yates*, London.

Anon (1798) *The Young and Thoughtless Criminal: Being a true and most affecting history of that unfortunate convict, Hannah Bromley*, London.

Anon (1799) *Observations on a Late Publication: Intituled A Treatise on the Police of the Metropolis*, London.

Anon (1799) *Reports from Select Committees, Respection The Arts-Masters and Apprentices of Bridewell Hospital*, London.

Anon (1799) *The Report of the Select Committee Appointed by the House of Commons, Relative to the Establishment of a New Police in the Metropolis, &c.*, London.

Anon (1799) *Thoughts on Means of Alleviating the Miseries attendant upon common Prostitution*, London.

Anon (1800) *Observations on the Duty and Power of Juries, as established by the Laws of England* (5th edn.), London.

Anon (1808) *The Constable's Assistant: being a compendium of the duties and powers of constables and other peace officers …* (2nd edn.), London: The Society for the Suppression of Vice.

Anon (1812) *Fairburn's Account of the Dreadful Murder of Mr. Marr and Family, … Including the Whole Investigation Before the Coroner's Inquest* (2nd edn.), London.

Anon (1815) *An Address to the Magistracy of the City of Middlesex and of the City and Liberties of Westminster*, London.

Anon (1821) *A Letter to a Member of Parliament, on the Police of the Metropolis*, London.

Anon (circa 1720) *The Great Grievance of Traders and Shopkeepers, by the Notorious Practise of Stealing their Goods out of their Shops and warehouses by persons commonly called shop-lifters*, London.

Archenholz, J. W. von (1789) *A Picture of England, Containing a description of the laws, customs and manners of England*, vol. 2, London.

Archenholz, J. W. von (1790) *A Picture of England, Containing a description of the laws, customs and manners of England*, Dublin.

Aylett, P. (1987) "A Profession in the Marketplace: The Distribution of Attorneys in England and Wales 1730-1800", *Law and History Review*, vol. 5, pp. 1-30.

B., N. (1718) *A Compleat Collection of Remarkable Tryals of the most Notorious Malefactors, at the Sessions-House in the Old Bailey, for near Fifty Years Past,* London: Printed by J. Phillips.

Babbington, A. (1999) *A House in Bow Street* (2nd edn.), Chichester: Barry Rose.

Bachiler, E. (1655) *To his Highness Oliver Lord Protector or the Commonwealth of England, Scotland, and Ireland,* London.

Bacon, F. (1641) *Cases of Treason,* London.

Baines, P. (2009) "Crime Histories", *Eighteenth-century Studies*, vol.41, issue 1, at pp. 166-170.

Baker, J. H. (1973) "Criminal Justice at Newgate 1616-1627", *The Irish Jurist,* vol. 8, pp.307-322.

Baldwin, R. (1776) *Considerations on some laws relating to the office of Coroner,* Newcastle.

Banks, S. (2008) ""Very Little Law in the Case": Contests of Honour and the Subversion of the English Criminal Courts, 1780-1845", *King's Law Journal,* vol. 19, pp. 575-594.

Barlow, T. (1745) *The Justice of Peace: A Treatise Containing the Power and Duty of that Magistrate,* London.

Barrie, D. G. (2008) "Patrick Colquhoun, The Scottish Enlightenment And Police Reform In Glasgow In The Late Eighteenth Century", *Crime, History & Societies,* vol. 12:2, pp. 59-79.

Barrington, G. (1795) *The Life and Extraordinary Adventures of George Barrington,* Darlington.

Bartlett, P. (1997) "Sodomites in the Pillory in Eighteenth-century London", *Social and Legal Studies,* vol. 6, pp. 553-572.

Beattie, J. M. (1986) *Crime and the Courts in England 1660-1800,* Oxford: OUP.

Beattie, J. M. (1988) "London Juries in the 1690s" in J. S. Cockburn and T.A. Green (Eds.), *Twelve Good Men and True: The Criminal Trial Jury in England 1200-1800,* Princeton: Princeton University Press.

Beattie, J. M. (1991) "Garrow for the Defence", *History Today,* vol. 41, issue 2, pp. 49-53.

Beattie, J. M. (1991) "Scales of Justice: Defense Counsel and the English Criminal Trial in the Eighteenth and Nineteenth Centuries", *Law and History Review,* vol. 9, no.2, pp. 221-267.

Beattie, J. M. (1995) "Crime and inequality in eighteenth-century London", in J. Hagan and R. D. Peterson (Eds.), *Crime and Inequality,* pp.116-139, Palo Alto: Stanford University Press.

Beattie, J. M. (2001) *Policing and Punishment in London, 1660-1750,* Oxford: CUP.

Beattie, J. M. (2006) "Early Detection: The Bow Street Runners in Late Eighteenth- century London" in C. Emsely et al (Eds.), *Police Detectives in History, 1750-1950,* at pp. 15-32, Farnham: Ashgate.

Beattie, J. M. (2007) "Garrow and the Detectives: lawyers and policemen at the Old Bailey in the late eighteenth century", *Crime, History and Societies,* vol. 11, issue 2, pp. 5-23.

Beattie, J. M. (2007) "Sir John Fielding and Public Justice: The Bow Street Magistrates' Court, 1754-1780", *Law and History Review*, vol. 25, no. 1, pp. 61-100.

Becket, A. (1785) *A Trip to Holland*, vols. 1-2, London.

Beier, A. L. (2005) "Identity, Language, and Resistance in the Making of the Victorian "Criminal Class": Mayhew's Convict Revisited", *Journal of British Studies*, vol. 44, issue 3, pp. 499-515.

Belcher, V. (1986) "A London Attorney of the Eighteenth Century: Robert Andrews", *The London Journal*, vol. 12, no 1, pp. 40-50.

Bellamy, M. (1728) *The Life of Martin Bellamy; with an account of all the several street robberies, burglaries, forgeries and other crimes by him committed, etc.*, London: J. Applebee.

Bellers, J. (1724) *An Abstract of George Fox's Advice and Warning, To The Magistrates of London, in the Year 1656*, London.

Bentley, D. (1998) *English Criminal Justice in the Nineteenth Century*, Hambledon: Hambledon Press.

Berman, H. J. (1983) *Law and Revolution: The Formation of the Western Legal Tradition*, Boston: Harvard University Press.

Bertelsen, L. (1997) "Committed by Justice Fielding: Judicial and journalistic Representation in the Bow Street Magistrate's Office: January 3-November 24, 1752", *Eighteenth-century Studies*, vol. 30, no. 4, pp. 337-363.

Bevell, J. (1764) *An Authentic Narrative of the Methods by which the Robbery Committed in The House of the Right Honourable the Earl of Harrington, in the Stable-Yard, St. James's, was discovered*, London.

Bird, J. B. (1799) *The Laws respecting parish matters*, London.

Blackerby, N. (1738) *The Speech of Nathaniel Blackerby Esq... To the Justices, High Bailiff, High Constable, and Petty constables of the City and Liberty of Westminster*, London.

Blackerby, S. (1715) *The Justice of Peace His Companion* (3rd edn.), London.

Blackstone, W. (1765-9) *Commentaries on the Laws of England*, Oxford: Clarendon Press , vols 1-4.

Blandy, M. (1752) *Genuine letters that pass'd between Miss Blandy and Miss Jeffries, before and after conviction*, London.

Blizard, W. (1785) *Desultory Reflections on Police: with an essay on the means of preventing crimes and amending criminals*, London.

Bodde, D. (1969) "Prison Life in Eighteenth-Century Peking", *Journal of the American Oriental Society*, vol. 89, no. 2, pp. 311-333.

Bohun, E. (1693) *The Justice of Peace His Calling and Qualifications*, London.

Bondeson, J. (2000) *The London Monster*, London: Free Association Books.

Bondeson, J. (2001) "Monsters and Moral Panic in 18th-and 19th-Century London", *History Today*, vol. 55, issue 5, at pp. 30-35.

Braddon, L. (1717) *The Miseries of the poor are a national sin..*, London.

Bramah, J. (1785) *A Dissertation on the Construction of Locks*, London.

Bray, T. (1709) *Sermon Preach'd at the Parish-Church of St. Clements Danes, Westminster on the 24th of March 1709 at the Funeral of Mr. John Dent,* London.

Bray, T. (1732). *The Tryals of Jeremy Tooley, William Arch, and John Clausson, Three Private Soldiers for the Murder of Mr. John Dent, Constable…*, London: J. Wilford.

Brooks, C. (1998) *Lawyers, Litigation and English Society since 1450,* London: The Hambledon Press.

Broughtan, T. (1763) *Serious Advice and Warning to Servants, More especially those of the Nobility and Gentry,* London.

Brown, J. (1758) *An Estimate of the Manners and Principles of the Times,* Belfast.

Browning, A. (Ed.) (1953-1977) *English Historical Documents, 1660-1714*, vol. viii, London: Eyre & Spottiswoode.

Brydall, J. (1700) *Non compos mentis: or, The law relating to natural fools, mad-folks, and lunatick persons: inquisited, and explained, for common benefit,* London: printed by the assigns of Richard and Edward Atkins.

Bulstrode, W. (1718) *The Charge of Whitlocke Bulstrode Esq to the Grand-Jury, and other Juries, of the County of Middlesex,* London.

Bulstrode, W. (1718) *The Charge of Whitlocke Bulstrode Esq to the Grand-Jury, and other Juries, of the County of Middlesex,* London.

Burdett, F. (1800) *An Impartial Statement of the Inhuman Cruelties Discovered! In the Coldbath-Fields Prison*, London.

Burn, R. (1755) *The Justice of the Peace and parish officer*, vols. 1 and 2, London: A. Millar

Cairns, D. J. A. (1998) *Advocacy and the Making of the Adversarial Criminal Trial, 1800-1865*, Oxford: Clarendon Press.

Calonne, M. D. (1801) *Proposal for Preventing Highway Robberies in the Environs of London: or, an Account of the Marechaussee in France,* London.

Cameron, I. A. (1977) "The Police of Eighteenth-century France", *European History Quarterly*, vol. 7, pp. 47-75.

Cannicott, W. (1756) *A Genuine Account of the Life and Actions of William Cannicott,* London.

Care, H. (1703) *English Liberties: or, the Free-Born Subject's Inheritance,* London.

Carrick, J. (1722) *A Compleat and True Account of all the Robberies Committed by James Carrick, John Malhoni, and their Accomplies,* London: Printed for J. Peele.

Chalkin, C. W. (Ed.) (2009) *Surrey Gaol and Session House, 1791-1824*, Woking: Surrey Record Society.

Chapman, R. W. (1904) *James Boswell's Life of Samuel Johnson, LL.D,* London.

Charlesworth, L., (1999) "Why Is It a Crime to be Poor", *Liverpool Law Review*, vol. 21, no. 2, pp. 149-167.

Childs, J. (1997) "War, crime waves and the English army in the late seventeenth century", *War and Society* , vol. 15, pp. 1-17.

Clayton, M. (2008) "The Life and Crimes of Charlotte Walker, Prostitute and Pickpocket", *The London Journal*, vol. 33, no. 1, 2008, pp. 3-19.

Clowes, W. (1819) *Leigh's New Picture of London*, London.

Cobbett, W. (1817) *The Parliamentary History of England from the Earliest Period to the Year 1803*, London.

Cockburn, J. S. (1994) "Punishment and Brutalization in the English Enlightenment", *Law and History Review*, vol. 12, no. 1, pp. 155-179.

Cockburn, J. S. (Ed.) (1977) *Crime in England 1550-1800*, London: Methuen.

Cockburn, J. S. and Green T. A. (Eds.), *Twelve Good Men and True: The Criminal Trial Jury in England 1200-1800*, Princeton: Princeton University Press.

Cocks, H. G. (2006) "Safeguarding Civility: Sodomy, Class and Moral Reform In early Nineteenth-century England", *Past and Present*, no. 190, pp. 121-146.

Cohen, S. (1972) *Folk Devils and Moral Panics: The Creation of the Mods and Rockers*, Oxford: Martin Robertson.

Coles, R. (1643) *An act of common counsel for the well-ordering and establishing of the watches within this city and payment of the beadle's salary*, London.

Coley, W. B. (1965) "Fielding's Two Appointments to the Magistracy". *Modern Philology*, vol. 63, no. 2, pp. 144-149.

Colquhoun, P. (1797) *An Account of a meat and soup charity established in the metropolis in the year 1797*, London.

Colquhoun, P. (1800) *A Treatise on the Police of the Metropolis* (6th edn.), London.

Colquhoun, P. (1803) *A Treatise on the Functions and Duties of a Constable*, London.

Colquhoun, P. (1806) *Treatise on Indigence*, London.

Cottu, C. (1820) *On the administration of the criminal code in England, and the spirit of the English government*, London.

Cottu, C. (1822) *On the administration of Criminal Justice in England*, London.

Cox, J. (1756) *A Faithful Narrative of the most wicked and inhuman Transactions of that Bloody-minded Gang of Thief-takers, alias Thief-makers, Macdaniel, Berry, Salmon, Eagan, alias Gahagan*, London.

Cox, W. (1773) *The Genuine Life of William Cox, Who is now under Sentence of Death in Newgate* (5th edn.), London.

Crittal, E. (Ed.), (1982) *The Justicing Notebook of William Hunt, 1744-1749,* Wiltshire: Wiltshire Record Society.

Cross, A. L. (1917) "The English Criminal Law and Benefit of Clergy during the Eighteenth and Early Nineteenth Century", *The American Historical Review*, vol. 22, no. 3, 1917, pp. 544-565.

Dabhoiwala, F. (2006) "Summary Justice in Early Modern London", *The English Historical Review*, vol. 121, no. 492, pp. 796-822.

Dagge, H. (1722) *Considerations on criminal law*, London.

Dalton, J., (1728) *A Genuine Narrative of all the Street Robberies Committed since October last, by James Dalton,* London.

Dalton, M. (1655) *The Country Justice,* London.

Daniels, T. (1761) *The Affecting Case of the Unfortunate Thomas Daniels*, London.

Davey, B. J. (1994) *Rural Crime in the Eighteenth Century: North Lincolnshire 1740-80,* Hull: The University of Hull Press.

Davis, J. (1984) "A Poor Man's System of Justice: The London Police Courts in the Second Half of the Nineteenth Century", *The Historical Journal*, vol. 27, no. 2, pp. 309-335.

Defoe, D. (1724) *The History of the Remarkable Life of John Sheppard,* London.

Defoe, D. (1725) *The True and Genuine Account of the Life and Actions of the late Jonathan Wild,* London.

Defoe, D. (1726) *Some considerations upon street-walkers. With a proposal for lessening the present number of them. In two letters to a Member of Parliament,* London.

Defoe, D. (1728) *Augusta Triumphans: Or, The Way to make London the most flourishing City in the Universe,* London.

Defoe, D. (1728) *Street Robberies Consider'd; the reason of their being so frequent, with probable means to prevent 'em,* London.

Defoe, D. (1728) *Street-Robberies, considered: The Reason of their being so Frequent, with Probable means to Prevent 'em,* London.

Defoe, D. (1927) *The Poor Man's Plea,* Oxford: Basil Blackwell.

Dekker, T. (1609) *The Gull's Horne-book,* London.

Denham, J. (1724) *A Sermon Preach'd to the Societies for Reformation of Manners, at Salter's-Hall, On Monday, June 29, 1724,* London.

Deveil, T. (1747) *Observations on the Practice of a Justice of the Peace,* London.

Deveil, T. (1748) *Memoirs of the Life and Times of Sir Thomas Deveil, Knight,* London.

Devereaux, S. (1999) "The Making of the Penitentiary Act, 1775-1779", *The Historical Journal*, vol. 42, issue 2, pp. 405-433.

Devereaux, S. (2007) "Imposing the Royal Pardon: Execution, Transportation, and Convict Resistance in London, 1789", *Law and History Review*, vol. 25, pp. 101-137.

Devereaux, S. (2007) "From Sessions to Newspaper? Criminal Trial Reporting, The Nature of Crime, and the London Press, 1770-1800", *The London Journal*, vol. 32, no. 1, pp. 1-27.

Devereaux, S. (2009) "Recasting the Theatre of Execution: The Abolition of the Tyburn Ritual", *Past and Present*, vol. 202, no. 1, pp. 127-174.

Disney, J. (1710) *An Essay Upon the Execution of the Laws Against Immorality and Prophaneness* (2nd edn.), London.

Disney, J. (1786) *An Address to Grand-Juries, Constables and Church Wardens*, London.

Dixon, S. (2007) "Quakers and the London Parish 1670-1720", *The London Journal*, vol. 32, no. 3, pp. 229-249.

Dodd, W. (1777) *Authentic Memoirs of the Life of William Dodd, LL.D. who was executed at Tyburn, on Friday, June 27, 1777*, Salisbury.

Dodsworth, F. M. (2008) "The Idea of Police in Eighteenth-century England: Discipline, Reformation, Superintendence, c. 1780-1800", *Journal of the History of Ideas*, vol. 64, issue 4, pp. 583-605.

Dogherty, T. (1787) *The Crown Circuit Assistant: Being a Collection of Precedents of Indictments*, London.

Dolins, D. (1726) *The Third Charge of Sir Daniel Dolins, Kt to the Grand–Jury, and other Juries of the County of Middlesex*, London.

Dornford, J. (1785) *Seven Letters to the Lords of the Privy Council, on the Police*, London.

Dowdell, E. G. (1932) *A Hundred Years of Quarter Sessions, The Government of Middlesex From 1660-1760*, Cambridge: CUP.

Drury, J. (1701) *An Account of the Progress of the Reformation of Manners*, London.

Dunton, J. (1703) *The Shortest Way With Whores and Rogues: Or a New Project for Reformation*, London.

Durston, G. (2005) "Magwitch's Forbears: Returning from Transportation in Eighteenth-century London", *Australian Journal of Legal History*, vol. 9(2), pp. 137-158.

Durston, G. (2007) *Victims and Viragos: metropolitan women, crime and the eighteenth-century justice system*, Ipswich: Abramis.

Dyer, J. (1729) *A Genuine Narrative of the Memorable Life and Actions of John Dyer*, London.

Eden, W. (1781) *Principles of Penal law*, London.

Eisner, M. (2001) "Modernization, Self-control and Lethal violence", *British Journal of Criminology*, vol. 41, pp. 618-638.

Eisner, M. (2003) "Long-Term Historical Trends in Violent Crime", *Crime and Justice: A Review of Research*, vol. 30, pp. 83-142.

Ekirch, A. R. (1985) "Bound for America: A Profile of British Convicts Transported to the Colonies, 1718-1775", *The William and Mary Quarterly*, vol. 42, no. 2, pp. 184-200.

Ekirch, A. R. (1987) *Bound for America: The Transportation of British Convicts to the Colonies, 1718-1775*, Oxford: Clarendon Press.

Emsley, C. (1987) *Crime and Society in England 1750-1900*, London: Longman.

Emsley, C. (2010) *Crime and Society in England 1750-1900* (4th edn.), London: Longman.

England, R. W. (1985) "Investigating Homicides in Northern England, 1800-1824", *Criminal Justice History*, vol. 6, pp. 105-123.

Espriella, M. A. (1814) *Letters from England* (3rd edn.), vol. 1, London: Longman.

Eure, S. (1739) *Trials per pais: or, the law of England concerning juries by nisi prius, &c., With a compleat Treatise of the evidence* (7th edn.), London.

Everett, C.W. (Ed.) (1927) *The Letters of Junius*, London: Faber and Gwyer.

Everett, J. (1730) *A Genuine Narrative of the Memorable Life and Actions of John Everett*, London.

Farr, S. (1788) *Elements of Medical Jurisprudence*, London.

Feeley, M. and Little, M. F. (1991) "The Vanishing Female: The Decline of Women in the Criminal Process, 1687-1912", *Law and Society Review*, vol. 25, pp. 719-757.

Fennor, W. (1617) *The Compters Commonwealth*, London.

Field, B. (1828) *A Vindication of the Practice of Not Allowing the counsel for Prisoners Accused of felony to make Speeches for Them*, London.

Fielding, H. (1749) *The Case of the Unfortunate Bosavern Penlez*, London.

Fielding, H. (1751) *An Enquiry into the causes of Late Increase of Robbers*, Dublin.

Fielding, H. (1752) *Examples of the Interposition of Providence in the Detection and Punishment of Murder*, Dublin

Fielding, H. (1753) *A Clear State of the Case of Elizabeth Canning* (2nd edn.), London.

Fielding, H. (1755) *Journal of a Voyage to Lisbon*, London: A. Millar.

Fielding, J. (1755) *A Plan for Preventing Robberies Within Twenty Miles of London*, London: A. Millar.

Fielding, J. (1758) *A Plan for A Preservatory and Reformatory for the Benefit of Deserted Girls, And Penitent Prostitutes*, London.

Fielding, J. (1762) *Extracts from such of the Penal Laws, As particularly relate to the Peace and Good Order of this Metropolis*, London.

Fielding, J. (1768) *Extracts from Such of the Penal Laws, As Particularly relate to the Peace and Good Order of this Metropolis… to which is added… a short Treatise on the Office of Constable*, London.

Fielding, J. (1776) *A Brief Description of the Cities of London and Westminster,* London.

Fielding, J. (1790) *The New London Spy or, a Modern twenty-four hours ramble through the great British metropolis,* London.

Fiennes, C. (1888) *Through England on a Side Saddle in the Time of William and Mary*, London: The Leadenhall Press.

Finnimore, H. (1779) *The trial of H. F.* [Humphrey Finnimore] *Esqr (reputed to be worth forty thousand pounds) who was tried … and convicted of felony in stealing of five turkies, the property of T. Humphries. With the pleading of the Counsel, etc.,* London.

Fisher, G. (1995) "The Birth of the Prison Retold", *Yale Law Journal*, vol. 104, pp. 1236-1252.

Fisher, G. (1997) "The Jury's Rise as Lie Detector", *Yale Law Review,* vol. 107, no. 3, pp. 575-713.

Fitzsimmonds, J. (1751) *Free and Candid Disquisitions on the Nature and Execution of the Laws of England, Both in Civil and Criminal Affairs,* London.

Foot, J. (1769) *An Appeal to the Public, Touching the Death of Mr. George Clarke* (2nd edn.), London.

Forbes, T. R. (1977) "Inquests into London and Middlesex Homicides, 1673-1782", *Yale Journal of Biology and Medicine*, vol. 50, pp. 207-220.

Foster, M. (1762) *A Report of some proceedings on the Commission of Oyer and Terminer and Goal [sic] Delivery for the trial of the Rebels in the year 1746 in the County of Surry, and of other Crown Cases. To which are added Discourses upon a few branches of the Crown Law,* Oxford: Clarendon Press.

Foucault, M. (1979) *Discipline and Punish: The Birth of the Prison*, New York: Vintage Books.

Foyster, E. (2007) "Introduction: Newspaper Reporting of Crime and Justice", *Continuity and Change*, vol. 22, pp. 9-12.

Frost, R. (1729) *The Folly and Danger of Drunkenness*, London.

Fuller, W. (1703) *Mr William Fuller's Trip to Bridewell: With a True Account of his Barbarous Usage in the Pillory,* London.

G.D., (1695) *Tryals Per Pais: or, the Law of England concerning Juries, By nisi prius, &c.* (3rd. edn.), London: Printed by Edward Atkins.

Gallanis, T. P. (1999) "The Rise of Modern Evidence Law", *Iowa Law Review,* vol. 84, pp. 499-560.

Gallanis, T. P. (2006) "The Mystery Of Old Bailey Counsel" *The Cambridge Law Journal*, 2006, vol. 65:1, pp. 159-173.

Galloway, R. (1773) *The Rat-Trap,* London.

Gardiner, R. (1710) *The Compleat Constable* (4th edn.), London.

Gardner, K. J. (2001) "George Farquhar's The Recruiting Officer: Warfare, Conscription, and the Disarming of Anxiety", *Eighteenth-century Life*, vol. 25, pp. 43-61.

Garnham, N. (1997) "How violent was eighteenth-century Ireland?", *Irish Historical Studies*, vol. 119, pp. 377-392.

Garrioch, D. (1994) "The People of Paris and their Police in the Eighteenth-Century: Reflections on the Introduction of a "modern" police Force", *European History Quarterly*, vol. 24, pp. 511-535.

Gatrell, V.A.C. (1996) *The Hanging Tree: Execution and the English People 1770-1868*, Oxford: OUP.

Gent, J. D. (1720) *An Humble Proposal to Prevent the Beginnings of Theft*, London.

George, D. (1965) *London Life in the Eighteenth Century*, London: Penguin.

Gery, C. (1750) *Mr. Gery's case With the Reforming Constables, Address'd to the members of the Honourable House of Commons*, London.

Gilbert, G. (1760) *The Law of Evidence* (2nd. edn.), London: Printed by Catherine Lintot.

Gilbert, T. (1735) *Observations Upon Orders and Resolutions of the House of Commons With Respect to the Poor, Vagrants and Houses of Correction*, London.

Gilboy, R. (1934) *Wages in Eighteenth-century England*, Cambridge: Harvard University Press.

Gillen, M. (1982) "The Botany Bay Decision, 1786: convicts, not empire", *English Historical Review*, vol. 97, pp. 740-766.

Gillespy, E. (1793) *A Disquisition upon the Criminal Laws; Shewing the Necessity of Altering and Amending them*, Northampton.

Gilmour, I. (1992) *Riot, Risings and Revolution: Governance and Violence in Eighteenth-century England*, London: Hutchinson.

Gisborne, T. (1794) *An Enquiry into the Duties of men in the Higher and Middle Classes of Society in Great Britain*, London.

Glassey, L. (1979) *Politics and Justices of the Peace, 1675-1720*, Oxford: Clarendon Press.

Goddard, K. S. (2004) "A Case of Injustice? The Trial of John Bellingham", *The American Journal of Legal History*, vol. XLVI, pp. 1-25.

Goldsmith, N. M. (1998) *The Worst of Crimes: Homosexuality and the Law in Eighteenth-Century London*, Aldershot: Ashgate.

Gonson, J. (1728) *The Charge of Sir John Gonson Knt. To the Grand Jury of the Royalty of the Tower of London, and Liberties and Precincts thereof*, London.

Gonzales, M. (1888) *London in 1731*, London: Cassell & Co.

Grant, F. (1701) *A Vindication of Informers of the Breaches of the Laws Against Prophaness and Immorality*, Edinburgh.

Grant, J. (1838) *Sketches in London*, London.

Gray, D. (2007) "The Regulation of Violence in the Metropolis; the Prosecution of Assault in the Summary Courts, c.1780-1820", *The London Journal*, vol. 32, no. 1, pp. 75-87.

Gray, D. (2008) "The People's Courts? Summary Justice and Social Relations in the City of London, c.1760-1800", *Family & Community History*, vol. 11/1, pp. 1-15.

Green, T. A. (1985) *Verdict According to Conscience*, Chicago: Chicago University Press.

Greenberg, D. (1975) "The Effectiveness of Law Enforcement in Eighteenth-century New York", *The American Journal of Legal History*, vol. 19, no. 3, pp. 173-207.

Griffiths, P. (2008) *Lost Londons: Change, Crime and Control in the Capital City, 1550-1660*, Cambridge: CUP.

Grose, F. (1811) *A Dictionary of the Vulgar Tongue*, London.

Grosley, P. J. (1772) *A Tour to London or, New Observations on England, And its inhabitants*, London.

Grubb, F. (2001) "The Market Evaluation of Criminality: Evidence from the Auction of British Convict Labor in America, 1767-1775", *The American Economic Review*, vol. 91, no. 1, pp. 295-304.

Guerrini, A. (2004) "Anatomists and Entrepreneurs in Early Eighteenth-century London", *Journal of the History of Medicine and Allied Sciences*, vol. 59:2, pp. 219-39.

Guthrie, J. (1742) *The Behaviour, Confession, and Dying Words of Thomas Homan, who was Executed on Thursday the 18th of this Instant November*, London.

Guthrie, J. (1746) *The Ordinary Of Newgate His Account Of The Behaviour, Confession, And Dying Words Of Matthew Henderson, Who Was Executed On Friday The 25th Of April, 1746*, London.

H, G. (1741) *Matchless Villany; or a full ... narrative of the robbery and murder of J. Penny. In a letter from a Gentleman in London*, London.

Hackman, J. (1779) *The Case and Memoirs of the Late Rev. Mr. James Hackman ... With an Appendix on the ill Effects Offices of Public Offices of Justices of the Peace*, London.

Hague, T. (1807), A *Letter to William Garrow, Esq.*, London.

Hale, M. (1713) *The History of the Common Law of England*, London: J. Walthoe.

Hale, M. (updated by G. Wilson and S. Emlyn) (1800) *The History of the Pleas of the Crown*, vol.1, London.

Halifax, C. (1791) *The Constable's sure guide; or every constable his own lawyer*, London.

Handler, P. (2007) "The Law of Felonious Assault in England, 1803-61", *Journal of Legal History*, pp. 183-206.

Hanway, J. (1776) *Solitude in imprisonment, with proper profitable labour and a spare diet, the most ... effectual means of bringing Malefactors ... to a right sense of their condition*, London.

Hanway, J. (1785) *The Defects of Police, the cause of immorality, and the continual robberies committed, particularly in and about the Metropolis*, London: Printed for J. Dodsley.

Harding, V. (2001) "Controlling a complex metropolis", *London Journal*, vol. 26, pp. 29-37.

Hardy, W. J. (1905) *Calender of the Sessions Books 1689 to 1709*, London: Richard Nicholson.

Hardy, W. J. (1937) *Middlesex Session Records, New Series, Volume III 1615-1616,* London: C. W. Radcliffe.

Harris, A. (2004) *Policing the City: Crime and Legal Authority in London, 1780-1840,* Columbus: Ohio State University Press.

Harrison, W. (1775) *A new and universal history, description and survey of London and Westminster,* London.

Hathaway, R. (1702) *The Tryal of Richard Hathaway,* London.

Havard, J. (1960) *The Detection of Secret Homicide,* London: Macmillan.

Hawles, J. (1680) *The Englishman's Right,* London: printed for Richard Jamesway.

Hay, D. (1976) "Property Authority and the Common Law", in P. Linebaugh et al (Eds.), *Albion's Fatal Tree: Crime and Society in Eighteenth-Century England,* London: Random House.

Hay, D. (1982) "War, Dearth and Theft in the Eighteenth Century: The Record Of the English Courts", *Past and Present,* vol. 95, pp. 117-160.

Hay, D. (2002) "Dread of the Crown Office: the English Magistracy and King's Bench 1740-1800", in Landau, N. (Ed.), *Law, Crime and English Society 1660-1830,* Cambridge: CUP, pp. 19-45.

Hay, D. and Rogers, N. (1997) *Eighteenth-century English Society: Shuttles and Swords,* Oxford: OUP.

Hay, D. and Snyder F. (Eds.). (1989) *Policing and Prosecution in Britain, 1750-1850,* Oxford: OUP

Hayhoe, J. D. (2003) "Neighbours Before the Court: Crime, Village Communities and Seigneurial Justice in Northern Burgundy, 1750-1790", *French History,* vol. 17, no. 2, pp. 127-148.

Hayter, A. J. (1978) *The Army and the Crowd in Mid-Georgian England,* London: Macmillan.

Hayward, A. L. (Ed.) (1926) *Captain Alexander Smith, A Complete History of the Highwaymen,* London: George Routledge.

Hayward, A. L. (Ed.) (1927) *Lives Of the Most Remarkable Criminals Who Have Been Condemned And Executed for Murder, The Highway, Housebreaking, Street Robberies, Coining Or Other Offences Collected from Original Papers and Authentic Memoirs, And Published In 1735,* New York: Routledge and Sons.

Henderson, T. (1999) *Disorderly-women in Eighteenth-century London,* London: Longmans.

Higgs, J. (1742) *A Guide to Justices or Modern English Precedents for the Direction of Justices of the Peace and their Clerks* (2nd edn.), London.

Highmore, A. (1783) *A Digest of the Doctrine of Bail in Civil and Criminal Cases,* London.

Hillier, B. (2003) "The Mysterious Case of Elizabeth Canning", *History Today,* vol. 53, issue 3, pp. 47-53.

Hindle, W. G. (2006) *A History of Bridewell Prison, 1553-1700,* Lampeter: The Edwin Mellen Press.

Hitchcock, T. (2005) "Begging on the Streets of Eighteenth-century London", *Journal of British Studies,* vol. 44:3, pp. 478-498.

Hitchcock, T. and Shore, H. (2003) "The Spatiality of the Poor in Eighteenth-century London, John Marriot" in *The Streets of London from the Great Fire to the Great Stink*, London: River Oram Press.

Hitchin, C. (1718) *A True Discovery of the Conduct of Receivers and Thief-Takers in and about the City of London*, London.

Holdsworth, W. (1938) *A History of English Law*, vol. 12, London: Sweet and Maxwell.

Horn D. and Ransome M. (Eds) (1957) *English Historical Documents*, vol. X, 1714-1783, London: Eyre and Spottiswoode.

Hostettler, J. (2009) *A History of Criminal Justice in England and Wales*, Winchester: Waterside Press.

Houston, R. (1986) "British Society in the Eighteenth Century", *The Journal of British Studies*, vol. 25, no. 4, pp. 436-466.

Howard, J. (1789) *An Account of the Principal Lazarettos in Europe*, London.

Howard, J. (1929) *The State of the Prisons in England and Wales* (1st pub. 1777), London: J.M. Dent.

Howel, J. (1657) *Londinopolis*, London.

Howson, G. (1970) *Thief-Taker General: The Rise and Fall of Jonathan Wild*, London: Hutchinson and Co.

Humfrey, P. (1998) "Female Servants and Women's Criminality in Early Eighteenth-century London", *Criminal Justice in the Old World and the New*, G.T. Smith et al (Eds.), Toronto: University of Toronto.

Hurl-Eamon, J. (2004) "Policing Male Heterosexuality: The Reformation of Manners Societies' Campaign Against the Brothels in Westminster, 1690-1720", *Journal of Social History*, vol. 37, pp. 1017-1035.

Hurl-Eamon, J. (2005) "The Westminster Impostors: Impersonating Law Enforcement in Early Eighteenth-century London", *Eighteenth-century Studies*, vol. 38, no. 3, pp. 461-483.

Hurl-Eamon, J. (2005) *Gender and Petty Violence in London, 1680-1720*, Columbus: Ohio State University Press.

Hutton, L. (1638) *The Discovery of a London Monster, Called, the Blacke Dogg of Newgate*, London: Printed by N. P.

Hutton, W. (1784) *A Dissertation on Juries; With a Description of the Hundred Court*, Birmingham.

Ilive, J. (1757) *Reasons offered for the reformation of the house of correction in Clerkenwell*, London.

Ilive, J. (1759) *A scheme for the employment of all persons sent as disorderly to the house of correction in Clerkenwell, … The whole proving, that the county by the execution of this scheme will soon save several hundred pounds a-year*, London.

Impey, J. (1800) *The Office and Duty of Coroners*, London.

Impey, J. (1982) *The New Instructor Clericalis, Stating the Authority, Jurisdiction, and Modern Practice of the Court of King's Bench,* London.

Innes, J. (1986) *Statute Law and Summary Justice in Early Modern England,* Unpublished paper: Privately circulated by the author.

Innes, J. (ND) *William Payne of Bell Yard, Carpenter c. 1718-1782: The Life and times of a London informing constable,* Unpublished paper (in original version): Privately circulated by the author.

Irwin, W. (1941) "An Attack on John Fielding", *Modern Language Notes*, vol. 56, no. 7, pp. 523-525.

Ivis, J. W. (2001) "Informers and Their Social Networks in Eighteenth-century London", *Social Science History*, vol. 25, no. 4, pp. 563-587.

Jackson, M. (1997) *New Born Child Murder,* Manchester: MUP.

Jackson, T. (Ed.) (1849) *The Journal of Charles Wesley to which are appended selections from his correspondence and poetry*, 2 vols, London.

Jackson, W. (1795) *New Newgate Calendar: or, Villany displayed, in all its branches,* vol. iv, London.

Jacob, G. (1718) *An Appendix to the modern Justice: Containing the particular Business of the Quarter Sessions,* London.

Jacob, G. (1719) *The Laws of Appeals and Murder,* London.

Jacob, G. (1750) *Everyman His own Lawyer: Or, A Summary of the Laws of England in a New and Instructive Method* (4th edn.), London.

James, L. (2006) *The Middle Class: A History,* London: Little Brown.

James, P. D. and Critchley, T. A. (1971) *The Maul and the Pear Tree: the Ratcliffe Highway murders, 1811*, London: Constable

Jeaffreson, J.C. (Ed.) (1892) *Middlesex County Records*, vol. iv, 1667-1689, London: Middlesex County Record Society.

Jenkins, P. (1986) "From Gallows to Prison? The Execution Rate in Early Modern England", *Criminal Justice History*, vol. 7, pp. 52-60.

Johnson, D. (1969) *Southwark and the City*, London: Corporation of London.

Johnson, S. (1953) *The Rambler,* London: J. M. Dent.

Jones, C. (1752) *Some Methods Proposed Towards putting a stop to the Flagrant Crimes of Murder, Robbery, and Perjury,* London.

Kalman, H. D. (1969) "Newgate Prison", *Architectural History*, vol. 12, pp. 50-62.

Kelying, J. (1661) *Directions for Justices of the Peace,* London.

Kelyng, J. (1734) *A Report of Divers Cases in Pleas of the Crown, Adjudged and Determined; In the Reign of the late King Charles II* (2nd edn.), London.

Kent, J. R. (1981) "The English Village Constable, 1580-1642: The Nature and Dilemmas of the Office", *Journal of British Studies*, vol. 20, no. 2, pp. 26-49.

Kent, J. R. (1986) *The English Village Constable 1580-1642*, Oxford: Clarendon.

Kent, J. R. (1995) "The Centre and the Localities State formation and Parish government in England, Circa 1640-1740", *The Historical Journal*, vol. 38, no. 2, pp. 363-404.

Kesselring, K. (2006) "Detecting 'Death Disguised'", *History Today*, vol. 56, no. 4, pp. 20-26.

Kesselring, K. (2009) "Felony Forfeiture in England, *c.* 1170-1870", *Journal of Legal History*, vol. 30.3, pp. 201-226.

Kesselring, K. (2010) "Felons' Effects and the Effects of Felony in Nineteenth-Century England", *Law and History Review*, vol. 28, issue 1, pp. 111-139.

Kilday, A. M. and Watson, K. (2005) "Child Murder in Georgian England", *History Today*, vol. 55, pp. 40-46.

King, P. (1990) "Female offenders, work and life-cycle change in late eighteenth-century London", *Continuity and Change*, vol. 11, at pp. 61-90.

King, P. (1992) "Legal Change, Customary Right, and Social Conflict in Late Eighteenth-century England: The Origins of the Great Gleaning Case of 1788", *Law and History Review*, vol. 10, issue 1, pp. 1-31.

King, P. (1996) "Punishing Assault: The Transformation of Attitudes in the English Courts", *Journal of Interdisciplinary History*, vol. 27, pp. 43-74.

King, P. (2000) *Crime, Justice and Discretion in England: 1740-1820*, Oxford: OUP.

King, P. (2004) "The Summary Courts and Social Relations in Eighteenth-century England", *Past & Present*, no. 183, pp. 125-172.

King, P. (2007) "Newspaper reporting and attitudes to crime and justice in late-eighteenth-and early-nineteenth-century London", *Continuity and Change*, vol. 22, pp. 73-112.

King, P. (2007), *Crime and Law in England, 1750-1840: Remaking Justice from the Margins*, Cambridge: CUP.

King, P. (2009) "Making Crime News: Newspapers, Violent Crime and the Selective Reporting of Old Bailey Trials in the late Eighteenth Century", *Crimes, Histoire & Societes*, vol. 13, no. 1, pp. 91-116.

King, R. (1780) *The New Cheats of London Exposed*, London.

Knapman, P. (1993) "The Crowner's Quest", *Journal of the Royal Society of Medicine*, vol. 86, pp. 716-720.

Knapp, A. and Baldwin, W. (1824) *Newgate Calendar Comprising Interesting Memoirs Of The Most Notorious Characters Who Have Been Convicted Of Outrages On The Laws Of England Since The Commencement Of The Eighteenth Century*, London.

Koslofsky, C. (2002) "Court Culture and Street Lighting in Seventeenth-Century Europe", *Journal of Urban History*, vol. 28, pp. 743-768.

L. B., (1724) *An Accurate Description of Newgate,* London.

Lacey, N. (2001) "In Search of the Responsible Subject: History, Philosophy and Social Sciences in Criminal Law Theory", *The Modern Law Review*, vol. 64.3, pp. 350-371.

Lambarde, W. (1640) *The Duties of Constables,* London: Printed by Miles Flesher.

Landau, N. (1984) *The Justices of the Peace 1679-1760,* Berkeley: University of California Press.

Landau, N. (1998) "Appearance at the Quarter Sessions of Eighteenth-century Middlesex", *London Journal*, vol. 23 (2), pp. 30-51.

Landau, N. (1999) "Indictment for Fun and Profit: A Prosecutor's Reward at Eighteenth-century Quarter Sessions", *Law and History Review*, vol. 17, no. 3, pp. 507-536.

Landau, N. (2002) "The Trading Justice's Trade", *Law, Crime and English Society: 1660-1830,* at pp. 47-65, Cambridge: CUP.

Landau, N. (2002) *Law, Crime and English Society 1660-1830,* Cambridge: CUP.

Landau, N. (2005) "Summary Conviction and the Development of the Penal Law", *Law and History Review*, vol. 23, no. 1, pp. 3-19.

Landers, J. and Mouzas, A. (1988) "Burial seasonality and Causes of death in London 1670-1819", *Population Studies*, vol. 42, pp. 59-83.

Landsman, S. (1990) "The rise of the contentious spirit: Adversary procedure in Eighteenth-Century England", *Cornell Law Review*, vol. 75, pp. 498-609.

Landsman, S. (1998) "One Hundred Years of Rectitude: Medical Witnesses at the Old Bailey, 1717-1817", *Law and History Review,* vol. 16, no. 3, pp. 445-494.

Langbein, J. H. (1983) "Shaping the Eighteenth-century Criminal Trial: A View from the Ryder Sources", *The University of Chicago Law Review*, vol. 50, no. 1, pp. 1-136.

Langbein, J. H. (1983) "Albion's Fatal Flaws", *Past & Present,* no. 98, pp. 96-120.

Langbein, J. H. (1994) "The historical origins of the privilege against self-incrimination at Common Law", *Michigan Law Review*, vol. 92, issue 5, pp. 1047-1085.

Langbein, J. H. (1996) "Historical Foundations of the Law of Evidence: A View From the Ryder Sources", *Columbia Law Review*, vol. 96, pp. 1168-1202

Langbein, J. H. (1999) "The Prosecutorial Origins of Defence Counsel in the Eighteenth Century: The Appearance of Solicitors", *Cambridge Law Journal,* vol. 58(2), pp. 314-365.

Langbein, J. H. (2003) *The Origins of Adversary Criminal Trial,* Oxford: OUP.

Langeluddecke, H. (1997) "Law and order in seventeenth-century England: the organisation of local administration during the personal rule of Charles I", *Law and History Review*, vol. 15, pp. 47-76.

Langeluddecke, H. (1998) "Patchy and Spasmodic'? The Response of Justices of the Peace to Charles I's Book of Orders", *English Historical Review*, vol. 113, no. 454, pp. 1231-1248 .

Langford, P. (1991) *Public Life and the Propertied Englishman: 1689-1798,* Oxford: Clarendon Press.

Laurie, P. (1832) *An Inquiry into the Use and Abuse of Grand Juries,* London: Smith, Elder and Co.

Lawrence, J. (2006) *The Middle Class: A History,* London: Little Brown.

Lea, J. (1999) "Social Crime Revisited", *Theoretical Criminology*, vol. 3, pp. 307-325.

Leigh, S. (1819) *Leigh's New Picture of London,* London: Printed for W. Clowes.

Lemmings, D and Walker, C (2009) *Moral Panics, the Media and the Law in Early Modern England,* Basingstoke: Palgrave MacMillan.

Lemmings, D. And Walker, C. (1998) "Blackstone and Law Reform by Education: Preparation for the Bar and Lawyerly Culture in Eighteenth-Century England", *Law and History*, vol. 16, pp. 211-225.

Lemmings, D. (2005) "Criminal trial procedure in eighteenth-century England: the impact of Lawyers", *The Journal of Legal History*, vol. 26, pp. 73-82.

Levack, B. et al (2007) *The West: Encounters & Transformations* (2nd edn.), London: Pearson

Linebaugh, P. (1975) "The Tyburn Riot Against the Surgeons", in P. Linebaugh et al (Eds.), *Albion's Fatal Tree: Crime and Society in Eighteenth-Century England,* London: Random House.

Linebaugh, P. (1985) "Social History and (Conservative) Legal History: A Reply To Professor Langbein", *New York University Law Review*, vol. 60, pp. 212-43.

Linebaugh, P. (1991) *The London Hanged: Crime and Civil Society in the Eighteenth Century*, London: Penguin.

Lloyd, T. (1794) *To The Grand Juries of the City of London and County of Middlesex, etc. [A memorial "respecting the improper conduct of the Jailer of Newgate, and the extortions and oppression practised by his connivance",* London.

Lobban, M. (1990) "From Seditious Libel to Unlawful Assembly: Peterloo and the Changing Face of Political Crime c1770-1820", *Oxford Journal of Legal Studies*, vol. 10, pp. 307-352,

Lopez-Lazaro, F. (2002) '"No Deceit Safe in Its Hiding Place": The Criminal Trial in Eighteenth-century Spain", *Law and History Review*, vol. 20, no. 3, pp. 449-487.

Lorraine, P. (1714) *The Ordinary Of Newgate, His Account of the Behaviour, Confession, and Last Speech of Thomas Douglas, that was Executed at Tyburn, on Wednesday the 27th October,* London.

Lorraine, P. (1707) *The Ordinary's Account of the Life and conversation, Birth, Parentage and Education of John Herman Bryan, The Switzer*, London.

Lorraine, P. (1715) *Declaration of Nathaniel Parkhurst, Esq; Who was executed at Tyburn on Friday the 20th of May, 1715,* London.

M., N. (1720) *A Letter to a Member of Parliament, Concerning the Bill for Regulating the Nightly Watch in the City of Westminster, and Liberties thereof,* London.

Mackay, L. (1999) "Why they stole: women in the Old Bailey, 1779-1789", *Journal of Social History,* vol. 32, pp. 623-639.

MacNally, L. (1802) *The rules of evidence on pleas of the Crown: illustrated from printed and manuscript trials and cases,* London.

Madan, M. (1785) *Thoughts On Executive Justice: With Respect To Our Criminal Laws, Particularly On The Circuits,* (2nd edn.), London.

Mainwaring, G. B. (1821) *Observations on the present state of the Police of the Metropolis,* London: John Murray.

Malcolm, S. (1732) *A True Copy of the Paper Delivered the Night Before Her Execution by Sarah Malcolm,* London.

Mandeville, B. D. (1725) *An Enquiry into the Causes of the Frequent Executions at Tyburn,* London.

Marriott, J. (2000) "Sweep them off the Streets", *History Today,* vol. 50, pp. 26-28.

Marriott, J. (2003) *The Spatiality of the Poor in Eighteenth-century London,* London: Rivers Oram Press.

Marryot, M. (1732) *An Account of Several Work-houses for Employing and Maintaining the Poor,* London.

May, A. N. (2003) *The bar and the Old Bailey, 1750-1850,* Chapel Hill: The University of North Carolina Press.

McGlynn, S (2008) "Violence and the Law in Medieval England", *History Today,* pp. 53-59.

McGowen, R. (1983) "The Image of Justice and Reform of the Criminal Law in Early Nineteenth-Century England", *Buffalo Law Review,* vol. 32, pp. 89-125.

McGowen, R. (2005) "The Bank of England and the Policing of Forgery, 1797-1821", *Past and Present,* no. 186, pp. 81-116.

McKenzie, A. (2005) "'This Death Some Strong and Stout Hearted Man Doth Choose': The Practice of Peine Forte et Dure in Seventeenth-and Eighteenth-century England", *Law and History Review,* vol. 23, no. 2, pp. 279-314.

McKenzie, A. (2003) "Martyrs in Low Life? Dying Game in Augustan England", *Journal of British Studies,* vol. 42, pp. 167-205.

McKenzie, A. (2006) 'God's Tribunal: Guilt, Innocence, and Execution in England, 1675–1775', *Cultural and Social History,* vol. 3, pp. 121–44.

McKenzie, A. (2007) *Tyburn's Martyrs,* London: Hambledon-Continuum.

McMahon, V. (2006) "Reading the Body: Dissection and the "Murder" of Sarah Stout, Hertfordshire, 1699", *Social History of Medicine,* vol. 19, no. 1, pp. 19-35.

McMullan, J. L. (1984) *The Canting Crew: London's Criminal Underworld 1550-1700*, New Brunswick: Rutgers University Press.

McMullan, J. L. (1996) "The New Improved Monied Police: Reform, Crime Control, and the Comodification of Policing in London", *British Journal of Criminology*, vol. 36, no. 1, pp. 85-108.

Melling, E. (Ed.) (1969) *Crime and Punishment* Maidstone: Kent County Council.

Mercer, E. D. and Goodacre, K. (1965) *Guide to the Middlesex Sessions Records, 1549-1884*, London: GLRO.

Mildmay, W. (1763) *The Police of France: Or, An Account of the Laws and Regulations Established in that Kingdom, for the Preservation of Peace and the Preventing of Robberies*, London.

Miles, W. A. (1773) *A Letter to Sir John Fielding, Knt. Occasioned by his Extraordinary Request to Mr. Garrick, for the Suppression of the Beggars Opera*, London.

Misodulus, S. H. (1713) *The Young-man's counselor or the way of the world displayd; in several profitable essays, serious and comical* (2nd edn.), London: Printed for Robert Gifford.

Misson, M. and Ozell, J. (Trans.) (1719) *Memoirs and Observations in his Travels over England*, London.

Moran, R. D. (1985) "The Origin of Insanity as a Special Verdict: The Trial For Treason of James Hadfield", *Law & Society Review*, vol. 19, no. 3, pp. 601-633.

Moreton, A. (1725) *Everybody's Business is Nobody's Business: With a proposal for Amendment of the same; as also for clearing the Streets of those Vermin called Shoe-Cleaners, and substituting in their stead many thousands of industrious Poor, now ready to starve* (5th edn.), London.

Moreton, A. (1727) *Parochial Tyranny*, London.

Moreton, A. (1729) *Second Thoughts are best: or, a Further Improvement of a Late Scheme to Prevent Street Robberies*, London.

Morgan, G. and Rushton, P. (1998) *Rogues, Thieves and the Rule of Law: The Problem of Law Enforcement in Northeast England*, London: University College London Press.

Morgan, K. (1989) "Petitions against Convict Transportation, 1725-1735", *The English Historical Review*, vol. 104, no. 410, pp. 110-113.

Moritz, C. (1965) *Journeys of a German in England in 1782*, London: Jonathan Cape.

Moritz, K. (1886) *Travels in England in 1782*, London: Cassell and Company.

Morris, C. (1751) *Observations on the Past Growth and Present State of the City of London*, London.

Morris, N. and Rothman, D. J. (Eds.) (1995) *The Oxford History of the Prison*, Oxford: OUP.

Muyden, M. V. (Ed.) (1902) *A Foreign View of England in the reigns of George I and George II; The letters of Monsieur Cesar de Saussure, to his Family*, London: John Murray.

Neaves, T. (1729) *The Life of Thomas Neaves*, London.

Neild, J. (1812) *State of the Prisons in England, Scotland and Wales,* London.

Nelson, W. (1717) *The Law of evidence*, London: R. Gosling.

O'Flannagan, J. R. (1870) *The Lives of the Lord Chancellors and Keepers of the Great Seal of Ireland–from the earliest times to the reign of Queen Victoria,* 2 vols, London.

Oldham, J. (2002) "The Limits of Discretion: Forgery and the Jury at the Old Bailey, 1818-1821", in Cairns, J. and McLeod, G. (Eds) *The Dearest Birth Right of the People of England: The Jury in the History of the Common Law,* Oxford: Hart Publishing, pp. 157-172.

Oldham, J. (1983) "The Origins of the Special Jury", *University of Chicago Law Review*, vol. 50, at pp. 142-144.

Oldham, J. (1987) "Law Reporting in the London Newspapers, 1756-1786", *The American Journal of Legal History,* vol.31, no.3, pp. 177-206.

Oldham, J. (1994) "Truth Telling in the Eighteenth-century English Courtroom", *Law and History Review*, vol. 12, no. 1, pp. 95-121.

Oliphant, J. (1768) *The Case of Mr James Oliphant, Surgeon, Respecting a Prosecution which He, together with his wife and maid servant, underwent in the Year 1764*, Newcastle upon Tyne.

Ollyffe, G. (1731) *An Essay Humbly offer'd, for An Act of Parliament to prevent Capital Crimes,* London.

Paleotti, F. (1718) *The Life, Actions, and Amours, of Ferdinando, Marquis of Palleotti, Lately Executed at Tyburn, for the Murther of his Servant,* London.

Paley, R. (1989) "An imperfect, inadequate and wretched system? Policing London before Peel", *Criminal Justice History*, vol. 10, pp. 95-130.

Paley, R. (1989) 'Thief-takers in London in the age of the McDaniel gang c.1745-1754' in Douglas Hay and Francis Snyder (eds.), *Policing and prosecution in Britain, 1750-1850*, Oxford: Clarendon Press.

Paley, R. (1991) *Justice in 18th-Century Hackney: the Justicing Notebook of Henry Norris and the Hackney Petty Sessions Book,* London: London Record Society.

Paley, W. (1814) *The Law and Practice of Summary Convictions on Penal Statutes by Justices of the Peace,* London.

Palk, D. (2006) *Gender, Crime and Judicial Discretion,* Woodbridge: Royal Historical Society/Boydell Press.

Palmer, S. H. (1988) *Police and Protest in England and Ireland 1780-1850,* Cambridge: CUP.

Parker, G. (1781) *A view of Society and Manners in High and Low Life,* London.

Paul, J. (1785) *The Compleat Constable,* London.

Pearce, T. (1756) *The compleat justice of the peace, and parish officer..,* London.

Peers, W. (1753) *The Genuine Lives of Christopher Johnson,* London.

Petty, W. (1685) *An Essay concerning the Multiplication of Mankind*, 2nd edn., London.

Petty, W. (1685) *An Essay concerning the Multiplication of Mankind; Together with another Essay in Political Arithmetick, concerning the Growth of the City of London* (2nd edn.), London.

Philipps, C. W. (1745) *The Charge of Sir Clifford Wm. Philipps, Knt. To the Grand Jury of the Royalty of the Tower of London, Liberties, and Precincts thereof. At the General Quarter Sessions of the Peace held for the Said Royalty, on Tuesday the Sixteenth Day of October, 1744, at the Court-House on Great Tower-Hill*, London.

Phillips, D. (2004) "A "Weak" State? The English State, the Magistracy and the Reform of Policing in the 1830s", *English Historical Review*, vol. cxix, no. 483, pp. 873-891.

Pike, R. (1983) *Penal Servitude in Early Modern Spain*, Madison: University of Wisconsin Press.

Pitofsky, A. (2000) "The Warden's Court Martial: James Oglethorpe and the Politics of Eighteenth-century Prison Reform", *Eighteenth-century Life*, vol. 24 pp. 88–102.

Pitt, W. M. (1804) *A Plan for the Improvement of the Internal Police of Prisons*, London.

Place, F. (1834) *Improvement of the Working People*, London: Charles Fox publishers.

Poussin, Father (1734) *Pretty Doings in a Protestant Nation*, London.

Prest, W. (1991) "Judicial Corruption in Early Modern England", *Past and Present*, vol. 133, pp. 67-95.

Prest, W. (1999) "Lay Legal Knowledge in Early Modern England", in A. Wijfells et al (Eds), *Learning the Law: Teaching and the Transmission of Law in England 1150-1900*, London: Hambledon, pp. 303-314.

Pue, W. W. (1983) "The Criminal Twilight Zone: Pre-Trial Procedures int he 1840s", *Alberta Law Review*, vol. 21, pp. 335-364.

Quarrell, W. H. and More, M. (Trans. and Eds.) (1934) *London in 1710 From the Travels of Zacharias Conrad Von Offenbach*, London: Faber & Faber Ltd.

Rabin, D. (2003) "Searching for the Self in Eighteenth-century English Criminal Trials, 1730-1800", *Eighteenth-century Life*, vol. 27, no. 1, pp. 85-106.

Rabin, D. (2004) *Identity, Crime, and Legal Responsibility in Eighteenth-century England*, Basingstoke: Palgrave Macmillan.

Rabin, D. (2005) "Drunkenness and Responsibility for Crime in the Eighteenth Century", *Journal of British Studies*, vol. 44.3, pp. 457-477.

Radzinowicz, L. (1948-56) *A History of English Criminal Law and its Administration from 1750*, vols. 1-3, London: Stevens & Sons.

Rastall, W. D. (1815) *A Practical Guide, to the Quarter and other, Sessions of the Peace*, London.

Rawlings, P. (1999) *Crime and Power: A History of Criminal Justice, 1688-1998*, London: Longman.

Rawlings, P. (2002) *Policing: A Short History*, Cullompton: Willan Publishing.

Rayner, J. L. and Crook, G. T. (Eds.) (1926) *The Complete Newgate Calender*, London: Privately printed for the Navarre Society, vols. 1-4.

Razzell, P. and Spence, C. (2007) "The History of Infant, Child and Adult Mortality in London, 1550-1850", *The London Journal*, vol. 32, no. 3, pp. 211-288.

Reinhardt, S. G. (1986) "The Selective Prosecution of Crime in Ancien Regime France: Theft in the Senechaussee of Sarlat", *European History Quarterly*, vol. 16, no. 3, pp. 3-21.

Reresby, J. (1734) *The Memoirs of Sir John Reresby*, London.

Reynolds, E. (1998) *Before the Bobbies, The Night Watch and Police Reform in Metropolitan London, 1720-1830*, Basingstole: Macmillan.

Reynolds, E. (2002) "Sir John Fielding, Sir Charles Whitworth, and the Westminster Night Watch Act, 1770-1775", *Criminal Justice History*, vol. 16, pp. 1-29.

Richardson, S. (1741) *Familiar letters on the most important occasions*, London.

Riddell, W. R. (1926) "Appeal of Death and Its Abolition", *Michigan Law Review*, vol. 24, no. 8. pp. 786-808.

Ritson, J. (1769) *A Digest of the Proceedings of the Court Leet of the Manor and Liberty of Savoy*, London.

Ritson, J. (1791) *The Office of Constable: being an entirely new compendium of the law concerning that ancient minister for the conservation of the peace, etc.*, London: Whieldon and Butterworth.

Ritson, J. (1809) *The Jurisdiction of the Court Leet* (2nd edn.), London.

Roberts, M. (1983) "The society for the Suppression of Vice and Its early Critics, 1802-1812", *The Historical Journal*, vol. 26, pp. 157-176.

Rock, P. (2005) "Chronocentrism and British Criminology", *British Journal of Sociology*, vol. 56(3), pp. 473-491.

Rogers, N. (1991) "Policing the Poor in Eighteenth-Century London: The Vagrancy Laws and Their Administration", *Histoire Sociale–Social History*, vol. 24, no. 47, pp. 127-147.

Romilly, S. (1786), *Observations on a Late Publication, Intituled, Thoughts of Executive Justice*, London.

Rosenheim, J. M. (1993) "Documenting Authority: Texts and Magistracy in Restoration Society", *Albion: A Quarterly Journal Concerned with British Studies*, vol. 25, no. 4, pp. 591-604.

Rude, G. (1971) *Hanoverian London, 1714-1808*, London: Secker & Warburg.

Rudolph, J. (2008) "That Blunderbuss of Law: Giles Jacob", *Studies in Eighteenth-century Culture*, vol. 37, pp. 196-215.

Ruffhead, O. (1763) *Statutes at Large: from Magna Carta to…1761*, London.

Rule, J. (1992) *Albion's People, English Society, 1714-1815*, London: Longman.

Rule, J. (1992) *The Vital Century: England's Developing Economy: 1714-1815*, London: Longman.

Rule, J. and Wells, R. (1997) *Crime, Protest and Popular Politic in Southern England 1740-1850*, Winchester: The Hambledon Press.

Rushton, P. and Morgan, G. (2003) "The Magistrate, the community and the maintenance of an orderly society in eighteenth-century England", *Historical Research*, vol. 76, no. 191, pp. 54-77.

Rushton, P. and Morgan, G. (2003) "Running Away And Returning Home: The Fate Of English Convicts In The American Colonies", *Crime, History & Societies*, vol. 7, no. 2, pp. 61-80.

Russell, S. (1742) *The Prisoner's Director*, London.

S., E. (1699) *A companion for debtors and prisoners, and advice to creditors in ten letters: from a gentleman in prison, to a member of Parliament: wherein, first, the villianies [sic] and insolencies [sic] of bayliffs, secondly, the evil practices of jaylers and pretended solicitors and thirdly the irregularities of prisons in general, are breifly [sic] detected and exposed,* London: A. Baldwin.

Sacerdote, B. and Glaeser, E. (1999) "Why is there more Crime in Cities?", *The Journal of Political Economy*, vol. 107, no. 6, part 2, pp. 225-258.

Sayer, E. (1784) *Observations on the Police or Civil Government of Westminster, with a Proposal for a Reform,* London.

Schwarz, L. (1979) "Income distribution and social structure in London in the late eighteenth century", *Economic History Review 2nd Series*, vol. 32, pp. 250-259.

Schwarz, L. (1985) "The Standard of Living in the Long Run: London, 1700-1860", *The Economic History Review*, vol. 38, pp. 24-41.

Scrimshaw, S. (1759) *The Trial of Samuel Scrimshaw and John Ross, For a Conspiracy, In Sending Threatening Letters To Humphry Morice, Esq: of Dover Street..*, London.

Seller, J. (1671) *A booke of the punishments of the common laws of England*, London.

Shapiro, B. J. (1986) "To A Moral Certainty: Theories of Knowledge and Anglo-American Juries 1600-1850", *Hastings Law Journal*, vol. 38, pp. 153-194.

Sharpe, J. A. (1983) *Crime in Seventeenth-Century England,* Cambridge: CUP.

Sharpe, J. A. (2002) "Crime and Punishment", in Dickinson, H. T. (Ed.), *A Companion to Eighteenth-Century Britain*, at pp. 358-366, Oxford: Blackwell.

Shaw, J. (1733) *Parish law: Or, a guide to justices of the peace, ministers, churchwardens,* London.

Sheppard, J. (1724) *A Narrative of all the Robberies, Escapes, &c. of Jack Sheppard* (2nd edn.), London.

Sheppard, W. (1652) *The Whole Office of the Country Justice of Peace,* London.

Sheppard, W. (1656) *The Court-Keepers Guide* (4th edn.), London.

Sheppard, W. (1669) *A Sure Guide for his Majesties Justices of Peace* (2nd edn.), London.

Shirley, L. (1760) *An Account of the Execution of the Late Laurence Earl Ferrers,* London.

Shoemaker, R. (1991) *Prosecution and Punishment: Petty Crime and the Law in London and Rural Middlesex, c. 1660-1725,* Cambridge: CUP.

Shoemaker, R. (2001) "Male Honour and the decline of public violence in eighteenth-century London", *Social History*, vol. 26, pp. 190-208.

Shoemaker, R. (2004) *The London Mob: Violence and Disorder in Eighteenth-century England,* London: Hambledon and London.

Shoemaker, R. (2006) "The Street Robber and the Gentleman Highwayman: Changing Representations and Perceptions of Robbery in London, 1690-1800", *Cultural and Social History*, vol. 3, pp. 381-405.

Shoemaker, R. (2008) "The Old Bailey Proceedings and the Representation of Crime and Criminal Justice in Eighteenth-century London", *Journal of British Studies*, vol.47:3, pp. 559-580.

Silverthorne, E. (1978) *Deposition Book of Richard Wyatt,* Guildford: Surrey Record Society.

Simpson, A. E. (2006) "The Ordeal of St. Sepulchre's: A Campaign Against Organised Prostitution in Early 19th-century London and the Emergence of Law Middle-Class Consciousness", *Social and Legal Studies*, vol. 15, pp. 363-387.

Simpson, A. E. (1996) ""The mouth of strange women is a deep pit": Male Guilt and Legal attitudes towards Prostitution in Georgian London", *Journal of Criminal Justice and Popular Culture,* vol. 4 (3), pp. 50-79.

Smith, A. (1984) *Lectures on Justice, Police, Revenue and Arms: reported by a student in 1763,* Manchester.

Smith, B. P. (2005) "The History of Wrongful Execution", *Hastings Law Journal,* vol. 56, pp. 1185–1233.

Smith, B. P. (2005) "The Presumption of Innocence and the English Law of Theft: 1750-1850", *Law and History Review* , vol. 23, no. 1, pp. 133-173.

Smith, B. P. (2006) "The Emergence of Public Prosecution in London, 1790-1850", *Yale Journal of Law and the Humanities* , vol. 18, pp. 29-62.

Smith, B. P. (2007) "English Criminal Justice Administration, 1650-1850", *Law and History Review,* vol. 25, no. 3, pp. 593-634.

Smith, G. T. (1996) "Civilized People Don't Want to See That Kind of Thing: The Decline of Public Physical Punishment in London, 1760-1840", in Strange, C. (Ed.), *Qualities of Mercy: Justice, Punishment, and Discretion*, Vancouver: UBC Press, at pp. 21-51.

Smith, G. T. (2007) "Expanding the compass of domestic violence in the Hanoverian Metropolis", *Journal of Social History*, vol. 41:1, pp. 31-54.

Smith, S. (1694) *A True Account Of The Behaviour, Confession, And Last Dying Speeches, Of The Criminals That Were Executed At Tyburn, On Wednesday The 24th of January, 1694,* London.

Smith, W. (1776) *State of the Gaols in London, Westminster, and Borough of Southwark*, London.

Smith, W. (1777) *Mild Punishments Sound Policy: Or Observations on the Laws Relative to Debtors and Felons*, London.

Smith, W. (1750) *An Authentic Account of the Life and Memoirs of Mr. William Smith* (4th edn.), London.

Somervill, R. (1960) *The Savoy; Manor: Hospital: Chapel,* London.

Speck, W. A. (1978) "Bernard Mandeville and the Middlesex Grand Jury", *Eighteenth-century Studies,* vol. 11, no. 3, pp. 362-374.

Spierenberg, P. (2006) "Democracy Came too Early: A Tentative Explanation for the Problem of American Homicide", *The American Historical Review,* vol. 111, pp. 104-114.

Spierenburg, P. (2008) *A History of Murder: Personal Violence in Europe from the Middle Ages to the Present,* Cambridge: Polity.

Spraggs, G. (2001) *Outlaws and Highwaymen: the Cult of the Robber in England from the Middle Ages to the Nineteenth Century,* London: Pimlico.

Sprinkle, R. H. (2001) "The Missing Politics and Unsettled science of the Trend towards earlier Puberty", *Politics and the Life Sciences,* vol. 20, pp. 43-66.

Squires, M. (1753) *The Controverted Hard Case: Or Mary Squires's Magazine of Facts Re-examin'd,* London.

Stanhope, G. (1701) *The Duty of Witnesses. A Sermon Preached at the Summer Assizes Holden at Maidstone in Kent...August the 5th, 1701,* London.

Storch, R. D. (1999) "The Old English Constabulary", *History Today,* vol. 49, issue 11, pp. 43-49.

Stow, W. (1722) *Remarks on London Being An Exact Survey of the Cities of London and Westminster,* London.

Strathern, M. (1985) "Discovering 'Social Control'", *Journal of Law and Society,* vol. 12, no. 2, pp.111-134.

Stubbs, W. (1762) *The Crown Circuit Companion; containing the practice on the crown side, and of the Courts of General and General Quarter Sessions..,* London.

Styles, J. (1982) "An Eighteenth-century magistrate as detective: Samuel Lister of Little Horton", *The Bradford Antiquary,* vol. 10, part 47, pp. 98-117.

Suzuki, A. (1992) "Lunacy in seventeenth-and eighteenth-century England: analysis of Quarter Sessions Records: Part 2", *History of Psychiatry,* vol. 3(9), pp. 29-44.

Tattle, T. (1720) *A Letter from Tom Tattle A Literate Watchman of Westminster to his Brother Jack Drydrub,* London.

Thomas, E. (1968) *The Making of the English Working Class,* Harmondsworth: Penguin Books.

Tosney, N. (2007) "Women and "False Coining" in Early Modern London", *The London Journal,* vol. 32, no. 2, pp. 103-123.

Toynbee, P. (Ed.) (1925) *Supplement to the Letters of Horace Walpole.* Oxford: Clarendon.

Toynbee, P. (Ed) (1905) *The Letters of Horace Walpole,* vol. 1, Oxford: Clarendon Press.

Tribe, J. (2009) "Bankruptcy and capital punishment in the 18th and 19th Centuries", *Insolvency Intelligence*, vol. 22, pp. 44-47.

Trusler, J. (1786) *The London Adviser and Guide: containing every instruction and information useful and necessary to persons living in London, and coming to reside there,* London.

Turpin, R. (1739) *The Genuine History of the Life of Richard Turpin,* London.

Villers, J. (1715) *The Case of Joseph Villers, Citizen of London,* London.

Villette, J. (1774) *A Genuine Account of the Behaviour, confession, and Dying-Words of William Hawke and William Jones,* London.

Villette, J. (1776) *A Genuine Account of the Behaviour, confession, and Dying-Words of Daniel Perreau and Robert Perreau,* London.

Voth, H. J. (1998) "Time and Work in Eighteenth-century London", *The Journal of Economic History,* vol. 58, pp. 29-58.

W. J. (1707) *A Compleat Guide for Justices of the Peace,* London.

Wales, T. (2000) "Thief-Takers and their Clients in later Stuart London", at pp. 67-84, in Griffiths, P. and Jenner, M., *Londinopolis: Essays in the cultural and social history of early modern London,* Manchester: MUP.

Ward, E. (1709) *The London-Spy Compleat in Eighteen Parts* (4th edn.), London.

Ward, G. A. (Ed.), (1864) *The Journal And Letters Of Samuel Curwen, An American In England, From 1775 To 1783* (4th edn.), London.

Warner, J. (1999) "Damn you, you informing bitch. Vox Populi and the unmaking of the Gin Act of 1736", *Journal of Social History,* vol. 33, no. 2, pp. 299-330.

Warner, J. (2000) "A Predatory Social Structure: Informers in Westminster, 1737-1741", *Journal of Interdisciplinary History,* vol. 30, no. 4, pp. 617-634.

Warner, J. (2003) "'My Pappa is out, and my Mamma is asleep': minors, their routine activities, and interpersonal violence in an early modern town, 1653-1781", *Journal of Social History,* vol. 35, issue 3, pp. 561-584.

Warner, J. (2003) "Violence against and amongst Jews in an Early Modern Town: Tolerance and its Limits in Portsmouth, 1718-1781", *Albion,* vol. 35, pp. 428-452.

Warner, J. and Her, M. *et al* (2001) "Can Legislation Prevent Debauchery? Mother Gin and Public Health in 18th-Century England", *American Journal of Public Health,* vol. 91(3), pp. 375-384.

Watson, K. (2006) "Medical and Chemical Expertise in English Trials for Criminal Poisoning, 1750-1914", *Medical History,* vol. 50, no. 3, pp. 373-390.

Welch, S. (1754) *Observations on the Office of Constable,* London.

Welch, S. (1758) *A Proposal to render effectual a Plan to remove the nuisance of Common Prostitutes from the Streets of the Metropolis,* London.

Welsh, A. (1990) 'Burke and Bentham on the Narrative Potential of Circumstantial Evidence,' *New Literary History: A Journal of Theory and Interpretation,* vol. 21, pp. 607-627.

Wesley, J. (1763) *A sermon preached before the Society for reformation of manners, etc.*, London.

Whatley, R. (1729) *A Friendly Admonition to Gentlemen in the Commission of the Peace* (2nd edn.), London.

White, J. (2003) "The Slow but sure Poyson: The Representation of Gin and Its Drinkers, 1736-1751", *Journal of British Studies,* vol. 42, pp. 35-64.

Whitlock, T. C. (2005) *Crime, Gender and Consumer Culture in Nineteenth-century England,* Aldershot: Ashgate.

Whitworth, C. (1773) *The Draught of an Intended Act, For the better Regulation of the Nightly Watch and Beadles within the City and Liberty of Westminster, and Parts Adjacent,* London.

Wiener, M. J. (1999) "Judges v Jurors: Courtroom Tensions in Murder Trials and the Law of Criminal Responsibility in Nineteenth-Century England", *Law and History Review*, vol. 17, no. 3, pp. 467-506.

Wiener, M. J. (2004) *Men of Blood: Violence, Manliness and Criminal Justice in Victorian England,* New York: CUP.

Willcock, J. W. (1827) *The Office of Constable,* London.

Williams, R. (1790) *An Appeal to the Public, by Rhynwick Williams, containing Observations and Reflections on Facts, relative to his Very Extraordinary Case,* London.

Williamson, S. (1775) *The Trial at Large of John Bolton, Gent. Of Bulmer, near Castle-Howard, for the wilful Murder of Elizabeth Rainbow*, York.

Willis, J. J. (2005) "Transportation versus Imprisonment in Eighteenth-and Nineteenth-Century Britain: Penal Power, Liberty, and the State", *Law & Society Review,* vol. 39, no. 1, pp. 171-210.

Willis, J. J. (2008) "Punishment and the cultural limits to state power in late 18th-century Britain", *Punishment & Society*, vol. 10, no. 4, pp. 401-428.

Wilner, A. F. (1988) "Henry Fielding and the Knowledge of Character", *Modern Language Studies*, vol. 18, no. 1, pp. 181-194.

Wilson, R. (1722) *A Full and Impartial Account of all the Robberies Committed by John Hawkins, George Sympson (lately Executed for Robbing the Bristol Mails) and their companions* (3rd edn.), London.

Wilson, T. (1736) *Distilled spirituous liquors the bane of the nation being some considerations humbly offered to the legislature,* London.

Wingate, E. ('E.W.') (1663) *The Exact Constable,* London.

Withers, E. (1747) *Sir T. Deveil, Observations on the Practice of a Justice of the Peace,* London.

Wood, J. C. (2003) "Self-Policing And The Policing Of The Self: Violence, Protection And the Civilizing Bargain In Britain", *Crime, Histoire & Sociétés/Crime, History and Societies*, vol. 7, no. 1, pp. 109-128.

Wood, J. C. (2007) "The Limits of Culture", *Cultural and Social History*, vol. 4, pp. 95-114.

Woodford, T. (1749) *A Discourse Concerning Some of the most important Branches, and Parts of the Office of the Justices of the Peace,* London.

Woodford, T. (1749) *A Discourse Concerning Some of the most important Branches, and Parts, of the Office of the Justices of the Peace, and of the Difficultys occurring to Them,* London.

Woodward, J. (1699) *An Account of the Societies for Reformation of Manners, in London and Westminster, and other parts of the Kingdom,* London.

Wright, D. E. (2004) "Female Crime and State Punishment in Early Modern Japan", *Journal Of Women's History*, vol. 16, no. 3, pp. 10-29.

Wrigley, E. A. (1985), "Urban Growth and Agricultural Change: England and the Continent in the Early Modern Period", *Journal of Interdisciplinary History*, vol. 15, pp. 683-728.

Wrigley, E. A. (1967) "A simple model of London's Importance in Changing English Society and Economy 1650-1750", *Past & Present*, vol. 37, pp. 44-70.

Zedner, L. (2006) "Policing Before and After the Police", *British Journal of Criminology* , vol. 46, pp. 78-96.

Zouch, H. (1779) *Observations upon a Bill, now depending in Parliament, entitled "A Bill ... to punish by imprisonment, and hard labour, certain offenders, and to establish proper places for their reception",* London.

Zouch, H. (1786) *Hints Respecting the Public Police,* London.

Contemporary Journals and Newspapers Cited

Adams's Weekly Courant

Applebee's Original Weekly Journal

Bingley's London Journal

British Mercury

British Journal or the Traveller

Country Journal or The Craftsman

Daily Gazetteer

Daily Journal

Daily Post

Diary or Woodfalls Register

English Post

Evening Mail

Evening Post

Flying Post

Fog's Weekly Journal

Gazetteer and New Daily Advertiser

General Advertiser

Grub-street Journal

Lloydes Evening Post and British Chronicle

London Chronicle

London Daily Post and General Advertiser

London Evening Post

London Post

Middlesex Journal or Chronicle of Liberty

Mist's Weekly Journal

Morning Post and Daily Advertiser

Old Common Sense

Old Common Sense: Or, the Englishman's Journal

Old England

Oracle and Daily Advertiser

Penny London Post

Parker's Penny Post

Porcupine

Public Advertiser

Review of the State of the British Nation

Royal Magazine; or, Quarterly Bee

Royal Gazette

The British Journal

The Calcutta Gazette

The Country Gentleman

The Covent Garden Journal

The Crisis

The Daily Journal

The Flying Post

The Gentleman's Magazine

The London Chronicle or Universal

The London Journal
The London Spy
The Middlesex Journal
The Morning Advertiser
The Observer
The Old Whig
The Post Angel or Universal Entertainment
The Post-Boy
The Spectator
The Tatler
The Times
The Weekly Oracle: or, Universal Library
The Whitehall Evening Post; Or, London Intelligencer
Weekly Journal, or The British Gazetteer
White-hall Evening-Post
World and Fashionable Advertiser
World

Law Reports Cited

Atkyns' Chancery Reports
Cobbett & Howell's State Trials
Douglas' King's Bench Reports
English Reports
Espinasse's Nisi Prius Reports
Keble's King's Bench Reports
Leach's Cases in Crown Law
Lord Raymond's King's Bench and Common Pleas Reports

INDEX

A

B

C

D

E

F

I

J

K

L

M

N

O

P

Q

R

S

T

W

Y

Z

Fields, Fens and Felonies

Crime and Justice in Eighteenth-Century East Anglia

by Gregory J Durston

A new work on Crime and Punishment in East Anglia (and other parts of Britain) during the eighteenth century. It was a time of highwaymen, footpads and desperate petty offenders accompanied by draconian penalties, extremes of wealth and poverty, corruption, developing laws, and rough and emerging forms of justice — often at a price.

The contents include justices of the peace, policing, crimes, courts and judicial personnel as well as such matters as summary trial and disposal, jury trial, execution (and reprieve), a variety of offences including murder (or other homicides), violence and sexual offences, smuggling, poaching, property crimes, riots and disturbances. It also looks at the various hierarchies that existed whether social, legal, judicial, religious, military or otherwise so as to exert a variety of social controls at a time of relative lawlessness. A fascinating and statistically absorbing account of crimes, responses and penal outcomes of the era. Neither a micro-history in the context of a parish, hundred, or small town nor national account, but a more unusual criminal-justice history of a major English region with its own correlation with London and the rest of England in addition to its local differences and 'quirks'.

By an acknowledged expert Fields, Fens and Felonies is a captivating social record, a colourful account that informs and entertains. Thoroughly researched, referenced and indexed.

2016 | Paperback & Ebook | ISBN 978-1-909976-11-5

WatersidePress.co.uk

Lightning Source UK Ltd.
Milton Keynes UK
UKOW05f1605111216
289693UK00001B/20/P

9 781909 976399